# MATHEMATICAL METHODS IN COMPUTER AIDED GEOMETRIC DESIGN

*Edited by*

**TOM LYCHE**
Institutt for informatikk
Universitetet i Oslo
Oslo, Norway

**LARRY L. SCHUMAKER**
Department of Mathematics
Vanderbilt University
Nashville, Tennessee

ACADEMIC PRESS, INC.
*Harcourt Brace Jovanovich, Publishers*
Boston   San Diego   New York
Berkeley   London   Sydney
Tokyo   Toronto

ACADEMIC PRESS, INC.
1250 Sixth Avenue, San Diego, CA 92101

*United Kingdom Edition published by*
ACADEMIC PRESS INC. (LONDON) LTD.
24-28 Oval Road, London NW1 7DX


**Library of Congress Cataloging-in-Publication Data**

Mathematical methods in computer aided geometric design / edited by
   Tom Lyche, Larry L. Schumaker.
       p.    cm.
   Papers originally presented at an international conference held
June 16–22, 1988, at the University of Oslo, Norway.
   Bibliography: p.
   ISBN 0-12-460515-X (alk. paper)
   1. Geometry – Data processing – Congresses.  I. Lyche, Tom.
II. Schumaker, Larry L., Date
QA448.D38M38  1989
516.15'028 – dc20                             89-32842
                                          CIP

Printed in the United States of America
89  90  91  92      9  8  7  6  5  4  3  2  1

# CONTENTS

## PREFACE

During the week of June 16 - 22, 1988, an international conference on *Mathematical Methods in Computer Aided Geometric Design* was held at the University of Oslo, Norway. Twelve one-hour survey lectures were presented along with 49 shorter research talks. The conference was attended by over 120 mathematicians from fifteen countries. This volume contains papers based on the survey lectures, along with 33 full-length research papers.

The conference was supported by grants from a number of international scientific organizations as well as several industrial concerns. Major support came from the Royal Norwegian Research Council for Science and the Humanities (NAVF), the Royal Norwegian Research Council for Scientific and Industrial Research (NTNF), the US Army European Research Office (London), the US Office of Naval Research (London), the US Air Force (EOARD), and the Center for Industrial Research, Oslo. We are also grateful for support from the Digital Equipment Corp. A/S, the Norsk Data A/S, the Veritas Sesam Systems A/S, the Moelven Bygg Gruppen A/S, and the Norwegian Contractors.

We would like to thank Morten Dæhlen and Knut Mørken for their help with organizing the program, accommodations, and entertainment as well as assisting with the preparation of the proceedings. We would also like to thank Erlend Arge, Sigurd Glærum, Ky Van Ha, Arne Laskå , Dag Nylund, Kyrre Strøm, Inger Ann Faye, Evy Madsen, and Lise Opsahl (all of the University of Oslo) for their help.

Our thanks are also due to the authors of the papers in this volume, both for submitting a paper, and for preparing it in TeX. Finally, we would like to express our appreciation to Ewald Quak and Gerda Schumaker who assisted in the preparation of the final manuscript.

Nashville, March 1, 1989

# PARTICIPANTS

Asle Aasen, *Moelven Bygg Gruppen A/S, P.O. Box 116, 2391 Moelv, NOR-WAY.*

Peter Alfeld, *University of Utah, Department of Mathematics, Salt Lake City, UT, 84112, USA.*

A. Andreev, *Bulgarian Academy of Sciences, Center of Mathematics and Mechanics, 1090 Sofia, P.O. Box 373, BULGARIA.*

Rémi Arcangéli, *Université de Pau, Laboraroire d'Analyse Numérique, Avenue de l'Université, 64000 Pau, FRANCE.*

Erlend Arge, *Universitetet i Oslo, Institutt for informatikk, P.O. Box 1080, Blindern, 0316 Oslo 3, NORWAY.*

Lise Wenstøp Arneberg, *Senter for Industriforskning, P.O. Box 350 Blindern, 0314 Oslo 3, NORWAY.*

Marc Atteia, *Université Paul Sabatier, Laboratoire d'Analyse Numérique, 118 Route de Narbonne, 31062 Toulouse Cédex, FRANCE.*

Lothar Bamberger, *Universität München, Mathematisches Institut, Siemens AG, Otto–Hahn–Ring 6, DAP 412, 8 München 83, W. GERMANY.*

Robert E. Barnhill, *Arizona State University, Dept. of Computer Science, Tempe, AZ 85287-5406, USA.*

Phillip Barry, *University of Waterloo, Dept. of Computer Science, Waterloo, Ontario, N2L 3G1, CANADA.*

Brian A. Barsky, *Univ. of California Berkeley, Computer Science Division, Elec. Eng. & Comp. Sci. Dept., Berkeley, CA 94720, USA.*

Richard Bartels, *University of Waterloo, Dept. of Computer Science, Waterloo, Ontario N2L 3G1, CANADA.*

Günter Baszenski, *Ruhr University, Computer Centre, Universitätstr. 150, 4630 Bochum 1, W. GERMANY.*

Marek Beśka, *Technical University of Gdańsk, Institut of Mathematics, 80–952 Gdańsk, Majakowskiego 11/12, POLAND.*

Louis J. Billera, *Rutgers University, Department of Mathematics, New Brunswick, NJ 08903, USA.*

Wolfgang Boehm, *Universität Braunschweig, Angewandte Geom. & Comp. Graphic, Pockelstr. 14, D-3300 Braunschweig, W. GERMANY.*

Mats Boholm, *Volvo Data AB, Dept 2930 DVF2, S-405 08 Gothenburg, SWEDEN.*

P. Brunet, *Univ. Polit. de Catalunya, ETSEIB, Dept. de Llenguatges i Sistemes Inform., Av. Diagonal 647, 8ena planta, 08028 Barcelona, SPAIN.*

M. D. Buhmann, *University of Cambridge, Dept. of Appl. Math. & Theor. Phys., Silver Street, Cambridge CB3 9EW, UK.*

Rosemary E. Chang, *Silicon Graphics Comp. Systems, M/S 3U-550, 2011 Stierlin Rd., Mountain View, CA 94043, USA.*

Elaine Cohen, *University of Utah, Dept. of Computer Science, Salt Lake City, UT 84112, USA.*

Morten Dæhlen, *Senter for Industriforskning, P.O. Box 124 Blindern, 0314 Oslo 3, NORWAY.*

Wolfgang Dahmen, *Freie Universität Berlin, Institut für Mathematik III, Arnimallee 2–6, 1000 Berlin 33, W. GERMANY.*

Anthony DeRose, *University of Washington, Dept. of Computer Science, FR-35, Seattle, WA 98195, USA.*

Flavia De Tisi, *Università di Milano, Dipartimento di Matematica, Via C. Saldini, 50-20133 Milano, ITALY.*

Paul Dierckx, *Katholieke Universiteit Leuven, Departement Computerwetenschappen, Celestijnenlaan 200 A, B-3030 Heverlee, BELGIUM.*

Tor Dokken, *Senter for Industriforskning, P.O. Box 124 Blindern, 0314 Oslo 3, NORWAY.*

Per Evensen, *Senter for Industriforskning, P.O. Box 124 Blindern, 0314 Oslo 3, NORWAY.*

Gerald Farin, *Arizona State University, Dept. of Computer Science, Tempe, AZ 85287-5406, USA.*

R. T. Farouki, *IBM T. J. Watson Research Center, P.O. Box 218, Yorktown Heights, NY 10598, USA.*

Thomas A. Foley, *Arizona State University, Dept. of Computer Science, Tempe, AZ 85287-5406, USA.*

Ferruccio Fontanella, Firenze, Dept. of Energetica, Facolta' di Ingegneria, Via di S. Marta 3, I 50139 Firenze, ITALY.

Richard Franke, Naval Postgrad. School, Monterey, Dept. of Mathematics, CA 93943-5100, USA.

Jean Gaches, Laboratorie d'Analyse Num., U.F.R./M.I.G., Université P. Sabatier, 118, Route de Narbonne, 31062 Toulouse Cédex, FRANCE.

Mariano Gasca, Universidad de Zaragoza, Departamento de Matematica Aplicada, 50009 Zaragoza, SPAIN.

Didier Girard, Université J. Fourier (Grenoble), TIM3. IMAG, B.P 68, 38402 St. Martin d' Hères Cédex, FRANCE.

Ronald Goldman, University of Waterloo, Dept. of Computer Science, Waterloo, Ontario N2L 3G1, CANADA.

Manfred v. Golitschek, Universität Würzburg, Institut für Angewandte Mathematik, Am Hubland, 8700 Würzburg, W. GERMANY.

T. N. T. Goodman, University of Dundee, Dept. of Maths. & Comp. Science, DD1 4HN, Scotland, UK.

John A. Gregory, Brunel University, Mathematics and Statistics Dept., Uxbridge, Middlesex UB8 3PH, UK.

Dag Gravningsbråten, Norsk Data A/S, Schwabesgt. 5, P.O. Box 489, 3601 Kongsberg, NORWAY.

Per Kristian Gurrik, Norsk Data A/S, Schwabesgt. 5, P.O. Box 489, 3601 Kongsberg, NORWAY.

Ernst Gschwind, Hewlett-Packard GmbH, Herrenbergerstrasse 130, 7030 Böblingen, W. GERMANY.

Monika Haase, Norsk Data A/S, Schwabesgt. 5, P.O. Box 489, 3601 Kongsberg, NORWAY.

Nils Terje Haavie, Raufoss A/S, P.B. 1, 2831 Raufoss, NORWAY.

Ky Van Ha, Universitetet i Oslo, Institutt for informatikk, P.O. Box 1080, Blindern, 0316 Oslo 3, NORWAY.

Hans Hagen, Universität Kaiserslautern, Institut für graph. Datenverarbeitung und Computergeometrie, D-6750 Kaiserslautern, W. GERMANY.

Øyvind Hjelle, Senter for Industriforskning, P.B. 124 Blindern, 0314 Oslo 3, NORWAY.

Klaus Höllig, Universität Stuttgart, Mathematisches Institut A, Pfaffenwaldring 57, 7000 Stuttgart 80, W. GERMANY.

G. L. Iliev, Bulgarian Academy of Sciences, Center of Mathematics and Mechanics, 1090 Sofia, P.O. Box 373, BULGARIA.

Thomas Jensen, Evans and Sutherland, Interactive Systems, P.O. Box 8700, Salt Lake City, UT 84108, USA.

Bo Johansson, Volvo Data AB, Dept 2930 DVF2, S-405 08 Gothenburg, SWEDEN.

Alain Kaufmann, Université J. Fourier (Grenoble), Lab. TIM3-IRMA, B.P. 53X, 38401 Grenoble Cédex, FRANCE.

Per Erik Koch, Norges Tekniske Høgskole, Institutt for Matematiske fag, 7034 Trondheim NTH, NORWAY.

Linde Wittmeyer-Koch, Linköping University, Department of Mathematics, S 58183 Linköping, SWEDEN.

Jernej Kozak, University of Ljubljana, Department of Mathematics, Jadranska 19, 61000 Ljubljana, YUGOSLAVIA.

Ulf Krystad, IDA, P.B 1163 Sentrum, 0107 Oslo 1, NORWAY.

Johannes Kåsa, Senter for Industriforskning, P.O. Box 124 Blindern, 0314 Oslo 3, NORWAY.

Dieter Lasser, Technische Hochschule Darmstadt, Fachbereich Mathematik, Schlossgartenstr. 7, 6100 Darmstadt, W. GERMANY.

Pierre-Jean Laurent, Université J. Fourier (Grenoble), TIM 3. IMAG, B.P. 68, 38402 Saint Martin d'Hères Cédex, FRANCE.

Alain Le Méhauté, Université de Lille, Laboratoire d'Analyse Numérique, et Optimisation, 59655 Villeneuve d'Ascq Cédex, FRANCE.

Charles Loop, University of Washington, Computer Science Dept., FR- 35 Seattle, WA 98195, USA.

J. Lorente, Universidad de Granada, Dpto. Matematica Aplicada, Facultad de Ciencias, Avda. Fuentenueva s/n, 18071 Granada,, SPAIN.

Rudolph Lorentz, Gesellschaft für Math. und Datenv., Postfach 1240, 5205 St. Augustin 1, W. GERMANY.

Tom Lyche, Universitetet i Oslo, Institutt for informatikk, P.O. Box 1080, Blindern, 0316 Oslo 3, NORWAY.

Carla Manni, *Istituto Matematico "U.Dini", Firenze, Viale Morgagni 67/A, Firenze, ITALY.*

Harry McLaughlin, *Rensselaer Polytechnic Inst., Department of Mathematical Sciences, Troy, NY 12181, USA.*

Steinar Meen, *Norsk Data A/S, Schwabesgt. 5, P.O. Box 489, 3601 Kongsberg, NORWAY.*

Ingrid Melinder, *Kungliga Tekniska Högskolan, NADA, 10044 Stockholm, SWEDEN.*

Charles Micchelli, *IBM T. J. Watson Research Center, Mathematical Sciences Department, P.O. Box 218, Yorktown Heights, NY 10598, USA.*

Ernest J. Mintel, *East Hartford, 15 Grant St., CT 06118, USA.*

Truls Engebret Moe, *Norsk Data A/S, Schwabesgt. 5, P.O. Box 489, 3601 Kongsberg, NORWAY.*

Knut Mørken, *Universitetet i Oslo, Institutt for informatikk, P.O. Box 1080, Blindern, 0316 Oslo 3, NORWAY.*

G. Müllenheim, *Katholische Universität Eichstätt, Mathematische Geographische Fakultät, Ostenstr. 18, 8078 Eichstätt, W. GERMANY.*

Udo Müller, *Technische Hochschule Darmstadt, Fachbereich Mathematik, Schloßgartenstraße 7, D-6100 Darmstadt, W. GERMANY.*

Edmond Nadler, *Wayne State University, Department of Mathematics, Detroit, MI 48202, USA.*

Norman W. Naugle, *Texas A&M University, Department of Mathematics, College Station, TX 77843-3368, USA.*

Gregory M. Nielson, *Arizona State University, Dept. of Computer Science, Tempe, AZ 85287-5406, USA.*

Geir Nilsen, *Raufoss A/S, P.B. 1, 2831 Raufoss, NORWAY.*

Carl S. Petersen, *Evans and Sutherland, Interactive Systems, P.O. Box 8700, Salt Lake City, UT 84108, USA.*

Pia Pfluger, *Univ. v. Amsterdam, Math. Institut, Roeterstr. 15, 1018 WB Amsterdam, THE NETHERLANDS.*

Hartmut Prautzsch, *Rensselaer Polytechnic Inst., Dept. of Math. Sciences, Troy, NY 12180-3590, USA.*

Ewald Quak,   *Vanderbilt University, Department of Mathematics, Nashville, TN 37235, USA.*

Christophe Rabut,   *Université Paul Sabatier,   Service de Mathématiques, I.N.S.A., Avenue de Rangueil, 31077 Toulouse Cédex, FRANCE.*

V. T. Rajan,   *T. J. Watson Research Center, Manufacturing Research, IBM Research Division, Yorktown Heights, NY 10510, USA.*

Ole Magnus Raff Reinemo,   *Norsk Data A/S, Schwabesgt. 5, P.O. Box 489, 3601 Kongsberg, NORWAY.*

Richard F. Riesenfeld,   *University of Utah, Dept. of Computer Science, Salt Lake City, UT 84112, USA.*

Dieter Roller,   *Hewlett–Packard GmbH, Herrenberger Strasse 130, 7030 Boeblingen, W. GERMANY.*

Hans Amund Rosbach,   *Veritas Sesam Systems, P.O. Box 300, Veritasveien 1, 1322 Høvik, NORWAY.*

Malcolm Sabin,   *FEGS Ltd., Oakington, Cambridge, CB4 5BA, UK.*

Paul Sablonnière,   *INSA Rennes, Laboratoire LANS, 20 Av. des Buttes de Coësmes, 35043 Rennes Cédex, FRANCE.*

K. Salkauskas,   *University of Calgary,   Dept. of Mathematics & Statistics, Calgary, Alberta, T2N 1N4, CANADA.*

Paolo Santarelli,   *Universität Kaiserslautern,   Inst. für graph. Datenv. & Comp.-geom., D-6750 Kaiserslautern, W. GERMANY.*

Ramon F. Sarraga,   *General Motors Research Labs., Computer Science Department, Warren, MI 48090, USA.*

Robert Schaback,   *Universität Göttingen, Inst. für Num. und Angew. Math., Lotzestrasse 16-18, D-3400 Göttingen, W. GERMANY.*

Karl Scherer,   *Universität Bonn,   Inst. für Angew. Math.,   Wegelerstasse 6, 5300 Bonn, W. GERMANY.*

Gerd Schmeltz,   *Technische Hochschule Darmstadt, Fachbereich Mathematik, Schloßgartenstraße 7, D-6100 Darmstadt, W. GERMANY.*

Guido Schulze,   *Universität Kaiserslautern, Inst. für graph. Datenv. & Comp.-geom., D-6750 Kaiserslautern, W. GERMANY.*

Larry L. Schumaker,   *Vanderbilt University,   Department of Mathematics, Nashville, TN 37235, USA.*

Hans-Peter Seidel, *Universität Tübingen, W.-Schickard-Inst. für Informatik, Graphisch-Interaktive Systeme, Auf der Morgenstelle 10 C9, D-7400 Tübingen, W. GERMANY.*

Vibeke Skytt, *Senter for Industriforskning, P.O. Box 124 Blindern, 0314 Oslo 3, NORWAY.*

Joachim Stoeckler, *Department of Mathematics, Texas A&M University, College Station, TX 77843, USA.*

Kyrre Strøm, *Universitetet i Oslo, Institutt for informatikk, P.O. Box 1080, Blindern, 0316 Oslo 3, NORWAY.*

J. P. Thiran, *University of Namur, Depart. Math. Fac., Rempart de la Vierge 8, B 5000 Namur, BELGIUM.*

Maria Bozzini Tirani, *Università di Milano, Dipartimento di Matematica, Via C. Saldini, 50-20133 Milano, ITALY.*

Romeo Tirani, *Università di Milano, Dipartimento di Matematica, Via C. Saldini, 50-20133 Milano, ITALY.*

C. R. Traas, *University of Twente, Faculty of Mathematics, P.O. Box 217, 7500 AE Enschede, THE NETHERLANDS.*

Keith Unsworth, *University of Dundee, Dept. of Maths. & Comp. Science, DD1 4HN, Scotland, UK.*

Alvar Vinacua, *Univ. Polit. de Catalunya, ETSEIB, Dept. de Llenguatges i Sistemes Inform., Av. Diagonal 647, 8ena planta, 08028 Barcelona, SPAIN.*

Mark Watkins, *Evans and Sutherland, Interactive Systems, P.O. Box 8700, Salt Lake City, UT 84108, USA.*

Andrew J. Worsey, *Univ. of N. Carolina Wilmington, Dept. of Mathematical Sciences, Wilmington, NC 28403–3297, USA.*

Anne-Marie Ytrehus, *Senter for Industriforskning, P.O. Box 124 Blindern, 0314 Oslo 3, NORWAY.*

# Scattered Data Interpolation
# in Three or More Variables

## Peter Alfeld

**Abstract.** This is a survey of techniques for the interpolation of scattered data in three or more independent variables. It covers schemes that can be used for any number of variables as well as schemes specifically designed for three variables. Emphasis is on breadth rather than depth, but there are explicit illustrations of different techniques used in the solution of multivariate interpolation problems.

## §1. Introduction

In this paper, we consider the following:

**Problem** (*Scattered data interpolation problem*). *Given*

$$(x_i, y_i) \in \Omega \times \mathbb{R}, \quad i = 1, 2, \cdots, N, \quad \Omega \subset \mathbb{R}^k, \tag{1}$$

*find* $s \in S(\Omega)$ *such that*

$$s(x_i) = y_i, \quad i = 1, 2, \cdots, N. \tag{2}$$

The points $(x_i, y_i)$ are the *data points* (or just *data*). We refer to the $x_i$ as *data sites* to separate them from the *function values* $y_i$. The integer $k$ is the number of independent variables. Our case of interest is

$$k > 2. \tag{3}$$

The integer $N$ is the number of data to be interpolated to, and $\Omega$ is a suitable domain containing the data sites. $S(\Omega)$ is the *interpolating space*; *i.e.*, a (usually finite dimensional) linear space of functions defined on $\Omega$. Usually, $S(\Omega) \subset C^1(\Omega)$.

Mathematical Methods in Computer Aided Geometric Design
Tom Lyche and Larry L. Schumaker (eds.), pp. 1–33.
Copyright ⊖ 1989 by Academic Press, Boston.
ISBN 0-12-460515-X.

It is often convenient (e.g., for describing an interpolation scheme) to think of the data as having been generated by a *primitive function f*; *i.e.*,

$$y_i = f(x_i), \quad i = 1, 2, \cdots, N. \tag{4}$$

However, we do not assume that any information about $f$ is available other than the data themselves.

A completely specified procedure of prescribing an interpolation space $S$ and an interpolant $s$ (for general $\Omega$ and general data) constitutes an interpolation *scheme*. This is distinguished from a *technique* which is used to build an interpolation scheme. An *algorithm* is a scheme that has been implemented in a commercially or freely available computer program. Emphasis in this paper is on techniques, and not on schemes or algorithms.

Multivariate scattered data interpolation problems arise in many different ways, as suggested by the following examples (others can be found in the literature listed at the end of this paper):

1. **Gravitational Field of the Earth [53].** Earth's gravitational field constitutes a vector-valued function of three components, which is the gradient of a scalar valued function, the potential function. This is generally regarded as being of significance when modelling the gravitational field. In particular, the problem is generally approached by modelling the potential function itself, but the approximation should be differentiable in order to be able to compute the force field. In fact, it should satisfy the 3–D Laplace Equation. The field has been measured with great accuracy at many points on the surface of the earth and in space. Yet no comprehensive model is currently available that is sufficiently accurate for all applications. Major difficulties in modeling the field are caused by the presence and significance of disparate spatial scales; on the surface of the planet the field may change appreciably within a few miles. It is affected—both in strength and direction—e.g., by the presence of mountain ranges. Gravitational effects on a larger scale affect a satellite in a typically low orbit of a few hundred kilometers. Finally, for the purposes of navigating a space craft in the vicinity of another planet, the earth can be thought of as a point source of gravity.

2. **Color Film Processing [48].** In generating color prints or slides, a processing system has to be corrected for effects, e.g., of film, chemistry, lenses, and filters. The correction is a (vector-valued) function of the intensities of three colors (Red, Green, Blue; *i.e.*, RGB) on certain test slides. Appropriate corrections can be determined for specific RGB values. Corrections for other RGB values can then be obtained by interpolation.

3. **Implicitly Defined Surfaces [73].** Tom Sederberg has explored the design and representation of (two-dimensional) surfaces as the contour surfaces of trivariate piecewise polynomial functions. Such functions can be constructed by interpolation. The data then serve as *Design Handles*.

4. **Oil exploration.** In exploratory oil drilling an abundance of data is obtained at each bore hole. The data are distributed in a peculiar fashion: they are dense along bore holes and widely scattered otherwise.

To make the scope of this paper manageable, a number of topics and issues had to be omitted:

1. **Approximation Problems.** Here the *residuals* $e_i = s(x_i) - y_i$ are to be made small in some appropriate sense. For practical applications, this is probably a more important objective than actual interpolation (which renders the residuals zero) since realistic data usually are comprised of measured values and include errors whose exact reproduction is pointless. Sometimes an approximation scheme can be turned into an interpolation scheme by choosing the dimension of the approximating space equal to the number of data. Used frequently, and related to some of the techniques described in this paper, are *smoothing splines* [82]; *i.e.*, functions that minimize

$$I(s) = \sum_{i=1}^{N} \left(s(x_i) - y_i\right)^2 + \lambda J(s), \tag{5}$$

where $\lambda$ is a parameter and $J(s)$ is a suitable semi-norm, measuring for example the strain energy in a clamped elastic plate (see Section 4.2.2). There are many additional references on smoothing splines in the bibliography [41].

2. **Interpolation Error.** This is the difference $\|s - f\|$ for some primitive function $f$ (and a suitable norm $\| \cdot \|$), usually considered a function of the density of the data sites. This is an issue in classical approximation theory.

3. **Multivariate B-Splines.** This is a large and fascinating area in its own right. However, to date multivariate B-splines do not appear to have been particularly competent in solving multivariate scattered data interpolation problems. There is a large number of papers on multivariate B-splines in the bibliography [41].

4. **Geometric Continuity.** In Computer Aided Geometric Design (of one and two dimensional surfaces embedded in $\mathbb{R}^3$) a central objective is to recognize, obtain, and represent properties of a surface that are independent of any particular parameterization. This allows a great degree of flexibility in the choice of the parameterization, and in the structure of the surfaces that can be designed. For higher dimensional surfaces this issue has not yet played a prominent role. The only reference on this topic known to the author is Dieter Lasser's recent thesis [50]. In this paper, we restrict ourselves to the functional case (1) (which of course includes *vector-valued* functions defined on $\Omega$).

I have attempted to cover existing techniques as widely as possible. However, only primary references are listed at the end of this paper. Their reference lists should be consulted for further information. For a recent extensive bibliography of 1107 entries on multivariate approximation and interpolation, see [41]. Recent collections of papers include [31,36], and the five volumes of the CAGD journal that have appeared to date. For a rich source of information and ideas, see the Winter, 1984 issue of *Rocky Mountain Journal of Mathemat-*

*ics* which is entirely devoted to multivariate interpolation and approximation problems.

It is unlikely that any multivariate interpolation schemes are going to emerge that are truly *general purpose* in the sense that they will solve satisfactorily the bulk of realistic problems. This observation applies to problems in three or more variables even more so than to the case of just two independent variables. There is a tremendous degree of variety and peculiarity present in multivariate interpolation problems. Thus, it is important to be aware of many different techniques for designing interpolation schemes, and for obtaining certain effects. Many such techniques are illustrated explicitly in this paper. The purpose of these illustrations is always the technique itself, and not a detailed description of the particular interpolation scheme to which it is applied.

In spite of the complexity of real problems, most of the schemes defined in this paper are *general purpose* in the sense that they are designed for generic situations rather than specific applications. (The exceptions are: tensor product schemes, interpolation on the sphere and other surfaces, and hypercubal methods). Calling a method *general purpose* requires certain underlying assumptions that should be made explicit:

1. There is no readily utilizable structure in the data that calls for the use of a more specific interpolation scheme. (In particular, it is hard to conceive of a situation where one would want to interpolate to tensor product data with a scattered data scheme.)

2. On the other hand, there is no *peculiar* structure that would upset a *general purpose method*. For example, a scheme based on a ($k$-dimensional) triangulation of the data sites is likely to perform poorly in a situation where data arise densely along scattered lines.

3. There is no appreciable noise in the data. (Otherwise one would use an approximation rather than an interpolation scheme.)

4. The representation of the data by a smooth (e.g., $C^1$) function is appropriate. This is often not the case. For example, in Computer Aided Tomography one is particularly interested in surfaces across which the density of the human body changes discontinuously (*i.e.*, the boundary of organs and bones). Similarly, in oil exploration a major issue is the location of *faults* (where subterranean layers of rock have been ruptured). The prediction and modeling of unknown discontinuities is an open and difficult problem that most likely will have to be addressed in the context of individual applications.

5. We will always assume that the data are such that the existence and uniqueness of an interpolant is assured. In several variables there are many settings where this is not the case. For example, it is impossible to interpolate to three data by a bivariate linear function if the data sites are situated along a straight line. Similarly, one cannot interpolate with a bivariate quadratic to six points whose sites lie on a conic section. Typically, such situations are *singular* in the sense that existence and uniqueness of the interpolant can be restored by an arbitrarily small perturbation of the

data sites. In this context, the opposite of *singular* is *generic*. For all of our interpolation schemes, existence and uniqueness are assured at least generically.

In designing, choosing, or using a multivariate interpolation scheme several issues may have to be considered:

1. How can a function of more than three variables be rendered?
2. Is the scheme *local* or *global*; *i.e.*, is the value of the interpolant at a given point dependent on all data or only a *small* subset of data sites close to the point of evaluation? A precise and general definition of these terms is not possible, but for any particular scheme it usually makes sense to classify it as local or global. Local schemes are more attractive for applications, while global schemes are easier to build and to design so as to possess other desirable properties (which depend on the particular problems that are to be solved).
3. What is the *degree of precision* of a scheme? This is the largest number $m$ such that $s = p$ whenever $p$ is polynomial of degree up to $m$ and $y_i = p(x_i)$, $i = 1, 2, \cdots, N$. The degree of precision is loosely related to the *shape fidelity* of a scheme. No precise statements can be made, but it is hard to envision viable schemes that do not have at least linear precision. On the other hand, a high degree of precision has no value in itself.
4. What is the *degree of smoothness* of the interpolant, *i.e.*, how often is it differentiable? Usually, first order differentiability is required.
5. What kind of data are required for the construction of the interpolant? As a rule, only functional data are provided by the problem, as indicated in (1). However, other data, e.g., values of derivatives at data sites, or function and derivative values at points other than data sites, may be required by the scheme to obtain properties such as localness, or increased precision. See Section 11 for a discussion of derivative generation techniques.
6. Is the scheme invariant under affine transformations? Let $A$ be a nonsingular $k \times k$ matrix, $\gamma$ a non-zero real number, and let $\bar{s}$ be the solution of the modified interpolation problem with the data $(Ax_i, \gamma y_i)$, $i = 1, 2, \cdots, N$. The interpolation scheme is *affinely invariant* if, for all data sets, and all points $x \in \Omega$, $\bar{s}(Ax) = \gamma s(x)$. Affine invariance implies for example that interpolated physical quantities are independent of the units chosen for expressing the data.
7. Does the interpolant depend continuously on the data sites? This property is clearly desirable, yet it is not present, e.g., for any triangulation based scheme since the triangulation itself depends discontinuously on the data sites.
8. A variety of properties may be desirable depending on the particular interpolation problem. For example, the value of the interpolant may be constrained to be bracketed by the minimum and maximum function values; the interpolant may have to be convex, or monotone with respect to some or all of the independent variables; or it may be required to minimize

a physically relevant variational principle over an affine space of potential interpolants.

We conclude this section by introducing a few terms and some notation that will be used throughout the paper. When it is necessary we will denote the components of $x \in \mathbb{R}^k$ by $\xi_i$, $i = 1, 2, \cdots, k$, to avoid confusion with the data sites. The *norm* $\| \cdot \|$ will be the *Euclidean Norm*; *i.e.*,

$$\|x\| = \sqrt{\sum_{i=1}^{k} \xi_i^2}. \tag{6}$$

The symbol $\mathbb{P}_d^k$ denotes the $\binom{d+k}{k}$-dimensional linear space of polynomials of $k$ variables of total degree $d$.

The interpolant $s$ will be sought in the finite dimensional linear interpolation space

$$S(\Omega) = \operatorname{span} \left\{ w_i \in C^1(\Omega) : \ i = 1, 2, \cdots, M \right\}, \tag{7}$$

where $M \geq N$. Thus, it will be of the form

$$s(x) = \sum_{i=1}^{M} \alpha_i w_i(x), \tag{8}$$

where the $\alpha_i$ are *coefficients* that are determined by the interpolation conditions (2) and, if $M > N$, by additional auxiliary conditions that are imposed to enforce certain useful properties of $s$. The $w_i$ are the *basis functions*.

We define the *Kronecker delta* as usual by

$$\delta_{ij} = \begin{cases} 1, & \text{if } i = j \\ 0, & \text{if } i \neq j. \end{cases} \tag{9}$$

A frequently arising special case is given when $M = N$ and

$$w_i(x_j) = \delta_{ij}. \tag{10}$$

In that case,

$$s(x) = \sum_{i=1}^{N} y_i w_i(x) \tag{11}$$

and the interpolant is said to be in *cardinal form*.

The generalization of a triangle to $k$-dimensional space is a *k-simplex* or just a *simplex*. A simplex $\mathcal{S}$ is the convex hull of $k+1$ points called the *vertices* of the simplex. $\mathcal{S}$ is *non-degenerate* if its $k$-dimensional volume is non-zero, and *degenerate* otherwise. The convex hull of any subset of $\kappa + 1$ vertices of a simplex is called a *$\kappa$-face* of the simplex. A face that is the convex hull of precisely $k$ vertices is also called a *facet*. A 1-face is also called an *edge*. Note that a $\kappa$-face of a simplex is itself a $\kappa$-dimensional simplex. (In [7] and [84], the meanings of the terms *facet* and *face* are interchanged. On the other hand, the usage proposed here is also employed, e.g., in [27] and [52]. There seem to be no linguistic reasons to prefer one usage over the other.)

The location of a point $x \in \mathbb{R}^k$ can be expressed uniquely in terms of *barycentric coordinates* $b_i$ with respect to a non-degenerate simplex $\mathcal{S}$ with vertices $V_i$, $i = 1, 2, \cdots, k+1$, as

$$x = \sum_{i=1}^{k+1} b_i V_i, \quad \text{where} \quad \sum_{i=1}^{k+1} b_i = 1. \tag{12}$$

A polynomial $p$ of degree $d$ can be expressed uniquely in *Bernstein-Bézier* form as

$$p(x) = \sum_{i_1+i_2+\cdots+i_{k+1}=d} c_{i_1 i_2 \cdots i_{k+1}} \frac{d!}{i_1! i_2! \cdots i_{k+1}!} b_1^{i_1} b_2^{i_2} \cdots b_{k+1}^{i_{k+1}}. \tag{13}$$

The Bernstein-Bézier form of a polynomial has many useful properties and is virtually indispensable in the design of piecewise polynomial multivariate interpolation schemes. For a recent survey of the properties of the Bernstein-Bézier form in a general number of variables, see [27].

## §2. Rendering of Trivariate Functions

The graphs of bivariate functions are frequently displayed as contour plots, three dimensional line drawings with or without hidden line elimination, or as shaded surfaces. Such surfaces reside in $\mathbb{R}^3$ and can be processed by the human mind as the familiar concept of a three dimensional object projected onto the two-dimensional retina. There is a fundamental biologic limit to similar renderings of higher dimensional objects. This seems to be the reason that pictorial displays of functions of more than two variables do not play nearly the same prominent role as for functions of two variables. However, some efforts have been made to render functions $s$ of precisely *three variables*. Two obvious approaches suggest themselves: 1.) Display a number of *cross sections* where one of the variables is held constant, or, 2.) display *contour surfaces* where the value of $s(x)$ equals some constant.

The latter approach is illustrated, e.g., in [16]. Particular schemes of displaying contour surfaces of a function $s$ are described in [61] and [74]. Petersen *et al* assume that $s$ is piecewise polynomial (of any degree) in Bernstein-Bézier form on a tetrahedral *tessellation* (but not necessarily a *triangulation*) of $\Omega$. Their scheme comes with an interpolation scheme of this character which is described in Section 8.1. The contouring scheme proceeds by approximating a polynomial $p$ on a given tetrahedron $t$ by another polynomial of degree one less than that of $p$. If the approximation is sufficiently accurate, it is accepted. Otherwise, $t$ is split (about its longest side) into two subtetrahedra $t_1$ and $t_2$, $p$ is restricted to each of $t_1$ and $t_2$, and the process is repeated on both $t_1$ and $t_2$. Eventually the approximation becomes a continuous piecewise linear function on a tetrahedral tessellation. The corresponding planar segments are then drawn to generate a *continuous piecewise linear* contour surface. The scheme has the advantage of spending computational effort only where it is needed, *i.e.*, it is *adaptive*. In an alternative approach, Sewell assumes that function values are given on a uniform three dimensional rectangular grid. (Of course, any interpolating function can be evaluated on such a grid.) The contour surfaces are drawn as frameworks of overlapping *bands* (*i.e.*, opaque lines of non-zero thickness). Bands in the background can be seen through gaps between bands in the foreground. Sewell's scheme has the advantage of being available as a FORTRAN algorithm [75].

## §3. Tensor Product Schemes

This section comprises a deviation from the main theme of this paper in that it assumes a very special distribution of the data sites. Suppose for simplicity that $k = 3$. Deviating momentarily from the notation defined in (1), suppose the data sites are of the form $(\zeta_i, \eta_j, \theta_\ell)$, $i = 1, \cdots, N_\zeta$, $j = 1, \cdots, N_\eta$, $\ell = 1, \cdots, N_\theta$, and we wish to find an interpolant of the form

$$s(\zeta, \eta, \theta) = \sum_{\mu=1}^{N_\zeta} \sum_{\nu=1}^{N_\eta} \sum_{\kappa=1}^{N_\theta} \alpha_{\mu\nu\kappa} p_\mu(\zeta) q_\nu(\eta) r_\kappa(\theta) \qquad (14)$$

satisfying the interpolation conditions

$$s(\zeta_i, \eta_j, \theta_\ell) = y_{ij\ell}, \quad i = 1, \cdots, N_\zeta, \quad j = 1, \cdots, N_\eta, \quad \ell = 1, \cdots, N_\theta. \qquad (15)$$

This is a *tensor product* problem. It can be reduced to a set of *univariate* interpolation problems. Suppose for simplicity that the basis functions for each variable are given in *cardinal form*; *i.e.*,

$$p_i(\zeta_j) = \delta_{ij}, \quad q_i(\eta_j) = \delta_{ij}, \quad r_i(\theta_j) = \delta_{ij}. \qquad (16)$$

The interpolant can then be written simply as

$$s(\zeta, \eta, \theta) = \sum_{\mu=1}^{N_\zeta} \sum_{\nu=1}^{N_\eta} \sum_{\kappa=1}^{N_\theta} y_{\mu\nu\kappa} p_\mu(\zeta) q_\nu(\eta) r_\kappa(\theta). \qquad (17)$$

Any set of (univariate) non-cardinal basis functions can be converted to cardinal form by calculating the inverse of the corresponding Vandermonde matrix, e.g., the matrix $[p_i(\zeta_j)]_{i,j=1,\cdots,N_\zeta}$ for the variable $\zeta$. In this manner, the effort of finding the coefficients of the interpolant is reduced from $O\big((N_\zeta N_\eta N_\theta)^3\big)$ to $O\big(N_\zeta^3 + N_\eta^3 + N_\theta^3\big)$ which constitutes a substantial saving. Tensor products do not have to be implemented in cardinal form, but in any case they can be reduced to univariate rather than truly multivariate interpolation problems. More detailed discussions of tensor product schemes are in [25] and [26]. See also [55] for a more abstract discussion of tensor product approximation.

## §4. Point Schemes

The term *Point Schemes* refers to interpolation schemes that are not based on a tessellation of the underlying domain $\Omega$.

### 4.1. Shepard's Methods

Shepard's method [76] may be the best known among all scattered data interpolants in a general number of variables. In its simplest form, it is given by

$$s(x) = \sum_{i=1}^{N} w_i(x) f(x_i) \quad \text{where} \quad w_i(x) = \frac{\|x - x_i\|^{-p}}{\sum_{j=1}^{N} \|x_i - x_j\|^{-p}}. \tag{18}$$

In this form, the evaluation of $s$ at a data site leads to a division by zero. However, the definition of $s$ can be extended continuously by the interpolation requirement $s(x_i) = y_i$.

Shepard's method is a particular example of a *convex combination* based scheme; *i.e.*, the weights $w_i$ are non-negative and sum to 1. The interpolant is arbitrarily often differentiable if $p > 1$. The most frequent choice is $p = 2$, in which case the basis functions $w_i$ are *rational*. If $p > 1$, the first derivatives vanish at the data points; *i.e.*, the interpolant has *flat spots*. The scheme is obviously global and has only constant precision. It does have the property

$$\min_{1 \leq i \leq N} \{y_i\} \leq s(x) \leq \max_{1 \leq i \leq N} \{y_i\} \quad \forall x \in \mathbb{R}^k \tag{19}$$

which is sometimes required. However, for most purposes Shepard's method in its unmodified form yields unacceptable interpolants. This is perhaps best illustrated by the fact that in the *univariate* case, where many other techniques are readily available, it has never been proposed as an interpolation scheme.

The deficiencies of Shepard's method can be overcome in various ways. We now describe some of them:

1. **Mollifying Basis Functions.** To localize Shepard's method one can multiply the basis functions $w_i$ by *mollifying functions* $\mu_i$ satisfying

$$\mu_i(x_i) = 1 \tag{20}$$

and having local support in some appropriate sense. For example, the *Franke-Little weights* [22] are given by

$$\mu_i(x) = \left( 1 - \frac{\|x - x_i\|}{R_i} \right)_+^{\nu} \tag{21}$$

where

$$x_+^{\nu} = \begin{cases} x^{\nu}, & \text{if } x > 0 \\ 0, & \text{if } x \leq 0, \end{cases} \tag{22}$$

and the $R_i$ are suitably chosen radii of circles around the data sites that constitute the support of the modified basis function. The smoothness of the multiplying factor is $\nu - 1$. This technique yields an interpolant

$$s(x) = \sum_{i=1}^{N} y_i \mu_i(x) w_i(x) \tag{23}$$

which is still in cardinal form. However, the (constant) precision of the scheme has been destroyed.

2. **Interpolation to Taylor operators.** To increase the precision of Shepard's method one can interpolate to Taylor expansions instead of function values. For example, the interpolant defined by

$$s(x) = \sum_{i=1}^{N} w_i(x) \left[ f(x_i) + \nabla f(x_i)^T (x - x_i) \right] \tag{24}$$

has linear precision (since the weights $w_i$ add to 1 and the individual Taylor operators have linear precision). Since $\nabla w_i(x_j) = 0$ for all $i$ and $j$, it also follows that $s$ interpolates to $\nabla f(x_i)$. The precision can be increased further by interpolating to Taylor operators of order greater than linear. However, for Shepard's method, if higher order Taylor operators were to be used, higher order derivatives would not be interpolated. Obviously, the technique calls for additional derivative values that are not normally available as data.

3. **Boolean sums.** Let $P$ and $Q$ be two linear operators defined on a suitable function space, and such that the composition $PQ$ is defined. The *Boolean sum* of $P$ and $Q$ is defined by

$$S = P \oplus Q = P + Q - PQ. \tag{25}$$

Barnhill and Gregory show in [18] that $S$ has (at least) the interpolation properties of $P$ and the precision properties of $Q$. Thus, one can obtain an interpolation scheme with an arbitrarily high degree of precision $m$, say, by letting $Pf$ be Shepard's interpolant and $Qf \in \mathbb{P}_m^k$ be a least squares approximation.

4. **Delta sums [38,39].** A Boolean sum can be formed only if the operator $Q$ can be applied when $f$ is represented solely by the given data. This fact rules out, e.g., tensor product based operators. This motivated Foley to define a *delta sum* of two operators $P$ and $Q$ as

$$S = P \triangle Q = P \oplus (QP) = QP + P(I - QP).$$

The process can be repeated to yield a *delta iteration*. Several Boolean sum and delta sum based interpolation schemes are described and discussed in [22].

For a recent survey of Shepard's method and analysis of its approximation order, see [37]. Other papers on implementations, modifications, and tests of Shepard's method include [15,17,40,42,49,56].

## 4.2. Radial Interpolants

The term *radial* is due to Rippa [68]. Radial interpolants are of the form

$$s(x) = \sum_{i=1}^{N} \alpha_i g(\|x - x_i\|) + p_m(x), \qquad (26)$$

where $g$ is a given univariate so-called *radial function*, and $p_m \in \mathbb{P}_m^k$. The coefficients of $s$ are determined by the interpolation condition (2) and the additional requirement that

$$\sum_{i=1}^{N} \alpha_i q(x_i) = 0 \qquad (27)$$

for all polynomials $q \in \mathbb{P}_m^k$. Obviously, if $y_i = p(x_i)$, $i = 1, 2, \cdots, N$ for some polynomial $p \in \mathbb{P}_m^k$, then the choice $\alpha_i = 0$, $i = 1, 2, \cdots, N$ and $p_m = p$ will satisfy all requirements. Thus, radial interpolants have degree of precision $m$.

Recent discussions of radial schemes can be found in [35,57,62]. Micchelli's paper [57] establishes, in particular, that for many radial schemes, including those described here, the interpolant exists and is unique for all data sets (provided only that the interpolation problem with $\mathbb{P}_m^k$ as interpolation space has at most one solution for all sets of function values). Remarkably, this fact was established only after Multiquadrics had been used with great success for fifteen years. Dyn and her co-workers in [35] and some of the references listed there develop particular radial schemes and numerical techniques to deal with the large and ill-conditioned linear system defining the interpolants.

The following subsections describe two specific choices of the radial function $g$.

### 4.2.1. Hardy Multiquadrics

These interpolants are defined by

$$g(t) = (h^2 + t^2)^\alpha, \quad \alpha = \pm\frac{1}{2}, \quad h > 0, \quad m = 0, \qquad (28)$$

and were first proposed by Hardy [44] in 1971. The parameter $h$ is at the user's disposal and its best choice is related to the distance between data points. Multiquadrics constitute one of the most successful and widely used general purpose interpolants for multivariate data. Until recently, that success was based entirely on numerical experiments. Further insight into the effectiveness of multiquadrics was gained by Buhmann [28,29], and Jackson [47] who study their approximation properties.

### 4.2.2. Duchon Thin Plate Splines

These interpolants were originally introduced by Duchon [34] for the case $k = 2$ as solutions of the variational problem

$$I_\mu s = \int_{\mathbb{R}^k} \|D^\mu(s)\|^2 \mathrm{d}x = \min, \tag{29}$$

where

$$D^\mu = \left( \frac{\partial^\mu}{\partial \xi_{i_1} \partial \xi_{i_2} \cdots \partial \xi_{i_\mu}} : \quad (i_1, i_2, \cdots, i_\mu) \in [1, d]^\mu \right), \quad \mu = m + 1 \tag{30}$$

over all admissible functions, subject to the interpolation conditions (2). In the special case $\mu = k = 2$,

$$I_2 s = \int_{\mathbb{R}^2} \left( s_{\xi_1 \xi_1}^2 + 2 s_{\xi_1 \xi_2}^2 + s_{\xi_2 \xi_2}^2 \right) \mathrm{d}\xi_1 \mathrm{d}\xi_2 \tag{31}$$

and the functional $I_2$ measures the strain energy in a clamped elastic plate, giving rise to the name *thin plate spline*.

The solution of the minimization problem (29) are radial interpolants, called *surface splines*, with

$$g(t) = \begin{cases} t^{(2\mu - k)} \log t, & \text{if } k \text{ is even} \\ t^{(2\mu - k)}, & \text{if } k \text{ is odd.} \end{cases} \tag{32}$$

## §5. Natural Neighbor Interpolation

This scheme was introduced by Sibson [77]. It is based on the *Dirichlet* (or *Thiessen* or *Voronoi*) *Tessellation* of $\Omega$. This is the collection of *tiles* of the form

$$\tau_i = \left\{ x \in \mathbb{R}^k : \|x - x_i\| \le \|x - x_j\|, \quad \forall j = 1, 2, \cdots, N \right\} \cap \Omega. \tag{33}$$

Obviously,

$$\Omega = \bigcup_{i=1}^N \tau_i, \tag{34}$$

and the tiles are disjoint except for parts of their boundaries.

We assume that the domain $\Omega \subset \mathbb{R}^k$ has finite volume. In order to evaluate the interpolant at a point $x \in \Omega$ we can think of adding $x$ to the set of data sites and carving its tile from the tiles of neighboring data sites. Thus, we let

$$\tau(x) = \left\{ z \in \mathbb{R}^k : \|z - x\| \le \|z - x_j\|, \quad \forall j = 1, 2, \cdots, N \right\}, \tag{35}$$

$$\tau_i(x) = \tau(x) \cap \tau_i \tag{36}$$

and

$$v(\tau) = \text{volume } (\tau). \tag{37}$$

Sibson's natural neighbor interpolant is then defined as

$$s(x) = \frac{\displaystyle\sum_{i=1}^{N} \lambda_i(x)\|x - x_i\|^{-1}\xi_i(x)}{\displaystyle\sum_{i=1}^{N} \lambda_i(x)\|x - x_i\|^{-1}}, \tag{38}$$

where

$$\xi_i(x) = f(x_i) + \nabla f(x_i)^T (x - x_i)$$
$$\lambda_i(x) = \frac{v\big(\tau_i(x)\big)}{v\big(\tau(x)\big)}. \tag{39}$$

Note that if we replace $\lambda_i(x)$ by $\|x - x_i\|^{-1}$, we obtain a linearly precise version of Shepard's method. However, $\lambda_i(x) \neq 0$ only for points close to $x$, which causes the scheme to be local. As for Shepard's method, we have to define $s(x_i) = y_i$ explicitly. The natural neighbor interpolant has some remarkable properties:

1. it has linear precision. In fact it also reproduces *spherical quadratics* (*i.e.*, quadratic functions whose matrix of second derivatives is a multiple of the identity matrix);
2. it is local;
3. in the special case $k = 1$ the function $s$ is piecewise cubic;
4. $s \in C^1(\Omega)$;
5. the value $s(x)$ depends continuously on the data sites $x_i$.

The proof of the last two properties is involved. Obviously, in order to construct the interpolant (38), gradient values have to be supplied. Sibson's paper describes a scheme in the spirit of natural neighbor interpolation that generates derivative values from given function values.

## §6. k-dimensional Triangulations

Many bivariate interpolation schemes are based on triangulations of the data set, and it is natural to use the same ideas in more than two variables. Let $\mathcal{T} = \{t_i : i = 1, 2, \cdots, T\}$ be a set of non-degenerate simplices, and let $\Omega = \bigcup_{i=1}^{T} t_i$. It is useful to allow for the possibility that $\Omega$ is not convex. The following definition is a slight variation of the definition in [52] (where $\Omega$ is the convex hull of the data sites). Denote the set of data sites by $\mathcal{X} = \{x_i : i = 1, 2, \cdots, N\}$. Then the set $\mathcal{T}$ is a *triangulation* of $\mathcal{X}$ if the following conditions are satisfied:

1. all vertices of each simplex are members of $\mathcal{X}$
2. the interiors of the simplices are pairwise disjoint

3. each facet of a simplex is either on the boundary of $\Omega$ or else is a common facet of exactly two simplices

4. each simplex contains no points of $\mathcal{X}$ other than its vertices

5. $\Omega$ is homeomorphic to $[0,1]^k$.

The last of the above conditions rules out degenerate triangulations consisting, for example, of two tetrahedra touching in just one vertex or edge.

There are some significant differences between bivariate and higher dimensional triangulations. These include for example:

1. Specification of $\mathcal{X}$ and $\Omega$ does not determine the number of simplices. Counterexamples are given in [19] and [52].

2. If $k > 3$, possible triangulations may not be distinguishable by information about connectivity of points; *i.e.*, by the specification of edges. For examples, see [52].

3. A standard technique for building *2-dimensional* triangulations consists of adding one triangle at a time, maintaining at each stage a valid triangulation. For some triangulations, this is not possible if $k > 2$. A simple counterexample (consisting of 14 points and 41 tetrahedra) is given in [69]. A more complicated one for many different triangulations of a particular domain is given in [24] and also described in [70], p. 17. If the construction is possible, the triangulation is said to be *shellable*.

Many criteria have been proposed for selecting particular *2-dimensional* triangulations. Perhaps the easiest to generalize is that of the *Delaunay triangulation*. This is the dual of the Thiessen tessellation: two points are connected if their tiles share a line segment. An equivalent requirement is that for any two neighboring triangles the circumcircle of one triangle does not contain the opposite vertex of the other triangle. This is the *local circle test*. It implies the stronger *global circle test*: the circumcircle of any triangle in the triangulation does not contain any other data site at all. (We ignore special cases where four or more points lie on the circumference of a circle.) Lawson [52] generalizes these concepts. He shows:

1. a set of $k+2$ points in $\mathbb{R}^k$ may be triangulated in at most 2 different ways;

2. the (local) sphere test (the obvious generalization of the local circle test) selects a preferred one of these two triangulations;

3. a triangulation that satisfies the local sphere test also satisfies the global sphere test;

4. a triangulation satisfying the global sphere test is dual to the Thiessen tessellation; *i.e.*, the tiles of two points connected by an edge share a $k-1$ dimensional boundary polygon (again we consider only the generic case).

Pascal codes for constructing $k$-dimensional triangulations are given in [45]. They contain facilities for forcing certain facets to be contained in the triangulation. This option can be used e.g., to generate non-convexities, holes, and cavities.

We now give a precise definition of the localness of triangulation-based schemes that is suitable for the purposes of this paper. More specifically, we generalize the term *minimally supported* defined in [13] for triangular schemes.

The *star* of a $\kappa$-face $\varphi$ is the union of all simplices that contain $\varphi$. A function $s$ defined on a $k$-dimensional triangulation is said to be *minimally supported* if there is a $\kappa$-face $\varphi$ in the triangulation such that the support of $s$ is contained in the star of $\varphi$. A linear space $S(\Omega)$ is *minimally supported* if it has a basis consisting of minimally supported functions. An interpolation scheme is *minimally supported* if the interpolation space $S$ is minimally supported.

Note that in spite of the term's negative connotation, it is highly desirable for a space or a scheme to be minimally supported.

If $S \subset C(\Omega)$ contains all constant functions, then for any face $\varphi$ there must be a function $s \in S$ whose support comprises all simplices containing $\varphi$. Otherwise, all functions $s \in S$ would have to vanish on $\varphi$. This fact gave rise to the term *minimally* supported. It is reasonable to consider a minimally supported scheme to be local. On the other hand, a scheme might also be called *local* without being minimally supported. It is, however, no easy task to find a reasonable more general definition of the word *local*. For example, in the case of 2-dimensional triangulations an easy fallacy would be to define a scheme to be local if for each basis function $w$ there exists a vertex $V$ such that the support of $w$ consists of the union of the stars of all vertices contained in the star of $V$. However, simple examples show that such a support set may not even be simply connected, which renders the utility of the definition doubtful. The problem is compounded for triangulations of dimension greater than two.

## §7. Tetrahedral Schemes

In this chapter, we consider schemes that have been specifically designed for interpolants on a *three-dimensional triangulation*. Interpolants that apply to triangulations of a general dimension are described in the next chapter.

The original motivation for defining interpolants piecewise on tetrahedra is the prospect of obtaining local schemes. Indeed, all schemes described in this chapter are minimally supported. However, with the increasing availability of *parallel processing*, tetrahedral (and, more generally, simplicial) schemes are likely to become even more attractive since individual simplices can be processed independently and simultaneously!

### 7.1. Polynomial Schemes

It is natural to consider the use of finite elements as an interpolant, particularly since there is a large and sophisticated machinery available for handling them. If a piecewise defined interpolant is to be polynomial on each tetrahedron and globally differentiable, then ([86]) its polynomial degree must be at least 9. Rescorla [67] gives an explicit description of such a scheme. It requires 220 (*i.e.*, the dimension of the space of trivariate nonic polynomials) data per tetrahedron. These include derivatives through fourth order at the vertices of the tetrahedron, as well as function and derivative values at various points on the faces and the centroid of the tetrahedron. The degree of precision of the scheme is nine. Rescorla's approach consists of constructing a basis of $\mathbb{P}_9^3$ (in terms of barycentric coordinates) that renders triangular the Vandermonde matrix associated with the data.

In the bivariate case, the minimal polynomial degree for a piecewise polynomial $C^1$ scheme is five. A well-known technique of reducing that degree, as well as the degree of the derivative values required as data, is to subdivide the triangle into subtriangles. Splitting a triangle about its centroid into three subtriangles and letting the polynomial degree be 3 gives rise to the widely used Clough-Tocher scheme [3,80], which requires only first order derivative data.

A similar approach to the trivariate problem is taken in [3]. The tetrahedron is split about its centroid into 4 subtetrahedra, the interpolant is *quintic* on each subtetrahedron, and the degree of the required derivative data is 2 (as opposed to 4 required for the nonic polynomial finite element). The scheme is such that perpendicular first order cross-boundary derivatives across a face of the tetrahedron have only quadratic precision. The overall degree of precision is therefore only cubic. A peculiarity of the scheme is that four of its coefficients are not needed for either interpolation or forcing global differentiability, and have to be *condensed*; *i.e.*, conditions have to be made up that eliminate them. The interpolant is given in Bernstein-Bézier Form. The MRC report [4] lists explicit expressions for the coefficients of the scheme.

An alternative approach is described in [85]. The bivariate Powell-Sabin split [63] is applied to each facet of the tetrahedron and all points obtained in this manner on the boundary of the tetrahedron are connected to a suitably chosen interior point. The interior points chosen on the facets need not be the centroids. The interpolant is *quadratic* on each of the resulting 24 subtetrahedra. (This low polynomial degree was originally motivated by the ease of contouring quadratic functions.) In order for the overall interpolant to be globally differentiable on a 3-dimensional triangulation, the interior points of the facets and the tetrahedra must satisfy certain geometric constraints. It is an open question whether the constraints can be satisfied in general. In the special case that the points about which edges, facets, and tetrahedra are split can be chosen to be the circumcenters of the corresponding faces, the constraints are satisfied. However, the circumcenters may not be interior points of their face. Worsey and Piper give a criterion for a triangulation to be such that all circumcenters are strictly interior.

## 7.2. Rational Schemes

Piecewise polynomial functions are usually preferred for applications because they are particularly easy to evaluate, differentiate, and integrate. However, they are *not* particularly easy to piece together smoothly. A great deal of flexibility can be gained by using *rational* functions.

A particularly serviceable class of basic interpolation operators on triangles and tetrahedra are *Barnhill-Birkhoff-Gordon (BBG)* projectors [2,19]. Here we discuss their application to a tetrahedron $t$. We denote the *edges* of $t$

by

$$e_{ij} = V_j - V_i, \quad i,j \in \{1,2,3,4\}, \quad i \neq j, \tag{40}$$

where the $V_j$ are the vertices of $t$. There is a BBG projector associated with each edge. For simplicity of notation, we describe only the projector associated with $e_{12}$. For a general point $x \in t$ we consider the line parallel to $e_{12}$ through $x$. That line intersects the facet $b_1 = 0$ in a point $X_1$ and the facet $b_2 = 0$ in a point $X_2$. Then we interpolate to function and derivative values at $X_1$ and $X_2$ and evaluate the so obtained *univariate* interpolant at $x$. Specifically, we define

$$
\begin{aligned}
P_{12}f = \ & h_0\left(\frac{b_2}{b_1 + b_2}\right)f(X_2) \\
&+ h_1\left(\frac{b_2}{b_1 + b_2}\right)f(X_1) \\
&+ \bar{h}_0\left(\frac{b_2}{b_1 + b_2}\right)(b_1 + b_2)\frac{\partial f}{\partial e_{12}}(X_2) \\
&+ \bar{h}_1\left(\frac{b_2}{b_1 + b_2}\right)(b_1 + b_2)\frac{\partial f}{\partial e_{12}}(X_1),
\end{aligned}
\tag{41}
$$

where

$$X_1 = (b_1 + b_2)V_2 + b_3 V_3 + b_4 V_4, \tag{42}$$

$$X_2 = (b_1 + b_2)V_1 + b_3 V_3 + b_4 V_4, \tag{43}$$

$$h_i, \ \bar{h}_i \in \mathbb{P}_3^1, \quad i \in \{0, 1\} \tag{44}$$

$$h_i(j) = \delta_{ij}, \ h_i'(j) = 0, \quad \bar{h}_i(j) = 0, \ \bar{h}_i'(j) = \delta_{ij}, \quad i, j \in \{0, 1\} \tag{45}$$

and the barycentric coordinates $b_i$ are defined in (12). The *directional derivatives* in (41) are defined for general directions $e \in \mathbb{R}^k$ by

$$\frac{\partial f}{\partial e}(x) = \frac{\mathrm{d}}{\mathrm{d}t}f(x + te)\Big|_{t=0}. \tag{46}$$

Note that these are *unnormalized* derivatives. Indeed, in dealing with a tetrahedron, the notion of *unit* length is not as appropriate as the concept of an edge providing a suitable length scale. If the gradient of the function $f$ is defined, then

$$\frac{\partial f}{\partial e}(x) = \nabla f(x) \circ e. \tag{47}$$

(Note that there is no conceptual difficulty in differentiating in the direction of the zero vector, $\partial f/\partial 0 = 0$.) Particularly simple are the edge derivatives of the barycentric coordinates:

$$\frac{\partial b_i}{\partial e_{jk}} = \delta_{ik} - \delta_{ij}. \tag{48}$$

Using these facts, it is easy to verify that

$$b_1 = 0 \text{ or } b_2 = 0 \quad \Longrightarrow \quad P_{12}f(x) = f(x) \text{ and } DP_{12}f(x) = Df(x), \quad (49)$$

where $D$ denotes any first order directional derivative. Thus $P_{12}f$ interpolates to function values and first order derivatives *everywhere* on the two facets not containing $e_{12}$. It is a *transfinite* interpolant.

The data required for a transfinite interpolant will not usually be available. However, the transfinite data are required on a *lower dimensional* face of the tetrahedron and can be *replaced* with a lower dimensional interpolant requiring lower dimensional data. This process is called *discretization*. For example, in (41) one might replace $f(X_1)$ by its linear interpolant

$$f\big((b_1 + b_2)V_2 + b_3V_3 + b_4V_4\big) \longleftarrow (b_1 + b_2)f(V_2) + b_3f(V_3) + b_4f(V_4). \quad (50)$$

Of course, in discretizing a transfinite interpolant one has to incorporate requirements such as global smoothness or a certain degree of polynomial precision. The above simple linear discretization would preclude any degree of precision greater than 1.

The operator $P_{12}$ discussed so far yields an interpolant on only two facets of the tetrahedron. In order to obtain an interpolant on the entire tetrahedron one has to combine several operators. This can be done in several ways. We discuss two of them, each leading to minimally supported discrete $C^1$ schemes.

**1. Boolean sums.** In [19], Barnhill and Little propose the Boolean sum

$$Qf = P_{12} \oplus P_{34}f. \quad (51)$$

The resulting scheme requires some second order derivative values as data and implies the *(twist) compatibility condition*

$$\frac{\partial^2 f}{\partial e_{12}\partial e_{34}}(x) = \frac{\partial^2 f}{\partial e_{34}\partial e_{12}}(x), \quad \forall x \in e_{13} \cup e_{14} \cup e_{23} \cup e_{24}. \quad (52)$$

This condition would be satisfied if we were actually given a sufficiently smooth primitive function $f$, but $f$ is used only as a conceptual vehicle towards obtaining a final discrete interpolant. The discretizations on two different facets sharing an edge will usually lead to a violation of the compatibility condition along the edge. However, this drawback can be overcome by adding a sophisticated rational correction term. The compatibility correction and the discretization are discussed at length in [19].

**2. Convex Combinations.** In [2], the transfinite interpolant

$$Sf = a_{12}P_{12}f + a_{34}P_{34}f \quad (53)$$

is proposed, where

$$a_{12} = \frac{b_3^2 b_4^2}{b_1^2 b_2^2 + b_3^2 b_4^2}, \quad a_{34} = 1 - a_{12}. \tag{54}$$

The scheme does not necessitate compatibility corrections, and can be discretized to result in a scheme requiring only function and gradient values at the vertices and having quadratic precision. Note that in (53) *discontinuous* blending functions $a_{12}$ and $a_{34}$ are used to yield a globally *differentiable* interpolant.

BBG projectors can be defined for higher degrees of smoothness than $C^1$. In [11] a *bivariate* $C^2$ scheme based on the Boolean sum of three BBG projectors is derived and discretized. In the trivariate case, however, the algebraic manipulations and the codes become too cumbersome to be useful [2,7]. In Section 8.2 an alternative technique for obtaining schemes of higher dimension and higher degrees of smoothness is described.

## §8. Simplicial Schemes

In this chapter, we discuss methods that are defined on $k$-dimensional triangulations of the data set. As for tetrahedral schemes, all of the schemes are minimally supported.

### 8.1. Polynomial Schemes

Finite element type piecewise polynomial schemes can be defined recursively on simplices of a general dimension [50]. The necessary polynomial degree $n$ increases exponentially with $k$. As in the bivariate and trivariate case, $n$ can be decreased by subdividing each simplex.

The latter approach is taken by Worsey and Farin [84] who propose a scheme with several remarkable properties: it is piecewise cubic, applicable to any $k$-dimensional triangulation, requires only function and first order derivative values, and has cubic precision. The key to obtaining the scheme is a particular triangulation of a $k$-simplex. More generally, the triangulation of a $\kappa$-simplex $\varphi$ ($\kappa \le k$) is defined recursively as follows:

1. If $\kappa = 1$, $\varphi$ is not split (in this case, $\varphi$ is an edge).
2. If $\kappa > 1$ then first all faces of $\varphi$ are split. Then an interior point $P$ of $\varphi$ is chosen and connected by a line segment to all boundary points of $\varphi$ and all previously chosen interior points on the faces of $\varphi$.

Thus, a $k$-simplex is split into $(k+1)!/2$ subsimplices. In the case $k = 2$ one obtains the Clough-Tocher split, except that the interior point need not be the centroid. If $k > 2$, the choice of the interior points of the various simplices and faces must satisfy the following geometric requirements:

1. Common faces between neighboring simplices are split identically on each simplex.

2. When splitting any two simplices sharing a facet in the triangulation, the
interior points chosen in each must be collinear with the interior point
chosen to split the common face.

Worsey and Farin [84] show that these objectives can indeed be accomplished. On the resulting split they construct their interpolant as a generalization of the bivariate Clough-Tocher split [80].

## 8.2. Rational Schemes

The most general discrete simplicial interpolation schemes are *perpendicular interpolants* described in [7]. The resulting interpolants are globally $m$ times differentiable and have polynomial degree of precision $m$ or $m + 1$, depending on the variant that is used. The parameter $m \geq 0$ can be chosen to suit the application. The only data requirements are function values and derivatives through $m$-th order at the vertices of the $k$-dimensional triangulation. Because of their intrinsic interest, and because their design illustrates several useful principles, we will discuss them in some detail.

A major difficulty in designing smooth local simplicial schemes is to enforce a certain degree of global differentiability without making reference to the geometry of neighboring simplices (otherwise the scheme would not be local). One therefore typically considers derivatives in directions *perpendicular* to a facet and requires that those derivatives are determined *uniquely* by the data given on the facet. Since neighboring simplices share the facet, the derivatives on the individual simplices are determined identically and agree on that facet; *i.e.*, they are continuous. The reason for choosing a perpendicular cross-direction is because it must be across the boundary and it must be chosen identically on neighboring simplices without knowledge of the geometric configuration of those simplices. This strategy is also used regularly in the finite element technique.

However, directions perpendicular to facets are intrinsically arbitrary as far as the geometry of the local simplex is concerned. A much more natural set of directions is given by the edges of the simplex. Thus, many simplicial interpolation schemes (such as the BBG schemes discussed above) are designed in terms of derivatives in the direction of edges, and global smoothness is enforced almost as an afterthought by expressing perpendicular cross-boundary derivatives in terms of edge derivatives. This makes the schemes exceedingly unwieldy, and is the sole reason that, e.g., the rational tetrahedral $C^1$ scheme [2] could not be modified to obtain a $C^2$ scheme.

The key idea in [7] is to incorporate perpendicular cross-boundary derivatives *directly*. Let $\mathcal{S}$ be the simplex in question, and let $F$ be a facet of $\mathcal{S}$. We think of all faces of $\mathcal{S}$ as embedded in low dimensional affine subspaces, so that any line can intersect a face even though the line may not intersect the simplex $\mathcal{S}$ itself. The *anchor* of $F$ is that facet other than $F$ that forms the smallest angle with $F$. With a point $x$ and the facet $F$ we associate the straight line through $x$ perpendicular to $F$. This is the *line of fixation* of $x$ with respect to $F$. $F$ is also called the *base face* of the line of fixation. The point $B_F(x)$ where the line of fixation intersects its base face is the base point of $x$ and the point $A_F(x)$ where it intersects the anchor is the *top point* of $x$ (all with respect to the base face). Note that the base point as well as the top point may lie outside the simplex $\mathcal{S}$.

Now, for any given point $x$, we obtain the value of the interpolant $s(x)$ by interpolating along each line of fixation through $x$ to function values and derivative values through $m$-th order perpendicularly to the base face at the base point. We may also interpolate to the function value at the top point. The $k+1$ values so obtained (one for each facet of $S$) are then blended together by forming a suitable convex combination. The resulting scheme is *transfinite*. It is discretized by replacing the transfinite data on faces of the simplex by lower-dimensional perpendicular interpolants. The scheme is thus defined recursively. Derivatives are interpolated to by less smooth interpolants. For the special case that a continuous function is required, we use linear interpolation, and for the special case that the dimension of the face is 1, we use polynomial Hermite interpolation of the appropriate degree.

For simplicity, we illustrate only the *unanchored* case where no interpolation takes place at the anchor. The interpolants are defined by

$$
P_{\mathcal{S}}^m(f)(x) = \begin{cases} \displaystyle\sum_{\mathcal{F}} c_{\mathcal{F}}^m(x) G_{\mathcal{F}}^m(f)(x), & \text{if } b_\mu(x) \neq 0, \quad \forall \mu = 1, \cdots, k+1 \\ P_{\mathcal{F}}^m(f)(x), & \text{if } x \in \text{ some face } \mathcal{F}. \end{cases}
\tag{55}
$$

Here, the summation is over all facets $\mathcal{F}$ of the simplex $\mathcal{S}$. For the definition of the blending functions $c_{\mathcal{F}}^m(x)$ we let $i$ be defined by $\mathcal{F} = \{x : b_i(x) = 0\}$ and let

$$
c_{\mathcal{F}}^m(x) = \frac{\displaystyle\prod_{r \neq i} b_r^{\eta(m)}}{\displaystyle\sum_{j=1}^{k+1} \prod_{r \neq j} b_r^{\eta(m)}},
\tag{56}
$$

where

$$
\eta(m) = \begin{cases} m+2, & \text{if } m \text{ is even,} \\ m+1, & \text{if } m \text{ is odd.} \end{cases}
\tag{57}
$$

Thus, the exponent in the blending functions is always even. This is required to maintain a convex combination, since some extrapolation may be necessary, leading to negative barycentric coordinates.

The operators $G_{\mathcal{F}}^m$ produce Taylor interpolants to derivatives perpendicular to the base face $\mathcal{F}$. They are defined by

$$
G_{\mathcal{F}}^m(f)(x) = \sum_{\nu=0}^m \frac{b_i^\nu}{\nu!} P_{\mathcal{F}}^{m-\nu} \left( \frac{\partial^\nu f}{\partial s_{\mathcal{F}}^\nu} \right) (B_{\mathcal{F}}(x)),
\tag{58}
$$

where $(B_{\mathcal{F}}(x))$ is the base point of the line of fixation with respect to $\mathcal{F}$ through $x$, and $s_{\mathcal{F}} = V_i - B_{\mathcal{F}}(V_i)$. Note that $G_{\mathcal{F}}^m$ is defined in terms of lower dimensional perpendicular interpolants. If the operators $P_{\mathcal{F}}^{m-\nu}$ were replaced by the appropriate identity operator, then a transfinite scheme (interpolating everywhere on the boundary of $\mathcal{F}$) would emerge. To complete the recursion, we also define:

$$P_{\mathcal{S}}^0(f)\left(\sum_{i=1}^{k+1} b_i V_i\right) = \sum_{i=1}^{k+1} b_i f(V_i), \tag{59}$$

$$\dim(\mathcal{S}) = 0 \quad\Longrightarrow\quad P_{\mathcal{S}}^m(f)(x) = f(V) \quad (\text{since } \mathcal{S} = \{V\}) \tag{60}$$

and

$$\dim(\mathcal{S}) = 1 \quad\Longrightarrow\quad P_{\mathcal{S}}^m(f)(tV_2 + (1-t)V_1) =$$

$$= \sum_{j=0}^{m}\left[h_{0,j}^m(t)\frac{\partial^j f}{\partial(V_2 - V_1)}(V_1) + h_{1,j}^m(t)\frac{\partial^j f}{\partial(V_2 - V_1)}(V_2)\right], \tag{61}$$

where the $h_{i,j}^m$ are cardinal polynomials of degree $2m+1$ defined uniquely by the properties

$$\left.\frac{\partial h_{i,s}^m(t)}{\partial x^\mu}\right|_{t=k} = \delta_{s\mu}\delta_{ik}, \tag{62}$$

$s, \mu \in \{0, 1, \cdots, m\}$, $i, k \in \{0, 1\}$.

See [7] for a more thorough discussion of perpendicular interpolants, including implementational details for $k \in \{2, 3\}$ and numerical examples.

### 8.3. A Transfinite Scheme

In [43], Gregory describes a transfinite simplicial scheme of arbitrary dimension $k$ and arbitrary degree of smoothness $m$. The scheme is a convex combination of Boolean sums of Taylor type operators. It requires derivative data up to order $m^k$ everywhere on the boundary of the simplex (and higher degree derivative data on lower dimensional faces). Its degree of precision is $k(m+1) - 1$. A remarkable aspect of the scheme is that the Taylor operators yield interpolants that are polynomial along lines parallel to certain edges, and the blending functions can be chosen to be polynomial. Gregory also describes a rational alternative of the polynomial blending functions. (However, a transfinite scheme cannot be classified as rational or polynomial since its boundary data may render the interpolant non-rational.) Because of its generality, the scheme is a natural candidate for discretization, particularly for the case $m = 1$.

### §9. Multivariate Splines

Perhaps the conceptually simplest approach to designing a multivariate interpolant is to generalize the concept of a *univariate spline*. Thus, we assume that $\Omega \subset \mathbb{R}^k$ has been tessellated by subregions $t_i$, $i = 1, 2, \cdots, T$, and define

$$S_d^r(\Omega) = \left\{s \in C^r(\Omega) : s|_{t_i} \in \mathbb{P}_d^k \quad \forall i = 1, 2, \cdots, k\right\}. \tag{63}$$

The elements of $S_d^r(\Omega)$ are $k$-variate splines (of polynomial degree $d$ and degree of smoothness $r$). We are of course particularly interested in the case that the subregions $t_i$ form a $k$-dimensional triangulation. The hope in using $S_d^r(\Omega)$ instead of a finite element space, say, would be the ability to decrease the local complexity of a scheme (e.g., lower its polynomial degree), in exchange for the need to determine the parameters of the interpolant globally.

However, the global structure of multivariate splines turns out to be extremely rich and complicated, and is at present only poorly understood. Even fundamental issues like the dimension and basis of spline spaces $S_d^r$ have not been resolved in general, yet similar questions in the univariate case can be answered trivially. One of the major differences to the univariate case is that the dimension of $S_d^r$ depends not just on the way in which simplices are connected, but also on the precise location of the data sites. Knowledge of *bivariate* splines is substantial and rapidly expanding. The subject was pioneered by Strang, [79], Morgan and Scott [54], and Schumaker [67,68]. The state of the art (as of this writing) is described in [14] and [46], and the references listed there.

A few results for trivariate splines are given in [8]. Following is a summary and an update: Suppose for the moment that the 3-dimensional triangulation is shellable and has been built by adding one tetrahedron at a time, maintaining at each step a valid triangulation. Thus, at each step we join the new tetrahedron to the developing triangulation at precisely 1,2, or 3 triangular facets. Let $a_i$, $i = 1, 2, 3$ denote the *number of times* that we joined at precisely $i$ facets. The values of $a_i$ are crucial in expressing dimensions. They can be generalized to non-shellable triangulations by the definition

$$a_1 = N - 4, \quad a_3 = I, \quad \text{and} \quad a_2 = T - 1 - a_1 - a_3, \tag{64}$$

where $T$ is the total number of tetrahedra and $I$ is the number of interior vertices.

Because of the paucity of trivariate results we deviate briefly from our plan of considering only differentiable functions. It can be shown quite easily, using the Bernstein-Bézier form of a polynomial, that

$$\dim S_d^0 = \binom{d+3}{3} + \binom{d+2}{3}a_1 + \binom{d+1}{3}a_2 + \binom{d}{3}a_3, \tag{65}$$

where

$$\binom{m}{n} = 0 \quad \text{if} \quad n > m \tag{66}$$

and $d \geq 1$. Let

$$P_d^r = \left\{ s \in S_d^0 : s \text{ is } r \text{ times differentiable at the vertices } x_i \right\}. \tag{67}$$

Then, for $d \geq 2r + 1$,

$$\dim P_d^r = \rho_0 + \sum_{i=1}^{3} \rho_i a_i, \tag{68}$$

where

$$\rho_0 = \dim \mathbb{P}_d^3 = \binom{d+3}{3}, \tag{69}$$

$$\rho_1 = \binom{d+2}{3} - 3\binom{r+2}{3}, \tag{70}$$

$$\rho_2 = \binom{d+1}{3} - 2\binom{r+1}{3} - 2\binom{r+2}{3}, \tag{71}$$

and

$$\rho_3 = \binom{d}{3} - \binom{r}{3} - 3\binom{r+1}{3}. \tag{72}$$

For $d \geq 3$

$$\dim S_3^1 \geq \max\left\{\rho_0, \rho_0 + \sum_{i=1}^{3} \tau_i a_i\right\}, \tag{73}$$

where

$$\tau_1 = \big(d(d^2 - 1)\big)/6, \tag{74}$$

$$\tau_2 = \big(d(d^2 - 6d + 5)\big)/6, \tag{75}$$

and

$$\tau_3 = (d^3 - 12d^2 + 29d - 18)/6. \tag{76}$$

The formulas in [8] also contain a term accounting for *singular edges* that may be incorrect if several singular edges emanate from one point. An analogous formula is given in [8] for the case $r = 2$.

The lower bound (73) gives the exact dimension in all cases where the dimension has been calculated explicitly [9], at least for the generic case. Note, however, that the lower bound is given as the maximum of $\rho_0 = \dim \mathbb{P}_d^3$ and another term $B$, say. The reason is that for some 3-dimensional triangulations $B$ may actually be less than $\rho_0$, whereas trivially $\dim S_d^1 \geq \dim \mathbb{P}_d^3 = \rho_0$. In [8] there is an example of a (large) triangulation where $B$ becomes negative if $r \in \{3, 4\}$.

No useful *upper bounds* are known (excluding trivial ones like $\dim S_d^r \leq \dim P_d^r$). Other wide open questions include the existence of local bases, and the ability to solve the interpolation problem (2).

Specific trivariate examples where the dimensions change with the geometry of the underlying triangulation are given in [9]. In addition, the author distributes periodically a *Multivariate Spline Newsletter* [10] that describes recent developments in the theory of multivariate splines, and lists further examples of geometric degeneracies.

The traditional approach to utilizing multivariate splines is to employ suitable subspaces of $S_d^r$. Finite elements constitute an extreme example where the polynomial degree is high, and the subspaces allow the construction of a minimally supported basis. A recently developed intermediate set of subspaces are those of *supersplines* [30,46] with minimally supported bases called *vertex splines*. These can be defined in any number of variables. A *superspline* is a spline $s \in S_d^r$ that is a specified number $R \geq r$ times differentiable at every vertex of the tessellation. For example, the finite element described in Section 7.1, applied to every tetrahedron of a triangulation, defines a spline in $s \in S_d^1$. Since it is four times differentable at each vertex, it is also a superspline with $R = 4$. Moreover, since it has nonic precision, every superspline in $S_9^1$ with $R = 4$ can be defined locally by the finite element. A $\kappa$-*vertex spline* $v$ (where $\kappa < k$) is a minimally supported superspline whose support is the star of a $\kappa$-face. Of particular interest for applications are spaces spanned by vertex splines. The finite element in Section 7.1 can be used to construct $\kappa$-vertex splines for $\kappa = 0, 1, 2$. Chui and Lai [30] also introduce supersplines and vertex splines defined on a tessellation comprised of a mixture of simplices and parallelepipeds.

## §10. Transfinite Hypercubal Methods

Occasionally there are applications in which transfinite schemes are appropriate. Examples include situations where a discretizing tool is moved across a surface, creating dense data along sparsely placed lines. We consider the case where the lines may be assumed to form a rectangular mesh. It is then reasonable to design schemes based on the assumption that functional data are given *everywhere* on the boundary of the tessellating rectangles. The natural generalization of a rectangle to higher dimension is a *hypercube* which can be scaled and represented by a cube $[0, 1]^k$. For the case $k = 2$, several transfinite schemes on rectangles have been proposed. In [23], Barnhill and Worsey generalize this concept of a rectangular $C^1$ transfinite patch to an arbitrary number $k \geq 2$ variables. The difficulty in designing such schemes is to satisfy compatibility requirements on mixed partial derivatives. This is accomplished by incorporating suitable rational correction terms. The resulting schemes can be discretized if desired. In [83], Worsey describes a transfinite hypercubal $C^2$ scheme.

## §11. Derivative Generation

It seems inevitable that in order to obtain an interpolant that is both local and smooth one has to supply derivative data. Typically, such data are not part of the interpolation problem and have to be made up from existing functional data. This process is usually referred as *derivative estimation*, but this is probably a misnomer. The objective is *not* to estimate existing but unknown values of derivatives. Instead, it is to generate values that will yield a *satisfactory interpolant*. Even if an underlying primitive function did exist it might be preferable to use derivative values that differ from the exact ones. (For example, a maximum error might be decreased by using the "wrong" derivative values.) Therefore, I prefer the term *derivative generation* rather than *derivative estimation*.

Most existing derivative generation schemes have been developed specifically for bivariate problems. However, most of the underlying ideas apply in more than two variables. It is desirable to generate derivative values locally in order to keep the overall scheme local. On the other hand, numerical experiments [40] suggest that global derivative generation schemes tend to yield better results. We now list a few specific local techniques:

1. Akima [1] discusses several versions of a gradient generation scheme that is based on averaging the normals defined by pairs of vectors connecting data points. Second derivatives can be obtained by applying the technique to gradient values.

2. Sibson [77] describes a specific scheme designed (for an arbitrary number of variables) in the spirit of his *natural neighbor* technique.

3. Stead [78] compares several techniques, including:
   — a Shepard-based method where, for each data point, Shepard's interpolant is computed for the six closest sites (excluding the data site itself), and differentiated at the data site.
   — a similar Hardy-multiquadric-based method where the interpolant is computed for twenty sites in a rectangular domain including the data site itself. That interpolant is then differentiated at the data site.
   — a weighted least squares approach where the gradients are obtained by differentiating a quadratic approximation to the data at the 10 closest sites plus the data site.
   — a similar linear least squares fit of nine points.
   — Little's method [8], which combines Shepard's method and triangulations.

On the basis of her experiments, Stead favors the multiquadric based generation technique.

All of the schemes described above have the significant advantage of being local. But they are also *ad hoc* schemes designed with a view to convenience and not towards desirable mathematical or physically meaningful properties. They may or may not perform well on specific problems, and choices must be based primarily on numerical experiments.

My own favorite approach is to select the interpolant from an affine space of many possible interpolants by requiring that a suitable functional be minimized. The *space* can be chosen conveniently to obtain interpolants with certain properties, such as being piecewise polynomial, easy to evaluate, or being of a structure that models behavior intrinsic in the physical problem (for example exponential decay). The *functional* can also be chosen to be meaningful in the context of the particular physical problem. For example, when building a ship by clamping metal plates to a framework, one might minimize the clamped elastic plate functional (31) over a space of multivariate splines or finite elements. The resulting interpolant can be used as such, or required derivative data can be obtained by differentiating and evaluating the interpolant. These data might then be exploited in the construction of a different, perhaps smoother, interpolant. The advantages of this technique are its flexibility, and its underlying physical motivation. Its severe disadvantage is that in its unmodified form the derivative generation scheme is global rather than local. Some bivariate implementations and numerical examples are given in [5] and [6].

## §12. Interpolation on the sphere and other surfaces

A special—but important and widely encountered—problem arises when the data sites lie on a 2-dimensional surface embedded in $\mathbb{R}^3$. Since we live on an approximately spherical planet, the most important instance of such a surface is a sphere. It is often unsatisfactory to project the surface, or different parts of it, into the plane. Instead, special methods have to be designed. Lawson [51], Renka [65], and Nielson and Ramaraj ([60] and [64]) independently propose schemes based on a triangulation of the surface of a sphere. In all of these schemes, the triangulations (by segments of great circles, rather than straight lines) are built by first constructing an initial triangulation and then swapping diagonals in convex quadrilaterals if required. Lawson's interpolant is the Clough-Tocher scheme [80]. His article also contains a detailed discussion of data structures, the triangulation procedure (yielding a generalization of the Delaunay triangulation), and a specific derivative generation scheme. Renka's scheme is a modification of his earlier planar scheme ([66] and [32]). His paper also contains algorithmic details. Nielson and Ramaraj use an interpolant based upon a minimal norm network (described for the planar case in [59]). Their paper contains several pictorial illustrations of their scheme. The surface can be rendered either as a shaded surface surrounding the sphere, or as a contour plot drawn on the sphere.

Wahba [81] describes an approach to *approximation* on the sphere that is based on *periodic* functions. Her technique can be specialized to interpolation. The paper also addresses the issues of noise in the data, smoothing splines, and cross-validation of results.

More general convex surfaces are considered by Barnhill *et al* ([20] and [21]). However, their main object of interest is the pressure on the wing of a particular aircraft. They propose a complex scheme, some of whose ingredients are: decomposition of the domain into two parts (the top and bottom of the wing), a multistage interpolation scheme yielding a bicubic map, Shepard's method, and Dirichlet tessellations.

## §13. Conclusions

The development of viable multivariate interpolation schemes is a rich and stimulating research area that is still in its infancy. The variety of problems requires a corresponding variety of techniques, schemes, and algorithms. Several techniques have been illustrated—or at least referenced—in this paper. These include, among others: tessellations of the domain; triangulations of the data sites; obtaining localness by expressing schemes solely in terms of data on a subdomain; using derivative data to increase the precision of a scheme, and to make it local; generating derivative data from functional data; Boolean sums; convex combinations; cardinal basis functions; blending partial schemes to obtain a complete one; the use of discontinuous ingredients to obtain smooth interpolants; transfinite schemes; discretization of transfinite schemes; the removal of compatibility conditions by adding rational correction terms; constructing high degree piecewise polynomial finite elements; constructing low degree finite elements on subdivided simplices; mollifying functions; interpolation to Taylor operators; recursion to obtain schemes on simplices of any dimension; judicious handling of perpendicular cross-boundary derivatives; radial functions; minimizing suitable linear functionals to select particular interpolants; the Bernstein-Bézier form of a (multivariate) polynomial. Naturally, there is a large number of sophisticated details to each of these techniques which could not be discussed in the given space.

We also encountered problems that do not arise in bivariate circumstances; for example, rendering difficulties, and the complexities of high-dimensional triangulations. The biggest difficulty in practical work has been the inability to adequately picture relevant phenomena. Whereas there is now a plethora of interpolation schemes for bivariate data, there exists only a handful of trivariate and higher-dimensional schemes, and in particular there is a paucity of algorithms.

One of the most significant phenomena in multivariate interpolation is that while there exist highly sophisticated, complex and powerful schemes with attractive properties such as localness and arbitrary precision, and yielding piecewise polynomial or rational interpolants, the schemes that are actually used by practitioners are mostly long known *ad hoc* schemes such as Shepard's method or Hardy multiquadrics. Without offense to these marvelous pioneering schemes, it seems there should be some promise and incentive in exploring simplex based schemes, particularly when considering the increasing availability of parallel processing. The reason why this opportunity has not been taken seems to be that the developers of complicated schemes, including this author, have failed to make the results of their work available as portable and well documented software. It is indeed unreasonable to expect a user—whose interests are in a field other than Mathematics—to spend the time and effort first to decipher the terse published description of a scheme and then program and debug it. On the other hand, the interests and abilities of the mathematicians who design their complicated schemes do not entice nor enable them to write the software themselves. What seems to be urgently required is the collaboration between a mathematician and a software engineer in producing widely usable software. This author would be interested in such collaboration.

Most schemes described here (and all of my own schemes) have been programmed as (often highly idiosyncratic and inefficient) research codes. The development of my own codes frequently uncovered subtle issues that had previously been overlooked, and sometimes outright errors and misconceptions. Indeed, I would be suspicious of any scheme that has not been actually tested on a computer. The FORTRAN software package MICROSCOPE [12] proved indispensable in my work. This is an interactive program that enables the examination of functions (including multivariate interpolants) with respect to smoothness, precision, polynomial degree, and bugs in the implementation. The package is available (free of charge) via electronic mail from the *netlib* software distribution center [33] (and of course also from the author).

Another interesting phenomenon is that the best *tetrahedral* schemes (in my opinion, the piecewise cubic generalized Clough-Tocher split and the arbitrarily smooth and precise piecewise rational perpendicular interpolants) are actually special cases of more general interpolation schemes of arbitrary dimension. It would be reasonable to expect that better schemes could be designed by exploiting the special case $k = 3$. That this has not been the case illustrates the value of generalization and abstraction as a research tool.

## Acknowledgments

I would like to thank the organizers of the Oslo conference for inviting me to present this survey at the conference, and to write this paper. The conference was very well run and a great pleasure to attend. My own work has benefitted over many years from the fruitful and constructive interaction with many people. In particular, I would like to thank Hiroshi Akima, Bob Barnhill, Nelson Beebe, Luis Billera, Carl de Boor, Ron DeVore, Gerald Farin, Tom Foley, Dick Franke, Fred Fritsch, Tom Grandine, Klaus Höllig, Tom Jensen, John Gregory, Chuck Lawson, Frank Little, Tom Lyche, Ed Nadeler, Greg Nielson, Bruce Piper, Paul Sablonnière, Kes Salkauskas, Ray Sarraga, Larry Schumaker, Frank Stenger, Keith Unsworth, and Andrew Worsey. In addition, my work has benefitted greatly from the congenial environment and the excellent computing facilities at the University of Utah.

## References

(Note: References not contained in the bibliography [41] in the form given here are marked with a superscript+.)

1. Akima, H., On estimating partial derivatives for bivariate interpolation of scattered data, Rocky Mountain J. Math. **14** (1984), 41–52.
2. Alfeld, P., A discrete $C^1$ interpolant for tetrahedral data, Rocky Mountain J. Math. **14** (1984), 5–16.
3. Alfeld, P., A trivariate Clough-Tocher scheme for tetrahedral data, Comput. Aided Geom. Design **1** (1984), 169–181.
4. Alfeld, P., A trivariate Clough-Tocher scheme for tetrahedral data, MRC Technical Summary Report #2702, Mathematics Research Center, University of Wisconsin–Madison, 1984.
5.+ Alfeld, P., Triangular extrapolation, MRC Technical Summary Report #2707, Mathematics Research Center, University of Wisconsin–Madison, 1984.
6. Alfeld, P., Derivative generation from multivariate scattered data by functional minimization, Comput. Aided Geom. Design **2** (1985), 281–296.
7. Alfeld, P., Multivariate perpendicular interpolation, SIAM J. Numer. Anal. **22** (1985), 95–106.

8.[+] Alfeld, P., On the dimension of multivariate piecewise polynomials, in *Numerical Analysis*, D. F. Griffiths and G. A. Watson (ed.), Longman Scientific and Technical, 1985, 1–23.

9.[+] Alfeld, P., A case study of multivariate piecewise polynomials, in [36], 149-160.

10.[+] Alfeld, P., The Multivariate Spline Newsletter, distributed periodically; to subscribe contact the author.

11. Alfeld, P., and R. E. Barnhill, A transfinite $C^2$ interpolant over triangles, Rocky Mountain J. Math. **14** (1984), 17–40.

12.[+] Alfeld, P. and B. Harris, Microscope: a smoothness tester for multivariate functions, MRC Rpt. 2701, Univ. Wisconsin-Madison, 1984.

13.[+] Alfeld, P., B. Piper, and L. L. Schumaker, Minimally supported bases for spaces of bivariate piecewise polynomials of smoothness $r$ and degree $d \geq 4r + 1$, Comput. Aided Geom. Design **4** (1987), 105–124.

14. Alfeld, P., B. Piper, and L. L. Schumaker, An explicit basis for $C^1$ quartic bivariate splines, SIAM J. Numer. Anal. **24** (1987), 891–911.                    •

15. Barnhill, R. E., Representation and approximation of surfaces, in *Mathematical Software III* J. R. Rice (ed.), Academic Press, New York, 1977, 68–119.

16. Barnhill, R. E., Surfaces in computer aided geometric design: A survey with new results, Comput. Aided Geom. Design **2** (1985), 1–17.

17. Barnhill, R. E., R. P. Dube, and F. F. Little, Properties of Shepard's surfaces, Rocky Mountain J. Math. **13**, 365–382.

18. Barnhill, R. E., and J. A. Gregory, Polynomial interpolation to boundary data on triangles, Math. Comp. **29** (1975), 726–735.

19. Barnhill, R. E., and F. F. Little, Three and four-dimensional surfaces, Rocky Mountain J. Math. **14** (1984), 77–102.

20. Barnhill, R. E., B. R. Piper, and K. L. Rescorla, Interpolation to arbitrary data on a surface, in [36], 281–290

21.[+] Barnhill, R. E., B. R. Piper, and S.E. Stead, A multidimensional surface problem: Pressure on a wing, Comput. Aided Geom. Design **2** (1985), 185–186.

22. Barnhill, R. E. and S. Stead, Multistage trivariate surfaces, Rocky Mountain J. Math. **14** (1984), 103–118.

23. Barnhill, R. E. and A. J. Worsey, Smooth interpolation over hypercubes, Comput. Aided Geom. Design **1** (1984), 101–113.

24.[+] Bing, R. H., Some aspects of the topology of 3-manifolds related to the Poincaré conjecture, in *Lectures on Modern Mathematics*, v. 2, Wiley, New-York, 1964, 93–128.

25. de Boor, C., *A Practical Guide to Splines*, Springer Verlag, New York, 1978.

26. de Boor, C., Efficient computer manipulation of tensor products, ACM Trans. Math. Software **5** (1979), 173–182.

27. de Boor, C., B-form Basics, in [36], 131–148.

28.[+] Buhmann, M. D., Convergence of univariate quasi-interpolation using multiquadrics, IMA J. Numer. Anal., to appear.

29.[+] Buhmann, M. D., Multivariate interpolation in odd dimensional Euclidean spaces using multiquadrics, preprint.

30. Chui, C. K., and M. Lai, On multivariate vertex splines and applications, in [31], 19–36.

31. Chui, C. K., L. L. Schumaker, and F. I. Utreras, 1987, *Topics in Multivariate Approximation*, Academic Press, New York, 1986.

32. Cline, A. K., and R. J. Renka, A storage efficient method for construction of a Thiessen triangulation, Rocky Mountain J. Math. **14** (1984), 119–140.

33.[+] Dongarra, J. J., and E. Grosse, Distribution of mathematical software via electronic mail, Numerical Analysis Manuscript 85-2, AT&T Bell Laboratories, Murray Hill, New Jersey 07974.

34. Duchon, J., Interpolation des Fonctions de deux variables suivant le principle de la flexion de plaques minces, R.A.I.R.O. Analyse Numeriques **10** (1976), 5–12.

35.[+] Dyn, D., Interpolation of scattered data by radial functions, in [31], 47–61.

36. Farin, G. E., (ed.) *Geometric Modeling: Algorithms and New Trends*, SIAM Publications, Philadelphia, 1987.

37. Farwig, R., Rate of convergence of Shepard's global interpolation formula, Math. Comp. **46** (1986), 577–590.

38. Foley, T. A., Smooth multivariate interpolation to scattered data, Ph.D. dissertation, Arizona State University, 1979.

39. Foley, T. A., Three-stage interpolation to scattered data, Rocky Mountain J. Math. **14** (1984), 141–150.

40. Franke, R. H., Scattered data interpolation: test of some methods, Math. Comp. **38** (1982), 181–200.

41.[+] Franke, R. H. and L. L. Schumaker, A bibliography of multivariate approximation, in [31], 275–335

42. Gordon, W. J., and J. A. Wixom, On Shepard's method of "metric interpolation" to bivariate and multivariate interpolation, Math. Comp. **32** (1978), 253–264.

43. Gregory, J. A. Interpolation to boundary data on the simplex, Comput. Aided Geom. Design **2** (1985), 43–52.

44. Hardy, R. L., Multiquadric equations of topography and other irregular surfaces, J. Geophysical Res. **76** (1971), 1905–1915.

45.[+] Hazelwood, C., A divide and conquer approach to $D$-dimensional triangulations, Ph.D. dissertation, Department of Computer Science, University of Texas at Austin, 1988.

46.[+] Ibrahim, A. K., and L. L. Schumaker, Super spline spaces of smoothness $r$ and degree $d \geq 3r + 2$, preprint.

47.[+] Jackson, I. R. H., Convergence properties of radial basis functions, Constr. Approx. **4** (1988), 243–264.

48.[+] Kirkpatrick, J., private communication, 1988.

49. Lancaster, P., and K. Salkauskas, Surfaces generated by moving least squares methods, Math. Comp. **37** (1981), 141–158.

50.+ Lasser, D., Bernstein-Bézier-Darstellung trivariater Splines, Ph.D. dissertation, Technische Hochschule Darmstadt, 1987.

51. Lawson, C. L., $C^1$ surface interpolation for scattered data on the surface of a sphere, Rocky Mountain J. Math. **14** (1984), 177–202.

52. Lawson, C. L., Properties of $n$-dimensional triangulations, Comput. Aided Geom. Design **3**, (1986), 231–247.

53.+ Lawson, C. L., private communication, 1988.

54. Le Méhauté, A., Unisolvent interpolation in $\mathbb{R}^n$ and the simplicial polynomial finite element method, in [28], 141–151.

55. Light, W. A. and E. W. Cheney, *Approximation Theory in Tensor Product Spaces*, Springer-Verlag Lecture Notes 1169, New York, 1985.

56. Little, F. F., Convex combination surfaces, in *Surfaces in Computer Aided Geometric Design*, R. E. Barnhill and W. Boehm (eds.), North-Holland, Amsterdam, 1983, 99–108.

57. Micchelli, C. A., Interpolation of scattered data: distance matrices and conditionally positive definite functions, Constr. Approx. **2** (1986), 11–22.

58. Morgan, J. and R. Scott, A nodal basis for $C^1$ piecewise polynomials in two variables, Math. Comp. **29** (1975), 736–740.

59. Nielson, G. M., A method for interpolating scattered data based upon a minimum norm network, Math. Comp. **40** (1983), 253–271.

60.+ Nielson, G. M., and R. Ramaraj, Interpolation over a sphere based upon a minimum norm network, Comput. Aided Geom. Design **4** (1987), 41–57.

61. Petersen, C. S., B. R. Piper and A. J. Worsey, Adaptive contouring of a trivariate interpolant, in [36], 385–396.

62. Powell, M. J. D., Radial basis functions for multivariable interpolation, in *Algorithms for Approximation*, J. C. Mason and M. G. Cox (eds.), Clarendon Press, Oxford, 1987, 143–168.

63. Powell, M. J. D., and M. A. Sabin, Piecewise quadratic approximations on triangles, ACM Trans. Math. Software **3** (1977), 316–325.

64. Ramaraj, R., *Interpolation and display of scattered data over a sphere*, M. S. Thesis, Arizona State University, 1986.

65. Renka, R. L., Interpolation of data on the surface of a sphere, ACM Trans. Math. Software **10** (1984), 417–436.

66. Renka, R. L., and A. K. Cline, A triangle based $C^1$ interpolation method, Rocky Mountain J. Math. **14** (1984), 223–238.

67.+ Rescorla, K. L., $C^1$ trivariate polynomial interpolation, Comput. Aided Geom. Design **4** (1987), 237–44.

68. Rippa, S., Interpolation and smoothing of scattered data by radial basis functions, M. Sc. Thesis, Tel Aviv University, 1984.

69.+ Rudin, M. E., An unshellable triangulation of a tetrahedron, Bull. Amer. Math. Soc. **64** (1958), 90–91.

70.+ Rushing, T. B., *Topological Embeddings*, Academic Press, 1973.

71. Schumaker, L. L., On the dimension of spaces of piecewise polynomials in two variables, in *Multivariate Approximation Theory*, W. Schempp and K. Zeller (eds.), Birkhäuser, Basel, 1979, 396–412.

72. Schumaker, L. L., Bounds on the dimension of spaces of multivariate piecewise polynomials, Rocky Mountain J. Math. **14** (1984), 251–264.

73. Sederberg, T. W., Piecewise algebraic surface patches, Comput. Aided Geom. Design **2** (1985), 53–59.

74.[+] Sewell, G., Plotting contour surfaces of a function of three variables, ACM Trans. Math. Software **14** (1988), 33–41.

75.[+] Sewell, G., Algorithm 657: Software for plotting contour surfaces of a function of three variables, ACM Trans. Math. Software **14** (1988), 33–41.

76. Shepard, D., 1968, A two-dimensional interpolation function for irregularly spaced data, Proc. 23 Nat. Conf. ACM, 517–524.

77. Sibson, R., A brief description of natural neighbor interpolation, in *Interpreting Multivariate Data*, D.V. Barnett (ed.), Wiley, New York, 1981, 21–36.

78. Stead, S., Estimation of gradients from scattered data, Rocky Mountain J. Math. **14** (1984), 265–280.

79. Strang, G., Piecewise polynomials and the finite element method, Bull. Amer. Math. Soc. **79** (1973), 1128–1137.

80. Strang, G, and J. Fix, *An Analysis of the Finite Element Method*, Prentice-Hall, Englewood Cliffs, N.J., 1973.

81. Wahba, G., Surface fitting with scattered noisy data on Euclidean $D$-space and on the sphere, Rocky Mountain J. Math. **14** (1984), 281–299.

82. Wahba, G. and J. Wendelberger, Some new mathematical methods for variational objective analysis using splines and cross validation, Monthly Weather Review **108** (1980), 36–57.

83. Worsey, A. J., $C^2$ interpolation over hypercubes, Comput. Aided Geom. Design **2** (1985), 107–115.

84. Worsey, A. J., and G. E. Farin, An $n$-dimensional Clough-Tocher interpolant, Constr. Approx. **3** (1987), 99–110.

85. Worsey, A. J., and B. Piper, A trivariate Powell-Sabin interpolant, Comput. Aided Geom. Design **5** (1988), 177–186.

86. Ženíšek, A., Polynomial approximation on tetrahedrons in the finite element method, J. Approx. Theory **7** (1973), 334–351.

Peter Alfeld
Department of Mathematics
University of Utah
Salt Lake City, Utah 84112
USA

Supported in part by NSF Grant DMS-8701121.

EMAIL: alfeld@ science.utah.edu

# Some Applications of Discrete $D^m$ Splines

## R. Arcangéli

**Abstract.** Given a suitable finite element space $V_h$, we define "$V_h$-discrete smoothing $D^2$-splines" belonging to $V_h$. Then we give three non-trivial examples of utilization of these splines: 1) construction of surfaces of class $C^1$ or $C^2$ from a large number of scattered Lagrange data, 2) approximation of non regular functions (a problem occurring in geophysics), and 3) spline fitting along a curve (an attempt to model the construction of surfaces from iso-valued curves).

## §1. $V_h$-Discrete Smoothing $D^m$-Splines

In this paper we concentrate on smoothing splines, although one can also define interpolating $D^m$-splines. For the sake of simplicity, we consider only the case of smoothing $D^m$-splines with

$$\begin{cases} m & = 2 \\ n & \text{(dimension of space)} = 2 \\ \Omega & = \text{bounded polygonal open subset of } \mathbb{R}^2, \end{cases}$$

but a generalization to the case $m > n/2$, $n \in \mathbb{N}^*$ and $\Omega$ any bounded connected subset of $\mathbb{R}^n$ with a Lipschitz-continuous boundary does not present any real difficulties. We begin by introducing some notation and definitions.

**Sobolev space $H^2(\Omega)$:**

We write $H^2(\Omega)$ for the Hilbert space of (classes of) all real functions $v$ which belong to $L^2(\Omega)$ together with all their partial derivatives $\partial^\alpha v = \dfrac{\partial^{|\alpha|} v}{\partial x_1^{\alpha_1} \partial x_2^{\alpha_2}}$, where $\alpha = (\alpha_1, \alpha_2) \in \mathbb{N}^2$ and $|\alpha| = \alpha_1 + \alpha_2$, of order $|\alpha| \le 2$, equipped with the norm

$$\|v\|_{2,\Omega} = \left( \sum_{|\alpha| \le 2} \int_\Omega (\partial^\alpha v)^2 \, dx \right)^{1/2}.$$

Mathematical Methods in Computer Aided Geometric Design
Tom Lyche and Larry L. Schumaker (eds.), pp. 35–44.

Moreover, we write

$$(u, v)_{2,\Omega} = \sum_{|\alpha|=2} \partial^\alpha u \, \partial^\alpha v \, dx, \qquad \forall u \in H^2(\Omega), \quad \forall v \in H^2(\Omega)$$

and

$$|v|_{2,\Omega} = (v, v)_{2,\Omega}^{1/2}, \qquad \forall v \in H^2(\Omega).$$

**Finite element (F.E.) space $V_h$:**

Suppose we are given :
- a subset $\mathcal{H}$ of $\mathbb{R}_+^*$ of which 0 is an accumulation point ;
- for any $h \in \mathcal{H}$ a "triangulation" $\mathcal{T}_h$ of $\overline{\Omega}$ made with rectangles or triangles $K$ with diameters $h_K \leq h$, such that (cf. [6])

  $$\text{the family } (\mathcal{T}_h) \text{ is regular (in the Ciarlet-Raviart/Strang sense)} \quad (1.1)$$

- for any $h \in \mathcal{H}$, a F.E. space $V_h$ constructed on $\mathcal{T}_h$ (a finite-dimensional subspace of $H^2(\Omega)$), such that

  $$\text{the generic F.E. } P_K \text{ of the family } (V_h) \text{ satisfies the}$$
  $$\text{inclusion : } P_K \supset P_{m'-1}(K) \text{ for some } m' > 2. \quad (1.2)$$

**Examples of F.E.:**

- of class $C^1$ (cf. for example [6]) : Argyris or Bell's triangles, Bogner-Fox-Schmit rectangle;
- of class $C^2$ : Argyris or Bell's triangles (cf. [14, 18]), Bogner-Fox- Schmit rectangle (cf. for example [2]).

**Interpolation conditions:**

Suppose we are given:
- a subset $\mathcal{D}$ of $\mathbb{R}_+^*$ of which 0 is an accumulation point;
- for any $d \in \mathcal{D}$, an (ordered) system $A^d$ of $N = N(d)$ points of $\overline{\Omega}$, such that

  $$\sup_{x \in \Omega} \delta(x, A^d) = d, \qquad (1.3)$$

  where $\delta$ denotes the Euclidean distance in $\mathbb{R}^2$, (notice that $\sup\alpha \in \Omega$ and that $\delta(x, A^d)$ is the Hausdorff distance between $\overline{\Omega}$ and $A^d$). For all $d \in \mathcal{D}$ and $v \in H^2(\Omega)$, we set $\rho^d v = (v(a))_{a \in A^d}$;
- an element $\beta^d$ of $\mathbb{R}^N$ for any $d \in \mathcal{D}$.

  Now we can define *discrete smoothing splines.* For any $\varepsilon > 0$, and any $d \in \mathcal{D}$, we set

  $$J_\varepsilon^d(v) = \|\rho^d v - \beta^d\|^2 + \varepsilon |v|_{2,\Omega}^2, \qquad \forall v \in H^2(\Omega),$$

where $\| \cdot \|$ denotes the Euclidean norm in $\mathbb{R}^N$. Then we consider the following problem:

**Problem.** *Find $\sigma_{\varepsilon h}^d \in V_h$ such that*

$$J_\varepsilon^d(\sigma_{\varepsilon h}^d) \leq J_\varepsilon^d(v_h), \qquad \forall v_h \in V_h. \tag{1.4}$$

**Theorem 1.1.** *For any $\varepsilon > 0$, any $h \in \mathcal{H}$, and any $d \in \mathcal{D}$ sufficiently small, Problem (1.4) has a unique solution $\sigma_{\varepsilon h}^d$, the $V_h$ –discrete smoothing $D^2$-spline relative to $A^d$, $\beta^d$ and $\varepsilon$, which is also the unique solution of the following problem: find $\sigma_{\varepsilon h}^d \in V_h$ satisfying*

$$\langle \rho^d \sigma_{\varepsilon h}^d, \rho^d v_h \rangle + \varepsilon(\sigma_{\varepsilon h}^d, v_h)_{2,\Omega} = \langle \beta^d, \rho^d v_h \rangle, \qquad \forall v_h \in V_h, \tag{1.5}$$

*where $\langle, \rangle$ is the Euclidean inner product in $\mathbb{R}^N$.*

**Proof:** We use the Lax-Milgram lemma and the equivalent (cf. [17]) norm $(\|\rho^d v\|^2 + |v|_{2,\Omega}^2)^{1/2}$. ∎

These splines should be compared with those of M. Atteia [4,5], P. J. Laurent [12], etc. For more information, cf. [3] and the lectures of R. Arcangéli which may appear in a series edited by SMAI. For approximation error bounds, see [15].

Now let $M = M(h)$ denote the dimension of $V_h$, and let $(w_j)_{1 \leq j \leq M}$ be a basis of $V_h$. Set

$$\sigma_{\varepsilon h}^d = \sum_{j=1}^M \alpha_j w_j,$$

with $\alpha_j \in \mathbb{R}$, $1 \leq j \leq M$. Let $a_1, \ldots, a_N$ be the points of $A^d$, and consider the matrices

$$\mathcal{A} = (w_j(a_i))_{i=1,j=1}^{N,M}, \qquad \mathcal{R} = ((w_j, w_i)_{2,\Omega})_{i=1,j=1}^{M,M}.$$

Then we see that (1.5) is equivalent to the problem: find $\alpha = (\alpha_j)_{j=1}^M \in \mathbb{R}^M$ satisfying

$$(\mathcal{A}^T \mathcal{A} + \varepsilon \mathcal{R})\alpha = \mathcal{A}^T \beta^d. \tag{1.6}$$

Notice that $\mathcal{A}^T \mathcal{A}$ is the least-squares matrix associated with the basis $(w_j)$. Now, we state a convergence result.

**Theorem 1.2.** *Under hypotheses (1.1), (1.2), and (1.3) and the additional condition that*

*there exists a constant $C$ such that for $d$ small enough $N(d) \leq C/d^2$* (1.7)

*and, if $f$ is a given function in $H^{m'}(\Omega)$, then for any $\varepsilon_0 > 0$ the solution $\sigma_{\varepsilon h}^d$ of (1.5) with $\beta^d = (f(a))_{a \in A^d}$ satisfies*

$$\lim_{\substack{0 \leq \varepsilon \leq \varepsilon_0 \\ d \to 0, h^{m'-2}/d\varepsilon^{1/2} \to 0}} \|\sigma_{\varepsilon h}^d - f\|_{2,\Omega} = 0.$$

**Proof:** We use compactness arguments. ∎

**Remark.** *If $m' \geq 4$, we can choose $h$ large enough so that we obtain a linear system of dimension $M$ much less than $N$.*

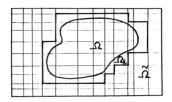

**Figure 1.** The domain.

## §2. Construction of Surfaces of Class $C^k$ from Lagrange Data

We now consider the following well-known problem (cf. for example [7,8]): given a function $f : \mathbb{R}^2 \supset \Omega \to \mathbb{R}$, sufficiently regular, and a set $\{a_j\}_{i=1}^N$ of points of $\overline{\Omega}$, construct an approximant $\Phi$ of class $C^k$, $k = 1, 2$, using only Lagrange data $\{f(a_j)\}_{1 \le j \le N}$. The number $N$ is supposed "large" (e.g. about several thousands ).

To solve this problem, we merely apply the method of Section 1; *i.e.*, we take $\Phi = \sigma_{\varepsilon h}^d$ for suitable $\varepsilon$ and $h$ (in the case of noisy data one can use the generalized cross validation method for the choice of $\varepsilon$).

**Advantages:**

- the matrix of the linear system is banded;
- there is possibility of local refinement;
- one can always use rectangular F.E. even if the geometry is not rectangular. More generally, we introduce (cf. Figure 1) a fixed rectangle $\tilde{\Omega}$ and, for any $h \in \mathcal{H}$, an open set $\Omega_h$, interior to a union of rectangles $K$, such that $\Omega \subset \Omega_h \subset \tilde{\Omega}$, and

$$\lim_{h \to 0} \text{meas}(\Omega_h \backslash \Omega) = 0.$$

Then we define $V_h$ as the vector space of all the restrictions to $\Omega_h$ of the functions of a space $\tilde{V}_h$ constructed over $\tilde{\Omega}$ following Section 1. (One can show that convergence is achieved as in Theorem 1.2).

**Disadvantage:**

- the method is more expensive than using bicubic splines, because the linear system is of larger dimension, although its construction is cheaper.

## §3. Approximation of non-Regular Functions (cf. [9,11,13,16])

We consider only the case of discontinuities of functions (faults), but the theory is valid for discontinuities of some partial derivative (creases). We need to modify the situation of Section 1.

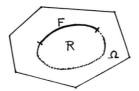

**Figure 2.** The set F.

First, we introduce a nonempty connected subset $F$ of $\Omega$ for which there exists an open set $R$ (cf. Figure 2) such that

  i) $R$ is connected with a Lipschitz-continuous boundary and $\overline{R} \subset \Omega$,

 ii) $F$ is the whole boundary or a part (open for the topology induced by $\mathbb{R}^2$) of the boundary of $R$,

(iii) the complement of $\overline{R}$ in $\Omega$ is connected.

Then we set

$$\Omega' = \Omega \backslash \overline{F},$$

and we introduce the spaces

 • $H^2(\Omega')$, a Sobolev space over $\Omega'$,

 • $C_F^0(\Omega')$, defined by

$$C_F^0(\Omega') = \left\{ v \in C^0(\Omega') : \quad v|_R \in C^0(\overline{R}), v|_{\tilde{R}} \in C^0(\overline{\tilde{R}}) \right\},$$

where $\tilde{R}$ is the complement of $\overline{R}$ in $\Omega$. Then, one can prove the following results:

**Theorem 3.1.** *$C_F^0(\Omega')$ is a Banach space with norm*

$$\|v\|_{C_F^0(\Omega')} = \max \left\{ \sup_R |v(x)|, \ \sup_{\tilde{R}} |v(x)| \right\}.$$

*Moreover, the space $C_F^0(\Omega')$ and norm $\|.\|_{C_F^0(\Omega')}$ are independent of the choice of $R$.*

**Theorem 3.2.** *$H^2(\Omega')$ is a subset of $C_F^0(\Omega')$ with continuous injection.*

The proofs of these theorems are due to R. Manzanilla [16]. Theorem 3.2 means that $H^2(\Omega')$ is included in a space whose functions have restrictions on "each side" of $F$ (and on the boundary $\partial\Omega$ of $\Omega$).

Next we change the interpolation conditions of Section 1. For any $d \in \mathcal{D}$, we introduce three finite sets of distinct points : $A_1^d \subset \overline{\Omega} \backslash F$, $A_+^d \subset F$, $A_-^d \subset F$, and we set

$$A^d = \{a \in A_1^d; \quad a \in A_+^d; \quad a \in A_-^d\}$$

which may contain repeated points (belonging to $F$). For all $d \in \mathcal{D}$ and $v \in H^2(\Omega')$, we define

$$v(a) = \begin{cases} \lim_{x \to a, \, x \in R} v(x), & a \in A_+^d \\ \lim_{x \to a, \, x \in \tilde{R}} v(x), & a \in A_-^d, \end{cases}$$

where as before, $\tilde{R}$ is the complement of $\overline{R}$ in $\Omega$. Let $N = \operatorname{card} A^d$, and (assuming that A is ordered) set

$$\rho^d v = (v(a))_{a \in A^d}.$$

We further suppose that

$$(\rho^d v = 0) \quad \Rightarrow \quad (v = 0) \qquad \forall v \in P_1(\Omega').$$

Finally, for all $h \in \mathcal{H}$ we introduce a F.E. space $V_h$ of functions defined over $\Omega'$. To simplify matters in the sequel, we assume that $F$ is **polygonal**. In this case it is necessary to use **triangles**. Furthermore, the construction of $V_h$ must be done carefully; it is crucial that triangles touching $F$ are **one-sided** (cf. Figure 3).

As in Section 1, we define

$$J_\varepsilon^d(v) = \|\rho^d v - \beta^d\|^2 + \varepsilon |v|_{2,\Omega'}^2 \qquad \forall v \in H^2(\Omega'),$$

and consider again problem (1.4): find $\sigma_h^d \in V_h$ such that

$$J_\varepsilon^d(\sigma_{\varepsilon h}^d) \leq J_\varepsilon^d(v_h), \qquad \forall v_h \in V_h.$$

In this new situation, we again get all of the results of Section 1; namely, existence and uniqueness of $\sigma_{\varepsilon h}^d$, and (under conditions (1.1), (1.2), (1.3) and (1.7)) convergence to $f \in H^{m'}(\Omega')$ of the $V_h$-discrete smoothing $D^2$-spline $\sigma_{\varepsilon h}^d$ relative to $A^d$, $\beta^d = (f(a))_{a \in A^d}$ and $\varepsilon$.

**Remark 3.3.** *Implementation of the method (with triangles) is more expensive than that of Section 1.*

**Remark 3.4.** *To deal with the case of discontinuities of derivatives, it suffices to notice (the proof is immediate) the following theorem, and then to apply the theory with $H^2(\Omega') \cap C^0(\overline{\Omega})$ in place of $H^2(\Omega')$.*

**Theorem 3.5.** *The subspace $H^2(\Omega') \cap C^0(\overline{\Omega})$ is closed in $H^2(\Omega')$.*

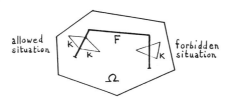

**Figure 3.** Conditions on the triangles.

## §4. Spline Fitting Along a Curve (cf. [1]).

The problem of constructing surfaces from iso-valued curves (and other problems) has the following abstract formulation: given

- a function $f \in H^2(\Omega)$

- an open polygonal set $\Omega \subset \mathbb{R}^2$;

- a subset $F$ of $\Omega$ defined as in §3 (by conditions (i) (ii) and (iii)), and such that

$$(p|_F = 0) \Rightarrow (p = 0), \qquad \forall p \in P_1(\Omega), \tag{4.1}$$

find a regular function $\Phi$ (e.g. $\Phi \in H^2(\Omega) \cap C^k(\overline{\Omega}), k = 1, 2$) that interpolates $f$ on $F$. Actually, this is a fitting problem along the curve

$$\left\{ (x_1, x_2, x_3) \in \mathbb{R}^3 \ : \ x_3 = f(x_1, x_2), \ (x_1, x_2) \in F \right\}.$$

This abstract problem clearly has solutions. Let us set

$$\rho v = v|_F \qquad \forall v \in H^2(\Omega), \tag{4.2}$$

(this has a meaning because $v \in C^0(\overline{\Omega})$). On the other hand, let us introduce the Hilbert space $L^2(F)$ of (classes of) all real functions which are square-integrable over $F$ (cf. [10,17]) and denote by $\|.\|_{0,F}$ some equivalent Hilbertian norm over $L^2(F)$. Then we consider the problem: find $\sigma$ solution of

$$\begin{cases} \sigma \in K \stackrel{\text{def}}{=} \left\{ v \in H^2(\Omega), \rho v = f \right\}, \\ \forall v \in K, \ |\sigma|_{2,\Omega} \le |v|_{2,\Omega}. \end{cases} \tag{4.3}$$

**Theorem 4.1.** *The problem (4.3) has a unique solution $\sigma$.*

**Proof:** $\sigma$ is the element of minimal norm

$$v \to (\|v\|_{0,F}^2 + |v|_{2,\Omega}^2)^{1/2}$$

in the subset $K$ that is convex, nonempty and closed in $H^2(\Omega)$. ∎

Thus, we can take $\Phi = \sigma$. Unfortunately, it is impossible to find $\sigma$ explicitly. Therefore, we must modify the initial abstract problem in such a way to obtain an approximation of $\sigma$. Suppose we are given

- a subset $\mathcal{E}$ of $\mathbb{R}_+^*$ of which 0 is an accumulation point
- for any $\eta \in \mathcal{E}$, a set $\{\xi_i\}_{1 \leq i \leq L}$ of $L = L(\eta)$ distinct points $\xi_i = \xi_i(\eta)$ of $\overline{F}$ such that $\max\limits_{1 \leq i \leq L-1} \delta(\xi_i, \xi_{i+1}) = \eta$ and a set $\{\lambda_i\}_{1 \leq i \leq L}$ of numbers $\lambda_i = \lambda_i(\eta) > 0$.

Then we set

$$\ell_\eta(v) = \sum_{i=1}^{L} \lambda_i v(\xi_i), \qquad \forall v \in C^0(\overline{F})$$

and assume that there exist $C > 0$, and $t > 0$ such that for all $\eta \in \mathcal{E}$ and all $v \in H^2(\Omega)$,

$$|\ell_\eta(v^2) - \|v\|_{0,F}^2| \leq C\eta^t \|v\|_{2,\Omega}^2. \tag{4.4}$$

**Remark 4.2.** *We have obtained a numerical integration formula for* $\|.\|_{0,F}^2$ :

$$\|v\|_{0,F}^2 \sim \ell_\eta(v^2), \qquad \forall v \in C^0(\overline{F}).$$

*Suppose, for simplicity, that $F$ is represented by a single equation*

$$x_2 = a(x_1), \qquad x_1 \in \Delta,$$

*and that $\|.\|_{0,F}$ is defined by*

$$\|v\|_{0,F}^2 = \int_\Delta v^2(x_1, a(x_1))(1 + a'^2(x_1))^{1/2} \, dx_1.$$

*Then we can take*

$$\ell_\eta(v) = \frac{1}{2}\delta(\xi_1, \xi_2)v(\xi_1)$$
$$+ \sum_{i=2}^{L-1} [\delta(\xi_{i-1}, \xi_i) + \delta(\xi_i, \xi_{i+1})]v(\xi_i)$$
$$+ \frac{1}{2}\delta(\xi_{L-1}, \xi_L)v(\xi_L)$$

*and verify that condition (4.4) is satisfied with $t = 1$ if $a$ is regular enough (of class $C^2$ for example).*

Next we introduce a family of F.E. spaces $V_h$ as in Section 1. We make the following assumptions

$$\text{the family of triangulations } (\mathcal{T}_h) \text{ is regular} \tag{4.5}$$

$$\text{the generic F.E. } P_K \text{ satisfy: } P_K \supset P_2(K). \tag{4.6}$$

Then for all $\varepsilon > 0$, $\eta \in \mathcal{E}$, and all $v \in H^2(\Omega)$, we define the functional

$$J_\varepsilon^\eta(v) = \ell_\eta((v - f)^2) + \varepsilon|v|_{2,\Omega}^2. \tag{4.7}$$

Now we consider the following minimization problem: find $\sigma_{\varepsilon h}^\eta \in V_h$ satisfying

$$J_\varepsilon^\eta(\sigma_{\varepsilon h}^\eta) \le J_\varepsilon^\eta(v_h), \qquad \forall v_h \in V_h, \tag{4.8}$$

and the variational problem: find $\sigma_{\varepsilon h}^\eta \in V_h$ satisfying

$$a_\eta(\sigma_{\varepsilon h}^\eta, v_h) + \varepsilon(\sigma_{\varepsilon h}^\eta, v_h)_{2,\Omega} = a_\eta(f, v_h), \qquad \forall v_h \in V_h, \tag{4.9}$$

where we have put $a_\eta(u_h, v_h) = \ell_\eta(u_h v_h)$ for all $u_h, v_h \in V_h$.

Our next result shows that the two problems have the same solution $\sigma_{\varepsilon h}^\eta$, and that we can take $\Phi = \sigma_{\varepsilon h}^\eta$ for suitable $\varepsilon$, $h$ and $\eta$.

**Theorem 4.3.** *Suppose that hypotheses (4.1) and (4.4) are satisfied. Then, for any $\varepsilon > 0$, any $h \in \mathcal{H}$, and any $\eta$ sufficiently small, the problems (4.8) and (4.9) have the same unique solution $\sigma_{\varepsilon h}^\eta$.*

**Proof:** We use the Lax-Milgram lemma. ∎

The function $\sigma_{\varepsilon h}^\eta$ is called the $V_h$-discrete smoothing $D^2$-spline of $f$ relative to $F$, $\eta$ and $\varepsilon$.

**Theorem 4.4.** *Suppose that hypotheses (4.1), (4.4), (4.5), and (4.6) are satisfied. Then the solution $\sigma_{\varepsilon h}^\eta$ of (4.8) and (4.9) satisfies*

*(i)*
$$\lim_{\varepsilon \to 0, h^{3-\theta}/\varepsilon \to 0, \eta^t/\varepsilon \text{ bounded}} \|\sigma_{\varepsilon h}^\eta - \sigma\|_{2,\Omega} = 0,$$

*where $\theta$ is any number in (0,3), and*

*(ii)*
$$\|\sigma_{\varepsilon h}^\eta - f\|_{0,F}^2 \le C(h^{3-\theta} + \eta^t o(1) + \varepsilon), \theta \in (0,3)$$

*when $\varepsilon \to 0$, $h^{3-\theta}/\varepsilon \to 0$, and $\eta^t/\varepsilon$ remains bounded.*

**Proof:** We use compactness arguments and results from F.E. theory. ∎

## References

1. Apprato, D. and R. Arcangéli, Ajustement spline le long d'une courbe, preprint.
2. Apprato, D., R. Arcangéli, and R. Manzanilla, Sur la construction de surfaces de classe $C^k$ à partir d'un grand nombre de données de Lagrange, RAIRO M²AN, **21** (1987), 529–555.

3. Arcangéli R., $D^m$-splines sur un domaine borné de $\mathbb{R}^n$, Publ. UA 1204 CNRS n°1986/2.

4. Atteia, M., Fonctions "splines" définies sur un ensemble convexe, Numer. Math. **12** (1968), 192–210.

5. Atteia, M, Fonctions "splines" et noyaux reproduisants d'Aronszajn-Bergman, RAIRO, $4^e$ année, R-3 (1970), 31–43.

6. Ciarlet P. G., *The Finite Element Method for Elliptic Problems*, North-Holland, Amsterdam, 1978.

7. Dierckx, P., An algorithm for surface-fitting with spline functions, IMA J. of Numer. Anal. **1** (1981), 267–283.

8. Franke, R., Scattered data interpolation: tests of some methods, Math. of Comp. **38** (1982), 181–200.

9. Franke, R. and G. Nielson, Surface approximation with imposed conditions, in *Surfaces in CAGD*, R. E. Barnhill and W. Boehm (eds.), North-Holland, 1983, 135–146.

10. Grisvard, P., *Elliptic Problems in Nonsmooth Domains*, Pitman, 1985.

11. Klein P., Thèse de $3^e$ cycle, Grenoble, 1987.

12. Laurent, P. J., *Approximation et Optimisation*, Hermann, Paris, 1972.

13. Laurent, P. J., Inf-convolution spline pour l'approximation de données discontinues, RAIRO **20** (1986), 89–111.

14. Le Méhauté A., Thèse d'état, Rennes, 1984.

15. Lopez de Silanes, M.C. and D. Apprato, Estimations de l'erreur d'approximation sur un domaine borné de $\mathbb{R}^n$ par $D^m$-splines d'interpolation et d'ajustement discrètes, Numer. Math. **53** (1988), 367-376.

16. Manzanilla, R., Thesis, Pau, 1986.

17. Necas, J., *Les Méthodes Directes en Théorie des Équations Elliptiques*, Masson, Paris, 1967.

18. Ženíšek, A., A general theorem on triangular finite $C^{(m)}$-elements, RAIRO R2 (1974), 119-127.

Rémi Arcangéli
Laboratoire d'Analyse Numérique, U.A. 1204 CNRS
Université de Pau
Avenue de l'Université
64000 Pau
FRANCE

# Spline Elastic Manifolds

## M. Atteia and M. N. Benbourhim

**Abstract.** This paper is intended to give the definition and main properties of a spline elastic manifold which minimizes the stored energy function of an isotropic hyperelastic material with local constraints.

## §1. Introduction

Consider a thin elastic rod fixed at its ends $a$ and $b$, whose deformation $u$ (from its initial configuration) is prescribed at $m$ points $x_0, x_1, ..., x_m \in [a, b] \subset \mathbb{R}$. It is known that if $u'$ is small, then $u$ is the solution of the following problem:

$(\mathcal{P}_0)$      Minimize    $\int_a^b | u''(x) |^2 \, dx$     over $U_2$,

where

$$U_2 = \{u \in H^2(a, b) \quad \text{with} \quad u(x_i) = z_i, \quad i = 1, 2, ..., m\}.$$

Here we assume $k \geq 2$. The function $u$ is called an interpolatory *cubic spline*.

Mathematical generalizations of $(\mathcal{P}_0)$ have been extensively studied. The (univariate or multivariate) $D^k$-splines are among the most useful. These are the solutions of

$(\mathcal{P}_1)$      Minimize     $\int_{\mathbb{R}^n} | D^k u(x) |^2 \, dx$     over $U_k$,

where

$$U_k = \{u \in D^{-k} L^2(\mathbb{R}^n) \; : \; u(x_i) = z_i, \quad i = 1, 2, ..., m\}$$

and

Mathematical Methods in Computer Aided Geometric Design
Tom Lyche and Larry L. Schumaker (eds.), pp. 45–50.

$$|D^k u(x)|^2 = \sum_{\alpha_1 + \cdots + \alpha_n = k} \left| \frac{\partial^k u(x)}{(\partial x^1)^{\alpha_1} \ldots \ldots (\partial x^n)^{\alpha_n}} \right|^2.$$

Here we assume that $m \geq \dim(Ker D^k)$.

Note that in problem $(\mathcal{P}_1)$, $u$ is a *scalar* deformation which is, in general, unrealistic. Therefore, we define and study elastic spline manifolds. Here we shall consider the simplest example of an elastic spline manifold. It is the solution of the following problem:

$(\mathcal{P})$     Minimize   $J(u) := \int_{\mathbb{R}^3} \sum_{i,j=1}^3 | \varepsilon_{ij}[u(x)] |^2 \, dx$     over $U$,

where

$$U = \{u \; : \; \rho_\ell(u) = z_\ell, \quad 1 \leq \ell \leq m\},$$

and

$$\rho_\ell(u) := \frac{1}{\text{mes } (\omega_\ell)} \int_{\omega_\ell} [a_\ell u_1(x) + b_\ell u_2(x) + c_\ell u_3(x)] dx.$$

Here $\omega_\ell$ is a bounded open subset of $\mathbb{R}^3$,

$$\varepsilon_{ij}(u) = \frac{1}{2}(\partial_i u_j + \partial_j u_i),$$

and

$$z_\ell, a_\ell, b_\ell, c_\ell \in \mathbb{R}, \quad 1 \leq \ell \leq m.$$

Moreover, assume that $m \geq \dim(\text{Ker } \varepsilon)$, where $\varepsilon(u) = (\varepsilon_{11}(u), \varepsilon_{12}(u), \varepsilon_{22}(u))$.

In problem $(\mathcal{P})$, the expression $J(u)$ represents the stored energy function of an isotropic hyperelastic material. For simplicity, and without loss of generality, we shall suppose that $u = (u_1, u_2, 0)$.

## §2. The Space $\mathcal{K}$

In order to study $(\mathcal{P})$, we must specify the space where $u$ lies. We shall denote this space by $\mathcal{K}$. First, we recall

**Lemma 1.** *(Korn inequality).* If $\Omega$ is a "regular" bounded open subset of $\mathbb{R}^2$, then:

(i) $\mathcal{V} := \{v = (v_1, v_2) \in (L^2(\Omega))^2; \quad \varepsilon(v) \in (L^2(\Omega))^3\} = (H^1(\Omega))^2$

(ii) There exists $c > 0$ such that

$$\forall v \in (H^1(\Omega))^2, \qquad \| v \|_{(H^1(\Omega))^2} \leq c[| v |^2_{(L^2(\Omega))^2} + | \varepsilon(v) |^2_{(L^2(\Omega))^3}].$$

**Theorem 2.** Let $\mathcal{K} = \{u \in (\mathcal{D}')^2 \; : \; u \in (L^2_{loc})^2 \text{ and } \varepsilon(u) \in (L^2)^3\}$. Then

$$(H^1)^2 \subset \mathcal{K} \subset (H^1_{loc})^2.$$

*In addition, if*

$$(\varepsilon(u) = 0 \ \text{and} \ \rho_k(u) = 0, \quad k = 1, 2, 3) \qquad \Leftrightarrow \qquad (u = 0),$$

*then $\mathcal{K}$ is a Hilbert space with respect to the inner-product*

$$\langle u \mid v \rangle := (\varepsilon(u) \mid \varepsilon(v))_{(L^2)^3} + \sum_{k=1}^{3} \rho_k(u)\rho_k(v).$$

*We write $\|.\|$ for the canonical norm associated with $\langle , \rangle$.*

**Proof:** Let $(v^n)$ be a Cauchy sequence in $(\mathcal{K}, \langle , \rangle)$. There exists $w \in (L^2)^3$ such that $\lim_{n \to \infty} \mid \varepsilon(v^n) - w \mid_{(L^2)^3} = 0$. Let $\Omega_j$ be an open ball centered at the origin and let $v(j), j \in \mathbb{N}$ be its radius. We suppose that

(*) $\qquad\qquad\qquad \Omega_{j_0} \supset \omega_k, \qquad k = 1, 2, 3$

(**) $\qquad\qquad\qquad\qquad \Omega_{j+1} \supset \Omega_j$

(***) $\qquad\quad \cup_j \Omega_j = \mathbb{R}^2 \qquad \Rightarrow \qquad \lim_{j \to \infty} v(j) = +\infty.$

We denote by $\tilde{v}_j{}^n$ (respectively, $\tilde{w}_j$) the restriction of $v^n$ (respectively, $w$) to $\Omega_j$. From Lemma 1, we deduce that $(\tilde{v}_j{}^n) \subset H^1(\Omega_j)$, $(\tilde{v}_j{}^n)$ is a Cauchy sequence in $H^1(\Omega_j)$, and $(\varepsilon(\tilde{v}_j{}^n))$ is a Cauchy sequence in $(L^2(\Omega_j))^3$. Then

$$\lim_{n \to \infty} \mid \varepsilon(\tilde{v}_j{}^n) - \tilde{w}_j \mid_{(L^2(\Omega_j))^3} = 0$$

and

$$\lim_{n \to \infty} \| \tilde{v}_j{}^n - \tilde{v}_j \|_{(H^1(\Omega_j))^2} = 0, \qquad \varepsilon(\tilde{v}_j) = \tilde{w}_j.$$

Since for all $t \in \Omega_j$, $\tilde{v}_j{}^n(t) = \tilde{v}_{j+1}^n(t)$, it is easy to prove that

$$\tilde{v}_j(t) = \tilde{v}_{j+1}(t) \qquad \forall t \in \Omega \qquad a.e.,$$

and

$$\rho_k(\tilde{v}_j) = \rho_k(\tilde{v}_{j+1}) \qquad \forall t \in \Omega \qquad a.e.$$

Let $v$ such that $v(t) = \tilde{v}_j(t)$ for all $t \in \Omega_j$, almost everywhere. Thus,

$$v \in (L^2_{loc})^2, \quad \rho_k(v) = \lim_{n \to \infty} \rho_k(v^n), \qquad k = 1, 2, 3.$$

Moreover,

$$\varepsilon(v) = w \quad \in (L^2)^3.$$

Hence,

$$v \in \mathcal{K} \quad \text{and} \quad \lim_{n \to \infty} \ \|v^n - v\| = 0. \quad \blacksquare$$

## §3. The Hilbert Kernel of $\mathcal{K}$

There is a close connection between the solution of $(\mathcal{P})$ and the Hilbert kernel $K$ of $\mathcal{K}$. We now give an explicit formulation of $K$.

**Lemma 3.** *The space $\mathcal{K}$ is a Hilbert subspace of $\mathcal{D}'$; i.e., for each $\varphi \in \mathcal{D}^2$, there exists $c(\varphi) > 0$ such that for each $u \in \mathcal{K}$,*

$$\mid \langle u, \varphi \rangle \mid = \mid \int_{\mathbb{R}^2} u\varphi dx \mid \leq c(\varphi) \|u\|.$$

**Theorem 4.**

(i) *There exists $K : \mathcal{D}^2 \to (\mathcal{D}')^2$ such that*

$$K\varphi = \begin{pmatrix} K_1\varphi \\ K_2\varphi \end{pmatrix} = \begin{pmatrix} K_{11} & K_{12} \\ K_{21} & K_{22} \end{pmatrix} \begin{pmatrix} \varphi_1 \\ \varphi_2 \end{pmatrix},$$

$$K_{ij}\varphi_k = \int_{\mathbb{R}^2} K_{ij}(.,s)\varphi_k(s)ds, \qquad K_{12} = {}^t K_{21}$$

(ii) *$K$ is characterized by the relation*

$$\int_{\mathbb{R}^2} (\varphi_1\psi_1 + \varphi_2\psi_2)ds = (\varepsilon(K\varphi) \mid \varepsilon(\psi))_{(L^2)^3} + \sum_{k=1}^{3} \rho_k(K\varphi) \cdot \rho_k(\psi)$$

*for all $(\varphi, \psi) \in \mathcal{D}^2$.*

**Proof:** The proof is classical (cf. [1]). ■

**Theorem 5.**

(i) *There exist linearly independent polynomials $\pi_k \in Ker\ \varepsilon, k = 1, 2, 3$ such that $\rho_j(\pi_k) = \delta_{jk}$, $j, k = 1, 2, 3$.*

(ii) *For $i,j = 1,2$, let*

$$H_{ij}(s) = -\frac{1}{2} \frac{s_i s_j}{\mid s \mid^2} + \frac{3}{2}\delta_{ij}Log \mid s \mid + \frac{5}{4}\delta_{ij},$$

*where*

$$\mid s \mid^2 = s_1^2 + s_2^2,$$

*and*

$$\delta_{ij} = \begin{cases} 1, & \text{if } i = j \\ 0, & \text{if } i \neq j. \end{cases}$$

*Then $K(s,t) = L(s,t) + N(s,t)$, where*

$$N(s,t) = \sum_{k=1}^{3} \pi_k(s)\pi_k(t),$$

$$L(s,t) = H(s,t) - \sum_{k=1}^{3} \pi_k(s)\rho_k(H(.,t)) - \sum_{\ell=1}^{3} \pi_\ell(t)\rho_\ell(H(s,.))$$

$$+ \sum_{k,\ell=1}^{3} \pi_k(s)\pi_k(t)(\rho_k^{(\theta)} \cdot \rho_\ell^{(\theta')})(H(\theta,\theta')).$$

**Proof:** Part (ii) is easy to prove if we notice that

$$\Delta H_{11}(.,t) + \partial_1[\text{div } H_{.1}(.,t)] = -\delta_t$$

$$\partial_2(\text{div } H_{.1}(.,t)) + \Delta H_{21}(.,t) = 0 \tag{1}$$

and

$$\Delta H_{12}(.,t) + \partial_1[\text{div } H_{.2}(.,t)] = 0$$

$$\partial_2(\text{div } H_{.2}(.,t) + \Delta H_{22}(.,t) = -\delta_t, \tag{2}$$

where $\Delta = \partial_1^2 + \partial_2^2$ and $\delta_t$ is the Dirac distribution. ∎

**Remark 6.** *H is the solution of the following problem:*

$$\frac{1}{4\pi} \{\Delta H(.,t) + \text{grad}(\text{div } H(.,t))\} = \delta_t I,$$

where $I$ is the unit tensor.

**Theorem 7.** *Let $\omega$ be a "regular" bounded open subset of $\mathbb{R}^2$ and suppose that for each $v \in \mathcal{K}$,*

$$\rho(v) = \int_\omega (av_1 + bv_2)dx, \qquad a, b \in \mathbb{R}.$$

*Then, for each $v \in \mathcal{K}$, we have $\rho(v) = \langle \chi \mid v \rangle$, where*

$$\chi_j = \int_\omega [aK_{1j}(t,.) + bK_{2j}(t,.)]dt, \qquad j = 1, 2.$$

**Proof:** The assertion that $\langle \chi \mid K\psi \rangle = \int_{\mathbb{R}^2}(\chi_1\psi_1 + \chi_2\psi_2)dt$ for all $\psi \in \mathcal{D}^2$, is equivalent to

$$\int_\omega [a(K_{11}\psi_1 + K_{12}\psi_2) + b(K_{21}\psi_1 + K_{22}\psi_2)]dt = \int_{\mathbb{R}^2}(\chi_1\psi_1 + \chi_2\psi_2)dt$$

for all $\psi \in \mathcal{D}^2$. ∎

## §4. Characterization of the elastic spline manifold

**Remark 8.** *Problem* $(\mathcal{P})$ *is equivalent to*

$$(\tilde{P}) \qquad \text{Minimize } \|u\| \qquad \text{over } u \in \mathcal{K} \quad \text{with } \rho_\ell(u) = z_\ell, \ 1 \le \ell \le m.$$

The proof of the following result is classical:

**Theorem 9.**

(i) $(\tilde{P})$ *has a unique solution* $\sigma$.

(ii) *If* $\chi^\ell$ *is such that:* $\forall v \in \mathcal{K}, \rho_\ell(v) = \langle \chi^\ell \mid v \rangle, 1 \le \ell \le m$, *then*

$$\sigma = \sum_{\ell=1}^{m} \mu_\ell \chi_\ell, \qquad \mu_\ell \in \mathbb{R}, \quad 1 \le \ell \le m,$$

*with* $\rho_j(\sigma) = z_j, \qquad 1 \le j \le m$.

(iii) $\sigma \in H_{loc}^2 \ \subset \ C^0$.

**Remark 10.** *The assertion* $\rho_j(\sigma) = z_j$ *is equivalent to* $\sum_{l=1}^{m} \mu_\ell \langle \chi^j \mid \chi^\ell \rangle = z_j$.

## References

1. Atteia, Marc, *Noyaux Hilbertiens et Fonctions Spline*, (book), to appear.
2. Benbourhim, Mohammed Najib, Doctoral thesis, to appear.
3. Duchon, Jean, Interpolation des fonctions de deux variables suivant le principe de la flexion des plaques minces, RAIRO Analyse Numérique **10** (1976), 5–12.
4. El Jihad, Jamal, Représentation des variétés à l'aide des fonctions splines de type moyenne locale, minimisant l'énergie de déformation élastique, Université Paul Sabatier, June, 1986.

M. Atteia and M. N. Benbourhim
Université Paul Sabatier
Laboratoire d'Analyse Numérique
118, route de Narbonne
31062 Toulouse Cédex
FRANCE

# Geometry Processing: Curvature Analysis and Surface-Surface Intersection

### Robert E. Barnhill

**Abstract.** Geometry Processing is the extraction of geometric features from an already constructed curve or surface. This paper concentrates on two aspects of geometry processing: curvature analysis and surface-surface intersections. Curvature analysis is a means of interrogating the higher order smoothness of curves and surfaces. A curve fairing method utilizing curvature plots is discussed. Curvature analysis for surfaces is used to determine the fairness of surfaces and to measure the effects of different choices of twists for bicubic patches. Surface-surface intersections of parametric patches is an important topic in geometric modelling. Our algorithm for surface-surface intersection is presented, including its application to offset surfaces.

## §1. Introduction to Geometry Processing

Geometry Processing is the extraction of geometric features from an already constructed curve or surface. Geometry processing arises in many applications such as detecting regions of high stress in finite element calculations and the modelling of automobile surfaces and engineering parts.

Geometry processing topics currently under consideration by the Computer Aided Geometric Design Group at Arizona State University include curve fairing, surface curvature analysis, surface-surface intersection, offset surfaces, and mass properties of surfaces. This paper is a survey of our recent progress on the first four of these topics. The fifth topic, mass properties, is discussed by Barnhill and Watson [5].

The outline of this paper is the following: Curve smoothing algorithms which make intrinsic use of curvature plots are presented in Section 2. Curvature analysis is used to interrogate the higher order smoothness of surfaces and to measure the effects of different choices of twists for bicubic patches in Section 3. One of the key elements in geometric modelling systems is a robust

Mathematical Methods in Computer Aided Geometric Design
Tom Lyche and Larry L. Schumaker (eds.), pp. 51–60.
ISBN 0-12-460515-X.

surface-surface intersection algorithm. Our surface-surface intersection algorithm for parametric patches is discussed, including its use to determine offset surfaces, in Section 4.

## §2. Curve Fairing

The "fairness" of a curve or surface has both esthetic (Birkhoff [7]) and practical applications (Nowacki [19]), examples being automobile and airplane surfaces, respectively. Surfaces are frequently built up from curves. Also, curves have some intrinsic value themselves, so we begin with curve fairing.

A difficulty: two curves may look almost identical, but one may be fairer than the other. How can fairness be measured? One approach is to consider a derivative of the curve. The second derivative of a planar curve $\mathbf{x}$ is related to the curvature $\kappa$ by

$$\kappa(t) = \frac{||\mathbf{x}'(t) \times \mathbf{x}''(t)||}{||\mathbf{x}'(t)||^3}. \tag{2.1}$$

A curvature plot may thus be used to interrogate higher order smoothness.

Farin, Rein, Sapidis, and Worsey [10] have developed a robust algorithm for planar cubic spline curves. A cubic spline curve is $C^2$, so its curvature is continuous. Two properties of a curve readily available from a plot of its curvature are the presence of inflection points and the variation of the curvature. Each can be "corrected" by means of the curve fairing algorithm. More precisely, the curve fairing algorithm identifies the "offending" knot, that is, the knot of largest discontinuity in the derivative of the curvature. The insertion of a $B$-spline knot (Boehm [8]) amounts to redefining a cubic over one interval as the same cubic over two subintervals. The inverse procedure, the removal of a knot, cannot be performed exactly (unless two cubic segments came from the same cubic polynomial). The fairing algorithm permits several possible approximations for removing the offending knot. The approximations are local, which means that changes affect the curve and hence its curvature only in the neighborhood of the change.

The local nature of the fairing algorithm makes it better for many applications than its predecessor algorithm, due to Kjellander [15]. Kjellander's algorithm removed an offending knot by creating the cubic Hermite interpolant to position and derivative data at the two knots surrounding the offending knot. Then the value of the Hermite interpolant at the offending knot was used as data for global cubic spline interpolation to all the positional data.

An example of a $B$-spline curve, its curvature plot and a faired version of the curve is illustrated in Figure 1. The original curve and smoothed curve look identical, but their curvature plots are different.

## §3. Surface Curvature Analysis

In the preceding section we used the curvature plot of a curve to detect geometric properties such as "fairness". Similarly, surfaces can be interrogated. Purposes of such interrogations include understanding the shape of a surface,

**Figure 1a.** Example curve.

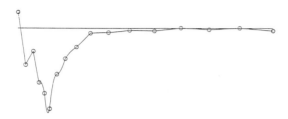

**Figure 1b.** Curvature plot of example curve.

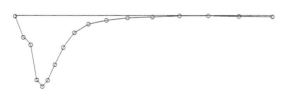

**Figure 1c.** Curvature plot after fairing at all the knots.

finding regions of convexity, and defining "twists" of certain surface forms. We use two surface interrogation tools to understand already constructed surfaces: reflection lines and curvatures.

*Reflection lines* are often used in computer graphics. So far as the surface **r** is concerned, reflection lines depend only on the surface normal **n** given by

$$\mathbf{n} = \frac{\mathbf{r}_u \times \mathbf{r}_v}{||\mathbf{r}_u \times \mathbf{r}_v||}. \tag{3.1}$$

Thus reflection lines depend upon the first derivatives of the surface. For examples of reflection lines, see the thesis of Fayard [12], and Color Plate 1 (inserted in this volume).

Surfaces have several curvatures. We focus on the principal curvatures, the derivation of which we now review. At a given point on surface $\mathbf{r}$ with normal $\mathbf{n}$, consider the ("normal section") curves on the surface formed by the intersection of the surface with planes containing $\mathbf{n}$. The curvature $k$ of a normal section curve can be decomposed into its normal and geodesic curvatures

$$k = k_n + k_g, \tag{3.2}$$

where $k_n$ is the projection of $k$ onto $\mathbf{n}$, and $k_g$ is then defined by equation (3.2). The curves resulting from setting $k_g = 0$ are called *geodesic curves*. Geodesic curves ("curves of shortest distance between points") are important in their own right in such applications as flat wrapping of airplane wings. For a discussion of geodesic curves for low order rectangular patches see the thesis by Whelan [20].

We focus here on the normal curvature $k_n$. The normal curvature can be calculated from the equation

$$k_n = \frac{-(\mathbf{u}')^T \, G \, \mathbf{u}'}{(\mathbf{u}')^T \, H \, \mathbf{u}'}, \tag{3.3}$$

where $\mathbf{u}' = [u', v']$ represents a direction in the parametric $uv$-plane and $G$ and $H$ are the first and second fundamental forms defined by

$$G = \begin{bmatrix} \mathbf{r}_u \cdot \mathbf{r}_u & \mathbf{r}_u \cdot \mathbf{r}_v \\ \mathbf{r}_v \cdot \mathbf{r}_u & \mathbf{r}_v \cdot \mathbf{r}_v \end{bmatrix} \tag{3.4}$$

$$H = \begin{bmatrix} \mathbf{n} \cdot \mathbf{r}_{uu} & \mathbf{n} \cdot \mathbf{r}_{vu} \\ \mathbf{n} \cdot \mathbf{r}_{uv} & \mathbf{n} \cdot \mathbf{r}_{vv} \end{bmatrix}. \tag{3.5}$$

The normal curvature is an extreme when

$$\frac{\partial k_n}{\partial u'} = 0, \quad \frac{\partial k_n}{\partial v'} = 0. \tag{3.6}$$

These conditions can be rewritten as the general eigenvalue-eigenvector equation

$$[G + k \, H]\mathbf{u}' = 0. \tag{3.7}$$

The extreme values of the principal curvature, called the *principal curvatures* $\kappa_1$ and $\kappa_2$, are the solutions of the quadratic equation

$$k^2 - 2bk + c = 0, \tag{3.8}$$

where $c = \frac{\det H}{\det G}$ and

$$b = (g_{12}h_{12} + g_{21}h_{21} - g_{11}h_{22} - g_{22}h_{11})/\det G.$$

The three curvatures used in Fayard's work are the *Gauss curvature* $\kappa_1\kappa_2$, the *mean curvature* $(\kappa_1 + \kappa_2)/2$ and the *absolute curvature* $|\kappa_1| + |\kappa_2|$. An example of Fayard's use of curvature analysis to study a surface follows. A wire frame drawing of the surface and two strip lighting reflections are shown in Color Plate 1. The curvature plot of the side curve is shown in Color Plate 2. Then the three surface curvatures, Gauss, mean, and absolute curvatures are displayed in color in Color Plate 3. Each of these curvatures shows different features of the surface. Color Plate 4 presents a black and white version showing local changes in the curvatures.

Next three points in the defining patch are altered by 1 part in 7,600. The resulting surface looks the same as the original surface, but the curvatures appear considerably different (see Color Plates 5 and 6).

These examples show the usefulness of curvature analysis in surface interrogation. For additional examples, see Fayard [12].

Surface curvatures have been considered by several authors. Forrest [13] suggests the use of Gauss curvature for surface interrogation. Nowacki and Reese [19] use Gauss curvature in the design and fairing of ship surfaces. Dill [9] uses Gauss and mean curvature on a torus, catenoid and car hood and fender. Munchmeyer [17,18] uses Gauss and mean curvature to study trigonometric functions. Beck, Farouki, and Hinds [6] use Gauss and mean curvature to study features of surfaces. Farouki [11] uses a curvature analysis in his offset surface algorithm.

## Curvature Analysis for Comparison of Twist Methods

Many design surfaces are constructed by means of a network of rectangular patches, because rectangular patches are easily interpreted and can be built up from curve schemes. Surfaces for most practical applications must be at least $C^1$. The most obvious way to build up a $C^1$ rectangular patch is from the tensor product of $C^1$ curves. However, this tensor product involves the $(1,1)$ derivative, called the "twist", at the four corners of the rectangular patch. Since the twist is a second derivative, and only first derivatives are specified as data, problems should and do arise.

Because tensor product patches are so important in applications, the problem of specifying twists has been considered by several authors. Barnhill, Brown, and Klucewicz [1] introduced the implied twist from "Adini's rectangle", a $C^0$ finite element which uses only first derivative data and has high accuracy. A second twist method is to use the implied twist from a bilinear patch; this is called the "FMILL twist". Finally, the original solution to the twist problem was to set all the twists equal to zero. These three methods can be compared by means of the surface curvature analysis. For additional information and examples on curvature analysis for twists, see Barnhill, Farin, Fayard, and Hagen [2] and Fayard [12].

## §4. Surface-Surface Intersection

Geometric modelling systems include Boolean operations such as finding the difference of two surfaces, which is equivalent to finding the intersection between two surfaces. Surface-surface intersection (SSI) also occurs in other applications such as design verification with interference checks of surfaces.

There are some algorithms for SSI that use a special structure of the surfaces. Such algorithms are efficient on the class of surfaces for which they are designed, e.g., polynomials, but may be either inapplicable or unreliable when applied to other surfaces. When integrating an SSI algorithm into a practical system, it is inconvenient to create algorithms for individual surface types. Thus Barnhill, Farin, Jordan, and Piper [3] developed a general SSI algorithm, which we now describe.

The problem specification is to find the intersection between two $C^1$ parametric rectangular patches for which positions and partial derivatives can be evaluated at any point.

The intersection of two smooth surfaces is either: (i) empty, (ii) a collection of points, (iii) a collection of smooth curves, (iv) a collection of smooth surfaces or (v) a combination of the above. We focus on (i) and (iii) hereafter, noting that (ii) is in general hopeless for any non-exhaustive algorithm. We can use our algorithm to detect (iv) and then take special measures.

Our criteria for success are:

1. The algorithm produces reasonable results on realistic examples

2. The algorithm is reasonably efficient.

A first idea is to exhaustively subdivide the surfaces until Criterion 1 is met. However, this would not produce an algorithm satisfying Criterion 2. We strike a balance between the two criteria for success by introducing four "tolerances" which control various aspects of the algorithm.

The algorithm proceeds in two stages: (1) find an initial point on an intersection curve and (2) follow this intersection curve by producing more points in a sequential fashion along the intersection curve.

**Step 1** (Finding an initial point on an intersection curve). Our plan is to intersect isoparametric curves of one surface with the second surface to find initial points of intersection curves between the two surfaces. (For symmetry, the roles of the two surfaces are interchanged later.) In fact, an isoparametric curve of the first surface is replaced by a suitably chosen (univariate) piecewise linear approximation and the second surface is replaced by a suitably chosen (bivariate) piecewise linear approximation. Both sets of approximations are controlled by the Search Refinement Tolerance (SRT). The intersections, if any, between the two types of piecewise linear functions are found. Such an intersection is made into a true intersection point by numerical analysis techniques of subdivision and Newton's method. These calculations are controlled by the user-specified Same Point Tolerance (SPT).

**Step 2** (Following an intersection curve). The intersection of the two tangent planes defines a direction in which we proceed, proportionally to the Curve Refinement Tolerance (CRT). Again, we must make points found into true intersection points by Newton's method. We stop following an intersection curve when we meet either with success or failure: "successes" include (i) the curve meets a boundary or meets itself, (ii) the curve meets the endpoint of a previously constructed intersection curve, (iii) the curve crosses an isoparametric curve at "nearly" the same point as a previously constructed intersection curve and "failure" means (iv) that the Newton's method and decreasing the length of the tangent vector failed to produce a new intersection point. In cases (iii) and (iv), we record the information as a "loose end" of the intersection curve to determine if subsequent intersection curves hook up with it.

A fourth tolerance, Optimization (OPT), simplifies the representation of intersection points on a line to only the endpoints of the line segment. This tolerance is applied at both local and global stages of the algorithm to compact the storage.

Efficiency of the algorithm is improved by deleting sections of isoparametric lines crossed by already-found intersection curves: this reduces the amount of searching for new intersection points.

Enhancements of the basic algorithm include a fast plane-patch intersection, surfaces with creases, and self-intersections.

Our SSI algorithm is illustrated with an example which has the following ingredients: a color picture of the two intersecting surfaces (see Color Plate 7) and a drawing of the intersection curves in the two parametric domains (see Figure 2). The first is a description of the problem and the second of the solution.

The only published algorithm of comparable generality to our algorithm is due to Houghton *et al.* [14]. Marchant's [16] master's thesis also implemented Houghton's algorithm. Barnhill and Kersey [4] are currently comparing the two SSI algorithms.

### §5. Offset Surfaces

Offset surfaces arise in geometric modelling for tolerancing and for the generation of tool paths for numerically controlled milling machines. The offset surface of the smooth parametric surface $\mathbf{r} = \mathbf{r}(u, v)$ has the equation

$$\mathbf{r}(u, v) + d(\mathbf{r}_u \times \mathbf{r}_v)/\text{length}(\mathbf{r}_u \times \mathbf{r}_v).$$

We observe that the offset surface is less smooth than its parent surface because of the derivatives and division by a square root. (A zero surface normal also can cause difficulties.) Farouki [11] has developed a curvature analysis for "non-degenerate" offset surfaces, "non-degenerate" meaning no cusps, ridges, or other tangent discontinuities, or self-intersections. Farouki's method has the following three steps: 1) A differential surface analysis is made to determine the extreme principal radii of curvature for each patch permissible without the offset's becoming degenerate. 2) The parametric domain of each patch is subdivided and the bicubic interpolant to the offset surface is computed. 3) A "tolerance analysis" on each patch of the offset surfaces determines its extreme deviation from the true offset.

For a possibly degenerate offset surface with creases or, more difficult, self-intersections, we have successfully applied our enhanced SSI algorithm. An example of the use of an SSI to detect a self-intersection is given in Color Plate 8 and Figure 3. This research is currently under further development.

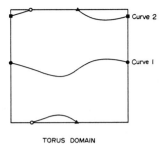

TORUS DOMAIN

**Figure 2a.** The pre-image of the intersection curves in the domain of the torus.

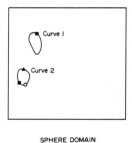

SPHERE DOMAIN

**Figure 2b.** The pre-image of the intersection curves in the domain of the sphere.

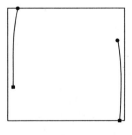

BICUBIC DOMAIN SELF INTERSECTION

**Figure 3.** The two pre-images of the intersection curve in the domain of the bicubic patch.

## Acknowledgments

This research was supported by the Department of Energy under grant DE-FG02-87ER25041 and by the National Science Foundation under grant DMC-8807747, both awarded to Arizona State University. The oral presentation of these results was made at the Mathematical Methods in CAGD conference in Oslo, June, 1988. We thank the organizers of the conference, Tom Lyche and Larry Schumaker, as well as their colleagues, for the pleasant and stimulating ambience of the conference.

## References

1. Barnhill, R. E., J. H. Brown, and I. M. Klucewicz, A new twist for CAGD, Computer Graphics and Image Processing **8** (1978), 78–91.
2. Barnhill, R. E., G. Farin, L. Fayard, and H. Hagen, Twists, curvatures and surface interrogation, Computer Aided Design **20** (1988), 341–346.
3. Barnhill, R. E., G. Farin, M. Jordan, and B. R. Piper, Surface-surface intersection, Comput. Aided Geom. Design **4** (1987), 3–16.
4. Barnhill, R. E. and S. N. Kersey, Two general methods for surface-surface intersection, preprint.
5. Barnhill, R. E. and S. H. Watson, Geometry processing: numerical multiple integration, in *Mathematics of Surfaces III*, Oxford University Press, to appear.
6. Beck, J., R. Farouki, and J. Hinds, Surface analysis methods, IEEE Computer Graphics & Applications **6** (1986), 18–36.
7. Birkhoff, G. D., *Aesthetic Measure*, Harvard University Press, Cambridge, MA, 1933.
8. Boehm, W., Inserting new knots into $B$-spline curves, Comput. Aided Design **12** (1981), 199–201.
9. Dill, J. C., An application of color graphics and ship hull surface curvature, Computer Graphics (Proc. SIGGRAPH 81) **15** (1981), 153–161.
10. Farin, G., G. Rein, N. Sapidis, and A. J. Worsey, Fairing cubic $B$-spline curves, Comput. Aided Geom. Design **4** (1987), 91–103.
11. Farouki, R., The approximation of non-degenerate offset surfaces, Comput. Aided Geom. Design **3** (1986), 15–43.
12. Fayard, L., The use of curvatures as a surface interrogation tool, Master's thesis, Arizona State University, 1988.
13. Forrest, A. R., On the rendering of surfaces, Computer Graphics (Proc. SIGGRAPH 79) **13** (1979), 253–259.
14. Houghton, E. G., R. F. Emnett, J. D. Factor, and C. L. Sabharwal, Implementation of a divide-and-conquer method for intersection of parametric surfaces, in *Surfaces in Computer Aided Geometric Design '84*, R. E. Barnhill and W. Boehm, (eds.), North-Holland, Amsterdam, 1985, 173–183.
15. Kjellander, J. A., Smoothing of cubic parametric splines, Comput. Aided Design **15** (1983), 175–179.

16. Marchant, P., A numerical method for intersection of parametric surfaces, Master's thesis, University of Utah, 1987.
17. Munchmeyer, F., On surface imperfections, in *Mathematics of Surfaces II*, R. R. Martin (ed.), Clarendon Press, Oxford, 1987, 459–474.
18. Munchmeyer, F., Shape Interrogation: a case study, in *Geometric Modeling: Algorithms and New Trends*, G. E. Farin (ed.), SIAM Publications, Philadelphia, 1987, 291–301.
19. Nowacki, H. and D. Reese, Design and fairing of ship surfaces, in *Computer Aided Geometric Design*, R. E. Barnhill and W. Boehm, (eds.), North-Holland, Amsterdam, 1983, 121–134.
20. Whelan, T. M., Geodesic curves on rectangular polynomial Bezier surface patches, Ph.D. dissertation, University of Utah, 1985.

Robert E. Barnhill
Computer Science Department
Arizona State University
Tempe, Arizona 85287
USA

# Three Examples of
# Dual Properties of Bézier Curves

## P. J. Barry and R. N. Goldman

**Abstract.** The dual functionals for the Bernstein basis are used to develop three examples of relationships between certain properties of Bézier curves. In particular, degree elevation is shown to be intimately related to differentiation; transformations to monomial form are essentially the same as transformations from monomial form; and evaluation by the de Casteljau algorithm is related to evaluation by nested multiplication.

## §1. Introduction

Bézier curves are mathematically elegant for many reasons. Bernstein polynomials appear not only in CAGD (computer aided geometric design), but also in such diverse areas as approximation theory and probability theory. Thus Bézier curves have links to several branches of mathematics. The reason that Bézier curves enjoy widespread use in CAGD is that they possess many useful geometric properties (see, for example, [3]). Few, if any other curve schemes, possess the same sheer number of properties. Moreover, there are nice interrelationships involving certain of these properties. For example, the de Casteljau evaluation algorithm can also be used for subdivision. If one views the de Casteljau algorithm primarily as a subdivision technique and remembers that Bézier curves interpolate their endpoints, this is not so surprising, but if one views it primarily as an evaluation algorithm, this is indeed astonishing.

In this paper we will expand on these connections by giving three examples of relationships between properties of Bézier curves. First, we will show that the two-term differentiation formula for Bézier curves is intimately related to the two-term degree elevation formula; secondly, that transformations to monomial form are essentially the same as transformations from monomial form; and thirdly, that evaluation by the de Casteljau algorithm is related to evaluation by Horner-type schemes (*i.e.*, nested multiplication).

Mathematical Methods in Computer Aided Geometric Design
Tom Lyche and Larry L. Schumaker (eds.), pp. 61–69.

The tool we will use to derive these examples is the dual basis for the Bernstein polynomials. Write $B_k^n(t) = \binom{n}{k}t^k(1-t)^{n-k}$. An important identity is

$$\sum_{r=0}^{n} \frac{(-1)^{n-r}[B_{n-j}^n(\tau)]^{(n-r)}[B_k^n(\tau)]^{(r)}}{n!(-1)^{n-j}\binom{n}{n-j}} = \delta_{jk}, \tag{1}$$

where $\tau$ is any number. This can be proved simply by showing first that the left hand side is indeed independent of the choice of $\tau$ (this can be done by showing that the derivative of the left hand side with respect to $\tau$ is identically 0), and then examining the $\tau = 0$ and $\tau = 1$ cases.

Equation (1) tells us that the dual basis for the Bernstein basis of degree $n$ consists of the linear functionals $\lambda_{n,j}$ on the space of polynomials of degree $n$ (or less) given by

$$\lambda_{n,j}f = \sum_{r=0}^{n} \frac{(-1)^{n-r}[B_{n-j}^n(\tau)]^{(n-r)}[f(\tau)]^{(r)}}{n!(-1)^{n-j}\binom{n}{n-j}}, \tag{2}$$

or in a slightly different form by

$$\lambda_{n,j}f = \sum_{r=0}^{n} \frac{(-1)^{n-r}}{n!}[((-\tau)^{n-j}(1-\tau)^j]^{(n-r)}[f(\tau)]^{(r)}. \tag{3}$$

*The crucial observation is that the dual basis is simply expressed in terms of the Bernstein basis functions themselves.* So relationships between the dual functionals give us relationships between the basis functions, and vice versa. Further, equation (1) can be interpreted either as applying $\lambda_{n,j}$ to $B_k^n(t)$, or as applying $\lambda_{n,n-k}$ to a constant multiple of $B_{n-j}^n(t)$. These are the two facts that are exploited in all of the examples below.

The dual functionals for the Bernstein basis functions are a special case of the de Boor-Fix form of the dual basis for B-splines [4]. Given a sequence of knots $t_i$, and letting $N_i^n(t)$ be the B-spline of degree $n$ (order $n + 1$) with leftmost point of support $t_i$, we can write the B-spline dual functionals as

$$\hat{\lambda}_{n,i}f = \sum_{r=0}^{n} \frac{(-1)^{n-r}}{n!}[\psi_i(\tau_i)]^{(n-r)}[f(\tau_i)]^{(r)}, \tag{4}$$

where $\psi_i(t) = (t_{i+1}-t)(t_{i+2}-t)\cdots(t_{i+n}-t)$, and $\tau_i$ is any point in $(t_i, t_{i+n+1})$. What allows this formula to specialize to equation (2) is the fact that not only are the Bernstein basis functions a special case of B-splines, but they are also a special case of the functions $\psi_i(t)$ (up to normalizing constants).

## §2. Example 1. Degree Elevation and Differentiation

Bézier curves possess a simple two-term degree elevation formula based on the identity

$$B_k^n(t) = \left(\frac{n+1-k}{n+1}\right)B_k^{n+1}(t) + \left(\frac{k+1}{n+1}\right)B_{k+1}^{n+1}(t), \tag{5}$$

and they also possess a simple two-term differentiation formula from the identity

$$[B_k^{n+1}(t)]' = (n+1)(B_{k-1}^n(t) - B_k^n(t)). \tag{6}$$

In our first example we will show that these identities are intimately related.

For the moment, let us put aside the fact that Bézier curves have *two-term* degree elevation and differentiation formulas. Instead, let us merely use the fact that that there exist matrices $A$ and $C$ such that

$$B_k^n(t) = \sum_{j=0}^{n+1} A_{jk} B_j^{n+1}(t) \tag{7}$$

and

$$[B_j^{n+1}(t)]' = \sum_{k=0}^{n} C_{kj} B_k^n(t). \tag{8}$$

That is, $A$ provides the transformation corresponding to degree elevation, and $C$ the transformation corresponding to differentiation. What we will show is that $A$ and $C$ are very nearly the same matrix.

Applying the linear functional $\lambda_{n+1,j}$ to equation (7), we get

$$A_{jk} = \sum_{r=0}^{n+1} \frac{(-1)^{n+1-r}[B_{n+1-j}^{n+1}(\tau)]^{(n+1-r)}[B_k^n(\tau)]^{(r)}}{(n+1)!(-1)^{n+1-j}\binom{n+1}{n+1-j}}. \tag{9}$$

Using the fact that $[B_k^n(t)]^{(n+1)} = 0$ and re-indexing, we can write this as

$$(n+1)(-1)^j \binom{n+1}{j} A_{jk} = \sum_{r=0}^{n} \frac{(-1)^{n-r}}{n!}[B_k^n(\tau)]^{(n-r)}[B_{n+1-j}^{n+1}(\tau)]^{(r+1)}. \tag{10}$$

Now applying $\lambda_{n,k}$ to (8) yields

$$C_{kj} = \sum_{r=0}^{n} \frac{(-1)^{n-r}[B_{n-k}^n(\tau)]^{(n-r)}[B_j^{n+1}(\tau)]^{(r+1)}}{n!(-1)^{n-k}\binom{n}{n-k}}. \tag{11}$$

We can rewrite this as

$$(-1)^k \binom{n}{k} C_{n-k,n+1-j} = \sum_{r=0}^{n} \frac{(-1)^{n-r}}{n!}[B_k^n(\tau)]^{(n-r)}[B_{n+1-j}^{n+1}(\tau)]^{(r+1)}. \tag{12}$$

Comparing (10) and (12) provides

$$A_{jk} = \frac{(-1)^{k-j}\binom{n}{k}}{(n+1)\binom{n+1}{j}} C_{n-k,n+1-j}. \tag{13}$$

Thus, up to a re-indexing and multiplication by some constants, the matrix $A$ and matrix $C$ are the same, so the coefficients used in degree elevation and the coefficients used in differentiation correspond. In particular, since (13) holds, the fact that Bézier curves have a two-term degree elevation formula is equivalent to the fact they have a two-term differentiation formula.

## §3. Example 2. Transformations to and from Monomial Form

Oftentimes, Bézier curves are transformed to or from monomial form. We will leave aside particular techniques for doing these transformations as well as the question of when such transformations are appropriate. Rather, our purpose in this example is to show that the relationship between these two transformations consists of more than the obvious fact that they are inverses of each other. Let the matrices $A$ and $C$ give the transformation to and from, respectively, the monomial basis:

$$t^k = \sum_{j=0}^{n} A_{jk} B_j^n(t) \tag{14}$$

$$B_j^n(t) = \sum_{k=0}^{n} C_{kj} t^k. \tag{15}$$

We can isolate $A_{jk}$ by applying $\lambda_{n,j}$ to the first of these equations to get

$$A_{jk} = \sum_{r=0}^{n} \frac{(-1)^{n-r}[B_{n-j}^n(\tau)]^{(n-r)}[\tau^k]^{(r)}}{n!(-1)^{n-j}\binom{n}{n-j}} \tag{16}$$

or

$$(-1)^{n-j}\binom{n}{j}A_{jk} = \sum_{r=0}^{n} \frac{(-1)^{n-r}}{n!}[B_{n-j}^n(\tau)]^{(n-r)}[\tau^k]^{(r)}. \tag{17}$$

We next wish to isolate $C_{kj}$. In order to do so, we use the dual basis for the monomial form. Rather than expressing these dual functionals in their usual representation as derivatives evaluated at 0 (which can also be used to derive our result), we shall express them in a form similar to the form for the Bernstein basis dual functionals in (2). The monomial basis satisfies an identity similar to (1):

$$\sum_{r=0}^{n} \frac{(-1)^{n-r}[\tau^{n-j}]^{(n-r)}[\tau^k]^{(r)}}{n!(-1)^{n-j}\binom{n}{n-j}^{-1}} = \delta_{jk} \tag{18}$$

and we can therefore write the dual basis for $1, t, \ldots, t^n$ as linear functionals $\xi_{n,j}$ given by

$$\xi_{n,j}f = \sum_{r=0}^{n} \frac{(-1)^{n-r}[\tau^{n-j}]^{(n-r)}[f(\tau)]^{(r)}}{n!(-1)^{n-j}\binom{n}{n-j}^{-1}}. \tag{19}$$

Applying $\xi_{n,k}$ to (15) gives us

$$C_{kj} = \sum_{r=0}^{n} \frac{(-1)^{n-r}[\tau^{n-k}]^{(n-r)}[B_j^n(\tau)]^{(r)}}{n!(-1)^{n-k}\binom{n}{n-k}^{-1}} \tag{20}$$

which, by reindexing, we can rewrite as

$$\frac{(-1)^{n-k}}{\binom{n}{k}}C_{n-k,n-j} = \sum_{r=0}^{n} \frac{(-1)^{n-r}}{n!}[\tau^k]^{(r)}[B_{n-j}^n(\tau)]^{(n-r)}. \tag{21}$$

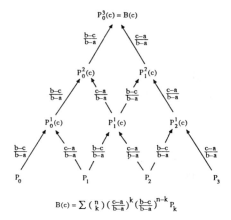

$$B(c) = \sum \binom{n}{k} \left(\tfrac{c-a}{b-a}\right)^k \left(\tfrac{b-c}{b-a}\right)^{n-k} P_k$$

**Figure 1.** The de Casteljau algorithm for the cubic case.

Comparing (17) and (21), we get

$$A_{jk} = \frac{(-1)^{k-j}}{\binom{n}{j}\binom{n}{k}} C_{n-k,n-j}. \tag{22}$$

Again, the matrices for these two transformations are the same up to re-indexing and multiplication by some constants. Since $A$ and $C$ are inverses, their relationship is somewhat akin to being orthogonal matrices.

## §4. Example 3. de Casteljau and Horner Evaluation

Our third example is slightly more involved. We will now show that the de Casteljau algorithm for evaluating a Bézier curve is related to Horner-type (*i.e.*, nested multiplication) evaluation techniques. For a discussion of the use of nested multiplication to evaluate Bézier curves and surfaces, see [5,6].

It will serve our purposes to give the de Casteljau algorithm for a Bézier curve

$$B(t) = \sum_{k=0}^{n} \binom{n}{k} \left(\frac{t-a}{b-a}\right)^k \left(\frac{b-t}{b-a}\right)^{n-k} P_k \tag{23}$$

parametrized over the interval $[a, b]$ rather than over the unit interval. To evaluate this curve at $t = c$, let

$$P_k^0(c) = P_k, \quad k = 0, \ldots, n$$

$$P_k^n(c) = \left(\frac{b-c}{b-a}\right) P_k^{r-1}(c) + \left(\frac{c-a}{b-a}\right) P_{k+1}^{r-1}(c), \quad r = 1, \ldots, n; \quad k = 0, \ldots, n-r. \tag{24}$$

Then $P_0^n(c) = B(c)$. This can be diagrammed as in Figure 1.

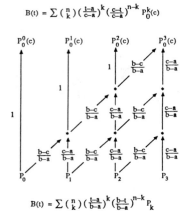

$$B(t) = \sum \left(\begin{array}{c}n\\k\end{array}\right)\left(\frac{t-a}{c-a}\right)^k\left(\frac{c-t}{c-a}\right)^{n-k}P_0^k(c)$$

$$B(t) = \sum \left(\begin{array}{c}n\\k\end{array}\right)\left(\frac{t-a}{b-a}\right)^k\left(\frac{b-t}{b-a}\right)^{n-k}P_k$$

**Figure 2.** The de Casteljau algorithm viewed as a transformation.

One way of interpreting the de Casteljau algorithm is that it is a transformation technique. The points $P_0^0(c), P_0^1(c), \ldots, P_0^n(c)$ provide the control
points for the segment of the original curve between $a$ and $c$, while the points
$P_0^n(c), P_1^{n-1}(c), \ldots, P_n^0(c)$ are the control points for the segment between $c$
and $b$. Let us focus on the first of these. We can then diagram the de
Casteljau algorithm as in Figure 2, as a transformation from a curve with
control points $P_0, P_1, \ldots, P_n$ and basis functions $\tilde{B}_k^n(t) = \left(\begin{array}{c}n\\k\end{array}\right)\left(\frac{t-a}{b-a}\right)^k\left(\frac{b-t}{b-a}\right)^{n-k}$
to a curve with control points $P_0^0(c), P_0^1(c), \ldots, P_0^n(c)$ and basis functions
$\hat{B}_k^n(t) = \left(\begin{array}{c}n\\k\end{array}\right)\left(\frac{t-a}{c-a}\right)^k\left(\frac{c-t}{c-a}\right)^{n-k}$.

This transformation induces a transformation in the dual space. However,
remember that since the Bernstein basis appears in its own dual basis, transformations between the dual functionals are actually transformations involving
the Bernstein basis itself. More specifically, since the dual basis for the $\tilde{B}_k^n(t)$
consists of $\tilde{\lambda}_{n,k}$ given by

$$\tilde{\lambda}_{n,k}f = \sum_{r=0}^{n} \frac{(-1)^{n-r}}{n!}[(a-\tau)^{n-k}(b-\tau)^k]^{(n-r)}[f(\tau)]^{(r)} \tag{25}$$

for any $\tau$, we replace $\tilde{B}_k^n(t)$ by $(a-t)^{n-k}(b-t)^k$, and similarly $\hat{B}_k^n(t)$ by
$(a-t)^{n-k}(c-t)^k$. Writing $Q_k = P_0^{n-k}(c)$, we then get the transformation
shown in Figure 3 from the curve

$$Q(t) = \sum_{k=0}^{n}(a-t)^{n-k}(c-t)^k Q_{n-k} \tag{26}$$

to a different representation

$$Q(t) = \sum_{k=0}^{n}(a-t)^{n-k}(b-t)^k P_k. \tag{27}$$

$$Q(t) = \sum \binom{n}{k} (a-t)^{n-k} (c-t)^k Q_{n-k}$$

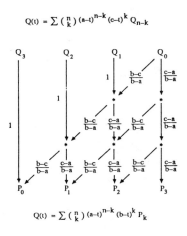

$$Q(t) = \sum \binom{n}{k} (a-t)^{n-k} (b-t)^k P_k$$

**Figure 3.** The dual transformation.

Thus, when we dualize the de Casteljau algorithm, we obtain a transformation between two unnormalized Bézier curves (which are over different intervals). Leaving aside the question of normalization for the moment, note from (27) that $Q(b) = (a-b)^n P_0$. Since $a, b, c$ are arbitrary, we can evaluate $Q(t)$ by applying the part of the dual transformation which finds $P_0$. This is shown in Figure 4.

From the figure it is not difficult to see that this process is equivalent to evaluating $Q(t)$ by using the nesting

$$Q(b) = (a-b)^n (Q_n + \frac{b-c}{b-a}(Q_{n-1} + \frac{b-c}{b-a}(Q_{n-2} +$$

$$\ldots + \frac{b-c}{b-a}(Q_1 + \frac{b-c}{b-a}Q_0)\cdots))). \qquad (28)$$

Thus we have essentially shown that by dualizing the de Casteljau algorithm we can derive a nested evaluation algorithm for Bézier curves. In a similar manner, if we start with the dual transformation, we can derive the de Casteljau algorithm.

There are many options for dealing with the normalization. One is to incorporate the constants into the control points. In such a case, if we are evaluating a Bézier curve over $[0,1]$ at $t = b$, the nesting in (28) becomes

$$Q(b) = (-b)^n (Q_n + \frac{b-1}{b}(Q_{n-1} + \frac{b-1}{b}(Q_{n-2} +$$

$$\ldots + \frac{b-1}{b}(Q_1 + \frac{b-1}{b}Q_0)\cdots))). \qquad (29)$$

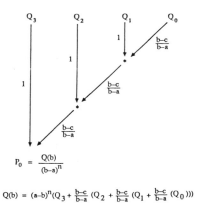

$$P_0 = \frac{Q(b)}{(b-a)^n}$$

$$Q(b) = (a-b)^n(Q_3 + \tfrac{b-c}{b-a}(Q_2 + \tfrac{b-c}{b-a}(Q_1 + \tfrac{b-c}{b-a}(Q_0))))$$

**Figure 4.** Evaluating an unnormalized Bézier
curve using part of the dual transformation.

Note that if $0 < b < 1$, this nesting will involve negative coefficients. This can
be remedied by using $(t-a)^{n-k}(c-t)^k$ and $(t-a)^{n-k}(b-t)^k$ as the basis
functions. In this case the nesting becomes

$$Q(b) = b^n(Q_n + \frac{1-b}{b}(Q_{n-1} + \frac{1-b}{b}(Q_{n-2} + \ldots + \frac{1-b}{b}(Q_1 + \frac{1-b}{b}Q_0)\cdots))).$$
$$(30)$$

Alternately, one can make sure that all the basis functions are normalized, in
which case evaluation can still be done by nested multiplication, although the
labels on the arrows in Figure 4 will take on different values.

It is also possible to nest an unnormalized Bézier curve as

$$B(b) = (1-b)^n(Q_0 + \frac{b}{1-b}(Q_1 + \frac{b}{1-b}(Q_2 + \ldots + \frac{b}{1-b}(Q_{n-1} + \frac{b}{1-b}Q_n)\cdots)).$$
$$(31)$$

In fact this is preferable for reasons of numerical stability if $0 < b < .5$.
This is the nesting one gets if, rather than viewing the de Casteljau algorithm
as a transformation to a Bézier curve between $a$ and $c$, one views it as a
transformation to a Bézier curve between $c$ and $b$.

An alternate way of viewing the above relationship is to consider Bézier
curves as special cases of B-splines and Pólya curves. The analysis is much the
same, although the perspective is somewhat different. For further details see
[1,2].

## §5. Concluding Remarks

We have used the dual functionals for the Bernstein basis functions to demonstrate three examples of the interconnectedness of various properties of Bézier curves. First, we showed that degree elevation and differentiation are closely related. Second, we showed that transformations to and from monomial form were linked in more than the obvious fashion. Third, we showed an intimate relationship between the de Casteljau evaluation algorithm and nested multiplication evaluation schemes. These three examples demonstrate the web of interconnectedness surrounding various properties of Bézier curves and give some insight into why Bézier curves have so many desirable properties.

Open questions for possible future research are whether additional connections exist for other properties of Bézier curves and whether or not a similar analysis applied to other curve schemes will yield any fruitful results.

### References

1. Barry, P. J., T. D. DeRose, and R. N. Goldman, B-splines, Pólya curves, and duality, preprint.
2. Barry, P. J. and R. N. Goldman, Knot deletion for Pólya curves, in preparation.
3. Boehm, W., G. Farin, and J. Kahmann, A survey of curve and surface methods in CAGD, Comput. Aided Geom. Design **1** (1984), 1–60.
4. de Boor, C. and G. Fix, Spline interpolation by quasi-interpolants, J. Approx. Theory **8** (1973), 19–45.
5. Farouki, R. T. and V. T. Rajan, Algorithms for polynomials in Bernstein form, Comput. Aided Geom. Design **5** (1988), 1–26.
6. Schumaker, L. L. and W. Volk, On the efficient evaluation of multivariate Bernstein polynomials, Comput. Aided Geom. Design **3** (1986), 149–154.

Phillip J. Barry and Ronald N. Goldman
Computer Graphics Laboratory
Computer Science Department
University of Waterloo
Waterloo, Ontario N2L 3G1
CANADA

Supported in part by the Natural Sciences and Engineering Research Council of Canada Grant OGP0036825

EMAIL: pjbarry@ watcgl.waterloo.edu
EMAIL: rngoldman@ watcgl.waterloo.edu

# What is the Natural Generalization
# of a Bézier Curve?

P. J. Barry and R. N. Goldman

**Abstract.** By splitting the standard properties of Bézier curves into three categories, we show that the question "what is the natural generalization of a Bézier curve?" has a particularly satisfying answer: both the B-spline curves and the Pólya polynomials are natural generalizations of Bézier curves because Bézier curves inherit all their nice features from one or the other or both of these schemes. Moreover, the B-splines and the Pólya polynomials are related by the de Boor-Fix dual functionals. We also examine the split of Bézier features into B-spline and Pólya properties and the interconnections between these two curve forms and their properties. This analysis sheds some new light on the origins of, and connections between, many of the standard features of Bézier curves.

## §1. Introduction

Bézier curves can be generalized in many ways. Since Bézier curves are polynomial, one might think about extending them either to rational polynomial or to piecewise polynomial schemes. In this sense both rational Bézier curves [16] and B-spline curves [6] are natural generalizations of Bézier curves. Or one might think of generalizing from curves to surfaces; and indeed both tensor product [5] and simplicial [11] extensions have been studied in some detail. Thus the answer to the question "what is the natural generalization of a Bézier curve?" seems to depend very much on what it is one is trying to generalize.

Typically, B-spline curves are considered to be *the* natural generalization of Bézier curves; that is, the Bernstein basis functions are viewed simply as B-splines with multiple knots. But even this perspective is somewhat limited, since Bézier curves have many interesting properties, not all of which extend readily to B-spline curves.

In this paper we will show that the question "what is the natural generalization of a Bézier curve?" does have a satisfying (and even elegant) answer. By

Mathematical Methods in Computer Aided Geometric Design
Tom Lyche and Larry L. Schumaker (eds.), pp. 71–85.
Copyright © 1989 by Academic Press, Boston.
ISBN 0-12-460515-X.

focusing on the properties of Bézier curves, we will show that those features not possessed by B-splines are possessed by another curve scheme, namely, Pólya polynomials [3]. Further, we will see that B-spline curves and Pólya polynomials are related in a very intimate way. Viewing B-spline curves and Pólya polynomials as natural generalizations of Bézier curves sheds some light on why Bézier curves have so many interesting properties, where these properties come from, and the interconnections between the various properties.

## §2. The Canonical Split

To generalize Bézier curves, we must first decide what precisely it is about Bézier curves that we want to generalize. In this section we will list the standard properties of Bézier curves and show how a couple of major properties extend to B-spline curves while a couple extend to Pólya polynomials. A more detailed analysis extending the other properties will be done in Section 3 and Section 4.

At first glance, Bézier curves seem to have a daunting array of properties. To introduce some order and to help focus our attention, we begin by grouping these features into three main categories:

I. Properties Essential for CAGD
- Affine Invariant
- Non-Degenerate
- Variation Diminishing
- Numerically Stable

II. Properties Desirable for CAGD
- Polynomial
  — Compact Explicit Formula
  — Horner Evaluation Algorithm (Nested Multiplication)
- Symmetry
- Special Conditions at End Points
  — Interpolates First and Last Control Points
  — Derivatives Depend Only on Nearby Control Points
- Convex Hull Property
- Subdivision Algorithm
- Dual Functionals
  — de Boor-Fix Formula
  — Blossoming Algorithm
- Probabilistic Interpretation

III. Properties which Generate Especially Nice Algorithms for CAGD
- Two Term Recursive Evaluation Algorithm (de Casteljau Algorithm)
- Two Term Differentiation Formula
- Two Term Degree Elevation Formula

If we try to extend the formulas in the last category, we find that the two-term differentiation formula generalizes readily to the B-spline basis functions,

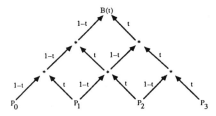

**Figure 1.** The de Casteljau algorithm for a cubic Bézier curve.

but that the two-term degree elevation formula does not. Rather, this degree raising formula generalizes naturally to the Pólya basis functions. Moreover, both the B-spline curves and the Pólya polynomials can be defined by recursive evaluation algorithms similar in structure to the de Casteljau algorithm (see, e.g., [5]) for Bézier curves. These algorithms can always be diagrammed, as is done in Figure 1 for the de Casteljau algorithm, as a triangle with the control points arranged at the bottom.

Each node in the diagram represents a value obtained by multiplying the values of the two nodes immediately below it by the labels on the connecting arrows, adding these products, and normalizing by dividing by the sum of the two labels. The value at the apex of the triangle will lie on the curve at parameter value $t$.

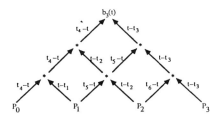

**Figure 2.** The de Boor algorithm for a cubic
B-spline curve with $t \in [t_3, t_4)$.

For the B-spline curves, the defining characteristic of the recursive evaluation algorithm is the *In/Out Property:* that is, the labels on edges that enter a vertex are the same as the labels on the edges that leave the vertex in the same direction (see the diagrams of the de Boor algorithm, Figures 2,3). Thus if we follow arrows along any straight line, the labels we observe are all identical. The above diagrams of the de Boor algorithm show two adjacent segments of a B-spline curve; an entire B-spline curve is obtained by pasting together many such individual curve segments. The main point about B-splines is that

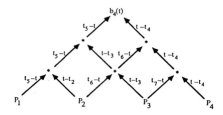

**Figure 3.** The de Boor algorithm for a cubic
B-spline curve with $t \in [t_4, t_5)$.

adjacent segments always fit together smoothly without any constraints on the
location of the control points.

The Pólya polynomials admit a similar recursive evaluation algorithm.
Again the algorithm has a triangular structure with the control points arranged as input at the base of the triangle and the point on the curve at
parameter $t$ emerging from the apex of the triangle. However, here the defining characteristic is the *Parallel Property*: that is, the labels on parallel edges
are identical (see Figure 4). Like Bézier curves, Pólya polynomials are polynomial curves, not splines; adjacent Pólya segments do not automatically join
together smoothly as do B-spline segments.

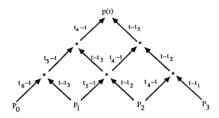

**Figure 4.** The recursive evaluation algorithm
for a cubic Pólya polynomial.

The standard properties of Bézier curves are split between the B-splines
and the Pólya polynomials. We have just seen how the three two-term formulas
are divided between these two schemes. We shall see below that all of the
properties of Bézier curves we listed as *essential* extend to both schemes, while
all the properties we listed as *desirable* are inherited by one or the other or
both. Moreover, the Pólya polynomials and the B-splines are related by the de
Boor-Fix dual functionals [2,7,8]. This connection leads to deeper relationships
which we shall also explore further below.

Another aspect of this split is a probabilistic interpretation of the basis functions. The Bernstein basis functions represent the binomial distribution which can be modeled by an urn containing balls of two colors using sampling with replacement. The Pólya basis functions represent the probabilities in a two color urn model where, after a specific color ball is selected and replaced, more balls of the *same* color are added to the urn [1,3,12]. The B-splines model the probabilities in a two color urn where balls of the *opposite* color are added to the urn [1,13]. Urn models where balls of the same color are added to the urn were originally studied by Pólya and are therefore called Pólya urn models [14]. It is from this urn model that the Pólya polynomials derive their name.

We call the split of the Bézier properties into B-spline and Pólya form the *canonical split*. This split and some of the connections between these two forms are summarized in Figure 5.

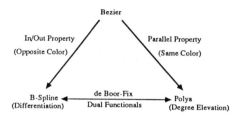

**Figure 5.** The canonical split.

## §3. B-Spline Properties

The B-splines are well known in CAGD, so here we shall only summarize their main properties and explain briefly how these B-spline properties generalize some standard features of Bernstein polynomials and Bézier curves.

B-spline curves are characterized recursively by the In/Out Property (see Figures 2,3), which is a generalization of the de Casteljau algorithm for Bézier curves (see Figure 1). Like the Bernstein basis, the B-spline basis functions satisfy a two term differentiation formula [6] which makes their smoothness properties particularly easy to analyze.

A B-spline curve of degree $n$ will interpolate the control point $P_k$ at the knot $t_k$ when $t_k = t_{k+1} = \ldots = t_{k+n}$. This interpolation property is a direct extension of Bézier interpolation at the end points.

Knot insertion algorithms are fundamental to many CAGD applications [10], and they play the same role for B-spline curves that subdivision plays for Bézier curves. Two distinct knot insertion algorithms are known: Boehm's algorithm [4] and the Oslo algorithm [10]. Boehm's algorithm is an explicit formula for inserting one or more knots at the same location; the Oslo algorithm is a recursive algorithm for simultaneously inserting an arbitrary number of knots at arbitrary locations.

To apply Boehm's algorithm at $t^*$, first evaluate the de Boor algorithm at $t = t^*$ (see Figure 2). Then to insert the knot $t^*$ exactly $k$ times, simply start at the lower left corner of the triangle and walk along the left edge to the $k^{th}$ level of the recursion. Then walk along this level and back down the right edge of the triangle. Collect all the points encountered along the way; these are the new control points for the spline with the knot $t^*$ inserted $k$ times and they replace the old control points at the base of the triangle (see Figure 6). Notice that to insert $t^*$ a total of $n$ times, we simply read the new control points off the left and right edges of the triangle. Of course, inserting a knot $n$ times subdivides the spline into two separate pieces. When applied to Bézier curves, this algorithm is precisely de Casteljau's subdivision algorithm (see, e.g., [5]).

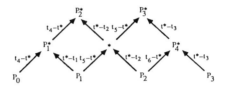

**Figure 6.** Boehm's algorithm for inserting a
double knot into a cubic B-spline curve.

The easiest way to understand the Oslo algorithm is in terms of blossoming. (For an extensive discussion of blossoming see Ramshaw [17,18]; here we shall simply summarize some of his main results). The *blossom* of a degree $n$ polynomial $p(t)$ is the unique symmetric multiaffine polynomial $P(u_1, \ldots, u_n)$ for which $P(t, \ldots, t) = p(t)$. Polynomial curves have the property that their blossom evaluated at $(0, \ldots, 0, 1, \ldots, 1)$, where 1 appears as an argument $k$ times and 0 $n - k$ times, is the $k^{th}$ Bézier control point.

B-spline segments extend this blossoming property of Bézier curves. They are characterized by the property that the blossom evaluated at the knots yields the B-spline control points. That is, if $B(u_1, \ldots, u_n)$ is the blossom of a B-spline segment $b(t)$ with control points $P_0, \ldots, P_n$ and knots $t_1, \ldots, t_{2n}$, then $P_k = B(t_{k+1}, \ldots, t_{k+n})$. Thus, blossoming is simply a representation of the dual functionals for B-splines in terms of symmetric multiaffine functions. Moreover, the blossom of a B-spline segment can be computed recursively by substituting $u_k$ for $t$ on the $k^{th}$ level of the de Boor algorithm (see Figure 7).

Now to insert an arbitrary collection of knots into a B-spline curve, let $u_1, \ldots, u_d$ be a refinement of the knot sequence $t_1, \ldots, t_m$. Then the new control points for the refined knot sequence can be computed recursively simply by evaluating the blossom at $u_{j+1}, \ldots, u_{j+n}$; *i.e.*, by computing $B(u_{j+1}, \ldots, u_{j+n})$ recursively by the blossoming algorithm. This recursive computation of the new control points is the Oslo algorithm.

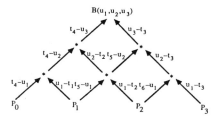

**Figure 7.** The blossoming algorithm for a cubic $B$-spline segment.

For B-splines, the knots are always assumed to be non-decreasing. However, the In/Out Property can be satisfied without this additional constraint. Thus, curves that we do not generally consider as B-spline segments retain many of the properties of B-splines, such as blossoming, as long as they satisfy the In/Out Property. In particular, curves written in terms of the normalized power basis $\{(t-t_k)^n\}$ at the knots $(t_0,\ldots,t_n)$ can be thought of as a B-spline segment with knots $(t_1,\ldots,t_n,t_0,\ldots,t_{n-1})$ (see Figure 8) and, if one neglects the normalization steps, the monomial basis can be thought of as a B-spline segment with knots $(0,\ldots,0,\infty,\ldots,\infty)$ (see Figure 9).

We summarize the special properties of B-splines in the following list:

- In/Out Property
- Two Term Differentiation Formula
  - Segments piece together smoothly to form polynomial splines
  - Local Control
  - Low Degree
- Interpolation at $P_k$
  - $t_k = t_{k+1} = \cdots = t_{k+n}$
- Knot Insertion Algorithms (Subdivision)
  - Boehm's Algorithm
  - Oslo Algorithm
- Blossoming (Dual Functionals)
- Special Cases
  - Bernstein Basis
  - Power Basis at Knots
  - Monomial Basis

## §4. Pólya Properties

The Pólya polynomials $p(t)$ are defined recursively by the Parallel Property (see Figure 4). The Pólya basis functions $p_k(t)$ are, by definition, the coefficients of the control points $P_k$. Thus, by construction, $p(t) = \Sigma p_k(t)P_k$. It follows from Figure 4 that $p_k(t)$ is the sum of all paths from $P_k$ to the apex of the triangle. But by the parallel property, it is easy to see that up to constant multiples

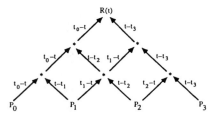

**Figure 8.** The evaluation algorithm for cubic curves in power form.

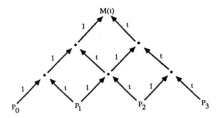

**Figure 9.** The evaluation algorithm for cubic curves in monomial form.

all paths from $P_k$ to the apex of the triangle are identical. Thus, the basis functions for an $n^{th}$ degree Pólya polynomial depending on knots $t_1, \ldots, t_{2n}$ can be written explicitly as

$$p_k(t) = \lambda_{n,k}(t - t_{n+1-k}) \cdots (t - t_{2n-k}),$$

where the $\lambda_{n,k}$ are normalizing constants chosen so that $\Sigma p_k(t) = 1$.

Many well known bases satisfy the Parallel Property. When $t_1 = t_2 = \cdots = t_n = 0$ and $t_{n+1} = t_{n+2} = \cdots = t_{2n} = 1$, then the Pólya basis functions reduce to the Bernstein basis functions (Figure 1), and when $t_1 = t_2 = \cdots = t_n = 0$ and $t_{n+1} = t_{n+2} = \cdots = t_{2n} = \infty$, the Pólya functions become the monomial basis (Figure 9). Another important special case occurs when $t_{2n-j+1} = t_{n-j}$ for all $j$. Then the Pólya basis functions become the Lagrange basis functions and the Parallel Property becomes Neville's algorithm (see, e.g., [9]) (Figure 10).

Pólya polynomials always interpolate their first and last control points. In fact, it follows immediately from the explicit formula that

$$p_k(t_n) = 0, \quad k \neq 0 \quad \Rightarrow \quad p(t_n) = P_0$$
$$p_k(t_{n+1}) = 0, \quad k \neq n \quad \Rightarrow \quad p(t_{n+1}) = P_n.$$

More generally, if $t_{2n-j+1} = t_{n-j}$, then $p_k(t_{n-j}) = 0$ for $j \neq k$ and $p(t_{n-j}) = P_j$. In particular, when $t_{2n-j+1} = t_{n-j}$ for all $j$, the Pólya basis functions

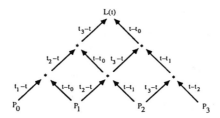

**Figure 10.** Neville's Algorithm for a cubic Lagrange polynomial.

become the Lagrange basis functions (see Figure 10). These interpolation properties of the Pólya polynomials are yet another extension of the Bézier property of interpolation at the end points.

The compact explicit formula for the Pólya basis functions leads to a Horner-like evaluation algorithm using nested multiplication. Observe that except for the first factor of $p_{k+1}(t)$ and last factor of $p_k(t)$, the polynomials $p_k(t)$ and $p_{k+1}(t)$ are composed of identical linear factors. Thus,

$$p_{k+1}(t) = \frac{\lambda_{n,k+1}(t - t_{n-k})}{\lambda_{n,k}(t - t_{2n-k})} p_k(t).$$

This observation leads to the following evaluation algorithms for $p(t)$ by nested multiplication:

$$p(t) = \frac{p_0(t)}{\lambda_{n,0}} \left( \lambda_{n,0} P_0 + \frac{t - t_n}{t - t_{2n}} \left( \lambda_{n,1} P_1 + \cdots + \frac{t - t_1}{t - t_{n+1}} (\lambda_{n,n} P_n) \cdots \right) \right)$$

$$p(t) = \frac{p_n(t)}{\lambda_{n,n}} \left( \lambda_{n,n} P_n + \frac{t - t_{n+1}}{t - t_1} \left( \lambda_{n,n-1} P_{n-1} + \cdots + \frac{t - t_{2n}}{t - t_n} (\lambda_{n,0} P_0) \cdots \right) \right).$$

Recursive evaluation requires $O(n^2)$ multiplications, whereas nested multiplication requires only $O(n)$ multiplications. Thus, we can evaluate Pólya polynomials more efficiently using nested multiplication than we can by recursion. Which nested multiplication formula we apply will depend on the relation of $t$ to the knots since we will wish to avoid division by $t - t_j$ when $t$ is near to $t_j$.

One of the most powerful tools for studying the Pólya polynomials is degree elevation. Writing the $n^{th}$ degree basis functions as $p_{n,k}(t)$ and the basis functions for a degree $n + 1$ Pólya polynomial with knots $t_1, \ldots, t_{2n+2}$ as $p_{n+1,k}(t)$, notice that

$$p_{n,k}(t) = \lambda_{n,k}(t - t_{n+1-k}) \cdots (t - t_{2n-k})$$

$$p_{n+1,k+1}(t) = \lambda_{n+1,k+1}(t - t_{n+1-k}) \cdots (t - t_{2n+1-k}).$$

Therefore, it follows that

$$(t - t_{2n+1-k})p_{n,k}(t) = \frac{\lambda_{n,k}}{\lambda_{n+1,k+1}}p_{n+1,k+1}(t)$$

$$(t - t_{n-k})p_{n,k}(t) = \frac{\lambda_{n,k}}{\lambda_{n+1,k+2}}p_{n+1,k+2}(t).$$

Subtracting the first of these formulas from the second and dividing by $(t_{2n+1-k} - t_{n-k})$, we obtain

$$p_{n,k}(t) = \frac{\lambda_{n,k}}{t_{2n+1-k} - t_{n-k}}\left[\frac{p_{n+1,k+2}(t)}{\lambda_{n+1,k+2}} - \frac{p_{n+1,k+1}(t)}{\lambda_{n+1,k+1}}\right],$$

which expresses the degree $n$ Pólya basis function as a linear combination of two degree $n+1$ Pólya basis functions. This two term degree elevation formula is a natural extension of the standard two term degree elevation formula for the Bernstein basis functions. We can use this two term degree elevation formula to represent a degree $n$ Pólya polynomial as a degree $n + 1$ Pólya polynomial and thereby introduce an extra degree of freedom into our curve [1,3].

However, these degree elevation formulas allow us to do much more than simply represent degree $n$ Pólya polynomials in terms of degree $n + 1$ Pólya polynomials; they can also be used to construct general change-of-basis matrices. Indeed, suppose we want to convert from a Pólya polynomial with knots $(t_1, \ldots, t_{2n}, \ldots)$ to one with knots $(u_1, \ldots, u_{2n}, \ldots)$. Since converting and then degree elevating is equivalent to degree elevating and then converting, we have the commutative diagram shown in Figure 11.

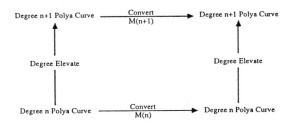

**Figure 11.** Pólya transformations by degree elevation.

Here the degree elevation can be performed by multiplying by any one of the factors $1, (t - t_{2n+1-k}), (t - t_{n-k})$. The advantage of multiplying by one of the factors $(t - t_{2n+1-k})$ or $(t - t_{n-k})$ is that we get to use a one term degree elevation formula in one of the degree elevation steps. Since the diagram commutes and since the Pólya blending functions form a basis, we can obtain a formula for the change-of-basis matrix $M(n + 1)$ in terms of the change-of-basis matrix $M(n)$ by collecting coefficients of the Pólya basis. Thus, we can build up the matrix $M(n+1)$ recursively in any number of ways, and we can perform conversion without resorting to matrix inversion. Explicit recursion formulas for $M(n+1)$ are given in [1]. This technique can be applied to convert from Pólya to Bézier or monomial form; to perform subdivision of Pólya polynomials; to compute the derivatives of Pólya polynomials; and to perform interpolation with Bézier or Pólya curves by converting from the Lagrange form. Moreover, we shall see that by applying dual functionals, this method can even be exploited to construct transformations between different B-spline bases (see Section 5).

Another transformation technique for Pólya polynomials is called *knot deletion*. Simple explicit formulas exist for expressing Pólya polynomials over any knot vector in terms of Pólya polynomials over a new knot vector obtained by removing one of the knots. Further details are found in [1]. This technique can be used to develop algorithms for converting one Pólya polynomial to another (including to Bézier and Lagrange form), subdividing Pólya polynomials, and evaluating points along Pólya polynomials.

We summarize the special properties of Pólya polynomials as follows:

- Parallel Property
- Compact Explicit Formula
- Horner Evaluation Algorithms (Nested Multiplications)
- Simple Degree Elevation Formulas (Transformations)
- Knot Deletion Algorithm
- Interpolation
  − At End Points — Always
  − At Interior Points — $t_{2n-j+1} = t_{n-j} \Rightarrow p(t_{n-j}) = P_j$
- Special Cases
  − Bernstein Basis
  − Lagrange Basis
  − Monomial Basis

## §5. Shared Properties and Dual Properties

Though some of the properties of Bézier curves are split between the B-splines and the Pólya polynomials, many are also shared by these two schemes. We now list these shared properties:

- Affine Invariant
- Non-Degenerate*
- Variation Diminishing*
- Numerically Stable*
- Symmetry
- Convex Hull Property*
- de Boor-Fix Dual Functionals

Here the * indicates that these properties do not hold for all knot sequences, but they are valid at least when the knots are nondecreasing.

Not only do B-spline curves and Pólya polynomials share some of the properties of Bézier curves and divide up the others, but these two curve schemes are themselves intimately related by the de Boor-Fix dual functionals [2,7,8]. Thus, the link between these two schemes actually goes much deeper than one would expect from a superficial splitting of the properties of Bézier curves. The de Boor-Fix dual functionals can be introduced in terms of a bilinear form on the polynomials of degree $n$. Specifically, let

$$[f(t), g(t)]_n = \Sigma_i (-1)^{n-i} c_n f^{(n-i)}(t) g^{(i)}(t),$$

where the $c_n$ are normalizing constants. It is simple to see that $[ \ , \ ]_n$ is bilinear. Moreover if $f(t), g(t)$ are polynomials of degree less than or equal to $n$, then it is easy to check that the derivative of $[f(t), g(t)]_n$ is zero. Thus, for polynomials of degree $n$, $[f(t), g(t)]_n$ is a constant independent of the value of $t$.

Now let $\{b_j(t)\}$ be a local B-spline basis of degree $n$ and let $\{p_k(t)\}$ be the corresponding Pólya basis. The main fact about the bilinear form $[ \ , \ ]_n$ is that with respect to $[ \ , \ ]_n$ the two bases $\{b_j(t)\}$ and $\{p_k(t)\}$ are essentially dual [7]. In particular,

$$[b_j(t), p_{n-k}(t)]_n = \begin{cases} 0, & j \neq k \\ \text{constant}, & j = k. \end{cases}$$

We shall not trouble ourselves about the exact value of the constant since we can always force it to be 1 by adjusting the normalizing constant $c_n$ and the coefficients of the Pólya basis $\lambda_{n,k}$. Because the bases $\{b_j(t)\}$ and $\{p_k(t)\}$ are dual with respect to $[ \ , \ ]_n$, the functionals $[\_\_\_, p_{n-k}(t)]_n$ and $[b_j(t), \_\_\_]_n$ are respectively the dual functionals for the B-spline and the Pólya bases. Important special cases of this duality occur when both $\{b_j(t)\}$ and $\{p_k(t)\}$ represent either the Bernstein basis or the monomial basis, and when $\{b_j(t)\}$ is the power basis at the knots while $\{p_k(t)\}$ is the Lagrange basis.

Now let $\{b_j^*(t)\}$ be another local B-spline basis of degree $n$ and let $\{p_k^*(t)\}$ be the corresponding Pólya basis. Suppose we want to transform between bases either from $\{b_j(t)\}$ to $\{b_j^*(t)\}$ or from $\{p_k^*(t)\}$ to $\{p_k(t)\}$. Then we need to compute the matrices $\{c_{kj}\}$ and $\{a_{jk}\}$ such that

$$b_k(t) = \Sigma c_{kj} b_j^*(t)$$

$$p_j^*(t) = \Sigma a_{jk} p_k(t).$$

By applying the bilinear form $[ \ , \ ]_n$, we find that, up to constant multiples,

$$c_{kj} = [b_k(t), p_{n-j}^*(t)]_n = a_{n-j,n-k}.$$

Thus, up to constant multiples and reordering of the elements, these two transformation matrices are identical. We formalize this observation in the following principle:

**The Principle of Duality.** *Transformations between B-spline bases are equivalent to transformations between corresponding Pólya bases in the opposite direction.*

But we have already seen that transformations between different Pólya bases are easy to compute either explicitly using knot deletion or recursively using degree elevation. Thus, it follows that it is simple to derive transformations between different B-spline bases by just applying the principle of duality to known transformations. Differentiation and degree elevation are dual in this precise sense [2,8]; so are transformations to and from Bézier or monomial form [1,2].

Another place where we can apply duality is to knot insertion algorithms. For example, the dual to the knot deletion algorithm for Pólya bases is Boehm's knot insertion algorithm for B-spline bases [2]. Similarly, suppose that we have two knot vectors where one is a refinement of the other. Then we can obtain the Oslo algorithm by dualizing the recursion formula for the transformation between the corresponding Pólya bases obtained by degree elevation [2,15].

In the following table we summarize the corresponding dual properties of B-spline and Pólya bases. For a further discussion of these properties in particular and duality in general see [1,2].

| **B-Spline** | **Pólya** |
| --- | --- |
| Differentiation | Degree Elevation |
| Knot Insertion | Knot Deletion |
| Conversion to Bézier | Conversion from Bézier |
| Conversion to Monomial | Conversion from Monomial |
| Conversion to Power Basis | Conversion from Lagrange Basis |
| Power Basis at Knots | Lagrange Basis at Knots |
| Exact Degree $N$ | Non-Degenerate |
| Knots | Roots |
| Opposite Color Urn | Same Color Urn |
| In/Out Property | Parallel Property |

## §6. Conclusions

The properties of Bézier curves split into three main categories: those which extend to B-splines, those which extend to Pólya polynomials, and those which extend to both. Turning this around, we may say that Bézier curves inherit their properties from these more general schemes. From the B-splines they inherit the two-term differentiation formula, the blossoming algorithm, and the de Casteljau subdivision algorithm (Boehm's knot insertion algorithm). From the Pólya polynomials they acquire the two-term degree elevation formula, evaluation by Horner's method (nested multiplication), and the knot deletion algorithm. From both schemes they receive affine invariance, the convex hull property, a recursive evaluation algorithm, interpolation of end points, non-degeneracy, the variation diminishing property, and the de Boor-Fix formula.

Both the B-spline curves and the Pólya polynomials are natural generalizations of Bézier curves. This is a particularly satisfying conclusion because each scheme extends certain specific features of the Bézier form and together they generalize almost all of the important properties of Bézier curves. Moreover, the B-spline and Pólya schemes are intimately related through the de Boor-Fix dual functionals. Using these dual functionals, we can derive the principle of duality, a principle which links transformations between B-spline bases to transformations between Pólya bases. Thus, many of the characteristic properties of the B-spline and Pólya schemes — such as differentiation and degree elevation or knot insertion and knot deletion — are linked and are essentially dual properties. Similarly many of the properties of Bézier curves are not independent but must also be related by duality.

By attempting to answer the question "what is the natural generalization of a Bézier curve?" we have gained some new insight into the origins of, and the connections between, the many properties of Bézier curves.

## References

1. Barry, P. J., *Urn Models, Recursive Curve Schemes, and Computer Aided Geometric Design*, Ph.D. dissertation, University of Utah, 1987.
2. Barry, P. J., T. D. DeRose, and R. N. Goldman, B-splines, Pólya curves, and duality, preprint.
3. Barry, P. J. and R. N. Goldman, Interpolation and approximation of curves and surfaces using Pólya polynomials, preprint.
4. Boehm, W., Inserting new knots into B-spline curves, Comput. Aided Design **12** (1980), 199–201.
5. Boehm, W., G. Farin, and J. Kahmann, A survey of curve and surface methods in CAGD, Comput. Aided Geom. Design **1** (1984), 1–60.
6. de Boor, C., *A Practical Guide to Splines*, Springer-Verlag, New York, 1978.
7. de Boor, C. and G. Fix, Spline approximation by quasi-interpolants, J. Approx. Theory **4** (1973), 19–45.
8. de Boor, C. and K. Höllig, B-splines without divided differences, in *Geometric Modeling: Algorithms and New Trends*, G. E. Farin (ed.), SIAM Publications, Philadelphia, 1987, 21–27.
9. Burden, R. L., J. D. Faires, and A. C. Reynolds, *Numerical Analysis*, Prindle, Weber, and Schmidt, Boston, 1978.
10. Cohen, E., T. Lyche, and R. Riesenfeld, Discrete B-splines and subdivision techniques in computer aided geometric design and computer graphics, Computer Graphics and Image Processing **14** (1980), 87–111.
11. Farin, G., Triangular Bézier-Bernstein patches, Comput. Aided Geom. Design **3** (1986), 83–127.
12. Goldman, R. N., Pólya's urn model and computer aided geometric design, SIAM Journal on Algebraic and Discrete Methods **6** (1985), 1–25.
13. Goldman, R. N., Urn models and B-splines, Constr. Approx. **4** (1988), 265–288.

14. Johnson, N. L. and S. Kotz, *Urn Models and Their Applications*, Wiley, New York, 1977.

15. Lyche, T., Note on the Oslo algorithm, Comput. Aided Design **20** (1988), 353–355.

16. Piegl, L., A geometric investigation of the rational Bézier scheme of computer aided design, Computers in Industry **7** (1986), 401–410.

17. Ramshaw, L., Béziers and B-splines as multiaffine maps, in: *Theoretic Foundations of Computer Graphics and CAD*, Proc. NATO International Advanced Study Institute, Lucca, Italy, Springer, New York, 1987.

18. Ramshaw, L., Blossoming: A connect the dots approach to splines, Digital Equipment Corporation Report 19, Palo Alto, California, 1987.

Phillip J. Barry and Ronald N. Goldman
Computer Graphics Laboratory
Department of Computer Science
University of Waterloo
Waterloo, Ontario N2L 3G1
CANADA

Supported in part by the Natural Sciences and Engineering Research Council of Canada Grant OGP0036825.

EMAIL: pjbarry@ watcgl.waterloo.edu
EMAIL: rngoldman@ watcgl.waterloo.edu

# Convexity and a Multidimensional Version of the Variation Diminishing Property of Bernstein Polynomials

M. Beśka

**Abstract.** We consider piecewise linear surfaces in $k$ variables defined over convex polyhedra. We give necessary and sufficient conditions for convexity, give formulae for total variation, and discuss variation diminishing properties of Bernstein polynomials.

## §1. Notation and Definitions

Let $\mathbb{R}^k$ be a $k$-dimensional real Euclidean space with the standard scalar product $\langle \ , \ \rangle$ which determines the norm $\|\cdot\|$. The $k$-dimensional Lebesgue measure is denoted by $\lambda_k$, and let $\mathbb{N} = \{0, 1, \ldots\}$. We treat $\mathbb{R}^k$ as an affine space. For given $P_1, \ldots, P_{k+1} \in \mathbb{R}^k$ we denote by $Q = [P_1, \ldots, P_{k+1}]$ the simplex with vertices $P_1, \ldots, P_{k+1}$. When the simplex $Q$ is non-degenerate (*i.e.*, $\lambda_k(Q) \neq 0$) then every point $P \in \mathbb{R}^k$ has barycentric coordinates $(u_1, \ldots, u_{k+1})$ in $\mathbb{R}^{k+1}$ with respect to $P_1, \ldots, P_{k+1}$ uniquely defined by

$$P = \sum_{j=1}^{k+1} u_j P_j, \qquad \text{where} \qquad \sum_{j=1}^{k+1} u_j = 1.$$

If these equalities hold, we simply write $P = (u_1, \ldots, u_{k+1})$. It is obvious that in this case, $P \in Q$ iff $u_j \geq 0$ for every $j = 1, \ldots, k + 1$. Without loss of generality, we may assume that the determinant

$$\det[(P_1 - P_{k+1}), \ldots, (P_k - P_{k+1})]$$

is positive. By $Q_\alpha$ ($1 \leq \alpha \leq k + 1$) we denote the $(k - 1)$-dimensional face of $Q$ which does not contain the vertex $P_\alpha$. By $Z := [T_1, \ldots, T_{k+1}]$ we denote

Mathematical Methods in Computer Aided Geometric Design
Tom Lyche and Larry L. Schumaker (eds.), pp. 87–92.

a simplex with the vertices $T_i := (\epsilon_{1,i}, \ldots, \epsilon_{k,i}) \in \mathbb{R}^k$ with $i = 1, \ldots, k+1$, where $\epsilon_{j,i} = 0$ for $j < i$ and $\epsilon_{j,i} = 1$ for $j \geq i$. Now let $S_n(Z)$ be the following triangulation of the simplex $Z$: a simplex $\Omega \subset Z$ belongs to $S_n(Z)$ iff

$$\Omega = \Delta_{i_1, \ldots, i_k}^n + \vec{v},$$

where

$$\Delta_{i_1, \ldots, i_k}^n := \{(x_1, \ldots, x_k) \in \mathbb{R}^k : 0 \leq x_{i_1} \leq \ldots \leq x_{i_k} \leq \frac{1}{n}\},$$

and the sequence $(i_1, \ldots, i_k)$ is a permutation of the set $\{1, \ldots, k\}$. The co-ordinates of the vector $\vec{v} = (v_1, \ldots, v_k) \in \mathbb{R}^k$ are such that the following conditions hold: i) $nv_i \in \mathbb{N}$ for $i = 1, \ldots, k$, and ii) $0 \leq v_1 \leq \ldots \leq v_k < 1$. For each permutation there is a numbering of the vertices $U_1, \ldots, U_{k+1}$ of $\Delta_{i_1, \ldots, i_k}^n$ such that $U_r$ does not lie on the plane $x_{i_{r-1}} = x_{i_r}$ for $r = 1, \ldots, k+1$, where $x_{i_0} := 0$ and $x_{i_{k+1}} := \frac{1}{n}$. This is our standard choice of the order for vertices of a subsimplex.

Now, let $L : \mathbb{R}^k \to \mathbb{R}^k$ be an affine transformation such that

$$L(T_i) = P_i \qquad \text{for} \qquad i = 1, \ldots, k+1. \tag{1}$$

Thus, $L$ transforms the triangulation $S_n(Z)$ of the simplex $Z$ into some triangulation of the simplex $Q$, denoted here by $S_n(Q)$. Moreover, for every $\Omega \in S_n(Q)$ the representation $\Omega = [U_1, \ldots, U_{k+1}]$ denotes the order of vertices of $\Omega$ induced by $L$ from the standard order of the corresponding subsimplex in $S_n(Z)$. It is easy to see that the barycentric coordinates of the vertices of $\Omega \in S_n(Q)$ with respect to the vertices of $Q$ have the form $\frac{\beta}{n}$ where $\beta \in \mathbb{N}^{k+1}$, $|\beta| = \sum_{i=1}^{k+1} \beta_i = n$.

## §2. Piecewise Linear Surface Over a Convex Polyhedron

Let $W \subset \mathbb{R}^k$ be a non-degenerate ($\lambda_k(W) \neq 0$) convex polyhedron, and let $S(W)$ be a triangulation of $W$. Assume that $m$ is a function numbering simplices of $S(W)$, and that $\mathcal{K}$ is the set of pairs of simplices with common $(k-1)$-dimensional face; i.e.,

$$\mathcal{K} := \{(\Omega, \Omega_0) \in S(W) \times S(W) : m(\Omega) < m(\Omega_0) \quad \text{and} \quad \lambda_{k-1}(\Omega \cap \Omega_0) \neq 0\}.$$

For a function $f : V \to \mathbb{R}$, where $V$ is the set of all vertices of $S(W)$, and for any $\Omega = [U_1, \ldots, U_{k+1}] \in S(W)$, we obtain $k+1$ points of the form $(U_i, f_{U_i}) \in \mathbb{R}^{k+1}$, where $f_U$ is the value of $f$ at $U$. Joining these $k+1$ points, we obtain a piecewise linear continuous surface $\hat{f}$ over $W$. The first theorem characterizes the convexity of $\hat{f}$.

**Theorem 1.** *The convexity of a piecewise linear surface $\hat{f}$ is equivalent to the following inequalities*

$$f_{U^0} - \sum_{i=1}^{k+1} u_i^0 f_{U_i} \geq 0 \quad \text{for} \quad (\Omega, \Omega_0) \in \mathcal{K}, \tag{2}$$

*where $\Omega = [U_1, \ldots, U_{k+1}] \in S(W)$ and $U^0 \notin \Omega \cap \Omega_0$ is a vertex such that its barycentric coordinates with respect to $U_1, \ldots, U_{k+1}$ are $(u_1^0, \ldots, u_{k+1}^0)$.*

For functions defined on $\mathbb{N}^{k+1}$, let us introduce formal shift operators

$$E_i(f_\beta) = f_{\beta+e_i}, \qquad \beta \in \mathbb{N}^{k+1}, \; i = 1, \ldots, k+1,$$

where $e_i = (\delta_{1,i}, \ldots, \delta_{k+1,i}) \in \mathbb{R}^{k+1}$ and $\delta_{j,i}$ is the Kronecker delta. In the case our polyhedron is equal to $Q$ we use the triangulation $S_n(Q)$ and define the piecewise linear continuous surface in the same way as in the convex polyhedron case. In this special case, this piecewise linear surface is called the *Bézier surface* and we denote it by $\hat{f}_n$. Now, by Theorem 1 we have

**Corollary 2.** *The Bézier surface $\hat{f}_n$ is convex iff*

$$D_{i.j}(f_\beta) := -(E_i - E_{i+1})(E_j - E_{j+1})(f_\beta) \geq 0, \qquad \forall \; 1 \leq i < j \leq k+1 \tag{3}$$

*and for all $\beta \in \mathbb{N}^{k+1}$ with $|\beta| = n - 2$, where $E_{k+2} := E_1$.*

**Remark 3.** *$|\beta| = n - 2$, but the resulting expression is a combination of $f_\gamma$ with $|\gamma| = n$ and $f_\gamma := \hat{f}_n(\frac{\gamma}{n})$.*

The function $\hat{f}$ defines a distribution on the convex polyhedron on $W$, which will be denoted by $\hat{f}$ as well. Then the Laplacian of $\hat{f}$ is defined by the following equality

$$\Delta \hat{f}(\phi) = \int_W \hat{f}(x) \Delta \phi(x) \lambda_k(dx) \qquad \text{for all} \quad \phi \in \mathcal{D}(\text{Int}(W)),$$

where $\mathcal{D}(\text{Int}(W))$ is the space of test-functions.

**Theorem 4.** *The Laplacian $\Delta \hat{f}$ of the distribution $\hat{f}$ is a measure and the total variation of $\Delta \hat{f}$ is equal to*

$$\text{Var}(\Delta \hat{f}) = \sum_{(\Omega, \Omega_0) \in \mathcal{K}} \frac{[\lambda_{k-1}(\Omega \cap \Omega_0)]^2}{k \lambda_k(\Omega)} |D_{(\Omega, \Omega_0)}(f)|, \tag{4}$$

*where*

$$D_{(\Omega, \Omega_0)}(f) = - \left( f_{U^0} - \sum_{j=1}^{k+1} u_j^0 f_{U_j} \right) \frac{1}{u_r^0},$$

if $\Omega = [U_1, \ldots, U_{k+1}] \in S(W)$ and $U_r \notin \Omega \cap \Omega_0$, $U^0$ is the vertex of $\Omega_0$ such that $U^0 \notin \Omega \cap \Omega_0$ and $U^0 = [u_1^0, \ldots, u_{k+1}^0]$ with respect to $U_1, \ldots, U_{k+1}$.

**Corollary 5.** *If* $\hat{f}_n$ *is the Bézier surface over* $Q$, *then the total variation of* $\Delta \hat{f}_n$ *is given by*

$$\frac{1}{kn^{k-2}\lambda_k(Q)} \sum_{|\beta|=n-2} \sum_{1 \leq i < j \leq k+1} C_{ij}^{\beta} |D_{ij}(f_\beta)| \cdot \| \sum_{\alpha=i+1}^{j} \overrightarrow{n_\alpha} \lambda_{k-1}(Q_\alpha) \|^2, \quad (5)$$

where $\overrightarrow{n_\alpha}$ will always be a unit vector normal to the face $Q_\alpha$ and directed outward from $Q$. The constant $C_{ij}^{\beta}$ is an integer which depends on $i, j, \beta$ satisfying $1 \leq C_{ij}^{\beta} \leq (k-1)!$ for $\beta \in \mathbb{N}^{k+1}$, $|\beta| = n-2$, $1 \leq i < j \leq k+1$.

For $k = 1, 2$ the total variation of $\Delta \hat{f}_n$ coincides with the variation of the Bézier surface which was considered by Goodman [5] and Chang and Hoschek [3] (see also [1]).

### §3. Variation Diminishing Property of Bernstein Polynomials

For a simplex $Q$, $n \in \mathbb{N}$, and a given function $f : Q \to \mathbb{R}$, we define

$$F_n := \left\{ f_\beta : \ f_\beta = f\left(\frac{\beta}{n}\right), \beta \in \mathbb{N}^{k+1}, |\beta| = n \right\}.$$

We define the Bernstein polynomial of degree $n$ as

$$B^n(f, P) := \sum_{|\beta|=n} f_\beta J_\beta^n(P), \qquad P \in Q, \quad (6)$$

where

$$J_\beta^n(P) = \frac{n!}{\beta_1! \cdots \beta_{k+1}!} u_1^{\beta_1} \cdots u_{k+1}^{\beta_{k+1}} \quad \text{for } P = (u_1, \ldots, u_{k+1}).$$

The polynomials $J_\beta^n(P)$ are called the *basic Bernstein polynomials*. The Bernstein polynomial $B^n(f, P)$ has the following probabilistic interpretation. Let $\{\overrightarrow{X}\}_{i=1}^n$ be a sequence of independent identically distributed random vectors. The distribution of $\overrightarrow{X}_i$ is defined as

$$\mathcal{P}\{\overrightarrow{X}_i = e_j\} = u_j \geq 0, \qquad j = 1, \ldots, k+1.$$

Hence, the Bernstein polynomial $B^n(f, P)$ is equal to

$$B^n(f, P) = E\left[f\left(\frac{\overrightarrow{S}_n}{n}\right)\right],$$

where $\vec{S}_n := \sum_{i=1}^n \vec{X}_i$ and $E[\vec{Y}]$ is the expectation of a random vector. It is easy to check that

$$E\left[\frac{\vec{S}_n}{n} \mid \vec{S}_{n+1}\right] = \frac{\vec{S}_{n+1}}{n+1}, \qquad \mathcal{P} - a.e.$$

Here $E[\vec{X} \mid \vec{Y}]$ is the conditional expectation of $\vec{X}$ with respect to the $\sigma$-algebra generated by $\vec{Y}$. Now by the above equation and Jensen's inequality, we obtain

**Theorem 6.** ([1,2,4]) *If $f : Q \to \mathbb{R}$ is a convex function, then*

$$B^n(f, P) \le B^{n+1}(f, P) \tag{7}$$

*for $P \in Q$, $n \ge 1$.*

By simple calculation we can obtain the following form of the second derivative of the Bernstein polynomial $B^n(\hat{f}_n, P)$

$$D^2 B^n(\hat{f}_n, P)(h, h) =$$

$$\frac{n(n-1)}{k^2[\lambda_k(Q)]^2} \sum_{|\beta|=n-2} \sum_{1 \le i < j \le k+1} \langle \sum_{\alpha=i+1}^j \vec{n}_\alpha \lambda_{k-1}(Q_\alpha), h \rangle^2 D_{ij}(f_\beta) J_\beta^{n-2}(P)$$

for $P \in Q$ and $h \in \mathbb{R}^k$.

Hence by Corollary 2 we get

**Corollary 7.** ([1,3]) *If the Bézier surface $\hat{f}_n$ over $Q$ is convex, then so is the Bernstein polynomial $B^n(\hat{f}_n, P)$.*

Now, we define (see [3]) the variation of $B^n(\hat{f}_n, P)$ by

$$V[B^n, Q] := \int_Q |\Delta B^n|, \tag{9}$$

where for simplicity $B^n$ stands for $B^n(\hat{f}_n, P)$. The distributional Laplacian of $B^n(\hat{f}_n, P)$ equals

$$(\Delta B^n)(\phi) = \int_Q \phi \Delta B^n \qquad \text{for} \quad \phi \in \mathcal{D}(\text{Int} Q).$$

Hence the total variation of the distributional Laplacian is equal to

$$V[B^n, Q] = \text{Var}(\Delta B^n). \tag{10}$$

By (8) we easily get the following formula

$$\Delta B^n(\hat{f}_n, P) = \frac{n(n-1)}{k^2[\lambda_k(Q)]^2} \cdot$$

$$\cdot \sum_{|\beta|=n-2} \sum_{1 \leq i < j \leq k+1} \| \sum_{\alpha=i+1}^{j} \overrightarrow{n}_\alpha \lambda_{k-1}(Q_\alpha) \|^2 D_{ij}(f_\beta) J_\beta^{n-2}(P) \qquad (11)$$

for $P \in Q$. Hence by Corollary 5, we can get the weak version of the variation diminishing property.

**Theorem 8.** *The Bernstein polynomial $B^n(\hat{f}_n, P)$ satisfies the inequality*

$$\mathrm{Var}(\Delta B^n) \leq (k-1)!\mathrm{Var}(\Delta \hat{f}_n).$$

*Here the constant $(k-1)!$ is the smallest possible constant.*

For $k = 1, 2$ this result was obtained by Chang and Hoschek [3].

### Acknowledgment

I would like to thank Prof. Z. Ciesielski for valuable comments and suggestions.

### References

1. Beśka, M., Convexity and variation diminishing property for Bernstein polynomials in higher dimensions, Banach Center Publications 22.
2. Chang, G., and P. Davis, The convexity of Bernstein polynomials over triangles, J. Approx. Theory **40** (1984), 11–28.
3. Chang, G., and J. Hoschek, Convexity and variation diminishing property of Bernstein polynomials over triangles, in *Multivariate Approximation Theory III*, W. Schempp and K. Zeller (eds.), Birkhäuser, Basel, 1985, 61–70.
4. Dahmen, W. and C. Micchelli, Convexity of multivariate Bernstein polynomials and box spline surfaces, Studia Scien. Math. Hun. **22** (1987).
5. Goodman, T., Variation diminishing properties of Bernstein polynomials on triangles, J. Approx. Theory **50** (1987), 111–126.

M. Beśka
Technical University of Gdańsk
Institut of Mathematics
Majakowskiego 11/12
80-952 Gdańsk
POLAND

# Gröbner Basis Methods for Multivariate Splines

## L. J. Billera and L. L. Rose

**Abstract.** For a finite polyhedral subdivision $\Delta$ of a region in $\mathbb{R}^d$, we consider the space $C_k^r(\Delta)$ consisting of all $C^r$ piecewise polynomial functions on $\Delta$. $C_k^r(\Delta)$ is a finite dimensional vector space, and we consider the problem of determining the dimension and a basis for this space. After summarizing some properties of the formal power series $\sum_{k \geq 0} \dim_{\mathbb{R}} C_k^r(\Delta)t^k$, we describe how the methods used to obtain these properties can be used to develop a computational scheme for obtaining this series as well as the desired vector space bases. Underlying this scheme is the Gröbner basis algorithm of computational commutative algebra. Computational experience with this method is discussed briefly at the end.

## §1. Dimensions of Spline Spaces

Let $\Delta$ be a finite polyhedral complex in $\mathbb{R}^d$ (*i.e.*, a finite collection of convex polyhedra such that the faces of any element of $\Delta$ are again in $\Delta$, and the intersection of any two elements of $\Delta$ is a face of each). We denote by $C^r(\Delta)$ the vector space of all $C^r$ piecewise polynomial functions over $\Delta$, and by $C_k^r(\Delta)$ the subspace consisting of all those elements involving only polynomials of degree at most $k$. For each $k$, $C_k^r(\Delta)$ is finite dimensional, and we are interested in determining its dimension in terms of combinatorial or geometric characteristics of the underlying complex $\Delta$.

Throughout this paper we assume certain regularity conditions on the complex $\Delta$. In particular, $\Delta$ is a *pure $d$-dimensional* complex in $\mathbb{R}^d$; *i.e.*, every maximal element of $\Delta$ is a $d$-polytope. One can think of $\Delta$ alternatively as a polyhedral subdivision of the region in $\mathbb{R}^d$ which is the union of these maximal elements. Referring to the polyhedra in $\Delta$ as *cells*, we call two $d$-cells *adjacent* if they intersect in a common face of dimension $d-1$. Given $d$-cells $\sigma$ and $\sigma'$, a *path* between them is a sequence of $d$-cells

$$\sigma = \sigma_1, \ldots, \sigma_k = \sigma'$$

Mathematical Methods in Computer Aided Geometric Design
Tom Lyche and Larry L. Schumaker (eds.), pp. 93–104.
Copyright © 1989 by Academic Press, Boston.
ISBN 0-12-460515-X.

such that for each $i$, $\sigma_i$ is adjacent to $\sigma_{i+1}$. We assume that $\Delta$ is *hereditary*, that is, for each cell $\tau \in \Delta$ (including $\tau = \emptyset$) any two $d$–cells containing $\tau$ can be joined by a path consisting only of $d$–cells containing $\tau$. Finally, we denote by $f_i(\Delta)$ the number of $i$–cells in $\Delta$, and by $f_i^o(\Delta)$ the number of interior $i$–cells in $\Delta$; *i.e.*, those not in the boundary of $\Delta$.

In [9], we studied the generating function of the numbers $\dim_{\mathbb{R}} C_k^r(\Delta)$, $k = 0, 1, 2, \ldots$, that is, the formal power series

$$\sum_{k \geq 0} \dim_{\mathbb{R}} C_k^r(\Delta) t^k.$$

We call this series the *dimension series* for $C^r(\Delta)$. In [9] we proved the following

**Theorem 1.1.** *For any $r$, we have*

$$\sum_{k \geq 0} \dim_{\mathbb{R}} C_k^r(\Delta) t^k = \frac{p(t)}{(1 - t)^{d+1}},$$

*where $p(t)$ is a polynomial in $t$ that satisfies*
  a. $p(1) = f_d(\Delta)$, *and*
  b. $p'(1) = (r + 1) f_{d-1}^o$.

The equality in the theorem is to be understood as equality of formal power series. The series on the right is evaluated by the usual multiplication of power series, with the understanding that

$$\frac{1}{1 - t} = 1 + t + t^2 + t^3 + \cdots .$$

See [19] for a discussion of generating function techniques. Given Theorem 1.1, to know the polynomial $p(t)$ is to know *all* the dimensions $\dim_{\mathbb{R}} C_k^r(\Delta)$. In fact, knowing only finitely many of these dimensions enables one to determine $p(t)$ and thus to determine all the rest. It is the aim of this paper to present an effective means to calculate $p(t)$.

We first consider several examples.

**Example 1.2.** *Consider the triangulation $\Delta$ of the interval $[-1, 1]$ in $\mathbb{R}^1$ into the two $1$–cells $[-1, 0]$ and $[0, 1]$. A $C^r$ piecewise polynomial function $F$ on $\Delta$ is given by a pair $(q_1, q_2)$ of one-variable polynomials, where $q_1 = F|_{[-1,0]}$ and $q_2 = F|_{[0,1]}$. It is easy to see that $C_k^r(\Delta)$ is the direct sum of the subspace consisting of elements of the form $(q_1, q_1)$ with the subspace consisting of elements of the form $(0, q_2)$. A basis for the former subspace is given by the elements $(1, 1), (x, x), \ldots, (x^k, x^k)$, while the elements $(0, x^{r+1}), \ldots, (0, x^k)$ form a basis for the latter. Thus*

$$\dim_{\mathbb{R}} C_k^r(\Delta) = \begin{cases} k + 1, & \text{if } k \leq r; \\ 2k - r + 1, & \text{if } k \geq r + 1. \end{cases}$$

A routine calculation with generating functions will verify that $p(t) = 1 + t^{r+1}$ in this case. Note $p(1) = 2$ and $p'(1) = r + 1$ as guaranteed by the theorem.

**Example 1.3.** Consider a triangulation $\Delta$ of a convex quadrilateral in the plane obtained by placing a new point in the interior of the quadrilateral and joining it to each of the boundary vertices. We consider the case $r = 1$, i.e., $C^1$ piecewise polynomials on $\Delta$. If the new point is the intersection of the two diagonals of the quadrilateral, then $p(t) = 1 + 2t^2 + t^4$; otherwise $p(t) = 1 + t^2 + 2t^3$. Notice that in each case, $p(1) = 4$, the number of triangles in $\Delta$, and $p'(1) = 8$, which is twice the number of interior edges in $\Delta$.

**Example 1.4.** Consider the Morgan-Scott example of a triangle in the plane triangulated into 7 triangles by adding 3 vertices in the interior. (The 1-skeleton of this triangulation is combinatorially that of the 3−dimensional octahedron.) See Alfeld [2] for a description of this triangulation and its embeddings in the plane. We consider $C^1$ piecewise polynomials for three of these embeddings: the generic (type 1 on Alfeld's list), the fully symmetric (Alfeld's type 6) and the singular (Alfeld's type 4). (For the purposes of considering $C^1$ splines, these are the only cases.) The polynomial $p(t)$ turns out to be $1 + 6t^3$ in the generic case, $1 + t^2 + 3t^3 + 3t^4 - t^5$ in the fully symmetric case, and $1 + t^2 + 4t^3 + t^4$ in the singular case. For each, $p(1) = 7$, the number of triangles, and $p'(1) = 18$, twice the number of interior edges.

**Example 1.5.** Let $\Delta$ be a general triangulated complex in $\mathbb{R}^d$, i.e., one in which all cells are simplices. Then for $C^0$ (i.e., continuous) piecewise polynomials, it follows from results in [6] and [16] that $p(t) = h_0 + h_1 t + \ldots + h_{d+1} t^{d+1}$, where

$$h_i = \sum_{j=0}^{i} (-1)^{i-j} \binom{d+1-j}{d+1-i} f_{j-1}.$$

The vector $h = (h_0, \ldots, h_{d+1})$ is called the *h-vector* of $\Delta$ and has received much attention in the combinatorial geometry literature. (See, for example [14; §5.2] or [8].) The quantities $h_i$ have also been considered by Alfeld in the context of multivariate splines; see [1; §4.1], where they are denoted $a_i$.

**Example 1.6.** Suppose $\Delta$ gives a triangulation of a 2−manifold (with boundary) embedded in the plane. It is a consequence of Strang's conjecture (proved in [7]) that for $C^1$ splines and generic embeddings of $\Delta$, we have $p(t) = 1 + (h_1 - h_2)t^2 + 2h_2 t^3$.

The key to the proof of Theorem 1.1, and to the computational method arising from it, is a characterization of $C^r(\Delta)$ (and $C_k^r(\Delta)$) as the null space of a matrix with polynomial entries, that is, the set of all polynomial relations on the columns of such a matrix.

To describe the matrix whose null space gives $C^r(\Delta)$, let $\tau_1, \ldots, \tau_m$ denote the $m = f_{d-1}^\circ$ interior $(d-1)$−cells in $\Delta$. The affine span of each $\tau_i$ is determined by the vanishing of a certain affine form $l_i$. The matrix in question, denoted $A(\Delta, r)$, will have $m$ rows and $s = f_d + m$ columns. The first $f_d$

columns make up the signed incidence matrix of the $m$ interior $(d - 1)$-cells in the $f_d$ $d$-cells (*i.e.*, the matrix of the usual oriented boundary operator on the $d$-cells of $\Delta$ (relative to the boundary of $\Delta$)). The remaining columns of $A(\Delta, r)$ make up an $m \times m$ diagonal matrix, the $i^{th}$ diagonal entry being $l_i^{r+1}$. Notice that in the case in which every maximal cell contains the origin in $\mathbb{R}^d$, each $\tau_i$ will also contain the origin, and so the $l_i$ will all be *homogeneous* linear forms.

**Example 1.7.** *Consider the quadrilateral in the plane having vertices* $v_1 = (1,0)$, $v_2 = (0,1)$, $v_3 = (-2,1)$ *and* $v_4 = (-1,-3)$. *Let* $\Delta$ *denote the triangulation of this quadrilateral formed by joining each boundary edge with the origin* $v_0 = (0,0)$. $\Delta$ *has four 2-cells (triangles):* $\sigma_1 = conv\{v_0, v_1, v_2\}$, $\sigma_2 = conv\{v_0, v_2, v_3\}$, $\sigma_3 = conv\{v_0, v_3, v_4\}$ *and* $\sigma_4 = conv\{v_0, v_4, v_1\}$, *and four interior 1-cells (edges)* $\tau_i = conv\{v_0, v_i\}$, $i = 1, \ldots, 4$. *Here* $l_1 = y$, $l_2 = x$, $l_3 = x + 2y$ *and* $l_4 = 3x - y$. *Then* $m = 4$, $s = 8$ *and* $A(\Delta, r)$ *is the matrix*

$$
\begin{pmatrix}
1 & 0 & 0 & -1 & y^{r+1} & 0 & 0 & 0 \\
-1 & 1 & 0 & 0 & 0 & x^{r+1} & 0 & 0 \\
0 & -1 & 1 & 0 & 0 & 0 & (x + 2y)^{r+1} & 0 \\
0 & 0 & -1 & 1 & 0 & 0 & 0 & (3x - y)^{r+1}
\end{pmatrix}.
$$

To see why $C^r(\Delta)$ is given by $\ker A(\Delta, r)$, consider the situation given by Example 1.7. Let $A = A(\Delta, r)$ and suppose $p = (p_1, \ldots, p_8)$ satisfies $Ap = 0$, where each $p_i \in \mathbb{R}[x, y]$, the ring of all polynomials in two variables. Then, for example, we have $p_1 - p_4 + y^{r+1}p_5 = 0$; *i.e.*, $p_1 - p_4$ is a multiple of $l_1^{r+1}$. Similarly, $p_2 - p_1$ is a multiple of $l_2^{r+1}$, $p_3 - p_2$ a multiple of $l_3^{r+1}$ and $p_4 - p_3$ a multiple of $l_4^{r+1}$. Thus, by a well-known criterion for smoothness, the piecewise polynomial function $F = (p_1, p_2, p_3, p_4)$, *i.e.*, $F$ such that $F \mid_{\sigma_i} = p_i$, is an element of $C^r(\Delta)$, and any element of $C^r(\Delta)$ arises in this way. (See [9] for details.)

## §2. Gröbner Bases

The technique of Gröbner bases provides a useful method of computation for ideals in polynomial rings. Applications of this method include solving systems of polynomial equations, deciding whether a polynomial is in a given ideal, and finding a canonical set of representatives for the quotient of the polynomial ring by an ideal. This technique also provides a highly effective method for computing the dimensions series for $C^r(\Delta)$ and finding vector space bases for the $C_k^r(\Delta)$'s. For a general introduction to Gröbner bases, see [10].

The idea behind the construction of Gröbner bases is to generalize the division algorithm to polynomials of several variables. To do this we need a total order on the monomials in a polynomial ring. Let $R = K[x_1, x_2, \ldots, x_d]$ be the polynomial ring in $d$ variables over a field $K$. Let $T$ be the set of monomials in $R$ and let $>$ be a total order on $T$ which refines the usual partial order. In addition, we require that $>$ be a *multiplicative order*; *i.e.*, $m > 1$ for all monomials $m \in T$, and if $m, n, p \in T$ and $m > n$, then $pm > pn$.

**Examples of multiplicative orders.**

1. The *lexicographic order* on $T$ is defined by $x_1^{a_1} \cdots x_d^{a_d} > x_1^{b_1} \cdots x_d^{b_d}$ if and only if the first place in which $a_i - b_i$ is non-zero is positive. For monomials in $x, y$ and $z$ up to degree 2 we have

$$x^2 > xy > xz > x > y^2 > yz > y > z^2 > z > 1$$

in the lexicographic order.

2. The *graduated lexicographic order* on $T$ is defined by $x_1^{a_1} \cdots x_d^{a_d} > x_1^{b_1} \cdots x_d^{b_d}$ if and only if $a_1 + \cdots + a_d > b_1 + \cdots + b_d$ or $a_1 + \cdots + a_d = b_1 + \cdots + b_d$ and the first place in which $a_i - b_i$ is non-zero is positive. For the monomials from (1) we have

$$x^2 > xy > xz > y^2 > yz > z^2 > x > y > z > 1$$

in the graduated lexicographic order.

3. The *(graduated) reverse lexicographic order* on $T$ is defined by $x_1^{a_1} \cdots x_d^{a_d} > x_1^{b_1} \cdots x_d^{b_d}$ if and only if $a_1 + \cdots + a_d > b_1 + \cdots + b_d$ or $a_1 + \cdots + a_d = b_1 + \cdots + b_d$ and the last place in which $a_i - b_i$ is non-zero is negative. For this order we have

$$x^2 > xy > y^2 > xz > yz > z^2 > x > y > z > 1.$$

There are infinitely many multiplicative orders, but these are the most common. For more about multiplicative orders (also called term orderings), see [15]. Given an order $>$ and an element $f$ in $R$, the *initial term* of $f$, $in(f)$, is the largest monomial under $>$ which appears in $f$. Let $S \subset R$ be any set. The initial ideal of $S$, $in(S)$ is the ideal generated by the initial terms of elements of $S$.

**Example.** If $f(x, y, z, w) = 5x + 3z^2 - yw + 2y$, where $x > y > z > w$, then $in(f) = x$ under the lexicographic order, $in(f) = yw$ under graduated lex, and $in(f) = z^2$ under reverse lex.

We can extend this notion to free modules over $R$ of finite rank $s$, viewed as sets of $s$-tuples of elements in $R$. A monomial in $R^s$ has the form $m\mathbf{e}_i$ where $m$ is a monomial in $R$ and $\mathbf{e}_i$ is the $i$th standard basis vector of $R^s$. The lexicographic order here is defined by $m\mathbf{e}_i > n\mathbf{e}_j$ if and only if $i > j$ or $i = j$ and $m > n$ under the lexicographic order on $R$. We can define the other orders in a similar manner. For $S \subset R^s$, $in(S)$ will be the submodule of $R^s$ generated by the initial terms of elements of $S$. With this set-up, we can now define Gröbner bases.

**Definition/Proposition 2.1.** Let $M$ be a submodule of $R^s$. (If $s = 1$, this is just an ideal.) A set $G = \{G_1, \ldots, G_n\}$ in $M$ is called a *Gröbner basis* for $M$ if any of the following equivalent conditions hold.

(1) $in(G) = in(M)$

(2) Any $F$ in $M$ has the form $\sum_{i=1}^{n} r_i G_i$ where $r_1, \ldots, , r_n$ are in $R$ and for all $i$, $in(r_i G_i) \leq in(F)$.

(3) The set $\Gamma = \{m G_i : m \text{ is a monomial in } x_1, \ldots, x_d, \text{ and } in(G_j) \text{ does not divide } in(m G_i) \text{ for all } j < i\}$ is a vector space basis for $M$ over $K$.

The first characterization says that the initial terms of all elements of M are determined by any Gröbner basis G. The second, the most useful in this work, says that any element F of M can be written in terms of lower or same degree elements of G. We can obtain this representation by subtracting from F an appropriate multiple of an element of G whose initial term divides the initial term of F, and then continuing this process with the remainder. For a description of the Gröbner basis algorithm, due to Buchberger, see [10]. The third characterization will be used to construct vector space bases for the $C_k^r(\Delta)$'s.

The equivalence of these conditions can be found in [20], which credits Lazard [12] and Bayer [3]. It follows from (2) that $G$ generates $M$. Given a generating set $S$ for $M$, the Gröbner basis algorithm constructs a (finite) Gröbner basis containing $S$. There is also an algorithm due to Spear [18] and Schreyer [17] which combined with Buchberger's algorithm, produces a Gröbner basis for the kernel of a map between free modules, that is, for the null space of a matrix with polynomial entries. (See also [21] and [22].) Let $A$ be an $m \times s$ matrix with entries in $R$ defining such a map. The kernel of $A$ is the set of all $s$-tuples $f = (f_1, \ldots, f_s)$ in $R^s$ such that $Af = 0$. This set is called the module of *syzygies* of the columns of A. In the case of splines, a Gröbner basis for this module is precisely what we want.

We can also use Gröbner bases to compute Hilbert series of homogeneous ideals and graded modules. Let $R_i$ be the set of homogeneous polynomials of degree $i$. A module $M$ over $R$ is *graded* if $M = \oplus_{j \geq 0} M_j$, where each $M_j$ is a vector space over $K$ and $R_i M_j \subset M_{i+j}$. If $M$ is finitely generated as an $R$-module, the dimensions of each $M_i$ over $K$ will be finite. In this case, the function $H(i) = \dim_K M_i$ is called the *Hilbert function* of $M$. It is well known that the generating function of $H(i)$, $\sum_{i \geq 0} H(i) t^i$, has the form of the rational function

$$\frac{P(t)}{(1-t)^d,}$$

where $P(t)$ is a polynomial in $t$ with integral coefficients. This series is called the *Hilbert series* of $M$. Using the following proposition (due to Macaulay [13]) and an inclusion-exclusion calculation we can compute this series.

**Proposition 2.2.** *If $H(M)$ denotes the Hilbert function of $M$, then $H(M) = H(inM)$.*

Recall that if $G$ is a Gröbner basis for $M$, $in(M) = in(G)$. Thus we need only to compute the Hilbert function of a module generated by the monomials $\{in(G_i) : G_i \in G\}$. This can be done using the following formula

$$H(\langle I \cup m \rangle) = H(I) + H(m) - H(I \cap \langle m \rangle),$$

where $I$ is any monomial ideal (or module), $m$ is a monomial and $\langle S \rangle$ denotes the ideal (or module) generated by the set $S$ [4].

These algorithms have been implemented on a number of computer algebra systems. In Section 4, examples computed using the program *Macaulay* will be given.

## §3. Computing Dimension Series and Bases of Splines

Let $\Delta$ be a hereditary $d$-complex and let $R = \mathbf{R}[x_1, \ldots, x_d]$. Since the spline modules $C^r(\Delta)$ can be realized as the kernels of maps between free modules, we can use the technique of Gröbner bases to make computations. Our primary interest is in computing the dimension series for $C^r(\Delta)$ as well as finding bases for the $C_k^r(\Delta)$'s as vector spaces over $\mathbf{R}$.

Recall from §1 that if $\Delta$ is hereditary, then $C^r(\Delta) \cong \ker A$ where $A = A(\Delta, r)$ is the matrix associated to $C^r(\Delta)$. We can view elements of $\ker A$ as $(n + m)$-tuples of polynomials, where $n$ is the number of $d$-dimensional faces of $\Delta$ and $m$ is the number of interior $(d - 1)$-dimensional faces of $\Delta$. Since $C^r(\Delta) \subset R^n$, this isomorphism will just be the projection onto the first $n$ components of elements of $\ker A$. Using the algorithms of Buchberger, Spear and Schreyer, we can find a Gröbner basis $G$ for $\ker A$, and by ignoring the last $m$ components of each $G_i$, we will have a Gröbner basis for $C^r(\Delta)$. By using the third characterization of Gröbner bases, we see that the set

$$\Gamma_k = \{mG_i : m \in T, \ deg(mG_i) \leq k, \ \text{and} \ in(G_j) \nmid in(mG_i) \ \forall j < i\}$$

gives a vector space basis for $C_k^r(\Delta)$, where $T$ is the set of all monomials in $x_1, \ldots, x_d$, and $deg(F)$ denotes the largest degree of a component of $F$.

Let $\hat{\Delta}$ denote the homogenization of $\Delta$, *i.e.*, the join of $\Delta$ with a vertex outside the affine span of $\Delta$. (Each cell of $\hat{\Delta}$ consists of a "cone" over some cell of $\Delta$ having this vertex as its apex.) $C^r(\hat{\Delta})$ is a graded $R$–module [9] so it has the form $\oplus_{k \geq 0} M_k$. It turns out that $M_k \cong C_k^r(\Delta)$ [9] so it follows that the dimension series, $\sum_{k \geq 0} \dim_{\mathbf{R}} C_k^r(\Delta) t^k$, is precisely the Hilbert series of $C^r(\hat{\Delta})$. This means we can find the dimensions of the $C_k^r(\Delta)$'s by finding the Hilbert series of $C^r(\hat{\Delta})$. This can be done using the techniques outlined in the previous section: finding a Gröbner basis for $C^r(\hat{\Delta})$ and considering the module generated by the initial terms of these elements.

If a vector space basis is not necessary, the dimensions of the $C_k^r(\Delta)$'s can be computed in a simpler manner. Let $\hat{A} = A(\hat{\Delta}, r)$. We have the following exact sequence:

$$0 \longrightarrow \ker \hat{A} \longrightarrow R^{m+n} \longrightarrow \operatorname{Im}\hat{A} \longrightarrow 0.$$

Using the additivity of the Hilbert function and the properties of graded modules we deduce the following:

$$P(t) = n + mt^{r+1} - P(\operatorname{Im}\hat{A}, t),$$

where

$$\frac{P(t)}{(1-t)^{d+1}}$$

is the Hilbert series of ker $\hat{A}$, and

$$\frac{P(\operatorname{Im}\hat{A}, t)}{(1-t)^{d+1}}$$

is the Hilbert series of the image of $\hat{A}$. (See [9] for details.) Using this, we can compute $P(t)$ and hence the dimension series for $C^r(\Delta)$ by computing the Hilbert series of $\operatorname{Im}(\hat{A})$, the submodule of $R^n$ generated by the columns of $\hat{A}$. To do this, we compute a Gröbner basis for $\operatorname{Im}(\hat{A})$ and use it to find the Hilbert series as in the previous case.

In the next section we will discuss the results of specific computations carried out using these techniques.

## §4. Example and Discussion

We discuss here the results obtained when applying Gröbner basis techniques to a certain 3−dimensional example considered by Alfeld [2; §3.2].

**Example 4.1.** *Let* $\Delta \subset \mathbb{R}^3$ *denote the trivariate Morgan/Scott example of Section 3.2 of* [2]. *This is a triangulation of a tetrahedron in* $\mathbb{R}^3$ *into* $f_3 = 15$ *tetrahedra, with 4 interior vertices, and* $f_2^\circ = 28$ *interior triangles.*

We note that $\Delta$ can be obtained from the $4-crosspolytope$ in $\mathbb{R}^4$ much as the Morgan-Scott triangulation of Example 1.4 is obtained from the octahedron in $\mathbb{R}^3$. (A *crosspolytope* in $\mathbb{R}^d$ is the convex hull of the $d$ unit vectors and their negatives; see [11] for further details.)

We considered only the *fully symmetric* embeddding described in [2]. The polynomial $p(t)$ defined in Theorem 1.1 was calculated for the cases $r = 0, \ldots, 4$. The case $r = 0$ also follows directly from Example 1.5 once one determines that the $h-$vector of $\Delta$ is $h = (1, 4, 6, 4, 0)$. The results are summarized below.

| $r$ | $p(t)$ |
|---|---|
| 0 | $1 + 4t + 6t^2 + 4t^3$ |
| 1 | $1 + t^2 + t^3 + 5t^4 + 7t^5 + 5t^6 - 5t^7 - t^8 + t^9$ |
| 2 | $1 + 3t^6 + 12t^7 + 9t^8 - 8t^9 - 3t^{10} + t^{12}$ |
| 3 | $1 + 2t^8 + 6t^9 + 18t^{10} - 2t^{11} - 10t^{12} - 2t^{13} + 2t^{15}$ |
| 4 | $1 + t^{10} + 3t^{11} + 9t^{12} + 21t^{13} - 5t^{14} - 19t^{15} - t^{16} + 3t^{17} + 2t^{18}$ |

One can check in each case that $p(1) = f_3 = 15$ and $p'(1) = (r+1)f_2^\circ = 28(r+1)$.

Alfeld computed $\dim_{\mathbb{R}} C_k^r(\Delta)$ for $(r,k) = (1,k)$, $k = 2,\ldots,7$ and for $(r,k) = (2,6)$ (see [2; Table 4]). Using the formula in Theorem 1.1 and the values of $p(t)$ above, one can verify that they give the values determined by Alfeld. Looking at the lowest term in $p(t)$ of positive degree in $t$, one can conclude that there are only global polynomials in $C_k^r(\Delta)$ for $r = 2,3,4$ and $k < 2r + 2$; for the case $r = 2$, this was observed by Alfeld. Looking at the coefficient of this term, one can conclude that, in addition to the global polynomials, there are 3, 2 and 1 linearly independent splines of degree $2r+2$, for $r = 2, 3$ and 4, respectively.

Some comments about the actual computations to produce the $p(t)$ are in order. They were all carried out on a Sun 3/60 using the computer algebra system *Macaulay*, which was designed specifically for computations of interest in algebraic geometry and commutative algebra. See [4] for a discussion of this program. *Macaulay* has a particularly efficient implementation of the Gröbner basis algorithm, and it is one of the few computer algebra systems to have implementations of the Gröbner basis algorithms for modules and for syzygies discussed in §2 and §3. In some sense, there is a bit of a cheat in these results, since *Macaulay* currently only uses arithmetic *mod p*; in this case $p$ was $31,991$, the largest value allowed. The times stated below are faster than they would have been had exact arithmetic been used. However, since when these calculations were carried out, *Macaulay* required homogeneous modules, the calculation was done for the complex $\hat{\Delta}$, requiring polynomials in 4 variables, not 3, resulting in a much more difficult calculation than necessary.

For $r \leq 3$, the full syzygy calculation was carried out, yielding a Gröbner basis for $C^r(\Delta)$ (and thus information to compute directly vector space bases for $C_k^r(\Delta)$ for every $k$ using part (3) of Proposition 2.1), as well as the dimension series for $C^r(\Delta)$. These calculations took about 6 minutes for $r = 1$, 91 minutes for $r = 2$, and more than 10 hours for $r = 3$. (For $r = 0$, the calculation was virtually instantaneous.) For $r \leq 4$, the dimension only calculation discussed at the end of §3 was carried out, taking .5, 11 and 22 minutes, respectively, for $r = 1, 2, 3$, and about 7 hours for $r = 4$.

Since we were working in the homogeneous case, the Gröbner basis algorithm could proceed one degree at a time, and so the polynomial $p(t)$ and any basis information could be obtained degree by degree, enabling one to stop the calculation once the desired degree was completed. We did this in the calculation for $C_6^2(\Delta)$, to compare these methods with those used by Alfeld. The only times mentioned in [2] were for the calculation of $\dim C_6^2(\Delta)$, which took over 10 hours by his methods. Most of this time was spent to compute symbolically a very large linear system, which was then solved quickly by methods of numerical linear algebra. To calculate dimension and basis information for $C_6^2(\Delta)$ by Gröbner basis methods took 8 minutes; the dimension alone required 3 minutes.

Admittedly, the computational experience cited here is quite limited, and much more would have to be done to make a reasonable case for the usefulness of these methods. However, the comparison between 3 minutes and 10 hours is enough to make this worth further study. The Gröbner basis algorithm is doubly exponential in the worst case [5], and so one would not expect that it would provide a good method for large practical problems. Yet, in this case there are some reasons that might make it at least comparable to other methods. Computing dimensions and bases for multivariate splines by linear algebra requires the calculation first of an extremely large linear system, which can then be solved quite efficiently (in terms of its size). Gröbner methods, on the other hand, work with a minimal description of the problem and do not require the preprocessing stage. Further, it is possible that, due to the extremely simple form of the matrix $A(\Delta, r)$, the Gröbner algorithm can be shown to perform much faster on this problem than in general.

Given the current state-of-the-art in applications of multivariate splines in geometric modeling, it would be of great interest to be able to compute effectively a basis for $C_k^r(\Delta)$ for $r$ small (say, $r = 1, 2, 3$) and $k$ small (say $k \leq 6$) for $\Delta$ in 2 or 3 dimensions. This would cover the case of modeling a smooth 2−dimensional surface by a low-degree piecewise polynomial function, or that of modeling a triangulated 3−dimensional object (such as an airplane). In each of these cases, it would be of interest to perform such calculations over subdivisions $\Delta$ having a large number of cells. This translates to the problem of fixing the dimension $d$, the smoothness $r$ and the degree $k$, but letting the size of the matrix $A(\Delta, r)$ grow. It is not known how the complexity of computing a Gröbner basis for the module generated by the columns of a matrix grows with the size of the matrix, but very preliminary computational experiments on a planar grid suggest that even polynomial growth may be possible in the spline case.

Finally, there is some reason to expect that significant gains might be obtainable by parallelizing the basic algorithm in this case.

### References

1. Alfeld, P., On the dimension of multivariate piecewise polynomials, in *Numerical Analysis*, D. F. Griffiths and G. A. Watson, (eds.), Longman Scientific & Technical, 1986, 1–23.

2. Alfeld, P., A case study of multivariate piecewise polynomials; in *Geometric Modeling: Algorithms and New Trends*, G. E. Farin (ed.), SIAM, Philadelphia, 1987, 149–160.

3. Bayer, D. A., The Division Algorithm and the Hilbert Scheme, Ph.D. Dissertation, Harvard University, 1982.

4. Bayer, D. A. and M. Stillman, The design of *Macaulay*: A system for computing in algebraic geometry and commutative algebra, Proceedings of the ACM SYMSAC '86 Conference, Association for Computing Machinery, 1986.

5. Bayer, D. A. and M. Stillman, On the complexity of computing syzygies, J. Symbolic Computation, to appear.

6. Billera, L. J., The algebra of continuous piecewise polynomials over a simplicial complex, Advances in Mathematics, to appear.

7. Billera, L. J., Homology of smooth splines: generic triangulations and a conjecture of Strang, Trans. Amer. Math. Soc. **310** (1988), 325–340.
8. Billera, L. J. and C. W. Lee, A proof of the sufficiency of McMullen's conditions for $f$−vectors of simplicial convex polytopes, Jour. Combinatorial Theory (A) **31** (1981), 237–255.
9. Billera, L. J. and L. L. Rose, A dimension series for multivariate splines, Discrete Comput. Geom., to appear.
10. Buchberger, B., Gröbner bases: An algorithmic method in polynomial ideal theory, in *Multidimensional Systems Theory*, N. K. Bose (ed.), D. Reidel Publishing Company, Dordrecht-Boston-Lancaster, 1985, 184–232.
11. Grünbaum, B., *Convex Polytopes*, Wiley-Interscience, London, 1967.
12. Lazard, D., Gröbner bases, Gaussian elimination and resolution of systems of algebraic equations, in *Computer Algebra, Proceedings EURO-CAL '83, London*, J.A. van Hulzen (ed.), Lecture Notes in Computer Science, Springer-Verlag, New York, 1983, 146–156.
13. Macaulay, F. S., Some properties of enumeration in the theory of modular systems, Proc. London Math. Soc. **26** (1927), 531–555.
14. McMullen, P. and G. Shephard, Convex Polytopes and the Upper Bound Conjecture, London Mathematical Lecture Notes No. 3, Cambridge University Press, Cambridge, 1971.
15. Robbiano, L., Term orderings on the polynomial ring, in *Proceedings of EUROCAL 85*, Lecture Notes in Computer Science No. 204, Springer-Verlag, New York, 1985, 513–517.
16. Rose, L. L., The Structure of Modules of Splines over Polynomial Rings, Ph.D. dissertation, Cornell University, 1988.
17. Schreyer, F.-O., Diplomarbeit am Fachbereich Mathematik der Universität Hamburg, 1980.
18. Spear, D. A., A constructive approach to commutative ring theory, in *Proceedings of the 1977 MACSYMA Users' Conference*, NASA CP-2012 (1977), 369–376.
19. Stanley, R., *Enumerative Combinatorics*, Vol. I, Wadsworth & Brooks/ Cole, Monterey, CA, 1986.
20. Sturmfels, B. and N. White, Gröbner bases and invariant theory, Adv. in Math., to appear.
21. Winkler, F., Solution of equations I: Polynomial ideals and Gröbner bases, in *Proc. Computers & Mathematics*, J. Davenport and R. Gebauer (eds.), Series in Computational Mathematics, Springer Verlag, to appear.
22. Winkler, F., A recursive method for computing a Gröbner basis of a module in $K[x_1, \ldots, x_\nu]^r$, $5^{th}$ Conference on Applied Algebra and Error Correcting Codes (AAECC-5), Menorca, Spain, June 1987.

Louis J. Billera
Department of Mathematics and Center for Operations Research
Rutgers University
New Brunswick, New Jersey 08903
USA

Lauren L. Rose
Department of Mathematics
Ohio State University
Columbus, Ohio 43210
USA

Supported in part by NSF Grant DMS-8703370/DMS-8896193.

EMAIL: billera@ math.rutgers.edu
EMAIL: llr@ osupyr.mast.ohio-state.edu

# On Finite Element Interpolation Problems

## J. M. Carnicer and M. Gasca

**Abstract.** Some practical aspects of a recursive method to solve Lagrange and Hermite multivariate interpolation problems are developed. As an example of application, the basic functions for the Argyris triangle interpolation problem are easily constructed.

## §1. Introduction

The technique of interpolation systems was introduced in [4] as a method to solve some multivariate interpolation problems by means of Newton-like interpolation formulae (see also [5-7]). In [4] several examples, arising in finite elements, were given.

One of the practical difficulties to apply the method was the efficient evaluation of directional derivatives of polynomials written in the form

$$\sum_{i=0}^{n} \sum_{j=0}^{m(i)} a_{ij} \prod_{h=0}^{i-1} r_h \prod_{k=0}^{j-1} r_{hk}, \qquad (1.1)$$

where $r_h, r_{hk}$ are polynomials in $x, y$ of total degree one. We have recently [2] obtained results on this problem and here show how they can be used to solve the Argyris triangle interpolation problem, well known to finite element practicioners.

## §2. Interpolation Systems in $\mathbb{R}^2$

In its simplest form (see [4,5]), an *interpolation system* in $\mathbb{R}^2$ is a set

$$S = \{(r_i, r_{ij}, u_{ij}) : (i, j) \in I\}, \qquad (2.1)$$

where

Mathematical Methods in Computer Aided Geometric Design
Tom Lyche and Larry L. Schumaker (eds.), pp. 105–113.
Copyright © 1989 by Academic Press, Boston.
ISBN 0-12-460515-X.

1) $I$ is a set of indices

$$I = \{(i,j): \ i = 0,1,\ldots,n; \quad j = 0,1,\ldots,m(i)\} \qquad (2.2)$$

lexicographically ordered,

2) $r_i, r_{ij}$ are straight lines given by

$$r_i \equiv \lambda_i x + \mu_i y + v_i = 0 \qquad (|\lambda_i| + |\mu_i| \neq 0) \qquad (2.3)$$

$$r_{ij} \equiv \lambda_{ij} x + \mu_{ij} y + v_{ij} = 0 \qquad (|\lambda_{ij}| + |\mu_{ij}| \neq 0) \qquad (2.4)$$

such that for each $(i,j) \in I$, $\lambda_i \mu_{ij} - \mu_i \lambda_{ij} \neq 0$.

3) $u_{ij}$ is the intersection point of $r_i$ and $r_{ij}$.

It must be remarked that neither the lines $r_i$ nor the lines $r_{ij}$ need be different, and that, accordingly, the points $u_{ij}$ may be repeated. We use the same symbols $r_i, r_{ij}$ to denote the polynomials of degree one in the left-hand sides of (2.3) (2.4) and the straight lines defined by those equations.

## §3. Interpolation Problem Associated to an Interpolation System

To each interpolation system we can associate an interpolation problem, defined by an interpolating space $F$ and a set of linear forms on $F$. The space $F$ is spanned by the polynomials

$$\Phi_{hk} = r_0 r_1 \ldots r_{h-1} r_{h0} r_{h1} \ldots r_{hk-1}, \quad (h,k) \in I \qquad (3.1)$$

where, as usual, empty products are taken as 1, and the linear forms $L_{ij}$, $(i,j) \in I$, are defined by

$$L_{ij} f = \frac{\partial^{T_{ij} + P_{ij}} f(u_{ij})}{\partial r_i^{T_{ij}} \partial r_{ij}^{P_{ij}}}, \qquad (3.2)$$

where

1) $T_{ij}$ (resp. $P_{ij}$) is the number of functions in the set

$$\{r_0, r_1, \ldots, r_{i-1}, r_{i0}, r_{i1}, \ldots, r_{ij-1}\}$$

which vanish at $u_{ij}$ and coincide (resp. do not coincide), up to a constant factor, with $r_i$.

2)

$$\frac{\partial f}{\partial r_i} = \mu_i \frac{\partial f}{\partial x} - \lambda_i \frac{\partial f}{\partial y}$$
$$\frac{\partial f}{\partial r_{ij}} = \mu_{ij} \frac{\partial f}{\partial x} - \lambda_{ij} \frac{\partial f}{\partial y}. \qquad (3.3)$$

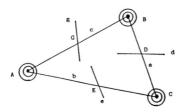

**Figure 1.** The Argyris triangle.

As shown in [4], the problem of finding $p \in F$ such that

$$L_{ij}p = z_{ij} \in \mathbb{R}, \qquad \forall(i,j) \in I \tag{3.4}$$

has a unique solution for any set of real numbers $z_{ij}$. In fact the solution can be constructed recursively, because

$$L_{ij}\Phi_{hk} = 0, \quad \forall(i,j) < (h,k) \tag{3.5}$$

$$L_{ij}\Phi_{ij} \neq 0, \quad \forall(i,j) \in I, \tag{3.6}$$

and writing $p$ in the form

$$p = \sum_{i=0}^{n} \sum_{j=0}^{m(i)} a_{ij}\Phi_{ij}, \tag{3.7}$$

the coefficients $a_{ij}$ are the solution of a lower triangular linear system, as is the case for the Newton formula for univariate interpolation problems.

## §4. Argyris Triangle

The well known Argyris triangle interpolation problem can be graphically described in the usual finite elements way by Figure 1.

The interpolating space is $\pi_5$, the space of polynomials of total degree not greater than 5, and the data are the values of the function, two derivatives of first order and three derivatives of second order at the vertices, and the value of a derivative of first order at each of the points $D, E, G$.

According to (3.1) (3.2), this problem is associated, for example, with the interpolation system defined by:

$$I = \{(i,j): \ i,j \in Z, \ i \geq 0, \ j \geq 0, \ i+j \geq 5\} \tag{4.1}$$

$$r_0 = a, \quad r_{00} = r_{01} = r_{02} = b, \quad r_{03} = r_{04} = r_{05} = c$$
$$r_1 = a, \quad r_{10} = r_{11} = b, \quad r_{12} = r_{13} = c, \quad r_{14} = e$$
$$r_2 = b, \quad r_{20} = r_{21} = r_{22} = c, \quad r_{23} = a$$
$$r_3 = b, \quad r_{30} = r_{31} = c, \quad r_{32} = d \tag{4.2}$$
$$r_4 = c, \quad r_{40} = b, \quad r_{41} = a$$
$$r_5 = c, \quad r_{50} = g.$$

For each $(i, j) \in I$ we have

$$\Phi_{ij} = \prod_{h=0}^{i-1} r_h \cdot \prod_{k=0}^{j-1} r_{hk}, \tag{4.3}$$

that is

$$\Phi_{00} = 1, \quad \Phi_{01} = b, \quad \Phi_{02} = b^2, \quad \Phi_{03} = b^3, \quad \Phi_{04} = b^3 c, \quad \Phi_{05} = b^3 c^2$$
$$\Phi_{10} = a, \quad \Phi_{11} = ab, \quad \Phi_{12} = ab^2, \quad \Phi_{13} = ab^2 c, \quad \Phi_{14} = ab^2 c^2$$
$$\Phi_{20} = a^2, \quad \Phi_{21} = a^2 c, \quad \Phi_{22} = a^2 c^2, \quad \Phi_{23} = a^2 c^3 \tag{4.4}$$
$$\Phi_{30} = a^2 b, \Phi_{31} = a^2 bc, \Phi_{32} = a^2 bc^2$$
$$\Phi_{40} = a^2 b^2, \Phi_{41} = a^2 b^3$$
$$\Phi_{50} = a^2 b^2 c$$

and the linear forms (3.2) are

$$L_{00}f = f(C), L_{01}f = \frac{\partial f(C)}{\partial a}, L_{02}f = \frac{\partial^2 f(C)}{\partial a^2},$$
$$L_{03}f = f(B), L_{04}f = \frac{\partial f(B)}{\partial a}, L_{05}f = \frac{\partial^2 f(B)}{\partial a^2}$$
$$L_{10}f = \frac{\partial f(C)}{\partial b}, L_{11}f = \frac{\partial^2 f(C)}{\partial a \partial b}, L_{12}f = \frac{\partial f(B)}{\partial c},$$
$$L_{13}f = \frac{\partial^2 f(B)}{\partial a \partial c}, L_{14}f = \frac{\partial f(E)}{\partial e},$$
$$L_{20}f = f(A), L_{21}f = \frac{\partial f(A)}{\partial b}, L_{22}f = \frac{\partial^2 f(A)}{\partial b^2}, L_{23}f = \frac{\partial^2 f(C)}{\partial b^2}, \tag{4.5}$$
$$L_{30}f = \frac{\partial f(A)}{\partial c}, L_{31}f = \frac{\partial^2 f(A)}{\partial b \partial c}, L_{32}f = \frac{\partial f(D)}{\partial d},$$
$$L_{40}f = \frac{\partial^2 f(A)}{\partial c^2}, L_{41}f = \frac{\partial^2 f(B)}{\partial c^2},$$
$$L_{50}f = \frac{\partial f(G)}{\partial g}.$$

As is easily seen, the space spanned by the $\{\Phi_{ij}\}$ in (4.4) is $\pi_5$, and therefore the Argyris interpolation problem consists of finding

$$p = \sum_{i=0}^{5} \sum_{j=0}^{5-i} a_{ij} \Phi_{ij} \tag{4.6}$$

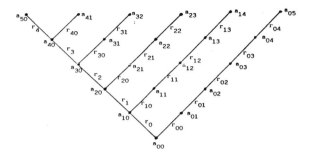

**Figure 2.** The algorithm of Section 5.

such that

$$L_{ij}p = z_{ij} \in \mathbb{R}, \quad i = 0, 1, \ldots, 5; \quad j = 0, 1, \ldots, 5 - i \tag{4.7}$$

with $L_{ij}$ defined by (4.5), where $z_{ij}$ are given real numbers.

## §5. Construction of the Solution of the Interpolation Problem

If we write

$$q_{ij} = \sum_{(h,k)<(i,j)} a_{ij}\Phi_{ij}, \tag{5.1}$$

taking into account (3.5), we have $a_{00} = z_{00}$ and

$$a_{ij} = \frac{z_{ij} - L_{ij}q_{ij}}{L_{ij}\Phi_{ij}}, \quad i = 0, 1 \ldots 5; \quad j = 0, 1, \ldots, 5 - i; \quad i + j > 0. \tag{5.2}$$

Therefore, for each $(i, j)$ one has to compute $L_{ij}q_{ij}$ and $L_{ij}\Phi_{ij}$; that is to evaluate two polynomials or some of their derivatives.

It was shown in [2] that if we denote

$$a_{ij}^{(0,0)} = a_{ij}, \quad i + j \le 5 \tag{5.3}$$

and $T \in \mathbb{R}^2$, then the algorithm

$$\begin{aligned}
&\text{For } i = 5, 4, \ldots, 1, 0 \\
&\text{For } j = 5 - i, \ldots, 1 \\
&\quad p_{ij}^{(0,0)} = a_{ij}^{(0,0)} + p_{ij+1}^{(0,0)}r_{ij}(T) \\
&\quad p_{i0}^{(0,0)} = a_{i0}^{(0,0)} + p_{i1}^{(0,0)}r_{i0}(T) + p_{i+10}^{(0,0)}r_i(T)
\end{aligned} \tag{5.4}$$

gives $p_{00}^{(0,0)}(T)$. This is straightforward from the representation of $p$ in the form given in Figure 2.

To compute

$$\frac{\partial^{v+w} p(T)}{\partial \rho^v \partial \sigma^w},$$

the same algorithm can be used:

For $i = 5, 4, \ldots, 0$

For $j = 5 - i, \ldots, 1$

$$p_{ij}^{(v,w)} = a_{ij}^{(v,w)} + p_{ij+1}^{(v,w)} r_{ij}(T) \tag{5.5}$$

$$p_{i0}^{(v,w)} = a_{i0}^{(v,w)} + p_{i1}^{(v,w)} r_{i0}(T) + p_{i+10}^{(v,w)} r_i(T)$$

with $a_{ij}^{(v,w)}, (i,j) \in I$, having been previously computed by (see [2])

For $i = 5, 4, \ldots, 0$

For $j = 5 - i, \ldots, 1$

$$a_{ij}^{(v,w)} = v p_{ij+1}^{(v-1,w)} \frac{\partial r_{ij}(T)}{\partial \rho} + w p_{ij+1}^{(v,w-1)} \frac{\partial r_{ij}(T)}{\partial \sigma}$$

$$a_{i0}^{(v,w)} = v p_{i1}^{(v-1,w)} \frac{\partial r_{i0}(T)}{\partial \rho} + w p_{i1}^{(v,w-1)} \frac{\partial r_{i0}(T)}{\partial \sigma} \tag{5.6}$$

$$+ v p_{i+10}^{(v-1,w)} \frac{\partial r_i(T)}{\partial \rho} + w p_{i+10}^{(v,w-1)} \frac{\partial r_i(T)}{\partial \sigma}.$$

In these schemes a term with negative upper index or lower index $i > 5$ or $j > 5 - i$ must be taken as 0. Finally, we get

$$p_{00}^{(v,w)} = \frac{\partial^{v+w} p(T)}{\partial \rho^v \partial \sigma^w}. \tag{5.7}$$

Observe that in (5.6), for $\rho = (\rho_1, \rho_2), \sigma = (\sigma_1, \sigma_2)$, one has

$$\frac{\partial r_{ij}(T)}{\partial \rho} = \rho_1 \lambda_{ij} + \rho_2 \mu_{ij}, \quad \frac{\partial r_i(T)}{\partial \rho} = \rho_1 \lambda_i + \rho_2 \mu_i, \tag{5.8}$$

with analogous formulae for

$$\frac{\partial r_{ij}(T)}{\partial \sigma}, \quad \frac{\partial r_i(T)}{\partial \sigma}.$$

These schemes allow the easy computation of any $L_{ij} q_{ij}$ and $L_{ij} \Phi_{ij}$ in (5.2). For example, if we have to compute $a_{13}$, we compute

$$L_{13} q_{13} = \frac{\partial^2 q_{13}(B)}{\partial a \partial c}, \quad L_{13} \Phi_{13} = \frac{\partial^2 \Phi_{13}(B)}{\partial a \partial c}. \tag{5.9}$$

For $L_{13} q_{13}$ we use schemes similar to (5.4) (5.5) (5.6) with $i = 1, 0; j = 3, 2, 1, 0$ and $T = B$. First (5.4), then (5.6) and (5.5) for $v = 1, w = 0$, and finally (5.6), (5.5) for $v = 1, w = 1$. The same computations can be used for $L_{13} \Phi_{13}$, with $a_{ij}, (i = 1, 0; j = 3, 2, 1, 0)$ replaced by 1 if $(i, j) = (1, 3)$ and by 0 elsewhere.

## §6. Basic Functions for the Argyris Triangle

Compute the solution $p$ of (4.7) for the 21 problems numbered $(k, l)$, $k = 0, 1, \ldots, 5; l = 0, 1, \ldots, 5 - k$, with respective data

$$z_{ij}^{(k,l)} = \delta_{ij} \cdot \delta_{jl} = \begin{cases} 1, & \text{if } (i, j) = (k, l) \\ 0, & \text{elsewhere.} \end{cases}$$

Then we get the 21 basic funtions for the Argyris triangle. If, for simplicity, we take $A = (0, 0), B = (1, 0), C = (0, 1), D = (0, 1/2), E = (1/2, 1/2), G = (1/2, 0)$, then we can take $a = 1 - x - y, b = x, c = y, e = y - x, d = y - 1/2, g = x - 1/2$ and therefore, by (3.3)

$$\frac{\partial p}{\partial a} = \frac{\partial p}{\partial y} - \frac{\partial p}{\partial x}, \frac{\partial p}{\partial b} = -\frac{\partial p}{\partial y}, \frac{\partial p}{\partial c} = \frac{\partial p}{\partial x}$$

$$\frac{\partial p}{\partial d} = \frac{\partial p}{\partial x}, \frac{\partial p}{\partial e} = \frac{\partial p}{\partial x} + \frac{\partial p}{\partial y}, \frac{\partial p}{\partial g} = -\frac{\partial p}{\partial y}.$$

Denoting by $B_{kl}$ the solution of the $(k, l)$-problem, that is the polynomial of total degree not greater than 5 such that

$$L_{ij}\Phi_{kl} = \delta_{ik} \cdot \delta_{jl}$$

with $L_{ij}$ defined by (4.5), we get

$$B_{00} = 1 - b^3 - 3b^3c - 6b^3c^2 - 3ab^2 - 9ab^2c - 3ab^2c^2 - a^2 - 2a^2c - 3a^2c^2$$
$$+ 6a^2c^3 - 2a^2b - 6a^2bc - 12a^2bc^2$$

$$B_{01} = -b + b^3 + 2b^3c + 3b^3c^2 + 2ab^2 + 4ab^2c - \frac{5}{2}ab^2c^2 + a^2b + 2a^2bc$$
$$+ 8a^2bc^2$$

$$B_{02} = \left(\frac{1}{2}\right)b^2 - \left(\frac{1}{2}\right)b^3 - \left(\frac{1}{2}\right)b^3c - \left(\frac{1}{2}\right)b^3c^2 - \left(\frac{1}{2}\right)ab^2$$
$$- \left(\frac{1}{2}\right)ab^2c + \left(\frac{3}{4}\right)ab^2c^2$$

$$B_{03} = b^3 + 3b^3c + 6b^3c^2 + 3ab^2 + 9ab^2c + 3ab^2c^2 - 3a^2b^2 + 6a^2b^3$$
$$- 12a^2b^2c$$

$$B_{04} = b^3c + 3b^3c^2 + 3ab^2c + \left(\frac{11}{2}\right)ab^2c^2 - 8a^2b^2c$$

$$B_{05} = \left(\frac{1}{2}\right)b^3c^2 + \left(\frac{5}{4}\right)ab^2c^2$$

$$B_{10} = a - ab^2 - 2ab^2c - 8ab^2c^2 - a^2 - a^2c - a^2c^2 + 3a^2c^3 - a^2b$$
$$\quad - 2a^2bc + 2a^2bc^2$$
$$B_{11} = -ab + ab^2 + ab^2c + 2ab^2c^2 + a^2b + a^2bc + 2a^2bc^2$$
$$B_{12} = -ab^2 - 2ab^2c + 8ab^2c^2 + a^2b^2 - 3a^2b^3 - 2a^2b^2c$$
$$B_{13} = -ab^2c + 2ab^2c^2 + 2a^2bc$$
$$B_{14} = -8ab^2c^2$$
$$B_{20} = a^2 + 2a^2c + 3a^2c^2 - 6a^2c^3 + 2a^2b + 6a^2bc + 12a^2bc^2 + 3a^2b^2$$
$$\quad - 6a^2b^3 + 12a^2b^2c$$
$$B_{21} = -a^2c - 2a^2c^2 + 3a^2c^3 - 2a^2bc - 6a^2bc^2 + 8a^2b^2c$$
$$B_{22} = \left(\frac{1}{2}\right)a^2c^2 - \left(\frac{1}{2}\right)a^2c^3 + a^2bc^2$$
$$B_{23} = \left(\frac{1}{2}\right)a^2c^3 + a^2bc^2$$
$$B_{30} = a^2b + 2a^2bc - 8a^2bc^2 + 2a^2b^2 - 3a^2b^3 + 6a^2b^2c$$
$$B_{31} = -a^2bc + 2a^2bc^2 + 2a^2b^2c$$
$$B_{32} = 16a^2bc^2$$
$$B_{40} = \left(\frac{1}{2}\right)a^2b^2 - \left(\frac{1}{2}\right)a^2b^3 + a^2b^2c$$
$$B_{41} = \left(\frac{1}{2}\right)a^2b^3 + a^2b^2c$$
$$B_{60} = -16a^2b^2c.$$

Other expressions for these functions can be found in [1].

## References

1. Bernadou, M., Sur l'Analyse Numérique du modèle linéaire de coques minces de Koiter, Doctoral dissertation, Univ. Paris VI, 1978.
2. Carnicer, J. M. and M. Gasca, Evaluation of multivariate polynomials and their derivatives, Univ. Zaragoza, 1987, preprint.
3. Ciarlet, P. G., *The Finite Element Method for Elliptic Problems*, North Holland, 1978.
4. Gasca, M. and J. I. Maeztu, On Lagrange and Hermite interpolation in $\mathbb{R}^k$, Numer. Math. **39** (1982), 1–14.
5. Gasca, M. and V. Ramírez, Interpolation systems in $\mathbb{R}^k$, J. Approx. Theory **42** (1984), 36–51.
6. Lorente, J. and V. Ramírez, On interpolation systems and $H$-reducible interpolation problems, in *Topics in Multivariate Approximation*,

C. K. Chui, L. L. Schumaker, and F. Utreras (eds.), Academic Press, 1987, New York, 153–163.

7. Maeztu, J. I. Divided differences associated with reversible systems in $\mathbb{R}^2$, SIAM J. Numer. Anal. **19** (1982), 1032–1040.

J. M. Carnicer and M. Gasca
Depto. Matemática Aplicada
Universidad Zaragoza
50009 Zaragoza
SPAIN

Supported by D.G.A. Res. Grant CB 3/85

# The Design of Curves and Surfaces
# by Subdivision Algorithms

### Alfred S. Cavaretta and Charles A. Micchelli

**Abstract.**    We present a survey of the basic principles and concepts associated with subdivision algorithms. Special attention is given to the convergence question for these algorithms, and the mathematical tools suitable for analysing convergence are presented.

## §1. Introduction

Subdivision methods consist of a class of numerically stable, easily implemented algorithms for the generation of parameterized curves and surfaces. These algorithms are sometimes referred to as corner cutting, recursive generation of curves, and the like; but always there is the underlying idea that a surface or curve is to be generated from a finite number of "control points" by iterative methods consisting predominantly of simple averaging processes. As the underlying parameters of these curves and surfaces are generally suppressed, and also since the surfaces depend on the control points in an entirely local fashion, the methods are imminently suited for use in interactive computer aided design systems; hence their popularity and wide applicability. We shall explore the evolution of subdivision from a mathematician's point of view. Beginning with a review of several simple instances for generating smooth curves, we will see how the basic structure and many of the geometric and algebraic features of these cases have lead to the development of other flexible, useful, and sophisticated methods.

So in general terms, what is a subdivision algorithm? We suppose we are given a sequence of control points $c = \{c_\alpha\}$ indexed over some easily described set such as the integer lattice $\mathbb{Z}^2$. If, for example, these control points are in the Euclidean space $\mathbb{R}^3$, then the subdivision algorithm will yield a surface $f$ in $\mathbb{R}^3$. This surface is approximated arbitrarily well by certain polygonal surfaces

Mathematical Methods in Computer Aided Geometric Design
Tom Lyche and Larry L. Schumaker (eds.), pp. 115–153.
Copyright © 1989 by Academic Press, Boston.
ISBN 0-12-460515-X.

$f_i$ which we call *control polygons*. The first control polygon $f_0$ interpolates the control points $c$; successive control polygons are then determined iteratively by the equation $f_i = S_i(f_{i-1})$ where $S_i$ is the subdivision operator at the $i^{th}$ level. It follows that

$$f = \lim_{i \to \infty} S_i S_{i-1} \cdots S_1 f_0.$$

So the key to the algorithm lies in the operators $S_i$ which most often are the same at every level except for a certain $i$-dependent scaling. Generally we require that the operation $S_i$ preserve constants, and often they are defined in terms of moving averages. In many cases the $S_i$ a: e locally determined so that if two control polygons $f_0$ and $g_0$ agree everywhere except in some bounded region $K_0$, then the resulting surfaces $f$ and $g$ are identical except in some neighborhood of $K_0$.

The present survey is organized more or less along historical lines. We will see that both geometric and algebraic ideas have contributed in equal measure to the development and understanding of subdivision. We have tried to tell the complete story, but of course within the scope of this short paper we cannot discuss all details or all papers. Nevertheless, the bibliography well represents papers in this field.

## §2. The Algorithms of de Casteljau and Chaikin

The simplest example of such a subdivision algorithm is the de Casteljau [10] subdivision for generating a single quadratic arc in space. We think of three control points $c = \{c_0, c_1, c_2\}$ as given in $\mathbb{R}^2$; the initial control polygon $f_0$ is simply the polygonal line joining $c_0 c_1 c_2$, parameterized linearly so that

$$f_0(0) = c_0, \quad f_0(\frac{1}{2}) = c_1, \quad f_0(1) = c_2.$$

The quadratic arc

$$B_2(t) = c_0(1-t)^2 + 2c_1 t(1-t) + c_2 t^2, \qquad 0 \le t \le 1$$

and $f_0$ are so situated that the curve $B_2$ is tangent to $f_0$ at each of its end points, as in Figure 1. Moreover

$$B_2(\frac{1}{2}) = \frac{1}{4}c_0 + \frac{1}{2}c_1 + \frac{1}{4}c_2$$
$$= \frac{1}{2}( \text{ midpoint } c_0 c_1 + \text{ midpoint } c_1 c_2).$$

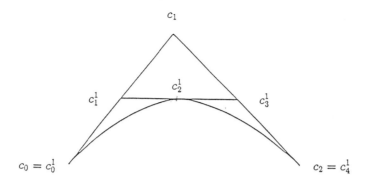

**Figure 1.** De Casteljau's algorithm.

This last equation is very suggestive of the de Casteljau algorithm for quadratics. From the control points $\{c_0, c_1, c_2\}$, compute $\{c_0^1, c_1^1, c_2^1, c_3^1, c_4^1\}$ by the rules

$$
\begin{aligned}
c_0^1 &= c_0, \\
c_1^1 &= \frac{1}{2}(c_0 + c_1), \\
c_2^1 &= \frac{1}{4}c_0 + \frac{1}{2}c_1 + \frac{1}{4}c_2, \\
c_3^1 &= \frac{1}{2}(c_1 + c_2), \\
c_4^1 &= c_2.
\end{aligned}
\tag{2.1}
$$

Then we define the new control polygon $f_1$ by

$$
f_1(t) = \sum_{j=0}^{4} c_j^1 \varphi(4t - j),
\tag{2.2}
$$

where $\varphi(t) = (1 - |t|)_+$ (here $u_+$ is $u$ if $u$ is positive, and zero otherwise). Thus, by connecting the midpoints of the two sides of $f_0$ by a secant line, we obtain $f_1$ from $f_0$. We notice that $c_0^1 c_1^1$ and $c_3^1 c_4^1$ are tangent to the arc $B_2$ at $t = 0$ and $t = 1$. Moreover, a little calculation reveals that the straight line segment $c_1^1 c_2^1 c_3^1$ is tangent to $B_2$ at $t = \frac{1}{2}$.

So the tangency relationship between $B_2$ and $f_0$ is preserved by one step of the de Casteljau algorithm (2.1), since the two subarcs of $B_2$ on the intervals $[0, \frac{1}{2}]$ and $[\frac{1}{2}, 1]$ are respectively inscribed in the two angles $c_0^1 c_1^1 c_2^1$ and $c_2^1 c_3^1 c_4^1$

of $f_1$. It follows that

$$B_2(t) = 4\left(c_0^1\left(\frac{1}{2}-t\right)^2 + 2c_1^1 t\left(\frac{1}{2}-t\right) + c_2^1 t^2\right),$$

$$B_2(t) = 4\left(c_2^1\left(1-t\right)^2 + 2c_3^1\left(t-\frac{1}{2}\right)\left(1-t\right) + c_4^1\left(t-\frac{1}{2}\right)^2\right).$$

(2.3)

So $f_1$ is related to the curve $B_2$ in two important ways. First it approximates $B_2$ in that there are three points of tangency, and second, the five vertices of $f_1$, taken in two groups $\{c_0^1, c_1^1, c_2^1\}$ and $\{c_2^1, c_3^1, c_4^1\}$, express $B_2$ in terms of the Bernstein bases relative to the intervals $[0, \frac{1}{2}]$ and $[\frac{1}{2}, 1]$, respectively.

The iteration which gives the complete algorithm should now be clear. At the $n^{th}$ stage, we obtain $2^{n+1}+1$ control points $c^n = \{c_j^n\}_{j=0}^{2^{n+1}}$, and the control polygon is

$$f_n(t) = \sum_{j=0}^{2^{n+1}} c_j^n \varphi(2^n t - j).$$

Just as with $f_1$, the polygon $f_n$ is tangent to $B_2$ at each of its evenly indexed vertices. Moreover, the three control points $c_{2j}^n, c_{2j+1}^n, c_{2j+2}^n$ are precisely the coefficients needed to express $B_2$ in terms of the Bernstein basis relative to the interval $[j/2^n, (j+1)/2^n]$. This suggests that

$$\lim_{n \to \infty} f_n(t) = B_2(t), \qquad 0 \le t \le 1,$$

since it clearly holds at every dyadic $\ell/2^k$ with $\ell, k \in \mathbb{Z}$.

In fact, the above limit can be shown to be uniform if we make one further observation about the control point sequences $\{c^n\}_{n=1}^{\infty}$. Clearly a quantity which measures the smoothness of the control polygon $f_n$ is

$$D(c^n) = \max_{|i-j| \le 1} |c_i^n - c_j^n|,$$

where $|\cdot|$ denotes Euclidean distance.

Observe that from (2.1),

$$c_1^1 - c_0^1 = \frac{1}{2}(c_1 - c_0),$$

$$c_2^1 - c_1^1 = \frac{1}{4}(c_2 - c_0) = \frac{1}{2}\left(\frac{1}{2}(c_1 - c_0) + \frac{1}{2}(c_2 - c_1)\right),$$

$$c_3^1 - c_2^1 = \frac{1}{4}(c_2 - c_0),$$

$$c_4^1 - c_3^1 = \frac{1}{2}(c_2 - c_1).$$

It follows then that

$$D(c^1) \le \frac{1}{2}D(c),$$

(2.4)

and more generally

$$D(c^n) \leq 2^{-n} D(c).$$

So $D(c^n)$ tends to zero as $n$ increases, and this fact combined with the tangency of $f_n$ and $B_2$ allows one to easily complete the proof of the uniform convergence.

Most of the features of the de Casteljau algorithm which we have just reviewed will be present in all the subdivision algorithms to be discussed. From a geometric view-point, the contraction property, as embodied in (2.4) for the de Casteljau algorithm, will play a fundamental role. Also the algebra of each algorithm can be analysed as the process of representing the desired curve or surface $f$ in terms of a "refinement" of a given basis. For the de Casteljau algorithm this rerepresentation is described by (2.3). The algorithm expresses $f$ in each of these bases; since the bases are increasingly locally supported, the coefficients, which in our terminology are the control points, become ever more accurate approximations to $f$ itself.

As a second and important example of subdivision techniques, we have the *Chaikin algorithm* [13]. Chaikin's interest in the algorithm was based on its high-speed generation of curves; Riesenfeld [45] then observed that Chaikin's algorithm in fact generated quadratic spline functions.

To describe the Chaikin algorithm, let the original control polygon $f_0$ have as vertices the points $c = \{c_0, c_1, \ldots, c_n\}$ where $c_i \in \mathbb{R}^2$. In the Chaikin algorithm, each vertex $c_i$ gets replaced by two vertices in a certain "corner cutting" construction as in Figure 2. Let $m_i$ be the midpoint of the side $c_i c_{i+1}$. Then according to Chaikin

$$p_i := \frac{1}{4}(m_{i-1} + 2c_i + m_i) \tag{2.5}$$

is a point on the curve $f$ which is to be generated. To advance the iteration we define the new control polygon $f_1$ to have as its vertices the $2n$ points

$$\left\{\frac{1}{2}(c_0 + m_0)\right\} \bigcup_{i=1}^{n-1} \left\{\frac{1}{2}(c_i + m_{i-1}), \frac{1}{2}(c_i + m_i)\right\} \bigcup \left\{\frac{1}{2}(c_n + m_{n-1})\right\}.$$

Then the midpoints of the sides of $f_1$ (which consists of the midpoints of the sides of $f_0$ and the points $p_i$) are all on the curve $f$. The algorithm then continues by the same corner cutting procedure applied now to $f_1$.

The algorithm can be viewed somewhat more simply as defined by

$$\begin{aligned} c_{2i}^1 &= \frac{3}{4}c_i + \frac{1}{4}c_{i+1}, \\ c_{2i+1}^1 &= \frac{1}{4}c_i + \frac{3}{4}c_{i+1}, \end{aligned} \qquad i = 0, \cdots, n-1, \tag{2.6}$$

cf. Figure 2. We then see that

$$f_1(t) = \sum_{i=0}^{2n-1} c_i^1 \varphi(2t - i), \tag{2.7}$$

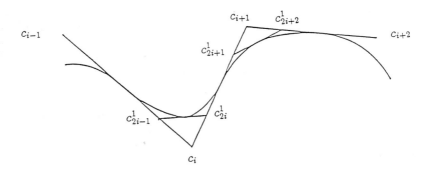

**Figure 2.** Chaikin's algorithm.

where as before $\varphi(t) = (1 - |t|)_+$.

Let $c^1 = \{c_0^1, \ldots, c_{2n-1}^1\}$ and define, as we did for the de Casteljau algorithm,

$$D(c) = \max_{|i-j|\leq 1} |c_i - c_j|.$$

Then it is easily seen that

$$D(c^1) \leq \frac{1}{2}D(c),$$

so that in this sense, the Chaikin subdivision is contractive.

The main observation of Riesenfeld [45] about the Chaikin construction is that the various midpoints of each control polygon $f_k$ always remain fixed as midpoints of successive control polygons $f_{k+j}$ for $j \geq 0$. From this he could conclude that the limiting curve $f$ is a quadratic spline curve whose knots occur at the midpoint of the sides of $f_0$. In fact, $p_i$ is on the parabolic arc inscribed in the angle $m_{i-1}c_im_i$. This is easy to see: observe that the inscribed parabolic arc is

$$g_i(t) = m_{i-1}(1 - t)^2 + 2c_it(1 - t) + m_it^2, \qquad 0 \leq t \leq 1,$$

since

$$g_i(0) = m_{i-1}, \qquad\qquad g_i(1) = m_i,$$
$$g_i'(0) = 2(c_i - m_{i-1}), \qquad g_i'(1) = 2(m_i - c_i).$$

This arc passes through $p_i$ since

$$g_i\left(\frac{1}{2}\right) = \frac{1}{4}(m_{i-1} + 2c_i + m_i).$$

Moreover,

$$g_i'\left(\frac{1}{2}\right) = m_i - m_{i-1}.$$

Let $f$ be the $C^1$ quadratic spline determined piecewise by each of the parabolic arcs $g_i(t)$. Then the above observations show that the control polygon $f_1$ defined by (2.7) is tangent to $f$ at the midpoints of every side of $f_1$. The same remains valid for every control polygon $f_k$, and this together with the contraction property yields

$$\lim_{k \to \infty} f_k(t) = f(t), \qquad 0 \le t \le n.$$

Very recently, M.J. Hejna [29] has used angle bisection on the control polygon to derive methods which compliment the Chaikin and de Casteljau algorithms.

## §3. De Rham's Construction of Certain Planar Curves

The Chaikin algorithm is a special case of a whole class of constructions considered many years earlier by the geometer de Rham [43,44]. In his detailed analyses, de Rham shows particular interest in two aspects of these curves. First, they are solutions of certain functional equations, and second, they are generally singular functions, in the sense of Lebesgue. Independently of de Rham and in a much wider context, Micchelli and Prautzsch [37] have shown the intimate connection of certain functional equations with matrix subdivision schemes for curves. We discuss this below in Section 10.

Given two affine transformations $A_0$ and $A_1$ of the plane into itself, de Rham's problem is to construct a curve $f(t)$ satisfying

$$\begin{aligned} f(t/2) &= A_0 f(t), \\ f((1+t)/2) &= A_1 f(t), \end{aligned} \qquad 0 \le t \le 1. \qquad (3.1)$$

Introducing the transformation $T_i t = (i+t)/2$ for $i = 0, 1$, we can write these equations more succinctly as

$$f(T_i t) = A_i f(t), \qquad 0 \le t \le 1, \quad i = 0, 1.$$

De Rham observes that one way to guarantee existence of a solution is to assume that $A_0$ and $A_1$ are contractions, in the sense that

$$|A_i x - A_i y| \le \gamma |x - y|, \qquad i = 0, 1,$$

holds for all $x, y \in \mathbb{R}^2$ and some fixed $\gamma \in (0, 1)$; here $|\cdot|$ denotes the Euclidean norm. Since $A_0$ and $A_1$ are contractions, they must have unique fixed points. Setting $t = 0$ and $t = 1$ in the first and second equation of (3.1) respectively, we identify these two fixed points as $f(0)$ and $f(1)$. Then reversing the values 0 and 1 in these same two equations, we obtain a *compatibility condition*

$$A_0 f(1) = A_1 f(0). \qquad (3.2)$$

Using binary expansions for $t \in [0, 1]$, de Rham then proves the following

**Theorem 3.1.** *If the affine transformations $A_0, A_1$ of the plane into itself are both contractive and if (3.2) holds where $f(0)$ and $f(1)$ are the fixed points of $A_0$ and $A_1$ respectively, then there exists a unique continuous curve $f(t)$ defined for $t \in [0, 1]$ satisfying (3.1).*

De Rham was first led to propose such a problem by the following considerations. Let a sequence of polygonal lines $f_n$ for $n = 0, 1, 2, \ldots$ be formed in the following manner: $f_0 = c_0 c_1 c_2$ is a broken line with two sides, and $f_{n+1}$ has as its vertices the points which divide each side of $f_n$ into three equal parts. Clearly each $f_n$ is convex, and in fact $f_{n+1}$ is derived from $f_n$ by corner cutting. As $n$ increases without bound, it can be seen geometrically that $f_n$ tends to a curve $C$ joining the midpoint of $c_0 c_1$ to the midpoint of $c_1 c_2$.

A little thought shows that the midpoints of each side of $f_n$ are again midpoints of certain sides of $f_{n+1}$, and hence are also midpoints of certain sides of all the polygons $f_{n+k}$ for $k = 1, 2, \ldots$. Therefore these very same points belong to the curve $C$. This observation also suggests a natural parameterization of the curve $C$. The polygonal line $f_n$ has $2^n + 1$ sides which we enumerate always in the same sense. The middle point of the $(i + 1)^{st}$ side of $f_n$ coincides with the middle point of the $(2i + 1)^{st}$ side of $f_{n+1}$, and, more generally, with the middle point of the $(2^k i + 1)^{st}$ side of $f_{n+k}$. Therefore we can justly denote this very point by $f_n(i2^{-n})$ for all $n$. So the curve $C$ is identified for every dyadic point $t$ as $f(t)$, and this parameterization of $C$ can be extended to the whole interval $[0, 1]$ by continuity.

To obtain the functional equations (3.1) for the function $f(t)$ as defined immediately above, let $c_0^1, c_1^1, c_2^1, c_3^1$ denote the vertices of $f_1$. Let $A_0 : \mathbb{R}^2 \to \mathbb{R}^2$ be the affine transformation which takes $c_0 c_1 c_2$ into $c_0^1 c_1^1 c_2^1$; then by linearity, $A_0$ maps $f_n$ into a polygon constructed from $c_0^1 c_1^1 c_2^1$ in exactly the same way as $f_n$ is constructed from $c_0 c_1 c_2$. But this means that $A_0$ must map $f_n$ to the polygon formed by the first $2^n + 1$ sides of $f_{n+1}$. It follows that

$$A_0 f(i/2^n) = f(i/2^{n+1}), \qquad i = 0, 1, \ldots, 2^n.$$

By continuity one deduces that

$$A_0 f(t) = f(t/2), \qquad 0 \le t \le 1.$$

Similarly one obtains that the affine map $A_1$ which maps $c_0 c_1 c_2$ to $c_1^1 c_2^1 c_3^1$ transforms $f(t)$ according to the equation

$$A_1 f(t) = f\big((1 + t)/2\big), \qquad 0 \le t \le 1.$$

De Rham then proposes a generalization of this particular construction which is amenable to exactly the same analysis given above. Again the vertices of $f_{n+1}$ divide each of the sides of $f_n$ into three parts, but now the two extreme segments are equal and the ratio of one of these segments to the middle segment is constant and denoted by a positive number $\gamma$. More precisely, given a fixed number $\alpha \in (1/2, 1)$, we define the new vertices from the old vertices of $f_n$ by

$$
\begin{aligned}
c_{2i}^1 &= \alpha c_i + (1 - \alpha) c_{i+1}, \\
c_{2i+1}^1 &= (1 - \alpha) c_i + \alpha c_{i+1}.
\end{aligned}
\tag{3.3}
$$

Then $\gamma = (1 - \alpha)/(2\alpha - 1)$. The resulting curve $C_\gamma$ again satisfies the functional equation (3.1) with appropriate $A_0$ and $A_1$, determined just as in the special case. Specializing $\gamma$, we easily see that $C_1 = C$ and if $\gamma = 2$ the de Rham construction is exactly the Chaikin algorithm (see (2.6) which should be compared to (3.3)).

Concerning the singular nature of the curves $C_\gamma$, de Rham gives a detailed analysis with results depending on the parameter $\gamma$. Clearly $C_\gamma$ is always convex, and so the curve must possess a tangent everywhere except possibly at countably many points. Expressing $m(t) = dy/dx$ as a continued fraction, of infinite length for non dyadics and of finite length for dyadics, de Rham is able to establish the following:

**Proposition 3.2.** *If $\gamma \geq 1$, the curve $C_\gamma$ has a tangent at each point and $m(t)$ is a continuous function of $t$. If $\gamma < 1$, the points $f_\gamma(t)$ for $t$ dyadic are angular points of $C_\gamma$; i.e., $m(t)$ has a jump discontinuity at these $t$ values.*

Concerning the second derivative $d^2y/dx^2$ at dyadic points, he proves that the curvature is zero if $\gamma < \sqrt{2} - 1$ or $\gamma > 2$ and infinite if $\sqrt{2} - 1 < \gamma < 2$. Thus $C_\gamma$ has no arc with a continuous second derivative, except for the curve $\gamma = 2$. So it appears that the Chaikin case $\gamma = 2$ is a truly exceptional case for the class of subdivision procedures considered by de Rham.

## §4. Algorithms for Surfaces

Motivated by the effectiveness of the Chaikin algorithm, Catmull, who had been devising recursive schemes for surfaces, refined his methods to generate piecewise bicubic surfaces. The idea of his scheme is to take a control polygon, defined as some configuration of points, edges, and faces, and to smooth it by cutting corners and replacing each of the faces by four smaller faces.

Many variants of this idea followed, but the most well known algorithms of this sort are due to Catmull-Clark [11], Doo [21,22], and Doo-Sabin [23]. When the configurations are regular in the sense that exactly four edges are incident at each vertex point, these algorithms yield biquadratic and bicubic surfaces. However, the algorithms allow for smoothing of an arbitrary polyhedron, where the vertices have varying valences, and some description of the limiting surface has been given, [23]. A common feature of these methods is that after several subdivision steps the polyhedron is primarily covered by four-sided faces. Therefore, the bulk of the surface can be described by a biquadratic or bi-cubic parametric surface. There are, however, a finite number of extraordinary points where four-sided faces are not sufficient for representing the surface. Furthermore, the smoothness of the surface at these points is difficult to determine, and in fact the surface may best be described as having "fractional" order smoothness at these points.

As an example of these algorithms, let us consider the biquadratic formulation of Catmull-Clark [11]. They reinterpret the tensor product version of Chaikin's algorithm (see Section 7) so that it is applicable to arbitrary configurations where the faces may have $n$ vertices with $n$ not necessarily equal to 4. Using (2.6) we find that a typical step of the tensor product of the Chaikin algorithm is

$$c_{00}^1 = \frac{9}{16}c_{00} + \frac{3}{16}c_{01} + \frac{3}{16}c_{10} + \frac{1}{16}c_{11}. \tag{4.1}$$

There are three other rules for $c_{ij}^1$ depending on the parity of $i$ and $j$. Interpreting these equations geometrically, Catmull-Clark propose the following rule for finding a new vertex $c_0^1$ in a face $F$ and near the old vertex $c_0$ of $F$:

$$c_0^1 = \frac{f}{n} + \frac{2e}{n} + \frac{c_0(n-3)}{n}. \tag{4.2}$$

Here $n$ is the number of vertices of $F$, while $f$ is the centroid of the $n$ vertices of $F$, and $e$ is the average of the midpoints of the two edges of $F$ which are incident at $c_0$. In the case when $n = 4$, equation (4.2) reduces to (4.1). The rule for joining the various new vertices $c_0^1$ together to form the new faces is simple and in fact is carried over from the tensor product construction. For details, the reader should consult [11].

## §5. The Subdivision Algorithm for Bernstein-Bézier Curves

Following the success of the early geometric approaches for the design of curves and surfaces by subdivision algorithms, Lane and Riesenfeld [30] presented extensions of the de Casteljau and Chaikin algorithms based on algebraic methods. To begin with the polynomal case, consider the Bernstein-Bézier curve of degree $m$ defined by

$$B_m(t \mid a, b) = \sum_{i=0}^{m} c_i b_i(t \mid a, b), \qquad a \leq t \leq b, \tag{5.1}$$

where $c_i \in \mathbb{R}^2$, and

$$b_i(t \mid a, b) = \binom{m}{i}(t-a)^i(b-t)^{m-i}/(b-a)^m.$$

The functions $b_i$ constitute the so-called Bernstein basis for $\pi_m$, the space of polynomials of degree $m$, relative to the interval $[a, b]$. The given control points $c_i$ are the vertices of the initial control polygon $f_0$. Observe that $B_m(a) = c_0$ and $B_m(b) = c_m$. A simple calculation also reveals that $c_1 - c_0$ is tangent to the curve $B_m$ at $t = a$ and $c_{m-1} - c_m$ is tangent at $t = b$.

By a subdivision procedure we wish to recover $B_m$. The de Casteljau algorithm has been analyzed from this point of view by Lane and Riesenfeld in [30], and we wish to highlight some of the details here. As in our introductory example when $m = 2$, the new control polygon $f_1$ has as its vertices the coefficients obtained by expressing $B_m(t)$ on each of the intervals $[a, (a+b)/2]$ and $[(a+b)/2, b]$ in the corresponding Bernstein bases of the same degree. The following proposition gives a closed form expression for these coefficients in terms of the old ones. We state the proposition for the interval $[0, 1]$, but these same formulas are valid for any interval $[a, b]$ which is halved.

**Proposition 5.1.** *For the polynomial $B_m$ given by (5.1), we have*

$$B_m(t \mid 0, 1) = \sum_{i=0}^{m} c_i^L b_i\left(t \mid 0, 2^{-1}\right),$$

*where*

$$c_i^L = 2^{-i} \sum_{j=0}^{i} \binom{i}{j} c_j, \qquad i = 0, 1, \ldots, m. \tag{5.2}$$

*Similarly*

$$B_m(t \mid 0, 1) = \sum_{i=0}^{m} c_i^R b_i(t \mid 2^{-1}, 1)$$

*where*

$$c_{m-i}^R = 2^{-i} \sum_{j=0}^{i} \binom{i}{j} c_{m-i+j}, \qquad i = 0, 1, \ldots, m. \tag{5.3}$$

**Proof:** If we set

$$B_m(t \mid 0, 1) = \sum_{k=0}^{m} t^k \left(\frac{1}{2} - t\right)^{m-k} q_k,$$

then we have

$$\sum_{k=0}^{m} \binom{m}{k} t^{m-k} (1-t)^k c_{m-k} = \sum_{k=0}^{m} t^{m-k} \left(\frac{1}{2} - t\right)^k q_{m-k}.$$

Dividing by $t^m$ and setting $x = (1 - 2t)/(2t)$, we obtain

$$\sum_{k=0}^{m} \binom{m}{k} (1 + 2x)^k c_{m-k} = \sum_{k=0}^{m} x^k q_{m-k}.$$

Equation (5.2) then follows by comparing coefficients of $x^k$. The proof of (5.3) is similar. ∎

We now display the steps of the de Casteljau subdivision in an array generated by successive averages from the original control points:

$$c_i^0 := c_i, \qquad i = 0, \ldots, m;$$

$$c_i^k := \frac{1}{2}\left(c_{i-1}^{k-1} + c_i^{k-1}\right), \qquad k = 1, \ldots, m; \quad i = k, \ldots, m. \tag{5.4}$$

$$
\begin{array}{cccccc}
c_0^0 & c_1^0 & c_2^0 & c_3^0 & \cdots & c_m^0 \\
 & c_1^1 & c_2^1 & c_3^1 & \cdots & c_m^1 \\
\downarrow & c_2^2 & c_3^2 & \cdots & \nearrow & \\
 & \vdots & & & & \\
 & c_m^m & & & &
\end{array} \tag{5.5}
$$

From the previous proposition, a straightforward induction on $m$ establishes

**Proposition 5.2.** *The new control polygon generated by the control points $c_i^L$ concatenated with $c_i^R$ is obtained from the first column and the lower diagonal of the de Casteljau array (5.5), as indicated by the two arrows. More generally we have*

$$c_n^k = 2^{-k} \sum_{j=0}^{k} \binom{k}{j} c_{n-k+j}, \qquad k = 0, 1, \ldots, n, \quad n = k, \ldots, m.$$

Denoting the sequence of new control points by $c^1$ and the original control points by $c^0$, Lane and Riesenfeld pointed out that

$$D(c^1) \le \frac{1}{2} D(c^0), \tag{5.6}$$

where as before

$$D(c) = \max_{|i-j| \le 1} |c_i - c_j|.$$

Indeed,

$$|c_{k-1}^{k-1} - c_k^k| = \frac{1}{2}|c_{k-1}^{k-1} - c_k^{k-1}|$$

and

$$|c_m^k - c_m^{k-1}| = \frac{1}{2}|c_{m-1}^{k-1} - c_m^{k-1}|,$$

since the array is constructed by successive averages (5.4). Then (5.6) follows by Proposition 5.2. Thus one step of the Casteljau algorithm as defined by the array (5.5) is contractive.

We now iterate, computing array after array, and generating the control polygons $f_j(t)$ determined by the $(2m + 1)$ entries of the first column and lower diagonal of each of the $2^j$ arrays. Note that $f_j$ interpolates, and in fact is tangent to, $B_m$ at the points $a + k(b - a)/2^j$ for $k = 0, \ldots 2^j$. From (5.6) it is clear that if $c^j$ denotes the control points of $f_j$, then

$$D(c^j) \le 2^{-j} D(c^0),$$

and so since the $f_j$ are piecewise linear, $\omega(f_j, h) = O(h)$ where $\omega$ is the modulus of continuity and the estimate is uniform in $j$. Therefore the sequence $\{f_j\}$ has a continuous limit on $[a, b]$; that this limiting curve must in fact be $B_m$ follows from the interpolation conditions. Thus we obtain

**Theorem 5.3.** *The sequence $\{f_j\}$ of control polygons given by the de Casteljau algorithm converges to $B_m(\cdot \mid a, b)$ uniformly on $[a, b]$.*

The de Casteljau algorithm has a generalization for Bernstein polynomials defined on simplices in $\mathbb{R}^s$. Thus with $s = 2$, surfaces in $\mathbb{R}^n$ can be generated. Details of such a generalization have been investigated successfully from a probabilistic point of view by Goldman [27] and recently by Seidel [49], using blossoming.

## §6. Subdivision Algorithms for Univariate Spline Functions

There are two important algorithms for spline functions of one variable. The first of these is a direct generalization of the Chaikin algorithm for quadratic splines and it generates splines of degree $n$ with equally spaced simple knots; the algorithm is due to Lane-Riesenfeld. The second, commonly called the Oslo algorithm, is much more general and can yield splines with arbitrary knot distributions; it also allows for multiple knots. Here we will give an outline of each algorithm and some specifics on their contractive properties.

Following Schoenberg [47], we define the cardinal $B$-spline of degree $n$ as

$$M_n(t) = \frac{1}{n!} \sum_{j=0}^{n+1} (-1)^j \binom{n+1}{j} (j - t)_+^n. \tag{6.1}$$

This function is positive on $(0, n + 1)$, has $n - 1$ continuous derivatives, and vanishes outside the interval $(0, n + 1)$. On each interval $(j, j + 1)$ with $j \in \mathbb{Z}$, the function $M_n$ is a polynomial of degree $n$, and $M_n$ satisfies the equation

$$\sum_{j=-\infty}^{\infty} M_n(t - j) = 1, \qquad x \in \mathbb{R}. \tag{6.2}$$

These properties of the $B$-spline are standard facts and can be found, for instance, in [8,48].

The space of *cardinal spline functions* is defined as the linear span of the integer translates of $M_n$; that is,

$$S_n = \left\{ f : f(t) = \sum_{j=-\infty}^{\infty} c_j M_n(t - j), \quad x \in \mathbb{R}, \quad c_j \in \mathbb{R} \right\}.$$

Alternatively, the space $S_n$ is the collection of all functions which are polynomials of degree at most $n$ on each interval $[j, j+1]$ with $j \in \mathbb{Z}$, and which have $n-1$ continuous derivatives on the domain $\mathbb{R}$.

To define the Lane-Riesenfeld algorithm, let the original control polygon $f_0$ be defined by $f_0(i) = c_i$ for $c_i \in \mathbb{R}^s$ and $i \in \mathbb{Z}$, and fix a natural number $n$. The first step of the algorithm is to "double up" the data by putting

$$d_{2i}^1 := c_i,$$
$$d_{2i+1}^1 := c_i. \tag{6.3}$$

The algorithm then calls for $n-1$ smoothing steps as defined by

$$d_i^\ell = \frac{1}{2}(d_i^{\ell-1} + d_{i-1}^{\ell-1}), \qquad \ell = 2, \ldots, n. \tag{6.4}$$

Set $c_i^1 := d_i^n$ and $c^1 = \{c_i^1\}$. Then $f_1$ is the control polygon satisfying

$$f_1(i/2) = c_i^1; \tag{6.5}$$

*i.e.*,

$$f_1(t) = \sum_{i=-\infty}^{\infty} c_i^1 \varphi(2t - i),$$

where $\varphi(t) = (1 - |t|)_+$. The change of scale in the argument of $f_1$ is best understood as the inverse operation of the doubling up which occurs in the first step of the algorithm. Repeating both steps of the algorithm, the doubling up and the averaging, we obtain after $k$ iterations the control polygon $f_k$ with vertices at the points $i/2^k$.

A simple check shows that if $n = 3$, so that two smoothing steps are done in each iteration of the algorithm, one obtains the Chaikin algorithm for cardinal quadratic splines.

The new control points $c_i^1$ generated in one pass of the above algorithm satisfy the equation

$$\sum_{j=-\infty}^{\infty} c_j^1 M_{n-1}(2t - j) = \sum_{j=-\infty}^{\infty} c_j M_{n-1}(t - j). \tag{6.6}$$

On the right hand side is the $B$-spline representation for cardinal splines; on the left side is the representation of the same function as a degree $n$ spline with knots at the half integers. Thus, just as we have observed with the de Casteljau algorithm, the subdivision algorithm can be viewed algebraically as a change of basis. We refer to (6.6) as the refinement property of the algorithm. Again letting

$$D(c) = \sup_{|i-j| \le 1} |c_i - c_j|,$$

we know from [30] that

$$D(c^1) \le \frac{1}{2}D(c), \tag{6.7}$$

which is easily seen from (6.4). So the algorithm is contractive just as in the de Casteljau case. Using these two observations one easily proves

**Theorem 6.1.** *Let $f_k(t)$ be the control polygon formed at the $k^{th}$ stage. Then*

$$\lim_{k \to \infty} f_k(t) = \sum_{j=-\infty}^{\infty} c_j M_{n-1}(t-j),$$

*uniformly in $t$.*

Denoting the control points of $f_k$ by $c^k = \{c_\ell^k\}_{\ell=-\infty}^{\infty}$, one has from (6.7)

$$D(c^k) \le \frac{1}{2^k} D(c),$$

which is the crucial step for establishing the theorem.

Let us make one more observation about the Lane-Riesenfeld algorithm. Let the space of splines of of degree $n$ with knot sequence $X = \{x_i\}$ satisfying $x_i < x_{i+1}$, be denoted by $\mathcal{S}_n(X)$. The Lane-Riesenfeld algorithm for cardinal splines just discussed is based on the inclusion $\mathcal{S}_n(\mathbb{Z}) \subset \mathcal{S}_n(\mathbb{Z}/2)$. From this containment $M_n \in \mathcal{S}_n(\mathbb{Z}/2)$, and therefore

$$M_n(t) = \sum_{j=-\infty}^{\infty} a_j^n M_n(2t-j)$$

for some coefficients $a_j^n$. By one step of the Lane-Riesenfeld algorithm we can compute $a_j^n$ as (6.6) shows. To see this, note that the control polygon for $M_n$ is simply the delta sequence

$$\delta_j = \begin{cases} 1, & \text{for } j = 0; \\ 0, & \text{otherwise.} \end{cases}$$

One easy way to keep track of the successive averaging called for by the algorithm in (6.3)–(6.4) is to use generating functions. In the first step of the algorithm we "double up" the $\delta$-sequence obtaining the sequence whose generating function is simply $1 + z$. Then we are to apply $n$ averaging steps, each of which means that the generating function should be multiplied by $\frac{1}{2}(1+z)$. Therefore, in this case we obtain

$$G(z) := \frac{1}{2^n}(1+z)^{n+1} = \sum_{j=0}^{n+1} a_j^n z^j, \tag{6.8}$$

which gives the formula

$$M_n(t) = \frac{1}{2^n} \sum_{j=0}^{n+1} \binom{n+1}{j} M_n(2t-j). \tag{6.9}$$

Summarizing, we see that the cardinal spline subdivision algorithm shares several nice features with the de Casteljau algorithm. It is numerically simple and stable, being essentially successive averages. The algorithm is contractive, and it is best understood and analyzed as a change of basis for the underlying spline space. Note that the change of basis, as in the de Casteljau algorithm, is effected by halving the independent variable.

A more flexible approach to univariate subdivision is available in the knot insertion algorithm of Boehm [6], and in the so called Oslo algorithm of Cohen, Lyche, Riesenfeld [14], both of which allow for arbitrary knot distributions. To describe the Oslo algorithm, let $N_{i,m}$ be the $B$-splines of degree $m-1$ for the knot sequence $X$ normalized so that

$$\sum_i N_{i,m}(t) = 1$$

for all $t$. Let $\hat{X} = \{\hat{x}_i\}$ be a finer knot sequence, that is $\hat{X} \supset X$, and let $\bar{N}_{i,m}$ be the corresponding normalized $B$-spline. Then, since $S_{m-1}(X) \subset S_{m-1}(\hat{X})$, each $B$-spline $N_{i,m}$ can be written in terms of the $B$-splines on the finer partition as

$$N_{i,m} = \sum_j a_{ij}^m \bar{N}_{j,m}.$$

Then any spline of the form

$$S(x) = \sum_i c_i N_{i,m}(x)$$

takes the form

$$S(x) = \sum_i c_i^1 \bar{N}_{i,m}(x),$$

where

$$c_i^1 = \sum_j a_{ji}^m c_j.$$

The coefficient sequences $\{a_{i,j}^m\}_j$ are called the *discrete B-splines* and an essential part of the Oslo algorithm is the recursive formula:

$$a_{ij}^{n+1} = \left( \frac{\bar{x}_{j+n} - x_i}{x_{i+n} - x_i} \right) a_{ij}^n + \left( \frac{x_{i+n+1} - \bar{x}_{j+m}}{x_{i+n+1} - x_{i+1}} \right) a_{i+1,j}^n, \tag{6.10}$$

where

$$a_{ij}^1 = \begin{cases} 1, & \text{for } x_i \leq \bar{x}_j < x_{i+1}; \\ 0, & \text{otherwise.} \end{cases}$$

In [40], Prautzsch offers a very nice proof of this recursion that uses a simple comparison of coefficients. Recently, the knot insertion algorithm was discussed by Seidel [50] who uses blossoming.

If we specialize to the cardinal spline case, then $x_i = i$ and $\bar{x}_i = i/2$, and so (6.10) becomes

$$a_{ij}^{(n+1)} = \frac{1}{n} \left( \left( \frac{j+n}{2} - i \right) a_{ij}^n + \left( i + n + 1 - \frac{j+n}{2} \right) a_{i+1,j}^n \right) \tag{6.11}$$

and

$$a_{ij}^1 = \begin{cases} 1, & \text{if } j = 2i \text{ or } j = 2i + 1; \\ 0, & \text{otherwise.} \end{cases}$$

Thus we have the same doubling up as in the Lane-Riesenfeld algorithm, but not the same averaging step. Therefore the two algorithms are distinct.

Discussions of the efficient computer implementation of these ideas appear in Boehm [1] and in Lyche and Mørken [33].

## §7. Cube Splines and the Line Average Algorithm

How can the concept of subdivision be extended in order to generate smooth surfaces? One successful approach, that of Catmull-Clark and Doo-Sabin, has already been discussed in §4. In the algorithms examined so far, two main features can be discerned. First, the algorithms generally consist of repeated averages. This feature gives an easy means to increase smoothness. Second, the underlying function spaces were somehow nested, as reflected for example by the simple structural characterization of univariate splines as piecewise polynomial arcs.

The first of these points has a natural enough extension to the multivariate setting. We can surely base an algorithm on repeated *line* averages; and the wider multivariate setting would naturally allow for variation in the directions of these line averages. Concerning the second point, it is far from obvious which multivariate spline space, if any, is appropriate for the convergence analysis of such a line average algorithm. To get some idea of what might be necessary, we return to (6.9), which is at the core of the convergence analysis of the Lane-Riesenfeld algorithm. In terms of the Fourier transform of $M_n$, the nesting means that $\hat{M}_n(2t)/\hat{M}_n(t)$ is a polynomial in $e^{it}$, as follows easily from (6.9), and this property carries over nicely to *cube splines*, which we now define.

In this section we let $X = \{x^1, \ldots, x^n\} \subset \mathbb{Z}^s - \{0\}$ denote a set of not necessarily distinct vectors, where $n \geq s$. For $i = 1, \ldots, s$ we assume that $x^i = e^i$, the $i^{th}$ coordinate vector, and so $\langle X \rangle := \operatorname{span} X = \mathbb{R}^s$. The symbol $X$ will also denote the $s \times n$ matrix whose $j^{th}$ column is $x^j$. Let $X_k = \{x^1, \ldots, x^k\}$ for $k = s, \ldots, n$, so that $X_n = X$. For $x = (x_1, \ldots, x_s)$, we make the following inductive definition,

$$M(x \mid X_s) := \begin{cases} 1, & 0 \leq x_i < 1 \text{ for all } i \in \{1, 2, \ldots, s\}; \\ 0, & \text{otherwise}; \end{cases}$$

$$M(x \mid X_k) := \int_0^1 M(x - tx^k \mid X_{k-1})dt \qquad \text{for } k = s+1, \ldots, n. \tag{7.1}$$

An easy induction establishes that for any continuous $f$,

$$\int_{\mathbb{R}^s} f(x)M(x \mid X_n)dx = \int_0^1 \cdots \int_0^1 f(t_1 x^1 + \cdots + t_n x^n)dt_1 \cdots dt_n. \tag{7.2}$$

This is the so-called distributional definition of the cube spline $M$, which was first presented by de Boor and DeVore [9]; special cases of this definition appeared earlier in Sabin [46]. Equation (7.2) shows that $M$ depends only on $X$ and not on its ordering. In the case where $n = s$, equation (7.2) is trivial since $x^i = e^i$ for $i = 1, \dots, s$. Assuming (7.2) for $n = k - 1$, we have

$$\int_{\mathbb{R}^s} f(x) M(x \mid X_{k-1}) dx = \int_0^1 \cdots \int_0^1 f(t_1 x^1 + \cdots + t_{k-1} x^{k-1}) dt_1 \cdots dt_{k-1}.$$

The left hand side equals

$$\int_{\mathbb{R}^s} f(x - tx^k) M(x - tx^k \mid X_{k-1}) dx,$$

and so using $g(x) := f(x - tx^k)$ we obtain

$$\int_{\mathbb{R}^s} g(x) M(x - tx^k \mid X_{k-1}) dx = $$
$$\int_0^1 \cdots \int_0^1 g(t_1 x^1 + \cdots + t_{k-1} x^{k-1} + tx^k) dt \cdots dt_{k-1}.$$

Integrating this last equation with respect to $t$ on $[0,1]$ gives equation (7.2) for $n = k$ and completes the induction.

From equation (7.2) we get that the Fourier transform of the cube spline is

$$\hat{M}(y) = \int_{\mathbb{R}^s} e^{ix \cdot y} M(x \mid X) dx = \prod_{j=1}^n \left( \frac{e^{iy \cdot x^j} - 1}{iy \cdot x^j} \right). \tag{7.3}$$

A straightforward calculation then shows that

$$2^s \frac{\hat{M}(2y \mid X)}{\hat{M}(y \mid X)} = \frac{1}{2^{n-s}} \prod_{j=1}^n \left( z^{x^j} + 1 \right) := \sum_{\alpha \in \mathbb{Z}^s} b_\alpha(X) z^\alpha, \tag{7.4}$$

where $z_j = e^{iy_j}, j = 1, \dots, s$, $z = (z_1, \dots, z_s)$, and $z^{x^j} := z_1^{x_1^j} \cdots z_s^{x_s^j}$. We note that a contribution of $z^\alpha$ appears in the product whenever $\alpha = \beta_1 x^1 + \cdots + \beta_n x^n$, where each $\beta_i$ is 0 or or 1; of course $b_\alpha(X) \geq 0$. We call the sequence $\{b_\alpha\}$, where $b_\alpha := b_\alpha(X)$, the *mask* of the subdivision algorithm. From (7.4),

$$2^s \hat{M}(2y \mid X) = \sum_{\alpha \in \mathbb{Z}^s} b_\alpha e^{iy\alpha} \hat{M}(y \mid X), \tag{7.5}$$

from which it follows that

$$M \left( \frac{x}{2} \mid X \right) = \sum_{\alpha \in \mathbb{Z}^s} b_\alpha M(x - \alpha \mid X). \tag{7.6}$$

The two functional equations (7.5) and (7.6) are in fact equivalent, and (7.6) should be compared to (6.9). We document specific instances of masks later.

Given the cube spline surface

$$f(x) = \sum_{\alpha \in \mathbb{Z}^s} c_\alpha M(x - \alpha \mid X), \qquad (7.7)$$

equation (7.6) allows us to represent it as

$$
\begin{aligned}
f(x) &= \sum_{\alpha \in \mathbb{Z}^s} c_\alpha \sum_{\beta \in \mathbb{Z}^s} b_\beta M(2x - 2\alpha - \beta \mid X) \\
&= \sum_{\beta \in \mathbb{Z}^s} c_\beta^1 M(2x - \beta \mid X),
\end{aligned}
\qquad (7.8)
$$

where

$$c_\beta^1 = \sum_{\alpha \in \mathbb{Z}^s} c_\alpha b_{\beta - 2\alpha}. \qquad (7.9)$$

Equation (7.8) gives the refinement property of the algorithm and (7.9) defines for us a single iteration of the subdivision algorithm. We wish to show that $\{c_\beta^1\}$ is obtained simply by certain line averages of $c_\alpha$. The set $X$ we assume fixed and ordered. The ordering is immaterial for the surface, though it will influence the course of the algorithm. To obtain these line averages, multiply the equation

$$\sum_{\alpha \in \mathbb{Z}^s} b_\alpha(X_{k-1}) z^\alpha = \frac{1}{2^{k-s-1}} \prod_{j=1}^{k-1} (z^{x^j} + 1)$$

by $\frac{1}{2}(z^{x^k} + 1)$ and obtain

$$\frac{1}{2} \sum_{\alpha \in \mathbb{Z}^s} \left( b_\alpha(X_{k-1}) + b_{\alpha - x^n}(X_{k-1}) \right) z^\alpha = \sum_{\alpha \in \mathbb{Z}^s} b_\alpha(X_k) z^\alpha.$$

So we see that

$$b_\alpha(X_k) = \frac{1}{2} (b_\alpha(X_{k-1}) + b_{\alpha - x^k}(X_{k-1})).$$

When this equation is used in (7.9), we obtain the recursion

$$c_\beta^1(X_k) = \frac{1}{2} \left\{ c_\beta^1(X_{k-1}) + c_{\beta - x^k}^1(X_{k-1}) \right\}. \qquad (7.10)$$

Note in the special case $X_s = \{e^1, \ldots, e^s\}$ that

$$\sum_{\alpha \in \mathbb{Z}^s} b_\alpha(X_s) z^\alpha = \prod_{j=1}^{s} (z_j + 1).$$

Thus

$$b_\alpha(X_s) = \begin{cases} 1, & \text{for } \alpha \in \text{ext}[0, 1]^s; \\ 0, & \text{otherwise.} \end{cases}$$

So using (7.9) in this case, we find that

$$c^1_\beta(X_s) = c_\alpha \text{ for } \beta = 2\alpha + \text{ ext } [0,1]^s. \tag{7.11}$$

This is the first expansion step of the line average algorithm, the succeeding steps being the line averages given by (7.10) for $k = s+1, \ldots, n$.

The algorithm replaces $c_\alpha$ with $c^1_\alpha(X_n)$ and then repeats (7.10) and (7.11), generating in this way $c^m_\alpha := c^m_\alpha(X_n)$, for $m \in \mathbb{Z}^+, \alpha \in \mathbb{Z}^s$. The control polygon at the $m^{th}$ stage is given by

$$f_m(x) := \sum_{\alpha \in \mathbb{Z}^s} c^m_\alpha \varphi(2^m x - \alpha), \tag{7.12}$$

where $\varphi$ is the tensor product linear B-spline satisfying

$$\varphi(\alpha) = \begin{cases} 1, & \text{if } \alpha = 0; \\ 0, & \text{if } \alpha \neq 0. \end{cases}$$

Thus on the fine lattice $2^{-m}\mathbb{Z}^s$, the control polygon $f_m$ interpolates the sequence $c^m_\alpha$; i.e.,

$$f_m\left(\frac{\alpha}{2^m}\right) = c^m_\alpha, \quad \text{for all } \alpha \in \mathbb{Z}^s.$$

This algorithm has been given independently both by Cohen, Lyche, and Riesenfeld [15] and by Dahmen and Micchelli [19,20]. Special cases appeared earlier in Boehm [2,3,4,5] and Prautzsch [41]. Concerning convergence of the algorithm we have

**Theorem 7.1.** [15,19] *The line average algorithm defined by (7.10), (7.11) converges at the rate* $O(2^{-m})$ *to $f$ given by (7.7).*

For a discussion of convergence for the line average algorithm based on contractivity properties, see Cavaretta, Dahmen, and Micchelli [12]. In summary, we have the following scheme:

$$\text{coarse lattice } \mathbb{Z}^s \qquad \text{fine lattice } 2^{-m}\mathbb{Z}^s$$
$$\downarrow \qquad\qquad\qquad \downarrow$$
$$\{c_\alpha : \alpha \in \mathbb{Z}^s\} \quad \rightarrow \quad \{c^m_{2^m\alpha} : \alpha \in \mathbb{Z}^s/2^m\}$$

Initialization: $c^0_\alpha := c_\alpha$;
For each $\ell = 1, \ldots, m$
$\quad$ set: $d^s_\beta := c^{\ell-1}_\alpha$ for $\beta = 2\alpha + \text{ ext } [0,1]^s$;
$\quad$ do for $k = s+1, \ldots, n$:
$\quad\quad d^k_\beta := \frac{1}{2}(d^{k-1}_\beta + d^{k-1}_{\beta-x^k})$;
$\quad$ Set $c^\ell_\alpha := d^n_\alpha$.

There are many examples of these line averages algorithms. We will give a few relatively simple ones that are used in practice.

1. Tensor product surfaces are obtained as special cases of the line average algorithm when $X$ consists of only coordinate directions. To achieve a desired smoothness, the coordinate directions $e^1, e^2 \in \mathbb{Z}^2$ are repeated $r$ and $q$ times respectively, so that $X_{r,q} = \{e^1, \ldots, e^1, e^2, \ldots, e^2\}$. Then

$$\frac{1}{2^{n+q-1}}(z_1 + 1)^r (z_2 + 1)^q = \frac{1}{2^{n+q-1}} \sum_{i=0}^{r} \sum_{j=0}^{q} \binom{r}{i} \binom{q}{j} z_1^i z_2^j$$

which determines the mask $\{b_{ij}\}$. When $r = q = 3$, we obtain the bivariate version of the Chaikin algorithm for $C^1$ biquadratic surfaces.

2. The masks of some non-tensor product subdivision algorithms are:

(i) $X = \{e^1, e^2, e^1 + e^2\}$. Then the product in (6.4) is

$$\frac{1}{2} \prod_{j=1}^{3} (z^{x^j} + 1) = \frac{1}{2}(z_1^2 z_2^2 + z_1 z_2^2 + z_1^2 z_2 + 2z_1 z_2 + z_1 + z_2 + 1)$$

and so the mask (modulo a factor of $\frac{1}{2}$) is as given in Figure 3.

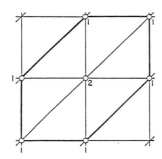

**Figure 3.** The mesh of Example (i).

(ii) $X = \{e^1, e^2, e^1 + e^2, e^1 - e^2\}$. Then the product in (7.4) is

$$\frac{1}{4}(z_1^3 z_2 + z_1^3 + z_1^2 z_2^2 + 2z_1^2 z_2 + 2z_1^2 + z_1^2 z_2^{-1}$$
$$+ z_1 z_2^2 + 2z_1 z_2 + 2z_1 + z_1 z_2^{-1} + z_2 + 1).$$

The mask in this case has the octagonal shape shown in Figure 4.

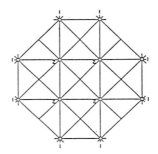

**Figure 4.** The mesh of Example *(ii)*.

There are a lot of special choices for the matrix $X \subset \mathbb{Z}^2$ which produce particularly nice cube splines. Recently, Loop [31] has given special attention to $X = \{e^1, e^1, e^2, e^2, e^1 + e^2, e^1 + e^2\}$. The cube spline in this case is of degree 4, in $C^2$, and has a certain trilateral symmetry. The associated line average algorithm when applied to the control polygon $\{c_\alpha : \alpha \in \mathbb{Z}^2\}$ produces a piecewise quartic surface which is everywhere $C^2$. Viewing this line average algorithm geometrically in the spirit of Catmull-Clark and Doo-Sabin, Loop proposes a subdivision algorithm applicable to control polygons which are not necessarily topologically equivalent to the triangular grid with vertices in $\mathbb{Z}^2$.

His algorithm has two rules, one for new points near the old vertices and another rule for generating new vertices near the middle of each of the edges of the given polygon. Let $c_0$ be a vertex joined by edges to $n$ other vertices $c_1, \ldots, c_n$. Let

$$q = \frac{1}{n} \sum_{i=1}^{n} c_i.$$

The new vertex $c_0^1$ is determined by

$$c_0^1 = \alpha_n c_0 + (1 - \alpha_n)q,$$

where $\alpha_n$ is to be determined. To be in agreement with the line average algorithm associated with $X$, we must have $\alpha_6 = \frac{5}{8}$. The second rule gives new "edge" points $e_i^1$ near the middle of the edge $c_0 c_i$. These points are defined by

$$e_i^1 = \frac{1}{8}c_{i-1} + \frac{3}{8}c_i + \frac{1}{8}c_{i+1} + \frac{3}{8}c_0, \quad i = 1, \ldots, n.$$

The new edges are those joining the new vertex $c_0^1$ to each $e_i^1$, in addition to those edges joining $e_i^1$ to $e_{i+1}^1$ and $e_n^1$ to $e_1^1$.

For this algorithm an extraordinary point is the limiting position of a vertex of valence other than 6. Clearly $c_0^1$ has valence equal that of $c$; moreover, it is easily seen that each new edge point $e_i^1$ will have valence 6. Thus the only extraordinary points are those which evolve from the original vertices of valence other than 6. Such vertices become isolated one from the other, and so the behavior of the algorithm can be analyzed separately at each one. Using the finite Fourier transform (a tool used previously in like circumstances by Doo-Sabin), Loop proves that the algorithm converges provided $-5/8 < \alpha_n < 11/8$. Further analysis shows that the surface will have a tangent plane at the extraordinary points provided $-1/4\cos(2\pi/n) < \alpha_n < 3/4 + 1/4\cos(2\pi/n)$. Analysis of the curvature at an extraordinary point is at the moment incomplete, although of course at all points other than extraordinary points the surface, being a cube spline surface, is $C^2$.

Another subdivision algorithm suitable for arbitrary triangular configurations is the "butterfly" scheme recently proposed by Dyn and Levin [26]. They were motivated by certain univariate schemes of theirs which are discussed below in Section 10. The butterfly scheme is a perturbation of the line average algorithm determined by $X = \{e^1, e^2, e^1 + e^2\}$, where $e^1$ and $e^2$ are the coordinate directions in $\mathbb{R}^2$. In this case, the cube spline surface is simply linear interpolation of the original control points $\{c_\alpha\}$ on the triangular grid generated by $X$. Thus the new control points are just the old ones together with the averages $\frac{1}{2}(c_\alpha + c_{\alpha-x})$ where $x \in X$. The butterfly algorithm selects as new control points all the old ones $\{c_\alpha\}$ plus new "edge" points $e$ defined for each edge $c_1 c_2$ by the formula

$$e = \frac{1}{2}(c_1 + c_2) - 2\omega(c_3 + c_4) + \omega(c_5 + c_6 + c_7 + c_8).$$

Here $c_3$ and $c_4$ are the other vertices of the two triangles $\triangle_1$ and $\triangle_2$ which share the edge $c_1 c_2$, and $c_5, c_6, c_7$, and $c_8$ are the remaining vertices of the triangles sharing a side with either $\triangle_1$ or $\triangle_2$. The tension parameter $\omega$ is at one's disposal; if $\omega = 0$, the subdivision will generate a piecewise linear surface as before. Exactly how the geometric continuity of the generated surface depends on $\omega$ is presently under consideration.

## §8. Rates of Convergence

Some comments on the rates of convergence of the algorithms so far discussed are in order. We expect that the convergence rate should be at least $O(h)$ where $h = 2^{-m}$ is the grid mesh size for the control polygon at the $m^{th}$ stage. However, for cardinal splines the convergence rate is $O(h^2)$. Under certain circumstances, Dahmen [17] and Dahmen, Dyn, and Levin [18] found that $O(h^2)$ can also be obtained for surfaces. To state one of the results, we need the notion of a *unimodular matrix* $X$, that is an $s \times n$ matrix all of whose $s \times s$ minors have values $\pm 1$ or 0.

**Theorem 8.1.** ([18]). *Let $X$ be unimodular, and suppose that for every $y \in X$, the vectors in $X - \{y\}$ span $\mathbb{R}^s$. Then the line average algorithm converges as $O(h^2)$ where $h = 2^{-m}$.*

Other sufficient conditions for quadratic convergence are given in [18]. A better convergence rate for the line average algorithm is only rarely possible, as the following theorem shows.

**Theorem 8.2.** ([35]). *If $f(x) = \sum_{\alpha \in \mathbb{Z}^s} c_\alpha M(x - \alpha \mid X)$ is a cube spline surface for which the line average algorithm converges at the rate $o(h^2)$, then $f$ is a polynomial.*

By interpreting the line average algorithm in terms of quadratures, the algorithm can be modified so that the convergence is accelerated; for details, see Prautzsch [42].

Along with the quadratic convergence of the line average algorithm for the case when $X$ is unimodular, there are two other cases of quadratically converging subdivision algorithms.

($i$) The subdivision algorithm for Bernstein-Bezier curves converges quadratically in $h = 2^{-m}$.

($ii$) If $S \in C^2(\mathbb{R})$ the Oslo algorithm converges quadratically in $\Delta_m :=$ $\max_i |t_{i+1}^m - t_i^m|$, where $\{t_i^m\}_{i \in \mathbb{Z}}$ is the knot sequence at the $m^{th}$ stage.

These facts are discussed by Cohen and Schumaker [16] and Dahmen [17].

As we have observed, each subdivision process is based on representing the desired function in "refined" bases, so that the $m^{th}$ iteration can be associated with a basis $\{p_\alpha^m\}$. For example, in the Lane-Riesenfeld algorithm for cardinal splines, the basis $p_i^m$ is simply the scaled and translated $B$-spline $M(2^m x - i)$. The rates of convergence of the algorithms can then be resolved in terms of the *uniform stability* of the bases, by which we mean the inequality

$$d^{-1}|c_\beta| \leq \| \sum_\alpha c_\alpha p_\alpha^m \|_\infty, \qquad \text{for all } \beta, \tag{8.1}$$

where $d$ is a positive constant independent of $m$. For the case of univariate splines with arbitrary knot sequences, the inequality is simply established with the help of the dual functionals; see for example [8,48].

To see how uniform stability bears on the convergence question, consider the Oslo algorithm based on the knot sequences $t^m = \{t_j^m\}$ for $m = 0, 1, \ldots$. Let $N_{j,m}$ be the $B$-spline of degree $k$ supported on $[t_j^m, t_{j+k+1}^m]$. Then as we have seen for a given function

$$f(x) = \sum_j c_j N_{j,m}(x),$$

the Oslo algorithm generates $\{c_j^m\}$ such that

$$f(x) = \sum_j c_j^m N_{j,m}(x). \tag{8.2}$$

Let $S_n(f; x)$ be the Marsden-Schoenberg operator defined by

$$S_n(f; x) = \sum_j f(\xi_j^m) N_{j,m},$$

where

$$\xi_j^m = \frac{t_{j+1}^m + \cdots + t_{j+k}^m}{k}.$$

If $f \in C^2$, then according to a result of Marsden and Schoenberg [34],

$$\|f - S_n\|_\infty \leq c \Delta_m^2 \|f''\|_\infty,$$

where $\Delta_m = \max_j |t_{j+k+1}^m - t_j^m|$ and $c$ is some positive constant. Applying this result to $f$ as given by (8.2), we obtain

$$\left\| \sum_j (c_j^m - f(\xi_j^m)) N_{jm} \right\| = O(\Delta_m^2), \tag{8.3}$$

and so using the uniform stability (8.1), we conclude that

$$|f(\xi_j^m) - c_j^m| = O(\Delta_m^2) \qquad \text{for all } j.$$

If we define the control polygon $f_m(x)$ as the piecewise linear function interpolating $c_j^m$ at $\xi_j^m$, then it follows that

$$\|f - f_m\| = O(\Delta_m^2),$$

as desired.

## §9. Subdivision as Corner Cutting

Renewed interest in the geometric approach to subdivision algorithms has suggested generating planar control polygons $f_n$ from $f_{n-1}$ by a "cut"; *i.e.*, by replacing some piecewise linear segment of the planar control polygon $f_{n-1}$ by the subtended secant to this segment and calling the result $f_n$. This is clearly a univariate procedure, and de Boor has presented a detailed analysis of such corner cutting when the original control polygon $f_0$ can be viewed as a function. The main idea is that the "local curvature" of $f_{n-1}$ is reduced by the construction which produces $f_n$. The least technical theorem of [7] to present is

**Theorem 9.1.** *If $f_0$ has finitely many vertices and $f_n$ is generated by corner cutting as described above, then $\lim_{n \to \infty} f_n$ exists uniformly and the limiting curve is Lipschitz continuous.*

**Proof:** The proof of this theorem is based on verifying convergence for the special case $\tilde{f}_0(t) = (t - u)_+$. Then the sequence $\tilde{f}_n$ naturally consists of convex functions. The approach can be generalized in the following way. We split the original control polygon $f_0$, defined on $[0, d]$, into linear, convex, and concave parts as follows

$$f_0 = f^0 + f^+ + f^-,$$

where

$$f^0(t) := f_0(0) + f_0'(0^+)(t),$$

and $f^+$ and $f^-$ are convex and concave respectively, both broken lines with the same breakpoints as $f_0$ and both satisfying $f^\pm(0) = (f^\pm)'(0^+) = 0$.

Now the corner cutting procedure leaves $f^0$ invariant (there are no corners), and when applied to $f^\pm$, the resulting sequences $\{f_n^\pm\}$ consist of convex and concave control polygons respectively. The sequence $\{f_n^+\}$ is monotone increasing and bounded above by the secant joining $f^+(0) = 0$ to $f^+(d)$. Moreover, the sequence of derivatives $\{f_n^{+\prime}\}$ is also bounded. So the sequence $\{f_n^+\}$ converges uniformly on $[0, d]$ to a convex function. Similarly $\{f_n^-\}$ is uniformly convergent. Now we view the corner cutting procedure as predetermined for all control polygons and hence given by a fixed sequence of linear operators $T_n$. Therefore

$$f_n = T_n T_{n-1} \cdots T_1 f_0 = f^0 + T_n T_{n-1} \cdots T_1 f^+ + T_n T_{n-1} \cdots T_1 f^-$$
$$= f^0 + f_n^+ + f_n^-.$$

It follows that $f_n$ is uniformly convergent on $[0, d]$, proving the theorem. ∎

Further analysis is given in [7] to handle the case of convergence of corner cutting procedures on infinite intervals as well as a discussion of corner cutting for periodic functions.

Lu Wei *et al.* [32] also take a geometric approach to corner cutting, although their definition is not quite as general as de Boor's. For them, the planar control points are generated by

$$c_{2i-1}^{n+1} = (1 - \lambda_{i,n})c_i^n + \lambda_{i,n} c_{i-1}^n,$$
$$c_{2i}^{n+1} = \mu_{i,n} c_{i+1}^n + (1 - \mu_{i,n})c_i^n.$$

By this method it is claimed that any smooth curve can be generated, given the freedom of the initial control polygon $f_0$ with $N$ vertices, and the cut parameter set

$$S_N = \{\, (\lambda_{i,n}, \mu_{i,n}) \ : \ \lambda_{i,n} \geq 0, \ \mu_{i,n} \geq 0,$$
$$0 \leq \lambda_{i+1,n} + \mu_{i,n} < 1, \ k = 0, \ldots, 2^n N \,\}.$$

Geometric $C^1$ continuity a.e., is assured given the de Boor point of view. Indeed, the limiting curve is the sum of concave and convex functions and hence has a tangent a.e.. Lu et al., in analyzing their construction, claim that the limiting curve is geometrically $C^1$ if $p_i \neq p_{i+1}$ and the set $S_N \subset \Omega$ where $\Omega = \{\, (\lambda, \mu) \ : \ 2\lambda + \mu < 1, \ \lambda + 2\mu < 1 \,\}$.

## §10. A Matrix Approach to Subdivision for the Univariate Case

In the previous sections, primary focus has been on the initial control polygon $c = \{c_\alpha\}$ and on the sequence $c^m$ which is determined iteratively from it. Most of the algorithms employ the same smoothing strategy at each iteration; in this sense the algorithms are examples of *regular* or *uniform* subdivision. The exceptions are the Catmull-Clark, Doo-Sabin, Loop algorithms where the formulas can vary slightly depending on the valences of the control points. In this section, we consider only univariate matrix subdivision, but we focus now on the curves rather than on the control polygons.

In a series of papers [36,37,38] Micchelli and Prautzsch study curves generated by matrix products and show that the curves are *uniformly refinable* in the sense that scaled versions of a curve can be represented in terms of the unscaled curve and its integer translates. To introduce this circle of ideas in a context we have already discussed, let $M_{n-1}$ be the cardinal $B$-spline of degree $n-1$, and introduce the curve $\Psi : [0,1] \to \mathbb{R}^n$ whose $i^{th}$ component $\psi_i$ is defined by

$$\psi_i(t) = M_{n-1}(t+i), \qquad 0 \leq t \leq 1, \quad i = 0, \cdots, n-1.$$

Then (6.1) written with $x$ replaced by $t+i$ gives

$$\psi_i(t) = \frac{1}{2^{n-1}} \sum_{j=0}^{n} \binom{n}{j} \psi_{2i-n+j}(2t)$$

$$= \frac{1}{2^{n-1}} \sum_{k=0}^{n-1} \binom{n}{n+k-2i} \psi_k(2t),$$

where the combinatorial symbol is zero if $n+k-2i < 0$ or $n+k-2i > n$. Thus

$$\Psi(t) = B_0 \Psi(2t), \qquad 0 \leq t \leq 1/2,$$

where the matrix $B_0$ is defined by

$$B_0 = \frac{1}{2^{n-1}} \left[ \binom{n}{n+k-2i} \right]_{i,k=0}^{n-1}.$$

Similarly we find that.

$$\Psi(t) = B_1 \Psi(2t-1), \qquad \frac{1}{2} \leq t \leq 1,$$

where

$$B_1 = \frac{1}{2^{n-1}} \left[ \binom{n}{n+k-2i-1} \right]_{i,k=0}^{n-1}.$$

These equations are called the refinement equations for the curve $\Psi$. If we inner product each equation with a control vector $c \in (\mathbb{R}^s)^n$, we obtain

$$c^T \Psi(t) = c^T B_i \Psi(2t-1), \qquad i \in \{0,1\},$$

which means that

$$c^T \Psi[i/2, (i+1)/2] = \left(B_i^T c\right)^T \Psi[0, 1].$$

Thus $B_0^T c$ and $B_1^T c$ constitute the new control polygon representing the curve $c^T \Psi(t)$ on the intervals $[0, 1/2]$ and $[1/2, 1]$ respectively.

These considerations led Micchelli and Prautzsch to define a matrix version of the subdivision process in the following way. Let $A_0$ and $A_1$ be $n \times n$ matrices. We define a curve $\Psi : [0, 1] \to \mathbb{R}^n$ by the limit process

$$\lim_{\ell \to \infty} A_{x_\ell} \cdots A_{x_1} c = (\Psi^T(t) \cdot c)v, \tag{10.1}$$

where $v = [1, \ldots, 1]^T$, the argument $t$ is given by $t = \sum_{i=1}^{\infty} x_i/2^i$ and $c \in \mathbb{R}^n$. Of course this algorithm is nothing more than a receipe which may or may not work; that the limit should exist will clearly depend on very special properties of the matrices $A_0$ and $A_1$. Moreover, that this limit should be expressed as a scalar multiple of the vector $e$ is characteristic of a subdivision process. In fact, as we have seen in the examples presented so far, each step of the subdivision contracts the control points bringing them closer together. Since each application of the matrices $A_0$ and $A_1$ represents another iteration, we expect that in the limit, all control points should be equal, hence the limit should be a multiple of $v$.

When does the very general algorithm given above converge? The following necessary conditions are easy to state, but hard to check. For every $k$ and every vector $(y_1, \ldots, y_k) \in \{0, 1\}^k$, the product matrix $A_{y_1} \cdots A_{y_k}$ has eigenvalues of modulus $\leq 1$, the only eigenvalue of modulus one is 1, and this is also a simple eigenvalue. For example, the matrices $A_0$ and $A_1$ for the Chaikin algorithm are

$$A_0 = \frac{1}{4} \begin{bmatrix} 1 & 3 & 0 \\ 0 & 3 & 1 \\ 0 & 1 & 3 \end{bmatrix} \quad \text{and} \quad A_1 = \frac{1}{4} \begin{bmatrix} 3 & 1 & 0 \\ 1 & 3 & 0 \\ 0 & 3 & 1 \end{bmatrix}.$$

Their eigenvalues are $1, \frac{1}{2}$, and $\frac{1}{4}$. For a sufficient condition, Micchelli and Prautzsch have given the following

**Theorem 10.1.** ([37]). *Suppose $A_0, A_1$ are stochastic matrices. Then*

$$\lim_{\ell \to \infty} A_{x_\ell} \ldots A_{x_1} c = \lambda v, \quad \lambda \in \mathbb{R}$$

*for all $(x_1, \ldots, x_\ell, \ldots) \in \{0, 1\}^\infty$ and $c \in \mathbb{R}^n$ (with $\lambda$ depending on both) if and only if there is a $k < 2^{n^2}$ such that $A_{y_1} \cdots A_{y_k}$ has a positive column for all $(y_1, \ldots, y_k) \in \{0, 1\}^k$. If in addition we let*

$$A_i^T f_i = f_i, \quad i \in \{0, 1\}, \tag{10.2}$$

and if it happens that

$$A_0^T f_1 = A_1^T f_0, \tag{10.3}$$

then $\lambda = \Psi^T(x) \cdot c$ for a unique continuous curve $\Psi : [0,1] \to \mathbb{R}^n$.

We can derive certain structural results about a convergent subdivision process. From (10.1) it follows that the function $\Psi$ satisfies the functional equation

$$\begin{aligned}
\Psi(t) &= A_0^T \Psi(2t), & t &\in [0,1/2]; \\
\Psi(t) &= A_1^T \Psi(2t-1), & t &\in [1/2,1].
\end{aligned} \tag{10.4}$$

Indeed, let $2t = \sum_{i=1}^{\infty} x_i/2^i$. Then by (10.1)

$$\lim_{\ell \to \infty} A_{x_\ell} \cdots A_{x_1} \tilde{c} = [\Psi(2t)^T \cdot \tilde{c}]v$$

for every $\tilde{c}$. Put $\tilde{c} = A_0 c$ and conclude that

$$(A_0^T \Psi(2t))^T \cdot c = \Psi(t)^T \cdot c$$

for all $c$. To establish the second equation of (10.4), observe similarly that if $t \in [1/2,1]$, then

$$2t - 1 = \sum_{i=1}^{\infty} \frac{x_i}{2^i} \quad \text{or} \quad t = \frac{1}{2} + \sum_{i=1}^{\infty} \frac{x_i}{2^{i+1}},$$

and so (10.4) follows.

Conversely, we have

**Theorem 10.2.** *If $\Psi$ is a continuous solution of the functional equation (10.4), and if $\Psi^T(x) \cdot v = 1$ and $\dim\{\operatorname{span}\{\Psi(t) : 0 \le t \le 1\}\} = n$, then the subdivision algorithm (10.1) converges.*

**Proof:** Let $B_i = A_i^T$ for $i \in \{0,1\}$. By repeated use of (10.4), we have for any $y \in [0,1]$

$$B_{x_\ell} \cdots B_{x_1} \Psi(y) = \Psi(x_1 + \frac{x_2}{2} + \cdots + \frac{x_\ell}{2^\ell} + \frac{y}{2^\ell}).$$

Then if $x = \sum_{i=1}^{\infty} x_i/2^i$, it follows that

$$\lim_{\ell \to \infty} B_{x_\ell} \cdots B_{x_1} \Psi(y) = \Psi(x),$$

since $\Psi$ is continuous. So choosing distinct points $y_i$ for $i = 1, \cdots, n$ and any numbers $u_i$, we obtain

$$\lim_{\ell \to \infty} (\lambda, B_{x_\ell} \cdots B_{x_1} \Psi(y_i)) = \Psi(x)^T \cdot \lambda,$$

and hence

$$\lim_{\ell \to \infty} (\lambda, B_{x_\ell} \cdots B_{x_1} (\sum_{i=1}^{n} \Psi(y_i) u_i)) = (\Psi^T(x) \cdot \lambda) \sum_{i=1}^{n} u_i.$$

Using the dimension hypothesis, it follows that for any $\delta \in \mathbb{R}^n$, there exists $u_i$ such that $\delta = \sum \Psi(y_i)u_i$, and therefore

$$\lim_{\ell \to \infty} (A_{x_\ell} \cdots A_{x_\ell}\lambda, \delta) = (\Psi^T(x) \cdot \lambda) \sum_{i=1}^{n} u_i.$$

Observe that

$$\delta^T \cdot v = \sum_{i=1}^{n} u_i \Psi^T(y_i) \cdot v = \sum_{i=1}^{n} u_i.$$

Hence

$$\lim_{\ell \to \infty} \delta^T A_{x_1} \cdots A_{x_1}\lambda = (\Psi^T(x) \cdot \lambda)\delta^T \cdot v,$$

which implies the desired result since $\delta$ was arbitrary. ■

**Remark.** For the case when $\text{span}\{\Psi^T c : c \in \mathbb{R}^n\} = \pi_{n-1}$, see Goldman and DeRose [28].

Note that from the sufficient conditions for a convergent scheme, we have

$$\lim_{\ell \to \infty} A_{x_\ell} \cdots A_{x_1}v = (\Psi^T(x) \cdot v) \cdot v$$

But $A_0 v = A_1 v = v$ since $A_0$ and $A_1$ are stochastic, and so we have that $\Psi^T(x) \cdot v = 1$, a condition which was hypothesized in Theorem 10.2.

While the notion of convergent subdivision here is very general, practical interests are directed most often to schemes which yield splines. In this regard, it is interesting to characterize those schemes for which the components of $\Psi$ are polynomials. In the univariate case, Micchelli and Prautsch have given several theorems in this direction.

In Micchelli and Prautzsch [36], subdivision schemes of the form $c_i^{k+1} = \sum_{j=-\infty}^{\infty} a_{i-2j}c_j^k$ were studied. The authors were concerned with the case $a_i > 0$ for $i = 0, \cdots, n$ and zero otherwise. By appealing to Theorem 10.1, they proved that the subdivision converges when $\sum_{i=-\infty}^{\infty} a_{2i} = \sum_{i=-\infty}^{\infty} a_{2i+1} = 1$.

Dyn, Gregory, and Levin [24] have also used matrix theory methods to analyse the four point interpolatory subdivision scheme defined by

$$c_{2i}^{k+1} = c_i^k$$

$$c_{2i+1}^{k+1} = (\frac{1}{2} + \omega)(c_i^k + c_{i+1}^k) - \omega(c_{i-1}^k + c_{i+2}^k),$$

where $\omega$ is a fixed real parameter. When $\omega = 0$, the scheme generates piecewise linear interpolation. Notice that this scheme is interpolatory in the sense that all control points lie on the limiting curve. Analysing the eigenvalues of an appropriate matrix, Dyn, Gregory and Levin [24] have proved that the scheme converges to a continuous function if $|\omega| < 1/4$ and does not converge if $|\omega| > 1/2$. Micchelli and Prautzsch [36] have proved that it is convergent provided that $-1/2 < \omega \le 0$. It was conjectured that the scheme is convergent for $|\omega| < 1/2$ and this has been proved recently by Powell [39]. If $0 < \omega < 1/8$, the limit curve was shown in [24] to be $C^1$, and therefore the subdivision is smoothing for small positive values of $\omega$. In general, the limit curve cannot be twice continuously differentiable.

Recently, Dyn, Gregory, and Levin [25] gave a useful characterization of subdivision schemes of the type in [36] in terms of the differenced scheme. They showed that the subdivision scheme is convergent if and only if the difference of the subdivision process converges uniformly to zero.

## §11. Regular Subdivision

As we have seen in this survey, until 1988 much of the study of subdivision has been univariate in character. The notable exceptions are the line average algorithm, so intimately connected to the multivariate cube spline, the Catmull-Clark and Doo-Sabin algorithms, and various tensor product schemes which have been used when surfaces are required. As of this writing, Cavaretta, Dahmen and Micchelli [12] are studying a general class of multivariate subdivision schemes which they refer to as *regular subdivision*. The essential feature of a regular subdivision is that it has certain shift invariant properties. To complete this survey, we wish to highlight some of their results on regular subdivision.

To determine a multivariate scheme, we fix a finitely supported multiindexed sequence $\{a_\alpha : \alpha \in \mathbb{Z}^s\}$. We define an operator $S : \ell^\infty(\mathbb{Z}^s) \to \ell^\infty(\mathbb{Z}^s)$ by

$$(S\lambda)_\alpha = \sum_{\beta \in \mathbb{Z}^s} \lambda_\beta a_{\alpha-2\beta}, \qquad \lambda \in \ell^\infty(\mathbb{Z}^s). \tag{11.1}$$

The subdivision scheme is then given by some iterates

$$\begin{aligned} \lambda^m &= S\lambda^{m-1}, \qquad m = 1, 2, \ldots; \\ \lambda^0 &= \lambda, \end{aligned} \tag{11.2}$$

for any $\lambda \in \ell^\infty(\mathbb{Z}^s)$. A concept of convergence is needed; one possibility is

**Definition 11.1.** *We say the subdivision scheme (11.2) converges if there exists a continuous function $f_\lambda$ defined on $\mathbb{R}^s$ such that*

$$\lim_{m \to \infty} \left\| f_\lambda \left( \frac{\cdot}{2m} \right) - \lambda^m \right\|_\infty = 0.$$

*The sequence $\{a_\alpha\}$ is called the mask, the sequence $\lambda$ is called the control polygon.*

Fundamental necessary conditions for convergence, proved in [12] and which have already appeared in the univariate examples discussed here, are the relations

$$\sum_{\beta \in \mathbb{Z}^s} a_{\alpha-2\beta} = 1, \qquad \alpha \in \mathbb{Z}^s. \tag{11.3}$$

This condition is stated without proof in [25] for the special case $s = 1$. We can express (11.3) in an equivalent form by introducing the set $E :=$ extreme points of $[0, 1]^s$ and for every $e \in E$ the sublattice $L_e := \{2\alpha + e : \alpha \in \mathbb{Z}^s\}$. Then (10.3) means $\sum_{\alpha \in L_e} a_\alpha = 1$ for all $e \in E$. These sublattices are basic to much of the theory as developed in [12].

If a subdivision scheme converges, then what does it converge to? More precisely how is $f_\lambda$ determined by $\lambda$? This is nicely answered by

**Theorem 11.2.** *Suppose the subdivision scheme (11.1) converges for all $\lambda \in \ell^\infty(\mathbb{Z}^s)$ and $f_\lambda \neq 0$ for some $\lambda \in \ell^\infty(\mathbb{Z}^s)$. Then its mask $\{a_\alpha : \alpha \subset \mathbb{Z}^s\}$ determines a unique compactly supported continuous function $\varphi$ with the following properties.*

(i)
$$\varphi(\alpha) = \sum_{\alpha \in \mathbb{Z}^s} \varphi(2x - \alpha), \qquad x \in \mathbb{R}^s$$

(ii)
$$\sum_{\alpha \in \mathbb{Z}^s} \varphi(x - \alpha) = 1.$$

*Moreover,*

$$f_\lambda(x) = \sum_{\alpha \in \mathbb{Z}^s} \lambda_\alpha \varphi(x - \alpha), \quad x \in \mathbb{R}^s, \quad \lambda \in \ell^\infty(\mathbb{Z}^s).$$

We refer to (i) as the *functional equation* associated with the mask $\{a_\alpha\}$.

Naturally enough, the proof of Theorem 11.2 is based on a study of the operator

$$(T\varphi)(x) = \sum_{\alpha \in \mathbb{Z}^s} a_\alpha \varphi(2x - \alpha)$$

which is well defined and of compact support for any $\varphi$ of compact support. Fixing any $\varphi \neq 0$, it is proved that

$$\lim_{m \to \infty} T^m \varphi_0$$

exists uniformly, and so this function provides the $\varphi$ of the theorem.

Clearly the $\varphi$ of Theorem 11.2 determines the character of the limit functions $f_\lambda$ which are obtained in the subdivision process. For example, there are limitations on the global smoothness of $\varphi$ and hence on the smoothness of $f_\lambda$; this limitation is determined by the size of the support of the mask. For example, if a univariate mask is supported on $[\nu, \nu + n + 1]$, then $\varphi$ has at most $(n - 1)$ continuous derivatives. To see this, suppose for simplicity that the mask is supported on $[0, n + 1]$ and so the same follows for $\varphi$. Then from the equation

$$\varphi\left(\frac{t}{2}\right) = \sum_{j=0}^{n+1} a_j \varphi(t - j) \tag{11.4}$$

follows the system

$$\varphi(1) = \sum_{j=0}^{n+1} a_j \varphi(2 - j)$$

$$\vdots$$

$$\varphi(n) = \sum_{j=0}^{n+1} a_j \varphi(2n - j).$$

These equations determine an $n \times n$ matrix mapping which evidently has the nonzero vector $\{\varphi(1), \ldots, \varphi(n)\}$ as an eigenvector with eigenvalue 1. If we differentiate (11.4) $j$ times and then evaluate the result for $x = 2\ell$ with $\ell = 1, \cdots, n$, we obtain as an eigenvector the nonzero vector $\{\varphi^{(j)}(1), \ldots, \varphi^{(j)}(n)\}$. Since an $n \times n$ matrix can have at most $n$ eigenvalues, we see that at most $n - 1$ differentiations are possible, as claimed.

Generally, there is of course no reason to expect any differentiability properties of $\varphi$; but if $\varphi$ has derivatives, then the subdivision scheme yields smooth functions with the same derivatives and it can be shown that the span of the integer translates of $\varphi$ contains certain polynomial subspaces. To give one instance of this, let

$$\Phi := \text{span} \{\varphi(\cdot - \beta) : \beta \in \mathbb{Z}^s\},$$

and as usual let $C_0^d(\mathbb{R}^s)$ denote those functions all of whose partial derivatives of order $d$ are continuous. Let $\pi_d(\mathbb{R}^s)$ be the space of all polynomials of total degree at most $d$.

**Theorem 11.3.** *Let $\varphi \in C_0^d(\mathbb{R}^s)$ be a nontrivial solution of the functional equation (11.4) associated with the mask $\{a_\beta : \beta \in \mathbb{Z}^s\}$. Then $\pi_d(\mathbb{R}^s) \subseteq \Phi$.*

For the multivariate case the proof is somewhat involved, but in the univariate case a simpler proof is available under the additional hypothesis of stability of the translates $\{\varphi(\cdot - j) : j \in \mathbb{Z}\}$. We wish to comment on the need for the stability hypothesis here. Let $\Delta_y$ be the first difference operator defined for fixed $y \in \mathbb{Z}^s$ by

$$(\Delta_y \lambda)_\alpha := \lambda_{\alpha+y} - \lambda_\alpha.$$

It was observed in [12] that if the subdivision scheme determined by $2\Delta_y S$ converges, then the function $\varphi(x + ty)$ is continuously differentiable in $t$ for every $x \in \mathbb{R}^s$; see also [25] for the case $s = 1$. However, as demonstrated in [12], the converse of this proposition is not clear unless we assume that the functions $\{\varphi(\cdot - \alpha) : \alpha \in \mathbb{Z}^s\}$ are algebraically independent. Fortunately, this independence is assured in many cases, for instance for interpolatory schemes. Therefore in such cases (e.g., the interpolatory schemes), the distinction between the convergence of the difference scheme and the smoothness of $\varphi$ need not be made. However in [25] this distinction clearly arises, as Theorem 11.3

is proved there for the case $s = 1$ under the assumption that the differences of the subdivision scheme converges.

Central to the discussion of multivariate schemes as developed in [12] is the concept of the contractability of the operator $S$ defined in (11.1). This in turn depends on a diameter function $D$ which should be defined for each control polygon $\lambda$. As already observed for most univariate schemes, the diameter

$$D(\lambda) = \sup_j |\lambda_j - \lambda_{j+1}|$$

is sufficient to analyse convergence. In the multivariate setting much more flexibility in the diameter function is desirable, and we only require that $D$ be nonnegative and defined for all $\lambda \in \ell_\infty(\mathbb{Z}^s)$. Then the contractivity notion is given by the

**Definition 11.4.** *We say that $S$ is contractive relative to $D$ if there exists a positive constant $\gamma < 1$ for which we have*

$$D(S\lambda) \leq \gamma D(\lambda), \qquad \lambda \in \ell^\infty(\mathbb{Z}^s).$$

With this concept and an appropriate convergent comparison subdivision scheme $T$ satisfying

$$\|S\lambda - T\lambda\| < cD(\lambda),$$

a convergence criterion is available. So it becomes essential to determine for any particular operator $S$ a diameter $D$ relative to which $S$ is contractive. This issue is discussed in detail in [12]. One tractable class of subdivision operators are those determined by masks which are strictly positive on a given rectangle in $\mathbb{Z}^s$. More generally, in place of the rectangle we can have certain zonotopes. To define this, let $X = \{x^1, \cdots, x^n\} \subset \mathbb{Z}^s$ and fix $t \in \mathbb{Z}^s$, all of whose components are positive. Then the zonotopes considered are given by

$$\mathbb{Z}_t(X) := \{Xu : -t \leq u \leq t\}$$

and their translates. In the following theorem we require that $X$ be unimodular, which simply means that every $s \times s$ submatrix of $X$ has determinant $-1, 0$, or $1$.

**Theorem 11.5.** *Let $\mathbb{Z}_t(X) \subseteq \mathbb{R}^s$ be a unimodular zonotope, and suppose $\{a_\alpha : \alpha \in \mathbb{Z}^s\}$ is a mask satisfying*

$$a_\alpha > 0 \quad \text{if and only if} \quad \alpha \in \Omega(X) := \mathbb{Z}^s \cap \mathbb{Z}_t(X),$$

*and*

$$\sum_{\beta \in \mathbb{Z}^s} a_{\alpha-2\beta} = 1, \qquad \alpha \in \mathbb{Z}^s.$$

*Then the subdivision operator (11.1) is contractive relative to the diameter*

$$D_X(\lambda) = \sup_{\alpha-\beta \in \Omega^0(x)} |\lambda_\alpha - \lambda_\beta|.$$

The proof is geometric in nature and focuses on cancellations which occur when sums such as

$$\sum_{\beta} |a_{\sigma-2\beta} - a_{\delta-2\beta}|$$

are computed.

Let $X = \{x^1, \ldots, x^n\} \subset \mathbb{Z}^s$, and as is our custom, let $X$ also stand for the $s \times n$ matrix whose $j^{th}$ column is $x^j$. Given a mask $\{a_\alpha : \alpha \in \mathbb{Z}^n\}$, we can define a new mask on a lower dimensional lattice $\mathbb{Z}^s$ for $s < n$, by the rule

$$b_\beta^X = 2^{s-n} \sum_{X\alpha=\beta} a_\alpha, \qquad \beta \in \mathbb{Z}^s. \tag{11.5}$$

This process we refer to as *compression*. It is a construction which can be motivated by considering the cube spline subdivision algorithm and abstracting its structure. In any case, it yields a great variety of convergent subdivision schemes. To state the relevant theorem, we let $L(X) := \{X\alpha : \alpha \in \mathbb{Z}^n\}$, where $X$ is assumed to be of full rank. Further, let $V$ denote any $n \times n$ nonsingular integer matrix whose $j^{th}$ column $v^j$ satisfies $v^j|_{\mathbb{Z}^s} = x^j$ for $j = 1, \ldots, n$.

**Theorem 11.6.** *Let* $\{a_\alpha : \alpha \in \mathbb{Z}^n\}$ *determine a convergent subdivision scheme whose associated functional equation is satisfied by* $\varphi \in C_0(\mathbb{R}^n)$. *Suppose* $X$ *is of full rank and* $L(X) = \mathbb{Z}^s$. *Then the compressed subdivision scheme determined by* $\{b_\beta^X : \beta \in \mathbb{Z}^s\}$ *converges for all* $\lambda \in \ell^\infty(\mathbb{Z}^s)$ *to*

$$f_\lambda^X = \sum_{\beta \in \mathbb{Z}^s} \lambda_\beta M_\varphi(x - \beta \mid X),$$

*where*

$$M_\varphi(x \mid X) := (\det V)^{-1} \int_{\mathbb{R}^{n-s}} \varphi(V^{-1}P_y)dy, \qquad \text{and} \qquad P_y := (x, y).$$

When $\varphi(x)$ with $x \in \mathbb{R}^n$ is a tensor product function, the compressed subdivision scheme can be computed by successive applications of univariate schemes. In fact, if $\varphi$ is the characteristic function

$$\varphi(x) = \chi_{[0,1]^n}(x),$$

then the scheme is the line average algorithm discussed previously in Section 6.

One other tool suitable for the analysis of multivariate subdivision is the representation of the subdivision process as matrix multiplication; the intent is then to generalize the results of Micchelli-Prautzsch, discussed in Section 10, to the multivariate setting. This approach keeps track of those control points $\lambda_\beta$ which are active on any lattice cube $\alpha + [0, 1]^s$, where $\alpha \in \mathbb{Z}^s$.

To this end we assume without loss of generality that the mask is supported in some rectangle; that is, $a_\beta = 0$ for

$$\beta \notin \Gamma_{n+1} := \{\alpha = (\alpha_1, \ldots, \alpha_s) : 0 \le \alpha_i \le n_i + 1, \alpha_i \in \mathbb{Z}_+, i = 1, \ldots, s\}.$$

We define, for every $e$ in the set $E$ of extreme points of $[0,1]^s$, the matrix $A_e$ by setting

$$(A_e)_{\beta,\gamma} := a_{e+2\gamma-\beta}, \qquad \beta, \gamma \in \Gamma_{n+1} \cap Z^s.$$

These matrices are square sections of the infinite Toeplitz matrix $a_{\alpha-\beta}$ for $\alpha, \beta \in Z^s$; their order is $N = \operatorname{card} \Gamma_{n+1} = \prod_{i=1}^s (n_i + 1)$. The following lemma shows the importance of these matrices.

**Lemma 11.7.** *Let $\alpha \in Z^s$ be any lattice point whose binary expansion is*

$$\alpha = e^m + 2^1 e^{m-1} + \cdots + 2^{m-1} e^1, \qquad \text{where } e^i \in E \text{ for } i = 1, \ldots, m.$$

*Let $\tilde{\alpha} = \frac{1}{2}(\alpha - e^m)$. Then the control points $\{(S\lambda)_{\alpha-\beta} : \beta \in \Gamma_n\}$ depend only on the set $\{\lambda_{\tilde{\alpha}-\beta} : \beta \in \Gamma_n\}$, and moreover*

$$(S\lambda)_{\alpha-\beta} = \sum_{\beta' \in \Gamma_n} (A_{e^m})_{\beta,\beta'} \lambda_{\tilde{\alpha}-\beta'}, \qquad \beta \in \Gamma_n.$$

For the proof, one must keep track of the non-zero terms in the series

$$(S\lambda)_{\alpha-\beta} = \sum_{\nu \subset Z^s} \lambda_\nu a_{\alpha-\beta-2\nu}.$$

With the lemma, the behavior of the subdivision at any point $x \in [0,1]^s$ can be analyzed in terms of its binary expansion

$$x = \sum_{k=1}^\infty 2^{-k} e^k, \qquad e^k \in E.$$

The analysis along these lines yields many interesting consequences, one being an alternative construction of the function $\varphi$ determined by the functional equation of Theorem 11.2. Specifically it is possible to build the function $\varphi$ locally with the matrices $A_e$. More immediate is the following necessary condition for convergent subdivision schemes:

**Proposition 11.8.** *If the subdivision algorithm (11.2) is convergent, then each of the matrices $A_{e^1}, \ldots, A_{e^{2^n}}$, and also each matrix which is a finite product of these must have spectral radius 1, and 1 must be a simple eigenvalue.*

## References

1. Boehm, W., On the efficiency of knot insertion algorithms, Comput. Aided Geom. Design **2** (1985), 141–143.
2. Boehm, W., Triangular spline algorithms, Comput. Aided Geom. Design **2** (1985), 61–67.
3. Boehm, W., Calculating with box splines, Comput. Aided Geom. Design **1** (1984), 149–162.

4. Boehm, W., The de Boor algorithm for triangular splines, in *Surfaces in Computer Aided Geometric Design*, R. E. Barnhill and W. Boehm (eds.), North-Holland, Amsterdam, 1983.

5. Boehm, W., Subdividing multivariate splines, Comput. Aided Design **15** (1983), 354–352.

6. Boehm, W., Inserting new knots into B-spline curves, Comput. Aided Design **12** (1980), 99–110.

7. de Boor, C., Cutting corners always works, Comput. Aided Geom. Design **4** (1987), 125–131.

8. de Boor, C., *A Practical Guide to Splines*, Springer-Verlag, New York, 1978.

9. de Boor, C. and DeVore, R., Approximation by smooth multivariate splines, Trans. Amer. Math. Soc. **276** (1983), 775–788.

10. de Casteljau, P., Outilage methodes calcul, Andre Citroën Automobiles, SA, Paris, 1959.

11. Catmull, E. E., and J. H. Clark, Recursively generated B-spline surfaces on arbitrary topological meshes, Comput. Aided Design **10** (1978), 350–355.

12. Cavaretta, A. S., C. A. Micchelli, and W. Dahmen, Regular subdivision, preprint.

13. Chaikin, G. M., An algorithm for high speed curve generation, Computer Graphics and Image Processing **3** (1974), 346–349.

14. Cohen, E., T. Lyche and R. F. Riesenfeld, Discrete B-splines and subdivision techniques in computer aided geometric design and computer graphics, Computer Graphics and Image Processing **14** (1980), 87–111.

15. Cohen, E., T. Lyche and R. F. Riesenfeld, Discrete box splines and refinement algorithms, Comput. Aided Geom. Design **1** (1984), 131–148.

16. Cohen, E. and L. L. Schumaker, Rates of convergence of control polygons, Comput. Aided Geom. Design **2** (1985), 229–235.

17. Dahmen, W., Subdivision algorithms converge quadratically, J. Comput. Appl. Math. **16** (1986), 145–158.

18. Dahmen, W., N. Dyn and D. Levin, On the convergence rates of subdivision algorithms for box splines, Constr. Approx. **1** (1985), 305–322.

19. Dahmen, W. and C. A. Micchelli, Subdivision algorithms for the generation of box spline surfaces, Comput. Aided Geom. Design **1** (1984), 115–129.

20. Dahmen, W. and C. A. Michelli, Line average algorithm: a method for the computer generation of smooth surfaces, Comput. Aided Geom. Design **2** (1985), 77–85.

21. Doo, D., A recursive subdivision algorithm for fitting quadratic surfaces to irregular polyhedrons, Ph.D. dissertation, Brunel University, 1978.

22. Doo, D. W. H., A subdivision algorithm for smoothing down irregularly shaped polyhedrons, in *Proceedings: Interactive Techniques in Computer Aided Design*, Bologna, 1978, 157–165.

23. Doo, D. and M. A. Sabin, Behavior of recursive subdivision of surfaces near extraordinary points, Comput. Aided Design **10** (1978), 356–360.

24. Dyn, N., J. A. Gregory, and D. Levin, A 4-point interpolation subdivision scheme for curve design, Comput. Aided Geom. Design **4** (1987), 257–268.
25. Dyn, N., J. A. Gregory, and D. Levin, Analysis of uniform subdivision schemes for curve design, preprint.
26. Dyn, N. and D. Levin, A butterfly subdivision scheme for surface interpolation with tension control, preprint.
27. Goldman, R. N., Subdivision algorithms for Bézier triangles, Comput. Aided Design **15** (1983), 159–166.
28. Goldman, R. N. and T. D. DeRose, Recursive subdivision without the convex hull property, Comput. Aided Geom. Design **3** (1986), 247–265.
29. Hejna, M. J., Curves constructed by geometrically based algorithms, dissertation, RPI, 1988.
30. Lane, J. M. and R. F. Riesenfeld, A theoretical development for the computer generation of piecewise polynomial surfaces, IEEE Trans. on Pattern Analysis and Machine Intelligence **2** (1980), 35–46.
31. Loop, Charles Teorell, Smooth subdivision surfaces based on triangles, Masters Thesis, University of Utah, 1987.
32. Lu Wei, Jin Tongun and Liang Youdong, A new method for curve and surface modelling, Comput. Aided Geom. Design , to appear.
33. Lyche, T. and K. Mørken, Making the Oslo algorithm more efficient, SIAM J. Numer. Anal. **23** (1986), 663–675.
34. Marsden, M. and I. J. Schoenberg, On a variation diminishing spline approximation method, Mathematica (Cluj) **8** (1966), 61–82.
35. Micchelli, C. A., Subdivision algorithms for curves and surfaces, Siggraph 86, Dallas, Texas.
36. Micchelli, C. A. and H. Prautzsch, Refinement and subdivision for spaces of integer translates of a compact by supported function, in *Numerical Analysis*, D. F. Griffiths and G. A. Watson (eds.), 1987, 192–222.
37. Micchelli, C. A. and H. Prautzsch, Uniform refinement of curves, Linear Algebra Appl. , to appear.
38. Micchelli, C. A. and H. Prautzsch, Computing curves invariant under halving, Comput. Aided Geom. Design **4** (1987), 133–140.
39. Powell, M. J. D., (private communication).
40. Prautzsch, H., A short proof of the Oslo algorithm, Comput. Aided Geom. Design **1** (1984), 95–96.
41. Prautzsch, H., Unterteilungsalgorithmen für multivariate splines — ein geometrischer zugang, Diss. T.U. Braunschweig, (1983/84).
42. Prautzsch, H., Generalized subdivision and convergences through quadrature, Comput. Aided Geom. Design **2** (1985), 69–75.
43. de Rham G., Sur une courbe plane, Journal de Mathématiques pures et appliquées **39** (1956), 25–42.
44. de Rham, G., Un peu de mathematiques á propos d'une courbe plane, Elem. Math. **2** (1947), 73–76, 89–97.
45. Riesenfeld, R. F., On Chaikin's algorithm, Computer Graphics and Image Processing **4** (1975), 304–310.

46. Sabin, M. A., The use of piecewise forms for the numerical representation of shapes, Ph.D. dissertation, Hungarian National Academy of Sciences, 1977.

47. Schoenberg, I. J., *Cardinal Spline Interpolation*, Regional Conference Series in Applied Mathematics **12**, SIAM, Philadelphia, 1973.

48. Schumaker, L. L., *Spline Functions: Basic Theory*, John Wiley & Sons, New York, 1981.

49. Seidel, H. P., A general subdivision theorem for Bézier triangles, in *Mathematical Methods in Computer Aided Geometric Design*, T. Lyche and L. Schumaker (eds.), Academic Press, N. Y., 1989, 573–581.

50. Seidel, H. P., Knot insertion from a blossoming point of view, Comput. Aided Geom. Design **5** (1988), 81–86.

Alfred S. Cavaretta
Dept. of Mathematics
Kent State University
Kent, Ohio 44242
USA

Charles A. Micchelli
Mathematical Sciences Department, IBM
Thomas J. Watson Research Center
P.O. Box 218
Yorktown Heights, New York 10598
USA

EMAIL: cam@ yktvmx
EMAIL: cavarett % kent.edu@ relay.cs.net

# A Data Dependent Parametrization
# for Spline Approximation

## E. Cohen and C. L. O'Dell

**Abstract.** When data is approximated with splines, the degree of the splines to be used, the number of knots, and their locations must be determined. When parametric curves are used, a parameter value must be assigned to each datapoint. As we shall see, the *goodness* of that value is critical to how good the least square fit can be. This paper presents a data dependent method for assignment of parameter values for curves with corners.

## §1. Introduction

In Computer Aided Geometric Design, it is often necessary to produce a smooth curve from data represented by an ordered set of data points such that the result captures the general shape of the data and comes very close to the ordered point set. Explicit approximation is used in many applications, yet curves used in design may not be explicit functions.

The general problem of explicit spline datafitting can be stated as needing to approximate an ordered set of points by an *appropriately* smooth spline curve in an *appropriate* norm using an *appropriate* measurement of error with an *appropriate* number of knots placed in *appropriate* locations. In trying to solve this problem for parametric data, we must add to that list the need to specify an *appropriate* parametrization.

Clearly, the number and placement of the knots will significantly effect the result of the spline fit. But just as significantly, if not more so, is the choice of the parametrization. If the parametrization is inappropriate, frequently the approximation may not represent the original shape well. A trial and error process is sometimes used to adjust parameter values and knot location and number in the search for a good curve fit.

If the problem is to be studied as a whole, then an automatic integrated

Mathematical Methods in Computer Aided Geometric Design
Tom Lyche and Larry L. Schumaker (eds.), pp. 155–166.
Copyright © 1989 by Academic Press, Boston.
ISBN 0-12-460515-X.

process would

1. *Find an initial parametrization*
2. *Specify an initial knot configuration*
3. *Find and mark the corners in the data so they will be kept*
4. *Find the best fit*
5. *Determine the error*
6. *If the error is too large, then (as appropriate)*
   a. *Reparametrize and/or*
   b. *Adaptively add knots and/or*
   c. *Optimize knot location (free knots)*
7. *Go to step 3.*

We have been developing an integrated approach to dealing with all of these issues. Data fitting is used as part of the effort to capture the shape intent of the designer. We have found that the integration of all of these topics into a unified approach is important in developing multistep solution techniques. Most research on data fitting has traditionally either been developed for explicit curves and surfaces, or has assumed the existence of a *good* parametrization. In Figure 1a, data is shown, connected by straight line segments, which was digitized from a raster device, like a range finder or a frame buffer. It looks very much as if the data point that is off to the right is a *bad* point, but actually it is not. This is an artifact of the view angle. The data was chord length parametrized. The initial least squares polynomial approximation had a loop. Knots were added adaptively where needed in several iterations, resulting in the least squares approximation of Figure 1b, with eight knots. The error in this fit is negligible in either the $L^2$ or $L^\infty$ norms; however, the loop that was present in the initial approximation has not disappeared. Adding knots lowered the error, but did not make the shape more faithful.

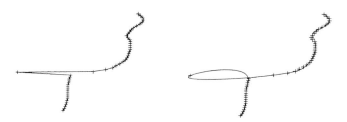

**Figure 1.** a) Digitized data.            b) Chord length least squares.

The work presented here is an approach to the first three steps of the ideal process discussed above; that is, to find corners, an initial parametrization, and initial knots. It was developed as part of our integrated approach. The effect of the method on the subsequent processes of reparametrization, adaptive knot placement, and optimizing free knot location will be demonstrated.

## §2. Background

To construct a parametric curve, $\gamma(t)$, as an approximation to a set of data points, it is necessary to associate a parameter value $t_i$ with each data point $(x_i, y_i)$. Unless the data is taken directly from a closed form representation, it is unlikely that appropriate parameter values are known. A slight change in the parametrization can have a great effect on the approximating curve [3,9].

Finding the minimal distance from a point to a parametric curve is not a linear problem, and even worse is the problem of selecting a parametric approximating curve to a set of data by minimizing the sum of the squares of the distances from the points in the set to the curve. Questions of convergence and uniqueness of the iterative methods used to find distance arise. So, in general the parametric least squares approximation is defined as finding the curve $\gamma(t) = (x(t), y(t))$ which minimizes the error

$$E = \sqrt{\sum \left( (x(t_i) - x_i)^2 + (y(t_i) - y_i)^2 \right)},$$

which we shall call the *pseudo-distance*. This sum clearly depends on the parameter values of the datapoints, so the parametrization strongly affects the calculated *best fit*.

Consider $\{(x_i, y_i)\}_{i=0}^{n}$. There are two widely used parametrizations for such data. The *uniform parametrization* sets $t_i = i$, and is inexpensive to compute, but it is unsuitable for data not prepared specifically with this parametrization in mind. The *chord length parametrization* sets

$$t_i = \begin{cases} 0, & \text{if } i = 0; \\ t_{i-1} + \sqrt{(x_i - x_{i-1})^2 + (y_i - y_{i-1})^2}, & \text{for } i > 0. \end{cases}$$

The *normalized chord length parametrization* is a slight modification of the chord length parametrization. If $L = t_n$, the total chord length, then the normalized parameter value at the $i^{th}$ point is $t_i/L$. These methods are discrete attempts to gain an approximating curve with an *arc length* parametrization. However, it does not work well in all cases, as our example showed. We will say an approximation is a *CL fit* if it is the least squares approximation in the chord length parametrization. It may be a single polynomial or a spline, as the situation requires.

In 1970 Grossman proposed a method for parametrizing a set of data for least squares fit with a single parametric polynomial. Initially the data set is given a chord length parametrization, and a least squares fit is found. The norm is minimized by finding an approximation to the distance from the point $p_i$ to the least square curve, which also serves to reparametrize the data by using the parameter value of the nearest point on the curve as the new parameter for $p_i$. Plass and Stone [9] used a similar approach on each piece of a $G^1$ parametric cubic curve after determining each segment's beginning and end. More recently, Hoscheck [5] proposed the use of reparametrization for polynomial data fitting. Reparametrization is used by O'Dell [8] and Cohen

and O'Dell [2] as part of the integrated approach to adaptively data fitting
with splines.

Since the chord length parametrization is a rough approximation to the
arc length parametrization, we felt that the variation in the magnitude of the
tangents of the approximating curves would be constrained. Experiments were
made using unevenly spaced data generated from known parametric cubics.
The magnitude of the first derivative of the approximating curves did not vary
as greatly, on the average, as the general B-spline curve. The approximations
seldom attained the extremes of curvature present in the generating curves,
and thus were not close to the data. Evidence supports that constraining the
first derivative in that way reduces the likelihood that a good fit will be found
for data in which the curvature of the underlying curve seems to have a large
dynamic range. Piecewise $G^1$ methods can constrain the curvature dynamic
range by using the chord length initial parametrization, approximating only
well behaved data on each piece, and having more pieces. A $C^2$ parametric
spline cannot do this, since the curvature is continuous across the polynomial
pieces.

In his work on interpolating a small number of data points with aesthetically pleasing curves, Manning observed that a chord length parametrization is
unsatisfactory if any segment of the curve turns through a large angle between
data points. Manning [6] developed a method of calculating the tangent direction at each data point, and the magnitudes on each side of that data point
to use for a piecewise $G^1$ parametric cubic curve. Similar effects can be seen
in approximation, and the parametrization method presented here adapts and
modifies his method of calculating tangent magnitudes as part of the basis for
its curvature calculation. We present the ideas.

At point $P_i$, denote the right and left derivatives by $P'_{i,l}$ and $P'_{i,r}$, respectively, and parametrize them uniformly by the integers. That is, $\gamma(i) = P_i$,
$\gamma'_i(i^+) = P'_{i,l}$, and $\gamma_i(i+1) = P_{i+1}$, $\gamma'_i((i+1)^-) = P'_{i+1,r}$. If the directions
of $P_{i,r}$ and $P_{i,l}$ are the same, that is, only their magnitudes differ, for each
$i$, then the resulting curve $\gamma$ is $G^1$. Further, it is well known that $\gamma$ can be
reparametrized to be a $C^1$ piecewise cubic curve. Manning assumed that the
tangent directions would be the same, and so do we for this discussion. Since
we shall not be estimating tangents, we also assume that the tangent direction
is known. Let the unit tangent at each data point $P_i$ be called $T_i$, and let the
vector from $P_i$ to $P_{i+1}$ be called $L_i$. We call $\theta_{i,l}$ the angle between $T_i$ and
$L_i$; and we call $\theta_{i+1,r}$ the angle between $L_i$ and $T_{i+1}$. These angles give some
measure of the *turning* of the underlying curve, the curvature, in the vicinity
of the data points and over the interval. The magnitudes of the tangents are
set to be

$$\|P'_{i,l}\| = \frac{2\|L_i\|}{1 + \alpha \cos \theta_{i+1,r} + (1 - \alpha) \cos \theta_{i,l}}$$

$$\|P'_{i+1,r}\| = \frac{2\|L_i\|}{1 + (1 - \alpha) \cos \theta_{i+1,r} + \alpha \cos \theta_{i,l}}.$$

If $\theta_{i,l} \approx \theta_{i+1,r} \approx 0$, then the denominator in each of the above equations is approximately equal to 2, and the tangent magnitudes are set equal to the distance between the data points. The less flat the piecewise linear interpolant is, the larger the magnitudes become. If for some reason $\theta_{i,l} = \theta_{i+1,r} = \pi$, then the method breaks down since the denominator would be 0. However, it is highly unlikely that this case would arise in any practical problem.

## §3. Finding an Initial Parametrization

Our goal is to identify the corners of the underlying curve and to find $C^2$ piecewise continuous spline approximations of arbitrary order between the corners. We use the term *corner* for a point on the curve which has a discontinuity in the first derivative direction. Manning's work is not directly applicable since we must find just a sequence of parameter values.

The curvature of a curve $\gamma$ is $\kappa = \|\gamma' \times \gamma''\|/\|\gamma'\|^3$, and empirically, the chord length approximation has problems where the dynamic range of the curvature is high. The inequality $\kappa\|\gamma'\|^2 \leq \|\gamma''\|$ is further support for the hypothesis that there is an inverse relationship between the curvature and the tangent magnitude. This would seem to support the Manning results. If $t_i$ is the parameter value of point $P_i$, then we call $t_{i+1} - t_i$ the *parametric interval* between $P_i$ and $P_{i+1}$. Increasing the relative size of one parametric interval relative to the others around it reduces the length of the first derivative of the approximating curve near that parameter value, permitting higher curvature, so that the curve may turn through a larger angle. Analogously, a relatively smaller interval increases the first derivative and tends to flatten the curve. Figure 2 shows these effects by scaling just the center interval. Figure 2a is the chord length approximation, while Figure 2b scales the center interval by a factor of 4 and Figure 2c scales the center interval by a factor of 9.

**Figure 2.** Study of magnifying the length of the center interval.
a) a *CL* fit    b) scale of 4    c) scale of 9.

We will use the parametrization to control the magnitudes of the first derivatives of the curve approximation. Our approach and algorithms will focus on methods to determine the spacing of the data parameters through a nonlinear scaling based on curvature information of a *quasi* chord length approximation. A first order approximation is derived and heuristics applied to identify corners in the underlying curves and to pinpoint potential regions of low and high curvature.

## A Piecewise Linear Approximation

The first stage of the method finds a piecewise linear approximation using subdivision techniques. Let $D$ be the set of data points, *minpts* the minimum number of points expected to be approximated by a single line, *eps* the maximum deviation of the data to the approximating lines, and $N$ the number of points in the data set. Finally, let $\mathcal{F}$ be the ordered list of data sets which are returned from FPiecewiselinearize.

FPiecewiselinearize creates the rough splitting of the data into subpieces and is presented algorithmically below.

Procedure FPiecewiselinearize($D$, *minpts*,*eps*,$\mathcal{F}$ )

1. find the least squares line fit to the entire data set;
2. if the true distance from the line to any point is
   more than $eps/2$, split the data sets into two parts:
   a. find the point with the maximum error
      that is near the center of the parametric range,
      and call its subscript $m$
   b. split the data set into two parts,
      $L = \{P_i : i \leq m\}$ and $R = \{P_i : i \geq m\}$,
   c. else, append $D$ to $\mathcal{F}$ , and return;
3. if $L$ has fewer than $(minpts + 1)/2$ points,
   append $L$ to $\mathcal{F}$
   else FPiecewiselinearize($L$, *minpts*,*eps*,$\mathcal{F}$ );
4. if $R$ has fewer than $(minpts + 1)/2$ points,
   append $R$ to $\mathcal{F}$
   else FPiecewiselinearize($R$, *minpts*,*eps*,$\mathcal{F}$ ).

The result of applying this algorithm is an ordered list of sets of ordered points. Two consecutive sets in the list have a single point in common. The algorithm is biased to split the data sets near the middle of the subscript range to assure that the data sets have roughly equal size, which is useful in the early stages when subdivision points cannot be picked reliably. On each segment, either the error is below tolerance, or the number of points is below minimum. The subdivision technique is not optimal, in the sense that the piecewise linear approximation resulting may not have the fewest number of line segments; however, the next step of the algorithm seeks to recombine elements of the list $\mathcal{F}$ to meet the minimality conditions and reduce the number of segments. Suppose the final list of datasubsets is $\mathcal{N}$, and let $\beta$ be the piecewise linear representation derived from the sets in $\mathcal{N}$. This method is unlike others in that there is no constraint that the first and last points of each set in $\mathcal{N}$ lies on the approximating lines.

## Determining the Parametrization

The process now determines a quasi chord length parametrization from $\beta$, and then proceeds to incorporate curvature information into the parametrization. There are two types of factors which are calculated. One is the *angle factor* which computes a factor based on the angle which $\beta$, the piecewise linear approximation, turns from one linear segment to the next. This factor has its basis in the work of Manning. For interpolation problems, the angle turned in the piecewise linear approximation at each data point is available, so tangent magnitude based on an angle factor was feasible. However, for approximation, many data points fall on a single line with no angles. Our method first derives angle factors for the ends of each subinterval, and then extends them to the interior data points using simple linear interpolation. In regions of high curvature of the underlying curve, not only might the curve turn through larger angles, but the piecewise linear approximation will have shorter segments, each of which either approximates fewer data points, or approximates more densely digitized points. We have derived the *length factor* to adjust the parametric interval for this phenomenon.

Denote by $S_i$ the $i^{th}$ line segment of $\beta$, which approximates the data subset $D_i = \{P_{i,j} : j = 0, \ldots, n_i\}$. Recall that $P_{i,n_i} = P_{i+1,0}$ and $P_{i-1,n_{i-1}} = P_{i,0}$ since the split points appear in consecutive fitting sets. Also, let $\theta_i$ be half the angle that $\beta$ turns through from $S_i$ to $S_{i+1}$. Half of the angle turned is used in the calculations instead of the whole angle since the angles tend to be more severe in a piecewise linear least square approximation than in a piecewise linear interpolant.

Call $q_{i,j}$ the nearest point on $S_i$ to $P_{i,j}$. The *working distance*, $\lambda_i$, along $S_i$ is defined as $\lambda_i = \|q_{i,n_i} - q_{i,0}\|$. Chord length along $\beta$ is not used directly, since $q_{i,n_i}$ and $q_{i+1,0}$ have different parametrizations on $\beta$, but represent the projections of the same point from the original dataset. This parametrization uses the working distances along each segment of the approximation. The initial parametrization for $P_{i,j}$ is then $\tau_{i,j} = \tau_{i,0} + \|q_{i,j} - q_{i,0}\|$. This initial parametrization is a sort of *flattened* chord length parametrization, since the projections are used. Since the approximation has the intrinsic shape of the underlying curve, using the projections serves to remove the noise from the parametrization.

Suppose there are $n + 1$ line segments of $\beta$, subscripted from 0 to $n$. The following steps are used to arrive at the new *variable speed* parametrization.
**Step 1:** An angle factor $a_i$ is computed for each vertex of $\beta$, even the end vertices, and so $a_i$ corresponds to $\theta_{i-1}$. We have

$$a_i = \begin{cases} 2/c_1, & i = 1 \\ 1/b_i + 1/c_i, & 2 \leq i \leq n - 1 \\ 2/b_n, & i = n, \end{cases}$$

where

$$b_i = 1 + (1 - \alpha) \cos \theta_{i-1} + \alpha \cos \theta_{i-2},$$

$$c_i = 1 + (1 - \alpha) \cos \theta_{i-1} + \alpha \cos \theta_i,$$

and

$$a_0 = a_{n+1} = \frac{\sum_{i=1}^n a_i}{n}.$$

**Step 2:** Compute the length factors. The length factors are a function of the average adjusted length of the intervals, $\mu$, and the lengths of the two intervals ad on either side of the vertex. For $\delta_j = \lambda_j + \max(.5 - \theta_{j-1}, 0)\lambda_{j-1} + \max(.5 - \theta_j, 0)\lambda_{j+1}$ and

$$\mu = \frac{\sum_{i=0}^n \delta_i}{n},$$

we define

$$s_i = \begin{cases} \frac{1}{2\delta_0 + \mu}, & i = 0 \\ \frac{1}{\delta_{i-1} + \delta_i + \mu}, & 1 \le i \le n \\ \frac{1}{2\delta_n + \mu}, & i = n + 1. \end{cases}$$

**Step 3:** Set the scale factors $f_i = s_i * a_i$.

**Step 4:** Find the final *variable speed parametrization* by the formula

$$t_{0,0} = 0,$$

$$t_{i,j} = t_{i,0} + \frac{\|q_{i,j} - q_{i,0}\|}{\lambda_i} * f_{i+1} + \frac{\|q_{i,n_i} - q_{i,j}\|}{\lambda_i} * f_i,$$

$$j = 0, \ldots, n_i, \text{ for each } i.$$

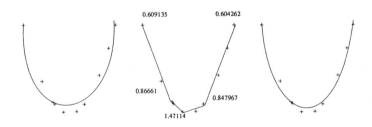

**Figure 3.** a) *CL fit*   b) $\beta$ *and* $f_i$   c) *VS fit*.

This defines the parametrization completely since $t_{i+1,0} = t_{i,n_i}$, which follows from the fact that there is only one parametrization for a single point. We call this parametrization the *variable speed parametrization*, and call any least squares approximation in that parametrization a *VS fit*. Figure 3 shows single polynomial approximation. In particular, Figure 3a shows the standard chord length approximation, Figure 3b shows $\beta$ and the $f_i$, and Figure 3c shows the variable speed parametrization approximation.

## Finding Corners

Data sets that come from points digitized from real models frequently have corners in them. While it is impossible to tell from data whether the underlying curve is $C^1$ or $C^2$, corners do occur and can be seen in data. There is no way to determine, however, if the data represents a corner or if it is in a region of extremely high curvature, so heuristics must be used. The user must have some input at the start of the process as to whether a particular use of this method allows corners or not.

The basic criteria for determining a corner was suggested by Plass and Stone [9], but is applied to the piecewise linear approximation derived in the subsection above. Suppose $v_j$ is a vertex of the piecewise linear approximation.

**Corner Finding Criteria.** *If the angle, $\phi_j$, between the vectors $v_j - v_{j-1}$ and $v_{j+1} - v_j$ is less than $3\pi/2$, then a corner occurs at $v_j$.*

The choice of $3\pi/2$ was heuristically determined, and the user might find that his data was more reflective of another value.

Subdividing at points of greatest distance from the local least squares approximation reinforces the goal of subdividing at potential corners. Further, oversubdividing and recombination performed in finding the piecewise linear approximation seems to help find an approximation which is more useful for corner detection.

The initial least squares approximation, then, has one of two forms. If the user has disallowed corners, then it will fit with a single polynomial piece. If the user has allowed corners, then the fit will be done for a single spline with $C^0$ continuity, and break points occurring at the parametric values of the designated *corner* vertices of $\beta$.

## §4. Experimental Results

The first example in Figure 4 is a comparison of the chord length approximation of Figure 1 with a variable speed approximation having the same number of knots. Criteria for adaptive knot placement were the same in both cases.

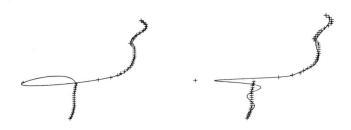

**Figure 4.** a) *CL fit*     b) *VS fit.*

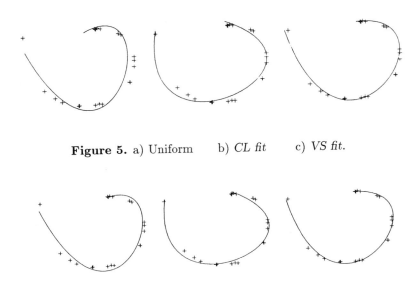

**Figure 5.** a) Uniform    b) *CL fit*    c) *VS fit.*

**Figure 6.** Reparametrized approximations with initial
a) Uniform    b) *CL fit*    c) *VS fit.*

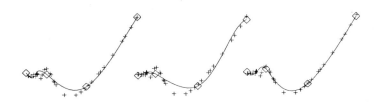

**Figure 7.** Effect of initial parametrization on adaptive knot selections
a) Uniform    b) *CL fit*    c) *VS fit.*

Figure 5 is a comparison of approximations done in the two standard parametrizations with the approximation for the variable speed parametrization.

Figure 6 shows the influence of the initial parametrization on the effectiveness of reparametrization. The figures show a single cubic approximating polynomial whose parametrization has undergone reparametrization one time. Part a) represents an initial uniform parametrization, part b) represents an initial chord length parametrization, and part c) represents an initial variable speed parametrization.

Figure 7 shows the influence of the initial parametrization on the placement of knots which have been added using *adaptive* criteria. The decisions were made on the same basis for all three parametrizations, and the same number of knots have been added to each. The little squares indicate the knot locations.

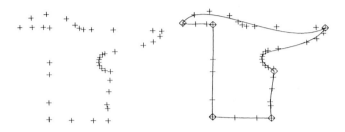

**Figure 8.** a) Data with corners.  b) The *VS* approximation.

Finally, Figure 8a shows data with corners, and Figure 8b shows the initial fit, which identified corners and parametrized the data. Between the corners, the curve has a single polynomial segment.

## §5. Remarks

We have presented a method for finding an initial parametrization for a spline curve which helps identify corners. Finding the piecewise linear approximation requires subdivision and distance calculations which take more time than just using the chord length parametrization directly. However, this method is based on allowing greater variation than is usually found in the chord length approximation in both the magnitudes of the tangents and the curvatures of the approximating curve. This approach gives promising results individually, and integrated with the other techniques of curve fitting, seems to enhance their approximating qualities.

### References

1. de Boor, C., *A Practical Guide to Splines*, Springer-Verlag, New York, 1978.
2. Cohen, E. and C. L. O'Dell, An integrated approach to approximating data with parametric B-splines, Technical Report, Computer Science, University of Utah, 1988.
3. Epstein, M. P., On the influence of parametrization in parametric interpolation, SIAM J. Numer. Anal. **13** (1976), 261–268.
4. Grossman, M., Parametric curve fitting, Computer J. **17** ( 1971), 169-172.
5. Hoschek, J., Intrinsic parametrization for approximation, Comput. Aided Geom. Design **5** (1988), 27 – 31.

6. Manning, J. R., Continuity conditions for spline curves, Computer J. **17** (1974), 181–183.
7. Marin, S. P., An approach to data parametrization in parametric cubic spline interpolation problems, J. Approx. Theory **41** (1984), 64–86.
8. O'Dell, C. L., Approximating data with parametric B-splines for Computer Aided Design, Masters Thesis, University of Utah, 1985.
9. Plass, M. and M. Stone, Curve-Fitting with piecewise parametric cubics, in ACM/SIGGRAPH, 1983, Peter Tanner (ed.), 229–239.

Elaine Cohen
Department of Computer Science
University of Utah
Salt Lake City, Utah 84112
USA

EMAIL: cohen% gr@ cs.utah.edu

Connie O'Dell
AT&T Bell Labs
2000 N. Naperville Rd
Naperville, IL
USA

Supported in part by DARPA (DAAK11-84-K0017). All opinions, findings, conclusions or recommendations expressed are those of the authors and do not necessarily reflect the views of the sponsoring agencies.

# On the Evaluation of Box Splines

## Morten Dæhlen

**Abstract.**    In this paper we develop an efficient method for computing $s$–variate box splines as combinations of $(s-1)$–variate simplex splines. On regular meshes in $\mathbb{R}^2$ and $\mathbb{R}^3$, simple and fast algorithms for computing all nonzero box splines at a fixed point are given. Numerical results on the stability and speed of the methods are presented.

## §1. Introduction

With $X = (x^1, \ldots, x^n)$, $x^i \in \mathbb{R}^s$, the box splines $B(x|X) : \mathbb{R}^s \to \mathbb{R}$ can be computed by the following recurrence relation, which was introduced in [2]:

$$B(x \mid X) = \frac{1}{n-s}\Big(\sum_{k=1}^{n} \lambda_k B(x \mid X_k) + (1-\lambda_k)B(x - x^k \mid X_k)\Big), \qquad (1)$$

where $x = \sum_{k=1}^{n} \lambda_k x^k$ and $X_k = (x^1, \ldots x^{k-1}, x^{k+1}, \ldots, x^n)$. The right hand side of this equation contains at least $n + 1$ terms, and thus a straightforward recursive implementation gives rise to an $\mathcal{O}((n+1)!)$ process in order to compute one box spline value. Moreover, box splines are defined as distributions, and the recurrence relation treats them as such. This makes the evaluation of box splines on joins between polynomial pieces very difficult. With the method to be presented here the latter problem does not occur.

It is known that box splines can be written as a difference of cone splines [7], and that $s$–variate cone splines can be expressed in terms of $(s-1)$–variate simplex splines [4]. This means, in the bivariate case, that evaluation of box splines can be reduced to the evaluation of univariate simplex splines; *i.e.*, B–splines. In the trivariate case the evaluation of box splines is reduced to the evaluation of bivariate simplex splines. Based on this observation, simple and fast algorithms for computing all nonzero box splines at a fixed point over a three–direction mesh in $\mathbb{R}^2$ and a four–direction mesh in $\mathbb{R}^3$ are given.

Mathematical Methods in Computer Aided Geometric Design
Tom Lyche and Larry L. Schumaker (eds.), pp. 167–179.

## §2. Boxes, Cones and Simplex Splines

In this section we give general definitions of box splines [1,2], cone splines [5] and simplex splines [13], and a review of necessary results on relations between these multivariate splines.

Let the integers $n \geq s \geq 1$ and the vectors $X = (x^1, \ldots, x^n)$ with $x^j \in \mathbb{R}^s$, $j = 1, \ldots, n$ be given. The *box spline* $B(x \mid X) : \mathbb{R}^s \to \mathbb{R}$ is defined as a distribution given by the rule

$$\int_{\mathbb{R}^s} B(x \mid X) f(x) \, dx = \int_{I^n} f(X\nu) \, d\nu_1 \ldots d\nu_n$$

for all $f \in C_0^\infty(\mathbb{R}^s)$, where $C_0^\infty(\mathbb{R}^s)$ denotes the space of all infinitely differentiable functions with compact support on $\mathbb{R}^s$. The integration on the right is over the unit cube $I^n = [0, 1]^n$ in $\mathbb{R}^n$, and $X\nu = \nu_1 x^1 + \ldots + \nu_n x^n$.

Similarly, the *cone spline* $C(x \mid X) : \mathbb{R}^s \to \mathbb{R}$ is a distribution given by the rule

$$\int_{\mathbb{R}^s} C(x \mid X) f(x) dx = \int_{\mathbb{R}_+^n} f(X\nu) d\nu_1 \ldots d\nu_n$$

for all $f \in C_0^\infty(\mathbb{R}^s)$. The integration on the right is over $\mathbb{R}_+^n = [0, \infty)^n$, and as before $X\nu = \nu_1 x^1 + \nu_2 x^2 + \ldots + \nu_n x^n$.

Finally, we recall the definition of simplex splines. The *simplex spline* $S(x \mid X) : \mathbb{R}^s \to \mathbb{R}$ is given by the following distribution

$$\int_{\mathbb{R}^s} S(x \mid X) f(x) dx = (n-1)! \int_{S^{n-1}} f(X\nu) d\nu_2 \ldots d\nu_n \tag{2}$$

for all $f \in C_0^\infty(\mathbb{R}^s)$. Here $X\nu = \nu_1 x^1 + \nu_2 x^2 + \ldots + \nu_n x^n$ and $\nu_1 = 1 - \sum_{j=2}^n \nu_j$. The integration on the right is over the standard simplex

$$S^{n-1} = \left\{ (\nu_2, \ldots \nu_n) : \nu_i \geq 0, \sum_{i=2}^n \nu_i \leq 1 \right\} \subset \mathbb{R}^{n-1}.$$

Next we give the equation relating box splines to cone splines. Let $\nabla_x$ be the backward difference operator given by $\nabla_x f(y) = f(y) - f(y - x)$. From [7] we have an expression which gives box spline as a backward difference of cone splines. The relation can be written

$$B(x \mid X) = \nabla_X C(x \mid X), \tag{3}$$

where $\nabla_X = \nabla_{x^1}, \ldots, \nabla_{x^n}$.

Furthermore, we have the relation between cone splines in $\mathbb{R}^s$ and simplex splines in $\mathbb{R}^{s-1}$, which was introduced in [4]. Let $V$ be a nonsingular $s \times s$ matrix with columns $v^1, \ldots v^s$ and $e = (1, \ldots, 1)^T \in \mathbb{R}^s$. We define a linear functional $\pi : \mathbb{R}^s \to \mathbb{R}$ and a function $\lambda : \mathbb{R}^s \to \mathbb{R}^s$ by

$$\pi(y) = e^T V^{-1} y$$

and

$$\lambda(y) = \begin{cases} V^{-1}y/\pi(y), & \pi(y) \neq 0, \\ V^{-1}y, & \text{otherwise.} \end{cases}$$

Moreover, we define the projection $P : \mathbb{R}^s \to \mathbb{R}^{s-1}$ by

$$P(y) = P(y_1, \ldots, y_s)^T = (y_2, \ldots y_s)^T. \tag{4}$$

Let $X = (x^1, \ldots x^n)$ be a set of nonzero vectors in $\mathbb{R}^s$, such that they span $\mathbb{R}^s$. For any nonsingular matrix $V$ such that $\pi(x^i) > 0$, $i = 1, 2, \ldots, n$, we have for $x \in R^s$ with $\pi(x) \neq 0$,

$$C(x \mid X) = K\pi(x)_+^{n-s} S(P\lambda(x) \mid P\lambda(X)), \tag{5}$$

where

$$K = \frac{1}{(n-1)!|\det(V)| \prod_{j=1}^n \pi(x^j)},$$

and $P\lambda(X) = (P\lambda(x^1), \ldots P\lambda(x^n))$.

## §3. Regular Meshes

Given $s$ linearly independent vectors $d^1, \ldots, d^s$ in $\mathbb{R}^s$, a uniform $(s+1)$-direction mesh is constructed by drawing straight lines in the $s+1$ directions $d^1, \ldots, d^s$ and $d^{s+1} = d^1 + \cdots + d^s$, through all points in $\mathbb{R}^s$ of the form $k_1 d^1 + \ldots + k_s d^s$, $k_1, \ldots k_s \in \mathbb{Z}^s$. The standard $(s+1)$-direction mesh in $\mathbb{R}^s$ is obtained by choosing $d^i$, $i = 1, \ldots, s$, equal to the standard unit vectors in $\mathbb{R}^s$, and this is the mesh we will work with in this paper. Translates of box splines on this mesh are linearly independent, see for example [2,6,12].

Let $m = (m_1, \ldots, m_{s+1})$ be $s+1$ given integers, such that $m_i > 0$, $i = 1, 2, \ldots, s$, and $m_{s+1} \geq 0$. Moreover, let $x = (x_1, \ldots, x_s) \in \mathbb{R}^s$. Then we have the following more simple definition of box splines on a $(s+1)$-direction mesh [8]:

$$B^{(m_1, \ldots, m_{s+1})}(x) = \begin{cases} M_{m_1}(x_1) \cdots M_{m_s}(x_s), & \text{if } m_{s+1} = 0, \\ \int_0^1 B^{(m_1, \ldots, m_s, m_{s+1}-1)}(x - \mathbf{t})dt, & \text{otherwise,} \end{cases}$$

where $\mathbf{t} = (t, \ldots, t) \in \mathbb{R}^s$. Here $M_k(y)$ is the univariate B-spline of order $k$ with knots $0, 1, \ldots, k$ normalized to have unit integral. Thus, $B^m(x) = B^{(m_1, \ldots, m_{s+1})}(x)$ is a tensor product B-spline if $m_{s+1} = 0$ and $B^m(x) = B(x \mid X)$, where

$$X = \{\overbrace{d^1, \ldots, d^1}^{m_1}, \ldots, \overbrace{d^s, \ldots, d^s}^{m_s}, \overbrace{d^{s+1}, \ldots, d^{s+1}}^{m_{s+1}}\}. \tag{6}$$

Moreover, let $\mu = \sum_{i=1}^{s+1} m_i$; i.e., the number of elements in $X$. Similarly, we write $C^m(x)$ for the cone spline and let

$$\nabla_m = \nabla_X = \overbrace{\nabla_{d^1} \cdots \nabla_{d^1}}^{m_1} \overbrace{\nabla_{d^{s+1}} \cdots \nabla_{d^{s+1}}}^{m_{s+1}}.$$

We now consider equation (5). With $X$ given by (6) we satisfy the condition $\pi(x^i) > 0$ simply by choosing $V = I$. In this case we have $\pi(y) = e^T V^{-1} y = \sum_{i=1}^{s} y_i$ and $\lambda(y) = y/\pi(y)$. We observe that $\pi(x) \neq 0$ for all $x$ where $B^m(x) \neq 0$. Equation (5) then takes the form

$$C^m(x) = \frac{1}{(\mu - 1)! \, s^{m_s+1}} \pi(x)_+^{\mu-s} S\left(\frac{P(x)}{\pi(x)} \mid Y\right), \tag{7}$$

where

$$Y = \{\overbrace{e^0, \ldots, e^0}^{m_1}, \overbrace{e^1, \ldots, e^1}^{m_2}, \ldots, \overbrace{e^{s-1}, \ldots, e^{s-1}}^{m_s}, \overbrace{u, \ldots, u}^{m_{s+1}}\}. \tag{8}$$

Here $e^0$ is the origin in $\mathbb{R}^{s-1}$, $e^1, \ldots, e^{s-1}$ are the standard unit vectors in $\mathbb{R}^{s-1}$ and

$$u = \frac{1}{s}(e^1 + e^2 + \ldots + e^{s-1}).$$

Combining (3) and (7) we have

$$B^m(x) = \frac{1}{(\mu - 1)! \, s^{m_s+1}} \nabla_m \left\{ \pi(x)_+^{\mu-s} S\left(\frac{P(x)}{\pi(x)} \mid Y\right) \right\}. \tag{9}$$

This is the formula which will be used to derive the algorithms in the next sections. It is possible to derive similar formulas for box splines on meshes in $\mathbb{R}^s$ other than the $(s+1)$–variate mesh considered here.

## §4. The Bivariate Case

In the bivariate ($s = 2$) case we consider translates of box splines on a three–direction mesh. The standard grid $G$ in $\mathbb{R}^2$ is obtained by choosing $d^1 = (1,0)^T$, $d^2 = (0,1)^T$ and $d^3 = (1,1)^T$. In this case the simplex spline on the right hand side of (9) will be a univariate B-spline. Moreover, since the simplex splines in (2) are normalized to have unit integral, we have

$$S\left(\frac{P(x)}{\pi(x)}\right) = (\mu - 1) M^m \left(\frac{x_2}{x_1 + x_2}\right),$$

where $\mu = m_1 + m_2 + m_3$, and where $M^m(x) = M^{(m_1, m_2, m_3)}(x) = [Y](\cdot - x)_+^{(\mu-2)}$ is a univariate B–spline of order $\mu - 1$ on the knotvector

$$Y = \{\overbrace{0, \ldots, 0}^{m_1}, \overbrace{1/2, \ldots, 1/2}^{m_3}, \overbrace{1, \ldots, 1}^{m_2}\}.$$

Equation (9) therefore takes the form

$$B^m(x) = \frac{1}{(\mu - 2)! \, 2^{m_3}} \nabla_m \left\{ (x_1 + x_2)_+^{\mu-2} M^m \left(\frac{x_2}{x_1 + x_2}\right) \right\}.$$

| $m_1$ | $m_2$ | $m_3$ | $\beta_0$ | $\beta_1$ | $\beta_2$ |
|-------|-------|-------|-----------|-----------|-----------|
| 1 | 1 | 1 | 1 | - | - |
| 2 | 1 | 1 | 1 | 3/2 | - |
| 1 | 2 | 1 | 1/2 | - | - |
| 1 | 1 | 2 | 1/2 | - | - |
| 1 | 1 | 3 | 1/6 | - | - |
| 1 | 1 | 4 | 1/24 | - | - |
| 2 | 2 | 1 | 1/2 | 2/3 | - |
| 2 | 1 | 2 | 1/2 | 5/6 | - |
| 1 | 2 | 2 | 1/6 | - | - |
| 2 | 2 | 2 | 1/6 | 1/4 | - |
| 3 | 2 | 2 | 1/12 | 1/4 | 23/120 |
| 2 | 3 | 2 | 1/24 | 7/120 | - |
| 2 | 2 | 3 | 1/24 | 1/15 | - |
| 3 | 3 | 1 | 1/12 | 5/24 | 2/15 |
| 3 | 3 | 2 | 1/48 | 7/120 | 1/24 |

**Table 1.** The coefficients $\beta_k = \beta_k^{(m_1,m_2,m_3)}$ in equation (10)
for various values of $m_1, m_2$ and $m_3$.

For computation it will be convenient to have an explicit expression for the
univariate B-spline in terms of the usual power functions. In order to simplify
the notation in the following lemma, let $n^{(p)} = (n(n+1)\ldots(n+p-1))/p!$,
with the convention that $n^{(0)} = 1$.

**Lemma 1.** *The B-spline*

$$M^m(x) = 2^{m_3}(\mu - 2)! \; x^{m_2+m_3-1} \sum_{k=0}^{m_1-1} (-1)^k \beta_k x^k \;, \quad 0 \le x \le \frac{1}{2} \qquad (10)$$

*where*

$$\beta_k = \beta_k^{(m_1,m_2,m_3)} = \frac{1}{(m_1-1-k)!(\mu-m_1+k-1)!} \sum_{j=0}^{k} 2^j m_3^{(j)} m_2^{(k-j)}.$$

*Moreover, we have*

$$M^{(m_1,m_2,m_3)}(x) = M^{(m_2,m_1,m_3)}(1-x). \qquad (11)$$

**Proof:** We prove this by using a representation for divided differences with
coalescent arguments, cf. [11]. Equation (10) follows from the relation

$$M^m(x) = g(0, \frac{1}{2}, 1)/[(m_1-1)!(m_2-1)!(m_3-1)!],$$

where

$$g(a, b, c) = \left(\frac{\partial}{\partial a}\right)^{m_1-1}\left(\frac{\partial}{\partial b}\right)^{m_2-1}\left(\frac{\partial}{\partial c}\right)^{m_3-1}[a, b, c](\cdot - x)_+^{(\mu-2)}.$$

Equation (11) follows directly from the divided difference definition of univariate B–splines. ∎

Table 1 gives the coefficients $\beta_k^{(m_1,m_2,m_3)}$, $k = 0, \ldots, m_1 - 1$, for the most common choices of multiplicities $m_1, m_2$ and $m_3$.

Let $a_k = \beta_k^{(m_1,m_2,m_3)}$, $k = 0, \ldots, m_1 - 1$, and $b_k = \beta_k^{(m_2,m_1,m_3)}$, $k = 0, \ldots,$ $m_2 - 1$ be coefficients given in Table 1. Moreover, let

$$\{x^1, \ldots, x^\mu\} = \{\overbrace{d^1, \ldots, d^1}^{m_1}, \overbrace{d^2, \ldots, d^2}^{m_2}, \overbrace{d^3, \ldots, d^3}^{m_3}\}.$$

In Algorithm 1 all bivariate non-zero translated box splines $B^m(y_1 - i, y_2 - j) = B_{i,j}$ at a fixed point $y = (y_1, y_2) \in \mathbb{R}^2$ are computed. Let us assume that $y$ is in the "half–open" unit square $[p, p + 1) \times [q, q + 1)$.

---

(i)
$$z_1 = y_1 - p + m_1 + m_3 - 1$$
$$z_2 = y_2 - q + m_2 + m_3 - 1$$
**for** $i = 0, \ldots, m_1 + m_3 - 1$
    **for** $j = 0, \ldots, m_2 + m_3 - 1$
    $u_1 = z_1 - i, \quad u_2 = z_2 - j,$
    $v_2 = u_1 + u_2$
    **if** $v_2 = 0.0$ **then** $v_1 = 0.0$ **else** $v_1 = \frac{u_2}{u_1 + u_2}$
    **if** $0 \le v_1 \le 1/2$ **then**
        $B_{i,j} = (v_2)^{m-2}(v_1)^{m_2+m_3-1}\sum_{k=0}^{m_1-1}(-1)^k a_k (v_1)^k$
    **else**
        $B_{i,j} = (v_2)^{m-2}(1 - v_1)^{m_1+m_3-1}\sum_{k=0}^{m_2-1}(-1)^k b_k (1 - v_1)^k$

(ii)
    **for** $n = 1, \ldots, \mu$
        **for** $i = 0, \ldots, m_1 + m_3 - 1$
            **for** $j = 0, \ldots, m_2 + m_3 - 1$
            $B_{i,j} = B_{i,j} - B_{i+x_1^n, j+x_2^n}$

---

**Algorithm 1.** The evaluation of bivariate box splines.

In Algorithm 1 we first translate $y$, such that the value $B_{0,0} = B^m(y)$, where the box spline $B^m(y)$ has lower left corner of the support at the origin in $\mathbb{R}^2$. In Part (i) all cone spline values are computed and stored in $B_{i,j}$. In Part (ii) the backward difference operation is performed such that $B^m(y_1 - i, y_2 - j) = B_{i,j}$. Figure 1 gives examples of cone splines which are involved in the evaluation of the box splines.

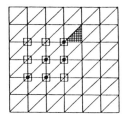 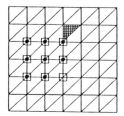

**Figure 1.** Cone splines involved in evaluation.

The circles in Figure 1 indicate the lower left corners of the support of the translated box splines which are nonzero at a fixed point $y$ given in the hashed regions. The squares indicate the lower left corners of the support of the cone splines which are involved in the evaluation of the box splines. The box splines $B^{(1,1,2)}$ and $B^{(2,2,1)}$ are shown on the left and right, respectively.

| $m_1$ | $m_2$ | $m_3$ | $B_A - B_R$ | $C_{max}$ |
|-------|-------|-------|-------------|-----------|
| 1 | 1 | 1 | 0.0 | 2.0 |
| 2 | 1 | 1 | 0.0 | 4.0 |
| 1 | 2 | 1 | 0.0 | 4.0 |
| 2 | 2 | 1 | 0.0 | 9.0 |
| 1 | 1 | 3 | 0.0 | 11 |
| 2 | 2 | 2 | $1.0 * 10^{-14}$ | 22 |
| 3 | 3 | 1 | $2.0 * 10^{-14}$ | 52 |
| 3 | 3 | 3 | $-2.8 * 10^{-13}$ | 333 |
| 4 | 4 | 3 | $1.2 * 10^{-11}$ | 2222 |
| 5 | 5 | 5 | $-5.4 * 10^{-10}$ | 115000 |
| 6 | 6 | 5 | $-4.6 * 10^{-9}$ | $8.1 * 10^5$ |
| 8 | 8 | 8 | $-2.7 * 10^{-5}$ | $9.5 * 10^8$ |

**Table 2.** Estimates on the error.

In Table 2, errors induced by using the backward difference algorithm are shown in the column marked $B_A - B_R$. The value $C_{max}$ gives an estimate on the largest value of the actual cone spline involved in the computations. The number of operations in Parts (i) and (ii) of Algorithm 1 are $O(\mu^3)$. We denote the box spline value evaluated by Algorithm 1 by $B_A$, and the result obtained by using a recursive implementation of (1) by $B_R$. The value $B_A(x) - B_R(x)$, where $x = (m_1 + m_3 - 10^{-4}, m_2 + m_3 - 10^{-4}/2)$, is given in Table 2 for various values of $m_1$, $m_2$ and $m_3$. The point $x$ lies near the upper right corner of the support of the box spline $B^{(m_1, m_2, m_3)}$. This is a point where the actual cone spline values are close to their largest values. Estimates of the largest cone spline values are given in the rightmost column of Table 2. All computations shown in Table 2 and in Table 3 in the next section are done in double precision on a SUN 3/60.

The main disadvantage of this method is of course that backward differencing might result in loss of accuracy. However, we observe that for the most common choices of multiplicities, the error is acceptable. The bivariate box spline with multiplicities $(m_1, m_2, m_3) = (6, 6, 5)$ is a piecewise polynomial of degree 15. The error in the evaluation is still within single precision accuracy.

## §5. The Trivariate Case

In the trivariate ($s = 3$) case we consider translates of box splines on a four-direction mesh. The standard grid $G$ in $\mathbb{R}^3$ is obtained by choosing $d^1 = (1, 0, 0)^T$, $d^2 = (0, 1, 0)^T$, $d^3 = (0, 0, 1)^T$ and $d^4 = (1, 1, 1)^T$. Trivariate box splines spanned by $d^j$, $j = 1, 2, 3, 4$ are piecewise polynomials on $G$. The partition $G$ is such that each unit-size cube is divided into six tetrahedra. This partition is in general known as *Kuhn's triangulation*. We recall that if $m_4 = 0$, we have a trivariate tensor product function, so let us assume $m_4 > 0$. In this case equation (9) takes the form

$$B^m(x) = \frac{1}{(\mu - 1)! \, 3^{m_4}} \nabla_m \left\{ (x_1 + x_2 + x_3)_+^{\mu - 3} S\left( \frac{(x_2, x_3)}{x_1 + x_2 + x_3} \mid Y \right) \right\}, \quad (12)$$

where $\mu = m_1 + m_2 + m_3 + m_4$, and where $S(y \mid Y)$ is a bivariate simplex spline spanned by the knot set given in (8). The support of $S(y \mid Y)$ is the unit triangle shown in Figure 2.

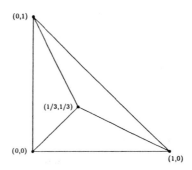

**Figure 2.** The support of the simplex splines given in (12).

As in the bivariate case we simplify the notation of Algorithm 2 by letting

$$\{x^1,\ldots,x^\mu\} = \{\overbrace{d^1,\ldots,d^1}^{m_1},\overbrace{d^2,\ldots,d^2}^{m_2},\overbrace{d^3,\ldots,d^3}^{m_3},\overbrace{d^4,\ldots,d^4}^{m_4}\}.$$

In Algorithm 2 all non-zero translated box splines $B^m(y_1 - i, y_2 - j, y_3 - k) = B_{i,j,k}$ at a fixed point $y = (y_1, y_2, y_3) \in \mathbb{R}^3$ are computed. Furthermore, let us assume that $y$ is in the "half–open" unit box $[p, p+1) \times [q, q+1) \times [r, r+1)$.

---

$$z_1 = y_1 - p + m_1 + m_4 - 1$$

$$z_2 = y_2 - q + m_2 + m_4 - 1$$

$$z_2 = y_2 - r + m_3 + m_4 - 1$$

(i)  **for** $i = 0, \ldots, m_1 + m_4 - 1$

 **for** $j = 0, \ldots, m_2 + m_4 - 1$

  **for** $k = 0, \ldots, m_3 + m_4 - 1$

   $u_1 = z_1 - i, \quad u_2 = z_2 - j, \quad u_3 = z_3 - k,$

   $B_{i,j,k} = \frac{1}{(\mu-1)!\,3^{m_4}}(u_1 + u_2 + u_3)_+^{\mu-3} S(\frac{(u_2,u_3)}{u_1+u_2+u_3} \mid Y)$

(ii) **for** $n = 1, \ldots, \mu$

 **for** $i = 0, \ldots, m_1 + m_4 - 1$

  **for** $j = 0, \ldots, m_2 + m_4 - 1$

   **for** $k = 0, \ldots, m_3 + m_4 - 1$

    $B_{i,j,k} = B_{i,j,k} - B_{i+x_1^n, j+x_2^n, k+x_3^n}$

---

**Algorithm 2.** The evaluation of trivariate box splines.

As in the bivariate case we first translate $y$, such that the value $B_{0,0,0} = B^m(y)$. In Part (i) all cone spline values are computed and stored in $B_{i,j,k}$. In Part (ii) the backward difference operation is performed such that we have $B^m(y_1 - i, y_2 - j, y_3 - k) = B_{i,j,k}$.

Let $N_m = N_{(m_1,\ldots,m_4)}$ denote the number of operations needed to evaluate the simplex spline $S(y \mid Y)$. Then the number of operations in Parts (i) and (ii) of Algorithm 2 are $\mathcal{O}(\mu^3) \times N_m$ and $\mathcal{O}(\mu^4)$, respectively.

In the computation of the trivariate box splines shown in the Figures 5, 6 and 7, we used the following recurrence relation for simplex splines [13]:

$$S(y \mid Y) = \left(\frac{\mu - 1}{\mu - 3}\right) \sum_{i=1}^{\mu} \lambda_i S(y \mid Y_i),$$

where $Y_i = \{y^1, \ldots y^{i-1}, y^{i+1}, \ldots y^\mu\}$. Moreover,

$$y = \sum_{i=1}^{\mu} \lambda_i y^i, \quad \sum_{i=1}^{\mu} \lambda_i = 1.$$

It is a problem to obtain correct values of $S(y \mid Y)$ on knotlines. To avoid the problem of uniqueness on knotlines, it is possible to take into acount the simple structure of the simplex splines appearing in Algorithm 2. The support of these simplex splines is shown in Figure 2. The problem of evaluation on knotlines is solved as follows:

- Avoid evaluation of constant simplex splines on the unit triangle $[(0,0),$ $(1,0)$, $(0,1)]$. This is always possible since $m_4 > 0$.

- Organize the three triangles $[(0,0),$ $(1/3,1/3),$ $(1,0)]$, $[(0,0),$ $(1/3,1/3),$ $(0,1)]$ and $[(0,1),$ $(1/3,1/3),$ $(1,0)]$, such that a common knotlines belong to only one of the triangles.

The rightmost column of Table 3 shows estimates on the number of operations needed to evaluate $S(y \mid Y)$ by the recurrence relation. The evaluation of multivariate simplex splines is extensively studied in [9] and [10]. We observe that the number $N_m$ has an $\mathcal{O}(\mu^2)$ behaviour.

Test results on the stability in the trivariate case are shown in Table 3, and as in the bivariate case, we observe that for the most common choices of multiplicities, the error is acceptable.

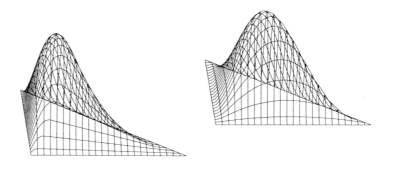

**Figure 3.**                                       **Figure 4.**

Figure 3 shows the $C^0$ quadratic simplex splines with knots $(0,0)$, $(0,0)$, $(0,1)$, $(0,1)$, $(1,0)$, $(1/3,1/3)$. Figure 4 shows the $C^1$ cubic simplex splines with knots $(0,0)$, $(0,0)$, $(0,1)$, $(0,1)$, $(1,0)$, $(1,0)$, $(1/3,1/3)$. Figures 5, 6 and 7 show projections of trivariate box splines $B^{m_1,\ldots,m_4}(x,y,z)$ into $\mathbb{R}^3$, where $x \in [0, m_1 + m_4]$, $y \in [0, m_2 + m_4]$ and where the values of $z$ are given in the figure captions. The $C^0$ quadratic simplex spline and the $C^1$ cubic simplex spline used in the evaluation of the trivariate box splines in Figures 6 and 7 are those shown in Figures 3 and 4, respectively.

| $m_1$ | $m_2$ | $m_3$ | $m_4$ | $B_A - B_R$ | $C_{max}$ | $N_m$ |
|---|---|---|---|---|---|---|
| 1 | 1 | 1 | 1 | 0.0 | 2.0 | 3 |
| 1 | 1 | 1 | 2 | 0.0 | 4.5 | 6 |
| 2 | 2 | 2 | 1 | $1.0 * 10^{-14}$ | 22 | 42 |
| 2 | 2 | 2 | 2 | $-0.2 * 10^{-13}$ | 55 | 58 |
| 3 | 2 | 2 | 2 | $-3.1 * 10^{-13}$ | 132 | 92 |
| 2 | 2 | 2 | 3 | $0.6 * 10^{-13}$ | 132 | 74 |
| 1 | 1 | 1 | 6 | $-0.7 * 10^{-13}$ | 170 | 18 |
| 3 | 3 | 3 | 1 | $-3.6 * 10^{-13}$ | 300 | 145 |
| 3 | 3 | 3 | 2 | $-1.9 * 10^{-13}$ | 880 | 184 |
| 3 | 3 | 3 | 3 | $5.4 * 10^{-12}$ | 2500 | 223 |
| 4 | 4 | 4 | 1 | $7.2 * 10^{-12}$ | 4520 | 342 |
| 4 | 4 | 4 | 4 | $1.5 * 10^{-9}$ | $1.5 * 10^5$ | 558 |
| 4 | 4 | 4 | 6 | $1.9 * 10^{-8}$ | $1.3 * 10^6$ | 702 |
| 6 | 6 | 6 | 6 | $-4.2 * 10^{-2}$ | $6.8 * 10^8$ | 1978 |

**Table 3.** Estimates on the error.

In Table 3, estimates of the error introduced by using the backward difference algorithm are shown in the column marked $B_A - B_R$. The value $C_{max}$ gives an estimate on the largest value of the actual cone spline involved in the computations. The rightmost column gives estimates on the number of operations necessary to compute the bivariate simplex splines with support as given in Figure 2.

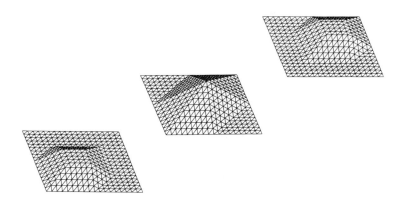

**Figure 5.** The linear box spline $B^{(1,1,1,1)}(x, y, z)$ for $x \in [0, 2]$, $y \in [0, 2]$ and $z$ equal to 0.5, 1.0 and 1.5, respectively.

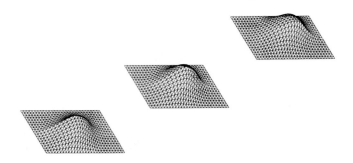

**Figure 6.** The $C^0$–quadratic box spline $B^{(2,1,2,1)}(x, y, z)$, $x \in [0, 3]$, $y \in [0, 2]$ and $z$ equal to 1.0, 1.5 and 2.0, respectively. Observe the discontinuity in the first derivative across the ridge.

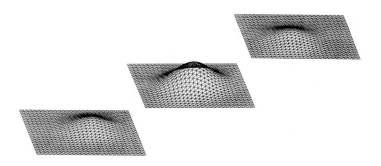

**Figure 7.** The $C^1$–cubic box spline $B^{(2,2,2,1)}(x, y, z)$ for $x \in [0, 3]$, $y \in [0, 3]$ and $z$ equal to 0.75, 1.5 and 2.25, respectively.

## Acknowledgment

The author wishes to thank Professor Tom Lyche for his helpful suggestions.

## References

1. de Boor, C. and R. DeVore, Approximations by smooth multivariate splines, Trans. Amer. Math. Soc. **276** (1983), 775–785.

2. de Boor, C. and K. Höllig, B–splines from parallelepipeds, J. Analyse Math. **42** (1982), 99–115.

3. de Boor, C. and K. Höllig, Bivariate box splines and smooth pp functions on a three direction mesh, J. Comput. Appl. Math. **9** (1983), 13–28.

4. Cohen, E., T. Lyche, and R. Riesenfeld, Cones and recurrence relations for simplex splines, Constr. Approx. **3** (1987), 131–142.

5. Dahmen, W., Multivariate B-splines — Recurrence relations and linear combinations of truncated powers, in *Multivariate Approximation Theory*, W. Schempp and K. Zeller (eds.), Birkhäuser, Basel, 1979, 64–82.

6. Dahmen, W. and C. A. Micchelli, Translates of multivariate splines, Linear Algebra Appl. **52/53** (1983), 217–234.

7. Dahmen, W. and C. A. Micchelli, Recent progress in multivariate splines, in *Approximation Theory IV*, C. Chui, L. L. Schumaker, and J. Ward (eds.), Academic Press, New York, 1983, 27–121.

8. Dæhlen, M. and T. Lyche, Bivariate interpolation by quadratic box splines, Math. Comp. **51** (1988), 219–230.

9. Grandine, T. A., The stable evaluation of multivariate simplex spline, Math. Comp. **50** (1988), 197–203.

10. Ha, K. V., On Multivariate Simplex B-Splines, dissertation, Institute for Informatics, Univ. of Oslo, 1988.

11. Isaacsen, E. and H. B. Keller, *Analysis of Numerical Methods*, John Wiley & Sons, New York, 1966.

12. Jia, R. Q., Linear independence of translates of box splines, J. Approx. Theory **40** (1984), 158–160.

13. Micchelli, C. A., A constructive approach to Kergin interpolation in $\mathbb{R}^k$, Multivariate B–splines and Lagrange interpolation, Rocky Mountain J. Math. **10** (1980), 485–497.

Morten Dæhlen
Center for Industrial Research
Box 124 Blindern
0314 Oslo 3
NORWAY

EMAIL: mortend@ ifi.uio.no

# Smooth Piecewise Quadric Surfaces

## Wolfgang Dahmen

**Abstract.** This paper is concerned with the construction of tangent plane continuous piecewise quadric surfaces that interpolate finite sets of essentially arbitrary points in $\mathbb{R}^3$ according to a given 'topology' which is described in terms of a piecewise linear interpolant. Moreover, within certain ranges depending on the topology and the location of data points, given normal directions at the points are also matched by the interpolating piecewise quadric surface.

## §1. Introduction

The use of *implicitly* defined surfaces in solid modeling or free form modeling has some principal advantages over parametric surface representations. For instance, ray-surface intersections are easily computed and one can immediately decide on which side of the surface a given point is located. However, the practical difficulties in dealing with such surface representations are known to increase dramatically with their degree. In fact, for instance, surface-surface intersections lead to curves of possibly very high degree. Keeping the degree low is also crucial when implicit representations are to be converted to parametric form. In order to still be able to represent complex shapes, it seems therefore reasonable, instead of raising the degree of the surface, to work with surfaces which are *composed* of several implicitly defined patches. A typical minimum smoothness requirement is that the entire surface should at least be *tangent plane continuous*. Again, to obtain a general scheme that is able to cope with complex shapes and surface topologies the construction should be *local*, i.e. each patch should be constructed only from 'nearby' data in such a way that any two adjacent patches *automatically* join with tangent plane continuity. Furthermore, one might wish the surface to pass through given points with suitably chosen normal directions.

Mathematical Methods in Computer Aided Geometric Design
Tom Lyche and Larry L. Schumaker (eds.), pp. 181–193.
Copyright © 1989 by Academic Press, Boston.
ISBN 0-12-460515-X.

The objective of this paper is to explore the possibility of constructing such piecewise implicit interpolating surfaces to essentially arbitrarily spaced data in $\mathbb{R}^3$ associated with a prescribed topology. Specifically, we will focus on realizing the above requirements for lowest possible degree, *i.e.*, for quadric patches. Taking up Sederberg's suggestion [7], we will use the *Bernstein-Bézier* representation of polynomials to define the patches which will allow to express the various interpolation and smoothness conditions in a convenient way. The key to actually realizing all these conditions by a local method is to construct appropriate *macro patches* which are designed somewhat in the spirit of the so called Powell-Sabin split for bivariate $C^1$-piecewise quadratics (cf. [5,6,2]). As one may expect, a definite choice of all the parameters involved in the proposed construction is hardly possible on the present level of generality. However, an attempt is made to bring possible constraints into focus that may arise from the underlying topology or from 'extreme' locations of data points.

The paper is organized as follows. In Section 2 we will fix some notation and terminology. In particular, we will discuss so called *transversal systems*, a geometric concept which is crucial for realizing the desired tangent plane continuity of the quadric patches. Section 3 will be devoted to the actual construction of the macro patches and to the discussion of their relevant properties.

## §2. Topology of Interpolating Surfaces and Transversal Systems

Throughout the following, $X = \{x^i : i = 1, \ldots, N\}$ will denote a fixed but arbitrary set of points $x^i = (x_1^i, x_2^i, x_3^i)$ in $\mathbb{R}^3$. Seeking an interpolating surface to these points only makes sense if, in addition, some information about the desired topology is given. For curves this can be done by fixing a polygon having the points as vertices or, in combinatorial terms, by prescribing an *ordering* of the points. Similarly, for surfaces, a topology can be described in terms of a collection $\mathcal{T}$ of triples $I \in \{1, \ldots, N\}^3$ with the following property: denoting for $I \in \mathcal{T}$ by $[I]$ the planar triangle spanned by the points $x^i$, $i \in I$, the intersection $[I] \cap [J]$, for any $I, J \in \mathcal{T}$, is empty or a vertex or a common edge of $[I]$ and $[J]$. Correspondingly, for $E \subset I$ with cardinality $\mid E \mid = 2$, the edge spanned by $x^i$, $i \in E$, is denoted by $[E]$. We will briefly refer to $\mathcal{T}$ as a triangulation of $X$. The corresponding piecewise linear interpolant to $X$ obtained by assembling the triangles $[I]$, $I \in \mathcal{T}$, will be denoted by $[\mathcal{T}]$. Any two triangles are called *adjacent* if they share an edge. An edge which belongs only to one triangle is called a *boundary* edge. It will sometimes be convenient to denote by $(I), (E), (A)$ the relative interior of the triangle $[I]$, of the edge $[E]$ or generally of the convex hull $[A]$ of a given set $A \in \mathbb{R}^3$, respectively. Similarly $\langle I \rangle, \langle E \rangle, \langle A \rangle$ will mean the respective affine hulls. Finally, a set $\mathcal{N} = \{n^i : i = 1, \ldots, N\}$ of unit vectors will stand for *normal directions* to be attained by the desired surface at the points in $X$. It is clear that $\mathcal{N}$ may not be completely arbitrary, but should be in some sense compatible with the given topology, and perhaps even with the particular location of data points. One could even think of $\mathcal{N}$ as being generated from $X$ and $\mathcal{T}$, for instance by forming (weighted) averages of normals to the planes $\langle I \rangle$ spanned by those triangles $[I]$ that share the respective vertex $x^i$. More concrete conditions on $\mathcal{N}$ will evolve from the subsequent discussion.

The first important step in the present approach is to construct for a given set $X$ a so called *transversal system* $\mathcal{L}$ which is defined as follows:

**Definition 2.1.** *A collection $\mathcal{L}$ of lines $L_I, I \in \mathcal{T}$, is called a transversal system if the following properties hold.*

*1) For each $I \in \mathcal{T}$, $L_I$ intersects $(I)$ in one point denoted by $y^I$.*

*2) For any two adjacent triangles $[I], [J]$ with common edge $[E]$, $E = I \cap J$, the lines $L_I$ and $L_J$ span a two-dimensional plane $P_E$ which intersects $(E)$ in some point $y^E$.*

It will be instructive to consider the following examples.

**Example 2.1.** *Suppose that for $X = \{x^0, \ldots, x^N\} \subset \mathbb{R}^3$ the set of triples $\mathcal{T} = \{(0, j, j+1) : j = 1, \ldots, N-1\}$ is a triangulation in the above sense. Choose planes $P_{(0,j)}$ which cut across $[(0,j)]$ in such a way that the line $L_j = P_{(0,j)} \cap P_{(0,j+1)}$, $j = 1, \ldots, N$ (counting mod N) intersects $(x^0, x^j, x^{j+1})$. The lines $L_j$, $j = 1, \ldots, N$ obviously form a transversal system.*

Applying such a strategy in a more general situation, eventually three planes would have to intersect in one line in order to satisfy requirement 2) in Definition 2.1. Roughly speaking, the smaller the number of edges relative to the number of triangles is, the less freedom one has in choosing the lines $L_I$. In this sense the following example is an extreme case as well.

**Example 2.2.** $\mathcal{T} = \{(i_1, i_2, i_3) : 1 \le i_1 < i_2 < i_3 \le 4\}$ *where $x^i$, $i = 1, \ldots, 4$, are affinely independent points; i.e., $\mathcal{T}$ represents a closed surface. Now fix any point $v$ in the open tetrahedron $(x^1, x^2, x^3, x^4)$ and let $y^I$ be any fixed point in the open face $(I)$, $I \in \mathcal{T}$, respectively. Setting $L_I = \langle v, y^I \rangle$ obviously yields a transversal system.*

Another explicit construction can be given for more general topologies under additional assumptions on the location of the points in $X$.

**Example 2.3.** *Suppose all the triangles $[I]$, $I \in \mathcal{T}$, are acute. Let $y^I \in (I)$ be the circumcenter of $[I]$, (i.e., the center of the circle containing $x^i, i \in I$). Let $L_I$ be the line that passes through $y^I$ and is perpendicular to $\langle I \rangle$. Noting that $y^I$ is the intersection of the orthogonal bisectors of the edges of $[I]$ one easily verifies that the $L_I$ form a transversal system.*

Finally, one should mention

**Example 2.4.** *Suppose the piecewise planar surface $[\mathcal{T}]$ is starlike, i.e., there exists a point $v$ in $\mathbb{R}^3$ such that any ray emanating from $v$ intersects $[\mathcal{T}]$ at most once. Now let $y^I$ be the incenter of $[I]$; i.e., the center of the largest circle contained in $[I]$ (cf. [6,2]). Then the lines $\langle v, y^I \rangle$ form a transversal system.*

Although the above examples cover many situations of practical interest, the construction of transversal systems for more general cases may require a combination of the above strategies. In fact, although the degrees of freedom involved in such a construction suggest that transversal systems always exist, there seems to be no obvious unified concrete recipe which works for any given situation.

## §3. Implicit Bézier Patches

The principal advantages of implicit surface representations in the context of solid modeling say, are often restricted by the difficulties of modeling surfaces of complex shape or topology. Raising the degree of the surface seems to cause, at least for the time being, prohibitive practical difficulties. The idea of building instead a surface by stitching several implicitly defined patches together was already mentioned in [7]. Here, an implicitly defined (algebraic) surface is understood to be the set of real zeros $\{x \in \mathbb{R}^3 : p(x) = 0\}$ of some polynomial $p \in \mathbb{R}[x_1, x_2, x_3]$. Any point $x$ in the zero set is called *regular* if $\nabla p(x) \neq 0$. Thus, for a portion of an implicit surface to have continuously varying tangent planes, it must contain only regular points. Confining such a zero set to some appropriate bounded set $B \subset \mathbb{R}^3$ creates what will be called in the following an *implicit patch*. Specifically, choosing $B$ to be a simplex has several advantages. Simplices are expected to offer most flexibility with regard to composing several patches. They also allow to use, as was suggested by Sederberg [7], the Bernstein-Bézier representation for the underlying polynomials which turns out to be, as in the parametric case, a convenient handle for shape control and design. So given any set $V$ of four affinely independent points $v^1, \ldots, v^4 \in \mathbb{R}^3$ generating the simplex $[V]$, and given any polynomial $p$, the set

$$S_{V,p} = \{x \in [V] : p(x) = 0\}$$

will be referred to as an *implicit patch* (which, at this point, may be empty). This setting also suggests the use of barycentric coordinates $\lambda = \lambda(x; V) = (\lambda_1, \ldots, \lambda_4)$ which are, as usual, defined by

$$x = \sum_{i=1}^{4} \lambda_i v^i, \quad \sum_{i=1}^{4} \lambda_i = 1.$$

To control such a patch, it is then convenient to use the Bernstein-Bézier representation

$$p(x) = \sum_{|\alpha|=k} c_\alpha B_\alpha(\lambda(x; V)). \tag{1}$$

Here for any $\alpha \in \mathbf{Z}_+^4$, standard multiindex notation is used; *i.e.*, $|\alpha| = \alpha_1 + \cdots + \alpha_4$, $\lambda^\alpha = \lambda_1^{\alpha_1} \cdots \lambda_4^{\alpha_4}$, $\alpha! = \alpha_1! \cdots \alpha_4!$ and the Bernstein basis functions are given by $B_\alpha(\lambda) := (|\alpha|!/\alpha!)\lambda^\alpha$. The coefficients $c_\alpha$ are usually referred to as *Bézier-* or *control-coefficients*. The fact that this latter terminology remains justified also for implicit representations is demonstrated by the following observations (cf. [7]). Associating the control coefficients in the usual

way with the grid points $v_\alpha = (1/|\alpha|) \sum_{j=1}^{4} \alpha_j v^j$, well-known properties of
the Bernstein representation immediately imply that for $W \subseteq V$ (cf. [1,3,4])

$$[W] \subset S_{V,p} \quad \text{iff} \quad c_\alpha = 0, \; v_\alpha \in [W]. \tag{2}$$

Specifically, one has for $|\alpha| = k$

$$v^j \in S_{V,p} \quad \text{iff} \quad c_{ke^j} = 0, \tag{3}$$

where $e_i^j = \delta_{ij}$, as well as

$$[v^i, v^j] \cap S_{V,p} \neq \emptyset \quad \text{iff} \quad c_{ke^i} c_{ke^j} \leq 0. \tag{4}$$

Noting that for any $x \in S_{V,p}$ the normal direction of $S_{V,p}$ at $x$ is given by $\nabla p(x)$ and recalling from [3] the formula

$$(v^i - v^j, \nabla p(x)) = k \sum_{|\alpha|=k-1} (c_{\alpha+e^i} - c_{\alpha+e^j}) B_\alpha(\lambda(x; V)), \tag{5}$$

where $(u, v) = \sum_{i=1}^{3} u_i v_i$ denotes the standard inner product on $\mathbb{R}^3$, one may summarize the above observations as follows.

**Proposition 3.1.** *Let* $S_{V,p} = \{x \in [V] : p(x) = 0\}$ *where* $p(x)$ *has the representation (1), and suppose that* $v^i \in S_{V,p}$, *i.e.,* $c_{ke^i} = 0$. *Then the vertex* $v^i$ *is a regular point and the tangent plane of* $S_{V,p}$ *at* $v^i$ *is given by*

$$T(v^i, n) = \{x \in \mathbb{R}^3 : (x - v^i, n) = 0\}, \tag{6}$$

*for some* $n \in \mathbb{R}^3 \backslash \{0\}$, *if and only if for some constant* $a \in \mathbb{R} \backslash \{0\}$

$$c_{(k-1)e^i+e^j} = a(n, v^j - v^i), \quad j = 1, \ldots, 4, \; j \neq i. \tag{7}$$

## §4. Macro Patches for Piecewise Quadric Surfaces

Suppose that the two sets $V = \{v^1, \ldots, v^4\}$, $V' = \{v^1, \ldots, v^3, v^5\}$ generate adjacent simplices in $\mathbb{R}^3$ with common face $[W]$, where $W = \{v^1, v^2, v^3\}$. The two patches $S_{V,p}$ and $S_{V',p'}$ are said to meet with $C^k$-continuity across $[W]$ if $S_{V,p} \cap [W] = S_{V',p'} \cap [W]$ is regular and if for some $C^k$-functions $r, q$ which do not vanish on $C := S_{V,p} \cap S_{V',p'}$ all partial derivatives of $rp$ and $qp'$ up to order $k$ agree on $C$. Specifically, choosing $r = q \equiv 1$ and recalling again well-known facts about Bernstein polynomials (cf. [3,4,1]), this implies that any two regular patches $S_{V,p}, S_{V',p'}$ form a tangent plane continuous composite patch $S := S_{V,p} \cup S_{V',p'}$ in $[V] \cup [V']$ if

$$c_\alpha = c'_\alpha, \quad \text{supp } \alpha \subseteq W, \tag{8}$$

and

$$c'_{\alpha+e^4} = \sum_{j=1}^{4} \lambda_j(v^5, V)c_{\alpha+e^j}, \ \ \text{supp}\, \alpha \subseteq W, \tag{9}$$

where $\text{supp}\, \alpha = \{v^j \in V : \alpha_j \neq 0\}$ and $\{c_\alpha\}_{|\alpha|=k}$, $\{c'_\alpha\}_{|\alpha|=k}$ are the Bézier nets of $p$ and $p'$, respectively.

According to the above definition, these conditions are of course not necessary, and the fact that they essentially lead to a construction of a scalar valued $C^1$-piecewise polynomial on a three dimensional triangulation in order to achieve a tangent plane continuous piecewise implicit surface may, at first glance, look discouraging. However, one should keep in mind that the three dimensional triangulation has to envelope only the surface to be built; *i.e.*, it essentially has to 'wrap' only around the piecewise linear interpolant $[\mathcal{T}]$ of the data $X$ which, roughly speaking, helps to maintain some bivariate features for the actual construction. In fact, to keep the construction local, one can form implicit *macro patches* which are somewhat reminiscent of bivariate so called split triangular methods for Hermite interpolation. The ideas apply in principle to implicit patches of any degree. For the reasons given in the introduction, the following discussion will focus, however, on piecewise *quadric* surfaces.

Adhering to the notation introduced in Section 2, $X, \mathcal{T}, \mathcal{N}$ as well as a transversal system $\mathcal{L}$ are assumed to be given.

To this end, defining as in (6) $T_i = \{x \in \mathbb{R}^3 : (x - x^i, n^i) = 0\}$, each line $L_I \in \mathcal{L}$ is assumed to intersect the planes $T_i$, $i \in I$. Choose two points $z^I, w^I$ on $L_I$ such that

$$\{T_i \cap L_I, y^I\} \subset [z^I, w^I], \ \ i \in I, \tag{10}$$

where (cf. 1) in Definition 2.1) $y^I$ is the intersection of $(I)$ and $L_I$. So $z^I$ and $w^I$ will, in general, be located on opposite sides of $\langle I \rangle$, but either one may agree with $y^I$. For any fixed $(i, j, k) \in \mathcal{T}$ and any adjacent $J$, let $P_{I \cap J}$ denote again the plane spanned by the lines $L_I, L_J \in \mathcal{L}$, and let $\{y^{I \cap J}\} = P_{I \cap J} \cap (I \cap J)$. Specifically, one can then write

$$y^{(i,j)} = \mu_1^1 x^i + \mu_2^1 x^j, \ y^{(j,k)} = \mu_1^2 x^j + \mu_2^2 x^k, \ y^{(k,i)} = \mu_1^3 x^k + \mu_2^3 x^i, \tag{11}$$

where $\mu_1^m + \mu_2^m = 1$, $\mu_l^m > 0$, $l = 1, 2$, $m = 1, 2, 3$.

As a first step, for each of the following six tetrahedra (see Figure 1)

$$[V_{I,1}] = [x^i, y^{(i,j)}, y^I, z^I], \ \ \ [V_{I,2}] = [x^j, y^{(i,j)}, y^I, z^I], \tag{12}$$

$$[V_{I,3}] = [x^j, y^{(j,k)}, y^I, z^I], \ \ \ [V_{I,4}] = [x^k, y^{(j,k)}, y^I, z^I],$$

$$[V_{I,5}] = [x^k, y^{(k,i)}, y^I, z^I], \ \ \ [V_{I,6}] = [x^i, y^{(k,i)}, y^I, z^I]$$

a quadratic polynomial

$$p_{I,j}(x) = \sum_{|\alpha|=2} d_\alpha^j B_\alpha(\lambda(x, V_{I,j})) \tag{13}$$

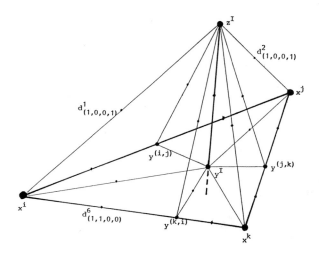

**Figure 1.** $\Delta_I$ formed by the tetrahedra $[V_{I,m}]$.

will be constructed in such a way that the function $p_I$ defined by

$$p_I \big|_{[V_{I,j}]} = p_{I,j}$$

has continuous first order derivatives on

$$\Delta_I := \bigcup_{j=1}^{6} [V_{I,j}].$$

Setting

$$d^j_{(2,0,0,0)} = 0, \quad j = 1, \ldots, 6, \tag{14}$$

yields, in view of (3),

$$p_I(x^l) = 0, \quad l \in I. \tag{15}$$

Moreover, choosing

$$d^1_{(1,1,0,0)} = \frac{1}{2}(n^i, y^{(i,j)} - x^i), \quad d^2_{(1,1,0,0)} = \frac{1}{2}(n^j, y^{(i,j)} - x^j),$$

$$d^3_{(1,1,0,0)} = \frac{1}{2}(n^j, y^{(j,k)} - x^j), \quad d^4_{(1,1,0,0)} = \frac{1}{2}(n^k, y^{(j,k)} - x^k), \tag{16}$$

$$d^5_{(1,1,0,0)} = \frac{1}{2}(n^k, y^{(k,i)} - x^k), \quad d^6_{(1,1,0,0)} = \frac{1}{2}(n^i, y^{(k,i)} - x^i),$$

and

$$d_{(1,0,1,0)}^m = \frac{1}{2}(n^i, y^I - x^i), \quad d_{(1,0,0,1)}^m = \frac{1}{2}(n^i, z^I - x^i), \ m = 1, 6,$$

$$d_{(1,0,1,0)}^m = \frac{1}{2}(n^j, y^I - x^j), \quad d_{(1,0,0,1)}^m = \frac{1}{2}(n^j, z^I - x^j), \ m = 2, 3, \qquad (17)$$

$$d_{(1,0,1,0)}^m = \frac{1}{2}(n^k, y^I - x^k), \quad d_{(1,0,0,1)}^m = \frac{1}{2}(n^k, z^I - x^k), \ m = 4, 5.$$

Proposition 3.1 guarantees that

$$\nabla p_I(x^m) \ = \ n^m, \quad m \in I. \qquad (18)$$

To assure that the piecewise quadratic $p_I$ is actually $C^1$ on $\Delta_I$, it suffices to satisfy (9). To this end, recall (11) and set

$$d_{(0,1,0,1)}^1 \ = \ d_{(0,1,0,1)}^2 \ = \ \mu_1^1 d_{(1,0,0,1)}^1 + \mu_2^1 d_{(1,0,0,1)}^2,$$

$$d_{(0,1,0,1)}^3 \ = \ d_{(0,1,0,1)}^4 \ = \ \mu_1^2 d_{(1,0,0,1)}^3 + \mu_2^2 d_{(1,0,0,1)}^4,$$

$$d_{(0,1,0,1)}^5 \ = \ d_{(0,1,0,1)}^6 \ = \ \mu_1^3 d_{(1,0,0,1)}^5 + \mu_2^3 d_{(1,0,0,1)}^5,$$

$$d_{(0,1,1,0)}^1 \ = \ d_{(0,1,1,0)}^2 \ = \ \mu_1^1 d_{(1,0,1,0)}^1 + \mu_2^1 d_{(1,0,1,0)}^2,$$

$$d_{(0,1,1,0)}^3 \ = \ d_{(0,1,1,0)}^4 \ = \ \mu_1^2 d_{(1,0,1,0)}^3 + \mu_2^2 d_{(1,0,1,0)}^4, \qquad (19)$$

$$d_{(0,1,1,0)}^5 \ = \ d_{(0,1,1,0)}^6 \ = \ \mu_1^3 d_{(1,0,1,0)}^5 + \mu_2^3 d_{(1,0,1,0)}^6,$$

$$d_{(0,2,0,0)}^1 \ = \ d_{(0,2,0,0)}^2 \ = \ \mu_1^1 d_{(1,1,0,0)}^1 + \mu_2^1 d_{(1,1,0,0)}^2,$$

$$d_{(0,2,0,0)}^3 \ = \ d_{(0,2,0,0)}^4 \ = \ \mu_1^2 d_{(1,1,0,0)}^3 + \mu_2^2 d_{(1,1,0,0)}^4,$$

$$d_{(0,2,0,0)}^5 \ = \ d_{(0,2,0,0)}^6 \ = \ \mu_1^3 d_{(1,1,0,0)}^5 + \mu_2^3 d_{(1,1,0,0)}^6.$$

Finally, by assumption $y^I$ can be written as

$$y^I \ = \ \sum_{m \in I} \gamma_m x^m, \ \sum_{m \in I} \gamma_m = 1, \ \gamma_m > 0, \ m \in I. \qquad (20)$$

This leads to

$$d_{(0,0,2,0)}^m = \gamma_i d_{(1,0,1,0)}^1 + \gamma_j d_{(1,0,1,0)}^3 + \gamma_k d_{(1,0,1,0)}^5, \ m = 1, \ldots, 6,$$

$$d_{(0,0,1,1)}^m = \gamma_i d_{(1,0,0,1)}^1 + \gamma_j d_{(1,0,0,1)}^3 + \gamma_k d_{(1,0,0,1)}^5, \ m = 1, \ldots, 6. \qquad (21)$$

So far all but the coefficients $d_{(0,0,0,2)}^m$, $m = 1, \ldots, 6$, corresponding to the vertex $z^I$ have been determined. One easily concludes from (19), (20), (21) that the coplanarity conditions (9) are satisfied for any choice of $d_I = d_{(0,0,0,2)}^m$, $m = 1, \ldots, 6$, so that for any value of $d_I$ the piecewise quadratic $p_I$ will be $C^1$ on $\Delta_I$. The parameter $d_I$ may therefore be used as a *shape parameter.* In fact, large absolute values of $d_I$ will push the zero set of $p_I$ and hence the implicit patch away from the vertex $z^I$.

Choosing $y^I$ as a common vertex of the tetrahedra $[V_{I,m}]$ resulted in simple expressions for the Bézier coefficients $d_\alpha^m$ and simplified the verification of the coplanarity conditions (9). However, in order to enclose appropriate portions of the zero set of $p_I$ by tetrahedra, one generally will have to replace the vertex $y^I$ in the sets $V_{I,m}$ (cf. (12)) by $w^I$. Calling these sets $W_{I,m}$, the construction assures that those faces of the $[V_{I,m}]$ having $[z^I, y^I]$ as a common edge are contained in corresponding faces of $[W_{I,m}]$ having now $[z^I, w^I]$ as a common edge. Consequently, $p_I$ still forms a $C^1$-piecewise quadratic on the larger polytope

$$\Sigma_I \ := \ \bigcup_{m=1}^{6} [W_{I,m}].$$

The new Bézier nets $\{c_\alpha^{I,m}\}_{|\alpha|=2}$ of the the quadratics $p_{I,m}$ relative to the tetrahedra $[W_{I,m}]$ could be either determined directly from the conditions (8) and (9) or by *subdivision*, i.e by applying de Casteljau's algorithm to the Bézier nets $\{d_\alpha^m\}_{|\alpha|=2}$ with respect to the new vertex $w^I$ (cf. [1,3]). Since $c_{(0,0,0,2)}^{I,m} = d_{(0,0,0,2)}^{I,m}$, $m = 1, \ldots, 6$, the above observations may be summarized as:

**Proposition 4.1.** *The piecewise quadratic function $p_I$ constructed above has for every value of $c_I = c_{(0,0,0,2)}^{I,m}$, $m = 1, \ldots, 6$, continuous first order derivatives on $\Sigma_I$ and satisfies the interpolation conditions*

$$p_I(x^m) \ = \ 0, \quad \nabla p_I(x^m) \ = \ n^m, \quad m \in I.$$

*Hence the corresponding implicit patch*

$$S_I \ := \ \{x \in \Sigma_I : \ p_I(x) = 0\}$$

*interpolates the positional data $x^r$ with unit normals $n^r$, $r \in I$.*

In order to be able to extend the $\Sigma_I$'s to an appropriate three-dimensional triangulation that envelopes $[\mathcal{T}]$, one has to assume in the following that for any two adjacent $I, J \in \mathcal{T}$, the polytopes $\Sigma_I, \Sigma_J$ satisfy

$$\Sigma_I \cap \Sigma_J \ = \ [I \cap J]. \tag{22}$$

Suppose again that $I = (i, j, k)$ and $J = (i, j, l)$ are adjacent with common edge $[E]$, where $E = (i, j)$. If for instance the points $x^l$, $x^k$ are relatively close to each other, some of the points $z^I, z^J, w^I, w^J$ may have to be chosen near $[I], [J]$, respectively, to make sure that (22) holds; *i.e.*, that the interiors of $\Sigma_I$ and $\Sigma_J$ do not intersect each other. Note that requiring both (22) as well as (10) may then impose constraints on $\mathcal{N}$. An appropriate choice of $\mathcal{N}$ is given by (31) below.

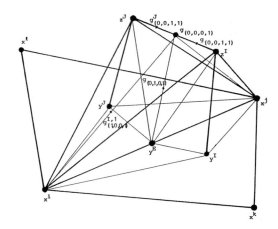

**Figure 2.** Filling gaps.

In view of (22), the patches $S_I, I \in \mathcal{T}$, cannot yet be expected to form a connected surface. To describe how to complete the surface, assume the points $z^I, z^J$ and $w^I, w^J$ are located relative to $[I], [J]$ as indicated in Figure 2.

If $\Sigma_I, \Sigma_J$ and

$$[\Gamma_{E,z}] := [x^i, x^j, z^I, z^J]$$

are essentially disjoint, this "gap" will be filled next by a patch $S_{E,z}$.

To this end, for $u := (z^I + z^J)/2$ let

$$G_{K,1} := \{x^i, y^E, z^K, u\}, \; G_{K,2} := \{x^j, y^E, z^K, u\}, \; K = I, J. \tag{23}$$

The objective is to construct for each set a polynomial

$$q_{K,m}(x) := \sum_{|\alpha|=2} g_\alpha^{K,m} B_\alpha(\lambda(x; G_{k,m})), \; K \in \{I, J\}, \quad m = 1, 2,$$

such that the patch

$$S_{E,z} := \cup\{S_{G_{K,m}, q_{K,m}} : K \in \{I, J\}, \quad m = 1, 2\}$$

joins $S_I$ and $S_J$ with tangent plane continuity. To this end, it is again more convenient to work with the Bézier nets $\{d_\alpha^{K,m}\}_{|\alpha|=2}$, $K \in \{I, J\}$, $m = 1, 2$, of the polynomials $p_{I,m}$, $p_{J,m}$ with respect to the sets $V_{I,m}$, $V_{J,m}$ (cf. (12)). Assume also that the $V_{I,m}, V_{J,m}$ are numbered so that for instance $V_{I,1} \cap V_{J,1} = \{x^i, y^E\}$. Setting

$$g_\alpha^{K,m} := d_\alpha^{K,m}, \; \text{supp}\,\alpha \subseteq G_{K,m} \cap V_{K,m}, \tag{24}$$

for $K = I, J, m = 1, 2$, ensures, in view of (8), that $S_{E,z}$ joins $S_I$ and $S_J$ continuously.

Next recall that by Definition 2.1 of a transversal system, the points $y^E, y^I, z^I, y^J, z^J, u$ (cf. Figure 2) are all located on the plane $P_E$ spanned by $L_I$ and $L_J$. Hence, one can write for $K = I, J$

$$u = \xi_1^K y^E + \xi_2^K y^K + \xi_3^K z^K, \quad \sum_{m=1}^{3} \xi_m^K = 1.$$

Moreover, by construction the two sets

$$\{(u+x^r)/2, (z^I+x^r)/2, (y^I+x^r)/2, (y^E+x^r)/2, (z^J+x^r)/2, (y^J+x^r)/2\}, \; r \in E,$$

span planes which are parallel to $P_E$. Hence, setting

$$g_{(1,0,0,1)}^{K,m} := \xi_1^K d_{(1,1,0,0)}^{K,m} + \xi_2^K d_{(1,0,1,0)}^{K,m} + \xi_3^K d_{(1,0,0,1)}^{K,m}, \; K = I, J, \, m = 1, 2, \quad (25)$$

one readily infers from (9) and (18) or Proposition 4.1 that

$$g_{(1,0,0,1)}^{I,m} = g_{(1,0,0,1)}^{J,m}, \quad m = 1, 2, \tag{26}$$

because by (25) one has

$$\nabla q_{I,1}(x^i) = \nabla q_{J,1}(x^i) = n^i, \quad \nabla q_{I,2}(x^j) = \nabla q_{J,2}(x^j) = n^j.$$

So it remains to determine the coefficients $g_{(0,1,0,1)}^{K,m}, g_{(0,0,1,1)}^{K,m}$ and $g_{(0,0,0,2)}^{K,m}$ for $K = I, J, m = 1, 2$ (see Figure 2). To this end, observe first

$$\begin{aligned}
\xi_1^I d_{(0,2,0,0)}^{I,1} + \xi_2^I d_{(0,1,1,0)}^{I,1} + &\xi_3^I d_{(0,1,0,1)}^{I,1} \\
&= \xi_1^J d_{(0,2,0,0)}^{J,1} \xi_2^J d_{(0,1,1,0)}^{J,1} + \xi_3^J d_{(0,1,0,1)}^{J,1}.
\end{aligned} \tag{27}$$

In fact, property 2) in Definition 2.1 of a transversal system ensures that the coefficients $\mu_I^m$ appearing in (11) are the same for $I$ and $J$. Hence, inserting (19) and reordering terms shows that

$$\begin{aligned}
\xi_1^K d_{(0,2,0,0)}^{K,1} + &\xi_2^K d_{(0,1,1,0)}^{K,1} + \xi_3^K d_{(0,1,0,1)}^{K,1} = \\
&\sum_{m=1}^{2} \mu_m^1 (\xi_1^K d_{(1,1,0,0)}^{K,m} + \xi_2^K d_{(1,0,1,0)}^{K,m} + \xi_3^K d_{(1,0,0,1)}^{K,m})
\end{aligned}$$

holds for $K = I, J$. The assertion (27) now follows from (25) and (26). Hence, setting for $K = I, J, m = 1, 2$

$$g_{(0,1,0,1)} = g_{(0,1,0,1)}^{K,m} := \xi_1^I d_{(0,2,0,0)}^{I,1} + \xi_2^I d_{(0,1,1,0)}^{I,1} + \xi_3^I d_{(0,1,0,1)}^{I,1} \tag{28}$$

as well as (see Figure 2)

$$g_{(0,0,1,1)}^{K,m} = g_{(0,0,1,1)}^{K} := \xi_1^K d_{(0,1,0,1)}^{K,1} + \xi_2^K d_{(0,0,1,1)}^{K,1} + \xi_3^K d_{(0,0,0,2)}^{K,1},$$
$$g_{(0,0,0,2)}^{K,m} = g_{(0,0,0,2)} := 1/2(g_{(0,0,1,1)}^I + g_{(0,0,1,1)}^J),$$

$$(29)$$

all the coefficients have been consistently defined. Moreover, elementary geometric considerations immediately confirm that the coplanarity conditions (9) hold. Hence the corresponding quadratics join with continuous first order derivatives.

Likewise, when the intersection of

$$[\Gamma_{E,w}] := [x^i, x^j, w^I, w^J]$$

with $\Sigma_I$ and $\Sigma_J$ is essentially disjoint, a corresponding patch $S_{E,w}$ is constructed in the same way.

Let $\Sigma$ denote the union of the polytopes $\Sigma_I$, $I \in \mathcal{T}$, and $\Gamma_{E,z}$, $\Gamma_{E,w}$, where $E$ ranges over the edges of the elements in $\mathcal{T}$. Clearly, one has $[\mathcal{T}] \subset \Sigma$. The above construction provides a $C^1$-piecewise quadratic $p$ on $\Sigma$ which satisfies

$$p(x^i) = 0, \ \nabla p(x^i) = n^i, \ i = 1, \dots, N.$$

Hence the piecewise quadric surface

$$S_X := \{x \in \Sigma : p(x) = 0\}$$

satisfies

i) $X \subset S_X$;

ii) The unit normal of $S_X$ at $x^i$ is $n^i$, $i = 1, \dots, N$.

Denoting by $\Delta_z$ and $\Delta_w$ the piecewise linear surfaces interpolating the points $x^i$, $i = 1, \dots, N$, $z^I$, $I \in \mathcal{T}$ and $w^I$, $I \in \mathcal{T}$, respectively, $S_X$ will indeed form a surface with the prescribed topology given by $\mathcal{T}$ if

$$S_X \cap \Delta_z = S_X \cap \Delta_w = X. \tag{30}$$

To this end, condition (10) insures that for each $i$ the tangent plane $T_i$ is locally contained in $\Sigma$; *i.e.*, there exists a neighborhood $U_i$ of $x^i$ such that

$$U_i \cap T_i \subset U_i \cap \Sigma. \tag{31}$$

Thus a judicious choice of the free parameters $c_I, I \in \mathcal{T}$, should allow to satisfy (30).

As mentioned above, the requirements (10) and (22) may interfere for certain choices of $\mathcal{N}$ and $\mathcal{L}$. $\mathcal{L}$ essentially should admit the construction of $\Sigma$ in such a way that in the sense of (31), near each $x^i$, $\Sigma$ contains *locally* some plane containing $x^i$. The corresponding normals would then allow to meet the conditions (10) and (22) which were assumed for the above construction. Finally, it should be mentioned that the flexibility in varying the normals in $\mathcal{N}$ as well as the parameters $c_I$, $I \in \mathcal{T}$, can be used to avoid the occurrence of singular points in the patches constructed above to ensure global tangent plane continuity.

The question arises whether the free parameters $d_I, I \in \mathcal{T}$, could be exploited for the purpose of *shape preservation*. For instance, convexity preserving interpolation will be discussed in a forthcoming paper.

Finally, it should be noted that a natural setting for piecewise third degree surfaces could be based on 'lifting' the Clough-Tocher split for bivariate cubics in a similar fashion as described above for the Powell-Sabin split.

## References

1. de Boor, C., B-form basics, in *Geometric Modeling: Algorithms and New Trends*, G. E. Farin (ed.), SIAM Publications, Philadelphia, 1987, 131–148.

2. Cendes, Z. J. and S. H. Wong, $C^1$ quadratic interpolation over arbitrary point sets, IEEE Computer Graphics and Applications (1987), 8–16.

3. Dahmen, W., Bernstein-Bézier representation of polynomial surfaces, Course Notes "Extension of B-spline curve algorithms to surfaces", ACM SIGGRAPH '86, 1986.

4. Farin, G., Bézier polynomials over triangles and the construction of piecewise $C^r$-polynomials, TR/91, Brunel University, Uxbridge, Middlesex, UK, 1980.

5. Powell, M. J. D. and M. A. Sabin, Piecewise quadratic approximations on triangles, ACM Trans. Math. Software **3** (1977), 316–325.

6. Sablonnière, P., Error bounds for Hermite interpolation by quadratic splines on an $\alpha$-triangulation, IMA J. Numer. Anal. **7** (1987), 495–508.

7. Sederberg, T.W., Piecewise algebraic surface patches, Comput. Aided Geom. Design **2** (1985), 53–59.

Wolfgang Dahmen
Fachbereich Mathematik
Freie Universität Berlin
Arnimallee 2-6
1000 Berlin 33
W. GERMANY

Supported in part by NATO Grant RG DJ 639/84

# Inserting New Knots Into Beta-Spline Curves

P. Dierckx and B. Tytgat

**Abstract.** The algorithm of Boehm is a well known recursive method for updating the B-spline representation of a spline curve when a single knot is added. We show how this algorithm can be adapted for cubic $\beta$-spline curves and discuss a number of applications in CAGD. Notably, we consider multiple insertion for a fixed parameter value, and obtain a fast and stable recursive scheme for computing the corresponding point on the curve, together with the tangent vector. The geometric interpretation of the presented insertion algorithm gives a good insight into the influence of the different shape parameters of the $\beta$-spline curve.

## §1. Introduction

In [2] Boehm describes a very simple algorithm for adding a knot to a B-spline curve. In the case of cubic spline curves, which are commonly used, the problem can be stated as follows. Let

$$\vec{s}(t) = \sum_{i=0}^{k-1} \vec{c}_i N_i(t), \qquad t_1 \leq t \leq t_{k-2} \tag{1.1}$$

be a cubic spline curve defined on the knot set $T = (t_j)_{-2}^{k+1}$ $(k \geq 4)$ where $N_i(t)$ denotes the normalized cubic B-spline defined on the knots $t_j$, $j = i-2, i-1, ..., i+2$. If we consider the extended knot set $\tilde{T} = (\tilde{t}_j)_{-2}^{k+2}$ with

$$
\begin{aligned}
\tilde{t}_j &= t_j, & j &= -2, ..., l \\
\tilde{t}_{l+1} &= z, & t_l &< z < t_{l+1}, \quad 1 \leq l \leq k-3 \\
\tilde{t}_{j+1} &= t_j, & j &= l+1, ..., k+1,
\end{aligned}
\tag{1.2}
$$

then obviously $\vec{s}(t)$ also has a representation

Mathematical Methods in Computer Aided Geometric Design
Tom Lyche and Larry L. Schumaker (eds.), pp. 195–205.

$$\vec{s}(t) = \sum_{i=0}^{k} \vec{d_i} \tilde{N}_i(t), \qquad \tilde{t}_1 \le t \le \tilde{t}_{k-1}, \tag{1.3}$$

with $\tilde{N}_i(t)$ the normalized cubic B-spline defined on the knots $\tilde{t}_j$, $j = i - 2, ..., i + 2$. The problem is then to determine the coefficients (control points) $\vec{d_i}$ from $\vec{c_i}$. Using properties of divided differences, Boehm proved that

$$N_i(t) = \begin{cases} \tilde{N}_i(t), & 0 \le i \le l - 2 \\ \frac{\tilde{t}_{l+1} - \tilde{t}_{i-2}}{\tilde{t}_{i+2} - \tilde{t}_{i-2}} \tilde{N}_i(t) + \frac{\tilde{t}_{i+3} - \tilde{t}_{l+1}}{\tilde{t}_{i+3} - \tilde{t}_{i-1}} \tilde{N}_{i+1}(t), & l - 1 \le i \le l + 2 \\ \tilde{N}_{i+1}(t), & l + 3 \le i \le k - 1 \end{cases} \tag{1.4}$$

and it immediately follows that

$$\vec{d_i} = r_i \vec{c_i} + (1 - r_i) \vec{c}_{i-1}. \tag{1.5$i$}$$

with

$$r_i = \begin{cases} 1, & 0 \le i \le l - 1 \\ \frac{\tilde{t}_{l+1} - \tilde{t}_{i-2}}{\tilde{t}_{i+2} - \tilde{t}_{i-2}}, & l \le i \le l + 2 \\ 0, & l + 3 \le i \le k. \end{cases} \tag{1.5$ii$}$$

A number of authors [4,5,8,16] have considered an extension of the problem by allowing the addition of more than one knot at a time. The algorithm, known as the Oslo algorithm, was first derived in Cohen, Lyche and Riesenfeld [8] using discrete B-splines and divided differences. In this paper we will generalize the algorithm of Boehm in a different direction. The curve (1.1) is $C^2$ continuous. However, in order for the design curve to appear visually smooth, it is sufficient for $\vec{s}(t)$ to satisfy the weaker $G^2$ continuity condition, *i.e.*, continuity of the curve, the unit tangent vector and the curvature vector. By introducing additional shape parameters at each knot, Barsky [1] and later Goodman [12] in a more general context, also derived a local support representation (1.1) for such curves with the so called $\beta$-splines replacing the B-splines. In Section 2 we will briefly recall the basic properties of these $\beta$-splines. Unlike the B-splines, these functions can no longer be expressed in terms of divided differences. Nevertheless, we will prove in Section 3 that they also satisfy a recurrence relation similar to (1.4). In Section 4 we will then discuss a number of applications in CAGD.

For a geometric approach to the problem of inserting knots into curvature continuous curves, we refer to a further paper of Boehm [6]. Very recently, Joe [15] also generalized the concept of discrete B-splines using his alternative explicit formulae for $\beta$-splines.

## §2. Generalized Cubic Splines and $\beta$-splines [12,13]

In this section we recall the basic properties of $\beta$-splines as described by Goodman [12]. We restrict ourself to the case of cubic splines. Take $k \geq 4$ and a strictly increasing sequence of knots $T = (t_j)_{-2}^{k+1}$. Also take sequences $B = (\beta_1^*(j))_{-1}^k$ and $\Gamma = (\beta_2^*(j))_{-1}^k$ with $\beta_1^*(j) > 0$ and $\beta_2^*(j) \geq 0$ called respectively the global bias and tension parameter at the knot $t_j$. Let $\zeta(T, B, \Gamma)$ denote the space of functions $f$ satisfying the following properties:

$$f(t) \equiv 0 \qquad \text{outside } (t_{-2}, t_{k+1}) \tag{2.1i}$$

$$f|_{[t_j, t_{j+1}]} \text{ is a cubic polynomial,} \qquad j = -2, -1, ..., k \tag{2.1ii}$$

$$f^{(\nu)}(t_{-2}^+) = f^{(\nu)}(t_{k+1}^-) = 0, \qquad \nu = 0, 1, 2 \tag{2.1iii}$$

$$f(t_j^+) = f(t_j^-), \qquad j = -1, ..., k \tag{2.1iv}$$

$$f'(t_j^+) = \beta_1^*(j) f'(t_j^-), \qquad j = -1, ..., k \tag{2.1v}$$

$$f''(t_j^+) = \beta_1^*(j)^2 f''(t_j^-) + \beta_2^*(j) f'(t_j^-), \qquad j = -1, ..., k. \tag{2.1vi}$$

Then every $f \in \zeta(T, B, \Gamma)$ has a unique representation in the form

$$f(t) = \sum_{i=0}^{k-1} C_i N_i(t), \tag{2.2}$$

with $N_i(t)$ the $\beta$-spline defined on the knots $t_j$, $j = i - 2, ..., i + 2$. These basis functions have local support; *i.e.*,

$$N_i(t) = 0 \quad \text{if } t \notin (t_{i-2}, t_{i+2}) \tag{2.3i}$$

$$N_i(t) > 0 \quad \text{if } t \in (t_{i-2}, t_{i+2}), \tag{2.3ii}$$

and, moreover, this support is minimal in the sense that if $f \in \zeta(T, B, \Gamma)$ is zero outside an interval $(t_l, t_{l+3})$, it will vanish everywhere. Finally, the $\beta$-splines also satisfy the normalizing condition

$$\sum_{i=0}^{k-1} N_i(t) = 1, \qquad t_1 \leq t \leq t_{k-2}. \tag{2.4}$$

If $\beta_1^*(j) = 1$, $\beta_2^*(j) = 0$ for $j = -1, ...k$, the $\beta$-splines reduce to the usual normalized cubic B-splines. If $t_j = j$ and $\beta_1^*(j) = \beta_1$, $\beta_2^*(j) = \beta_2$, they reduce to the $\beta$-splines as considered by Barsky [1]. Finally, we will also need an explicit expression for $N_i(t)$. If we define the local bias and tension parameters as

$$\beta_1(j) = \beta_1^*(j)\frac{t_{j+1} - t_j}{t_j - t_{j-1}}, \qquad j = -1, ..., k \qquad (2.5)$$

and

$$\beta_2(j) = \beta_2^*(j)\frac{(t_{j+1} - t_j)^2}{t_j - t_{j-1}}, \qquad j = -1, ..., k \qquad (2.6)$$

and introduce the notation

$$\alpha_j = \beta_1(j)^2 + \beta_1(j) + \frac{1}{2}\beta_2(j), \qquad j = -1, ..., k \qquad (2.7)$$

$$\beta_j = \beta_1(j), \qquad j = -1, ..., k \qquad (2.8)$$

$$\delta_j = \alpha_j(\beta_{j+1}^3 + \beta_{j+1}^2) + \alpha_{j+1}(\beta_j + 1) + \alpha_j\alpha_{j+1}, \qquad j = -1, ..., k-1 \quad (2.9)$$

the formula is [13,14]

$$N_i(t) = \delta_{i-1}^{-1}\alpha_i u^3, \qquad u = \frac{(t - t_{i-2})}{t_{i-1} - t_{i-2}}, \quad t_{i-2} \le t \le t_{i-1} \qquad (2.10\mathrm{i})$$

$$\begin{aligned} N_i(t) = {}&\delta_{i-1}^{-1}\alpha_i + 3\delta_{i-1}^{-1}\alpha_i\beta_{i-1}u + 3\delta_{i-1}^{-1}\alpha_i(\alpha_{i-1} - \beta_{i-1})u^2 \\ &+ \delta_{i-1}^{-1}(\alpha_i\beta_{i-1} + \alpha_{i-1}\beta_i^2 - 2\alpha_{i-1}\alpha_i)u^3 - \delta_i^{-1}\alpha_{i+1}u^3, \\ u = {}&\frac{(t - t_{i-1})}{t_i - t_{i-1}}, \ t_{i-1} \le t \le t_i \end{aligned} \qquad (2.10\mathrm{ii})$$

$$\begin{aligned} N_i(t) = {}&\delta_i^{-1}\alpha_i\beta_{i+1}^3 + 3\delta_i^{-1}\alpha_i\beta_{i+1}^2 u + 3\delta_i^{-1}\alpha_i(\alpha_{i+1} - \beta_{i+1}^2)u^2 \\ &+ \delta_i^{-1}(\alpha_{i+1}\beta_i + \alpha_i\beta_{i+1}^2 - 2\alpha_i\alpha_{i+1})u^3 - \delta_{i-1}^{-1}\alpha_{i-1}\beta_i^3 u^3, \\ u = {}&\frac{t_{i+1} - t}{t_{i+1} - t_i}, \ t_i \le t \le t_{i+1} \end{aligned} \qquad (2.10\mathrm{iii})$$

$$N_i(t) = \delta_i^{-1}\alpha_i\beta_{i+1}^3 u^3, \qquad u = \frac{t_{i+2} - t}{t_{i+2} - t_{i+1}}, \qquad t_{i+1} \le t \le t_{i+2}. \qquad (2.10\mathrm{iv})$$

## §3. Knot Insertion

In this section we will prove in a constructive way that the $\beta$-splines also satisfy a recursive relation similar to (1.4). If we consider the extended knot set $\tilde{T}$ in (1.2), and denote all corresponding parameters (knots, shape parameters, etc.) by tilde, it follows that every function $f(t)$ belonging to $\zeta(T, B, \Gamma)$ will also belong to $\zeta(\tilde{T}, \tilde{B}, \tilde{\Gamma})$ if the new global shape parameters are chosen as follows:

$$\tilde{\beta}_1^*(j) = \beta_1^*(j), \qquad j = -1, ..., l \tag{3.1i}$$

$$\tilde{\beta}_1^*(l+1) = 1 \tag{3.1ii}$$

$$\tilde{\beta}_1^*(j+1) = \beta_1^*(j), \qquad j = l+1, ..., k \tag{3.1iii}$$

and

$$\tilde{\beta}_2^*(j) = \beta_2^*(j), \qquad j = -1, ..., l \tag{3.2i}$$

$$\tilde{\beta}_2^*(l+1) = 0 \tag{3.2ii}$$

$$\tilde{\beta}_2^*(j+1) = \beta_2^*(j), \qquad j = l+1, ..., k. \tag{3.2iii}$$

Indeed, the function $f(t)$ and all its derivatives are continuous at $z = \tilde{t}_{l+1}$. The $\beta$-splines $\tilde{N}_i(t)$ on the extended knot set $\tilde{T}$ have the same explicit expression (2.10), provided we put tildes where possible. Moreover, if we introduce the notation

$$\mu = (z - t_l)/(t_{l+1} - t_l) \tag{3.3i}$$
$$\nu = 1 - \mu, \tag{3.3ii}$$

it is easily checked that the new $\tilde{\beta}_j$ and $\tilde{\alpha}_j$ are related to the old $\beta_j$ and $\alpha_j$ in the following way:

$$\tilde{\beta}_j = \beta_j, \qquad j = -1, ..., l-1 \tag{3.4i}$$
$$\tilde{\beta}_l = \mu\beta_l \tag{3.4ii}$$
$$\tilde{\beta}_{l+1} = \nu\mu^{-1} \tag{3.4iii}$$
$$\tilde{\beta}_{l+2} = \nu^{-1}\beta_{l+1} \tag{3.4iv}$$
$$\tilde{\beta}_{j+1} = \beta_j, \qquad j = l+2, ..., k \tag{3.4v}$$

and

$$\tilde{\alpha}_j = \alpha_j, \qquad j = -1, ..., l-1 \tag{3.5i}$$
$$\tilde{\alpha}_l = \mu^2\alpha_l + \mu\nu\beta_l \tag{3.5ii}$$
$$\tilde{\alpha}_{l+1} = \nu\mu^{-2} \tag{3.5iii}$$
$$\tilde{\alpha}_{l+2} = \nu^{-1}\alpha_{l+1} + \mu\nu^{-2}\beta_{l+1}^2 \tag{3.5iv}$$
$$\tilde{\alpha}_{j+1} = \alpha_j, \qquad j = l+2, ..., k. \tag{3.5v}$$

The $\tilde{\delta}_j$ parameters are also related to the old $\beta_j$, $\alpha_j$ and $\delta_j$ values, but it is cheaper to use (2.9) (in terms of the new $\tilde{\beta}_j$ and $\tilde{\alpha}_j$) for calculating the non-trivial $\tilde{\delta}_j$, i.e., for $j = l - 1, l, l + 1, l + 2$. We can then prove

**Theorem 1.**

$$N_i(t) = \tilde{N}_i(t), \qquad i = 0, 1, ..., l - 2 \tag{3.6i}$$

$$N_{l-1}(t) = \tilde{N}_{l-1}(t) + \left(1 - \frac{\alpha_l \tilde{\delta}_{l-1}}{\tilde{\alpha}_l \delta_{l-1}}\right) \tilde{N}_l(t) \tag{3.6ii}$$

$$N_l(t) = \left(\frac{\alpha_l \tilde{\delta}_{l-1}}{\tilde{\alpha}_l \delta_{l-1}}\right) \tilde{N}_l(t) + \left(1 - \frac{\alpha_{l+1} \tilde{\delta}_l}{\tilde{\alpha}_{l+1} \delta_l}\right) \tilde{N}_{l+1}(t) \tag{3.6iii}$$

$$N_{l+1}(t) = \left(\frac{\alpha_{l+1} \tilde{\delta}_l}{\tilde{\alpha}_{l+1} \delta_l}\right) \tilde{N}_{l+1}(t) + \left(\frac{\alpha_{l+1} \tilde{\delta}_{l+2}}{\tilde{\alpha}_{l+2} \, \delta_{l+1}}\right) \tilde{N}_{l+2}(t) \tag{3.6iv}$$

$$N_{l+2}(t) = \left(1 - \frac{\alpha_{l+1} \tilde{\delta}_{l+2}}{\tilde{\alpha}_{l+2} \delta_{l+1}}\right) \tilde{N}_{l+2}(t) + \tilde{N}_{l+3}(t) \tag{3.6v}$$

$$N_i(t) = \tilde{N}_{i+1}(t), \qquad i = l + 3, ..., k - 1. \tag{3.6vi}$$

**Proof:**

(A) [Expressions (3.6i) and (3.6vi)]. The $\beta$-splines on the left and right hand side are defined on the same knots with the same corresponding shape parameters.

(B) [Expression (3.6ii)]. We prove that there exists a constant $a$ such that $N_{l-1}(t) = \tilde{N}_{l-1}(t) + a\tilde{N}_l(t)$ on the whole interval $[\tilde{t}_{-2}, \tilde{t}_{k+2}]$.

(B1) $[t \leq \tilde{t}_{l-3} = t_{l-3}$ or $t \geq \tilde{t}_{l+2} = t_{l+1}]$. From (2.3i) it follows that $N_{l-1}(t) = \tilde{N}_{l-1}(t) = \tilde{N}_l(t) = 0$

(B2) $[t_{l-3} = \tilde{t}_{l-3} \leq t \leq \tilde{t}_{l-2} = t_{l-2}]$. From (2.3i) it follows that $\tilde{N}_l(t) = 0$ and from (2.10i), (3.4) and (3.5) we find that

$$N_{l-1}(t) = \frac{\alpha_{l-1}}{\delta_{l-2}} \left(\frac{t - t_{l-3}}{t_{l-2} - t_{l-3}}\right)^3 = \frac{\tilde{\alpha}_{l-1}}{\tilde{\delta}_{l-2}} \left(\frac{t - \tilde{t}_{l-3}}{\tilde{t}_{l-2} - \tilde{t}_{l-3}}\right)^3 = \tilde{N}_{l-1}(t)$$

(B3) $[z = \tilde{t}_{l+1} \leq t \leq \tilde{t}_{l+2} = t_{l+1}]$. From (2.3i) it follows that $\tilde{N}_{l-1}(t) = 0$ and from (2.10iv), (3.3), (3.4) and (3.5) we find that

$$N_{l-1}(t) = \frac{\alpha_{l-1}}{\delta_{l-1}} \beta_l^3 \left(\frac{t_{l+1} - t}{t_{l+1} - t_l}\right)^3 = \frac{\alpha_{l-1}}{\delta_{l-1}} \beta_l^3 \nu^3 \left(\frac{\tilde{t}_{l+2} - t}{\tilde{t}_{l+2} - \tilde{t}_{l+1}}\right)^3$$

$$= \frac{\alpha_{l-1}}{\delta_{l-1}} \frac{\tilde{\delta}_l}{\tilde{\alpha}_l} \frac{\beta_l^3 \nu^3}{\tilde{\beta}_{l+1}^3} \tilde{N}_l(t) = a\tilde{N}_l(t)$$

with

$$a = \frac{\alpha_{l-1}\tilde{\delta}_l}{\delta_{l-1}\tilde{\alpha}_l}\tilde{\beta}_l^3 = 1 - \frac{\alpha_l\tilde{\delta}_{l-1}}{\delta_{l-1}\tilde{\alpha}_l}$$

The last equality can be proved by a simple (but tedious) verification. A nicer proof using property (2.4) is given in [10].

(B4) $[t_{l-2} = \tilde{t}_{l-2} \leq t \leq \tilde{t}_{l+1} = z]$ From (B1), (B2) and (B3) we already know that the function $f(t) = N_{l-1}(t) - \tilde{N}_{l-1}(t) - a\tilde{N}_l(t)$, which belongs to $\zeta(\tilde{T}, \tilde{B}, \tilde{\Gamma})$ is zero outside $(\tilde{t}_{l-2}, \tilde{t}_{l+1})$. From the minimal support property (see Section 2) it follows then that $f(t) = 0$ everywhere.

(C) [Expressions (3.6iii), (3.6iv) and (3.6v)]. These are proved in a very similar way. For more details we refer to [10]. ■

## §4. Applications in CAGD

### 4.1. The New Control Vertices

From (3.6) it immediately follows that if we have a $\beta$-spline curve of the form (1.1) and want to represent it in the form (1.3), the new control points $\vec{d}_i$ will again be determined from the old control points $\vec{c}_i$ by formula (1.5i) but now with

$$r_i = 1, \qquad i = 0, 1, ..., l - 1 \qquad (4.1\text{i})$$

$$r_l = (\alpha_l\tilde{\delta}_{l-1})/(\tilde{\alpha}_l\delta_{l-1}) \qquad (4.1\text{ii})$$

$$r_{l+1} = (\alpha_{l+1}\tilde{\delta}_l)/(\tilde{\alpha}_{l+1}\delta_l) \qquad (4.1\text{iii})$$

$$r_{l+2} = 1 - (\alpha_{l+1}\tilde{\delta}_{l+2})/(\tilde{\alpha}_{l+2}\delta_{l+1}) \qquad (4.1\text{iv})$$

$$r_i = 0, \qquad i = l + 3, ..., k. \qquad (4.1\text{v})$$

As for the B-spline curves, we can show that all $r_i \in [0, 1]$. Using (2.9), (3.4i), (3.4ii), (3.5i), (3.5ii) and (3.3ii), we find that

$$r_l(\mu) = \frac{\alpha_l}{\delta_{l-1}}\left(1 + \alpha_{l-1} + \beta_{l-1} + \frac{\alpha_{l-1}\beta_l^2\mu(1 + \mu\beta_l)}{\beta_l(1 - \mu) + \mu\alpha_l}\right). \qquad (4.2)$$

It is now easily verified that $r_l'(\mu) > 0$. So $r_l(\mu)$ is strictly increasing on $[0,1]$ while

$$\lim_{\mu \to 0+} r_l(\mu) = \frac{\alpha_l}{\delta_{l-1}}(1 + \alpha_{l-1} + \beta_{l-1}) > 0 \qquad (4.3\text{i})$$

$$= \frac{\delta_{l-1} - \alpha_{l-1}\beta_l^2(1 + \beta_l)}{\delta_{l-1}} < 1 \qquad (4.3\text{ii})$$

and

$$\lim_{\mu \to 1-} r_l(\mu) = 1. \qquad (4.4)$$

In a similar way we can also prove that $r_{l+1}$ and $r_{l+2} \in [0,1]$, (see [10]). For this, we use the following explicit expressions:

$$r_{l+1}(\mu) = \frac{\alpha_{l+1}}{\delta_l}(1 + \beta_l + \alpha_l \mu), \tag{4.5}$$

and

$$r_{l+2}(\nu) = 1 - \frac{\alpha_{l+1}}{\delta_{l+1}}\left(\beta_{l+2}^2 + \beta_{l+2}^3 + \alpha_{l+2} + \frac{\alpha_{l+2}\nu(\nu + \beta_{l+1})}{\nu\alpha_{l+1} + (1 - \nu)\beta_{l+1}^2}\right). \tag{4.6}$$

Thus, we may conclude that the new control points $\vec{d}_i$ are obtained by taking convex linear combinations of the old control points $\vec{c}_i$. It is therefore a stable procedure. The process of knot insertion may be repeated. If the refined partition is dense in $[t_1, t_{k-2}]$, the resulting sequence of control polygons will converge to the $\beta$-spline curve there as follows from (2.3) and (2.4) (see e.g. [9] in a more general context).

### 4.2. Multiple Insertion

It is a well known result for cubic B-spline curves (see e.g. [3]) that if we add a triple knot at $t = z$, the new control polygon will be tangent to the curve at the point $\vec{s}(z)$. We prove that this property is still valid for cubic $\beta$-spline curves. For simplicity, we first consider the case that $z = t_l$ and we add two more knots at this point. The parameters of the curve after the second addition will be denoted by $\hat{\ }$, those after the first insertion by $\tilde{\ }$ as before.

**Theorem 2.** *Let*

$$\vec{s}(t) = \sum_{i=0}^{k-1} \vec{c}_i N_i(t) = \sum_{i=0}^{k} \vec{d}_i \tilde{N}_i(t) = \sum_{i=0}^{k+1} \vec{e}_i \hat{N}_i(t).$$

*Then*

$$\vec{s}(t_l) = \vec{e}_{l+1} \tag{4.7}$$

*and*

$$D_t \vec{s}(t_{l+}) = \frac{3\beta_l}{(1 + \beta_l)(t_{l+1} - t_l)}(\vec{d}_{l+1} - \vec{d}_l). \tag{4.8}$$

**Proof:** It immediately follows from (1.5i), (4.1), (4.3i), (4.5) and (4.6) that if we add a knot at $z = t_l$,

$$\vec{d}_i = \vec{c}_i, \qquad i = 0, 1, ..., l-1 \tag{4.9i}$$

$$\vec{d}_l = \delta_{l-1}^{-1}\alpha_l(1 + \alpha_{l-1} + \beta_{l-1})(\vec{c}_l - \vec{c}_{l-1}) + \vec{c}_{l-1} \tag{4.9ii}$$

$$\vec{d}_{l+1} = \delta_l^{-1}\alpha_{l+1}(1 + \beta_l)(\vec{c}_{l+1} - \vec{c}_l) + \vec{c}_l \tag{4.9iii}$$

$$\vec{d}_i = \vec{c}_{i-1}, \qquad i = l+2, ..., k. \tag{4.9iv}$$

In a similar way, if at the second step we add a knot at $z = \tilde{t}_{l+1}$, we find that

$$\vec{e}_i = \vec{d}_i, \qquad i = 0, 1, ..., l \tag{4.10i}$$

$$\vec{e}_{l+1} = \tilde{\delta}_l^{-1} \tilde{\alpha}_{l+1}(1 + \tilde{\alpha}_l + \tilde{\beta}_l)(\vec{d}_{l+1} - \vec{d}_l) + \vec{d}_l \tag{4.10ii}$$

$$\vec{e}_{l+2} = \tilde{\delta}_{l+1}^{-1} \tilde{\alpha}_{l+2}(1 + \tilde{\beta}_{l+1})(\vec{d}_{l+2} - \vec{d}_{l+1}) + \vec{d}_{l+1} \tag{4.10iii}$$

$$\vec{e}_i = \vec{d}_{i-1}, \qquad i = l+3, ..., k+1. \tag{4.10iv}$$

Now, from (3.4), (3.5) and (2.9) we get for $\mu \to 0$ that $\tilde{\beta}_l \sim \mu\beta_l$, $\tilde{\beta}_{l+1} \sim \mu^{-1}$, $\tilde{\beta}_{l+2} \sim \beta_{l+1}$, $\tilde{\alpha}_l \sim \mu\beta_l$, $\tilde{\alpha}_{l+1} \sim \mu^{-2}$, $\tilde{\alpha}_{l+2} \sim \alpha_{l+1}$, $\tilde{\delta}_l \sim \mu^{-2}(1 + \beta_l)$, $\tilde{\delta}_{l+1} \sim \mu^{-2}(\alpha_{l+1} + \beta_{l+1}^2 + \beta_{l+1}^3)$, and (4.10) simply becomes

$$\vec{e}_i = \vec{d}_i, \qquad i = 0, 1, ..., l \tag{4.11i}$$

$$\vec{e}_{l+1} = (1 + \beta_l)^{-1}(\vec{d}_{l+1} - \vec{d}_l) + \vec{d}_l \tag{4.11ii}$$

$$\vec{e}_i = \vec{d}_{i-1}, \qquad i = l+2, ..., k+1. \tag{4.11iii}$$

Thus, from (4.11ii), (4.9ii), (4.9iii) and using (2.9) we find that

$$\vec{e}_{l+1} = \delta_{l-1}^{-1} \alpha_{l-1} \beta_l^3 \vec{c}_{l-1} + (1 - \delta_l^{-1} \alpha_{l+1} - \delta_{l-1}^{-1} \alpha_{l-1} \beta_l^3) \vec{c}_l + \delta_l^{-1} \alpha_{l+1} \vec{c}_{l+1}. \tag{4.12}$$

By using (2.10iv), (2.10iii) for $u = 1$, (2.10ii) for $u = 0$, and again by using (2.9) it is straightforward then to verify (4.7). Expression (4.8) can then be proved in a very similar way [10]. ∎

In [11] we show that $\vec{d}_l$, $\vec{e}_{l+1}$ and $\vec{d}_{l+1}$ are Bézier points associated with the $\beta$-spline curve. Now, if $z$ doesn't coincide with a knot, we first add a knot at this point by using the formulae of Section 4.1, and then we can again proceed as described above. Summarizing, if we have a $\beta$-spline curve

$$\vec{s}(t) = \sum_{i=0}^{k-1} \vec{b}_i N_i(t), \qquad t_1 \le t \le t_{k-2} \tag{4.13}$$

and want to find $\vec{s}(z)$ and $\vec{s}'(z)$, $t_{l-1} < z < t_l$, $2 \le l \le k-2$, we can set up the following triangular scheme (see [10] for an illustration)

$$\begin{array}{cccc} \vec{b}_{l-2} & & & \\ \vec{b}_{l-1} & \vec{c}_{l-1} & & \\ \vec{b}_l & \vec{c}_l & \vec{d}_l & \\ \vec{b}_{l+1} & \vec{c}_{l+1} & \vec{d}_{l+1} & \vec{e}_{l+1}. \end{array}$$

The control points $\vec{c}_i$ are found as

$$\vec{c}_i = r_i \vec{b}_i + (1 - r_i)\vec{b}_{i-1}, \qquad i = l-1, l, l+1 \tag{4.14}$$

with the $r_i$ computed by (4.1ii), (4.1iii) and (4.1iv) replacing $l$ by $l - 1$. The points $\vec{d}_l$, $\vec{d}_{l+1}$ and $\vec{e}_{l+1}$ are computed by using (4.9ii), (4.9iii) and (4.11ii) putting tildes where possible. It also implies that on the way we have to compute $\tilde{\beta}_i$ and $\tilde{\alpha}_i$, $i = l-1, l, l+1$ using (3.4) and (3.5) with $l$ replaced by $l - 1$, and must also compute $\tilde{\delta}_i$, $i = l-2, l-1, l, l+1$ using (2.9). All computations are numerically stable.

### 4.3. Influence of the Shape Parameters

In [13,14], Goodman and Unsworth discuss the effect on the design curve of changing the shape parameters. By an interpretation of the results of Section 4.2, we can come to similar conclusions in a very straightforward manner. Let us first consider the effect of increasing one tension parameter $\beta_2(l)$ while keeping the control vertices and the other parameters fixed. Let $q = \beta_2(l)/2 \to \infty$. Then from (2.7) and (2.9) it follows that $\alpha_l \sim q$, $\delta_{l-1} \sim q(1 + \alpha_{l-1} + \beta_{l-1})$ and $\delta_l \sim q(\alpha_{l+1} + \beta_{l+1}^2 + \beta_{l+1}^3)$. We then see from (4.9ii), (4.9iii) and (4.11ii) that $\vec{d}_l \to \vec{c}_l$, $\vec{d}_{l+1} \to \vec{c}_l$ and therefore also that $\vec{s}(t_l) = \vec{e}_{l+1} \to \vec{c}_l$. Thus, the effect of increasing $\beta_2(l)$ is to pull part of the design curve towards the control vertex $\vec{c}_l$. Next, suppose we increase both $\beta_2(l)$ and $\beta_2(l+1)$. We show that the effect is to pull a section of the design curve towards the line segment joining $\vec{c}_l$ and $\vec{c}_{l+1}$. Let $q = \beta_2(l)/2 = \beta_2(l+1)/2 \to \infty$. Then again from (2.7) and (2.9) it follows that $\alpha_l \sim q$, $\alpha_{l+1} \sim q$, $\delta_{l-1} \sim q(1 + \alpha_{l-1} + \beta_{l-1})$, $\delta_l \sim q^2$ and $\delta_{l+1} \sim q(\alpha_{l+2} + \beta_{l+2}^2 + \beta_{l+3}^3)$. Using (4.9ii), (4.9iii) and (4.11ii) we find that $\vec{s}(t_l) \to \vec{c}_l$ and using the same formulae for $l = l+1$, that $\vec{s}(t_{l+1}) \to \vec{c}_{l+1}$. Moreover, if we add a knot at the point $z$, with $t_l < z < t_{l+1}$ it follows from (4.2), (4.5) and (4.6) that $r_l(\mu) \to 1$, $r_{l+1}(\mu) \to \mu$ and $r_{l+2}(\nu) \to 0$. So, our triangular scheme for determining $\vec{s}(z)$ (see Section 4.2) will now become

$$
\begin{array}{llll}
\vec{c}_{l-1} & & & \\
\vec{c}_l & & \vec{c}_l & \\
\vec{c}_{l+1} & \mu\vec{c}_{l+1} + (1-\mu)\vec{c}_l & \vec{d}_{l+1} & \\
\vec{c}_{l+2} & \vec{c}_{l+1} & \vec{d}_{l+2} & \vec{s}(z)
\end{array}
$$

and we may conclude indeed that $\vec{s}(z)$ will tend to a point on the line segment joining $\vec{c}_l$ and $\vec{c}_{l+1}$. In a similar way, we can also consider the effect of changing just a bias parameter $\beta_l = \beta_1(l)$. It follows that if $\beta_l \to \infty$, the curve segment between $\vec{s}(t_{l-1})$ and $\vec{s}(t_l)$ will tend to the line segment joining $\sigma\vec{c}_{l-2} + (1-\sigma)\vec{c}_{l-1}$ and $\vec{c}_{l-1}$ with $\sigma = \delta_{l-2}^{-1}\beta_{l-1}^3\alpha_{l-2} = N_{l-2}(t_l)$. If $\beta_l \to 0$ and $\beta_2(l) = 0$, the curve segment between $\vec{s}(t_l)$ and $\vec{s}(t_{l+1})$ will tend to the line segment joining $\vec{c}_{l+1}$ and $(1-\tau)\vec{c}_{l+1} + \tau\vec{c}_{l+2}$ with $\tau = \delta_{l+1}^{-1}\alpha_{l+2} = N_{l+2}(t_{l+1})$.

### References

1. Barsky, B. A. , The Beta-spline : A local representation based on shape parameters and fundamental geometric measures, Ph.D. dissertation, University of Utah, 1981.

2. Boehm, W. , Inserting new knots into B-spline curves, Comput. Aided Design **12** (1980), 199–201.

3. Boehm, W., G. Farin, and J. Kahmann, A survey of curve and surface methods in CAGD, Comput. Aided Geom. Design **1** (1984), 1–60.

4. Boehm, W. and H. Prautzsch, On the efficiency of knot insertion algorithms, Comput. Aided Geom. Design **2** (1985), 141–143.

5. Boehm, W. and H. Prautzsch, The insertion algorithm, Comput. Aided Design **17** (1985), 58–59.

6. Boehm, W., Curvature continuous curves and surfaces, Comput. Aided Geom. Design **2** (1985), 313–323.

7. Cohen, E., A new local basis for designing with tensioned splines, ACM Trans. Graphics **6** (1987), 81–122.

8. Cohen, E., T. Lyche, and R. F. Riesenfeld, Discrete B-splines and subdivision techniques in computer aided geometric design and computer graphics, Computer Graphics and Image Processing **14** (1980), 87–111.

9. Dahmen, W., Subdivision algorithms - Recent results, some extensions and further developments, in *Algorithms for Approximation*, J. C. Mason and M. G. Cox (eds.), Clarendon Press, Oxford, 1987, 21–49.

10. Dierckx, P. and B. Tytgat, Inserting new knots into $\beta$-spline curves, Report TW108, Dept. of Computer Science, K. U. Leuven, 1988.

11. Dierckx, P. and B. Tytgat, Generating the Bézier points of a $\beta$-spline curve, Report TW 109, Dept. of Computer Science, K. U. Leuven, 1988.

12. Goodman, T. N. T. , Properties of $\beta$-splines, J. Approx. Theory **44** (1985), 132–153.

13. Goodman, T. N. T. and K. Unsworth, Generation of $\beta$-splines curves using a Recurrence Relation, in *Fundamental algorithms for Computer Graphics*, NATO ASI Series, Series F, **17** (1985), 325–353.

14. Goodman, T. N. T. and K. Unsworth, Manipulating shape and producing geometric continuity in $\beta$-spline curves, IEEE Comp. Graph. Appl. **6** (1986), 50–56.

15. Joe, B., Discrete Beta-splines, SIGGRAPH '87 Conference Proceedings, Computer Graphics **21** (1987), 137–144.

16. Lyche, T. and K. Mørken, Making the Oslo algorithm more efficient, SIAM J. Numer. Anal. **23** (1986), 663–675.

P. Dierckx and B. Tytgat
Department of Computer Science
K. U. Leuven
Celestijnenlaan 200A, B-3030 Leuven
BELGIUM

EMAIL: pol@ kulcs.bitnet, pol@ kulcs.uucp

# Recursive Subdivision and Iteration in Intersections and Related Problems

Tor Dokken, Vibeke Skytt, and Anne-Marie Ytrehus

**Abstract.** The intersection algorithms discussed here use recursive subdivision to decide the number of solutions, while iterative techniques are used to calculate the geometry of the solutions within a user specified tolerance. The framework developed supports a wide class of problems covering all intersection variants of curves and surfaces, closest point calculations and extremal point calculations. The algorithms aim to meet the requirements for correct topology and high accuracy originating from integrated sculptured surfaces and volume modellers.

## §1. Introduction

As soon as the Oslo Algorithm was available to us in 1979, we started implementing intersection algorithms based on recursive subdivision. In the initial attempts, we combined iteration and recursive subdivision techniques, trying to make efficient algorithms. However, at this stage, the use of iteration inside the recursive subdivision did not give us any improved performance. The reason for this was the accuracy requirements and the small address space of the computers available to us. Until 1986, we followed a strategy for intersection algorithms only utilizing recursive subdivision; this gave us a unique opportunity to understand the nature of recursive subdivision and its limitations. Although the geometry is represented mathematically by nonuniform B-splines, any other parametric representation of the geometry can be used, provided the interrogation requirements described in Section 4 are fulfilled.

When the recursive subdivision algorithm for surface/surface intersection was extensively tested in 1986, we found that the functionality was good, but that the performance needed improvements in order to satisfy industrial demands. Knowing that iterative algorithms are fast, we measured the performance of the algorithms, and detected that the introduction of iteration in

Mathematical Methods in Computer Aided Geometric Design
Tom Lyche and Larry L. Schumaker (eds.), pp. 207–214.
Copyright © 1989 by Academic Press, Boston.
ISBN 0-12-460515-X.

surface/curve intersection increased the performance significantly. In a similar way, tracing out intersection curves by marching is much faster than generating the same number of intersection points by recursive subdivision. Thus, we now combine recursive subdivision to detect all intersection curves with marching to produce the geometry within the required tolerances. We have been able to match the increasing industrial demand for high accuracy intersection algorithms and correct handling of the intersection curve topology close to and at singularities. Our aim is to handle relative tolerances of the magnitude $10^{-11}$.

During the years of research we made a number of observations that we now use for improving the performance of the intersection algorithms:

- Recursion depth is often unpredictable in recursive subdivision
- Subdivision borders going through singularities often create simple subproblems
- Subdivision lines going through "near" singularities create simple subproblems
- The distribution of intersection points resulting from subdivision borders should not be clustered along the curve
- Optimal solutions for subalgorithms often slow down the total performance of the algorithm.

The outline of the paper is as follows. In Section 2 we will describe the nature of iteration and recursive subdivision, focusing on the strong and weak properties of the two approaches. Then, in Section 3 we will give a general layout of the intersection strategy we follow. Section 4 will go into subalgorithms that are critical to the total performance, and focus on possible improved strategies for these problems. We conclude the paper with some remarks on future work. More information on the general approach to surface/surface intersection can be found in [3].

## §2. Comparison of Iteration and Recursive Subdivision

In algorithms based on recursive subdivision, the problem is viewed from a global viewpoint to determine if it has a simple solution. If not, the problem is divided into subproblems and these are solved separately. From the solutions of the subproblems we construct the solution of the initial problem. The subproblems are each viewed as an intital problem and solved in the same recursive way. It is assumed that all problems can be subdivided recursively into problems with simple solutions.

In iterative techniques a local view is taken, utilizing information at the present location, and extrapolating this information to determine the next step in the process. In most cases the step is successful, but there is no guarantee of success or that a seemingly successful step is really successful.

The properties of iteration and recursion used for the intersection type of algorithms are summarized in Table 1. The quality of the algorithms implemented depend to a large extent on internal strategies in the algorithms; thus it is possible to implement the intersection algorithms in such a way that their quality deviates from Table 1.

|  | Iteration | Recursion |
|---|---|---|
| **Finding all solutions** | No | Yes |
| **High performance** | Yes | No |
| **Accuracy** | Yes | Yes |
| **Sensitive to erroneous data** | No | Yes |

**Table 1.** Classification of the properties of iteration and recursion when used in intersection algorithms.

Since the recursive subdivision strategy applies a "divide and conquer" technique, we can always continue the subdivision until the problem can be classified as simple within a user specified tolerance. Thus, we can find all solutions within a user specified tolerance. In iterative techniques, we don't have any strategy for deciding if more solutions exist. However, by combining the recursive and iterative technique, we can get the quality of recursion combined with the speed of iteration. The reason why iterative techniques are faster than the recursive techniques is that it is much cheaper to extract the local data necessary in iteration than the global properties necessary in the recursive subdivision.

There is, however, another computational penalty in the recursive techniques. Since conclusions to a large extent are based on the results of subproblems, errors in a subproblem solution will affect the conclusions based on them. For example, a simple problem can be misclassified as a complex problem. Because the behaviour of the problem along boundaries is inherited by subproblems, the algorithm will spread this erroneous conclusion to those subproblems. In the worst case, this inheritance is stopped by the fact that we reach the computer resolution, and thus isolate the problem. The result of the algorithm will be correct; however, the time spent to isolate the problem will be extensive. If double precision is used, the number of subdivisions to reach the computer resolution in a parameter direction will typically be 50. If this type of subdivision down to the computer resolution is necessary in a surface/surface intersection we will have to apply the subdivision in four parameter directions. The space needed for just taking care of the current branch in the subdivision tree for fourth order Bézier patches will be 9600 double precision numbers for storage of the Bézier vertices. The formula to use for this calculation is: 2 patches × point dimension × polynomial order × polynomial order × 100 levels.

## §3. General Layout of the Intersection Strategy

The intersection strategy is tailored to cover algorithms of the following types:

- Object/Object intersection, where the objects are parametric curves or parametric surfaces
- Finding zeros of one or more parallel functions in one or two parameter directions. By putting a curve or surface into the implicit description of a straight line, plane, sphere, cylinder, conic surface or torus surface, etc., such functions can be made
- Extremal value calculations, where the absolute extremal of a parametric function in one or two parameter variables is to be found. Extremal point calculations and some closest point calculations can be reformulated in this way.

A vast number of problems can be reformulated to fit into these two classes of problems. For example, a closest point problem can be reformulated as finding the minimum of the distance function. A silhouette line calculation can be reformulated as finding an intersection curve ([2]).

The intersection strategy is a two stage process:

**1.** Find the topology of the solution of the problem. The result of this process is either points or intervals in the parameter range of a curve. Correspondingly, we have points, curves or areas in the parameter plane of a surface.

**2.** Generate geometry of each topological element in the solution. Based on the dimensionality of the intersection elements of the first stage, different actions are taken:

- Points: Evaluate the curve or surface at the given parameter value.
- Curves: Trace of the geometry of the curve within specified resolution.
- Areas : Pick out the relevant part of the surface

The strategy for finding intersection topology assumes that the following questions can be answered:

- Is an intersection impossible?
- Is the problem simple?

In addition we must be able to:

- Subdivide the problem
- Find the behaviour of the problem along its boundaries
- Find the subdivision boundary between subproblems
- Combine results from subparts with behaviour along a problem boundary and subdivision boundary.

The layout of the recursive part of the intersection algorithms is as shown in Figure 1.

The actual contents of the different stages in the topology interrogation process depends on the dimensionality of the space the geometry objects lie in, compared with the number of parameter directions. In case the number of parameter directions is equal to the number of dimensions, we can expect

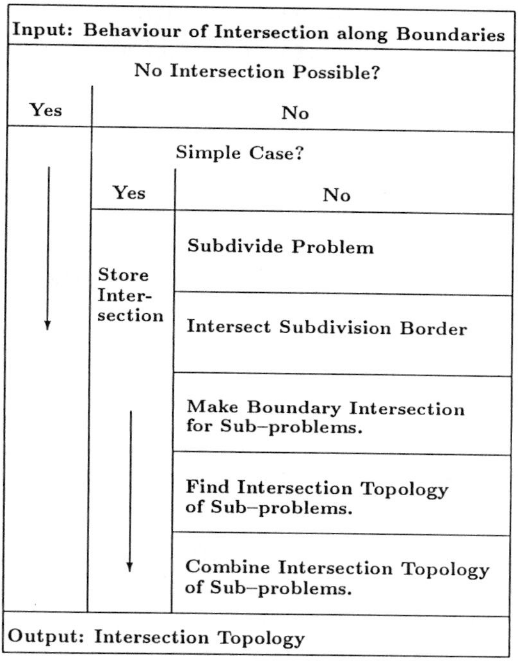

| Input: Behaviour of Intersection along Boundaries | | | |
|---|---|---|---|
| No Intersection Possible? | | | |
| Yes | No | | |
| ↓ | Simple Case? | | |
| | Yes | No | |
| | Store Inter-section | Subdivide Problem | |
| | | Intersect Subdivision Border | |
| | ↓ | Make Boundary Intersection for Sub–problems. | |
| | | Find Intersection Topology of Sub–problems. | |
| | ↓ | Combine Intersection Topology of Sub–problems. | |
| Output: Intersection Topology | | | |

**Figure 1.** The recursive part of the intersection algorithm.

points to be found; in such cases the test for the simple case will be oriented towards points. If the number of dimensions of the space the geometry lies in is one greater than the number of parameter directions, then curves are expected to be found. The test for simple cases will be oriented towards curves.

In a similar way we know that if the object being subdivided is a curve, the borders are points. In the case the object is a surface, the subdivision border is a curve. The calculation of the intersection of the subdivision border includes reducing the number of parameter directions by one, and thus the mathematical complexity is reduced; a simpler subproblem is solved than the initial problem. At the stage where we find the intersection topology of the subproblems, we retain the mathematical complexity of the problem, but reduce the size of the geometrical objects, thus reducing the geometric size of the problem. The other steps of the algorithm relate to data administration problems which depend on the dimensionality of the solution elements found. For points, we have to check for double storage, for curves we have to chain segments together and check for double storage, and for areas we have to check for double storage and chain areas together. An approach to surface/surface intersection only using recursive subdivision can be found in [5].

## §4. Critical Subalgorithms

A number of subalgorithms influence the performance of the algorithms significantly:

- Test for possibility of intersection
- Test for simple problem
- Where to position subdivision borders
- Step length generation for marching algorithms.

The main problem with these subalgorithms is that they are used to classify the properties of the relationships between geometric objects, not to classify the properties of one object. Thus, if the properties are calculateded independently of the other objects involved, then we will get a crude estimate. This will in many cases be satisfactory. However, it is important to notice that objects with a "simple" geometry can have a complex intersection with many separate intersection points and intersection curves. The quality of the result of these tests depends to a large extent on which level the geometrical relationships being investigated are taken into consideration. Thus if we make axes-parallel property boxes for the geometric elements, crude estimates will be made.

### TEST FOR POSSIBILITY OF INTERSECTIONS

The simplest way of testing for the possibility of intersections is to use traditional box–tests based on axes-parallel boxes. This is not optimal from the geometrical viewpoint, but it is a simple calculation. The penalty of choosing such a strategy is that in cases where geometry elements cannot be separated by axis parallel straight lines, planes, or hyperplanes, the subdivision depth will be large. Thus, more optimal strategies must be employed. By using boxes that are oriented optimally with respect to the geometry, more cases will be ruled out. Still, in cases where two geometric objects are close, e.g. B-spline approximations of two concentric circles with almost the same radius, a plane is not suitable for separating the geometries. In such cases a more sculptured separator of the geometries is needed; here the concept of parabolic hull can be a solution [4].

### TEST FOR THE SIMPLE CASE

A critical stage in the algorithms is to determine if a single intersection point or curve can be isolated. Strategies based on boxes for tangent vectors for curves, and boxes for normal vectors for surfaces is the first natural choice. Depending on the dimensionality of the problems and the geometries involved, a number of different simple case tests can be made. The following examples illustrate some of these tests:

- If two curves have tangent boxes that do not overlap, there is only one possible intersection point between the two curves.
- If the tangent box of a curve and the normal box of a surface point in the same direction (*i.e.*, all their possible scalar products all have the same sign and are different from zero), only one intersection point is possible.

   – If the normal boxes of two surfaces have no overlap, then only one intersection curve is possible.

Making tangent direction boxes for curves is straightforward. To make the
normal vector boxes for surfaces involve much more calculations. There is,
however, another possibility for analyzing the number of intersection branches
possible in a surface/surface intersection of parametric surfaces. In addition to
the space in which the surfaces lie, we have the parameter planes of the surfaces.
A complex intersection problem may, when projected into the parameter planes
of the surfaces, be identified as a simple problem. This can be done by finding
the tangent direction boxes of the projections into the parameter planes of
intersection curves. If the tangent direction boxes of the projection of the
intersection curves into the parameter plane have an opening of less than $\pi/2$
then a simple intersection problem has been found. The main advantage of
this approach is elimination of the dependencies of the coordinate system of
the intersection problem. However, the computation involved to make these
projections is expensive.

## WHERE TO POSITION SUBDIVISION BORDERS

During our implementation of recursive subdivision algorithms we have had
considerable experience concerning the positioning of subdivision borders.

   – If the subdivision results in a clustering of intersection points on an intersection curve, then numerical unstabilities can occur.

   – A subdivision going through a singularity often create simple subproblems.
A singularity is a point of intersection where the geometries being inter-
sected are parallel. For a curve/curve intersection this implies that the
curves have parallel tangents in the intersection point. For surface/surface
intersections this implies that the surfaces normals are parallel at the intersection point.

   – A subdivision going through a "near" singularity often creates simple subproblems. A "near" singularity is a point where the geometries are parallel
and the distance is "small".

   – If we only subdivide in the direction in a surface that is most curved, the
subpatches will in some cases be long and narrow, which can result in
many subdivisions and slow algorithms.

The subdivision strategy will influence the total performance of the intersection
algorithm. A strategy can be devised to give fast solutions in most cases, but
that will in a number of cases be extremely slow. Another strategy will give a
lower average performance, but have fewer cases that are slow. It seems that
any subdivision strategy should search for singularities or near singularities to
minimize the number of recursive levels necessary.

## STEP LENGTH GENERATION

The marching algorithms are based on the traditional Newton iteration. However, we have put emphasis on the interaction between the accuracy of the

Hermite interpolation approximating the true intersection curve, and the step length in the marching. By accurate control of tangent lengths, Hermite interpolation can approximate a curve with an error term of $O(h^6)$. One such technique is described in [1].

## §5. Conclusion

Although extensive work has been put into intersection algorithms so far, more work has to be done to handle the rising industrial demand for high quality intersection algorithms; especially the handling of regions with singularities in surface/surface intersection has to be addressed. When doing Boolean operations on volume objects, the surfaces of the objects will often be near parallel and almost coincident. Applying traditional intersection strategies will in many cases produce undesired results. A vast number of closed intersection loops are detected, while the result needed is an area in the parameter plane of the surface where the surfaces are closer than a specified geometric tolerance. Algorithms have to be devised that can trace the contour of such areas. These new algorithms will have to be combined with the existing surface/surface intersection algorithms to enable the handling of singularities, "near" singularities and intersection problems without singularities in one overall algorithm.

## References

1. de Boor, C., K. Höllig, and M. Sabin, High accuracy geometric Hermite Interpolation, Comput. Aided Geom. Design **4** (1987), 269–278.
2. Dokken, T., Finding intersections of B-spline represented geometries using recursive subdivision techniques, Comput. Aided Geom. Design **2** (1985), 189-195.
3. Barnhill, R. E., G. Farin, M. Jordan, and B. R. Piper, Surface/Surface intersection, Comput. Aided Geom. Design **4** (1987), 3–16.
4. Rajan, V. T., S. R. Klinkner, and R. T. Farouki, Root isolation and root approximation for polynomials in Bernstein form, preprint.
5. Thomas, S. W., Boolean operations on freeform surfaces, Ph.D. dissertation, University of Utah, 1984.

Tor Dokken, Vibeke Skytt and Anne-Marie Ytrehus
Center for Industrial Research
Box 124, Blindern, 0314 Oslo 3
NORWAY

EMAIL: dokken % si.uninett @ tor.nta.no

# Rational Curves and Surfaces

## Gerald Farin

**Abstract.** This article is both a survey and a tutorial on the theory and use of rational Bézier curves and rational B-spline curves, as well as the corresponding surface schemes.

## §1. Introduction

If one asks a person in the CAD/CAM industry or in graphics about the most promising curve or surface form, the current answer is invariably "NURBS", or non-uniform rational B-splines. In this paper, we shall describe the main features of this curve and surface representation; we will also discuss their main advantages as well as point to some drawbacks and unresolved problems.

It is assumed that the reader is fluent with the concepts of integral (*i.e.*, nonrational) Bézier and B-spline curves and surfaces, as described in Boehm *et al* [10] or Farin [19]. More material on rational curve and surface schemes is in Piegl [30], Piegl and Tiller [34], and Tiller [40].

## §2. Conics as Rational Quadratics

Conics are the simplest rational B-spline curves; in considering them we can study most properties of the general case. Many equivalent ways exist to define a conic section; for our purposes the following one is very useful:

*A conic section in $\mathbb{E}^2$ is the projection of a parabola in $\mathbb{E}^3$ into a plane.*

Here, $\mathbb{E}^2$ and $\mathbb{E}^3$ denote Euclidean two- and three-space, respectively. One typically chooses the center of the projection to be the origin **0** of a 3D cartesian coordinate system. The plane into which one projects is taken to be the plane $z = 1$. Since we will study planar curves in this section, we may think of this

Mathematical Methods in Computer Aided Geometric Design
Tom Lyche and Larry L. Schumaker (eds.), pp. 215–238.
Copyright © 1989 by Academic Press, Boston.
ISBN 0-12-460515-X.

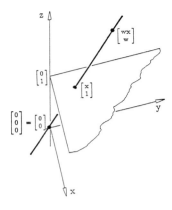

**Figure 1.** A projection into the plane $z = 1$.

plane as a copy of $I\!E^2$, thus identifying points $[x \ \ y]^T$ with $[x \ \ y \ \ 1]^T$. Our special projection is characterized by

$$\begin{bmatrix} x \\ y \\ z \end{bmatrix} \rightarrow \begin{bmatrix} x/z \\ y/z \\ 1 \end{bmatrix} \equiv \begin{bmatrix} x/z \\ y/z \end{bmatrix} \in I\!E^2.$$

Note that a point $[x \ \ y]^T$ is the projection of a whole family of points: every point on the straight line $[wx \ \ wy \ \ w]^T$ projects to $[x \ \ y]^T$. In the following, we will use the more convenient notation $[w\mathbf{x} \ \ w]^T$, where $\mathbf{x} \in I\!E^2$ for $[wx \ \ wy \ \ w]^T$. Sometimes the set of all points $[wx \ \ wy \ \ w]^T$ is called *homogeneous form* or *homogeneous coordinates* of $[x \ \ y]^T$. An illustration of this special projection is given in Figure 1.

We shall now show that every conic may be written as a rational quadratic Bézier curve.

**Theorem 2.1.** *Let* $\mathbf{c}(t) \in I\!E^2$ *be a point on a conic. Then there exist numbers* $w_0, w_1, w_2 \in I\!R$ *and points* $\mathbf{b}_0, \mathbf{b}_1, \mathbf{b}_2 \in I\!E^2$ *such that*

$$\mathbf{c}(t) = \frac{w_0\mathbf{b}_0 B_0^2(t) + w_1\mathbf{b}_1 B_1^2(t) + w_2\mathbf{b}_2 B_2^2(t)}{w_0 B_0^2(t) + w_1 B_1^2(t) + w_2 B_2^2(t)}, \tag{1}$$

*where the* $B_i^n(t) = \binom{n}{i} t^i (1-t)^{n-i}$ *are Bernstein polynomials.*

**Proof:** We may identify $\mathbf{c}(t) \in I\!E^2$ with $[\mathbf{c}(t) \ \ 1]^T \in I\!E^3$. This point is the projection of a point $[w(t)\mathbf{c}(t) \ \ w(t)]^T$ which lies on a 3D parabola. The third component $w(t)$ of this 3D point must be a quadratic function in $t$, and may be expressed in Bernstein form:

$$w(t) = w_0 B_0^2(t) + w_1 B_1^2(t) + w_2 B_2^2(t).$$

Having determined $w(t)$, we may now write

$$w(t) \begin{bmatrix} \mathbf{c}(t) \\ 1 \end{bmatrix} = \begin{bmatrix} \mathbf{c}(t) \sum w_i B_i^2(t) \\ \sum w_i B_i^2(t) \end{bmatrix}.$$

Since the left hand side of this equation denotes a parabola, we may write

$$\sum_{i=0}^{2} \begin{bmatrix} \mathbf{p}_i \\ w_i \end{bmatrix} B_i^2(t) = \begin{bmatrix} \mathbf{c}(t) \sum w_i B_i^2(t) \\ \sum w_i B_i^2(t) \end{bmatrix}$$

with some points $\mathbf{p}_i \in I\!E^2$. Thus

$$\sum_{i=0}^{2} \mathbf{p}_i B_i^2(t) = \mathbf{c}(t) \sum_{i=0}^{2} w_i B_i^2(t), \qquad (2)$$

and hence

$$\mathbf{c}(t) = \frac{\mathbf{p}_0 B_0^2(t) + \mathbf{p}_1 B_1^2(t) + \mathbf{p}_2 B_2^2(t)}{w_0 B_0^2(t) + w_1 B_1^2(t) + w_2 B_2^2(t)}.$$

Setting $\mathbf{p}_i = w_i \mathbf{b}_i$ proves (1). ∎

We call the points $\mathbf{b}_i$ the *control polygon* of the conic $\mathbf{c}$; the numbers $w_i$ are called *weights* of the corresponding control polygon vertices. Thus the conic control polygon is the projection of a control polygon with vertices $[\, w_i \mathbf{b}_i \quad w_i \,]^{\mathrm{T}}$, which is the control polygon of a 3D parabola that we projected onto $\mathbf{c}$. The form (1) is called the *rational quadratic form* of a conic section. If all weights are equal, we recover integral quadratics, *i.e.*, parabolas. Note that a common nonzero factor in the $w_i$ does not affect the conic at all. If $w_0 \neq 0$, one may therefore always achieve $w_0 = 1$ by a simple scaling of all $w_i$.

There are other changes of the weights that leave the curve shape unchanged: these correspond to *rational linear parameter transformations*. Let us set

$$t = \frac{\hat{t}}{\hat{\rho}(1 - \hat{t}) + \hat{t}}, \qquad \text{and} \qquad (1 - t) = \frac{\hat{\rho}(1 - \hat{t})}{\hat{\rho}(1 - \hat{t}) + \hat{t}}.$$

We may insert this into (1) to obtain:

$$\mathbf{c}(\hat{t}) = \frac{\hat{\rho}^2 w_0 \mathbf{b}_0 B_0^2(\hat{t}) + \hat{\rho} w_1 \mathbf{b}_1 B_1^2(\hat{t}) + w_2 \mathbf{b}_2 B_2^2(\hat{t})}{\hat{\rho}^2 w_0 B_0^2(\hat{t}) + \hat{\rho} w_1 B_1^2(\hat{t}) + w_2 B_2^2(\hat{t})}. \qquad (3)$$

Thus the curve shape is not changed if each weight $w_i$ is replaced by $\hat{w}_i = \hat{\rho}^{2-i} w_i$. If, for a given set of weights $w_i$, we select

$$\hat{\rho} = \sqrt{\frac{w_2}{w_0}},$$

we obtain $\hat{w}_0 = w_2$, and, after dividing all three weights by $w_2$, we even have $\hat{w}_0 = \hat{w}_2 = 1$. A conic that satisfies this condition is said to be in *standard form*. All conics with $w_0, w_2 > 0$ may be rewritten in standard form with the above choice of $\hat{\rho}$. The above short derivation is due to Sederberg [37]; more detailed treatments are in Patterson [28] and Farin and Worsey [22].

We finish this section with a theorem that will be useful in the later development of rational curves:

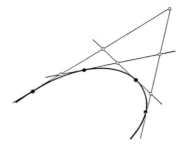

**Figure 2.** The four tangent theorem. The four cross ratios
on the tangents shown equal each other.

**Theorem 2.2.** *Any four tangents to a conic intersect each other in the same
cross ratio.*

The theorem is illustrated in Figure 2. The proof of this *four tangent theorem* is straightforward: one shows that it is true for (nonrational) parabolas.
It then follows for all conics by their definition as a projection of a parabola
and by the fact that cross ratios are invariant under projections. The theorem
is due to J. Steiner.

## §3. Derivatives

In order to find the derivative of a conic section; *i.e.*, the vector $\dot{\mathbf{c}}(t) = d\mathbf{c}/dt$,
we may employ the quotient rule. For a simpler derivation, let us rewrite (2)
as

$$\mathbf{p}(t) = w(t)\mathbf{c}(t).$$

We apply the product rule

$$\dot{\mathbf{p}}(t) = \dot{w}(t)\mathbf{c}(t) + w(t)\dot{\mathbf{c}}(t)$$

and solve for $\dot{\mathbf{c}}(t)$:

$$\dot{\mathbf{c}}(t) = \frac{1}{w(t)}[\dot{\mathbf{p}}(t) - \dot{w}(t)\mathbf{c}(t)]. \tag{4}$$

We may evaluate (4) at the endpoint $t = 0$:

$$\dot{\mathbf{c}}(0) = \frac{2}{w_0}[w_1\mathbf{b}_1 - w_0\mathbf{b}_0 - (w_1 - w_0)\mathbf{b}_0].$$

After some simplifications we obtain

$$\dot{\mathbf{c}}(0) = \frac{2w_1}{w_0}\Delta\mathbf{b}_0. \tag{5}$$

Similarly, we obtain

$$\dot{\mathbf{c}}(1) = \frac{2w_1}{w_2}\Delta\mathbf{b}_1. \tag{6}$$

**Figure 3.** The complementary segment: the original segment
and the complementary segment, both evaluated for all
parameter values $t \in [0, 1]$, comprise the whole conic.

Let us now consider two conics, one defined over the interval $[u_0, u_1]$ with
control polygon $\mathbf{b}_0, \mathbf{b}_1, \mathbf{b}_2$ and weights $w_0, w_1, w_2$, and the other defined over
the interval $[u_1, u_2]$ with control polygon $\mathbf{b}_2, \mathbf{b}_3, \mathbf{b}_4$ and weights $w_2, w_3, w_4$.
The two segments form a $C^1$ curve if

$$\frac{w_1}{\Delta_0} \Delta \mathbf{b}_1 = \frac{w_3}{\Delta_1} \Delta \mathbf{b}_2, \tag{7}$$

where the appearance of the interval lengths $\Delta_i$ is due to the application of the
chain rule, which is necessary since we now consider a composite curve with a
global parameter $u$.

## §4. Classification

In a projective environment, all conics are equivalent: projective maps map
conics to conics. In affine geometry, conics fall into three classes, namely
hyperbolas, parabolas, and ellipses. Thus, ellipses are mapped to ellipses under
affine maps, parabolas to parabolas, and hyperbolas to hyperbolas. How can
we tell of what type a given conic is?

Before we answer this question, (following Lee [27]) let us consider the
*complementary segment* of a conic. Given a conic in standard form, the complementary segment is obtained by reversing the sign of $w_1$. If $\mathbf{c}(t)$ is a point
on the original conic and $\hat{\mathbf{c}}(t)$ is a point on the complementary segment, one
easily verifies that $\mathbf{b}_1, \mathbf{c}(t)$, and $\hat{\mathbf{c}}(t)$ are collinear, as shown in Figure 3.

If we assume that $w_1 > 0$, then the behavior of the arc $\hat{\mathbf{c}}(t)$ determines
of what type the conic is: if $\hat{\mathbf{c}}(t)$ has no singularities in $[0, 1]$, it is an ellipse,
if it has one singularity, it is a parabola, and if it has two singularities, it is a
hyperbola.

The singularities corresponding to points at infinity of $\hat{\mathbf{c}}(t)$ are determined
by the real roots of the denominator $\hat{w}(t)$ of $\hat{\mathbf{c}}(t)$. There are at most two real
roots, given by

$$t_{1,2} = \frac{2 \pm \sqrt{w_1^2 - 1}}{2 + 2w_1}.$$

Thus, a conic is an ellipse if $w_1 < 1$, a parabola if $w_1 = 1$, and a hyperbola if
$w_1 > 1$. The three types of conics are shown in Figure 4.

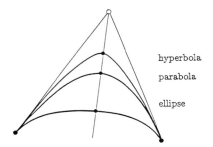

**Figure 4.** Conic classification: depending on the middle
weight, the three types of conics are obtained.

### §5. Conic splines

In the context of piecewise polynomials, $C^1$ piecewise quadratics are well understood; for instance, we know that any such curve has a B-spline representation
with simple knots. In the rational case, a surprising complication arises.

In accordance with our definition of rational quadratic Bézier curves, we
may define a rational quadratic B-spline curve as the *projection of a 4D integral
quadratic B-spline into* $I\!\!E^3$. A rational quadratic B-spline curve then takes the
form

$$s(u) = \frac{\sum w_i \mathbf{d}_i N_i^2(u)}{\sum w_i N_i^2(u)}, \tag{8}$$

where the $N_i^2(u)$ are quadratic B-splines over some knot sequence $\{u_i\}$. If
all knots are simple, the $4D$ integral curve is $C^1$, resulting in a $C^1$ rational
quadratic B-spline curve.

We know that every $C^1$ piecewise quadratic integral curve possesses a B-
spline representation over a knot sequence that has only simple knots. This is
not true in the rational case: not every $C^1$ piecewise quadratic may be written
in the form (8). Recall that a curve of the form (8) is the projection of a
$C^1$ curve, which has a $C^1$ component $w(t)$. With the notation from equation
(7) (assuming for simplicity that our spline is defined over two intervals, with
lengths $\Delta_0$ and $\Delta_1$), this necessitates

$$\text{ratio}(w_1, w_2, w_3) := \frac{w_2 - w_1}{w_3 - w_2} = \frac{\Delta_0}{\Delta_1}. \tag{7a}$$

Inspection of (7), however, reveals that $C^1$ continuity does not depend on the
weight $w_2$ at all. Thus the class of $C^1$ piecewise quadratics is larger than
the class of projections of integral $C^1$ quadratics, a situation that persists for
higher order curves.

As an example, let us consider a circle. It may be represented by three
rational quadratic arcs, as shown in Figure 5. The weights of the junction

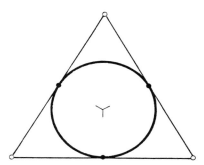

**Figure 5.** Conic splines: a circle may be represented
as a piecewise rational quadratic Bézier curve.

Bézier points are unity; the interior Bézier points have weight $1/2$. This curve
satisfies the $C^1$ condition (7), but not (7a); thus it is not the projection of a
$C^1$ curve.

In order to handle those $C^1$ curves that are not projections as B-spline
curves, we have to introduce knot multiplicities. Since a quadratic B-spline
curve with double knots has its piecewise Bézier polygon as its B-spline control
polygon, we see that the piecewise Bézier form is the most advantageous when
dealing with conic splines.

More material on conic splines, including their use as interpolatory curves,
may be found in Pavlidis [29], Pratt [35], and Farin [18].

## §6. Rational Bézier Curves

The definition of rational Bézier curves is quite straightforward: a rational
Bézier curve of degree $n$ in $I\!\!E^3$ is the projection of an $n^{\text{th}}$ degree Bézier curve
in $I\!\!E^4$ into the hyperplane $w = 1$. We may view this 4D hyperplane as a copy of
$I\!\!E^3$; we assume that a point in $I\!\!E^4$ is given by its coordinates $[\,x \quad y \quad z \quad w\,]^{\text{T}}$.
Proceeding in exactly the same way as we did for conics, we can show that an
$n^{\text{th}}$ degree rational Bézier curve is given by

$$\mathbf{x}(t) = \frac{w_0\mathbf{b}_0 B_0^n(t) + \cdots + w_n\mathbf{b}_n B_n^n(t)}{w_0 B_0^n(t) + \cdots + w_n B_n^n(t)}; \qquad \mathbf{x}(t), \mathbf{b}_i \in I\!\!E^3. \tag{9}$$

The $w_i$ are again called *weights*; the $\mathbf{b}_i$ form the *control polygon*. It is the projection of the 4D control polygon $[\,w_i\mathbf{b}_i \quad w_i\,]^{\text{T}}$ of the nonrational 4D preimage
of $\mathbf{x}(t)$.

If all weights equal one (or if they are all equal – a common factor does
not matter), we obtain the standard nonrational Bézier curve; in this case, the
denominator is identically equal to one. If some $w_i$ are negative, singularities
may occur; we will therefore deal only with nonnegative $w_i$. Rational Bézier
curves enjoy all the properties that their integral counterparts possess; for

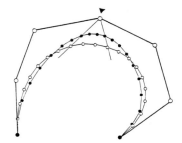

**Figure 6.** Influence of the weights: The curve marked by open circles
is an integral Bézier curve. The one marked by solid circles is
obtained by increasing the weight of the indicated Bézier point.

example, they are affinely invariant. We can see this by rewriting (9) as

$$\mathbf{x}(t) = \sum_{i=0}^{n} \mathbf{b}_i \frac{w_i B_i^n(t)}{\sum_{i=0}^{n} w_i B_i^n(t)}.$$

We see that the basis functions

$$\frac{w_i B_i^n(t)}{\sum_{i=0}^{n} w_i B_i^n(t)}$$

sum to one identically, thus assuring affine invariance. We have invariance
under projective maps, since we know how to modify the weights accordingly:
the projective map consists of an affine map of the 4D preimage, followed by
a projection. If all $w_i$ are nonnegative, we have the convex hull property.
We also have symmetry, invariance under affine parameter transformations,
endpoint interpolation, and the variation diminishing property. Obviously, the
conic sections from the preceding section are included in the set of all rational
Bézier curves.

The $w_i$ are typically used as *shape parameters*. If we increase one $w_i$, the
curve is pulled toward the corresponding $\mathbf{b}_i$, as illustrated in Figure 6.

## §7. The de Casteljau Algorithm

A rational Bézier curve may be evaluated by applying the de Casteljau algorithm to both numerator and denominator and dividing through. A warning
is in order: while simple and usually effective, this method is not always numerically stable. If some of the $w_i$ are large, the intermediate control points
$[w_i \mathbf{b}_i]^r$ are no longer in the convex hull of the original control polygon; this
may result in a loss of accuracy.

An expensive yet more accurate technique is to project every intermediate
de Casteljau point $[\, w_i \mathbf{b}_i \quad w_i \,]^{\mathrm{T}}$ with $\mathbf{b}_i \in I\!\!E^3$ into the hyperplane $w = 1$. This
yields the rational de Casteljau algorithm (see Farin [17]):

$$\mathbf{b}_i^r(t) = (1-t)\frac{w_i^{r-1}}{w_i^r}\mathbf{b}_i^{r-1} + t\frac{w_{i+1}^{r-1}}{w_i^r}\mathbf{b}_{i+1}^{r-1}, \qquad (10)$$

with
$$w_i^r(t) = (1 - t)w_i^{r-1}(t) + tw_{i+1}^{r-1}(t).\tag{11}$$

An explicit form for the intermediate points $\mathbf{b}_i^r$ is given by

$$\mathbf{b}_i^r(t) = \frac{\sum_{j=0}^r w_{i+j}\mathbf{b}_{i+j}B_j^r(t)}{\sum_{j=0}^r w_{i+j}B_j^r(t)}.$$

Note that for positive weights, the $\mathbf{b}_i^r$ are all in the convex hull of the original $\mathbf{b}_i$, thus assuring numerical stability.

The rational de Casteljau algorithm has a nice geometric interpretation. While the standard de Casteljau algorithm makes use of ratios of three points, this one makes use of the *cross ratio of four points*. The cross ratio, cr, of four collinear points is defined as a ratio of ratios:

$$\mathrm{cr}(\mathbf{a}, \mathbf{b}, \mathbf{c}, \mathbf{d}) = \frac{\mathrm{ratio}(\mathbf{a}, \mathbf{b}, \mathbf{d})}{\mathrm{ratio}(\mathbf{a}, \mathbf{c}, \mathbf{d})}.\tag{12}$$

Let us define auxiliary points $\mathbf{q}_i^r(t)$ that are located on the straight lines joining $\mathbf{b}_i^r$ and $\mathbf{b}_{i+1}^r$, subdividing them in the ratio

$$\mathrm{ratio}(\mathbf{b}_i^r, \mathbf{q}_i^r, \mathbf{b}_{i+1}^r) = \frac{w_{i+1}^r}{w_i^r}.$$

Then all of the following cross ratios are equal:

$$\mathrm{cr}(\mathbf{b}_i^r, \mathbf{q}_i^r, \mathbf{b}_i^{r+1}, \mathbf{b}_{i+1}^r) = \frac{1 - t}{t} \qquad \text{for all} \quad r, i.$$

For $r = 0$, the auxiliary points

$$\mathbf{q}_i = \mathbf{q}_i^0 = \frac{w_i\mathbf{b}_i + w_{i+1}\mathbf{b}_{i+1}}{w_i + w_{i+1}}$$

are directly related to the weights $w_i$: given the weights, we can find the $\mathbf{q}_i$, and given the $\mathbf{q}_i$, we can find the weights $w_i$, except for an immaterial common factor. Thus the $\mathbf{q}_i$ may be used as *shape parameters*: moving a $\mathbf{q}_i$ along the polygon leg $\mathbf{b}_i, \mathbf{b}_{i+1}$ influences the shape of the curve. It may be preferable to let a designer use these geometric handles rather than requiring him or her to input numbers for the weights.

As in the nonrational case, the de Casteljau algorithm may be used to *subdivide* a curve. The (integral) de Casteljau algorithm subdivides the 4D preimage of our 3D rational Bézier curve $\mathbf{x}(t)$. The intermediate 4D points $[w_i^r\mathbf{b}_i^r \quad w_i^r]^{\mathrm{T}}$ with $\mathbf{b}_i^r \in I\!\!E^3$ may be projected into the hyperplane $w = 1$ to provide us with the control polygons for the "left" and "right" curve segment: the control vertices and weights corresponding to the interval $[0, t]$ are given by

$$\mathbf{b}_i^{\mathrm{left}} = \mathbf{b}_0^i(t), \quad w_i^{\mathrm{left}} = w_0^i,\tag{13}$$

where the $\mathbf{b}_0^i(t)$ and the $w_0^i$ are computed from (10). The control points and weights corresponding to the interval $[t, 1]$ are given by

$$\mathbf{b}_i^{\text{right}} = \mathbf{b}_{n-i}^i(t), \quad w_i^{\text{right}} = w_{n-i}^i. \tag{14}$$

Note that now, just as in the integral case, subdivision is a "byproduct" of evaluation. The more straightforward evaluation method – evaluating numerator and denominator separately and then dividing – does not have this advantage.

## §8. Derivatives

For the first derivative of a rational Bézier curve, we obtain

$$\dot{\mathbf{x}}(t) = \frac{1}{w(t)}[\dot{\mathbf{p}}(t) - \dot{w}(t)\mathbf{x}(t)], \tag{15}$$

where we have set

$$\mathbf{p}(t) = w(t)\mathbf{x}(t), \qquad \mathbf{p}(t), \mathbf{x}(t) \in I\!\!E^3 \tag{16}$$

in complete analogy to the development in Section 3. For higher derivatives, we differentiate (16) $r$ times:

$$\mathbf{p}^{(r)}(t) = \sum_{j=0}^{r} \binom{r}{j} w^{(j)}(t)\mathbf{x}^{(r-j)}(t).$$

We can solve for $\mathbf{x}^{(r)}(t)$:

$$\mathbf{x}^{(r)}(t) = \frac{1}{w(t)}[\mathbf{p}^{(r)} - \sum_{j=1}^{r} \binom{r}{j} w^{(j)}(t)\mathbf{x}^{(r-j)}(t)]. \tag{17}$$

This is a recursive formula for the $r^{\text{th}}$ derivative of a rational Bézier curve. It only involves taking derivatives of polynomial curves.

For the first derivative at the endpoint of a rational Bézier curve, we find

$$\dot{\mathbf{x}}(0) = \frac{nw_1}{w_0}\Delta\mathbf{b}_0.$$

Let us now consider two rational Bézier curves, one defined over the interval $[u_0, u_1]$ with control polygon $\mathbf{b}_0, \ldots, \mathbf{b}_n$ and weights $w_0, \ldots, w_n$ and the other defined over the interval $[u_1, u_2]$ with control polygon $\mathbf{b}_n, \ldots, \mathbf{b}_{2n}$ and weights $w_n, \ldots, w_{2n}$. The two segments form a $C^1$ curve if

$$\frac{w_{n-1}}{\Delta_0}\Delta\mathbf{b}_{n-1} = \frac{w_{n+1}}{\Delta_1}\Delta\mathbf{b}_n,$$

where the appearance of the interval lengths $\Delta_i$ is due to the application of the chain rule, which is necessary since we now consider a composite curve with a global parameter $u$.

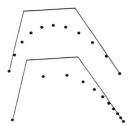

**Figure 7.** Reparametrization: top, a rational Bézier curve evaluated
at parameter values $0, 0.1, 0.2, \ldots$. Bottom, the same curve and
parameter values but after a reparametrization with $c = 3$.

### §9. Reparametrization and Degree Elevation

Arguing exactly as in the conic case (see the end of Section 2), we may
*reparametrize* a rational Bézier curve by changing the weights according to

$$\hat{w}_i = c^i w_i, \qquad i = 0, \ldots, n,$$

where $c$ is any nonzero constant. Figure 7 shows how the reparametrization
affects the parameter spacing on the curve; note that the curve shape remains
the same. We may always transform a rational Bézier curve to *standard form*
by using the rational linear parameter transformation resulting from the choice

$$c = \sqrt[n]{\frac{w_0}{w_n}}.$$

This results in $\hat{w}_n = w_0$; after dividing all weights through by $w_0$, we have
the standard form $\hat{w}_0 = \hat{w}_n = 1$. A different derivation of this result is in
Patterson [28].

We may perform *degree elevation* by degree elevating the 4D polygon with
control vertices $[\, w_i \mathbf{b}_i \quad w_i \,]^{\mathrm{T}}$ and projecting the resulting control vertices into
the hyperplane $w = 1$. Let us denote the control vertices of the degree elevated
curve by $\mathbf{b}_i^{(1)}$; they are given by

$$\mathbf{b}_i^{(1)} = \frac{w_{i-1}\alpha_i \mathbf{b}_{i-1} + w_i(1 - \alpha_i)\mathbf{b}_i}{w_{i-1}\alpha_i + w_i(1 - \alpha_i)}, \qquad i = 0, \ldots, n+1 \tag{19}$$

and $\alpha_i = i/(n+1)$. The weights $w_i^{(1)}$ of the new control vertices are given by

$$w_i^{(1)} = w_{i-1}\alpha_i + w_i(1 - \alpha_i), \qquad i = 0, \ldots, n+1.$$

Let us now consider the following procedure: take any rational Bézier
curve in standard form and degree elevate it. Next, take the original curve,
reparametrize it, and then degree elevate it and standardize it. We end up

**Figure 8.** Different curve representations: the two solid polygons represent the same rational quartic. The dashed polygon shows the the rational cubic from which they were obtained.

with two different polygons (and two sets of standardized weights) which both describe the same curve. This situation is very different from the integral case! Figure 8 gives an illustration.

How can we detect if two curve representations are related by the above procedure? Let us denote the two polygons by $\{\mathbf{b}_i\}$ and $\{\mathbf{c}_i\}$, and the weights by $\{w_i\}$ and $\{v_i\}$, respectively. We assume that $\mathbf{b}_0 = \mathbf{c}_0$ and $\mathbf{b}_n = \mathbf{c}_n$. If we draw straight lines through corresponding points $\mathbf{b}_i$ and $\mathbf{c}_i$, we may obtain a new polygon, with vertices $\mathbf{a}_i$. The straight line segments need not intersect, in which case the two given curve representations did not arise by applying degree elevation and reparametrizations to a curve of degree $n-1$. In case the $\mathbf{a}_i$ do exist, we need to check that the following cross ratios are all equal:

$$\mathrm{cr}(\mathbf{a}_i, \mathbf{b}_{i+1}, \mathbf{c}_{i+1}, \mathbf{a}_{i+1}) = \text{constant}, \quad \text{all } i.$$

If they are, we still need to calculate weights $u_i$ of the vertices $\mathbf{a}_i$. They may be found from

$$\mathrm{ratio}(u_i, w_{i+1}, u_{i+1}) = \mathrm{ratio}(\mathbf{a}_i, \mathbf{b}_{i+1}, \mathbf{a}_{i+1}),$$

but also from

$$\mathrm{ratio}(u_i, v_{i+1}, u_{i+1}) = \mathrm{ratio}(\mathbf{a}_i, \mathbf{c}_{i+1}, \mathbf{a}_{i+1}),$$

thus providing a last check if in fact the two given curve representations are equivalent. We note that two curves may come from a common lower degree curve, yet they are not related by a rational linear parameter transformation.

As a corollary, we can state that if two cubic rational Bézier curves with coincident first and last polygon vertices are equivalent; *i.e.*, they both define the same curve (in a point set context), then they must both define a conic section.

### §10. Functional Rational Bézier Curves

A functional integral Bézier curve is defined by

$$y = \sum b_i B_i^n(x).$$

It may be shown (see e.g. Farin [19]) that it has a representation as a parametric Bézier curve; its Bézier points are given by $\mathbf{b}_i = [i/n, b_i]^{\mathrm{T}}$.

The situation in the rational case is somewhat more complicated, as we shall see. Let

$$y = \frac{\sum w_i b_i B_i^n(x)}{\sum w_i B_i^n(x)} \tag{20}$$

be a function. Can we write it as a rational Bézier curve, and if so, what are its Bézier points $\mathbf{b}_i$ and the corresponding weights $v_i$? Written in parametric form, (20) takes the form

$$\begin{bmatrix} x(u) \\ y(u) \end{bmatrix} = \frac{1}{\sum w_i B_i^n(u)} \begin{bmatrix} u \sum w_i B_i^n(u) \\ \sum w_i b_i B_i^n(u) \end{bmatrix}.$$

Using the identity $u B_i^n(u) = \left(\frac{i+1}{n+1}\right) B_{i+1}^{n+1}(u)$ and degree elevation, we obtain

$$\begin{bmatrix} x(u) \\ y(u) \end{bmatrix} = \frac{\sum_{i=0}^{n+1} v_i \mathbf{b}_i B_i^{n+1}(u)}{\sum_{i=0}^{n+1} v_i B_i^{n+1}(u)},$$

where

$$\mathbf{b}_i = \frac{1}{v_i} \begin{bmatrix} iw_{i-1} \\ iw_{i-1}b_{i-1} + (n+1-i)w_i b_i \end{bmatrix}, \qquad i = 0, \ldots, n+1$$

and

$$v_i = iw_{i-1} + (n+1-i)w_i, \qquad i = 0, \ldots, n+1.$$

While in the nonrational case the abscissae of the Bézier points of a functional Bézier curve do not depend on the function, they now depend on the weights of the function under consideration. Also, a rational function $y = a(x)/b(x)$ with both $a$ and $b$ polynomials of degree $n$ in general has a rational parametric representation of degree $n + 1$.

The abscissae $iw_{i-1}/v_i$ are, as expected, in the range $[0, 1]$. But note that they do not necessarily have to be increasing! For example, if the original weight sequence $\{w_i\}$ is $1, 10, 1, 10$, then the abscissae sequence $\{iw_{i-1}/v_i\}$ is $0, 1/31, 10/11, 3/13, 1$.

We give an example of the computation of the Bézier points of a functional curve: the function $y = 1/(1 + x)$ may be written as

$$y = \frac{1 \cdot 1 \cdot B_0^1(x) + 2 \cdot \frac{1}{2} \cdot B_1^1(x)}{1 \cdot B_0^1(x) + 2 \cdot B_1^1(x)},$$

thus conforming with (20). Written as a rational quadratic, its Bézier points are

$$\mathbf{b}_i = \begin{bmatrix} 0 \\ 1 \end{bmatrix}, \begin{bmatrix} 1/3 \\ 2/3 \end{bmatrix}, \begin{bmatrix} 1 \\ 1/2 \end{bmatrix},$$

and the corresponding weights are

$$v_i = 2, 3, 4.$$

We may standardize this curve and obtain weights

$$\hat{v}_i = 1, \frac{3}{4}\sqrt{2}, 1.$$

The middle weight is larger than one, indicating that our example function represents a hyperbola. This is always the case for functions of the form $y = a(x)/b(x)$ with both $a$ and $b$ linear in $x$.

In summary: the rational parametric representation of functional rational polynomials is of degree

$$\max (\text{degree numerator, degree denominator} + 1).$$

Thus we should, in particular, not expect rational quadratic functions (as for example in Delbourgo and Gregory [16]) to be conic sections.

## §11. Rational Cubic B-spline Curves

A 3D rational cubic B-spline curve over a knot sequence $\{u_i\}$ is the projection through the origin of a 4D nonrational cubic B-spline curve into the hyperplane $w = 1$. The control polygon of the rational B-spline curve is given by vertices $\mathbf{d}_{-1}, \ldots, \mathbf{d}_{L+1}$; each vertex $\mathbf{d}_i \in I\!\!E^3$ has a corresponding weight $w_i$. The rational B-spline curve has a piecewise rational cubic Bézier representation. It may be obtained by projecting the corresponding 4D Bézier points into the hyperplane $w = 1$. Thus we obtain

$$\mathbf{b}_{3i-2} = \frac{w_{i-1}(1 - \alpha_i)\mathbf{d}_{i-1} + w_i\alpha_i\mathbf{d}_i}{v_{3i-2}} \tag{21}$$

$$\mathbf{b}_{3i-1} = \frac{w_{i-1}\beta_i\mathbf{d}_{i-1} + w_i(1 - \beta_i)\mathbf{d}_i}{v_{3i-1}}, \tag{22}$$

where all points $\mathbf{b}_j, \mathbf{d}_k$ are in $I\!\!E^3$,

$$\Delta = \Delta_{i-2} + \Delta_{i-1} + \Delta_i,$$
$$\alpha_i = \frac{\Delta_{i-2}}{\Delta},$$
$$\beta_i = \frac{\Delta_i}{\Delta},$$

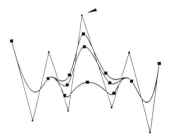

**Figure 9.** Rational B-splines: the weight of the indicated control point is changed (assuming values 2.0, 1.0, 0.2). The resulting changes are only local.

and $\Delta_i = u_{i+1} - u_i$. The weights of these Bézier points are given by

$$v_{3i-2} = w_{i-1}(1 - \alpha_i) + w_i \alpha_i, \tag{23}$$

$$v_{3i-1} = w_{i-1}\beta_i + w_i(1 - \beta_i). \tag{24}$$

For the junction points, we obtain

$$\mathbf{b}_{3i} = \frac{\gamma_i v_{3i-1}\mathbf{b}_{3i-1} + (1 - \gamma_i)v_{3i+1}\mathbf{b}_{3i+1}}{v_{3i}}, \tag{25}$$

where

$$\gamma_i = \frac{\Delta_i}{\Delta_{i-1} + \Delta_i}$$

and

$$v_{3i} = \gamma_i v_{3i-1} + (1 - \gamma_i)v_{3i+1}$$

is the weight of the junction point $\mathbf{b}_{3i}$.

Designing with rational B-spline curves is not very different from designing with their nonrational counterparts. We now have the added freedom of being able to change weights. A change of only one weight affects a rational B-spline curve only locally, as shown in Figure 9.

This development follows the general philosophy of computing with rational curves: we are given 3D points $\mathbf{x}_i$ and their weights $w_i$. Transform them to 4D points $[\,w_i\mathbf{x}_i \quad w_i\,]^{\mathrm{T}}$ and perform 4D nonrational algorithms (for example, finding the Bézier points of a B-spline curve). The result of these operations will be a set of 4D points $[\,\mathbf{y}_i \quad v_i\,]^{\mathrm{T}}$. From these, obtain 3D points $\mathbf{y}_i/v_i$. The weights of these 3D points are the numbers $v_i$.

Let us close this section with a result that somewhat limits the use of $C^2$ rational B-spline curves.

**Theorem 11.1.** *There is no symmetric periodic representation of a circle as a $C^2$ rational cubic B-spline curve.*

**Proof:** If such a representation existed, it would be of the form

$$\mathbf{x}(u) = \sum w_i \mathbf{d}_i N_i^3(u) / \sum w_i N_i^3(u),$$

where all $w_i$ are equal by symmetry. Then the $w_i$ cancel out, leaving us with an integral B-spline curve, which is not capable of representing a circle. Note, however, that we can represent any *open* circular arc by $C^2$ rational cubics. ∎

## §12. Rational B-splines of Arbitrary Degree

It is now straightforward to generalize the concept of general B-spline curves to the rational case. A 3D rational B-spline curve is the projection through the origin of a 4D nonrational B-spline curve into the hyperplane $w = 1$. It is thus given by

$$s(u) = \frac{\sum w_i \mathbf{d}_i N_i^n(u)}{\sum w_i N_i^n(u)}. \tag{26}$$

A rational B-spline curve is given by its knot sequence, its 3D control polygon, and its weight sequence. The control vertices $\mathbf{d}_i$ are the projections of the 4D control vertices $[\, w_i \mathbf{d}_i \quad w_i \,]^{\mathrm{T}}$.

To evaluate a rational B-spline curve at a parameter value $u$, we may apply the de Boor algorithm to both numerator and denominator of (26) and finally divide through. This corresponds to the evaluation of the 4D nonrational curve with control vertices $[\, w_i \mathbf{d}_i \quad w_i \,]^{\mathrm{T}}$ and to projecting the result into $I\!\!E^3$. Just as in the case of Bézier curves, this may lead to instabilities, and so we give a rational version of the de Boor algorithm that is more stable but also computationally more involved:

**Rational de Boor algorithm.** *Let* $u \in [u_I, u_{I+1}]$. *Define*

$$d_i^k(u) = \left[ (1 - \alpha_i^k) w_{i-1}^{k-1} \mathbf{d}_{i-1}^{k-1}(u) + \alpha_i^k w_i^{k-1} \mathbf{d}_i^{k-1}(u) \right] / w_i^k \tag{27}$$

*for* $k = 1, \ldots, n - r$, *and* $i = I - n + k + 1, \ldots, I + 1$, *where*

$$\alpha_i^k = \frac{u - u_{i-1}}{u_{i+n-k} - u_{i-1}}$$

*and*

$$w_i^k = (1 - \alpha_i^k) w_{i-1}^{k-1} + \alpha_i^k w_i^{k-1}.$$

*Then*

$$s(u) = \mathbf{d}_{I+1}^{n-r}(u) \tag{28}$$

*is the point on the B-spline curve at parameter value* $u$.

Here, $r$ denotes the multiplicity of $u$ in case it was already one of the knots. If it was not, set $r = 0$. As usual, we set $\mathbf{d}_i^0 = \mathbf{d}_i$ and $w_i^0 = w_i$.

Knot insertion is, as in the nonrational case, performed by executing just one step of the de Boor algorithm; *i.e.*, by fixing $k = 1$ in the above algorithm. The original polygon vertices $\mathbf{d}_{I-n+2}, \ldots, \mathbf{d}_I$ are replaced by the $\mathbf{d}_{I-n+2}^{(1)}, \ldots, \mathbf{d}_{I+1}^{(1)}$; their weights are the numbers $w_{I-n+2}^{(1)}, \ldots, w_{I+1}^{(1)}$.

A rational B-spline curve, being a piecewise rational polynomial, has a piecewise rational Bézier representation. We can find the Bézier points and their weights for each segment by inserting every knot until it has multiplicity $n$; *i.e.*, by applying the de Boor algorithm to each knot.

## §13. Reparametrizations of Rational B-spline Curves

We have seen that we may reparametrize a rational Bézier curve by a rational linear transformation of the parameter, thus changing the weights but not the shape of the curve. This is not possible for rational B-spline curves:

**Theorem 13.1.** *Let* $\mathbf{r}$ *be a rational B-spline curve with knot sequence* $\{u_i\}$. *Let* $\phi : u \to \phi(u)$ *be a rational linear parameter transformation. Then the transformed curve* $\hat{\mathbf{r}}(\phi u)$ *is not a rational B-spline curve over the transformed knot sequence* $\{\phi u_i\}$.

**Proof:** Suppose such a transformation exists. Then let $u_k$ be a breakpoint of the original knot sequence and let $\mathbf{a} = \mathbf{r}(u_k)$ be the corresponding point on the original curve. After the transformation $\phi$ is applied, the point $\mathbf{a}$, still being on the curve, will now correspond to the parameter value $\phi^{-1}u_k$. In general, $\phi^{-1}u_k$ will not be a breakpoint of the new knot sequence; thus the transformed curve, being analytic at $\phi^{-1}u_k$, will possess continuous derivatives of all orders at $\mathbf{a}$. Hence the original and the transformed curve have different graphs at $\mathbf{a}$, contradicting our assumption. ■

## §14. Interpolation with Rational Cubics

The interpolation problem in the context of rational B-splines is the following:

**Problem.** *Given 3D data points* $\mathbf{x}_0, \ldots, \mathbf{x}_L$, *parameter values* $u_0, \ldots, u_L$, *and weights* $w_0, \ldots, w_L$, *find a* $C^2$ *rational B-spline curve with control vertices* $\mathbf{d}_{-1}, \ldots, \mathbf{d}_{L+1}$ *and weights* $v_{-1}, \ldots, v_{L+1}$ *that interpolates to the given data and weights.*

For the solution of this problem, we follow the philosophy outlined at the end of the last section: solve a 4D interpolation problem to the data points $[\, w_i \mathbf{x}_i \quad w_i \,]^{\mathrm{T}}$ and parameter values $u_i$. All we have to do is to solve the standard linear spline system, where input and output are now 4D instead of the usual 3D. We will obtain a 4D control polygon $[\, \mathbf{e}_i \quad v_i \,]^{\mathrm{T}}$, from which we now obtain the desired $\mathbf{d}_i$ as $\mathbf{d}_i = \mathbf{e}_i / v_i$. The $v_i$ are the weights of the control vertices $\mathbf{d}_i$.

We have not yet addressed the problem of how to choose the weights $w_i$ for the data points $\mathbf{x}_i$. No known algorithms exist for this problem. It seems reasonable to assign high weights in regions where the interpolant is expected to curve sharply. There is a limit to the assignment of weights: if all of them are very high, this will not have a significant effect on the curve since a common factor in all weights will simply cancel out. Also, care must be taken to prevent the denominator of the interpolant from being zero. This is not a trivial task, as spline interpolation can exhibit undulations, and thus assigning positive weights to the data points does not guarantee positive weights for the control vertices of the interpolating spline curve (see Figure 10).

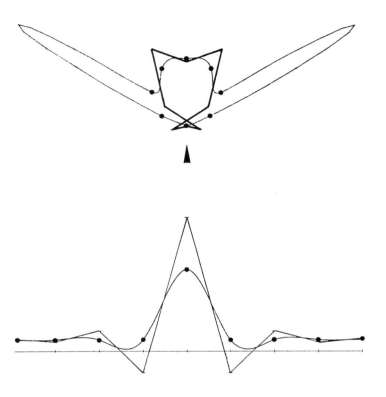

**Figure 10.** Rational spline interpolation: the indicated data point has
a weight of 7, while all other data weights are unity. The resulting
control polygon has negative weights. The bottom part of the figure
shows the weight function $w(t)$ with its control polygon.

Integral cubic spline interpolation has *cubic precision*: if the data points
and the parameter values come from one global cubic, the interpolant reproduces that cubic. In the context of rational spline interpolation, an analogous
question is that of *conic precision*: if the data points and the parameter values
come from one global conic, can we reproduce it? We must also require that the
data points have weights assigned to them. With them, we may view the rational spline interpolation problem as an integral spline interpolation problem in

$I\!E^4$. There, cubic splines have quadratic precision; *i.e.*, we may recapture any parabola. The projection of the parabola yields a conic section. Thus, if our data points, parameter values, and weights were taken from a conic, rational cubic spline interpolation will reproduce the conic.

We should also note that this argument is limited to open curves; for closed curves, we have already seen that we cannot represent a circle as a $C^2$ symmetric periodic B-spline curve.

## §15. Rational B-spline Surfaces

A rational B-spline surface **s** is defined by

$$\mathbf{s}(u,v) = \frac{\sum_i \sum_j w_{i,j} \mathbf{d}_{i,j} N_i^m(u) N_j^n(v)}{\sum_i \sum_j w_{i,j} N_i^m(u) N_j^n(v)}; \tag{29}$$

*i.e.*, as the projection of a 4D tensor product B-spline surface. It is a common misconception to call (29) a tensor product surface itself. Recall that a tensor product surface is of the form $\mathbf{x}(u,v) = \sum_i \sum_j \mathbf{c}_{i,j} F_{i,j}(u,v)$, where the basis functions $F_{i,j}$ may be expressed as products $F_{i,j}(u,v) = A_i(u) B_j(v)$. The basis functions for (29) are of the form

$$F_{i,j}(u,v) = \frac{w_{i,j} N_i^m(u) N_j^n(v)}{\sum_i \sum_j w_{i,j} N_i^m(u) N_j^n(v)}. \tag{30}$$

Because of the structure of the denominator, this may in general not be factored into the required form $F_{i,j}(u,v) = A_i(u) B_j(v)$.

But even though a rational B-spline surface does not possess a tensor product structure, we may utilize many tensor product algorithms for its manipulation, namely all those algorithms that operate on the 4D preimage of the given surface. For example, we may perform knot insertion in 4D and then project the resulting new control net down. Similarly, we may evaluate using a tensor product de Boor algorithm. If each knot is inserted to maximum multiplicity, we have obtained the piecewise rational Bézier form of the surface.

Currently, rational B-spline surfaces are used for two reasons: they allow the exact representation of surfaces of revolution and of quadric surfaces. Let us briefly discuss both.

## §16. Surfaces of Revolution

A surface of revolution is given by

$$\mathbf{x}(u,v) = \begin{bmatrix} r(v)\cos u \\ r(v)\sin u \\ z(v) \end{bmatrix}. \tag{31}$$

For fixed $v$, the isoparametric line $v = const$ traces out a circle of radius $r(v)$, called a *meridian*. Since a circle may be exactly represented by rational quadratic arcs, we may find an exact rational representation of a surface of revolution provided we can represent $r(v)$, $z(v)$ in rational form.

The most convenient way to define a surface of revolution is to prescribe the (planar) generating curve, or *generatrix*, given by

$$\mathbf{g}(v) = \begin{bmatrix} r(v) \\ 0 \\ z(v) \end{bmatrix} \tag{32}$$

and by the *axis of revolution*, in the same plane as $\mathbf{g}$. Suppose $\mathbf{g}$ is given by its control polygon, knot sequence, and weight sequence. We can construct a surface of revolution such that each meridian consists of three rational quadratic arcs, as shown in Figure 5. For each vertex of the generating polygon, construct an equilateral triangle (perpendicular to the axis of revolution) as in Figure 5. Assign the given weights of the generatrix to the three polygons corresponding to the triangle edge midpoints; assign half those weights to the three control polygons corresponding to the triangle vertices.

Instead of breaking down each meridian into three arcs, we might have used four or more. This would have resulted in a larger number of patches; for an illustration, see Piegl and Tiller [34].

Note that although the generatrix may be defined over a knot sequence $\{v_j\}$ with only simple knots, this is not possible for the knots of the meridian circles: we have to use double knots, thereby essentially reducing it to the piecewise Bézier form.

## §17. Quadric Surfaces

We defined a conic section as the projective map of a parabola, the only conic allowing a polynomial parametrization. For surfaces, we again consider those quadrics that permit polynomial parametrizations: these are the paraboloids, consisting of elliptic, parabolic, and hyperbolic paraboloids. Every quadric surface may be defined as a (real) projective image of one of these paraboloids. (I am grateful to W. Boehm for bringing this fact to my attention).

A paraboloid may be represented by a parametric polynomial surface of degree two. However, not every parametric quadratic is a paraboloid. We need an extra condition, which is easily formulated if we write the quadratic surface in triangular Bézier form (see Boehm *et al* [10], Farin [20], or [19]):

**Theorem 17.1** (Boehm [8]). *A quadratic Bézier triangle is an elliptic or hyperbolic paraboloid if and only if the second derivative vectors of the three boundary curves are parallel to each other. It is a cylindrical paraboloid if those three vectors are only coplanar.*

**Proof:** We give our own proof: first, we observe that nonparametric or functional (*i.e.*, of the form $z = f(x, y)$ ) quadratic polynomials include all three types of paraboloids, all satisfying the conditions of the theorem. Next, we observe that every paraboloid may be obtained as an affine map of a paraboloid of the same type. Thus every paraboloid may be obtained as an affine map of a functional quadratic surface. Consequently, the control net of any paraboloid must be an affine image of the control net of a functional quadratic Bézier triangle. This is exactly what Boehm's theorem states. ■

We may now obtain the following characterization of a quadric surface (Boehm [8]):

**Theorem 17.2.** *A rational quadratic Bézier triangle is a quadric if all three boundary curves meet in a common point and have coplanar tangents there.*

Clearly, not every rational quadratic surface is a quadric surface, a situation quite different from that of the curve case.

Also, not every triangle-shaped region on a quadratic surface has a rational quadratic representation: if specific boundaries are required, one might have to resort to higher degrees. An example follows.

Probably the most important quadric is the sphere. Several rational polynomial representations exist for it. The sphere may be written as an assembly of eight octants, each represented by a rational biquadratic (and having singularities at the north and south poles), see [34]. A representation as two rational bicubics (Piegl [32]) turned out to be incorrect (see Cobb [12]).

Or, it may be written as eight octants, each represented as a rational quartic Bézier triangle, see [21]. This representation has the advantage of avoiding singularities at the poles. Note that all (valid) representations are of degree four. One can easily see that rational quadratics are not sufficient to represent an octant of the sphere (Arner [1]).

## §18. Conclusion

Rational B-splines (NURBS) enjoy considerable popularity, yet they are not used to the full extent of their potential power.

Presently, many CAD systems use rational B-spline curves to represent "exactly" surfaces of revolution or conic sections. Since we all know that there is no such thing as "exact" on a digital computer, this is not as advantageous as it sounds. These curve and surface types may equally well be approximated by piecewise polynomial schemes – even with the rational form, we cannot do better than machine accuracy.

If conic sections and surfaces of revolution are all that rational B-spline curves are going to be used for, they constitute a serious overkill: all algorithms in a CAD system must be able to handle the full variety of NURB curves and surfaces, a task that certainly involves more effort than the integral case.

A simple example: if second derivatives are desired of a rational surface (necessary for any kind of curvature analysis), their computation is considerably slower than for the integral case. Integral curves and surfaces, when represented as rational ones, will be as tedious to handle! The remedy of flagging the integral cases (and maybe not even storing their unity weights) and branching to different algorithms will lead to a proliferation of case distinctions, which is not desirable.

In summary: it does not seem to be a viable option to introduce NURBS just in order to be able to handle conic sections and surfaces of revolution "exactly". The overhead that is thus created does not justify the alleged payoff. It seems therefore that the present popularity of NURBS is more of a trend than a real necessity.

Should we conclude that we should return to integral splines and abandon the rational ones? I do not think so. Rational curves and surfaces have a lot more to offer than just conics and surfaces of revolution. They speed up realistic perspective maps in graphics and they offer designers more flexibility through the use of weights. Also, as of now, they are the most general surface description, thus offering themselves as a flexible tool in the conversion of geometry data from one CAD system to another.

Also, it is by no means the case that rational curves and surfaces in CAGD are fully understood. Several open questions remain, among them reparametrization of rational B-spline curves and surfaces, the representation of quadric surfaces, and general $G^k$ conditions or even general $C^k$ conditions.

Typically, $C^k$ NURBS are conceived as the projection of a $C^k$ integral 4D curve or surface. As we have seen, not every $C^k$ piecewise rational curve or surface can be obtained in this way. While the description of curve schemes that are derived from projections is now straightforward, discussion of piecewise rational schemes that are not generated in this way is more involved. As an example of the first kind of curve schemes, we cite the projective generation of beta-splines (Barsky [6]); as an example of the second kind, we mention the more general derivation of rational gamma-splines (Boehm [7]).

Finally, we point out the absence of algorithms that fully exploit the flexibility inherent in rational schemes. For instance, it seems likely that offset curves or surfaces may be obtained using rational schemes – it is to be expected that they would have fewer segments than would be needed in the integral case. An attempt in that direction can be found in Farin [18]. Rational schemes are well understood in approximation theory. It is conceivable that those concepts can find their way into CAGD.

## §19. Acknowledgements

This research was supported by NSF grant DMC-8807747 and by DoE grant DE-FG02-87ER25041 to Arizona State University. Thanks to T. DeRose for a discussion of nonparametric rational curves and to P. Chan for helping with Figures 9 and 10.

## References

1. Arner, P., Quadratics as rational polynomials, Utah Math CAGD seminar, 1985.
2. Ball, A., Consurf I, Comput. Aided Design **6** (1974), 237–242.

3. Ball, A., Consurf II, Comput. Aided Design **7** (1975), 237–242.

4. Ball, A., Consurf III, Comput. Aided Design **9** (1977), 9–12.

5. Ball, A., The parametric representation of curves and surfaces using rational polynomial functions, in *The Mathematics of Surfaces II*, R. Martin (ed), Oxford University Press, 1987, 39–62.

6. Barsky, B., Introducing the rational beta-spline, in *Proceedings of the third Int. Conf. on Engineering Graphics and Descriptive Geometry,*, Vienna, Austria, 1988.

7. Boehm, W., Bézier presentations of airfoils, Comput. Aided Geom. Design **4** (1987), 17–22.

8. Boehm, W., Private communication, 1988.

9. Boehm, W., Rational geometric splines, Comput. Aided Geom. Design **4** (1987), 67–78.

10. Boehm, W., G. Farin, and J. Kahmann, A survey of curve and surface methods in CAGD, Comput. Aided Geom. Design **1** (1984), 1–60.

11. Bookstein, F., Fitting conic sections to scattered data, IEEE Computer Graphics and Applications **9** (1979),56–71.

12. Cobb, J. E., Letter to the editor, Comput. Aided Geom. Design **6** (1989), 85–86.

13. Coolidge, J., *A History of the Conic Sections and Quadric Surfaces*. Oxford University Press, 1945.

14. Coons, S., Surfaces for computer aided design, Technical Report, M.I.T., 1964. Available as AD 663 504 from the National Technical Information Service, Springfield, VA 22161.

15. Degen, W., Some remarks on Bézier curves, Comput. Aided Geom. Design **5** (1988), 259–268.

16. Delbourgo, R., and J. Gregory, $C^2$ rational quadratic spline interpolation to monotonic data, IMA J. Numer. Anal. **3** (1983), 141–152.

17. Farin, G., Algorithms for rational Bézier curves, Comput. Aided Geom. Design **15** (1983), 73–77.

18. Farin, G., Curvature continuity and offsets for piecewise conics, ACM Transactions on Graphics, to appear.

19. Farin, G., *Curves and Surfaces for Computer Aided Geometric Design*, Academic Press, New York, 1988.

20. Farin, G., Triangular Bernstein-Bézier patches, Comput. Aided Geom. Design **3** (1986), 83–128.

21. Farin, G., B. Piper, and A. Worsey, The octant of a sphere as a nondegenerate triangular Bézier patch, Comput. Aided Geom. Design **4** (1988), 329–332.

22. Farin, G., and A. Worsey, Reparametrization and degree elevation of rational Bézier curves, preprint.

23. Forrest, A., Curves and surfaces for computer-aided design, PhD dissertation, Cambridge, 1968.

24. Forrest, A., The twisted cubic curve: a computer-aided geometric design approach, Comput. Aided Design **12** (1980), 165–172.

25. Gossing, T., Bulge, shear and squash: a representation for the general conic arc, Comput. Aided Design **13** (1981), 81–84.

26. Hands, J., Reparametrisation of rational surfaces, in *The Mathematics of Surfaces II*, R. Martin (ed.), Oxford University Press, 1987, 87–100.

27. Lee, E., The rational Bézier representation for conics, in *Geometric Modeling: Algorithms and New Trends*, G. E. Farin (ed.), SIAM Publications, Philadelphia, 1987, 3–19.

28. Patterson, R., Projective transformations of the parameter of A rational Bernstein-Bézier curve, ACM Transactions on Graphics, **4** (1986), 276–290.

29. Pavlidis, T., Curve fitting with conic splines, ACM Transactions on Graphics **2** (1983), 1–31.

30. Piegl, L., A geometric investigation of the rational Bézier scheme in computer aided geometric design, Computers in Industry **7** (1987), 401–410.

31. Piegl, L., On the use of infinite control points in CAGD, Comput. Aided Geom. Design **4** (1987), 155–166.

32. Piegl, L., The sphere as a rational Bézier surface, Comput. Aided Geom. Design **3** (1986), 45–52.

33. Piegl, L., A technique for smoothing scattered data with conic sections, Computers in Industry **9** (1987), 223–237.

34. Piegl, L., and W. Tiller, Curve and surface constructions using rational B-splines, Comput. Aided Design **19** (1987), 485–498.

35. Pratt, V., Techniques for conic splines, in *SIGGRAPH '85 Proceedings*, 1985, 151–159.

36. Sederberg, T., Improperly parametrized rational curves, Comput. Aided Geom. Design **1** (1986), 67–75.

37. Sederberg, T., Lecture notes on CAGD, Brigham Young Univ., 1987.

38. Sederberg, T. and X. Wang, Rational hodographs, Comput. Aided Geom. Design **4** (1988), 333–336.

39. Shantz, M. and S. Chang, Rendering trimmed NURBS with adaptive forward differencing, Computer Graphics **22** (1988), 189–198.

40. Tiller, W., Rational B-splines for curve and surface representation, IEEE Computer Graphics and Applications **3** (1983).

41. Vesprille, K., Computer aided design application of the rational *B*-spline approximation form, PhD dissertation, Syracuse University, 1975.

Gerald Farin
Computer Science Department
Arizona State University
Tempe, Arizona 85287
USA

EMAIL: farin@ asuvax.csnet

# Hierarchical Segmentations of Algebraic Curves and Some Applications

## Rida T. Farouki

**Abstract.**     We describe a pre-processing scheme for algebraic curves which dissects them into segments exhibiting an increasing simplicity of their intrinsic geometry. The segmentation is based on identifying points of a curve where successive differential characteristics vanish, and facilitates a variety of applications such as the shape analysis, polygonal approximation, localization and intersection of curves, and the approximation of offset curves.

## §1. Introduction

The *intrinsic equation* of a plane curve is a familiar notion of elementary differential geometry, giving the (signed) curvature $\kappa$ as an explicit function $\kappa(s)$ of the cumulative arc length $s$ [11]. A given $\kappa(s)$ determines a *unique* curve, apart from a rigid motion, which may be fixed by specifying a start point $(x_0, y_0)$ and tangent $\mathbf{t}_0$ at $s = 0$.

Although intrinsic equations have been invoked in the *design* of curves, by integrating simple prescribed forms for $\kappa(s)$ [1,12], the converse problem of *deriving* the intrinsic equations of given curves, and usefully employing them in practical applications, has received little attention. Clearly this is because most algebraic curves, whether defined by parametric (polynomial or rational) forms $\{x(t), y(t)\}$, or more generally by implicit equations $f(x, y) = 0$, do not possess simple closed-form expressions for $\kappa(s)$ – apart from the trivial case $\kappa(s) = constant$ for a circle or straight line.

However, much of the information contained in $\kappa(s)$ may be extracted and employed to advantage without writing down an explicit form for it. In this paper we propose a *hierarchical segmentation* procedure for algebraic curves, based on identifying points where $\kappa(s)$ and its successive derivatives vanish. These points dissect a (bounded) curve into a sequence of contiguous segments

Mathematical Methods in Computer Aided Geometric Design
Tom Lyche and Larry L. Schumaker (eds.), pp. 239–248.

characterized by a certain simplicity of their intrinsic geometry – and thus especially amenable to diverse curve-processing functions. The split points are themselves algebraic, requiring only standard polynomial arithmetic and root approximation techniques for their determination.

The procedure bears only superficial resemblance to familiar *subdivision* methods (e.g., the de Casteljau and knot-insertion algorithms for Bézier and B-spline curves, respectively [4]) frequently used in rendering, intersecting, and approximating parametric curves). Hierarchical segmentation should be regarded essentially as a *pre-processing* step in such applications, furnishing simple elements on which traditional algorithms operate with enhanced speed and robustness. Whether this strategy proves cost-effective will depend on the extent to which a curve is to be processed.

Finally, we emphasize that the segmentation scheme is based on the curve *geometry* and not an arbitrary *parameterization* of that geometry, as is the case with customary subdivision techniques.

## §2. Characteristic Points

In the interest of brevity, we concentrate at present on curves specified by a polynomial parameterization $\mathbf{r}(t) = \{x(t), y(t)\}$. We consider the bounded segment $t \in [0, 1]$ and assume that $|\mathbf{r}'(t)| \neq 0$ on that interval. Then $t$ bears a monotone relation to the arc length $s$, but otherwise it is impossible that $t = s$ when $\mathbf{r}(t)$ is of degree $n \geq 2$ (*i.e.*, not a straight line). For numerical stability, it is preferable that $\mathbf{r}(t)$ be specified and processed in Bernstein-Bézier form [6,7], although the segmentation is obviously quite independent of this.

Arc-length and parametric derivatives along $\mathbf{r}(t)$ are related by

$$\frac{d}{ds} = \frac{1}{|\mathbf{r}'|} \frac{d}{dt} .$$

In particular, $\mathbf{t} = d\mathbf{r}/ds$ is the unit tangent and $\mathbf{n} = \mathbf{t} \times \mathbf{z}$ the unit normal ($\mathbf{z}$ being a unit vector orthogonal to the plane of the curve); these vectors satisfy the *Frenet* equations

$$\frac{d\mathbf{t}}{ds} = -\kappa \mathbf{n} , \qquad \frac{d\mathbf{n}}{ds} = \kappa \mathbf{t} ,$$

the quantity $\kappa$ being the *curvature* [11]. Thus, all arc-length derivatives of $\mathbf{r}(t)$ may be expressed in terms of $\mathbf{t}$, $\mathbf{n}$ and $\kappa(s)$ and its derivatives

$$\frac{d\mathbf{r}}{ds} = \mathbf{t} , \qquad \frac{d^2\mathbf{r}}{ds^2} = -\kappa \mathbf{n} , \qquad \frac{d^3\mathbf{r}}{ds^3} = -\kappa^2 \mathbf{t} - \frac{d\kappa}{ds} \mathbf{n} , \qquad \dots$$

where $\mathbf{t}, \kappa, d\kappa/ds, \dots$ are given in terms of the *parametric* derivatives $\mathbf{r}'$, $\mathbf{r}''$, $\mathbf{r}'''$, $\dots$ by

$$\mathbf{t} = \frac{\mathbf{r}'}{|\mathbf{r}'|} , \qquad \kappa = \frac{(\mathbf{r}' \times \mathbf{r}'') \cdot \mathbf{z}}{|\mathbf{r}'|^3} ,$$

$$\frac{d\kappa}{ds} = \frac{|\mathbf{r}'|^2(\mathbf{r}' \times \mathbf{r}''') \cdot \mathbf{z} - 3(\mathbf{r}' \cdot \mathbf{r}'')(\mathbf{r}' \times \mathbf{r}'') \cdot \mathbf{z}}{|\mathbf{r}'|^6}, \quad \ldots$$

The numerator components of **t** are the polynomials $\{x'(t), y'(t)\}$. We note that the numerator terms of $\kappa$, $d\kappa/ds$, ... are also polynomials in $t$, which we denote by $P_2(t)$, $P_3(t)$, ....

**Definition 2.1.** *Turning points of* $\mathbf{r}(t)$ *occur at real roots of the polynomials* $x'(t)$ *and* $y'(t)$, *of degree* $n-1$ *at most.*

**Definition 2.2.** *Inflections of* $\mathbf{r}(t)$ *occur at real roots of the polynomial* $P_2(t)$, *of degree* $2n-4$ *at most.*

**Definition 2.3.** *Vertices of* $\mathbf{r}(t)$ *occur at real roots of the polynomial* $P_3(t)$, *of degree* $4n-7$ *at most.*

Turning points, inflections, and vertices are *characteristic points* of order 1, 2, and 3, respectively. In general, characteristic points of order $r$ $(\geq 2)$ occur at the real roots of the polynomial $P_r(t)$, the numerator of the expression for $d^{r-2}\kappa/ds^{r-2}$.

**Lemma 2.4.** *For a polynomial curve* $\mathbf{r}(t)$ *of degree* $n$, *the* $(r-2)$-*th derivative of the intrinsic equation has the form* $d^{r-2}\kappa/ds^{r-2} = P_r(t)/|\mathbf{r}'|^{3(r-1)}$, *where* $P_r(t)$ *is a polynomial of degree* $2(r-1)n-3r+2$, *at most, for* $r \geq 2$.

**Proof:** We note $\kappa$ has the form $P_2(t)/|\mathbf{r}'|^3$, with $P_2$ of degree $2n-4$ in $t$ due to a cancellation of leading terms, and apply induction with the arc-length derivative operator $d/ds = |\mathbf{r}'|^{-1}d/dt$. ∎

The degrees of the polynomials $\{x'(t), y'(t)\}$, $P_2(t)$, $P_3(t)$, ... impose upper bounds on the number of real characteristic points of corresponding order. These degrees are not unreasonable for curves in common use (e.g., $2, 2, 5, \ldots$ and $4, 6, 13, \ldots$ for cubics and quintics, respectively). Note that characteristic points of a given order are not necessarily distinct from those of lower order.

For a *rational* curve of degree $n$, the characteristic points also occur at the roots of univariate polynomials in the parameter $t$, although these are of somewhat higher degree (and considerably more cumbersome to derive) than for polynomial curves; cf. [8].

## §3. Hierarchical Segmentations

The *distinct* characteristic points of order $\leq r$ for $r = 1, 2, 3, \ldots$ induce a hierarchical segmentation of $\mathbf{r}(t)$; the segments delineated by these points are distinguished by a certain simplicity of their intrinsic geometry

**Definition 3.1.** *A monotone segment* $\{\mathbf{r}(t), t \in [a_1, b_1]\}$ *is a regular segment of* $\mathbf{r}(t) = \{x(t), y(t)\}$ *such that* $x' \neq 0$ *and* $y' \neq 0$ *on* $t \in (a_1, b_1)$.

**Definition 3.2.** *A convex segment* $\{\mathbf{r}(t), t \in [a_2, b_2]\}$ *is a monotone segment of* $\mathbf{r}(t)$ *such that* $\kappa \neq 0$ *on* $t \in (a_2, b_2)$.

**Definition 3.3.** *A primitive segment* $\{\mathbf{r}(t), t \in [a_3, b_3]\}$ *is a convex segment of* $\mathbf{r}(t)$ *such that* $d\kappa/ds \neq 0$ *on* $t \in (a_3, b_3)$.

These definitions are motivated primarily by their utility in various practical applications. (Note, for example, that our notion of a *convex* segment is more restrictive than generally accepted.) Note also that monotone segments are not intrinsic to the curve, being determined by the orientation of the axes (however, any orientation suffices to define a valid monotone segmentation).

Monotone, convex, and primitive segments will also be called 1-, 2-, and 3-segments, and in general we have

**Definition 3.4.** *An* $r$-*segment* $\{\mathbf{r}(t), t \in [a_r, b_r]\}$ *is an* $(r-1)$-*segment such that* $d^{r-2}\kappa/ds^{r-2} \neq 0$ *on* $t \in (a_r, b_r)$, *for* $r \geq 2$.

We will be concerned here mainly with segmentations of order $r \leq 3$. The following simple observation will prove valuable in a number of situations:

**Remark 3.5.** *Any subsegment of an* $r$-*segment is also an* $r$-*segment.*

Finally, we note that the *identity* of the $r$-segments on a rational curve is immediately apparent from the partition $[0, t_1, \ldots, t_N, 1]$ of the parameter interval $[0, 1]$ by the distinct real roots $\{t_i\}$ of the polynomials $x'(t)$, $y'(t)$, $P_2(t)$, $\ldots$, $P_r(t)$, sorted in ascending order. This fact is not trivial, since for general algebraic curves the absence of a simple global parameterization renders the identification much more difficult.

## §4. Implicit Curves

It is well-known [15] that rational curves are a special class of algebraic curves, and cannot describe precisely many loci of practical interest (e.g., surface intersections). We now examine segmentation in the context of general plane algebraic curves, as specified by implicit equations $f(x, y) = 0$.

Along $f(x, y) = 0$, the arc-length total derivative operator is

$$\frac{d}{ds} = \frac{\pm 1}{|\nabla f|} \left[ f_y \frac{\partial}{\partial x} - f_x \frac{\partial}{\partial y} \right],$$

where $|\nabla f| = \sqrt{f_x^2 + f_y^2}$. By repeated differentiation we deduce that

$$\mathbf{t} = \pm \frac{(f_y, -f_x)}{|\nabla f|}, \quad \kappa = \frac{H}{|\nabla f|^3}, \quad \frac{d\kappa}{ds} = \pm \frac{K}{|\nabla f|^6}, \quad \cdots$$

the choice of sign corresponding to the sense in which $s$ increases, and $H$, $K$, $\ldots$ being given in terms of partial derivatives of $f$

$$H = 2 f_x f_y f_{xy} - f_x^2 f_{yy} - f_y^2 f_{xx},$$

$$K = |\nabla f|^2 (f_x^3 f_{yyy} - 3 f_x^2 f_y f_{xyy} + 3 f_x f_y^2 f_{xxy} - f_y^3 f_{xxx})$$
$$- 3H (f_x f_y (f_{xx} - f_{yy}) - (f_x^2 - f_y^2) f_{xy}), \quad \cdots$$

**Lemma 4.1.** *Turning points, inflections, vertices, etc., of $f(x, y) = 0$ occur at real solutions of the simultaneous bivariate equations $\{f = f_x = 0,\ f = f_y = 0\}$, $f = H = 0$, $f = K = 0$, etc., within the domain of interest.*

In order to identify these characteristic points algorithmically, we must have recourse to the resultant calculations of classical elimination theory [14], or the Gröbner basis reduction method [5]. In either case, the computational complexity greatly exceeds that of simply identifying the roots of univariate polynomials, as in the case of rational curves.

We note also that the expressions for $\mathbf{t}$, $\kappa$, $d\kappa/ds$, $\ldots$ on $f(x, y) = 0$ are all indeterminate whenever $f_x = f_y = 0$

**Definition 4.2.** *A point of $f(x, y) = 0$ is singular if $f_x = f_y = 0$ there.*

Such singular points must always be included among the characteristic points of $f(x, y) = 0$; they may be identified without further computation as the solutions common to both $f = f_x = 0$ and $f = f_y = 0$, already determined. The curve may have several real branches at a singular point, and the quantities $\mathbf{t}$, $\kappa$, $d\kappa/ds$, $\ldots$ must be determined separately for each by means of power-series developments (cf. [8] for further details).

One final point about implicit curves: the identification of characteristic points does not, on its own, establish a segmentation since we do not know which pairs of points actually delineate an $r$-segment. This ambiguity may be resolved by appealing to a numerical *curve-tracing* procedure [3], but in general such methods are quite difficult to implement in a robust manner.

**Example 4.3.** *Consider the quartic curve given by $f(x, y) = 36x^2(x^2 + y^2) - 12(6x^3 + 3x^2y + 5xy^2 + y^3) + 59x^2 + 60xy + 43y^2 - 29x - 34y + 9 = 0$ on $[0, 1] \times [0, 1]$. Solving the systems $f = f_x = 0$, $f = f_y = 0$, $f = H = 0$, and $f = K = 0$, we find 3 turning points with horizontal tangent, 3 with vertical tangent, 1 singular point, 4 inflections, and 6 vertices; a turning point and inflection coincide at $(5/6, 1/2)$. By tracing the curve between these characteristic points, we identify 18 primitive segments (Figure 1).*

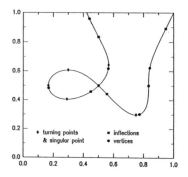

**Figure 1.** Characteristic points.

The difficulty of segmenting implicit curves is illustrated by the resultant degrees encountered in Example 4.3 (as computed in the SCRATCHPAD II computer algebra system): 10 and 11 for turning points, 24 for inflections, and 45 for vertices, although $f(x, y) = 0$ itself is only of degree 4.

An immediate application of hierarchical segmentations is the analysis of "shape" and topological configuration. Since the characteristic points at all stages of the hierarchy are algebraic, the method may be regarded as an extension of established algebraic procedures for these purposes [2]. We briefly discuss below some other practical applications arising from the differential approach to processing algebraic curves.

## §5. Localization and Intersections

The efficiency and reliability of iterative curve-intersection procedures is dramatically improved by furnishing them with close starting approximations. The segmentation procedure yields relatively simple localizing regions for each segment which are refined at each stage of the hierarchy. Bounds for starting approximations are then indicated by the overlap of such regions. Elementary geometric considerations lead to the following results:

**Lemma 5.1.** *A monotone segment between* **a** *and* **b** *is confined to the rectangle* $\mathcal{R}$ *with the chord from* **a** *to* **b** *as diagonal.*

**Lemma 5.2.** *A convex segment between* **a** *and* **b** *is confined to the triangle* $\mathcal{T}$ *with vertices* **a**, **b** *and* **c**, *the intersection of the tangent lines at* **a** *and* **b**.

**Lemma 5.3.** *A primitive segment between* **a** *and* **b** *(where* $|\kappa_a| > |\kappa_b|$*) is confined to a region* $\mathcal{V}$ *defined thus: follow the circle of curvature at* **a** *until it meets the chord from* **a** *to* **b**; *follow this chord to* **b**; *follow the circle of curvature at* **b** *until it meets the tangent at* **a**; *follow this tangent back to* **a**.

**Remark 5.4.** *For a primitive segment, it may be readily verified that the confining regions satisfy* $\mathcal{V} \subset \mathcal{T} \subset \mathcal{R}$.

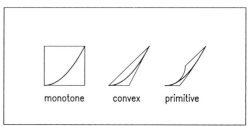

**Figure 2.** Confinement of a parabolic arc.

In principle, further confinement may be achieved by proceeding to higher order segmentations. However, it is questionable whether any practical benefit will ensue, since the diminished area of the confining region is mitigated by the complexity of its boundary.

**Example 5.5.** *The parabolic segment* $\mathbf{r}(t) = (t, t^2)$ *on* $t \in [0, 1]$ *is primitive, since* $x' = 1$, $y' = 2t$, $\kappa = 2/(1 + 4t^2)^{3/2}$, *and* $d\kappa/ds = -24t/(1 + 4t^2)^3$ *do not vanish on its interior (the point* $t = 0$ *is both a turning point and a vertex). Figure 2 illustrates confinements of this segment, considered successively as monotone, convex, and primitive, by the regions* $\mathcal{R}, \mathcal{T}, \mathcal{V}$.

Finally, note that convex segments may have at most two intersections.

## §6. Offset Curves

Let $\mathbf{r}(t)$ be a (regular) rational plane curve, the "generator," defined on $t \in [0, 1]$. If $\mathbf{n}(t)$ denotes the unit normal along $\mathbf{r}(t)$, the *offset curve* to $\mathbf{r}(t)$ at (signed) distance $d$ is defined by

$$\mathbf{r}_o(t) = \mathbf{r}(t) + d\,\mathbf{n}(t), \quad t \in [0, 1].$$

The offset $\mathbf{r}_o(t)$ is (a segment of) an algebraic curve, but in general is *not* rational itself because of the radical term arising in the normal $\mathbf{n}(t)$. Offset curves are thus usually approximated by piecewise-rational forms [9,10,13].

Segmentations with $r = 3$ are quite useful in approximating offset curves. The derivative operator with respect to arc length $s_o$ along the offset is simply

$$\frac{d}{ds_o} = \frac{1}{|\mathbf{r}'_o|} \frac{d}{dt},$$

and by repeated application we can express the differential properties $\mathbf{t}_o$, $\kappa_o$, $d\kappa_o/ds_o$, ... of the offset in terms of those $\mathbf{t}$, $\kappa$, $d\kappa/ds$, ... of the generator

$$\mathbf{t}_o = \frac{1 + \kappa d}{|1 + \kappa d|}\mathbf{t}, \quad \kappa_o = \frac{\kappa}{|1 + \kappa d|}, \quad \frac{d\kappa_o}{ds_o} = \frac{1 + \kappa d}{|1 + \kappa d|^4}\frac{d\kappa}{ds}, \quad \cdots$$

at points of corresponding parameter value $t$.

**Definition 6.1.** *If* $\mathbf{r}(t)$ *has curvatures* $\kappa_1, \ldots, \kappa_N$ *at vertices* $t_1, \ldots, t_N$ *and* $\kappa_0, \kappa_{N+1}$ *at* $t = 0, 1$ *the offset* $\mathbf{r}_o(t)$ *is said to be* degenerate *if* $\min(\kappa_i d) \leq -1$.

**Definition 6.2.** *A point on a degenerate offset curve* $\mathbf{r}_o(t)$ *corresponding to a point of curvature* $\kappa = -1/d$ *on the generator* $\mathbf{r}(t)$ *is called a* cusp.

From the expressions for the differential characteristics of the offset, it is evident that the tangent $\mathbf{t}_o$ suffers a reversal at a cusp, while the curvature and its derivatives $\kappa_o$, $d\kappa_o/ds_o$, ... are not well defined there.

**Lemma 6.3.** *If we include points of curvature* $\kappa = -1/d$ *on the generator and cusps on the offset among the characteristic points,* $r$*-segments of the generator and offset curves are in one-to-one correspondence for* $r \leq 3$.

**Proof:** From the expressions for the differential characteristics of the offset, it is evident that a necessary and sufficient condition for any of the quantities $x'_o, y'_o, \kappa_o, d\kappa_o/ds_o$ to vanish at parameter value $t$ is that the corresponding quantity for the generator, $x', y', \kappa, d\kappa/ds$, should vanish at $t$. The points of curvature $\kappa = -1/d$ on $\mathbf{r}(t)$ and corresponding cusps on $\mathbf{r}_o(t)$ are included because $\mathbf{t}_o, \kappa_o, d\kappa_o/ds_o$ are not well defined at a cusp. ∎

The importance of Lemma 6.3 lies in the fact that a segmentation of the offset into simple elements – amenable to various approximation procedures – is achieved by an analysis of the generator curve only. The correspondence does not extend to higher orders, however, since by further differentiation we deduce that

$$\frac{d^2\kappa_o}{ds_o^2} = \frac{1 + \kappa d}{|1 + \kappa d|^5} \frac{d^2\kappa}{ds^2} - \frac{3d}{|1 + \kappa d|^5} \left(\frac{d\kappa}{ds}\right)^2,$$

so points where $d^2\kappa_o/ds_o^2$ and $d^2\kappa/ds^2$ vanish are *not* in simple correspondence.

**Example 6.4.** *For the parabolic segment* $\mathbf{r}(t) = (t, t^2)$ *on* $t \in [-2, +2]$*, we have unit normal* $\mathbf{n}(t) = (2t, -1)/\sqrt{1 + 4t^2}$ *and curvature* $\kappa = 2/(1 + 4t^2)^{3/2}$*. Taking offset distance* $d = -1$*, we identify two points of curvature* $\kappa = -1/d$*, at* $t = \pm0.38321\ldots$*, and a turning point/vertex at* $t = 0$*. Figure 3 illustrates corresponding primitive segments on the generator and offset curves.*

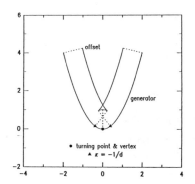

**Figure 3.** Primitive segments on generator and offset curves.

As evident in Figure 3, degenerate offsets usually suffer self-intersections in the vicinity of their cusps. In practical applications (e.g., N.C. machining, where the offset describes the center-line path of a cylindrical tool cutting the generator), the loops induced by these intersections must usually be trimmed off. To each self-intersection of the offset there are two *distinct* values $u \neq v$ of the parameter $t$; these may also be included among the characteristic points of the generator and offset, to ensure that the correspondence of primitive segments is retained after trimming.

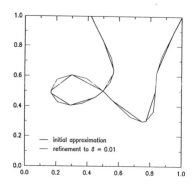

**Figure 4.** Polygonal approximations.

## §7. Polygonal Approximations

The $r = 3$ segmentations are also valuable in computing piecewise-linear approximations of algebraic curves to a prescribed tolerance $\delta$, facilitating "intelligent" use of the following standard result from approximation theory:

**Lemma 7.1.** *Let $C$ be a regular curve segment between* **a** *and* **b**, *$s$ the arc length measured from* **a**, *$S$ the total arc length, and $\sigma = s/S$ the fractional arc length. Then the distance $d(\sigma)$ between points of equal fractional distance $\sigma$ along $C$ and along the chord from* **a** *to* **b** *satisfies the bound*

$$d(\sigma) \leq \frac{1}{8} S^2 \sup_{\sigma \in [0,1]} |\kappa(\sigma)| \quad \text{for all} \quad \sigma \in [0, 1].$$

**Proof:** See [8]. ∎

Since $d\kappa/ds \neq 0$ over the interior of a primitive segment – *i.e.*, $\kappa$ does not attain an intermediate extremum – we can simply replace $\sup |\kappa(\sigma)|$ above by $\max(|\kappa_a|, |\kappa_b|)$. We also take advantage of this property in the subdivision of a primitive segments since the subsegments are necessarily primitive, new error bounds for them require only the evaluation of the curvature at the split point. (If $\delta$ is quite small, we may substitute the chord length $L = |\mathbf{b} - \mathbf{a}|$ in place of $S$, since $S/L$ approaches unity rapidly as subdivision proceeds.)

In particular, subdivision strategies may be formulated for primitive segments which economize on the number of chords required to achieve the given tolerance $\delta$. These are described in some detail in [8].

**Example 7.2.** *Consider again the quartic curve of Example 4.1. Replacing each primitive segment by its chord, we obtain the initial approximation shown in Figure 4. Determining the error bound for each chord requires only the evaluation of end-point curvatures $\kappa_a, \kappa_b$ for the corresponding segment, and a numerical quadrature for its total arc length $S$ (or we may simply use the* *chord length L). The dashed lines indicate a refinement to tolerance $\delta = 0.01$, obtained by an optimal split of segments with large chordal deviation (cf. [8]).*

## References

1. Adams, J. A., The intrinsic method for curve definition, Comput. Aided Design **7** (1975), 243–249.
2. Arnon, D. S., G. E. Collins, and S. McCallum, Cylindrical algebraic decomposition I. The basic algorithm; II. An adjacency algorithm for the plane, SIAM J. Comput. **13** (1984), 865-889.
3. Bajaj, C., C. Hoffmann, and J. Hopcroft, Tracing planar algebraic curves, CSD-TR-637 (1987), Computer Sciences Dept., Purdue University.
4. Boehm, W., G. Farin, and J. Kahmann, A survey of curve and surface methods in CAGD, Comput. Aided Geom. Design **1** (1984), 1–60.
5. Buchberger, B., Gröbner bases: an algorithmic method in polynomial ideal theory, in *Multidimensional Systems Theory*, N.K. Bose (ed.), Reidel, Dordrecht, 1985,184–232.
6. Farouki, R. T. and V. T. Rajan, On the numerical condition of polynomials in Bernstein form, Comput. Aided Geom. Design **4** (1987), 191–216.
7. Farouki, R. T. and V. T. Rajan, Algorithms for polynomials in Bernstein form, Comput. Aided Geom. Design **5** (1988), 1–26.
8. Farouki, R. T., Concise piecewise linear approximation of algebraic curves, IBM Research Report RC13724, 1988.
9. Hoschek, J., Spline approximation of offset curves, Comput. Aided Geom. Design **5** (1988), 33–40.
10. Klass, R., An offset spline approximation for plane cubic splines, Comput. Aided Design **15** (1983), 297–299.
11. Kreyszig, E., *Differential Geometry*, University of Toronto Press, 1959.
12. Nutbourne, A. W., P. M. McLellan, and R. M. L. Kensit, Curvature profiles for plane curves, Comput. Aided Design **4** (1972), 176–184.
13. Tiller, W. and E. G. Hanson, Offsets of two-dimensional profiles, IEEE Comp. Graph. Appl. **4** (Sept. 1984), 36-46.
14. van der Waerden, B. L., *Modern Algebra*, Vol. 2, Ungar, New York, 1950.
15. Walker, R. J., *Algebraic Curves*, Springer-Verlag, New York, 1978.

Rida T. Farouki
IBM Thomas J. Watson Research Center
P.O. Box 218, Yorktown Heights, NY 10598
USA

EMAIL: farouki @ yktvmx

# An Algorithm for Shape Preserving Parametric Interpolating Curves with $G^2$ Continuity

## T. A. Foley, T. N. T. Goodman and K. Unsworth

**Abstract.** In [3], Goodman and Unsworth describe a parametric shape preserving $G^2$ interpolation scheme for planar curves, obtained by patching together cubic segments and straight lines, and requiring both a tangent direction and curvature value to be assigned at each interpolation point. The generation of a cubic segment generally requires a positive solution of a system of two non-linear quadratic equations, and in order to guarantee the existence of a unique positive solution, lower bounds are placed upon the magnitude of the curvature at each relevant interpolation point. In this paper, a modification is proposed to the way in which the curvature values are selected. This leads to an algorithm which may require a number of passes until a unique positive solution of each non-linear system is guaranteed.

## §1. Introduction

In [3], a parametric interpolation scheme for planar curves is described, obtained by patching together cubic segments and straight lines. The scheme has a number of desirable properties which include the following:

— it is local convexity preserving (l.c.p.) (see [2]),

— in the event that the given data arise from a function, it can generate a single-valued curve which is local monotonicity preserving (l.m.p.),

— in general, the unit tangent vector and the curvature vary continuously along the curve; *i.e.*, the curve has, in general, $G^2$ continuity,

— it is a local scheme,

— it is invariant under a rotation or change of scale in any direction,

— it is, in general, stable; *i.e.*, small changes in the data lead to small changes in the curve.

Mathematical Methods in Computer Aided Geometric Design
Tom Lyche and Larry L. Schumaker (eds.), pp. 249–259.

In addition, de Boor *et al* [1] have considered interpolation using $G^2$ parametric cubics and have established that an interpolating curve with non-zero curvature is $6^{th}$-order accurate, although possibly only $4^{th}$-order accurate near points of zero curvature.

The scheme described in [3] requires a positive solution of a system of two non-linear quadratic equations for each cubic segment which is not joined to a linear segment. In order to guarantee the existence of a unique positive solution of such a system, lower bounds are placed upon the magnitude of the curvatures at the interpolation points at each end of the relevant curve segment, and the values of these curvatures are subsequently chosen in order to satisfy these bounds. However, experience with using the method indicates that the recommended choice of curvature values may be unnecessarily large, and it is the purpose of this paper to describe an alternative algorithm which offers a wider choice of curvature values based upon results obtained in [1].

The remainder of the paper is divided into five sections. In Section 2, an overview of the scheme described in [3] is presented, and the proposed modifications which form the basis of the new algorithm are explained in Section 3. Details of the new algorithm are then given in Section 4. Output from the algorithm is presented in Section 5 and the final section, Section 6, provides a summary and conclusions based upon the work.

## §2. Overview of the Interpolation Scheme

In its most general form, the algorithm can deal with arbitrary data sets, and can generate either functional or open or closed multi-valued curves. However, for the purposes of this exposition, it will be assumed that the given data set contains no consecutive collinear points and does not arise from a function. It will also be assumed that an open curve is to be generated. The details of the algorithm which relate to closed curves, collinear data points and functional data are described in Sections 3,4,5 of [3].

Let $I_i = (x_i, y_i), i = 0, \ldots, N$, be given data points in the plane. Suppose that tangent directions $T_i, i = 1, \ldots, N - 1$, are specified, these being of the form

$$T_i = a_i(I_i - I_{i-1}) + b_i(I_{i+1} - I_i), \quad a_i, b_i \geq 0. \tag{2.1}$$

A rule for choosing $a_i, b_i$ in order that the resulting curve is l.c.p. and satisfies the stability and invariance properties referred to in Section 1 is,

$$\left. \begin{array}{l} a_i = |P_{i+1}|, \quad i = 1, \ldots, N - 2, \quad a_{N-1} = |P_{N-1}|, \\ b_1 = |P_1|, \quad b_i = |P_{i-1}|, \quad i = 2, \ldots, N - 1, \end{array} \right\} \tag{2.2}$$

where

$$P_i = (x_i - x_{i-1})(y_{i+1} - y_i) - (x_{i+1} - x_i)(y_i - y_{i-1}), \quad i = 1, \ldots, N - 1.$$

Values for $T_0, T_N$ can be chosen using some suitable end conditions.

Having specified the tangent directions at each interpolation point, the curve $Q(t) = (Q_1(t), Q_2(t))$, may be represented between $I_i$ and $I_{i+1}$, $i = 0, \ldots, N-1$, by a cubic polynomial which may be written in Bézier form as

$$Q(t) = A(1-t)^3 + 3B(1-t)^2 t + 3C(1-t)t^2 + Dt^3, \quad (0 \le t \le 1), \quad (2.3)$$

where $\lambda_i, \mu_i > 0$, $A = I_i$, $B = I_i + \lambda_i |T_i|$, $C = I_{i+1} - \mu_i |T_{i+1}|$, $D = I_{i+1}$. Thus $Q(t)$ interpolates $I_i, I_{i+1}, T_i, T_{i+1}$. Values for $\lambda_i, \mu_i$ must now be selected on each curve segment in order to locate the two corresponding interior Bézier points. These values are chosen so that the curve interpolates specified curvature values at the interpolation points, thereby ensuring curvature continuity. Now suppose, given two vectors $A = (A_1, A_2), B = (B_1, B_2)$, we write

$$A \times B := A_1 B_2 - A_2 B_1 = |A||B| \sin \theta,$$

where $\theta$ represents the angle from $A$ to $B$ in an anti-clockwise direction. Suppose also that $\kappa_i, \kappa_{i+1}$ represent the curvatures at $I_i, I_{i+1}$ respectively. Then, it is shown in [3] that in order for the curve to interpolate these values, $\lambda_i, \mu_i$ must satisfy the following equations:

$$\left. \begin{array}{l} \mu_i \gamma_i = \alpha_i - 1.5 \kappa_i |T_i|^3 \lambda_i^2, \\ \lambda_i \gamma_i = \beta_i - 1.5 \kappa_{i+1} |T_{i+1}|^3 \mu_i^2, \end{array} \right\} \quad (2.4)$$

where

$$\lambda_i, \mu_i > 0, \quad \alpha_i = T_i \times (I_{i+1} - I_i), \quad \beta_i = (I_{i+1} - I_i) \times T_{i+1}, \quad \gamma_i = T_i \times T_{i+1}.$$

Values for $\kappa_i, \kappa_{i+1}$ must now be chosen so that at $I_i$ and $I_{i+1}$ the curve should turn towards the straight line joining $I_i$ to $I_{i+1}$ and so that (2.4) should have a unique positive solution. It is shown in Section 2 of [3] that it is sufficient to choose $\kappa_i, \kappa_{i+1}$ so that

$$\kappa_i \alpha_i > 0, \quad \kappa_{i+1} \beta_i > 0, \quad (2.5)$$

$$|\kappa_i| > |\alpha_i| \gamma_i^2 / (1.5 |T_i|^3 \beta_i^2), \quad (2.6)$$

$$|\kappa_{i+1}| > |\beta_i| \gamma_i^2 / (1.5 |T_i|^3 \alpha_i^2). \quad (2.7)$$

In the event that $\gamma_i = \gamma_{i-1} = 0$, however, conditions (2.6) and (2.7) could allow $\kappa_i$ to be arbitrarily close to zero, and consequently $\lambda_i$ could be arbitrarily large, which in turn would allow the portion of the curve between $I_i$ and $I_{i+1}$ to have arbitrarily large length. To avoid this possibility, stronger restrictions are imposed on the curvatures by defining

$$\delta_i = |T_i|^2 \beta_i^2 + |T_{i+1}|^2 \alpha_i^2, \quad i = 0, \ldots, N-1, \quad (2.8)$$

and choosing the curvature values as follows:

$$\kappa_i \alpha_i > 0, \quad i = 0, \ldots, N-1, \quad \kappa_N \beta_{N-1} > 0, \quad (2.9)$$

$$|\kappa_i| = \max \left( \frac{2|\alpha_i|\delta_i}{1.5|T_i|^3\beta_i^2|I_{i+1} - I_i|^2}, \frac{2|\beta_{i-1}|\delta_{i-1}}{1.5|T_i|^3\alpha_{i-1}^2|I_i - I_{i-1}|^2} \right), \quad i = 0, \ldots, N,$$

$$(2.10)$$

with the second term on the right-hand side of (2.10) ignored if $i = 0$, and the first term ignored if $i = N$.

In the event that $\gamma_i = 0$, it can be shown using (2.10) that

$$|\lambda_i T_i| \leq |I_{i+1} - I_i|/\sqrt{2}, \quad |\mu_i T_{i+1}| \leq |I_{i+1} - I_i|/\sqrt{2}.$$

Having specified $T_i, \kappa_i, i = 0, \ldots, N$, using (2.1), (2.2), (2.9) and (2.10), the unique positive values of $\lambda_i, \mu_i$ which are solutions of (2.4) can be found for each curve segment, and each curve segment may then be defined using (2.3).

## §3. Modifications to the Scheme

Experience with using the above interpolation scheme indicates that in a number of cases the curves produced were not always "visually pleasing", due to the fact that the magnitude of the curvature values generated by (2.10) were unnecessarily large. Hence, ways of possibly reducing the values of $|\kappa_i|, i = 0, \ldots, N$, are now described.

We first consider the quantity $\delta_i$ as defined in (2.8). The restrictions on the curvatures imposed by (2.8) and (2.10) can be relaxed by defining a new $\delta_i, \tilde{\delta}_i$, by

$$\tilde{\delta}_i = (|T_i||\beta_i| + |T_{i+1}||\alpha_i|)^2, \quad i = 0, \ldots, N-1, \quad (3.1)$$

and replacing (2.10) by

$$|\kappa_i| = \max \left( \frac{|\alpha_i|\tilde{\delta}_i}{1.5|T_i|^3\beta_i^2|I_{i+1} - I_i|^2}, \frac{|\beta_{i-1}|\tilde{\delta}_{i-1}}{1.5|T_i|^3\alpha_{i-1}^2|I_i - I_{i-1}|^2} \right). \quad (3.2)$$

In the event that $\gamma_i = 0$, it is now found that using (3.2),

$$|\lambda_i T_i| \leq |I_{i+1} - I_i|, \quad |\mu_i T_{i+1}| \leq |I_{i+1} - I_i|.$$

Note, however, that the condition which necessitates the use of (3.2), viz. $\gamma_i = \gamma_{i-1} = 0$, amounts to requiring three consecutive tangent directions to be parallel. In practice it is unlikely that this situation will occur very often. Thus it is suggested that (3.2) should only be used on a selective basis; i.e., only when this particular condition occurs, rather than for all curvature values, as in the original algorithm.

As a consequence of the above, the use of (2.6) and (2.7) in assigning curvature values at the interpolation points which do not use (3.2) must be considered. These two conditions arise from three possible cases involving the given data and the specified tangent directions. Thus for the curve segment between $I_i$ and $I_{i+1}$, these are

1. $\alpha_i\beta_i < 0$,     $\alpha_i\gamma_i > 0$,

2. $\alpha_i \beta_i < 0, \qquad \alpha_i \gamma_i < 0,$

3. $\alpha_i \beta_i > 0, \qquad \alpha_i \gamma_i > 0.$

The condition $\alpha_i \beta_i > 0, \alpha_i \gamma_i < 0$ requires no constraints on the curvature values. These three cases will now be considered individually.

**Case 1** $(\alpha_i \beta_i < 0, \alpha_i \gamma_i > 0)$. It is shown in [3] that (2.5) and (2.7) are sufficient conditions for the existence of a unique positive solution of (2.4), and it can be easily shown using either simple geometry or an algebraic argument similar to the one in [3], that these conditions are also necessary.

**Case 2** $(\alpha_i \beta_i < 0, \alpha_i \gamma_i < 0)$. Remarks similar to Case 1 are also appropriate in this case, with (2.5) and (2.6) the corresponding conditions.

**Case 3** $(\alpha_i \beta_i > 0, \alpha_i \gamma_i > 0)$. In this case, (2.5)–(2.7) are the corresponding sufficient conditions used in [3], but de Boor *et al* [1] have studied this case in some detail and have shown that a wider range of possible curvature values may be used while still guaranteeing a unique positive solution of (2.4), and it is these values that are now considered. Assume that (2.5) is true. Adopting the same notation as [1], let

$$(R_0)_i = 1.5|\kappa_i||T_i|^3 \beta_i^2/(|\alpha_i|\gamma_i^2), \quad (R_1)_i = 1.5|\kappa_{i+1}||T_i|^3 \alpha_i^2/(|\beta_i|\gamma_i^2).$$

Then (2.6) and (2.7) correspond to

$$P = ((R_0)_i, (R_1)_i) \in T, \qquad (3.3)$$

where $T = (1, \infty) \times (1, \infty)$. In addition, however, de Boor *et al* [1] show that a unique positive solution of (2.4) also exists if

$$P \in S, \qquad (3.4)$$

where $S \subset U = [0, 1] \times [0, 1]$, and is bounded by two curves which meet in a cusp at $(0.75, 0.75)$; see Figure 3 of [1]. Thus, the new algorithm could allow as possible curvature values those values which satisfy either (3.3) or (3.4). For computational ease, however, a relatively small region of $S$ in the vicinity of the cusp is ignored, so that (3.4) is replaced by

$$P \in \tilde{S}, \qquad (3.5)$$

where $\tilde{S} = U - ([0.75, 1] \times [0.75, 1])$. In addition, it follows from Cases 1 and 2 above that if $\alpha_i \beta_i < 0$, then

$$P \notin U. \qquad (3.6)$$

## §4. A Modified Algorithm

The changes described in Section 3 have been included in an interactive algorithm in which the user supplies possible curvature value(s) at each interpolation point, $I_i, i = 0, \ldots, N$, via the input of values for $(R_1)_{i-1}$ and/or $(R_0)_i$. Acceptable values for these parameters will depend upon the signs of $\alpha_j \beta_j$ and $\alpha_j \gamma_j$ for $j = i - 1, i$ as discussed in the previous section. $\kappa_i$ is then initialized in order to satisfy (3.3), (3.5) or (3.6) as appropriate. In particular, the version of the algorithm below attempts to choose $P$ in order to satisfy (3.5) for all convex segments (*i.e.*, those for which $\alpha_i \beta_i > 0$), though clearly this is something that can be decided by the user. For inflection segments (*i.e.*, $\alpha_i \beta_i < 0$) the curvature values must be chosen in order to satisfy (3.6). When a value has been assigned to each $\kappa_i$, a check is performed to ensure that sufficient conditions for the existence of a unique positive solution of (2.4) are satisfied on each curve segment for which $\alpha_i \beta_i > 0$ and $\alpha_i \gamma_i > 0$. If, for any one curve segment, these are not satisfied (this may occur, for example, if such a segment is adjacent to an inflection segment), the relevant curvature value(s) are modified accordingly. This check is repeated until, in a sweep through all the curvature values, no further modifications are necessary, and the final choices for $\kappa_i, i = 0, \ldots, N$ are then provided as input for solving (2.4).

The interactive selection of the curvature values is now described for open, non-functional curves with no consecutive collinear points. Modifications are needed to deal with a totally arbitrary, possibly functional, data set, but the basic approach remains the same. Comments included in the pseudo-code are enclosed in $\{\ldots\}$. For the purposes of the explanation, the following notation is introduced for appropriate $i \in [0, N]$:

$$C0 := \frac{|\alpha_i|\gamma_i^2}{1.5|T_i|^3\beta_i^2}, \quad C1 := \frac{|\beta_{i-1}|\gamma_{i-1}^2}{1.5|T_{i-1}|^3\alpha_{i-1}^2},$$

$$R0 := (R_0)_i, \quad R1 := (R_1)_{i-1}.$$

**Algorithm**
{Assign value to $\kappa_0$ according to value of $\gamma_0$ and sign of $\alpha_0\beta_0$}
    $i := 0$
    **if** $\gamma_0 = 0$ **then**
        assign first term on right-hand side of (3.2) to $\kappa_0$
    **else**
    **begin**
{Input $R0$, $> 1$ if $\alpha_0\beta_0 < 0$, arbitrary otherwise}
        **read** $R0$;
        $\kappa_0 := R0 * C0$
    **end**;
{Enforce condition $\alpha_0\kappa_0 > 0$}
    **if** $\alpha_0 < 0$ **then** $\kappa_0 := -\kappa_0$;
{Set $i = N$ and perform analogous operations to assign value to $\kappa_N$}
    **for** $i := 1$ **to** $N - 1$ **do**

{Assign curvature values at all remaining interpolation points}
    **begin**
        **if** $\gamma_i = \gamma_{i-1} = 0$ **then**
{Case of three consecutive parallel tangent directions}
           use right-hand side of (3.2) to assign value to $\kappa_i$
        **else**
          **if** $(\alpha_i\beta_i > 0$ **and** $\alpha_{i-1}\beta_{i-1} > 0)$ **then**
{Join of two convex segments}
           **if** $(\gamma_i = 0$ **or** $\gamma_{i-1} = 0)$ **then**
{Must avoid possibility of zero curvature when taking minimum of two quantities below}
             use right-hand side of (3.2) to assign value to $\kappa_i$;
           **else**
           **begin**
{Input values for $R0, R1$ - may be arbitrary but this version of algorithm expects both $< 1$}
             **read** $(R1, R0)$;
             $\kappa_i := \min(R0 * C0, R1 * C1)$
           **end**
        **else**
           **if**$(\alpha_i\beta_i < 0$ **and** $\alpha_{i-1}\beta_{i-1} < 0)$**then**
{Join of two inflection segments - input $R0, R1 > 1$}
           **begin**
             **read** $(R1, R0)$;
             $\kappa_i := \max(R0 * C0, R1 * C1)$
           **end**
           **else**
           **if**$(\alpha_i\beta_i > 0$ **and** $\alpha_{i-1}\beta_{i-1} < 0)$**then**
{Join of inflection segment(on the left) with convex segment(on the right) }
           **begin**
{Input $R1 > 1$ and $R0$ which may be arbitrary, but this version of algorithm expects $R0 < 1$}
             **read** $(R1, R0)$
             **if** $(\alpha_{i-1}\gamma_{i-1} < 0)$ **then**
{No constraint on $\kappa_i$ from inflection segment}
               $\kappa_i := R0 * C0$
             **else**
{Assign value based upon inflection segment)}
               $\kappa_i := R1 * C1$
           **end**
           **else**
{Join of convex segment(on the left) with inflection segment(on the right). Input $R0 > 1$ and $R1$ which may be arbitrary, but this version of algorithm expects $R1 < 1$}
{Assign value to $\kappa_i$ in analogous manner to inflection/convex join above}

{Enforce condition $\alpha_i \kappa_i > 0$}
    **if** $\alpha_i < 0$ **then**
        $\kappa_i := -\kappa_i$
   **end**;
{Check that conditions for unique positive solution are satisfied for all curve segments for which $\alpha_i \beta_i > 0$ and $\alpha_i \gamma_i > 0$}
   **repeat**
     $finish := true$;
     **for** $i := 0$ **to** $N - 1$ **do**
     **begin**
       **if** $\alpha_i \beta_i > 0$ **and** $\alpha_i \gamma_i > 0$ **then**
       **begin**
{Calculate values for $R0$ and $R1$ for each segment}
       $R0 := \kappa_i / C0$;
{In all future references to $R1, C1$ replace $i$ by $i + 1$ in above definitions}
       $R1 := \kappa_{i+1} / C1$;
       $invalid1 := (1 - R0)(1 - R1) \leq 0$;
       $invalid2 := (0.75 \leq R0 \leq 1)$**and** $(0.75 \leq R1 \leq 1)$;
       **if** $(invalid1$ **or** $invalid2)$ **then**
       **begin**
        **if** $(R0 < R1)$ **then**
{Input new (larger) value for $R0$ and modify $\kappa_i$}
         **begin**
          **read**(R0);
          $\kappa_i := R0 * C0$;
          **if** $\alpha_i < 0$ **then**
            $\kappa_i := -\kappa_i$
         **end**
         **else**
         **begin**
{Input new (larger) value for $R1$ and modify $\kappa_{i+1}$}
          **read**(R1);
          $\kappa_{i+1} := R1 * C1$;
          **if** $\alpha_{i+1} < 0$ **then**
            $\kappa_{i+1} := -\kappa_{i+1}$
         **end**
        **end**;
{If any modifications have been made all values have to be re-checked}
        $finish := false$
      **end**
     **end**
   **until** finish;

The need to re-check all curvature values, following modifications in the second **for** loop, arises because any such modifications may have a non-local effect. For example, if for some $i$, **invalid1** is **true**, and $\kappa_i$, say, is modified

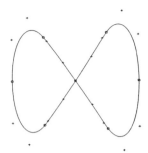

**Figure 1.** A closed curve: (○ = interpolation points, + = Bézier points).

accordingly, this change may cause **invalid1** to become **true** for $i - 1$, when previously it may have had the value **false**. The necessary modification for $i - 1$ may then affect values for $i - 2$ and so on.

The above description should be considered as a shortened version of a more versatile algorithm which can deal with arbitrary data sets and allow almost as wide a range of curvature values as possible. The full algorithm is too detailed to be included here, but has been used to generate the results described in Section 5.

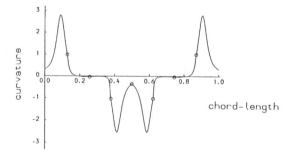

**Figure 2.** Curvature plot for Figure 1: (○ = interpolation points).

## §5. Numerical Results

Three sets of output are presented using the data of Table 1 of [3]. A closed curve is presented in Figure 1, and the corresponding curvature plot in Figure 2. These should be compared with Figures 6 and 7 of [3]. Note that the curvature values have been chosen in order to generate a smoother curvature plot than that of [3]. Two examples of open curves, using quadratic end conditions, are shown in Figure 3. Each curve is represented by one inflection segment and five convex segments. In Figure 3(a), curvature values which are relatively large

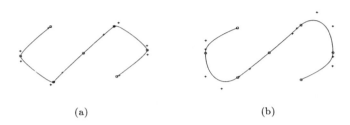

(a)                              (b)

**Figure 3.** Examples of open curves. Symbols as in Figure 1.

in magnitude have been assigned at each interpolation point, so that in this case (3.3) is satisfied on every curve segment. In Figure 3(b) the magnitudes of these curvature values have been reduced to produce a "looser" curve. In this case (3.6) is satisfied on the end segments, while (3.3) is still satisfied on the remaining segments.

## §6. Summary and Conclusions

In this paper, an algorithm for the generation of planar parametric interpolating curves has been presented. The resulting curves are l.c.p. (and may be single-valued and l.m.p. for data arising from a function), and in general have $G^2$ continuity. The interpolation scheme requires, for each cubic segment which is not adjacent to a linear segment, a positive solution of the system of equations (2.4). In order to guarantee a unique positive solution of such a system, the curvature values at the relevant interpolation points must be chosen to satisfy certain constraints. In Section 4, an algorithm is described in which these values are chosen interactively. Note, however, that they could also be chosen in a "black box" manner with no user interaction, the curvature values being assigned so that (3.3) is automatically satisfied on all curve segments. In this case, of course, only a subset of the available curvature values would be available.

It follows from the above discussion that an improved scheme would be one which did not require solutions of (2.4), but still retained the properties listed in Section 1. The removal of the need for (2.4) should clearly reduce computation time, and should also remove any curvature constraints. A study is currently in progress to try and develop such a scheme and it is hoped that the results of this study will be the subject of a future paper.

## Acknowledgment

This research was performed while one of the authors (K.U.) was visiting the Department of Computer Science, Arizona State University, on leave from the

University of Dundee. He would like to thank all members of the CAGD group at A.S.U. for many stimulating discussions he had with them during the visit, and Professor R.E. Barnhill, in particular, for making the visit possible.

### References

1. de Boor, C., K. Höllig and M. Sabin, High accuracy geometric Hermite interpolation, Comput. Aided Geom. Design 4 (1987), 269–278.
2. Goodman, T.N.T. and K. Unsworth, Shape preserving interpolation by parametrically defined curves, SIAM J. Numer. Anal., to appear.
3. Goodman, T.N.T. and K. Unsworth, Shape preserving interpolation by curvature continuous parametric curves, Comput. Aided Geom. Design 5 (1988), 323–340.

T. A. Foley*
Department of Computer Science
Arizona State University
Tempe, Arizona, 85287
USA

EMAIL: foley@ asuvax.csnet

T. N. T. Goodman and K. Unsworth*
Department of Mathematics and Computer Science
University of Dundee
Dundee DD1 4HN
SCOTLAND

EMAIL: t.goodman@ uk.ac.dundee (janet)

* Supported by the U.S. Department of Energy under contract DE–FG02–87ER25041 to Arizona State University.

K.U. also acknowledges the financial support given to him by The Royal Society and The Carnegie Trust for the Universities of Scotland.

# Knot Selection for Parametric
# Spline Interpolation

## Thomas A. Foley and Gregory M. Nielson

**Abstract.** We present a new method for the selection of knot sequences for parametric spline curves. The method takes into consideration the geometry of the control points and produces quality results for a wide variety of curve fitting problems. In addition, this method is invariant with respect to affine transformations of the control points.

## §1. Introduction

In many CAGD applications, a user wishes to construct a smooth and visually pleasing parametric curve passing through some given 2D or 3D control points. Although the techniques presented here apply to a variety of curve fitting schemes in many dimensions, it will suffice to describe them for the case of planar $C^2$ cubic splines. Given $n$ control points $P_i = (x_i, y_i)$ and a knot sequence $t_1 < t_2 < \cdots < t_n$, we wish to compute a parametric cubic spline interpolant $S(t) = (x(t), y(t))$ that satisfies $S(t_i) = (x_i, y_i)$, for $i = 1, ..., n$. Without loss of generality, it can be assumed that $t_1 = 0$, and thus the knot sequence is determined by the knot spacing vector $H = (h_1, ..., h_{n-1})$, where $h_i = t_{i+1} - t_i$. Since the knot sequence is arbitrary, we address the problem of selecting the knot spacing vector $H$ so that $S(t)$ has certain desirable properties. In particular, the knot spacing should be effective for poorly scaled data, and for data where there are sudden changes in direction.

The two most commonly used parametrizations or knot spacings are the *chord length* spacing, where $h_i = |P_{i+1} - P_i|$ (Euclidean distance), and the *uniform* spacing, where $h_i = 1$ (or $h_i =$ some constant). It is easy to construct examples where the uniform knot spacing yields poor results by having two data points near each other and the next point significantly farther away. Examples are given in de Boor [2] and Farin [4] where the $P_i$ are unequally

Mathematical Methods in Computer Aided Geometric Design
Tom Lyche and Larry L. Schumaker (eds.), pp. 261–271.

spaced on gentle curves, yet loops or oscillations occur between data points. Several authors (for example [1] and [2]) have suggested using chord length knot spacing partially because it approximates the arc length of a parametric curve. Another motivating factor for chord length is the result of Epstein [3] which guarantees that there will be no cusps for the case of a closed periodic curve. As noted in Foley [5] and in several examples presented here, the chord length knot spacing often produces visually poor results when the data is poorly scaled, or when the direction of the data changes abruptly.

A nonlinear optimization problem is solved in Marin [10] in order to determine a knot sequence for interpolation, and another optimization problem is solved in Hoschek [7] to select a parametrization for an approximation (not interpolation) problem. A knot spacing recently developed by Lee [9] and discussed in Farin [4], termed the *centripetal* model, is given by $h_i = \sqrt{|P_{i+1} - P_i|}$. This model was motivated by the paradigm of a car traveling through the data points $P_i$, and it works well on some data sets. An interesting note related to the car paradigm is that this knot sequence, (also the chord and uniform methods), disregard the angles formed by the control polygon $P_1, ..., P_n$. The method presented here takes these angles into consideration.

We feel that in addition to distance, the relative shape of the control polygon should be considered when motivated by the car paradigm because you would like to slow down for corners and travel at a constant speed on linear stretches. Another aspect that we incorporate is the affine invariant metric described in [12] and [13]. By using this metric, poorly scaled data generally cause no problems. More importantly, it should not matter if the $x$-axis is measured in seconds, minutes or hours, and the $y$-axis is measured in inches, feet or meters. The interpolating curve should be independent of these arbitrary choices.

## §2. Desirable Properties

In applications involving robot motion and animation, if $P_i \rightarrow P_{i+1}$ and the other data points remain fixed, then it is desirable for $h_i \rightarrow 0$, because $h_i$ represents the time it takes to travel the distance between these two points. The chord length and centripetal parametrizations satisfy this property, but the uniform spacing does not. Uniform spacing often yields poor results when the data points are unevenly distributed because it does not take into account any measure of distance between points. The chord length knot spacing has a property which is useful in motion applications in that the average speed between data points is constant in linear regions. In terms of ratios, if $P_{i-2}, ..., P_{i+2}$ are collinear and the average speed from $P_{i-1}$ to $P_i$ is equal to the average speed from $P_i$ to $P_{i+1}$, then $|P_i - P_{i-1}|/h_{i-1} = |P_{i+1} - P_i|/h_i$. Since there are possibly corners to negotiate at $P_{i-2}$ and $P_{i+2}$, we would not expect to have similar ratios involving $h_{i-2}$ and $h_{i+1}$. The centripetal and uniform methods do not have this property, and these methods may yield extraneous oscillations in regions where the data points are not equally spaced and the points are linear or gently curved. A property that all three of these methods have is that the parametric spline curves are continuous with respect to small changes in the data.

The three spline interpolation methods which use the chord length, uniform and centripetal parametrizations, are each invariant under rotations, translations and equal scaling in the $x$ and $y$ coordinates. However, the chord length and the centripetal methods are not scale invariant when the $x$ and $y$ coordinates of the data are scaled differently. Figure 1 demonstrates this using the chord length parametrization on six data points scaled by different values in the $y$ coordinate. The geometric properties of scale, rotation and translation invariance are important in character font applications where characters are stored as a sequence of control points which are transformed to the desired position, and a parametric spline interpolant is formed to represent the character. The shape of the characters should be consistent if the defining data points are scaled differently in $x$ and $y$, rotated, translated or sheared. Another justification for wanting scale invariance is that the resulting curve should be the same regardless of whether the $x$-axis is measured in seconds, minutes or hours, and the $y$-axis is measured in inches, feet or meters, for example. An easy solution to having a scale invariant method would be to form the bounding box of the data points and map this rectangle to the unit square. Such a scheme, however, would not be rotation invariant.

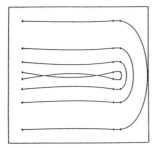

**Figure 1.** The chord length method is not affine invariant.

In order to prove formal statements about affine invariant spline interpolation methods, some representation is needed. Here, the Hermite form is used. On the interval $[t_i, t_{i+1}]$, the parametric $C^2$ cubic spline interpolant $S[P, H](t)$ to the points $P = (P_1, ..., P_n)^T$ can be represented by

$$S[P, H](t) = P_i B_1(\bar{t}) + P_{i+1} B_2(\bar{t}) + h_i D_i B_3(\bar{t}) + h_i D_{i+1} B_4(\bar{t}), \qquad (1)$$

where $\bar{t} = (t - t_i)/h_i$, $B_i(s)$ are the Hermite basis functions on $[0, 1]$, and the tangent vectors $D_i = (dx_i, dy_i)$ satisfy the following tridiagonal linear system of $n - 2$ vector equations:

$$D_{i-1}/h_{i-1} + 2(h_{i-1}^{-1} + h_i^{-1})D_i + D_{i+1}/h_i = 3\Delta P_i/h_i^2 + 3\Delta P_{i-1}/h_{i-1}^2 \qquad (2)$$

for $i = 2, ..., n - 1$, where $\Delta P_i = P_{i+1} - P_i$. Two additional vector equations are needed which generally represent user defined end conditions.

Returning to the concept of affine invariance, suppose that $P_i' = P_i A + b$ is an affine image of the points $P_i$, where $A$ is a $2 \times 2$ matrix and $b$ is a $1 \times 2$ vector. Let $P' = (P_1', ..., P_n')^T$, let $H' = (h_1', ..., h_{n-1}')$ be the knot spacing for the transformed points, and let the knot sequence be $\{u_i\}$, where $u_1 = 0$ and $u_{i+1} = u_i + h_i'$. The parametric spline interpolation method is said to be *affine invariant* if for every affine map of the form $P' = PA + b$,

$$(S[P, H](t))A + b = S[P', H'](u) \tag{3}$$

when $(t - t_i)/h_i = (u - u_i)/h_i'$. This formal statement says that if an affine invariant method is used, then the left side of (3), which represents the transformation of the original curve, is equal to the spline interpolant applied to the transformed data. Equality in (3) is based on specific parameter values $t$ and $u$ because we want more than equality of point sets, particularly in applications involving robot motion or animation.

In order for a method to be affine invariant, the following theorem characterizes the parametrizations that can be used. Since the parametric spline is affected by its end conditions, for the discussion which follows, assume that either natural, periodic or finite difference approximated first derivative end conditions are used.

**Theorem 2.1.** *A parametric spline interpolation method is affine invariant if and only if there exists a constant $c$ such that $h_i' = c h_i$ for $i = 1, ..., n - 1$.*

**Proof:** Assume that the method is affine invariant. From (1), if $t_i \leq t \leq t_{i+1}$,

$$(S[P, H](t))A + b = P_i A B_1(\bar{t}) + P_{i+1} A B_2(\bar{t}) + h_i D_i A B_3(\bar{t}) + h_i D_{i+1} A B_4(\bar{t}) + b \tag{4}$$

where $\bar{t} = (t - t_i)/h_i$. Since $B_1(s) + B_2(s) = 1$, it follows that

$$S[P', H'](u) = P_i A B_1(\bar{u}) + P_{i+1} A B_2(\bar{u}) + h_i' D_i' B_3(\bar{u}) + h_i' D_{i+1}' B_4(\bar{u}) + b \tag{5}$$

for $u_i \leq u \leq u_{i+1}$, where $\bar{u} = (u - u_i)/h_i'$ and the $D_i'$ satisfy equation (2) with $D, P$ and $h$ all replaced with primes. Since (4) and (5) are equal when $\bar{t} = \bar{u}$, we have that $h_i D_i A = h_i' D_i'$ and $h_i D_{i+1} A = h_i' D_{i+1}'$. Since this holds on all intervals, we also have that $h_{i-1} D_i A = h_{i-1}' D_i'$; hence, $h_i/h_i' = h_{i-1}/h_{i-1}'$ for all $i$, and thus $h_i'$ is proportional to $h_i$.

Suppose that $h_i' = c h_i$ for all $i$. Denote the system of equations in (2) in matrix form by $LD = R$, where $L$ is a $n \times n$ tridiagonal matrix, $D = (D_i, ..., D_n)^T$ is the $n \times 2$ unknown derivative matrix, and $R$ is the $n \times 2$ right side matrix. Since $\Delta P_i' = \Delta(P_i A)$ and $h_i' = c h_i$, equation (2) for the transformed data is $LD' = c^{-1} RA$. Combined with $LD = R$, it follows that $L(c^{-1} DA) = c^{-1} RA$, thus $D_i' = c^{-1} D_i A$. Therefore, equations (4) and (5) are equal when $\bar{t} = \bar{u}$, and so the method is affine invariant. ∎

**Corollary 2.2.** *If all knot sequences are normalized so that $t_1 = 0$ and $t_n = 1$, then a parametric cubic spline interpolation method is affine invariant if and only if the same knot spacing is used for all affine images of the data.*

Some additional desirable properties for automatic curve fitting algorithms include the preservation of local convexity and monotonicity. Unfortunately, these properties are unattainable for the present situation using $C^2$ splines. If the addition of knots or the relaxation of $C^2$ continuity to $G^2$ continuity is allowed, then shape preservation is possible using techniques such as those in [8] and [6].

## §3. Affine Invariant Methods

The previous theorem and corollary imply that an affine invariant spline interpolation method must use the same knot spacing if the data is transformed by an affine map. The uniform spacing satisfies this property, but it often performs poorly when the data are unevenly spaced because the distance between points is never considered. An affine invariant metric was recently introduced in Nielson [12], and several applications of it are given in Nielson and Foley [13]. We will briefly describe the metric, and then give two new affine invariant knot spacings that generally yield visually pleasing results.

Given a set of points $P = (P_1, ..., P_n)^T$, define the $2 \times 2$ matrix $Q = [q_{ij}]$ by $q_{11} = \sigma_Y/g$, $q_{22} = \sigma_X/g$ and $q_{12} = q_{21} = -\sigma_{XY}/g$, where

$$\bar{x} = \sum_{i=1}^{n} x_i/n, \ \ \bar{y} = \sum_{i=1}^{n} y_i/n, \ \ \sigma_X = \sum_{i=1}^{n}(x_i - \bar{x})^2/n, \ \ \sigma_Y = \sum_{i=1}^{n}(y_i - \bar{y})^2/n,$$

$$\sigma_{XY} = \sum_{i=1}^{n}(x_i - \bar{x})(y_i - \bar{y})/n, \ \ g = \sigma_X \sigma_Y - (\sigma_{XY})^2.$$

If $U$ and $V$ are two points, define

$$M[P](U, V) = \sqrt{(U - V)Q(U - V)^T}.$$

The metric $M[P](U, V)$ is affine invariant in that

$$M[P](U, V) = M[PA + b](UA + b, VA + b)$$

for all nonsingular $2 \times 2$ matrices $A$ and $1 \times 2$ vectors $b$. An interesting geometric property of this metric is that the set of points equidistant from a fixed point is an ellipse. If the points $P_i$ do not all fall on a line, then $g$ is nonzero. If all the points are on a line, then simply use chord length knot spacing; thus, for the discussion that follows, assume that the data points are not all collinear.

The first method that we present will be called the *affine invariant chord knot spacing*, and it is simply defined by $h_i = M[P](P_i, P_{i+1})$. This approach is affine invariant, it satisfies all of the properties stated in the previous section, and it generally yields visually pleasing curves. Since this metric induces a norm, the results of Epstein [3] hold, and there are no cusps when forming a closed periodic planar interpolant. However, the affine invariant chord method does not involve any local geometry, such as the angles or corners implied by the data. The method which we will call the *affine invariant angle* knot spacing involves this local geometry and it is defined by

$$h_i = d_i \left[ 1 + \frac{1.5\theta_i d_{i-1}}{d_{i-1} + d_i} + \frac{1.5\theta_{i+1} d_{i+1}}{d_i + d_{i+1}} \right], \tag{6}$$

where $d_i = M[P](P_i, P_{i+1})$, $\theta_i = min[\alpha_i, \pi/2]$ and

$$\alpha_i = \pi - \arccos \left[ \frac{d_{i-1}^2 + d_i^2 - M^2[P](P_{i-1}, P_{i+1})}{2 d_i d_{i-1}} \right] \tag{7}$$

If $\alpha_i < \pi/2$, then $\theta_i = \alpha_i$, and it represents the exterior angle shown in Figure 2. Angles and scalar (dot) products are generally not invariant under affine transformations. However, since the computation of the angle in (7) is done using the Law of Cosines, the angular measure in (7) is affine invariant. Since the distance $d_i$ is computed using the affine invariant metric, the knot spacing in (6) is affine invariant. It is straightforward to show that the other properties discussed in the previous section are also satisfied.

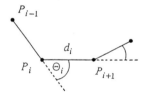

**Figure 2.** Geometry of the affine invariant angle method.

The affine invariant angle knot spacing is motivated by having an affine invariant method that adheres to the paradigm involving a car traveling through the data points. With all distances fixed, as $\theta_i$ increases from 0 to 90 degrees, the knot spacing $h_i$ increases. This larger value of $h_i$ corresponds to the car slowing down when there are corners to negotiate. The maximum of 90 degrees for the computed angle corresponds to not wanting to slow down more than you would for a right angle corner. The maximum of 90 degrees was selected after many experiments, as was the constant 1.5. In fact, the constant 1.5 could be replaced with a variable that acts as a shape control parameter. Since $\theta_i \leq \pi/2$ and the ratio terms $d_{i-1}/(d_{i-1} + d_i)$ and $d_{i+1}/(d_i + d_{i+1})$ are less than one, we have that the affine invariant angle knot spacing $h_i$ is linearly bounded by $d_i \leq h_i \leq 5.7 d_i$. With $d_i$ and the angles fixed, the above two ratio terms also insure that short neighboring intervals will increase $h_i$ less than large neighboring intervals will. That is, if $d_{i-1}$ and $d_{i+1}$ are small relative to $d_i$, then $h_i \approx d_i$ regardless of the size of the angles.

In each of the following figures, first derivative end conditions are used based on one sided three point divided difference approximations. In most of these examples, the first three points and the last three points are chosen to be collinear so that the end conditions will have minimal effect on the resulting curves. In the situation where they are collinear, the end conditions simplify to $D_1 = (P_2 - P_1)/h_1$ and $D_n = (P_n - P_{n-1})/h_{n-1}$.

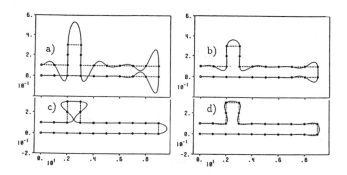

**Figure 3.** a) chord length, b) centripetal, c) affine invariant chord, d) affine invariant angle

The four curves in Figure 3 are parametric spline interpolants using the following knot spacings: a) chord length, b) centripetal, c) affine invariant chord and d) affine invariant angle. The chord length and centripetal methods have problems because the scale in the $y$-direction is significantly smaller than the scale in the $x$-direction. Another reason for these problems is that the spline function components $x(t)$ and $y(t)$ often have trouble when there is a large change in the slope from one interval to the next, for example, when $(x_i - x_{i-1})/h_{i-1}$ is significantly different than $(x_{i+1} - x_i)/h_i$. This occurs when there is a large angle $\theta_i$ (see Figure 2). A motivating factor in the development of the affine invariant angle knot spacing is that it attempts to reduce the change in the chord slopes in the data for the spline function components $x(t)$ and $y(t)$.

Figure 4a) uses chord length knot spacing, while 4b) uses the affine invariant angle parametrization. Figure 4c) and d) are the $y(t)$ function components of the parametric spline $S(t) = (x(t), y(t))$ using the chord length method and the affine invariant angle knot spacing, respectively, on the data shown in Figure 4a) and b).

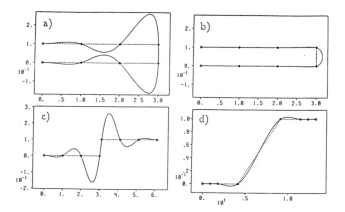

**Figure 4.** Parametric spline $(x(t), y(t))$ using a) chord length and b) affine invariant angle. Function component $y(t)$ using c) chord length and d) affine invariant angle on the y-data in a) and b).

Figure 5 is an example where $\alpha_4$ and $\alpha_5$ in (7) exceed $\pi/2$ and thus the affine invariant angle method in b) sets $\theta_4 = \theta_5 = \pi/2$. When $\theta_4$ and $\theta_5$ were allowed to exceed $\pi/2$ in this example, the interpolating curve "ballooned" out an excessive amount on the fourth interval. Figure 5a) uses the chord length knot spacing and this curve is very similar to the curves which use the centripetal and uniform knot spacings, thus they are omitted. Figure 6 uses functional data from [8] and the parametric curves use a) chord length, b) uniform , c) centripetal and d) affine invariant angle knot spacings.

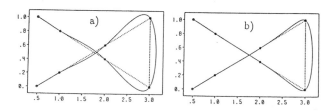

**Figure 5.** a) chord length, b) affine invariant angle

Our final example interpolates the very poorly scaled data where $x_i = i$ and $y_i = 0$ except that $y_5 = 100$. Figure 7a) uses chord length spacing, b) uses the centripetal method and c) uses the affine invariant knot spacing. Figure 7d) uses the affine invariant angle method applied to the sheared data where $P_5 = (-1, 100)$. Since this method is affine invariant, the curve in Figure 7d) is equal to the shearing of Figure 7c).

We have applied these affine invariant knot spacings to many other data sets and the results are consistent with the examples given here. We have also combined the affine invariant metric with the centripetal method. The cost of computing the knot spacings using either of the affine invariant methods is linear in the number of data points; thus, the order of computing the parametric spline does not increase, although the actual time will increase somewhat. The affine invariant methods apply to 3-D and higher dimensional space curves because the affine invariant metric can be generalized in this case [12], and because (6) and (7) only depend on these distances in the calculation of the angles. Since there is no guarantee that any parametrization will yield a curve that a designer has in mind, splines with tension controls (c.f. [5] and [11]) can be interactively used to obtain the desired shape. When using these tension splines, the initial or default curve with no tension applied is a $C^2$ cubic spline, thus the affine invariant parametrizations can save the designer time by constructing a reasonably shaped initial curve.

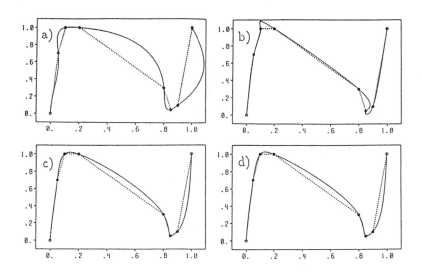

**Figure 6.** a) chord length, b)uniform,
c) centripetal, d) affine invariant angle

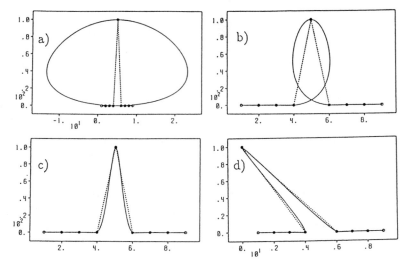

**Figure 7.** a) chord length, b) centripetal, c) affine invariant angle, and d) affine invariant angle method applied to sheared data.

## Acknowledgements

A portion of this research was performed at Lawrence Livermore National Laboratory and supported by a grant from Associated Western Universities and by the U.S. Dept. of Energy contract W-7405-ENG-48. We wish to thank Fred Fritsch of LLNL for hosting our visit and for his valuable discussions. This work was also supported by the U.S. Dept. of Energy contract DE-FG-02-87ER25041 at Arizona State University and by NATO RG. 0097/88.

## References

1. Ahlberg, J. H., E. N. Nilson and J. L. Walsh, *The Theory of Splines and Their Applications*, Academic Press, New York, 1967.
2. de Boor, C., *A Practical Guide to Splines*, Springer-Verlag, N.Y., 1978.
3. Epstein, M. P., On the influence of parameterization in parametric interpolation, SIAM J. Num. Anal. **13** (1976), 261–268.
4. Farin, G. E., *Curves and Surfaces for CAGD*, Academic Press, N.Y., 1988.
5. Foley, T. A., Interpolation with interval and point tension controls using cubic weighted $\nu$-splines, ACM Trans. Math. Soft. **13** (1987), 68–96.
6. Foley, T. A., T. N. T. Goodman and K. Unsworth, An algorithm for shape preserving parametric curves with $G^2$ continuity, in *Mathematical Methods in Computer Aided Geometric Design*, T. Lyche and L. Schumaker (eds.), Academic Press, N. Y., 1989, 249–259.
7. Hoschek, J., Intrinsic parametrization for approximation, Comput. Aided Geom. Design **5** (1988), 27–31.

8. Irvine, L. D., S. P. Marin and P. W. Smith, Constrained interpolation and smoothing, Constr. Approx. **2** (1985), 129–151.

9. Lee, E. T., On choosing nodes in parametric curve interpolation, presented at the SIAM Conference on Applied Geometry, Albany, N.Y., 1985.

10. Marin, S. P., An approach to data parameterization in parametric cubic spline interpolation, J. Approx. Theory **41** (1984), 64–86.

11. Nielson, G. M., Some piecewise polynomial alternatives to splines under tension, in *Computer Aided Geometric Design*, R. E. Barnhill and R. F. Riesenfeld, Eds., Academic Press, New York, 1974, 209–235.

12. Nielson, G. M., Coordinate free scattered data interpolation, in *Topics in Multivariate Approximation*, C. Chui, L. L. Schumaker and F. Utreras (eds.), Academic Press, New York, 1987, 175–184.

13. Nielson, G. M. and T. A. Foley, A survey of applications of an affine invariant norm, in *Mathematical Methods in Computer Aided Geometric Design*, T. Lyche and L. Schumaker (eds.), Academic Press, N. Y., 1989, 445–467.

Thomas A. Foley and Gregory M. Nielson
Computer Science Department
Arizona State University
Tempe, Arizona 85287
USA

Supported in part by NATO RG. 0097/88 and DOE DE-FG-02-87ER25041

EMAIL: foley@ asuvax.csnet
EMAIL: nielson@ asuvax.csnet

**Plate 2.** A curvature plot of the side boundaries of the "trunk lid".

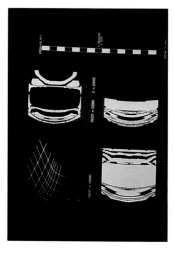

**Plate 4.** Curvature plots of the "trunk lid" with alternating black and white bands.

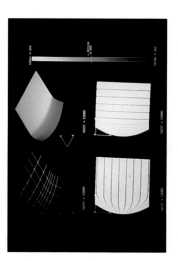

**Plate 1.** An automobile "trunk lid" wire frame, shaded rendering and two reflection line patterns.

**Plate 3.** Curvature plots of the "trunk lid" with a "blue" color map.

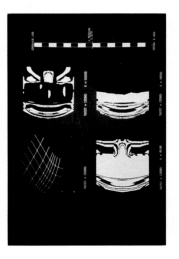

**Plate 5.** Curvature plots of the "trunk lid" with three points perturbed 0.1 mm. using a "blue" color map.

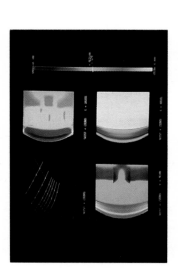

**Plate 6.** Curvature plots of the "trunk lid" with three points perturbed 0.1 mm. using wide black and white bands.

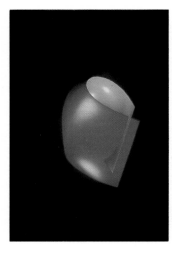

**Plate 8.** A self-intersecting bicubic patch.

**Plate 7.** The torus-sphere intersection problem.

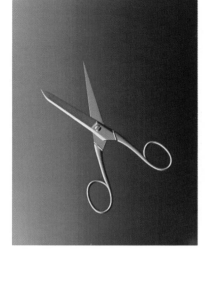

**Plate 9.** Alpha_1 Logo.

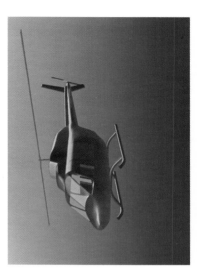

**Plate 10.** Swept Scissors.

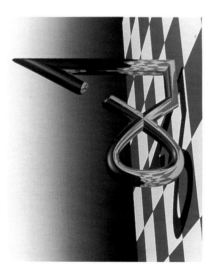

**Plate 11.** Turbine Blade Root.

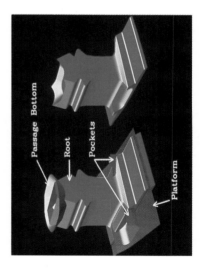

**Plate 12.** The Helicopter.

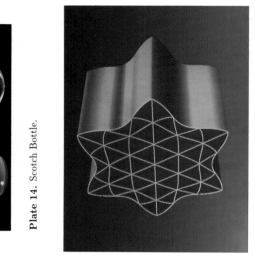

**Plate 14.** Scotch Bottle.

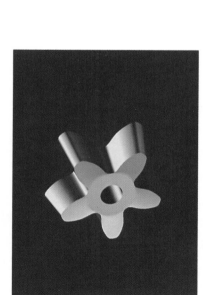

**Plate 16.** Box Spline Cap.

**Plate 13.** Sculpted Spoon.

**Plate 15.** Nonplanar Cap.

# Splines and Estimation
# of Nonlinear Parameters

## D. Girard and P. J. Laurent

**Abstract.** Given the approximate values $z_i$ at points $t_1, \cdots, t_n$ of a function $f$ having some particular features (determined by $\alpha$), the purpose is to smooth the data and simultaneously to estimate $\alpha$. For example, $\alpha$ might be the location of peaks or discontinuities, the value of a period, etc. The idea is to use the smoothing spline corresponding to a well chosen quadratic smoothness criterion $L_\alpha$. Such a criterion can be built using the inf-convolution of several quadratic functionals. Characterizations and computational methods for the resulting splines are presented here. In addition, we discuss the use of the generalized cross-validation method for choosing both the smoothing parameter and $\alpha$. Several algorithms are given and the efficiency is illustrated on several types of numerical examples.

## §1. Introduction

Suppose that $t_1, \cdots, t_n$ are given points in a domain $D$ of $\mathbb{R}^d$, and that approximate values $z_i$ of an unknown function $f$ are given at these points; *i.e.*,

$$z_i = f(t_i) + \varepsilon_i, \qquad i = 1, \cdots, n, \tag{1.1}$$

where $\varepsilon_i$ are random errors. To simplify the presentation, we assume that the $\varepsilon_i$'s are independent, zero mean, random variables with common (unknown) standard deviation.

Furthermore, we assume that certain particular *a priori* information on the shape of $f$ is also given. Generally, such information will only be qualitative. To fix the ideas, we first briefly describe three typical examples:

1. The first example is the following: we know only that the univariate function $f$ is smooth except that there probably exist breaks in its slope at a small number of locations. The unknown number and locations of these

Mathematical Methods in Computer Aided Geometric Design
Tom Lyche and Larry L. Schumaker (eds.), pp. 273–298.

derivative discontinuities will be denoted by $m$ and $\alpha_1, \cdots, \alpha_m$, respectively.

2. In our second example, the a priori information is that $f$ is the sum of a smooth function and a narrow Gaussian peak whose location $\alpha$ is unknown; in other applications the unknown non-linear parameter may be the width of the peak or both its location and its width (such a vector parameter will still be denoted in short by $\alpha$).

3. The third example concerns functions which are known to be periodic and for which the observed data correspond to more than one period; here $\alpha$ will denote the unknown period.

The problem of interest in this paper may be now expressed in the following general form: assuming that the data satisfy (1.1) and that the essential features of $f$ are not exactly determined; i.e., the non-linear parameter $\alpha$ (cf. the previous examples) is unknown, we wish to smooth the data and, simultaneously, to estimate $\alpha$.

To start with, we assume that we know the essential features of $f$ (i.e., the true value $\alpha$). The first idea of our approach consists in choosing a subspace $X$ of the space of real-valued functions on $D$, and a smoothness criterion $L :$ $X \to \mathbb{R}$ related to the expected particular form of the solution (and the value of $\alpha$); i.e., such that $L$ is small on $f$ (and large for unsuitable functions!). An approximation of $f$ is then classically obtained by solving the minimization problem:

$$\min_{x \in X} \quad L(x) \; + \; \rho \sum_{i=1}^{n} [x(t_i) - z_i]^2. \tag{1.2}$$

In this paper we essentially use the concept of inf-convolution of several quadratic functionals in order to build, from standard smoothness criteria, a large variety of much less standard criteria $L$ which will be able to take into account particular features of $f$.

Let us describe the three examples in more detail:

**Example 1.1.** Suppose that $f : [a, b] \to \mathbb{R}$ is smooth except for $m$ discontinuities of the first derivative at points $\alpha_j, j = 1, \cdots, m$, with $\alpha_0 = a < \alpha_1 < \cdots < \alpha_m < b = \alpha_{m+1}$. We will then consider functions $x$ of the form

$$x = x_1 + x_2, \tag{1.3}$$

where $x_1 \in H^2[a, b]$ is smooth and $x_2 \in V = \text{Span}(p_1, \cdots, p_m)$ with $p_j(t) = (t - \alpha_j)_+$ for $j = 1, \cdots, m$; i.e.,

$$x_2(t) = \sum_{j=1}^{m} d_j(t - \alpha_j)_+. \tag{1.4}$$

We remark that $d_j$ is simply the jump of the derivative of $x$ (or $x_2$) at $\alpha_j$, and the decomposition (1.3) is then unique. Set

$$X = H^2[a, b] + V, \tag{1.5a}$$

and for any $x = x_1 + x_2 \in X$, set

$$L(x) = \int_a^b (x_1''(t))^2 dt. \tag{1.5b}$$

It is easy to show that $X$ consists of those functions of $H^1[a, b]$ whose restriction on each subinterval $[\alpha_j, \alpha_{j+1}]$ is in $H^2[\alpha_j, \alpha_{j+1}], j = 0, \cdots, m$, and that in fact $L(x) = \int_a^{\alpha_1} (x''(t))^2 dt + \int_{\alpha_1}^{\alpha_2} (x''(t))^2 dt + \cdots + \int_{\alpha_m}^b (x''(t))^2 dt$ (cf. [17]). It is then intuitively reasonable to approximate $f$ by finding a solution of a minimization problem of the form (1.2).

**Example 1.2.** *Suppose that $f$ is smooth except for $m$ Gaussian peaks at points $\alpha_j, j = 1, \cdots, m$. We then consider functions $x$ of the form $x = x_1 + x_2$, where $x_1 \in H^q[a, b]$ is smooth and $x_2 \in V = \mathrm{Span}(p_1, \cdots, p_m)$ with*

$$p_j(t) = \exp(-(t - \alpha_j)^2 / \beta_j^2) \quad j = 1, \cdots, m. \tag{1.6}$$

*But now, since $p_j \in H^q[a, b]$, the decomposition is not unique. Here we will take, as an estimate of $f$, a solution of (1.2) with $X = H^q[a, b]$ and $L$ defined by*

$$L(x) = \min_{\substack{x_1 \in H^q[a,b], x_2 \in V \\ x_1 + x_2 = x}} \int_a^b (x_1^{(q)}(t))^2 dt, \quad x \in X. \tag{1.7}$$

*It will be easily shown (Section 2) that the solution $(x_1, x_2)$ of this minimization problem (1.7) is unique.*

**Example 1.3.** *Suppose $f$ is a periodic function with period $\alpha$, having zero mean over the period. Set $\omega = \frac{2\pi}{\alpha}$. We consider quadratic functionals on $X = H^2[a, b]$ of the form*

$$L_j(x) = \int_a^b (x''(t) + \omega_j^2 x(t))^2 dt, \quad \text{with } \omega_j = j\omega, \ j = 1, \cdots, k, \tag{1.8}$$

*and we define*

$$L(x) = \min_{\substack{x_j \in X, j=1, \cdots, k \\ x_1 + \cdots + x_k = x}} (L_1(x_1) + \cdots + L_k(x_k)). \tag{1.9}$$

*Obviously, $L(x) = 0$ if $x$ is a trigonometric polynomial of degree at most $k$ and period $\alpha$, whose mean value over one period is zero; i.e.,*

$$x(t) = \sum_{j=1}^k (\lambda_j \cos(j\omega t) + \mu_j \sin(j\omega t)).$$

*Now, to recover $f$ from the data $z_i$, we will find a minimizer $x^*$ of $L(x) + \rho \sum_{i=1}^n [x(t_i) - z_i]^2$ or equivalently a $k$-tuplet $(x_1^*, \cdots, x_k^*)$ which minimizes*

$$L_1(x_1) + \cdots + L_k(x_k) + \rho \sum_{i=1}^n [x_1(t_i) + \cdots + x_k(t_i) - z_i]^2,$$

and we will have $x^* = \sum_{j=1}^{k} x_j^*$.

The expression (1.9) is known in convex analysis as an *inf-convolution*, and is usually written $L = \overset{k}{\underset{j=1}{\nabla}} L_j$ (cf. [15,18,19]). Note that the functional $L$ in the second example can also be defined by a similar expression. If we introduce the notations

$$L_1(x_1) = \int_a^b (x_1^{(q)}(t))^2 dt, \quad x_1 \in X_1 = H^q[a,b], \qquad (1.10a)$$

$$L_2(x_2) = 0, \quad x_2 \in X_2 = V, \qquad (1.10b)$$

we can write

$$L(x) = \min_{\substack{x_1 \in X_1, x_2 \in X_2 \\ x_1 + x_2 = x}} (L_1(x_1) + L_2(x_2)),$$

and we have $L = L_1 \nabla L_2$. (The first example can also be put in this form, but the decomposition $x = x_1 + x_2$ being unique, the minimization becomes trivial).

This is the reason why the previous splines were called inf-convolution splines when they were introduced by Laurent [13-16]. The formulation there was quite general, and included interpolation or smoothing of data corresponding to a function of one or several variables with *singularities* like faults, discontinuities of normal derivatives along a specified curve, etc. Many numerical applications have been studied in [23,11].

A similar approach, although restricted to the first two examples, was recently considered by some authors in a more statistical context (cf. for example, Wahba [25], Shiau, Wahba and Johnson [21], Eubank [3]). There, these very particular examples of inf-convolution splines were called *partial splines*. Other approaches to the problem of interpolating data with discontinuities at specified locations can be found in [4] and the references cited therein.

In the present paper, unicity, characterization, and computational methods for inf-convolution splines (ICS) are discussed. We show that a simple scheme readily provides the characterization of such a smoothing ICS, starting from the (usually well known) characterizations of the standard spline (or least squares) approximations associated with each of the $L_j$'s. Several algorithms are given for the computation of ICS functions, among these, an iterative algorithm which is very simple to implement if we have at hand procedures for computing each one of the $k$ smoothing splines associated with the $L_j$.

It is now classical to choose the smoothing parameter $\rho$ by minimizing the generalized cross-validation (GCV) function, see [1,9,20,22,24] and [17]. The second idea of our approach is to choose the parameter $\alpha$ also by minimizing the GCV function. In the case of polynomial smoothing splines of order $q$, the GCV method was previously proposed for choosing $q$, see Wahba [24,25]. In the problems discussed here, a good choice of $\alpha$ seems to be much more critical.

For the first example, it is well known that a corner (a break in the derivative) which is not well taken into account (if the location $\alpha$ is badly specified) will be *over-smoothed* in the resulting spline function and will cause unexpected oscillations. As a likely result, a datum near the true discontinuity will then not be well predicted by the spline computed without this datum. Thus, having in mind that the GCV function is a (suitably) weighted average of such prediction errors, it is clear that GCV should be a good method for choosing the discontinuity location $\alpha$. For the other examples, it is intuitive that the GCV function should still have a minimum at (or near) the true $\alpha$ as long as choosing $\alpha$ in this neighborhood is necessary to provide a good recovery of the underlying $f$.

A well known difficulty in using GCV is the evaluation of the trace of the smoothing operator at a reasonable cost. In this paper several algorithms are given. In the case of ICS with a finite dimensional subspace (or partial spline case) we give a very useful relation between the required trace and the trace of the associated standard spline problem. For the sake of completeness, we also review the simple general Monte-Carlo algorithm proposed by Girard [6,7] for computing an approximation of the trace term. This algorithm is particularly suitable in cases where the inf-convolution splines are computed by the iterative algorithm mentioned above.

In Section 2 inf-convolution splines are presented as in [14-16], but in a slightly simplified form. We give a simple characterization result in Theorem 2.1. Several algorithms are then presented for the computation of inf-convolution splines. In Section 3 we show that the GCV function can be efficiently computed by several types of algorithms. Numerical experiments demonstrate that the fast Monte-Carlo type algorithm is quite reliable. Numerical applications of our approach are then presented in Section 4 corresponding to the examples outlined above.

## §2. Inf-convolution Splines and their Computation

### 2.1. Some Notation, Assumptions and Definitions

Let $E$ denote the space of real-valued functions on a domain $D$ of $\mathbb{R}^d$ (with the topology of pointwise convergence) and $X_j, j = 1, \cdots, k$, a family of semi-Hilbertian subspaces (s.H.s) of $E$.

Recall that a subspace $X_j$ with a semi-scalar product $(\cdot, \cdot)_j$ and the associated semi-norm $|x|_j^2 = (x, x)_j$ is called s.H.s if the null-space $N_j$ of the semi-norm is finite dimensional and if the quotient space $X_j/N_j$ is complete and topologically included in $E/N_j$ (this latter assumption is in fact satisfied in most of useful examples).

We define the functionals $L_j : X_j \to \mathbb{R}$, $j = 1, \cdots, k$, by

$$L_j(x) = |x|_j^2, \quad \text{for } x \in X_j.$$

**Definition 2.1.** *The inf-convolution of the functionals $L_1, \cdots, L_k$ is the functional $L$ defined for any $x \in X = X_1 + \cdots + X_k$ by*

$$L(x) = \min_{\substack{x_1 \in X_1, \cdots, x_k \in X_k \\ x_1 + \cdots + x_k = x}} (L_1(x_1) + \cdots + L_k(x_k)), \tag{2.1}$$

*and is denoted by* $L = L_1 \nabla \cdots \nabla L_k = \overset{k}{\underset{j=1}{\nabla}} L_j$.

It can be proved (cf. [14,16]) that a semi-scalar product $(\cdot, \cdot)$ and a corresponding semi-norm $|\cdot|$ can be defined on $X$ for which $X$ is again a s.H.s and $L(x) = |x|^2$. The null space $N$ of this semi-norm is easily shown to be

$$N = \sum_{j=1}^{k} N_j. \tag{2.2}$$

Now, for a given $\rho > 0$, we consider the following minimization problem

$$\min_{x \in X} \quad L(x) + \rho \sum_{i=1}^{n} [x(t_i) - z_i]^2, \quad \text{where } L = \overset{k}{\underset{j=1}{\nabla}} L_j, \tag{2.3}$$

whose solution will be called a *smoothing "inf-convolution spline"* corresponding to the $L_j$'s. (Interpolating or smoothing splines based on inf-convolution of $k$ arbitrary semi-Hilbertian functionals $L_j$ are studied in detail in [14-16]).

Problem (2.3) is equivalent to the following minimization in the product space $X_1 \times \cdots \times X_k$

$$\min_{x_j \in X_j, j=1, \cdots, k} \quad L_1(x_1) + \cdots + L_k(x_k) + \rho \sum_{i=1}^{n} [x_1(t_i) + \cdots + x_k(t_i) - z_i]^2. \tag{2.4}$$

The solution $x^*$ of (2.3) is equal to $\sum_{j=1}^{k} x_j^*$ if $x_1^*, \cdots, x_k^*$ is a solution of (2.4).

## 2.2. A System of $k$ Connected Linear Systems

We suppose that for every $j$ the standard problem

$$\min_{x \in X_j} \quad L_j(x) + \rho \sum_{i=1}^{n} [x(t_i) - z_i]^2, \tag{2.5}$$

associated with $X_j, L_j$ has a unique solution $s_j(\mathbf{z})$, called the smoothing $L_j$-spline approximation of $\mathbf{z} = (z_1, \cdots, z_n)^T$. Let $s_j$ denote the approximation operator ($\mathbb{R}^n \to X_j$) associated with this $j$th problem.

We denote by $S_j$ the associated smoothing spline operator; *i.e.*, $S_j : \mathbb{R}^n \to \mathbb{R}^n$ is defined by

$$S_j(\mathbf{z}) = (s_j(\mathbf{z})(t_1), \cdots, s_j(\mathbf{z})(t_n))^T;$$

that is, the vector of the smoothed (or predicted) values obtained by this $L_j$-spline. $S_j$ is also called the $L_j$-*influence matrix*.

In practice, each one of these $k$ problems will be either a simple least-square approximation problem (case of a finite dimensional subspace), or a standard smoothing spline problem for which computational procedures already exist. Now we have the following result:

**Theorem 2.2.** *An element $(x_1^*, \cdots, x_k^*)$ of $X_1 \times \cdots \times X_k$ is a solution of (2.4) if and only if*

$$x_j^* = s_j(\mathbf{z} - \sum_{\substack{l=1 \\ l \neq j}}^{k} \mathbf{y}_l^*), \quad j = 1, \cdots, k, \qquad (2.6)$$

*where $\mathbf{y}_l^* = (x_l^*(t_1), \cdots, x_l^*(t_n))^T$ .*

**Proof:** The function $(x_1^*, \cdots, x_k^*) \in X_1 \times \cdots \times X_k \to L_1(x_1) + \cdots + L_k(x_k) + \rho \sum_{i=1}^{n} [x_1(t_i) + \cdots + x_k(t_i) - z_i]^2$ is convex and differentiable. Thus, an element $(x_1^*, \cdots, x_k^*)$ is a minimizer of (2.4) if and only if each of the $x_j^*$ is a solution of the partial minimization problem

$$\min_{x_j \in X_j} \quad L_j(x_j) \; + \; \rho \sum_{i=1}^{n} \left[ x_j(t_i) - (z_i - \sum_{\substack{l=1 \\ l \neq j}}^{k} x_l^*(t_i)) \right]^2,$$

*i.e., $x_j^* = s_j(\mathbf{z} - \sum_{l \neq j} \mathbf{y}_l^*)$.* ∎

This theorem says in a concise way that our inf-convolution spline $x^* = x_1^* + \cdots + x_k^*$ will in fact be a sum of $k$ functions, where $x_j^*$ is a spline corresponding to the $j$th smoothing criterion, and that $(\mathbf{y}_1^*, \cdots, \mathbf{y}_k^*)$ satisfy the following system of $k$ connected linear equations:

$$\mathbf{y}_j^* = S_j \left( \mathbf{z} - \sum_{\substack{l=1 \\ l \neq j}}^{k} \mathbf{y}_l^* \right), \quad j = 1, \cdots, k. \qquad (2.7)$$

### 2.3. The Case of a Finite Dimensional Subspace

Assume that $k = 2$, that $L_1$ is a standard smoothness criterion on a space $X_1$ (for which we generally know how to compute the related smoothing spline $s_1(\mathbf{y})$, the smoothing parameter $\rho$ being fixed), and that $L_2$ is the indicator functional of a finite dimensional subspace $V = \mathrm{Span}(p_1, \cdots, p_m)$.

Then, for any $\mathbf{y}$, $s_2(\mathbf{y})$ is now the function $x$ in $V$ which minimizes $\sum_{i=1}^{n} [x(t_i) - y_i]^2$. Let $P$ denote the $n \times m$ matrix

$$P = (\mathbf{p}_1, \cdots, \mathbf{p}_m), \text{ with columns } \mathbf{p}_j = (p_j(t_1), \cdots, p_j(t_n))^T, j = 1, \cdots, m.$$

The assumption of unicity of $s_2(\mathbf{y})$ is easily shown to be equivalent to the assumption that $P$ is a matrix of full rank, and the vector of the smoothed values given by this least square fit of $\mathbf{y}$ is obviously

$$S_2(\mathbf{y}) = P(P^T P)^{-1} P^T \mathbf{y}.$$

Now, from the previous theorem, it follows that

$$x_1^* = s_1(\mathbf{z} - \mathbf{y}_2^*), \tag{2.8a}$$
$$x_2^* = s_2(\mathbf{z} - \mathbf{y}_1^*). \tag{2.8b}$$

Thus $x_2^*$ is simply the solution of the least square fit of $\mathbf{z} - \mathbf{y}_1^*$ in the space $V$, and there exist $\mathbf{d}^*$ in $\mathbb{R}^m$ such that

$$\mathbf{y}_2^* = P\mathbf{d}^*, \quad \text{with } P^T P \mathbf{d}^* = P^T (\mathbf{z} - \mathbf{y}_1^*).$$

Replacing $\mathbf{y}_1^*$ by its value $S_1(\mathbf{z} - P\mathbf{d}^*)$ from (2.8a), we obtain the $m \times m$ linear system

$$P^T (I - S_1) P \mathbf{d}^* = P^T (\mathbf{z} - S_1 \mathbf{z}),$$

which is clearly non-singular if and only if there is no nonzero combination of the $m$ columns of $P$ belonging to the nullspace of the symmetric nonnegative definite matrix $I - S_1$ ( this nullspace is easily shown to be $\{(p(t_1), \cdots, p(t_n))^T : p \in N_1\}$ ).

This yields the following simple algorithm for computing this inf-convolution spline:

### Algorithm 2.3.

1. *compute the $n \times m$ matrix $Q = S_1 P$ (computation of $m$ $L_1$-splines)*
2. *compute $S_1 \mathbf{z}$ (one spline)*
3. *compute the $m \times m$ matrix $R = P^T (P - Q)$ and $\mathbf{b} = P^T (\mathbf{z} - S_1 \mathbf{z})$ ($m^2 n + mn$ operations)*
4. *compute $\mathbf{d}^*$ from $R\mathbf{d}^* = \mathbf{b}$ (a $m \times m$ linear system)*
5. *$\mathbf{y}^* = \mathbf{y}_1^* + \mathbf{y}_2^* = (S_1 \mathbf{z} - Q \mathbf{d}^*) + P \mathbf{d}^*$ (mn operations).*

Note that the smoothing inf-convolution spline is thus given by

$$x^*(t) = x_1^*(t) + x_2^*(t) = s_1(\mathbf{z})(t) - \sum_{j=1}^{m} d_j^* s_1(\mathbf{p}_j)(t) + \sum_{j=1}^{m} d_j^* p_j(t).$$

An attractive feature of this simple algorithm is that it may be readily implemented as soon as we have a procedure that computes a smoothing $L_1$-spline. Note that in practice ($m \ll n$), its cost is essentially the cost for $m + 1$ runs of this $L_1$-spline procedure with different sets of data.

### 2.4. The General Case

To simplify the presentation, we assume in this section that the first $k - 1$ $L_j$-splines are standard splines; *i.e.*, that we can define the associated energy matrices $\Omega_j, j = 1, \cdots, k - 1$, by

$$\min_{\substack{x \in X_j \\ x(t_i) = z_i, i = 1, \cdots, n}} L_j(x) = \mathbf{z}^T \Omega_j \mathbf{z}, \quad \text{for all } \mathbf{z} \in \mathbb{R}^n, \quad j = 1, \cdots, k - 1,$$

and we assume that only the $k^{th}$ spline is a least square approximation in $V = \text{span}(p_1, \cdots, p_m)$. $P$ will still denote the regression matrix (of full rank) associated with $V$.

The minimization (2.4) then has a unique solution if and only if the system (2.7) has a unique solution, where the $S_j$'s are

$$S_j = \left(I + \frac{1}{\rho}\Omega_j\right)^{-1}, \quad j = 1, \cdots, k-1, \text{ and } S_k = P(P^T P)^{-1} P^T. \quad (2.10)$$

Now substituting $P\mathbf{d}$ for $\mathbf{y}_k$, it can easily be checked that (2.7) is equivalent to

$$\begin{bmatrix} S_1^{-1} & I & \cdots & I & P \\ I & S_2^{-1} & \cdots & I & P \\ \vdots & \vdots & \ddots & \vdots & \vdots \\ I & I & \cdots & S_{k-1}^{-1} & P \\ P^T & P^T & \cdots & P^T & P^T P \end{bmatrix} \begin{bmatrix} \mathbf{y}_1 \\ \mathbf{y}_2 \\ \vdots \\ \mathbf{y}_{k-1} \\ \mathbf{d} \end{bmatrix} = \begin{bmatrix} \mathbf{z} \\ \mathbf{z} \\ \vdots \\ \mathbf{z} \\ P^T \mathbf{z} \end{bmatrix}. \quad (2.11)$$

Denoting by $M$ the matrix of this system, it is easy to verify that $M$ is non-negative definite, and we have

**Theorem 2.4** (Unicity). *The solution of (2.4) (or of (2.11)) is unique if and only if the sum of the subspaces* $\{(p(t_1), \cdots, p(t_n))^T : p \in N_j\}, j = 1, \cdots, k-1,$ *and of range(P) is a direct sum in* $\mathbb{R}^n$.

**Proof:** A necessary and sufficient condition for unicity is that $M$ is positive definite. We have

$$[\mathbf{y}_1^T, \cdots, \mathbf{y}_{k-1}^T, \mathbf{d}^T] M \begin{bmatrix} \mathbf{y}_1 \\ \mathbf{y}_2 \\ \vdots \\ \mathbf{y}_{k-1} \\ \mathbf{d} \end{bmatrix} = \sum_{j=1}^{k-1} \mathbf{y}_j^T [(I + \frac{1}{\rho}\Omega_j)\mathbf{y}_j + \sum_{\substack{l=1 \\ l \neq j}}^{k-1} \mathbf{y}_l + P\mathbf{d}]$$

$$+ \mathbf{d}^T [\sum_{j=1}^{k-1} P^T \mathbf{y}_j + P^T P\mathbf{d}]$$

$$= \frac{1}{\rho} \sum_{j=1}^{k-1} \mathbf{y}_j^T \Omega_j \mathbf{y}_j + \|\sum_{j=1}^{k-1} \mathbf{y}_j + P\mathbf{d}\|^2.$$

Thus we see that $M$ is positive definite if and only if $\{\mathbf{y}_j^T \Omega_j \mathbf{y}_j = 0, j = 1, \cdots, k-1$ and $\sum_{j=1}^{k-1} \mathbf{y}_j + P\mathbf{d} = 0\}$ implies that $\{\mathbf{y}_1 = \cdots = \mathbf{y}_{k-1} = P\mathbf{d} = 0\}$. Since the null space of $\Omega_j$ is easily seen (from the definition of $\Omega_j$) to be $\{(p(t_1), \cdots, p(t_n))^T : p \in N_j\}$, we then have unicity of the solution of (2.4) if and only if, for any $\mathbf{y}_j \in \{(p(t_1), \cdots, p(t_n))^T : p \in N_j\}, j = 1, \cdots, k-1,$ and $\mathbf{d} \in \text{range}(P)$, $\{\sum_{j=1}^{k-1} \mathbf{y}_j + P\mathbf{d} = 0\}$ implies $\{\mathbf{y}_1 = \cdots = \mathbf{y}_{k-1} = 0$ and $\mathbf{d} = 0\}$. ∎

## 2.5. A General Characterization

Consider again the $j^{th}$ problem (2.5) associated with $X_j, L_j(\ ) = (\ ,\ )_j$. Suppose that $K_j : \mathbb{R}^d \times \mathbb{R}^d \to \mathbb{R}$ is a semi-reproducing function for $X_j, (\ ,\ )_j$. Then it is known that for any $\mathbf{z} \in \mathbb{R}^n$ the solution $x_j = s_j(\mathbf{z})$ of (2.5) has the following representation:

$$x_j(t) = \sum_{i=1}^{n} \lambda_{j,i} K_j(t_i, t) + q_j(t), \qquad q_j \in N_j,$$

where the $n$ coefficients $\lambda_{i,j}$ and the function $q_j$ are determined by the equations

$$\sum_{i=1}^{n} \lambda_{j,i} q(t_i) = 0, \quad \forall q \in N_j$$

$$\lambda_{j,i} + \rho(x_j(t_i) - z_i) = 0, \quad \forall i.$$

Note that such a representation is still correct (although unusual) if we have a least squares problem (*i.e.*, $L_j \equiv 0$, on $X_j = V$) by choosing $K_j \equiv 0$ since the previous characterization is then equivalent to

$$s_j(\mathbf{z}) = q_j, \ q_j \in N_j, \quad \text{with } \sum_{i=1}^{n} (q_j(t_i) - z_i) q(t_i) = 0, \quad \forall q \in N_j.$$

Our inf-convolution spline is now characterized by the following:

**Theorem 2.5.** *An element $(x_1^*, \cdots, x_k^*)$ of $X_1 \times \cdots \times X_k$ is a solution of (2.4) if and only if there exist $n$ coefficients $\lambda_i^*$ and $k$ functions $q_j^*$, each $q_j^* \in N_j$, such that for $j = 1, \cdots, k$*

$$x_j^* = \sum_{i=1}^{n} \lambda_i^* K_j(t_i, \cdot) + q_j^*, \tag{2.12}$$

*with*

$$\sum_{i=1}^{n} \lambda_i^* q(t_i) = 0, \quad \forall q \in \sum_{j=1}^{k} N_j$$

$$\lambda_i^* + \rho((x_1^* + \cdots + x_k^*)(t_i) - z_i) = 0, \quad \forall i.$$

**Proof:** By a straightforward application of Theorem 2.2 and using the $k$ previous characterizations, we see that $(x_1^*, \cdots, x_k^*) \in X_1 \times \cdots \times X_k$ is a solution of (2.4) if and only if the following $k$ connected representations hold: for $j = 1, \cdots, k$,

$$x_j^* = \sum_{i=1}^{n} \lambda_{j,i}^* K_j(t_i, \cdot) + q_j^*, \qquad q_j^* \in N_j$$

with

$$\sum_{i=1}^{n} \lambda_{j,i}^* q(t_i) = 0, \quad \forall q \in N_j$$

$$\lambda_{j,i}^* + \rho\big(x_j^*(t_i) - (z_i - \sum_{l \neq j} x_l^*(t_i))\big) = 0, \quad \forall i.$$

To complete the proof, it suffices now to observe that the latter equation implies that the $\lambda_{j,i}^*$'s do not depend on $j$. ∎

We remark that the connection between the $x_j^*$'s is that they have the same coefficients $\lambda_{j,1}^*, \cdots, \lambda_{j,n}^*$. Assuming that we know the semi-reproducing functions $K_j$ for $j = 1, \cdots, k$, and a basis for each null space $N_j, j = 1, \cdots, k$, we see that the coefficients in the representation (2.12) of our inf-convolution spline can be computed by solving a linear system of order $n + \sum_{j=1}^{k} m_j$, where $m_j$ denotes the dimension of $\{(p(t_1), \cdots, p(t_n))^T : p \in N_j\}$.

However, it is well known that characterizations using semi-reproducing functions yield linear systems in which the $n \times n$ matrix with $(i, j)^{th}$ entry $K_j(t_i)$ is generally not sparse. Therefore, in most of the typical one-dimensional problems, computation of inf-convolution splines using the previous linear system will be far from the most efficient method. A typical example of an efficient algorithm is described in the following:

**Example 2.6.** *(Inf-convolution of trigonometric splines as in Example 1.1). Let us recall first some basic facts on trigonometric splines. For a given $\omega$, let $X$ be the set of real functions $x : \mathbb{R} \to \mathbb{R}$ such that*

$$L_\omega(x) = \int_{\mathbb{R}} (x''(t) + \omega^2 x(t))^2 dt \ < \infty,$$

*and consider the problem*

$$\min_{x \in X} \quad L_\omega(x) \ + \ \rho \sum_{i=1}^{n} [x(t_i) - z_i]^2 , \tag{2.13}$$

*where $t_1 < \cdots < t_n$ $(n \geq 2)$.*

It is known (see Laurent [12], p. 229) that a semi-reproducing function for $X, |.| = L_\omega$ can be defined by

$$K(t, t') = \Theta_\omega(t - t')$$

with

$$\Theta_\omega(t) = \frac{1}{2\omega^3} [\sin(\omega t)_+ - (\omega t)_+ \cos \omega t], \tag{2.14}$$

and that the (unique) solution $x = s_\omega(\mathbf{z})$ of (2.13) has the representation

$$x(t) = \sum_{i=1}^{n} \lambda_i \Theta_\omega(t - t_i) + \mu \cos \omega t + \nu \sin \omega t, \tag{2.15}$$

where the $n + 2$ coefficients $\lambda_i, i = 1, \cdots, n$, and $\mu, \nu$ are determined by the $n + 2$ equations

$$\sum_{i=1}^{n} \lambda_i \cos(\omega t_i) = 0, \qquad \sum_{i=1}^{n} \lambda_i \sin(\omega t_i) = 0$$
$$\lambda_i + \rho(x(t_i) - z_i) = 0, \quad i = 1, \cdots, n.$$

Note that $\lambda_i$ in (2.15) is actually the discontinuity of the third derivative of $x$ at $t_i$.

Now, it is easy to see that this characterization is not suitable for computational purposes. In fact, it is known that efficient algorithms can be obtained by observing that the set $\{s_\omega(\mathbf{z}) : \mathbf{z} \in \mathbb{R}^n\}$ is exactly the $n$-dimensional subspace of those functions $x$ that satisfy the following properties:

1. in each interval $(t_i, t_{i+1})$, $x$ is a linear combination of the four functions $\sin(\omega t), \cos(\omega t), (\omega t) \sin(\omega t), (\omega t) \cos(\omega t)$,

2. in $(-\infty, t_1)$ and $(t_n, \infty)$, $x$ is a linear combination of $\sin(\omega t), \cos(\omega t)$,

3. $x, x'$ and $x''$ are continuous.

A classical algorithm (e.g. [12]) is then to express each piece of such a trigonometric spline $x$ in terms of its values $y_i$, $y_{i+1}$ at $t_i$, $t_{i+1}$ and its first derivatives $y_i'$, $y_{i+1}'$ at $t_i$, $t_{i+1}$, respectively. These $2n$ parameters are then determined by imposing the following $2n$ conditions: for $i = 1, \cdots, n$,

$$\text{disc}(x''')(t_i) + \rho(x(t_i) - z_i) = 0$$
$$x''(t_i^+) = x''(t_i^-),$$

where $\text{disc}(x''')(t_i) = x'''(t_i^+) - x'''(t_i^-)$. It can be checked that this yields a $2 \times 2$ block tridiagonal linear system of order $2n$ which, in the case of equally spaced data $t_{i+1} - t_i = h$, can be easily written

$$B'\Lambda_1 + C\Lambda_2 \qquad\qquad = \begin{bmatrix} uwz_1 \\ 0 \end{bmatrix},$$

$$A\Lambda_{i-1} + B\Lambda_i + C\Lambda_{i+1} = \begin{bmatrix} uwz_i \\ 0 \end{bmatrix}, \quad i = 2, \cdots, n-1, \qquad (2.16)$$

$$A\Lambda_{n-1} + B''\Lambda_n = \begin{bmatrix} uwz_n \\ 0 \end{bmatrix},$$

where $\Lambda_i = \begin{bmatrix} y_i \\ hy_i' \end{bmatrix}$ and $A, B, B', B''$ and $C$ are $2 \times 2$ matrices given by

$$A = \begin{bmatrix} d & -c \\ c & 1 \end{bmatrix}, \quad B = \begin{bmatrix} 2b + uw & 0 \\ 0 & 2a \end{bmatrix}, \quad C = A^T$$
$$B' = \begin{bmatrix} b + uw & e \\ e & a \end{bmatrix}, \quad B'' = \begin{bmatrix} b + uw & -e \\ -e & a \end{bmatrix}, \qquad (2.17a)$$

with

$$a = (p - \sin p \cos p)/e$$
$$b = p^2(p + \sin p \cos p)/e$$
$$c = (p^2 \sin p)/e$$
$$d = -p^2(\sin p + p \cos p)/e \qquad (2.17b)$$
$$u = (p^2 - \sin^2 p)/(p \cdot e)$$
$$w = \frac{\rho h^3}{2}$$

and $p = \omega h$, $e = \sin p - p \cos p$.

Let us consider now the inf-convolution of $k$ trigonometric splines; *i.e.*, the minimization of

$$L_{\omega_1}(x_1) + \cdots + L_{\omega_k}(x_k) + \rho \sum_{i=1}^{n} [x_1(t_i) + \cdots + x_k(t_i) - z_i]^2 .$$

From Theorem 2.3 and definition (2.14), $x_1^*, \cdots, x_k^*$ is a solution of this minimization problem if and only if for $j = 1, \cdots, k$

$$x_j^*(t) = \sum_{i=1}^{n} \lambda_i \Theta_{\omega_j}(t - t_i) + \mu_j \cos \omega_j t + \nu_j \sin \omega_j t,$$

where the $n + 2k$ coefficients $\lambda_i, i = 1, \cdots, n,$ and $\mu_j, \nu_j, j = 1, \cdots, k$ are determined by the $n + 2k$ equations

$$\sum_{i=1}^{n} \lambda_i \cos(\omega_j t_i) = 0, \qquad \sum_{i=1}^{n} \lambda_i \sin(\omega_j t_i) = 0, \quad j = 1, \cdots, k,$$
$$\lambda_i + \rho(x_1^*(t_i) + \cdots + x_k^*(t_i) - z_i) = 0, \quad i = 1, \cdots, n.$$

The previous remark implies here that the $x_j^*$'s have a common jump of the third derivative at each $t_i$.

The above computation method for trigonometric splines can be easily generalized for inf-convolution of $k$ trigonometric splines. It suffices to observe that the $i^{th}$ piece of each $x_j^*$ is again determined by its values $y_{j,i}$, $y_{j,i+1}$ at $t_i$, $t_{i+1}$ and its first derivatives $y_{j,i}'$, $y_{j,i+1}'$ at $t_i$, $t_{i+1}$, respectively, and that we can write, for $j = 1, \cdots, k$, for $i = 1, \cdots, n,$

$$\text{disc}(x_j^{*'''})(t_i) + \rho(y_{1,i} + \cdots + y_{k,i} - z_i) = 0$$
$$x_j^{*''}(t_i^+) = x_j^{*''}(t_i^-).$$

This again yields a block tridiagonal linear system where the blocks are certain matrices of order $2k$. For example, in the case $k = 2$ we obtain

$$\begin{bmatrix} A_1 & 0 \\ 0 & A_2 \end{bmatrix} \begin{bmatrix} \Lambda_{i-1}^1 \\ \Lambda_{i-1}^2 \end{bmatrix} + \begin{bmatrix} B_1 & 0 \\ 0 & B_2 \end{bmatrix} \begin{bmatrix} \Lambda_i^1 \\ \Lambda_i^2 \end{bmatrix} + \begin{bmatrix} C_1 & 0 \\ 0 & C_2 \end{bmatrix} \begin{bmatrix} \Lambda_{i+1}^1 \\ \Lambda_{i+1}^2 \end{bmatrix} = \begin{bmatrix} u_1 w(z_i - y_{2,i}) \\ 0 \\ u_2 w(z_i - y_{1,i}) \\ 0 \end{bmatrix},$$

where $\Lambda_i^1$ (resp. $\Lambda_i^2$) and the $2 \times 2$ matrices $A_1$, $B_1$, $C_1$ (resp. $A_2$, $B_2$, $C_2$) are defined as in (2.17) with $\omega_1$ (resp. $\omega_2$) in place of $\omega$.

We note that such a block tridiagonal linear system of order $2n$ is in fact simply the characterization that was given in Theorem 2.1, where each of the $k$ equations (2.6) is replaced by the corresponding block tridiagonal linear system (2.16) of order $2n$.

## 2.6. A Gauss-Seidel Block Iteration

From the $k$ connected linear equations (2.7), it is natural to propose the following iterative scheme for the computation of $(\mathbf{y}_1^*, \cdots, \mathbf{y}_k^*)$:

for $j = 1, \cdots, k$ do

$$\mathbf{y}_j^{(r+1)} := S_j(\mathbf{z} - (\mathbf{y}_1^{(r+1)} + \cdots + \mathbf{y}_{j-1}^{(r+1)} + \mathbf{y}_{j+1}^{(r)} + \cdots + \mathbf{y}_k^{(r)}))$$

In fact, we recognize here the block Gauss-Seidel iteration applied to the corresponding linear system, in a form similar to (2.11). Assuming the unicity of the solution, the matrix of this system is a symmetric positive definite matrix, and, as is well known, such a block Gauss-Seidel iteration will always converge (see e.g. Young [26]). In practice it has been observed that this iterative scheme is quite efficient in typical examples of trigonometric inf-convolution splines. Indeed a few iterations are always sufficient, provided that all of the $\omega_j$'s are sufficiently distinct, and that the desired smoothing is not too strong.

We do not claim, however, that such an iterative scheme will always be efficient. For some other problems, its convergence may be prohibitively slow. This is the case, for example, for inf-convolution with break functions as mentioned for functions with discontinuities (Example 1.1).

## §3. Computation of the Generalized Cross-validation Function

In this section we discuss the use of the method of generalized cross-validation (GCV) for choosing $\rho$ and $\alpha$ at a reasonable cost. In each of the previous problems, we could define, for a given $\rho$ and $\alpha$, the corresponding smoothing operator $A_{\rho,\alpha}$ by

$$\mathbf{y}_{\rho,\alpha}^* = (x^*(t_1), \cdots, x^*(t_n))^T = A_{\rho,\alpha}\mathbf{z}.$$

GCV then consists of choosing the main parameters determining the fit of $\mathbf{z}$ (here $\rho$ and $\alpha$) so as to minimize the GCV function defined by

$$V(\rho, \alpha) = \frac{\frac{1}{n}\|\mathbf{y}_{\rho,\alpha}^* - \mathbf{z}\|^2}{\left[\frac{1}{n}\mathrm{tr}(I - A_{\rho,\alpha})\right]^2}. \tag{3.1}$$

As the minimization of this function with respect to $\rho$ and $\alpha$ requires a global search method, it is essential to have a fast algorithm for its evaluation with different values of $\rho$ and $\alpha$.

We have seen in Section 2 that there exist efficient algorithms for the computation of $\mathbf{y}^*_{\rho,\alpha}$. The (usual) difficulty is to compute the trace-term at a reasonable cost. Let us recall first some standard algorithms.

In these problems, for given $\alpha$, $A_{\rho,\alpha}$ can always be written in the form

$$A = \left( I + \frac{1}{\rho}\Omega \right)^{-1},$$

where $\Omega$ is the real symmetric non-negative definite matrix associated with the smoothness criterion

$$\min_{\substack{x \in X \\ x(t_i)=z_i, i=1,\cdots,n}} L(x) = \mathbf{z}^T \Omega \mathbf{z}.$$

The standard algorithms essentially consist of first computing the eigenvalues $\nu_1, \cdots, \nu_n$ of $\Omega$. Then the expression

$$\mathrm{tr}(A) = \sum_{i=1}^{n} \left( 1 + \frac{1}{\rho}\nu_i \right)^{-1}$$

allows repeated computations of $\mathrm{tr}(A)$ for different values of $\rho$ at a low cost.

Except for some well structured problems (periodic splines [1] or rotation invariant tomography [7]), such an algorithm requires order $n^3$ operations and order $n^2$ storage locations. Fortunately, for the classical problems of fitting data by a polynomial smoothing spline or similarly for banded least squares problems, there exist some much more economical algorithms based on a nice recursive formula for calculating the trace of the inverse of a banded matrix (see Elden [2], Hutchinson, de Hoog [10]).

Let us recall also some approximation formulae that have been derived for the trace in one-dimensional polynomial spline problems. In the case of equally spaced data points $\{t_1, \cdots, t_n\} = \{(i-0.5)/n, i = 1, \cdots, n\}$ and splines of order $q$ , Utreras [22] has shown that the eigenvalues of $\Omega$ are

$$\lambda_1 = \cdots = \lambda_q = 0, \qquad \lambda_i \approx c(i - 1.5)^{2q}, \; i = q+1, \cdots, n. \tag{3.2}$$

In [20], Silverman gives a similar approximation and proposes a generalization for nonequally spaced $t_i$'s.

## 3.1. The Case of a Finite Dimensional Subspace

We now consider the case discussed in Section 2.2. Such an approach with a standard smoothing spline criterion $L_1$ and a subspace $V$ of singularities has many practical applications. We will show here that the required trace of the ICS smoothing operator can be simply related to the trace of the standard $L_1$-smoothing operator.

Let us denote this smoothing operator associated with $L_1$ by
$$A_\rho = S_1.$$
In Section 2.2 we saw that the ICS fit of $\mathbf{z}$ is $\mathbf{y}^* = \mathbf{y}_1^* + \mathbf{y}_2^*$, where
$$\mathbf{y}_1^* = A_\rho(\mathbf{z} - \mathbf{y}_2^*)$$
$$\mathbf{y}_2^* = P\mathbf{d}^* \text{ with } P^T(I - A_\rho)P\mathbf{d}^* = P^T(\mathbf{z} - A_\rho\mathbf{z}).$$
We then have the following expression for the ICS smoothing operator $S$ transforming $\mathbf{z}$ into $\mathbf{y}^* = S(\mathbf{z})$, which we will now call the *P-preserving smoothing operator* and denote by $B_{\rho,P} = S$:

$$B_{\rho,P} = A_\rho(I - R_{\rho,P}) + R_{\rho,P}, \tag{3.3}$$

where $R_{\rho,P}$ is the operator which transforms $\mathbf{z}$ into the singular part $\mathbf{y}_2^*$
$$R_{\rho,P} = P(P^T(I - A_\rho)P)^{-1}P^T(I - A_\rho). \tag{3.4}$$

A simple and very useful relation between the trace of $B_{\rho,P}$ and the trace of $A_\rho$, as shown in [8], can now be stated in the following theorem:

**Theorem 3.1.** *If $B_{\rho,P}$ denotes the P-preserving smoothing operator, then*

$$\text{tr}(B_{\rho,P}) - \text{tr}(A_\rho) = \text{tr}(\ (P^T(P - Q))^{-1}\ (P - Q)^T(P - Q)\ ), \tag{3.5}$$

*where $Q$ is the $n \times m$ matrix defined by $Q = A_\rho P$.*

**Proof:** From (3.3) we have $B_{\rho,P} - A_\rho = (I - A_\rho)R_{\rho,P}$, and thus
$$\text{tr}(B_{\rho,P} - A_\rho) = \text{tr}(\ (I - A_\rho)\ P(P^T(I - A_\rho)P)^{-1}P^T(I - A_\rho)\ ).$$
The relation (3.5) can now be obtained by using the fact that $\text{tr}(M_1 M_2) = \text{tr}(M_2 M_1)$ with $M_1 = (I - A_\rho)P$ and $M_2 = (P^T(I - A_\rho)P)^{-1}P^T(I - A_\rho)$. ∎

In many problems there already exist efficient algorithms for computing the classical $\text{tr}(A_\rho)$ and the number $m$ of singularity parameters is much less than $n$. Furthermore, the computation of one inf-convolution spline by the algorithm of Section 2.2 already needs the computation of the $n \times m$ matrix $Q$ and of $P^T(P - Q)$. Thus, this theorem yields a very economical formula for $\text{tr}(B_{\rho,P})$ requiring only $m^2 n$ operations (for $(P - Q)^T(P - Q)$) plus some computations of order $m^3$.

In the case of a single singularity (*i.e.*, $m = 1$, and $P = \mathbf{p}$), we see that (3.5) becomes

$$\text{tr}(B_{\rho,\mathbf{p}}) - \text{tr}(A_\rho) = \frac{||(I - A_\rho)\mathbf{p}||^2}{\mathbf{p}^T(I - A_\rho)\mathbf{p}} \tag{3.6a}$$

$$= \frac{\mathbf{q}^T(I - A_\rho)\mathbf{q}}{||\mathbf{q}||^2}, \tag{3.6b}$$

where we have set $\mathbf{q} = (I - A_\rho)^{1/2}\mathbf{p}$. Then if $\lambda_{\min}(I - A_\rho)$ (resp. $\lambda_{\max}(I - A_\rho)$) denotes the smallest (resp. the largest) eigenvalue of $I - A_\rho$ we have, from the well known properties of Raleigh quotients

$$0 \le \lambda_{\min}(I - A_\rho) \le \text{tr}(B_{\rho,\mathbf{p}}) - \text{tr}(A_\rho) \le \lambda_{\max}(I - A_\rho) \le 1.$$

More generally, we have the following bounds [8] for an arbitrary $m$:

**Corollary 3.2.** *The following inequality holds:*

$$0 \le \mathrm{tr}(B_{\rho,P} - \mathrm{tr}(A_\rho) \le m \cdot \lambda_{\max}(I - A_\rho) \le m.$$

**Proof:** This can be easily obtained in the following way: if $\lambda$ is any one of the $m$ eigenvalues of the symmetric matrix on the right-hand side of (3.5), then there exist $\mathbf{v} \in \mathbb{R}^n$ such that

$$P^T(I - A_\rho)(I - A_\rho)P\mathbf{v} = \lambda P^T(I - A_\rho)P\mathbf{v}.$$

Multiplying this equation by $\mathbf{v}^T$ and setting $\mathbf{q} = (I - A_\rho)^{1/2}P\mathbf{v}$ (that is non-zero since $P^T(I - A_\rho)P$ is nonsingular), we obtain that $\lambda = \frac{\mathbf{q}^T(I - A_\rho)\mathbf{q}}{\|\mathbf{q}\|^2}$ is still a Rayleigh quotient of $I - A_\rho$. ∎

This corollary implies that the quantities $\frac{1}{n}\mathrm{tr}(B_{\rho,P})$ and $\frac{1}{n}\mathrm{tr}(A_\rho)$, which both belong to [0,1], are very close if $m \ll n$. Therefore, the denominator of the GCV function in (3.1) does not depend very much on $\alpha$ (*i.e.*, on the locations of discontinuities, the shape parameters of peaks, etc.). This important remark means that the partial minimization of $V(\rho, \alpha)$ with respect to $\alpha$ is approximately equivalent to the minimization of the numerator of $V(\rho, \alpha)$; in other words for a fixed $\rho$ the optimal $\alpha$ is found so that the ICS fit $\mathbf{y}^*_{\rho,\alpha}$ will be the best least-squares approximation of the data $\mathbf{z}$.

### 3.2. Monte-Carlo Approximation of the Trace

Suppose that $\mathbf{w} = (w_1, \cdots, w_n)^T$ is a vector of $n$ independent random variables with zero mean and common variance $\sigma^2 = 1$. It is straightforward to derive that for any $n \times n$ matrix $B$,

$$E(\mathbf{w}^T B\mathbf{w}) = \mathrm{tr}(B),$$

where E denotes the mean value. Furthermore, if we assume that each $w_i$ has a Gaussian probability distribution, it can be easily shown (e.g. [6,7]) that

$$E\left(\frac{\mathbf{w}^T B\mathbf{w}}{\mathbf{w}^T \mathbf{w}}\right) = \frac{1}{n}\mathrm{tr}(B).$$

Note that when we have a fast algorithm, say of order $n$, to compute the product $B\mathbf{w}$, Monte-Carlo simulations of the previous quantities are cheap.

Consider now the case $B = I - A_\rho$, where $A_\rho = \left(I + \frac{1}{\rho}\Omega\right)^{-1}$. A somewhat surprising property, noted by Girard [7], of the random quantities $\mathbf{w}^T B\mathbf{w}$ or $\mathbf{w}^T B\mathbf{w}/\mathbf{w}^T\mathbf{w}$, is that their variance is relatively very small as compared to their mean when $n$ is large enough, and that in most of the practical examples we can compute a reliable approximation of $\mathrm{tr}(I - A_\rho)$ with only a few (or even only one) Monte-Carlo simulations of these quantites. In fact, if we define $c(\rho)$ by

$$\frac{\sigma(\mathbf{w}^T(I - A_\rho)\mathbf{w})}{\mathrm{tr}(I - A_\rho)} = \sqrt{\frac{2}{n}}c(\rho),$$

where $\sigma(\cdot)$ denotes the standard deviation (the left side is thus the *relative* standard deviation of $\mathbf{w}^T(I - A_\rho)\mathbf{w}$), then in many problems $c(\rho)$ is a quantity which is never much bigger than 1. More precisely, the following theorem has been shown in [7]:

**Theorem 3.2.** *The relative standard deviation of* $\mathbf{w}^T(I - A_\rho)\mathbf{w}$ *is* $\sqrt{\frac{2}{n}}c(\rho)$, *where* $c(\rho)$ *is an increasing function on* $(0, +\infty)$ *bounded by*

$$c_{min} = \lim_{\rho \to 0+} c(\rho) = \sqrt{\frac{n}{n-q}}, \qquad c_{max} = \lim_{\rho \to \infty} c(\rho) = \frac{\sqrt{\frac{1}{n}\operatorname{tr}(\Omega^2)}}{\frac{1}{n}\operatorname{tr}(\Omega)},$$

*where* $q$ *denotes the dimension of the null-space of* $\Omega$.

### 3.3. Examples

(i) For one-dimensional polynomial splines of order $q$, asymptotic values for the upper bound can be easily computed by using the eigenvalues (3.2) and approximating the following sums by integrals:

$$c_{\max} = \frac{\sqrt{\frac{1}{n}\operatorname{tr}(\Omega^2)}}{\frac{1}{n}\operatorname{tr}(\Omega)} \approx \frac{\sqrt{\frac{1}{n}\sum_{i=q+1}^{n}(\frac{i-1.5}{n})^{4q}}}{\frac{1}{n}\sum_{i=q+1}^{n}(\frac{i-1.5}{n})^{2q}} \approx \frac{\sqrt{\int_0^1 t^{4q}dt}}{\int_0^1 t^{2q}dt} \approx \frac{2q+1}{\sqrt{4q+1}}.$$

Some similar expressions can also be obtained for the case of nonequally spaced data, see [7]. A complete experimental study of these Monte-Carlo approximations is presented in [6],[7]. There, it has been shown that such approximations yield simple GCV procedures which are as efficient as the recently published algorithms in [22,2,10].

(ii) A similar study has also been done in [7] for a simple two-dimensional discretized version of standard thin-plate approximation. A very reasonable value for the previous bounds has been obtained there, and numerical experiments have confirmed the reliability of this Monte-Carlo technique.

(iii) We now present some experimental comparisons for trigonometric splines. With $n$ equally spaced data points $t_i = (i-1)h$, $h = 1/(n-1)$, $i = 1, \cdots, n$, and $\omega = 0.25$, we have computed the exact trace of the smoothing operator associated with the trigonometric spline problem (2.13), for 21 equispaced values of $w = \frac{\rho h^3}{2}$ (in log scale) in $[10^{-5}, 10^3]$, and we have computed its Monte-Carlo approximation (with a single run) for 81 equispaced values of $w$ in $[10^{-5}, 10^3]$. We see in Figure 1 that the Monte-Carlo approximations are quite reliable for these trigonometric splines.

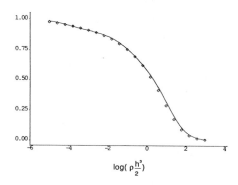

**Figure 1.** Exact traces $\frac{1}{n}\mathrm{tr}(I - A_\rho)$ ($\diamond$) and
Monte-Carlo approximations $\frac{\mathbf{w}^T(I-A_\rho)\mathbf{w}}{\mathbf{w}^T\mathbf{w}}$ (-).

## §4. Numerical Applications

We now present three kinds of numerical applications, corresponding to the three examples described in the introduction, to illustrate the abilities of the above methods to recover a function with unknown discontinuities, peaks or periods, respectively.

In all the following applications, the (easily implemented) Monte-Carlo approximation was used to compute the required traces, each time with a single simulation. Note also that we have used a common pseudo-random $\mathbf{w}$ for all the evaluations with different $\rho$'s or $\alpha$'s.

Computational strategies for minimization of the GCV function are not discussed in detail here. We only point out that, in the case of equally spaced data points, a fast algorithm (of order $n$) for the estimation of the number of discontinuities (or local singularities) and their location by GCV has been proposed by Girard [8]; this will be published elsewhere.

In each of the examples, we have used artificial data of the form $z_i = f(t_i) + \varepsilon_i$, $i = 1, \cdots, n$, where $f$ is a given test function on $[a, b]$, $t_i$ are equally spaced points $t_i = a + (i - 1)(b - a)/(n - 1)$, and $\varepsilon_i$ normally distributed pseudo-random numbers with mean 0 and a given variance $\sigma^2$. Of course, $f$, $\sigma^2$ and $n$ are chosen so that the particular features we want to recover are still more or less implied by the data $z_i$.

### 4.1. Derivative Discontinuities

The scheme we consider in this subsection is the modelling of $f$ by the sum of a smooth cubic spline plus a break function $d(t - \alpha)_+$. Thus, we use the

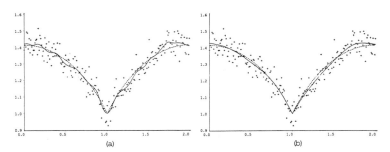

**Figure 2.**(a)Standard cubic spline, (b) ICS using the true location $\alpha = 1$.

criterion (1.5) with $m = 1$. We take

$$f(t) = \begin{cases} \sqrt{2 - t^2}, & \text{if } t \le 1 \\ \sqrt{2 - (t-2)^2}, & \text{if } t > 1, \end{cases}$$

on $[a, b] = [0, 2]$, $n = 201$ and $\sigma = 0.05$.

Figure 2a shows the test function $f$ (in dashed line), the data $\mathbf{z}$, and the solid curve is the classical cubic spline fit of the data with smoothing parameter chosen by GCV. In Figure 2b we present $\mathbf{z}$ and $f$ and the solid curve which is the result of fitting such a ICS spline to the data, assuming the true discontinuity location ($\alpha = 1$) is given, and using the smoothing parameter $\rho_{opt}$ that minimizes $V(\rho, 1)$; $i.e.$, the GCV function for $\alpha = 1$. Obviously, the oscillations in the classical cubic spline can be reduced by another choice of $\rho$, but the corner in $f$ will then be even more 'over-smoothed'.

In order to assess the ability of GCV to choose $\alpha$, we studied the variation of $V(\rho_{opt}, \alpha)$ with $\alpha \in [0.8, 1.2]$. Figure 3 shows that this function has a local minimum at a value, say $\alpha_{opt}$, which is very close to $\alpha = 1$. With these values of $\rho_{opt}, \alpha_{opt}$, we obtained the ICS fit presented in Figure 4. We see that this approximation of $f$ is almost as good as the one we obtained with the true $\alpha$ in Figure 2.

### 4.2. Peaks

We now consider the inf-convolution spline with a smooth cubic spline plus a Gaussian peak. The test function $f$ is

$$f(t) = \cos 2\pi t + \frac{1}{4} \sin 4\pi t + 4 \exp(-(t - 0.4)^2/0.025^2),$$

on $[a, b] = [0, 0.8]$, $n = 201$ and $\sigma = 0.1$. Figures 5a and 5b show $f$ (in dashed line) and the data $\mathbf{z}$. In Figure 5a the solid curve is the standard cross-validated cubic spline fit. In Figure 5b the solid curve is the ICS fit assuming the true location $\alpha = 0.4$ and width $\beta = 0.025$ are known, and using the smoothing parameter $\rho_{opt}$ which minimizes $V(\rho, \alpha, \beta)$ for these fixed values of $\alpha, \beta$. The

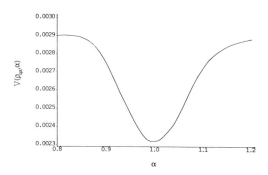

**Figure 3.** The GCV function $V(\rho_{\mathrm{opt}}, \alpha)$.

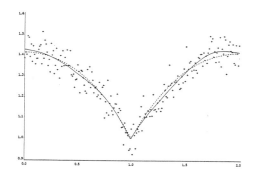

**Figure 4.** ICS with $\rho_{\mathrm{opt}}, \alpha_{\mathrm{opt}}$ 'chosen' by GCV.

remark we have previously made about the choice of $\rho$ for the standard cubic spline in Figure 2a clearly holds again in Figure 5a.

We have computed the variation of $V(\rho_{\mathrm{opt}}, \alpha, 0.025)$ with respect to $\alpha \in [0.3, 0.5]$, and the variation of $V(\rho_{\mathrm{opt}}, 0.4, \beta)$ with respect to $\beta \in [0.02, 0.03]$. As Figure 6 shows, the GCV function $V(\rho_{\mathrm{opt}}, \cdot, \cdot)$ has a minimum at $(\alpha_{\mathrm{opt}}, \beta_{\mathrm{opt}})$ which is very near $(0.4, 0.025)$. Indeed, with these values $(\rho_{\mathrm{opt}}, \alpha_{\mathrm{opt}}, \beta_{\mathrm{opt}})$, we obtained an ICS fit (not presented here) which was as good as the one we had obtained using the true $\alpha, \beta$ in Figure 5.

### 4.3. Periods

We now present two experiments involving trigonometric splines and ICS of trigonometric splines. In the first, we study the ability of standard trigono-

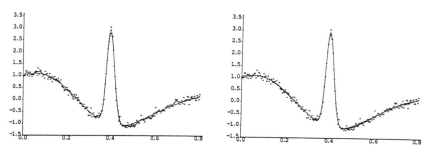

**Figure 5.** (a) Standard cubic spline,    (b) ICS fit using
the true location $\alpha = 0.4$ and width $\beta = 0.025$.

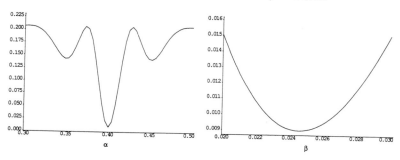

**Figure 6.** (a)The GCV function $V(\rho_{\text{opt}}, \alpha, 0.025)$,    (b) $V(\rho_{\text{opt}}, 0.4, \beta)$.

metric splines and GCV to recover a 'pseudo-period'. The test function is a
damped sine curve

$$f(t) = \frac{\sin 2\pi t}{t+1}$$

observed over 8 pseudo-periods ($[a,b] = [0,8]$) with $n = 201$ and $\sigma = 0.1$.

A plot of the data $\mathbf{z}$ and $f$ (in dashed line) is given in Figures 7a and
7b. In Figure 7a the solid curve is the standard cross-validated cubic spline
fit. In Figure 7b the solid curve is the trigonometric spline fit (solution of
(2.13)) assuming the true pseudo-period $\alpha = \frac{2\pi}{\omega} = 1$ is known, and using the
smoothing parameter $\rho_{\text{opt}}$ which minimizes $V(\rho, 1)$.

To investigate the ability of GCV to choose $\alpha$, we computed (by a golden
section search) $V(\alpha) = \min_\rho V(\rho, \alpha)$ for 21 values of the period $\alpha$ equispaced
in $[0.8, 1.2]$. Figure 8 indicates that we were able to recover a good estimate of
the underlying pseudo-period by a global minimization of the GCV function.

The second experiment concerns the third example described in the introduction. The test function, whose period is to be estimated, is simply

$$f(t) = \sin 2\pi t + \frac{1}{4} \cos 4\pi t,$$

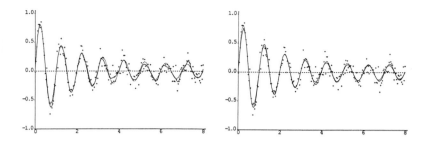

**Figure 7.** (a) Standard cubic spline,  (b) Trigonometric
spline using the true pseudo-period $\alpha = 1$.

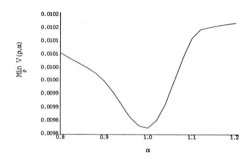

**Figure 8.** $V(\alpha) = \min_\rho V(\rho, \alpha)$.

with $[a, b] = [0, 4]$, $n = 201$ and $\sigma = 0.2$. We use the ICS criterion (1.9) with
$k = 2$. Plots of the data $\mathbf{z}$ and $f$ (in dashed line) are given in Figures 9.a and
9.b. In Figure 9.a the solid curve is the standard cross-validated cubic spline
fit. In Figure 10.b the solid curve is the trigonometric ICS fit assuming the
true period $\alpha = \frac{2\pi}{\omega} = 1$ is known, and $\rho$ chosen by GCV.

Then, we computed (by a golden section search) $V(\alpha) = \min_\rho V(\rho, \alpha)$ for
21 values of the period $\alpha$ equispaced in $[0.8, 1.2]$. Again, Figure 10 indicates
that we can recover a good approximation of an underlying period by the GCV
method.

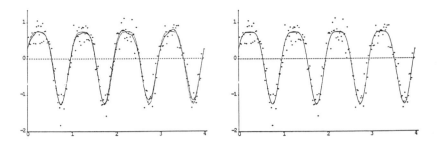

**Figure 9.** (a) Standard cubic spline,    (b) Trigonometric
ICS fit with the true period $\alpha = 1$.

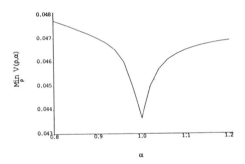

**Figure 10.** $V(\alpha) = \min_\rho V(\rho, \alpha)$.

## References

1. Craven, P. and G. Wahba, Smoothing noisy data with spline functions, Numer. Math. **31** (1979), 377–403.
2. Eldén, L., A note on the computation of the generalized cross-validation function for ill-conditioned least squares problems, BIT **24** (1984), 467–472.
3. Eubank, R. L., A note on smoothness priors and nonlinear regression, J. Amer. Statist. Assoc. **81** (1986), 514–517.
4. Franke, R. and G. Nielson, Surface approximation with imposed conditions, in *Surfaces in Computer Aided Geometric Design*, R.E. Barnhill and W. Boehm (eds.), North-Holland, Amsterdam, 1984, 135–146.
5. Girard, D. A., Optimal regularized reconstruction in computerized tomography, SIAM J. Sci. Statist. Comput. **8** (1987), 934–950.
6. Girard, D., Un algorithme rapide pour le calcul de la trace de l'inverse

d'une grande matrice, Rapport de recherche RR 665-M, TIM3-IMAG, Université de Grenoble, 1987.

7. Girard, D., A fast 'Monte-Carlo cross-validation' for large least squares problems with noisy data, RR 687-M, TIM3-IMAG, Université de Grenoble, 1987.

8. Girard, D., Détection de discontinuités dans un signal (ou une image) par Inf-Convolution Spline et Validation Croisée: un algorithme rapide non paramétré, RR 702-I-M, TIM3-IMAG, Université de Grenoble, 1988.

9. Golub, G. H., M. Heath, and G. Wahba, Generalized cross-validation as a method for choosing a good ridge parameter, Technometrics **21** (1979), 215–224.

10. Hutchinson, M. F. and F. R. de Hoog, Smoothing noisy data with spline functions, Numer. Math. **47** (1985), 99–106.

11. Klein, P., Sur l'approximation et la représentation de surfaces explicites en présence de singularités, Thèse, Université de Grenoble, IMAG, 29 Sept., 1987.

12. Laurent, P. J., *Approximation et Optimisation*, Hermann, Paris, 1972.

13. Laurent, P. J., Spline functions using inf-convolution, Colloquium talk, International Workshop on Approximation Theory, Technion, Haifa, Israel, June 1–6, 1980.

14. Laurent, P. J., Inf-convolution spline pour l'approximation de données discontinues, Rapport de Recherche IMAG 270 (1981); see also M2AN, RAIRO, Anal. Num. **20** (1986), 89–111 .

15. Laurent, P. J., Quadratic convex analysis and splines, Proc. of the Intern. Conf. *Methods of Functional Analysis in Approximation Theory* (Bombay, Dec. 16–20, 1985), Birkhauser Verlag, ISNM 76, 1986, 17–43.

16. Laurent, P. J., Inf-convolution splines, Rapport de Recherche TIM3-IMAG, 1988.

17. Laurent, P. J. and F. Utreras, Optimal smoothing of noisy broken data, J. of Approx. Theory and its Appl. **2** (1986), 71–94.

18. Maury, S., Inf-convolution de formes quadratiques positives, Séminaire d'Analyse Unilatérale de Montpellier, 2, 1969.

19. Moreau, J. J., Fonctionnelles convexes, Séminaire du Collège de France, 1966–67.

20. Silverman, B. W., A fast and efficient cross-validation method for smoothing parameter choice in spline regression, J. Amer. Statist. Assoc. **79** (1984), 584–589 .

21. Shiau, J. J., G. Wahba and D. R. Johnson, Partial spline models for the inclusion of tropopause and frontal boundary information in otherwise smooth two- and three-dimensional objective analysis, J. Atmospheric and Oceanic Technology **3** (1986), 714–725.

22. Utreras, F., Sur le choix du paramètre d'ajustement dans le lissage par fonctions spline, Numer. Math. **34** (1980), 15–28.

23. Valera Garcia, D., Application de l'inf-convolution spline au traitement des chromatogrammes de gasoils, Thèse, Université de Grenoble, 1984.

24. Wahba, G., The approximate solution of linear operator equations when the data are noisy, SIAM J. Numer. Anal. **14** (1977), 651–667.

25. Wahba, G., Partial and Interaction spline models for the semiparametric estimation of functions of several variables, Computer Science and Statistics, T. J. Boardman (ed.), Proc. of the 18th Symposium on the Interface, Fort Collins, March 1986.

26. Young, D. M., *Iterative Solution of Large Linear Systems*, Academic Press, New York, 1971.

D. Girard and P. J. Laurent
Lab. TIM3, Institut IMAG
Université Joseph Fourier
B.P. 68
38402 St. Martin d' Hères
FRANCE

# On Beta-continuous Functions and Their Application to the Construction of Geometrically Continuous Curves and Surfaces

R. N. Goldman and B. A. Barsky

**Abstract.** A function is said to be $\beta$-continuous if it satisfies the Beta-constraints for the fixed values $\beta = (\beta_1, \ldots, \beta_n)$. Sums, differences, products, quotients, and scalar multiples of $\beta$-continuous functions are shown to be $\beta$-continuous. These basic results are applied to various standard constructions of parametrically continuous curves and surfaces — such as rational splines, Catmull-Rom splines, affine combinations of curves, as well as ruled, lofted, tensor product, and Boolean sum surfaces — to generate geometrically continuous analogues. This analysis for geometric continuity defined by the Beta-constraints (reparametrization) is contrasted with a corresponding investigation for Frenet frame continuity.

## §1. Introduction

One theme with many variations will occupy our attention here. Our theme: to generalize standard constructions for parametrically continuous curves and surfaces to geometrically continuous curves and surfaces. The variations: rational splines, Catmull-Rom splines [11], affine combinations of curves, and ruled, lofted, tensor product, or Boolean sum surfaces [25].

Consider first rational curves or surfaces. Let $b_0(t), \ldots, b_m(t)$ be the B-spline basis functions for some knot vector $\mathbf{T}$, let $\mathbf{V}_0, \ldots, \mathbf{V}_m$ be a collection of control vertices, and let $w_0, \ldots, w_m$ be a set of scalar weights. The standard construction of a parametrically continuous rational B-spline curve is given by setting

$$\mathbf{r}(t) = \sum_j \frac{w_j \mathbf{V}_j b_j(t)}{\sum_k w_k b_k(t)}.$$

Mathematical Methods in Computer Aided Geometric Design
Tom Lyche and Larry L. Schumaker (eds.), pp. 299–311.
Copyright © 1989 by Academic Press, Boston.
ISBN 0-12-460515-X.

Question: what happens if we replace the B-spline basis functions with basis functions for geometrically continuous curves and surfaces? Answer: we shall see below that this depends upon our definition of geometric continuity.

What about Catmull-Rom splines? Here we begin with a set of B-spline basis functions $b_0(t), \ldots, b_m(t)$ of degree $p$ and a collection of Lagrange polynomials $\mathbf{L}_0(t), \ldots, \mathbf{L}_m(t)$ of degree $q$, where $\mathbf{L}_j(t)$ interpolates the control vertices $\mathbf{V}_{j-q}, \ldots, \mathbf{V}_j$. The Catmull-Rom spline is defined by

$$\mathbf{c}(t) = \sum_j b_j(t) \mathbf{L}_j(t).$$

These splines are $C^{p-1}$ continuous curves which interpolate their control vertices $V_j$ if $q \geq p$; see [7,11]. Again we would like to know what happens if we replace the B-splines and the Lagrange polynomials by their geometrically continuous analogues [14]. We shall see that here too the answer depends on our definition of geometric continuity.

For our next problem, let $\mathbf{c}_1(t)$ and $\mathbf{c}_2(t)$ be two parametrically continuous curves and let $\alpha$ be a fixed scalar. Then the affine combination

$$\mathbf{a}(t) = (1 - \alpha)\mathbf{c}_1(t) + \alpha \mathbf{c}_2(t)$$

is again a parametrically continuous curve. However, if $\mathbf{c}_1(t)$ and $\mathbf{c}_2(t)$ are only geometrically continuous, then it is known that $\mathbf{a}(t)$ need not be geometrically continuous.

A related problem concerns the ruled surface

$$\mathbf{r}(s,t) = (1 - s)\mathbf{c}_1(t) + s\mathbf{c}_2(t)$$

joining the curves $\mathbf{c}_1(t)$ and $\mathbf{c}_2(t)$. If the curves $\mathbf{c}_1(t)$ and $\mathbf{c}_2(t)$ are parametrically continuous, then so is the surface $\mathbf{r}(s,t)$. However, if $\mathbf{c}_1(t)$ and $\mathbf{c}_2(t)$ are only geometrically continuous, then again it is known that the ruled surface $\mathbf{r}(s,t)$ need not be geometrically continuous [20]. Is there anything more we can say here? Are there any restrictions we can make to force the curve $\mathbf{a}(t)$ or the surface $\mathbf{r}(s,t)$ to be geometrically continuous?

We can extend these questions to lofted surfaces, tensor product surfaces, and Boolean sum surfaces. When the original curves and blending functions are parametrically continuous, so are the resulting surfaces, but this inheritance generally fails for geometric continuity. What is to be done?

We plan to address these questions more fully in Section 4, after reviewing the concept of geometric continuity in Section 2, and developing some basic results about $\beta$-continuous functions in Section 3.

## §2. Geometric Continuity

*Geometric continuity* is a measure of smoothness which has recently been proposed as an alternative to *parametric continuity*, the conventional measure of smoothness for parametric curves and surfaces. In this section we review notions of geometric continuity for curves; geometric continuity for surfaces will be reviewed briefly in Section 4.2.

For parametric curves there are two competing concepts of $n^{th}$ order geometric continuity in the literature today: one based on the notion of *reparametrization* or the *Beta-constraints* [4,5,6,7,12,13], and the other based on the continuity of the *Frenet frame* or *higher order curvatures* [15,16,17,26]. Both of these notions of geometric continuity have their roots in first and second order geometric continuity (that is, continuity of the unit tangent and curvature vectors) which appeared in various forms in [1,2,18,19,21,32,33,34]. Geometric continuity has become an important topic of research, and recent work has been reported in [7,8,23,24,27,28].

We begin here with the concept of geometric continuity that is based on the notion of reparametrization. Recall that a parametrization is said to be *regular* if its derivative is never zero. A piecewise regular curve $\mathbf{r}(t)$, $\mathbf{r}$ : $[t_{min}, t_{max}] \to \mathbb{R}^d$, $d > 1$, is said to be $n^{th}$ order geometrically continuous, or $G^n$, at $\mathbf{r}(\tau)$ if there exists a regular reparametrization $t : [\tilde{t}_{min}, \tilde{t}_{max}] \to [t_{min}, t_{max}]$ such that $\mathbf{r}(t(\tilde{t}))$ is $n^{th}$ order parametrically continuous, or $C^n$, at $\mathbf{r}(\tau)$. This characterization of geometric continuity based on the *existence* of a $C^n$ parametrization can be summarized as follows: *Do not base smoothness on the parametrization at hand; reparametrize if necessary to find one that is $C^n$ continuous.* Notice that like parametric continuity, geometric continuity is a local property.

The preceding definition characterizes geometric continuity in terms of the existence of a regular $C^n$ parametrization. This characterization is rather theoretical and hard to apply in practice. What we would like is a more concrete characterization of geometric continuity based on the parametrization at hand. This can be done in terms of the Beta-constraints [6,12] which we now recall.

Intuitively, since the parametrization $\mathbf{r}(t(\tilde{t}))$ is $C^n$ at $\mathbf{r}(\tau)$, we can use the chain rule to calculate the $j^{th}$ right hand derivative of $\mathbf{r}(t)$ at $\tau$ in terms of the first $j$ left hand derivatives of $\mathbf{r}(t)$ at $\tau$. To simplify our notation, let $\beta = (\beta_1, \dots, \beta_n)$ and let $\sum M_{jk}(\beta)\mathbf{r}^{(k)}(t)$, $j = 0, 1, \dots, n$, denote the expression for the chain rule applied to $\mathbf{r}^{(j)}(t(\tilde{t}))$ with $\beta_i$ substituted for $t^{(i)}(\tilde{t})$, $i \geq 1$. Notice that $M(\beta) = \{M_{jk}(\beta)\}$ is a lower triangular matrix and that one new $\beta$ parameter appears in each new row of $M(\beta)$. Moreover $M_{0k} = M_{k0} = \delta_{0k}$, $M_{j1}(\beta) = \beta_j$, $j \geq 1$, and $M_{jj}(\beta) = \beta_1^j$. The other entries of $M(\beta)$ are polynomials in $\beta_1, \dots, \beta_n$. Both explicit and recursive formulas for the entries of the $M(\beta)$ are given in [31]. Now the following theorem (see [4,6,12]) uses the matrix $M(\beta)$ to characterize precisely when a piecewise regular curve $\mathbf{r}(t)$ is $G^n$ at $\mathbf{r}(\tau)$.

**Theorem 1.** *(Beta-Constraints) Suppose that $\mathbf{r}(t)$ is a piecewise regular $C^n$ parametrization. Then the following statements are equivalent:*
1. *$\mathbf{r}(t)$ is $G^n$ continuous at $\mathbf{r}(\tau)$.*
2. *There exists a regular reparametrization $t : [\tilde{t}_{min}, \tilde{t}_{max}] \to [t_{min}, t_{max}]$*

*such that* $\mathbf{r}(t(\tilde{t}))$ *is* $C^n$ *continuous at* $\mathbf{r}(\tau)$.

3. *There exists real numbers* $\beta_1, \ldots, \beta_n$ *with* $\beta_1 > 0$ *such that*

$$\mathbf{r}^{(j)}(\tau^+) = \sum M_{jk}(\beta)\mathbf{r}^{(k)}(\tau^-), \quad j = 0, 1, \ldots, n. \tag{1}$$

Equations (1) are called the *Beta-constraints*; the values $\beta_1, \beta_2, \ldots, \beta_n$ are the *shape parameters* which are found in the Beta-spline. It follows from the Beta-constraints that $G^1$ continuity is equivalent to the continuity of the unit tangent vector, and $G^2$ continuity is equivalent to continuity of the unit tangent and curvature vectors [4,5,6,12].

Using matrix multiplication, we can rewrite the Beta-constraints (1) as

$$(\mathbf{r}(\tau^+), \mathbf{r}^{(1)}(\tau^+), \ldots, \mathbf{r}^{(n)}(\tau^+))^T = M(\beta)(\mathbf{r}(\tau^-), \mathbf{r}^{(1)}(\tau^-), \ldots, \mathbf{r}^{(n)}(\tau^-))^T, \tag{2}$$

where $M(\beta) = \{M_{jk}(\beta)\}$ is the matrix expressing the Beta-constraints. When a curve $\mathbf{r}(t)$ satisfies (2) for the specific values $\beta = (\beta_1, \beta_2, \ldots, \beta_n)$, we shall say that it is $\beta$-continuous.

More generally, we shall say that a piecewise regular curve $\mathbf{r}(t)$ is $M$-continuous at $\mathbf{r}(\tau)$ for a fixed matrix $M$, if it satisfies the matrix equation

$$(\mathbf{r}(\tau^+), \mathbf{r}^{(1)}(\tau^+), \ldots, \mathbf{r}^{(n)}(\tau^+))^T = M(\mathbf{r}(\tau^-), \mathbf{r}^{(1)}(\tau^-), \ldots, \mathbf{r}^{(n)}(\tau^-))^T. \tag{3}$$

The matrix $M$ is called a *connection matrix*. We shall see directly that Frenet frame continuity can be characterized in terms of $M$-continuity.

Given a curve $\mathbf{r}(s)$ in $\mathbb{R}^d$, where $s$ is the arc length parametrization, the Frenet frame of orthonormal vectors $\mathbf{v}_1(s), \ldots, \mathbf{v}_d(s)$ and the higher order scalar curvatures $\kappa_1(s), \ldots, \kappa_{d-1}(s)$ can be defined recursively by

$$\mathbf{v}_1(s) = \mathbf{r}'(s), \qquad\qquad \kappa_0(s) = 0$$

$$\mathbf{v}_{i+1}(s) = \frac{\mathbf{v}_i'(s) + \kappa_{i-1}(s)\mathbf{v}_{i-1}(s)}{\kappa_i(s)}, \qquad i = 1, 2, \ldots, d-1.$$

When $d = 3$, then $\kappa_1(s)$ is the curvature and $\kappa_2(s)$ is the torsion. For further details and explanation, see [35]. Using connection matrices, the following theorem (see [15]) precisely characterizes when a piecewise regular curve $\mathbf{r}(t)$ is Frenet frame continuous at $\mathbf{r}(\tau)$.

**Theorem 2.** *(Frenet Frame Continuity) A piecewise regular curve* $\mathbf{r}(t)$ *is Frenet frame continuous at* $\mathbf{r}(\tau)$ *if and only if it is* $M$-*continuous at* $\mathbf{r}(\tau)$ *for a lower triangular connection matrix* $M$ *such that* $M_{0k} = M_{k0} = \delta_{0k}$ *and* $M_{jj} = M_{11}^j$.

It follows from Theorem 2 that the concept of Frenet frame continuity is somewhat weaker than the notion of continuity based on reparametrization. That is, a curve may be Frenet frame continuous and not be continuous in the sense of reparametrization, but not conversely.

## §3. Some Basic Results on $\beta$-Continuous Scalar-Valued Functions

Before proceeding with our study of curves in $\mathbb{R}^d$, $d > 1$, we need to digress somewhat and focus our attention on scalar-valued functions $f : [t_{min}, t_{max}] \rightarrow \mathbb{R}^1$. As with curves, we say that a scalar-valued function $f(t)$ is $\beta$-continuous at $\tau$ if it satisfies the Beta-constraints (2) for some $\beta = (\beta_1, \beta_2, \ldots, \beta_n)$, $\beta_1 > 0$, at $f(\tau)$; that is, if

$$(f(\tau^+), f^{(1)}(\tau^+), \ldots, f^{(n)}(\tau^+))^T = M(\beta)(f(\tau^-), f^{(1)}(\tau^-), \ldots, f^{(n)}(\tau^-))^T. \tag{4}$$

Notice that unlike curves in $\mathbb{R}^d$, $d > 1$, if $f(\tau^-)$ and $f(\tau^+)$ are regular $C^n$ scalar-valued functions at $\tau$, then there always *exists a unique* $\beta$ for which $f(t)$ is $\beta$-continuous at $\tau$ because exactly one new $\beta$ parameter is introduced in each new Beta-constraint as the coefficient of $f'(\tau^-)$. The point in the following lemmas is that we shall fix the value of $\beta$.

Analogously, we say that a scalar-valued function $f(t)$ is $M$-continuous at a parameter $\tau$ if

$$(f(\tau^+), f^{(1)}(\tau^+), \ldots, f^{(n)}(\tau^+))^T = M(f(\tau^-), f^{(1)}(\tau^-), \ldots, f^{(n)}(\tau^-))^T \tag{5}$$

for some fixed connection matrix $M$. Note $M$-continuity, like $\beta$-continuity, is a local property. However, unlike the vector $\beta$, the matrix $M$ is not unique; a scalar-valued function $f(t)$ may be $M$-continuous for a wide range of matrices $M$. Again we shall focus our attention on $M$-continuity for fixed matrices $M$.

We are now going to study various combinations of $\beta$-continuous and $M$-continuous functions.

### Lemma 1.
1. If $f(t)$ is $M$-continuous at $\tau$, then $cf(t)$ is $M$-continuous at $\tau$.
2. If $f(t)$ and $g(t)$ are $M$-continuous at $\tau$, then $f(t) \pm g(t)$ are $M$-continuous at $\tau$.

**Proof:** These results follow immediately from the linearity of differentiation and matrix multiplication. ∎

Comparable results are not, in general, valid for multiplication and division of $M$-continuous functions. Here, we must specialize our results to $\beta$-continuous functions.

**Proposition 1.** *The following two statements are equivalent:*
1. *The functions $f_1(t), \ldots, f_d(t)$ are all $\beta$-continuous at $\tau$ for some fixed $\beta$.*
2. *There exists a reparametrization $t : [\tilde{t}_{min}, \tilde{t}_{max}] \rightarrow [t_{min}, t_{max}]$ for which the functions $f_1(t(\tilde{t})), \ldots, f_d(t(\tilde{t}))$ are all $C^n$ at $\tilde{\tau}$, where $t(\tilde{\tau}) = \tau$.*

**Proof:** Let $\mathbf{r}(t) = (f_1(t), \ldots, f_d(t))$ be a curve in $\mathbb{R}^d$. We shall apply Theorem 1. If the functions $(f_1(t), \ldots, f_d(t))$ are all $\beta$-continuous at $\tau$, then $\mathbf{r}(t)$ satisfies the Beta-constraints at $\tau$. Therefore by Theorem 1, there exists a reparametrization $t : [\tilde{t}_{min}, \tilde{t}_{max}] \rightarrow [t_{min}, t_{max}]$ for which $\mathbf{r}(t(\tilde{t}))$ is $C^n$ at

$\mathbf{r}(\tau)$. Hence the component functions $f_1(t(\tilde{t})), \ldots, f_d(t(\tilde{t}))$ must all be $C^n$ at $\tilde{\tau}$.

Conversely, if a reparametrization $t : [\tilde{t}_{min}, \tilde{t}_{max}] \to [t_{min}, t_{max}]$ exists for which the functions $f_1(t(\tilde{t})), \ldots, f_d(t(\tilde{t}))$ are all $C^n$ at $\tilde{\tau}$, then $\mathbf{r}(t(\tilde{t}))$ is $C^n$ at $\mathbf{r}(\tau)$. Therefore by Theorem 1, $\mathbf{r}(\tau)$ satisfies the Beta-constraints at $\mathbf{r}(\tau)$. Hence, the component functions $f_1(t), \ldots, f_d(t)$ must all be $\beta$-continuous functions at $\tau$ for the same fixed value of $\beta$. ∎

**Lemma 2.** *Suppose that $f(t)$ and $g(t)$ are $\beta$-continuous at $\tau$. Then*

1. $f(t)g(t)$ is $\beta$-continuous
2. $f(t)/g(t)$ is $\beta$-continuous at $\tau$ (provided that $g(\tau) \neq 0$).

**Proof:** By Proposition 1, since $f(t)$ and $g(t)$ are both $\beta$-continuous at $\tau$, there exists a reparametrization $t : [\tilde{t}_{min}, \tilde{t}_{max}] \to [t_{min}, t_{max}]$ for which $f(t(\tilde{t}))$ and $g(t(\tilde{t}))$ are both $C^n$ continuous at $\tilde{\tau}$, where $t(\tilde{\tau}) = \tau$. Therefore $f(t(\tilde{t}))g(t(\tilde{t}))$ and $f(t(\tilde{t}))/g(t(\tilde{t}))$ are also $C^n$ continuous at $\tilde{\tau}$. Thus by Proposition 1, $f(t)g(t)$ and $f(t)/g(t)$ are also $\beta$-continuous at $\tau$. ∎

What is remarkable is that Lemma 2 holds only for $\beta$-continuous functions and not for any other form of $M$-continuity.

**Lemma 3.**
1. *If $f(t)$ and $g(t)$ are $M$-continuous at $\tau$ implies $f(t)g(t)$ is $M$-continuous at $\tau$, then $M = M(\beta)$ for some value of $\beta$.*
2. *If $f(t)$ and $g(t)$ are $M$-continuous at $\tau$ implies $f(t)/g(t)$ is $M$-continuous at $\tau$, then $M = M(\beta)$ for some value of $\beta$.*

**Proof:** See [22]. ∎

We shall see below that the preceding result has certain important consequences for constructions involving Frenet frame continuous curves.

## §4. Constructions of Geometrically Continuous Curves and Surfaces

We shall now apply our results on $\beta$-continuity and $M$-continuity to study some standard constructions of parametric curves and surfaces. Our goal is to determine under what conditions these constructions remain valid if we replace parametric continuity by geometric continuity.

### 4.1. Curves

Here we will consider three standard curve constructions: rational curves, Catmull-Rom splines, and affine combinations of curves. We will begin with rational curves.

Let $b_0(t), \ldots, b_m(t)$ be a collection of basis functions which are all $M$-continuous at $\tau$ . Let $\mathbf{V}_0, \ldots, \mathbf{V}_m$ be a collection of control vertices, and let

$w_0, \ldots, w_m$ be a set of scalar weights. The standard construction of a rational curve is given by setting

$$\mathbf{r}(t) = \sum_j \frac{w_j \mathbf{V}_j b_j(t)}{\sum_k w_k b_k(t)}, \qquad \Sigma_k w_k b_k(t) \neq 0.$$

If we introduce the rational blending functions

$$R_j(t) = \frac{w_j b_j(t)}{\sum_k w_k b_k(t)}, \qquad j = 0, 1, \ldots, m, \qquad (6)$$

then we can rewrite $\mathbf{r}(t)$ simply as

$$\mathbf{r}(t) = \sum R_j(t) \mathbf{V_j}.$$

When the integral basis functions $b_0(t), \ldots, b_m(t)$ are parametrically continuous ($M$ is the identity), the rational blending functions $R_0(t), \ldots, R_m(t)$ are also parametrically continuous , and hence so is the rational curve $\mathbf{r}(t)$. By Lemmas 1 and 2, this property also extends to $\beta$-continuous blending functions; that is, when the integral basis functions $b_0(t), \ldots, b_m(t)$ are $\beta$-continuous ($M = M(\beta)$ for some fixed value of $\beta$), then the rational blending functions $R_0(t), \ldots, R_m(t)$ are also $\beta$-continuous, and hence so is the rational curve $\mathbf{r}(t)$. Since rational Beta-spline curves are defined in precisely this manner [3,29], it follows that rational Beta-spline curves are geometrically continuous. Moreover, the values of the shape parameters for the rational Beta-spline basis functions and the rational Beta-spline curves are exactly the same as the values of the shape parameters for the corresponding integral basis functions and integral curves.

Notice, however, that because of the division in equation (6), it follows by Lemma 3 that $M$-continuity cannot be preserved by this rational construction unless $M = M(\beta)$. That is, the rational blending functions $R_0(t), \ldots, R_m(t)$ are not, in general, $M$-continuous and hence neither is the rational curve $\mathbf{r}(t)$. In particular, if the integral blending functions are Frenet frame continuous, then the rational curve will not, in general, be Frenet frame continuous *for the same connection matrix $M$*. However, this does not imply that the rational blending functions and the rational curve cannot be Frenet frame continuous *for a different connection matrix $N$* — that is, for new values of the shape parameters which depend on the original values of the shape parameters as well as on the values of the weights. In fact, Goldman and Micchelli have shown that this is precisely what happens; that is, the rational blending functions and the rational curves are indeed still Frenet frame continuous but for a different connection matrix than the corresponding integral blending functions and integral curve [22]. This result was first observed by Boehm in [10], where he proved it for geometric continuity of order 3. A geometric construction for rational torsion continuous curves is given by Boehm in [9].

Next, let us consider Catmull-Rom splines. Here we begin with a set of $M$-continuous basis functions $b_0(t), \ldots, b_m(t)$ of degree $p$ and a collection of $M$-continuous analogues of the Lagrange polynomials $L_0(t), \ldots, L_m(t)$ of degree $q$ where $L_j(t)$ interpolates the control vertices $V_{j-q}, \ldots, V_j$. The Catmull-Rom spline is defined by setting

$$c(t) = \sum b_j(t) L_j(t). \tag{7}$$

When the basis functions and the Lagrange polynomials are parametrically continuous, these splines are also parametrically continuous. By Lemmas 1 and 2 applied to the components of $c(t)$, this property extends to $\beta$-continuous functions. Thus when the basis functions $b_0(t), \ldots, b_m(t)$ and the analogues of the Lagrange polynomials $L_0(t), \ldots, L_m(t)$ are $\beta$-continuous ($M = M(\beta)$ for some fixed value of $\beta$), then the Catmull-Rom spline $c(t)$ is also $\beta$-continuous. In particular, if we replace the B-spline basis functions by the Beta-spline basis functions and the Lagrange polynomials by their $\beta$-continuous analogues, then the Catmull-Rom spline is a geometrically continuous curve and the values of its shape parameters are exactly the same as the values of the shape parameters of the Beta-spline basis functions.

Again because of the multiplication in Equation (7), it follows by Lemma 3 that $M$-continuity cannot be preserved by the Catmull-Rom construction unless $M = M(\beta)$. Thus the Catmull-Rom spline $c(t)$ is not, in general, $M$-continuous. In particular, if the blending functions and Lagrange functions are Frenet frame continuous, then the Catmull-Rom curve will not, in general, be Frenet frame continuous *for the same connection matrix* $M$. Whether it is possible for the Catmull-Rom curve to be Frenet frame continuous for a *different connection matrix* $N$ is still an open question.

Affine combinations of curves are somewhat better behaved. Let $c_1(t)$ and $c_2(t)$ be two curves which are $M$-continuous at $\tau$ and let $\alpha$ be a fixed scalar. Then by Lemma 1 applied to the component functions, the affine combination

$$a(t) = (1 - \alpha) c_1(t) + \alpha c_2(t)$$

is again $M$-continuous at $\tau$. In particular, if $c_1(t)$ and $c_2(t)$ are geometrically continuous at $\tau$ and satisfy the Beta-constraints for the *same values* of $\beta$, then $a(t)$ is also geometrically continuous at $\tau$ and satisfies the Beta-constraints for these same values of $\beta$. Notice, however, that if $c_1(t)$ and $c_2(t)$ are geometrically continuous but satisfy the Beta-constraints for *different values* of $\beta$ at $\tau$, then $a(t)$ will not be geometrically continuous at $\tau$. In particular, the affine combination of two curvature continuous curves need not be a curvature continuous curve. Identical results hold for Frenet frame continuous curves.

## 4.2. Surfaces

For parametric surfaces there are many different definitions of geometric continuity [12,13,30,36], but, unlike parametric curves, these definitions are all equivalent to reparametrization [12]. Thus, a parametric surface $\mathbf{p}(s,t)$ is $n^{th}$ order geometrically continuous, or $G^n$, at $\mathbf{p}(\sigma,\tau)$ if and only if there exists a regular reparametrization $\mathbf{h}(\tilde{s},\tilde{t})$ such that $\mathbf{p}(\mathbf{h}(\tilde{s},\tilde{t}))$ is $n^{th}$ order parametrically continuous, or $C^n$, at $\mathbf{p}(\sigma,\tau)$.

If we begin with curves that are simply Frenet frame continuous, many of the standard parametric surface constructions fail to yield geometrically continuous surfaces. Indeed, ruled surfaces, lofted surfaces, tensor product surfaces, and Boolean sum surfaces that each begin with Frenet frame continuous curves do not generate geometrically continuous surfaces. This occurs because the original curves cannot be reparametrized into $C^n$ continuous curves so neither can the newly constructed surfaces be reparametrized into $C^n$ continuous surfaces. Therefore, in the following discussion we shall restrict our attention to geometrically continuous curves that can be reparametrized into parametrically continuous curves — that is, to $\beta$-continuous curves.

Consider first ruled surfaces. Let $\mathbf{c}_1(t)$ and $\mathbf{c}_2(t)$ be two curves which are $\beta$-continuous at $\tau$ , and let

$$\mathbf{r}(s,t) = (1 - s)\mathbf{c}_1(t) + s\mathbf{c}_2(t)$$

be the ruled surface joining these two curves. Since $\mathbf{c}_1(t)$ and $\mathbf{c}_2(t)$ satisfy the Beta-constraints at $\tau$ for the *same values* of $\beta$, by Proposition 1 the same reparametrization makes them both into $C^n$ curves at $\tau$. Therefore, the surface $\mathbf{r}(s,t)$ is geometrically continuous at $(\sigma,\tau)$ since it can be reparametrized into a $C^n$ surface. However, if the curves $\mathbf{c}_1(t)$ and $\mathbf{c}_2(t)$ are geometrically continuous at $\tau$ but satisfy the Beta-constraints for *different values* of $\beta$, then the surface $\mathbf{r}(s,t)$ will not be geometrically continuous at $(\sigma,\tau)$, see [20]. Thus, to construct geometrically continuous ruled surfaces from Beta-spline curves, we must make sure that these curves satisfy the Beta-constraints for the same values of $\beta$ at corresponding joints.

For lofted, tensor product, or Boolean sum surfaces, we have much the same results. Let $\mathbf{u}_0(s),\ldots,\mathbf{u}_k(s)$ and $\mathbf{v}_0(t),\ldots,\mathbf{v}_m(t)$ be two sets of curves, and let $f_0(t),\ldots,f_k(t)$ and $g_0(s),\ldots,g_m(s)$ be two sets of scalar blending functions. Let $\mathbf{P}_{ij}$ be the intersection of the $\mathbf{u}_i(s)$ and $\mathbf{v}_j(t)$. If the curves $\mathbf{u}_0(s),\ldots,\mathbf{u}_k(s)$ all satisfy the Beta-constraints for the *same values* of $\beta = (\beta_1,\ldots,\beta_n)$ at $\sigma$, and the blending functions $f_0(t),\ldots,f_k(t)$ all satisfy the Beta-constraints for the *same values* of $\beta^* = (\beta_1^*,\ldots,\beta_n^*)$ at $\tau$, then by Proposition 1 the lofted surface

$$\mathbf{l}_u(s,t) = \sum_i f_i(t)\mathbf{u}_i(s)$$

can be reparametrized into a $C^n$ surface at $(\sigma,\tau)$ by reparametrizing independently in $s$ and $t$. Therefore, in this case, the lofted surface $\mathbf{l}_u(s,t)$ will be geometrically continuous at $(\sigma,\tau)$. Similarly, if the curves $\mathbf{v}_0(t),\ldots,\mathbf{v}_m(t)$ all satisfy the Beta-constraints for the *same values* of $\beta^* = (\beta_1^*,\ldots,\beta_n^*)$ at $\tau$, and the blending functions $g_0(s), \ldots, g_m(s)$ all satisfy the Beta-constraints for the same values of $\beta = (\beta_1, \ldots, \beta_n)$ at $\sigma$, then the lofted surface

$$\mathbf{l}_v(s,t) = \sum_j g_j(s)\mathbf{v}_j(t)$$

will be geometrically continuous at $(\sigma, \tau)$. Moreover, under these conditions the tensor product surface

$$\mathbf{t}_{uv}(s,t) = \sum_{i,j} f_i(t)g_j(s)\mathbf{P}_{ij}$$

is also geometrically continuous at $(\sigma, \tau)$.

Finally, to force the Boolean sum surface

$$\mathbf{b}_{uv}(s,t) = \mathbf{l}_u(s,t) + \mathbf{l}_v(s,t) - \mathbf{t}_{uv}(s,t)$$

to be geometrically continuous at $(\sigma, \tau)$, it is not enough for all three surfaces $\mathbf{l}_u(s,t)$, $\mathbf{l}_v(s,t)$, and $\mathbf{t}_{uv}(s,t)$ to be geometrically continuous; they must also satisfy the Beta-constraints for exactly the same values of $\beta$ and $\beta^*$. For this to occur, the curves $\mathbf{u}_0(s), \ldots, \mathbf{u}_k(s)$ and the blending functions $g_0(s), \ldots, g_m(s)$ must all satisfy the Beta-constraints for the *same values* of $\beta$ at $\sigma$, and the curves $\mathbf{v}_0(t), \ldots, \mathbf{v}_m(t)$ and the blending functions $f_0(t), \ldots, f_k(t)$ must all satisfy the Beta-constraints for the *same values* of $\beta^*$ at $\tau$. When this occurs, the Boolean sum surface $\mathbf{b}_{uv}(s,t)$ will be geometrically continuous at $(\sigma, \tau)$.

Thus, to construct geometrically continuous ruled, lofted, or Boolean sum surfaces from Beta-spline curves, we must put severe restrictions on the curves. In particular, we must ensure that they satisfy the Beta-constraints for identical values of $\beta$ at corresponding joints. Notice, however, that if we use the Beta-spline basis functions as our blending functions, the tensor product construction always yields a geometrically continuous surface. Indeed, even the rational tensor product Beta-spline surface is geometrically continuous by an argument similar to the one given in Section 4.1 for the rational Beta-spline curve.

## §5. Summary

To study geometric continuity more carefully, the notions of $\beta$-continuity and $M$-continuity were introduced. Sums, differences, products, quotients, and scalar multiples of $\beta$-continuous scalar-valued functions were shown to be $\beta$-continuous. However, for arbitrary connection matrices $M$, only sums, differences, and scalar multiples of $M$-continuous scalar-valued functions are always $M$-continuous; products and quotients of $M$-continuous scalar-valued functions are not, in general, $M$-continuous unless $M = M(\beta)$ for some value of $\beta$.

These properties of $\beta$-continuity and $M$-continuity were applied to extend various standard constructions of parametric curves and surfaces to the realm of geometric continuity. For curves, rational splines, Catmull-Rom splines, and affine combinations were examined; for surfaces, ruled, lofted, tensor product, and Boolean sum constructions were investigated.

Results for geometric continuity defined by reparametrization (the Beta-constraints) were contrasted with the corresponding results for Frenet frame continuity. In particular, it was shown that for rational splines *only* the rational Beta-spline will preserve the *same values* of the shape parameters as the corresponding integral splines. Moreover, in order to form geometrically continuous surfaces, the curves used in the construction must satisfy the Beta-constraints (reparametrization); Frenet frame continuous curves do not generate geometrically continuous surfaces.

## References

1. Barsky, B. A., The Beta-spline: A Local Representation based on Shape Parameters and Fundamental Geometric Measures, Ph.D. dissertation, University of Utah, 1981.
2. Barsky, B. A., *Computer Graphics and Geometric Modeling Using Beta-splines*, Springer-Verlag, Heidelberg, 1988.
3. Barsky, B. A., Introducing the rational Beta-spline, Proceedings of the Third International Conference on Engineering Graphics and Descriptive Geometry, **1** Vienna, 1988, 16-27.
4. Barsky, B. A. and T. D. DeRose, Geometric continuity of parametric curves, Technical Report UCB/CSD 84/205, Computer Science Division, Electrical Engineering and Computer Sciences Department, University of California, Berkeley, 1984.
5. Barsky, B. A. and T. D. DeRose, Three characterizations of geometric continuity for parametric curves, Technical Report UBC/CSD 88/417, Computer Science Division, Electrical Engineering and Computer Sciences Department, University of California, Berkeley, 1988. Also notes for ACM/Siggraph '88 Course 25, Atlanta, Georgia, 1988.
6. Barsky, B. A. and T. D. DeRose, Geometric continuity of parametric curves: developing the Beta-constraints, preprint.
7. Bartels, R. H., J. C. Beatty, and B. A. Barsky, *An Introduction to Splines for Use in Computer Graphics and Geometric Modeling*, Morgan Kaufmann Publishers, Inc., San Mateo, California, 1987.
8. Boehm, W., Curvature continuous curves and surfaces, Comput. Aided Geom. Design **2** (1985), 313–323.
9. Boehm, W., Rational geometric splines, Comput. Aided Geom. Design **4** (1987), 67–77.
10. Boehm, W., Letter to the Editor, Comput. Aided Design **20** (1988), 372–374.
11. Catmull, E. E. and R. J. Rom, A class of local interpolating splines, in *Computer Aided Geometric Design*, R. Barnhill and R. Riesenfeld (eds.), Academic Press, New York, 1974, 317–326.

12. DeRose, T. D., Geometric Continuity: A Parametrization Independent Measure of Continuity for Computer Aided Geometric Design, PhD dissertation, University of California, Berkeley, 1985.

13. DeRose, T. D. and B. A. Barsky, An intuitive approach to geometric continuity for parametric curves and surfaces, Proceedings of Graphics Interface '85, Montreal, 343–351. Revised version published in *Computer-Generated Images — The State of the Art*, N. Magnenat-Thalmann and D. Thalmann (eds.), Springer-Verlag, 1985, 159–175.

14. DeRose, T. D. and B. A. Barsky, Geometric continuity, shape parameters, and geometric constructions for Catmull-Rom splines, Trans. Graph. **7** (1988), 1–41.

15. Dyn, N., A. Edelmann, and C. Micchelli, On locally supported basis functions for the representation of geometrically continuous curves, Analysis **7** (1987), 313–341.

16. Dyn, N. and C. Micchelli, Shape preserving parametric representation of curves with local control for computer aided geometric design, Numerische Math., to appear.

17. Dyn, N. and C. Micchelli, Piecewise polynomial spaces and geometric continuity of curves, RC 11390, IBM T.J. Watson Research Center, Yorktown Heights, New York, 1985.

18. Farin, G., Visually $C^2$ cubic splines, Comput. Aided Design **14** (1982), 137–139.

19. Faux, I. D. and M. J. Pratt, *Computational Geometry for Design and Manufacture*, Ellis Horwood Ltd., 1979.

20. Filip, D. and T. Ball, Procedurally represented lofted surfaces, preprint.

21. Fowler, A. H. and C. W. Wilson, Cubic spline, a curve fitting routine, Union Carbide Corporation Report Y-1400 (Rev. I), 1966.

22. Goldman, R. N., and C. A. Micchelli, Algebraic aspects of geometric continuity, in *Mathematical Methods in Computer Aided Geometric Design*, T. Lyche and L. Schumaker (eds.), Academic Press, N. Y., 1989, 313–332.

23. Goodman, T., Properties of Beta-splines, J. Approx. Theory **44** (1985), 132–153.

24. Goodman, T. and K. Unsworth, Manipulating shape and producing geometric continuity in Beta-spline curves, IEEE Comp. Graph. Appl. **6** (1986), 50–56.

25. Gordon, W., Spline-blended surface interpolation through curve networks J. Math. Mech **18** (1969), 931–952.

26. Hagen, H., Geometric spline curves, Comput. Aided Geom. Design **2** (1985), 223–227.

27. Herron, G., Techniques for visual continuity, in *Geometric Modeling: Algorithms and New Trends*, G. E. Farin (ed.), SIAM Publications, Philadelphia, 1987, 163–174.

28. Höllig, K., Geometric continuity of spline curves and surfaces, Computer Science Department, University of Wisconsin, Madison, Wisconsin, 1986.

29. Joe, B., Rational Beta-spline curves and surfaces and discrete Beta-splines,

Technical Report TR8704, Department of Computer Science, University of Alberta, Edmonton, Alberta, 1987.

30. Kahmann, J., Continuity of curvature between adjacent Bézier patches, in *Surfaces in Computer Aided Geometric Design*, R. Barnhill and W. Böhm (eds.), North Holland Publishing, 1983, 65–75.

31. Knuth, D. E., *The Art of Computer Programming: Volume 1/Fundamental Algorithms*, Addison-Wesley Publishing Company, Reading, Massachusetts, Second Edition, 1973.

32. Manning, J. R., Continuity conditions for spline curves, Computer J. **17** (1974), 181–186.

33. Nielson, G. M., Some piecewise polynomial alternatives to splines under tension, in *Computer Aided Geometric Design*, R. Barnhill and R. Riesenfeld, (eds.), Academic Press, New York, 1974, 209–235.

34. Sabin, M. A., Parametric splines in tension, Tech. Report VTO/MS/160, British Aircraft Corporation, Weybridge, Surrey, England, (1970).

35. Spivak, M., *Differential Geometry*, Publish or Perish, Inc., Boston, 1975.

36. Veron, M., G. Ris, and J. Musse, Continuity of biparametric surface patches, Comput. Aided Design **8** (1976), 267–273.

Ronald N. Goldman
Computer Graphics Laboratory
Department of Computer Science
University of Waterloo
Waterloo, Ontario, N2L 3G1
CANADA

EMAIL: rngoldman@ watcgl.waterloo.edu

Supported in part by the Natural Sciences and Engineering Research Council of Canada Grant OGP0036825

Brian A. Barsky
Computer Science Division
Department of Electrical Engineering and Computer Sciences
University of California
Berkeley, California 94720
USA

EMAIL: barsky@ berkeley.edu

Supported in part by the National Science Foundation Grant CCR-8451997, the Control Data Corporation, AT&T Bell Laboratories, and an IBM Faculty Development Award

# Algebraic Aspects of Geometric Continuity

## R. N. Goldman and C. A. Micchelli

**Abstract.** Let $C(M, \tau)$ denote the set of all scalar valued functions with connection matrix $M$ at $\tau$. We show that $C(M, \tau)$ is closed under multiplication and division if and only if $M$ is a reparametrization matrix. We conclude that reparametrization is the most general form of geometric continuity for which the shape parameters remain invariant under lifting and projection. We go on to show that Frenet frame continuity is also invariant under projection, even though the shape parameters are not preserved. We also investigate curves which are not smooth, but which become smooth under projection.

## §1. Introduction

Two alternative notions of geometric continuity for parametric curves are current in computer aided geometric design. The first is based on standard parametric continuity after a suitable reparametrization [2,6,10,15]; the second on continuity of the Frenet frame or higher order curvatures [3,4,7,8,9,13, 14]. Both of these geometric concepts have algebraic interpretations in terms of connection matrices. For reparametrization, the connection matrix must take the form of the chain rule or the *Beta-constraints* [2,6]; for Frenet frame continuity the connection matrix must simply be lower triangular with the first column $(1, 0, \ldots, 0)^T$ and the diagonal entries increasing powers of some fixed positive scalar [9].

During the Oslo Conference on Mathematical Methods in Computer Aided Geometric Design, these two notions of geometric continuity were widely discussed. Early in the conference, Gregory gave a survey talk carefully defining and contrasting these two competing concepts [12]. Later on, Goldman and Barsky presented a paper where they generalized many of the standard analytic constructions for parametrically continuous curves and surfaces to geometrically continuous curves and surfaces [11]. They observed that when the notion of geometric continuity based on reparametrization is used in the standard

Mathematical Methods in Computer Aided Geometric Design
Tom Lyche and Larry L. Schumaker (eds.), pp. 313–332.
Copyright © 1989 by Academic Press, Boston.
ISBN 0-12-460515-X.

construction for rational curves, the connection matrices — or equivalently the shape parameters — remain invariant under projection.

Goldman and Barsky conjectured that reparametrization was the most general form of geometric continuity for which the shape parameters would remain unchanged under projection. They actually had a proof of this result for geometric continuity of order 3, but their proof was highly computational. Originally they had planned to try to extend this computational proof to geometric continuity of arbitrary order. However, during the conference, we discovered a novel proof which was much more general, much less computational, and provided much more insight into the problem.

The purpose of this paper is to present this new proof and then to apply these same techniques to study several additional problems related to geometric continuity. The proof is given in Section 3 after the proper algebraic foundation is laid in Section 2. In Section 4 we show that Frenet frame continuity is also invariant under projection, even though the shape parameters are not preserved. In Section 5 we go on to investigate curves which are not smooth, but which become smooth under projection.

The focus of this paper is on the essential algebraic aspects of geometric continuity. Unlike many previous approaches to constraint equations and shape parameters which were highly computational [2,5,6,16], the approach taken here simplifies the study of geometric continuity by adopting a more abstract, less computational, higher-level perspective.

## §2. Some Algebraic Aspects of Geometric Continuity

We begin with some notation. Let $f$ be an $n$-times differentiable function and let $\tau$ be a parameter value. We write

$$D_n(f)(\tau) = (f(\tau), f'(\tau), \ldots, f^{(n)}(\tau))^T.$$

A continuous piecewise $n$-times differentiable function $f$ is said to have *connection matrix* $M = (M_{ij})$ $i, j = 0, 1, \ldots, n$ at the parameter value $\tau$ if and only if

$$D_n(f^+)(\tau) = M D_n(f^-)(\tau). \tag{1}$$

Here $f^-$ denotes the function $f$ to the left of $\tau$ and $f^+$ denotes $f$ to the right of $\tau$. Now we define the set

$$C(M, \tau) = \{f : \ f \text{ has connection matrix } M \text{ at } \tau\}.$$

From here on, when we say that $f$ is a differentiable function we shall mean that $f$ is at least $n$ times differentiable.

Since the functions $f$ in $C(M, \tau)$ are continuous, $f^+(\tau) = f^-(\tau)$; therefore we shall always take $M_{0j} = \delta_{0j}$. Also, to assure that the constant functions lie in $C(M, \tau)$, we shall generally take $M_{i0} = \delta_{i0}$, though we shall relax this restriction in Sections 4 and 5.

Let $F(t) = (f_1(t), \ldots, f_d(t))$ be a parametric curve. Then $F$ is said to be *geometrically continuous* at $\tau$ if all of its coordinate functions $f_k$ have the same connection matrix $M$ at $\tau$. A curve is said to be geometrically continuous of order $n$ at $\tau$ if its connection matrix is an $(n+1) \times (n+1)$ matrix. We shall write $F \in C(M, \tau)$ to denote that $f_1(t), \ldots, f_d(t) \in C(M, \tau)$. The entries of $M$ are called *shape parameters* because they affect the shape of the curve.

A parametric curve is Frenet frame continuous at some parameter value if and only if it has a lower triangular connection matrix $M$ with $M_{i0} = \delta_{i0}$ and $M_{jj} = M_{11}^j > 0$, see [9]. Such matrices are called *Frenet frame connection matrices*. For a discussion of the geometric significance of Frenet frame continuity, see [9]. If we relax the condition $M_{jj} = M_{11}^j$ and permit arbitrary non-zero values along the diagonal of $M$, then instead of Frenet frame continuity we simply get continuity of the first $n$ osculating linear spaces. By relaxing the condition that $M$ is lower triangular, we can get even weaker forms of geometric continuity.

Fix a differentiable function $h$ and a parameter $\tau$, and let $f$ be an arbitrary differentiable function. We shall use the notation $f \circ h$ to denote $f$ composed with $h$ — that is, $(f \circ h)(t) = f(h(t))$. Now by the chain rule, there is a constant matrix $R(h)$ such that

$$D_n[f \circ h](\tau) = R(h)D_n(f)[h(\tau)]. \tag{2}$$

If $h(\tau) = \tau$, the matrix $R(h)$ is called a *reparametrization matrix*. A parametric curve will, by definition, be geometrically continuous in the sense of reparametrization if and only if its connection matrix is a reparametrization matrix [2,6]. Every reparametrization matrix is a Frenet frame connection matrix, but not conversely. Therefore, geometric continuity in the sense of reparametrization is a stronger condition than Frenet frame continuity. When $f$ is a parametric curve and $M = R(h)$, equation (1) is often called the *Beta-constraints* and the entries $R(h)_{j1}$ are the *Beta parameters* that appear in the *Beta-spline* curves [2,6].

Because differentiation and matrix multiplication are linear operations, the set $C(M, \tau)$ forms a vector space under the usual operations of addition and scalar multiplication. Thus, the set $C(M, \tau)$ is closed under addition and scalar multiplication. Our purpose here is to discover for what kind of matrices $M$ the set $C(M, \tau)$ is also closed under multiplication and division.

To proceed, notice that if $h(\tau) = \tau$, then $f \in C(R(h), \tau)$ if and only if $f^-$ can be reparametrized by $h$ so that $f^- \circ h$ meets $f^+$ at $\tau$ with $C^n$ continuity. Therefore, clearly $f, g \in C(R(h), \tau) \Rightarrow fg, f/g \in C(R(h), \tau)$ — that is, $C(R(h), \tau)$ is closed under multiplication and division. Our first important result is that reparametrization matrices are, in fact, the only connection matrices for which $C(M, \tau)$ is closed under multiplication and division.

**Theorem 1.** *If $M$ is a connection matrix, then $f \in C(M, \tau) \Rightarrow P \circ f \in C(M, \tau)$ for every polynomial $P$ if and only if $M$ is a reparametrization matrix — that is, if and only if there is a function $h$ such that $h(\tau) = \tau$ and $M = R(h)$.*

**Proof:** First we show that if $h(\tau) = \tau$, then $f \in C(R(h), \tau) \Leftrightarrow P \circ f \in C(R(h), \tau)$ for every polynomial $P$. Now $f \in C(R(h), \tau)$ if and only if

$$D_n(f^+)(\tau) = R(h)D_n(f^-)(\tau).$$

But by the chain rule (2),

$$D_n(f^- \circ h)(\tau) = R(h)D_n(f^-)(\tau).$$

Therefore, $f \in C(R(h), \tau)$ if and only if

$$D_n(f^+)(\tau) = D_n(f^- \circ h)(\tau).$$

However, from the product rule for differentiation it follows easily that

$$D_n(f^+)(\tau) = D_n(f^- \circ h)(\tau) \Leftrightarrow D_n(f^{k+})(\tau) = D_n(f^{k-} \circ h)(\tau) \text{ for all } k.$$

Now let $P(t) = \Sigma a_k t^k$ be an arbitrary polynomial. Then by the linearity of differentiation

$$D_n(f^+)(\tau) = D_n(f^- \circ h)(\tau) \Leftrightarrow D_n(\Sigma a_k f^{k+})(\tau) = D_n(\Sigma a_k f^{k-} \circ h)(\tau).$$

Therefore,

$$D_n(f^+)(\tau) = D_n(f \circ h^-)(\tau) \Leftrightarrow D_n(P \circ f^+)(\tau) = D_n(P \circ f^- \circ h)(\tau)$$

for every polynomial $P$. Hence $f \in C(R(h), \tau)$ if and only if $P \circ f \in C(R(h), \tau)$ for every polynomial $P$.

Conversely, suppose that $f \in C(M, \tau)$ implies $P \circ f \in C(M, \tau)$ for every polynomial $P$. If $f \in C(M, \tau)$, then

$$D_n(P \circ f^+)(\tau) = MD_n(P \circ f^-)(\tau).$$

Now define $h(t)$ by setting

$$h^-(t) = t$$

$$h^+(t) = \tau + \sum_{j=0}^{n} M_{j1}(t - \tau)^j/j!.$$

Then clearly

$$D_n(h^+)(\tau) = (\tau, M_{11}, \ldots, M_{n1})^T = M(\tau, 1, 0, \ldots, 0)^T = MD_n(h^-)(\tau)$$

so certainly $h \in C(M, \tau)$. Therefore, for all polynomials $P$,

$$D_n(P \circ h^+)(\tau) = MD_n(P \circ h^-)(\tau) = MD_n(P)(\tau).$$

But by the chain rule (2),

$$D_n(P \circ h^+)(\tau) = R(h^+)D_n(P)(\tau).$$

Hence, for all polynomials $P$,

$$MD_n(P)(\tau) = R(h^+)D_n(P)(\tau). \tag{3}$$

Let $P_k(t) = (t - \tau)^k/k!$. Substituting $P_k(t)$ into (3), we obtain

$$k^{th} \ column \ M = k^{th} \ column \ R(h^+), \quad k = 0, 1, \ldots, n.$$

Therefore, we conclude that $M = R(h^+)$. ■

Theorem 1 requires us to check $f \in C(M, \tau) \Rightarrow P \circ f \in C(M, \tau)$ for every polynomial $P$ in order to conclude that $M$ is a reparametrization matrix. However, we can see from the proof of Theorem 1 that, in fact, it is only necessary to check $f \in C(M, \tau) \Rightarrow P \circ f \in C(M, \tau)$ for the polynomials $P_k(t) = (t - \tau)^k/k!$, $k = 0, 1, \ldots, n$. We shall now show that it is only necessary to check that $f \in C(M, \tau) \Rightarrow P \circ f \in C(M, \tau)$ for any single arbitrary non-linear polynomial $P$ in order to conclude that $M$ is a reparametrization matrix. To prove this result, we need the following proposition.

**Proposition 1.** *Let $S$ be a set of polynomials in $t$ which satisfies the following axioms:*

   (A1). $1, t \in S$
   (A2). $P, Q \in S \Rightarrow aP + bQ \in S$
   (A3). $P, Q \in S \Rightarrow P \circ Q \in S$
   (A4). $\exists P \in S$ *with degree* $P > 1$.

*Then $S$ is the set of all polynomials in $t$.*

**Proof:** First, notice that $S$ contains polynomials of arbitrarily high degree. This observation follows from the fact that by (A4), $S$ contains a polynomial $P$ of degree greater than 1. Composing $P$ with itself arbitarily many times, we obtain polynomials of arbitrarily high degree which by (A3) are in the set $S$.

Next, suppose that $Q_n$ is a polynomial of degree $n$ which is in the set $S$; we shall show that all polynomials $Q$ with degree $Q \le$ degree $Q_n$ are also in $S$. Applying (A2), we can assume without loss of generality that $Q_n$ is a monic polynomial. Let

$$Q_{n-1}(t) = Q_n(t + 1/n) - Q_n(t).$$

Then $Q_{n-1}(t)$ is a monic polynomial of degree $n - 1$. Moreover, (A1), (A2), (A3) $\Rightarrow Q_{n-1} \in S$. Iterating this construction, we obtain a sequence of $n + 1$ polynomials $\{Q_k(t)\}$ such that $Q_k(t)$ is a monic polynomial of degree $k$ and $Q_k \in S$. But these polynomials certainly form a basis for all polynomials of degree less than or equal to $n$. Therefore by (A2), $S$ contains all polynomials $Q$ with degree $Q \le$ degree $Q_n$. Since we have shown that $S$ contains polynomials of arbitrarily high degree, it follows that $S$ must be the set of all polynomials in $t$. ∎

**Theorem 2.** *Let $M$ be a connection matrix and let $P$ be any polynomial with degree $P > 1$. Then $f \in C(M, \tau)$ implies $P \circ f \in C(M, \tau)$ if and only if $M$ is a reparametrization matrix — that is, if and only if there is a function $h$ such that $h(\tau) = \tau$ and $M = R(h)$.*

**Proof:** If $M$ is a reparametrization matrix, then by Theorem 1, we have $f \in C(M, \tau) \Rightarrow P \circ f \in C(M, \tau)$.

Conversely, suppose that $f \in C(M, \tau) \Rightarrow P \circ f \in C(M, \tau)$. Define

$$S = \{\text{polynomials } Q : \ f \in C(M, \tau) \Rightarrow Q \circ f \in C(M, \tau)\}.$$

We shall show that $S$ satisfies axioms (A1-A4) and therefore that $S$ is actually the set of all polynomials in $t$. Axiom (A1) is satisfied since clearly $1, t \in S$. Axiom (A2) is satisfied by the linearity of differentiation and matrix multiplication. Axiom (A3) is satisfied because if $Q, R \in S$, then $f \in C(M, \tau) \Rightarrow Q \circ f \in C(M, \tau) \Rightarrow R \circ Q \circ f \in C(M, \tau)$ so $R \circ Q \in S$. Finally, Axiom (A4) is satisfied since by assumption $P \in S$. Therefore, it follows by Proposition 1 that $S$ is the set of all polynomials in $t$. Hence by Theorem 1, $M$ is a reparametrization matrix. ∎

**Corollary 1.** *If $M$ is a connection matrix, then $f, g \in C(M, \tau) \Rightarrow fg \in C(M, \tau)$ if and only if $M$ is a reparametrization matrix.*

**Proof:** Let $P(t) = t^2$. Then by assumption $f \in C(M, \tau) \Rightarrow P \circ f = f^2 \in C(M, \tau)$. Therefore, this result follows immediately from Theorem 2. ∎

**Corollary 2.** *If $M$ is a connection matrix, then $f, g \in C(M, \tau) \Rightarrow f/g \in C(M, \tau)$ if and only if $M$ is a reparametrization matrix.*

**Proof:** Again let $P(t) = t^2$. By assumption $f \in C(M, \tau) \Rightarrow f, 1/f \in C(M, \tau) \Rightarrow P \circ f = f^2 = f/(1/f) \in C(M, \tau)$. Therefore, this result also follows immediately from Theorem 2. ∎

We can extend Theorem 1 in yet another fashion. We need not consider only polynomials. As the following result shows, other simple functions may do as well.

**Theorem 3.** *Let $M$ be a connection matrix, and let $P(t) = t^{-m}$, $m \geq 1$. Then $f \in C(M, \tau) \Rightarrow P \circ f \in C(M, \tau)$ if and only if $M$ is a reparametrization matrix.*

**Proof:** Let $R(h)$ be a reparametrization matrix. We showed in Theorem 1 that

$$f \in C(R(h), \tau) \Leftrightarrow D_n(f^+)(\tau) = D_n(f^- \circ h)(\tau).$$

But by the quotient rule

$$D_n(f^+)(\tau) = D_n(f^- \circ h)(\tau) \Rightarrow D_n(1/(f^+)^m)(\tau) = D_n(1/(f^- \circ h)^m)(\tau).$$

Hence if $P(t) = t^{-m}$, then $f \in C(R(h), \tau) \Rightarrow P \circ f \in C(R(h), \tau)$.

Conversely, suppose $f \in C(M, \tau) \Rightarrow P \circ f \in C(M, \tau)$. Then $f \in C(M, \tau) \Rightarrow P \circ P \circ f \in C(M, \tau)$. But for $m \geq 2$, $(P \circ P)(t) = t^{m^2}$ is a polynomial of degree $> 1$. Therefore, by Theorem 2, $M$ must be a reparametrization matrix.

It remains only to consider the case $m = 1$. Suppose that $f \in C(M, \tau) \Rightarrow 1/f \in C(M, \tau)$. Since $1, f \in C(M, \tau)$, we have $f + 1, f - 1 \in C(M, \tau)$. Therefore, $1/(f + 1), 1/(f - 1) \in C(M, \tau)$. Subtracting and dividing by 2, we obtain that $1/(f + 1)(f - 1) \in C(M, \tau)$. Taking the reciprocal, we conclude that $f \in C(M, \tau) \Rightarrow f^2 - 1 \in C(M, \tau)$. Thus for $P(t) = t^2 - 1$, we have $f \in C(M, \tau) \Rightarrow P \circ f \in C(M, \tau)$. Therefore, by Theorem 2, $M$ must be a reparametrization matrix. ∎

Theorem 3 suggests yet further possible extensions of Theorem 1. By Theorem 2, we can conclude that $M$ is a reparametrization matrix if there is a single nonlinear polynomial $P$ such that $f \in C(M, \tau) \Rightarrow P \circ f \in C(M, \tau)$. Theorem 3 suggests that we can replace the polynomial $P$ with a rational polynomial $R$ or perhaps even with some yet more exotic function of $t$. A general result of this type is the following theorem.

**Theorem 4.** *Let $M$ be an $(n + 1) \times (n + 1)$ connection matrix, and let $B$ be a non-linear function which is at least $(n + 2)-$times differentiable. Then $f \in C(M, \tau) \Rightarrow B \circ f \in C(M, \tau)$ if and only if $M$ is a reparametrization matrix.*

**Proof:** Let $R(h)$ be a reparametrization matrix. We showed in Theorem 1 that

$$f \in C(R(h), \tau) \Leftrightarrow D_n(f^+)(\tau) = D_n(f^- \circ h)(\tau).$$

But by the chain rule for differentiation it follows easily that

$$D_n(f^+)(\tau) = D_n(f^- \circ h)(\tau) \Leftrightarrow D_n(B \circ f^+)(\tau) = D_n(B \circ f^- \circ h)(\tau)$$

for every differentiable function $B$. Hence $f \in C(R(h), \tau) \Leftrightarrow B \circ f \in C(R(h), \tau)$ for every differentiable function $B$.

Conversely, let $B$ be any non-linear function which is at least $(n + 2)-$times differentiable and suppose that $f \in C(M, \tau) \Rightarrow B \circ f \in C(M, \tau)$; we need to show that $M$ is a reparametrization matrix. Because $B$ is non-linear, there must be some constant value $c$ for which $B''(c) \neq 0$. Let $f \in C(M, \tau)$ and define a 1-parameter family of functions $g(x, t)$ by setting

$$g(x, t) = x f(t) + c.$$

Since $C(M, \tau)$ is a vector space and both 1 and $f$ are in $C(M, \tau)$, it follows that for any fixed value of $x$, $g(x, \cdot) \in C(M, \tau)$. Therefore, by hypothesis, for every $x$, $(B \circ g)(x, \cdot) \in C(M, \tau)$. Consequently for every value of $x$

$$D_n(B \circ g^+)(x, \tau) = M D_n(B \circ g^-)(x, \tau).$$

Differentiating both sides of this equation twice with respect to $x$ and using the fact that the derivatives with respect to $x$ and $t$ commute, we find that

$$D_n\left(\frac{\partial^2(B \circ g^+)}{\partial x^2}\right)(x, \tau) = MD_n\left(\frac{\partial^2(B \circ g^-)}{\partial x^2}\right)(x, \tau).$$

(Here we need the assumption that $B$ is at least $(n+2)$−times differentiable.) Hence, for all $x$, $\partial^2(B \circ g)/\partial x^2 \in C(M, \tau)$. But by the chain rule

$$\frac{\partial^2(B \circ g)}{\partial x^2}\Big|_{x=0} = B''(c)f(t)^2.$$

Therefore, we have shown that $f \in C(M, \tau) \Rightarrow B''(c)f^2 \in C(M, \tau)$. Now let $P(t) = B''(c)t^2$. Then $f \in C(M, \tau) \Rightarrow P \circ f \in C(M, \tau)$. Hence by Theorem 2, $M$ must be a reparametrization matrix. ∎

## §3. The Invariance of Shape Parameters Under Projection

The unique algebraic properties of the sets $C(R(h), \tau)$, derived in the preceding section, have analytic consequences regarding the invariance of the shape parameters under certain geometric operations. Here we explore some of these consequences.

We shall consider two operations: *projection* and *lifting*. Given a parametric curve

$$F(t) = (x_1(t), \ldots, x_d(t), w(t))$$

in $d+1$ space, we can project it into $d$ space by dividing all the coordinate functions by $w(t)$ to obtain the curve

$$P[F](t) = (x_1(t)/w(t), \ldots, x_d(t)/w(t), 1)$$

which lies in the $d$ dimensional hyperplane $x_{d+1} = 1$. Conversely, given a curve

$$G(t) = (x_1(t), \ldots, x_d(t), 1)$$

in the hyperplane $x_{d+1} = 1$, we can lift it into $d+1$ space by multiplying each coordinate function by a fixed function $w(t)$ to obtain the curve

$$L[G](t) = (x_1(t)w(t), \ldots, x_d(t)w(t), w(t))$$

which lies on the cone joining $G(t)$ and the origin. Like multiplication and division, projecting and lifting are inverse operations since

$$P[L[G]](t) = G(t)$$

$$L[P[F]](t) = F(t).$$

Now suppose that the curves $F(t)$ and $G(t)$ are geometrically continuous. What can we conclude about the curves $P[F](t)$ and $L[G](t)$?

**Theorem 5.** *If $M$ is a connection matrix, then $F \in C(M, \tau) \Rightarrow P[F] \in C(M, \tau)$ if and only if $M$ is a reparametrization matrix.*

**Proof:** This result is an immediate consequence of Corollary 2. ∎

**Corollary 3.** *Reparametrization is the most general form of geometric continuity for which the shape parameters remain invariant under projection.*

**Theorem 6.** *Suppose $M$ is a connection matrix. Then $(G, w) \in C(M, \tau) \Rightarrow L[G] \in C(M, \tau)$ if and only if $M$ is a reparametrization matrix.*

**Proof:** This result is an immediate consequence of Corollary 1. ∎

**Corollary 4.** *Reparametrization is the most general form of geometric continuity for which the shape parameters remain invariant under lifting.*

### §4. The Invariance of Frenet Frame Continuity Under Projection

Even though by Corollary 3 reparametrization is the most general form of geometric continuity for which the shape parameters remain invariant under projection, it is not the most general form of geometric continuity which is preserved under projection. In fact, Boehm has shown that Frenet frame continuity of order 3 — that is, continuity of unit tangent, curvature, and torsion — is preserved under projection, and he goes on to claim that Frenet frame continuity of arbitrary order will also be preserved under projection [5]. However, his method of analysis is computational and would ultimately lead to a technically complicated proof. We shall now confirm his intuition and give a simple proof of this result. As we shall see, in spite of Theorem 5, this result is not paradoxical, because for Frenet frame continuity the connection matrix changes under projection. To prove this general result, we need to introduce the following matrices.

Fix both a differentiable function $w$ and a parameter $\tau$, and let $f$ be an arbitrary differentiable function. Then by Leibniz's rule there is a constant matrix $L(w)$ such that

$$D_n(fw)(\tau) = L(w)D_n(f)(\tau). \tag{4}$$

Notice the strong similarity in structure between equation (4), Leibniz's rule, and equation (2), the chain rule. From (4) it is easy to verify that

$$L(w_1 w_2) = L(w_1)L(w_2), \tag{5}$$

so, in particular,

$$L(w)^{-1} = L(1/w). \tag{6}$$

Using Leibniz's rule, we can actually find $L(w)$ explicitly. In fact,

$$L(w) = \begin{pmatrix} w & 0 & 0 & \cdots & 0 & 0 \\ w' & w & 0 & \cdots & 0 & 0 \\ w'' & 2w' & w & \cdots & 0 & 0 \\ & & \vdots & & & \\ w^{(n)} & \cdots & & \cdots & nw' & w \end{pmatrix}.$$

**Theorem 7.** *Let $M$ be a connection matrix and fix any continuous piecewise differentiable function $w$ with $w(\tau) \neq 0$. Then*

$$f \in C(M, \tau) \Leftrightarrow f/w \in C(L(1/w^+)ML(w^-), \tau).$$

**Proof:** If $f \in C(M, \tau)$, then

$$D_n(f^+/w^+)(\tau) = L(1/w^+)D_n(f^+)(\tau) = L(1/w^+)MD_n(f^-)(\tau).$$

But by (4),

$$D_n(f^-)(\tau) = D_n(w^- f^-/w^-)(\tau) = L(w^-)D_n(f^-/w^-)(\tau).$$

Therefore, for all $f \in C(M, \tau)$

$$D_n(f^+/w^+)(\tau) = L(1/w^+)ML(w^-)D_n(f^-/w^-)(\tau).$$

Hence $f \in C(M, \tau) \Rightarrow f/w \in C(L(1/w^+)ML(w^-), \tau)$.

Conversely, if $f/w \in C(L(1/w^+)ML(w^-), \tau)$, then by what we have just proved,

$$f = (f/w)/(1/w) \in C(L(w^+)L(1/w^+)ML(w^-)L(1/w^-), \tau).$$

But by (6),

$$L(w^+)L(1/w^+)ML(w^-)L(1/w^-) = M.$$

Therefore, $f/w \in C(L(1/w^+)ML(w^-), \tau) \Rightarrow f \in C(M, \tau)$. ∎

**Theorem 8.** *Let $M$ be a connection matrix and fix any continuous piecewise differentiable function $w$ with $w(\tau) \neq 0$. Then*

1. *$M$ lower triangular $\Rightarrow L(1/w^+)ML(w^-)$ is lower triangular*
2. *$M$ lower triangular $\Rightarrow [L(1/w^+)ML(w^-)]_{jj} = M_{jj}$*
3. *$w \in C(M, \tau) \Rightarrow [L(1/w^+)ML(w^-)]_{i0} = \delta_{i0}$.*

**Proof:** 1. The matrices $L(w)$ are lower triangular, and the product of lower triangular matrices is again a lower triangular matrix. Therefore, $M$ lower triangular $\Rightarrow L(1/w^+)ML(w^-)$ is lower triangular.

2. If $M$ is lower triangular, then

$$j^{th} \text{ column } [ML(w^-)] = (0, \ldots, 0, M_{jj}w^-, *, \ldots, *)^T.$$

Therefore, since by assumption $w$ is continuous

$$[L(1/w^+)ML(w^-)_{jj}] =$$
$$= (*, \ldots *, 1/w^+, 0, \ldots, 0)(0, \ldots, 0, M_{jj}w^-, *, \ldots, *)^T$$
$$= M_{jj}w^-/w^+ = M_{jj}.$$

3. If $w \in C(M, \tau)$, then

$$D_n(w^+) = MD_n(w^-).$$

Since the first column of $L(w^-)$ is $D_n(w^-)$, it follows that

$$1^{\text{st}} \text{ column } [ML(w^-)] = MD_n(w^-) = D_n(w^+).$$

Therefore by (4),

$$1^{\text{st}} \text{ column } [L(1/w^+)ML(w^-)] = L(1/w^+)D_n(w^+)$$
$$= D_n(1) = (1, 0, \ldots, 0)^T. \quad \blacksquare$$

**Corollary 5.** *Let $M$ be a Frenet frame connection matrix, and fix any function $w \in C(M, \tau)$ with $w(\tau) \neq 0$. Then $L(1/w^+)ML(w^-)$ is also a Frenet frame connection matrix.*

**Corollary 6.** *Let $M$ be a Frenet frame connection matrix, and fix any function $w \in C(M, \tau)$ with $w(\tau) \neq 0$. Then $g \in C(M, \tau) \Rightarrow g/w \in C(N, \tau)$, where $N$ is a Frenet frame connection matrix that depends only on $M$ and $w$.*

**Corollary 7.** *If $M$ is a Frenet frame connection matrix, then $F \in C(M, \tau) \Rightarrow P[F] \in C(N, \tau)$, where $N$ is a Frenet frame connection matrix that depends only on $M$ and $w$.*

**Corollary 8.** *Frenet frame continuity is invariant under projection, but the shape parameters are not generally preserved.*

Much the same arguments can be used to show that continuity of the first $n$ osculating linear spaces is invariant under projection even though the shape parameters are not generally preserved. Again, this result is just a simple consequence of Theorems 7 and 8.

Given a set of scalar blending functions $\{B_k(t)\}$ and a set of control vertices $\{V_k\}$ in $d$ space, *rational curves* $R(t)$ in $d$ space are generally defined by first introducing a set of scalar weights $\{w_k\}$ and then projecting the integral curve with control vertices $\{(w_kV_k, w_k)\}$ from $d+1$ space onto $d$ space. That is,

$$R(t) = \Sigma_j\{w_jV_jB_j(t)/\Sigma_k w_kB_k(t)\} = P[\Sigma_j(w_jV_j, w_j)B_j(t)].$$

If the blending functions $\{B_k(t)\}$ are Beta-spline basis functions, then the curves $R(t)$ are called *rational Beta-spline curves* [1]. Now it follows by Theorem 5 that rational Beta-spline curves have the same shape parameters as the corresponding (unprojected) integral Beta-spline curves. Thus the weights and the Beta parameters have independent geometric effects. In contrast, even though Frenet frame continuity is preserved under projection, rational Frenet frame continuous splines have different shape parameters than the corresponding integral (unprojected) splines because, by Corollary 8, projection alters the connection matrix. Hence the weights actually influence the shape parameters; changing a weight will also change some shape parameters. Thus for Frenet frame continuity, the weights and the shape parameters do not behave independently.

Reparametrization is actually the most general form of Frenet frame continuity which is invariant under lifting. Knowing Corollary 7, one might be somewhat surprised by this assertion. That is, one might have expected a result for lifting somewhat similar to Corollary 7: that if $M$ is a Frenet frame connection matrix, then $(G, w) \in C(M, \tau) \Rightarrow L[G] \in C(N, \tau)$, where $N$ is a Frenet frame connection matrix that depends only on $M$ and $w$. In fact, as we shall see, it is a consequence of Corollary 6 that this cannot be the case. To demonstrate the difference between lifting and projecting, we shall need the following proposition.

**Proposition 2.** *If* $C(N, \tau) \supset C(M, \tau)$, *then* $N = M$.

**Proof:** Suppose that $C(N, \tau) \supset C(M, \tau)$. Then if $f \in C(M, \tau)$,

$$D_n(f^+)(\tau) = M D_n(f^-)(\tau)$$

$$D_n(f^+)(\tau) = N D_n(f^-)(\tau).$$

Therefore, for all $f \in C(M, \tau)$, we have

$$N D_n(f^-)(\tau) = M D_n(f^-)(\tau). \tag{7}$$

Now define $f_k(t)$ by setting

$$f_k^-(t) = (t - \tau)^k / k!$$

$$f_k^+(t) = \Sigma_j M_{jk}(t - \tau)^j / j!.$$

Then

$$D_n(f_k^+)(\tau) = (M_{0k}, \ldots, M_{nk})^T = M(0, \ldots, 1, \ldots, 0)^T = M D_n(f_k^-)(\tau)$$

so certainly $f_k \in C(M, \tau)$. Hence by (7), we have

$$N D_n(f_k^-)(\tau) = M D_n(f_k^-)(\tau).$$

Therefore,

$$k^{th} \text{ column } N = k^{th} \text{ column } M, \quad k = 0, 1, \ldots, n,$$

so we conclude that $N = M$. ∎

**Theorem 9.** *Let $M$ be a Frenet frame connection matrix. Suppose that for any $w \in C(M, \tau)$ there exists a Frenet frame connection matrix $N$ which depends only on $M$ and $w$ such that $g \in C(M, \tau) \Rightarrow gw \in C(N, \tau)$. Then $M$ is a reparametrization matrix and $N = M$.*

**Proof:** Let $M$ be a Frenet frame connection matrix and fix any $w \in C(M, \tau)$ with $w(\tau) \neq 0$. Suppose that $g \in C(M, \tau) \Rightarrow gw \in C(N, \tau)$, where $N$ is a Frenet frame connection matrix that depends only on $M$ and $w$. Then since both 1 and $f$ lie in $C(M, \tau)$, it follows that both $w$ and $wf$ lie in $C(N, \tau)$. Now because $N$ is a Frenet frame connection matrix and $w \in C(N, \tau)$, it follows from Corollary 6 that $g \in C(N, \tau) \Rightarrow g/w \in C(N^*, \tau)$, where $N^*$ is a Frenet frame connection matrix that depends only on $N$ and $w$. Hence clearly $C(N^*, \tau) \supset C(M, \tau)$ since $f \in C(M, \tau) \Rightarrow wf \in C(N, \tau) \Rightarrow f \in C(N^*, \tau)$. Therefore, by Proposition 2, $N^* = M$. But $1 \in C(N, \tau) \Rightarrow 1/w \in C(N^*, \tau) = C(M, \tau)$. Thus we have shown that $w \in C(M, \tau) \Rightarrow 1/w \in C(M, \tau)$. Now it follows from Theorem 3 that $M$ must be a reparametrization matrix in which case certainly $N = M$. ∎

**Corollary 9.** *Suppose $M$ is a Frenet frame connection matrix. Further suppose $(G, w) \in C(M, \tau) \Rightarrow L[G] \in C(N, \tau)$ where $N$ is a Frenet frame connection matrix that depends only on $M$ and $w$. Then $M$ is a reparametrization matrix and $N = M$.*

**Corollary 10.** *Reparametrization is the most general form of Frenet frame continuity that is invariant under lifting.*

By Theorem 4, geometric continuity based on reparametrization is preserved under all differential transformations, but as we can see from Corollary 10, this fails to be true for Frenet frame continuity. For additional concrete examples and further geometric insight into this phenomenon, see [17].

The distinction between lifting and projecting can be explained geometrically. Consider torsion continuous curves in 3 space. Every planar curve has zero torsion; thus every smooth planar curve is torsion continuous. Now if a curve is torsion continuous in 3 space, certainly its projection will be torsion continuous in 2 space. However, there is no geometric reason to expect that lifting an arbitrary smooth planar curve into 3 space will result in a torsion continuous curve. What we have shown, in fact, is that lifting will not generally result in a torsion continuous curve unless the original curve was geometrically continuous in the strong sense of reparametrization.

Lifting by $w$ is equivalent to projecting by $1/w$. Therefore, we do have the following analog to Corollary 7.

**Corollary 11.** *Let $M$ be a Frenet frame connection matrix. Then $(G, 1/w) \in C(M, \tau) \Rightarrow L[G] \in C(N, \tau)$, where $N$ is a Frenet frame connection matrix that depends only on $M$ and $w$.*

## §5. Some Further Algebraic Aspects of Geometric Continuity

If $f \in C(L(w), \tau)$, then $wf^-$ and $f^+$ meet with $C^n$ continuity. Thus multiplication by $w$ on the left makes these functions smooth. Therefore if $f, g \in C(L(w), \tau)$, then $f/g$ must actually be $C^n$. Similarly, if $f, g \in C(R(h)L(w), \tau)$, then $f/g \in C(R(h), \tau)$. Recently Hohmeyer and Barsky have examined curves which are not smooth but which become smooth upon projection, and they proved that the converses of these two statements are also true [16]. In fact, they proved results equivalent to Theorem 10 and Corollary 12 below. To derive these results using the methods employed here, we shall make use of the following proposition.

**Proposition 3.** $R(h)L(w) = L(w \circ h)R(h)$.

**Proof:** Let $f$ be any differentiable function. Then by applying equations (4) and (2), we obtain

$$\begin{aligned}
D_n[(fw) \circ h](\tau) &= D_n[(f \circ h)(w \circ h)](\tau) \\
&= L(w \circ h)D_n(f \circ h)(\tau) \\
&= L(w \circ h)R(h)D_n(f)(h(\tau)).
\end{aligned}$$

On the other hand, applying equation (2) first and then equation (4), we obtain

$$\begin{aligned}
D_n[(fw) \circ h](\tau) &= R(h)D_n(fw)(h(\tau)) \\
&= R(h)L(w)D_n(f)(h(\tau)).
\end{aligned}$$

Hence for all differentiable functions $f$,

$$R(h)L(w)D_n(f)(h(\tau)) = L(w \circ h)R(h)D_n(f)(h(\tau)).$$

Consequently,

$$R(h)L(w) = L(w \circ h)R(h). \quad \blacksquare$$

**Theorem 10.** Let $R(h)$ be a reparametrization matrix — that is, $h(\tau) = \tau$. Then $P[F] \in C(R(h), \tau) \Leftrightarrow F \in C(L(\gamma)R(h), \tau)$ for some function $\gamma$.

**Proof:** Let $F(t) = (x_1(t), \ldots, x_d(t), w(t))$, and suppose that $F$ belongs to $C(L(\gamma)R(h), \tau)$ for some function $\gamma$. Then by (2) and (4)

$$D_n(x_k^+)(\tau) = L(\gamma)R(h)D_n(x_k^-)(\tau) = D_n[(x_k^- \circ h)\gamma](\tau)$$

$$D_n(w^+)(\tau) = L(\gamma)R(h)D_n(w^-)(\tau) = D_n[(w^- \circ h)\gamma](\tau).$$

Therefore, for all $k$,

$$\begin{aligned}
D_n(x_k^+/w^+)(\tau) &= D_n[(x_k^- \circ h)\gamma/(w^- \circ h)\gamma](\tau) \\
&= D_n[(x_k^- \circ h)/(w^- \circ h)](\tau) \\
&= R(h)D_n(x_k^-/w^-)(\tau),
\end{aligned}$$

and so $P[F] \in C(R(h), \tau)$.

Conversely, suppose that $P[F] \in C(R(h), \tau)$. Then for all $k$,

$$D_n(x_k^+/w^+)(\tau) = R(h)D_n(x_k^-/w^-)(\tau) = R(h)L(1/w^-)D_n(x_k^-)(\tau).$$

Multiplying both sides by $L(w^+)$ and applying (4), we obtain

$$D_n(x_k^+)(\tau) = L(w^+)R(h)L(1/w^-)D_n(x_k^-)(\tau).$$

But by Proposition 3,

$$R(h)L(1/w^-) = L(1/w^- \circ h)R(h).$$

Hence by (5), for all $k$

$$\begin{aligned}
D_n(x_k^+)(\tau) &= L(w^+)L(1/w^- \circ h)R(h)D_n(x_k^-)(\tau) \\
&= L(w^+/w^- \circ h)R(h)D_n(x_k^-)(\tau).
\end{aligned}$$

Moreover, by (2) and (4)

$$\begin{aligned}
D_n(w^+)(\tau) &= D_n[w^+(w^- \circ h/w^- \circ h)](\tau) \\
&= L(w^+/w^- \circ h)D_n(w^- \circ h)(\tau) \\
&= L(w^+/w^- \circ h)R(h)D_n(w^-)(\tau).
\end{aligned}$$

Therefore, $F \in C(L(w^+/w^- \circ h)R(h), \tau)$. ■

**Corollary 12.** $P[F]$ *is* $C^n \Leftrightarrow F \in C(L(\gamma), \tau)$ *for some function* $\gamma$.

**Proof:** This result follows immediately from Theorem 10 with $h(t) = t$. ■

By Proposition 3, Theorem 10 remains valid if we replace $L(\gamma)R(h)$ by $R(h)L(\gamma^*)$. Together, Corollary 7 and Theorem 10 suggest the following result for Frenet frame connection matrices.

**Theorem 11.** *If $N$ is a Frenet frame connection matrix, then $P[F] \in C(N, \tau)$ $\Leftrightarrow F \in C(ML(\gamma), \tau)$ for some Frenet frame connection matrix $M$ and some function $\gamma$.*

**Proof:** Let $F(t) = (x_1(t), \ldots, x_d(t), w(t))$ and suppose that $F \in C(ML(\gamma), \tau)$ for some Frenet frame connection matrix $M$ and some function $\gamma$. Then by (4),

$$D_n(x_k^+)(\tau) = ML(\gamma)D_n(x_k^-)(\tau) = MD_n(\gamma x_k^-)(\tau)$$

$$D_n(w^+)(\tau) = ML(\gamma)D_n(w^-)(\tau) = MD_n(\gamma w^-)(\tau).$$

Now since $M$ is a Frenet frame connection matrix, it follows by Corollary 6 that there is a Frenet frame connection matrix $N$ such that for all $k$

$$D_n(x_k^+/w^+)(\tau) = ND_n(\gamma x_k^-/\gamma w^-)(\tau) = ND_n(x_k^-/w^-)(\tau),$$

so $P[F] \in C(N, \tau)$.

Conversely, suppose that $P[F] \in C(N, \tau)$. Then for all $k$,

$$D_n(x_k^+/w^+)(\tau) = ND_n(x_k^-/w^-)(\tau) = NL(1/w^-)D_n(x_k^-)(\tau).$$

Multiplying both sides by $L(w^+)$ and applying (4), we obtain

$$D_n(x_k^+)(\tau) = L(w^+)NL(1/w^-)D_n(x_k^-)(\tau).$$

Moreover since $1 \in C(N, \tau)$, it follows easily from (4), (5), (6), that

$$D_n(w^+)(\tau) = L(w^+)NL(1/w^-)D_n(w^-)(\tau).$$

Now define a function $\mu \in C(N, \tau)$ by setting

$$\mu^+ = 1/w^+$$

$$(\alpha_0, \ldots, \alpha_n)^T = N^{-1}D_n(\mu^+)(\tau)$$

$$\mu^-(t) = \sum_{k=0}^{n} \alpha_k(t - \tau)^k/k!.$$

Then by construction

$$D_n(\mu^-)(\tau) = (\alpha_0, \ldots, \alpha_n)^T = N^{-1}D_n(\mu^+)(\tau)$$

$$D_n(\mu^+)(\tau) = ND_n(\mu^-)(\tau)$$

so $\mu \in C(N, \tau)$. Now by (5) and (6) and the relations derived above,

$$D_n(x_k^+)(\tau) = L(1/\mu^+)NL(\mu^-)L(1/\mu^- w^-)D_n(x_k^-)(\tau)$$

$$D_n(w^+)(\tau) = L(1/\mu^+)NL(\mu^-)L(1/\mu^- w^-)D_n(w^-)(\tau).$$

Let $M = L(1/\mu^+)NL(\mu^-)$. Then by Corollary 5, $M$ is a Frenet frame connection matrix. Thus for all $k$,

$$D_n(x_k^+)(\tau) = ML(1/\mu^- w^-)D_n(x_k^-)(\tau),$$

$$D_n(w^+)(\tau) = ML(1/\mu^- w^-)D_n(w^-)(\tau).$$

Therefore, $F \in C(ML(1/\mu^- w^-), \tau)$. ∎

Like Theorem 10, Theorem 11 remains valid if we replace $ML(\gamma)$ by $L(\gamma^*)M$; again the proof is much the same.

Because of the results of Hohmeyer and Barsky, we have strong geometric motivation for studying the algebraic structure of the sets $C(L(w), \tau)$. Moreover, the matrices $L(w)$ also appeared in our proof that Frenet frame continuity is preserved under projection. Our final theme is that there is a major parallel between the Leibniz matrices $L(w)$ and the reparametrization matrices $R(h)$ — that is, $L(w)$ is to multiplication as $R(h)$ is to composition. Indeed for the matrices $L(w)$, we have the following analog of Theorem 1.

**Theorem 12.** *If $M$ is a connection matrix, then $f \in C(M, \tau) \Rightarrow Pf \in C(M, \tau)$ for every polynomial $P$ if and only if $M = L(w)$ for some function $w$.*

**Proof:** The proof is identical to the proof of Theorem 1. Simply replace composition by multiplication, $R(h)$ by $L(w)$, and the functions $h^-(t)$ and $h^+(t)$ by the functions

$$w^-(t) = 1$$

$$w^+(t) = \Sigma_j M_{j0}(t - \tau)^j / j!.$$

Then proceed exactly as in the proof of Theorem 1. ∎

Again the statement of Theorem 12 requires us to check $f \in C(M, \tau) \Rightarrow Pf \in C(M, \tau)$ for every polynomial $P$ in order to conclude that $M = L(w)$. However, it is sufficient simply to test the one polynomial $P_0(t) = t$ since if $f \in C(M, \tau) \Rightarrow P_0 f \in C(M, \tau)$, then clearly $f \in C(M, \tau) \Rightarrow Pf \in C(M, \tau)$ for every polynomial $P$.

Our next two theorems are analogs of Corollary 1.

**Theorem 13.** *Suppose $M$ is a non-singular matrix. Then $f, g \in C(M, \tau) \Rightarrow fg \in C(M^2, \tau)$ if and only if $M = L(w)$ for some function $w$.*

**Proof:** If $f, g \in C(L(w), \tau)$, then by (4),

$$D_n(f^+)(\tau) = L(w)D_n(f^-)(\tau) = D_n(wf^-)(\tau)$$

$$D_n(g^+)(\tau) = L(w)D_n(g^-)(\tau) = D_n(wg^-)(\tau).$$

Therefore by (5),

$$D_n(f^+g^+)(\tau) = D_n(w^2 f^- g^-)(\tau)$$

$$= L(w^2)D_n(f^- g^-)(\tau) = L(w)^2 D_n(f^- g^-)(\tau).$$

Hence $f, g \in C(L(w), \tau) \Rightarrow fg \in C(L(w)^2, \tau)$.

Conversely, suppose that $f, g \in C(M, \tau) \Rightarrow fg \in C(M^2, \tau)$. Define $w(t)$ by setting

$$w^-(t) = 1$$

$$w^+(t) = \Sigma_j M_{j0}(t - \tau)^j / j!.$$

Then

$$D_n(w^+)(\tau) = (M_{00}, \ldots, M_{n0})^T = MD_n(w^-)(\tau),$$

so clearly $w \in C(M, \tau)$. Therefore, for any $f \in C(M, \tau)$

$$D_n(w^+ f^+)(\tau) = M^2 D_n(w^- f^-)(\tau) = M^2 D_n(f^-)(\tau).$$

But by (4),

$$D_n(w^+ f^+)(\tau) = L(w^+)D_n(f^+)(\tau) = L(w^+)MD_n(f^-)(\tau).$$

Hence for all $f \in C(M, \tau)$

$$M^2 D_n(f^-)(\tau) = L(w^+)M D_n(f^-)(\tau).$$

Therefore, we conclude that $M^2 = L(w^+)M$. Since $M$ is non-singular it follows that $M = L(w^+)$. ∎

**Theorem 14.** *Let $M$ and $N$ be non-singular matrices. Then $f \in C(M, \tau)$ and $g \in C(N, \tau) \Rightarrow fg \in C(MN, \tau)$ if and only if $M = L(w_1)$ and $N = L(w_2)$ for some functions $w_1$ and $w_2$.*

**Proof:** The proof of this result is much the same as the proof of Theorem 13 so we omit the details. ∎

If we replace multiplication by division, then we get the following analog of Corollary 2.

**Theorem 15.** *Let $M$ be a connection matrix. Then $f, g \in C(M, \tau) \Rightarrow f/g$ is $C^n$ if and only if $M = L(w)$ for some function $w$.*

**Proof:** If $f, g \in C(L(w), \tau)$, then multiplication on the left makes $f$ and $g$ into $C^n$ functions. Hence $f/g$ is certainly $C^n$. To prove the converse, define $w \in C(M, \tau)$ as in Theorem 13. If $f \in C(M, \tau)$, then

$$D_n(f^+/w^+)(\tau) = D_n(f^-/w^-)(\tau) = D_n(f^-)(\tau).$$

Therefore, for all $f \in C(M, \tau)$,

$$D_n(f^+)(\tau) = D_n(w^+ f^+/w^+)(\tau) = D_n(w^+ f^-)(\tau) = L(w^+)D_n(f^-)(\tau).$$

But for all $f \in C(M, \tau)$,

$$D_n(f^+)(\tau) = M D_n(f^-)(\tau).$$

Therefore, for all $f \in C(M, \tau)$,

$$M D_n(f^-)(\tau) = L(w^+)D_n(f^-)(\tau).$$

Hence we conclude that $M = L(w^+)$. ∎

**Corollary 13.** *Suppose $M$ is a connection matrix. Then $F \in C(M, \tau) \Rightarrow P[F]$ is $C^n$ if and only if $M = L(w)$ for some function $w$.*

Finally, very similar arguments can be used to prove the following two analogous results for geometric continuity. Again, since the proofs are much the same, we omit the details.

**Theorem 16.** *Suppose $M$ is a connection matrix. Then $f, g \in C(M, \tau) \Rightarrow f/g \in C(R(h), \tau)$ if and only if $M = R(h)L(w)$ for some function $w$.*

**Corollary 14.** *Suppose $M$ is a connection matrix. Then $F \in C(M, \tau) \Rightarrow P[F] \in C(R(h), \tau)$ if and only if $M = R(h)L(w)$ for some function $w$.*

## §6. Conclusion

We have investigated some of the algebraic properties of the sets $C(M, \tau)$ of all scalar valued functions with connection matrix $M$ at $\tau$. In particular, we have shown that the set $C(M, \tau)$ is closed under multiplication and division if and only if $M$ is a reparametrization matrix. Rather than being computational and *ad hoc*, our proofs tried to emphasize the essential algebraic structure of these problems.

Using these results, we were able to prove that reparametrization is the most general form of geometric continuity for which the shape parameters remain invariant under projection. We went on to show that Frenet frame continuity is also invariant under projection, even though the shape parameters are not necessarily preserved.

Finally, we investigated curves which are not smooth, but which become smooth under projection. This investigation led to the study of the algebraic structure of the sets $C(M, \tau)$, where $M$ is a matrix generated by Leibniz's rule.

## References

1. Barsky, B. A., Introducing the rational Beta-spline, Proceedings of the Third International Conference on Engineering Graphics and Descriptive Geometry, Vienna **1** (1988), 16–27.
2. Barsky B. A. and T. D. DeRose, Geometric continuity of parametric curves: Developing the Beta-constraints, preprint.
3. Boehm, W., Curvature continuous curves and surfaces, Comput. Aided Geom. Design **2** (1985), 313–323.
4. Boehm, W., Rational geometric splines, Comput. Aided Geom. Design **4** (1987), 67–77.
5. Boehm, W., On the definition of geometric continuity, Letter to the Editor, Comput. Aided Design **20** (1988), 370–372.
6. DeRose, T. D., Geometric Continuity: A Parametrization Independent Measure of Continuity for Computer Aided Geometric Design, PhD dissertation, University of California, Berkeley, 1985.
7. Dyn, N., A. Edelmann, and C. Micchelli, On locally supported basis functions for the representation of geometrically continuous curves, Analysis **7** (1987), 313–341.
8. Dyn, N. and C. Micchelli, Shape preserving parametric representation of curves with local control for computer aided geometric design, RC 10931, IBM T. J. Watson Research Center, Yorktown Heights, New York, 1985.
9. Dyn, N. and C. Micchelli, Piecewise polynomial spaces and geometric continuity of curves, Numerische Math., to appear.
10. Farin, G., Visually $C^2$ cubic splines, Comput. Aided Design **14** (1982), 137–139.
11. Goldman, R. N. and B. A. Barsky, Some basic results on $\beta$-continuous functions and their application to the construction of geometrically continuous curves and surfaces, in *Mathematical Methods in Computer Aided*

*Geometric Design*, T. Lyche and L. Schumaker (eds.), Academic Press, N. Y., 1989, 299–311.

12. Gregory, J., Geometric continuity in CAGD, in *Mathematical Methods in Computer Aided Geometric Design*, T. Lyche and L. Schumaker (eds.), Academic Press, N. Y., 1989, 353–371.

13. Hagen, H., Geometric spline curves, Comput. Aided Geom. Design **2** (1985), 223–227.

14. Hagen, H., Bézier curves with curvature and torsion continuity, Rocky Mountain Journal of Mathematics **16** (1986), 629–638.

15. Höllig, K., Geometric continuity of spline curves and surfaces, Computer Science Department, University of Wisconsin, Madison, Wisconsin, 1986.

16. Hohmeyer, M. E. and B. A. Barsky, Rational continuity: Parametric and geometric continuity of rational polynomial curves, Trans. on Graphics, to appear.

17. Pottman, H., On the invariance of geometric continuity under certain transformations, Letter to the Editor, Comput. Aided Design, to appear.

Ronald N. Goldman
Computer Science Department
University of Waterloo
Waterloo, Ontario N2L 3G1
CANADA

EMAIL: rngoldman@ watcgl.waterloo.edu

Charles A. Micchelli
Mathematical Sciences Department, IBM
Thomas J. Watson Research Center
P.O. Box 218
Yorktown Heights, New York 10598
USA

EMAIL: cam@ yktvmx

Supported in part by the Natural Sciences and Engineering Research Council of Canada Grant OGP0036825.

# Shape Preserving Representations

## T. N. T. Goodman

**Abstract.** Given appropriate functions $\phi_1,\ldots,\phi_n$ on an interval, we consider how the shape of a curve $\Sigma A_i\phi_i$ can mimic or *preserve* the shape of the polygonal arc joining the points $A_1,\ldots,A_n$ in $\mathbb{R}^2$. The best known example is when the functions $\phi_i$ are the Bernstein polynomial basis functions (where the points $A_i$ are known as Bézier points), but many other bases share similar properties. Corresponding properties for surfaces are also discussed.

## §1. Introduction

When defining a curve or surface from a given finite dimensional space of functions, it is important which basis we use. As a simple example, consider the space of polynomials of degree $n$ on $[a, b]$. Writing

$$p(x) = \sum_{i=0}^{n} a_i x^i, \qquad a \leq x \leq b,$$

the coefficients $a_i$ do not give much immediate information on the shape of the curve $p$. However, if we write

$$p(x) = \sum_{i=0}^{n} b_i \binom{n}{i} \left(\frac{x-a}{b-a}\right)^i \left(\frac{b-x}{b-a}\right)^{n-i}, \qquad a \leq x \leq b,$$

then the coefficients $b_i$ give very simply a great deal of information about the shape of the curve $p$. To give just one example, we note that if the sequence $(b_0,\ldots,b_n)$ is increasing, then $p$ is increasing.

Mathematical Methods in Computer Aided Geometric Design
Tom Lyche and Larry L. Schumaker (eds.), pp. 333–351.
Copyright Ⓒ 1989 by Academic Press, Boston.
ISBN 0-12-460515-X.

To consider this in more detail, we start with Descartes' Rule of Signs, so named because of its use by Descartes in the third book of his Géométrie of 1637. This says that given any polynomial

$$p(x) = \sum_{i=0}^{n} a_i \binom{n}{i} x^i, \qquad x > 0, \tag{1}$$

then the number of times it changes sign on $(0, \infty)$ is bounded by the number of changes of sign in the sequence $a_0, \ldots, a_n$. (We shall not be concerned here with counting zeros.) Letting $V(\cdot)$ denote the number of sign changes of a function or sequence, this result can be written as

$$V(p) \leq V(a_0, \ldots, a_n). \tag{2}$$

For applications in CAGD, we are concerned more with finite than semi-infinite intervals, so without loss of generality, we shall consider $[0, 1]$. Following Schoenberg [41], we put $x = t/(1 - t)$ in (1) and then multiply by $(1 - t)^n$ to give

$$p(t) = \sum_{i=0}^{n} a_i \binom{n}{i} t^i (1 - t)^{n-i}, \qquad 0 < t < 1, \tag{3}$$

which is the usual Bézier representation. Since in going from (1) to (3) we have not changed the sign of $p$, inequality (2) still holds.

Again with an eye to CAGD, we now consider a parametrically defined curve

$$p(t) = (p_1(t), p_2(t)) = \sum_{i=0}^{n} A_i \binom{n}{i} t^i (1 - t)^{n-i}, \qquad 0 < t < 1, \tag{4}$$

where for $i = 0, \ldots, n$, $A_i = (x_i, y_i) \in \mathbb{R}^2$. The analogue and consequence of inequality (2) for the curve (4) is

**Theorem 1.** *The number of times any straight line crosses the curve $p$ given by (4) is no more than the number of times it crosses the polygonal arc $A_0 \ldots A_n$.*

**Proof:** Take any line $ax + by + c = 0$. Then the number of times it crosses the curve $p$ is

$$V(ap_1 + bp_2 + c) = V\left( a \sum x_i \binom{n}{i} t^i (1 - t)^{n-i} + b \sum y_i \binom{n}{i} t^i (1 - t)^{n-i} \right.$$
$$\left. + c \sum \binom{n}{i} t^i (1 - t)^{n-i} \right)$$
$$= V\left( \sum (ax_i + by_i + c) \binom{n}{i} t^i (1 - t)^{n-i} \right)$$
$$\leq V(ax_0 + by_0 + c, \ldots, ax_n + by_n + c).$$

Since this last expression is the number of times the line crosses the arc $A_0 \ldots A_n$, this completes the proof. ∎

To see the significance of Theorem 1, we consider some simple consequences. First, suppose the polygonal arc $A_0 \ldots A_n$ is convex. Then any straight line crosses it at most twice. Thus, by Theorem 1, any straight line crosses the curve $p$ at most twice and so the curve $p$ is convex. Next suppose that the arc $A_0 \ldots A_n$ is increasing in the y-direction; *i.e.*, $y_0 \leq y_1 \leq \ldots \leq y_n$. Then any straight line parallel to the x-axis crosses it at most once. So from Theorem 1, any such line crosses the curve $p$ at most once and so the curve $p$ is increasing in the y-direction; *i.e.*, $p_2$ is an increasing function. Thus, Theorem 1 shows that the shape of the curve $p$ closely mimics the shape of the *Bézier polygon* $A_0 \ldots A_n$.

To sum up, we have found a particular basis for the space of polynomials of given degree on a finite interval with the property that the polygon of coefficients, or *control polygon*, of a parametrically defined curve with respect to this basis gives us a good guide to the shape of the curve. Thus, we can predict or manipulate the shape of the curve by suitably choosing or changing the control polygon.

In the next three sections we are going to extend this idea to certain bases of various spaces of functions, and to consider further ways in which the control polygon can indicate the shape of the curve or, to put it another way, the curve can *preserve* the shape of the control polygon. Section 2 introduces the important concept of total positivity and considers various bases which possess this property. The next section shows how total positivity leads to shape-preserving properties, and Section 4 mentions some shape-preserving properties that do not follow from total positivity. The final section discusses how these ideas can be extended to surfaces.

## §2. Total Positivity

A matrix is said to be *totally positive* (TP) if all its minors are non-negative. This important property has been widely studied and applied. A standard reference book is [34]. It does not seem to be well-known that there is a simple alternative characterization of TP matrices which we now describe. We shall say a matrix $A = (A_{ij})_{1,1}^{m,n}$ is *one-banded* if one of the following holds:

a) $m = n$ or $n + 1$ and $A_{ij} = 0$ unless $i = j$ or $i = j + 1$,
b) $m = n$ or $n - 1$ and $A_{ij} = 0$ unless $i = j$ or $i = j - 1$.

It is easily seen that a positive one-banded matrix is TP and, since a product of TP matrices is TP, any product of positive one-banded matrices is TP. The converse was proved for non-singular square matrices in [11], and the proof can easily be extended to arbitrary matrices. Thus, we have

**Theorem 2.** *A matrix is totally positive if and only if it is a product of positive one-banded matrices.*

**Definition.** *We shall say a sequence* $(\phi_0,\dots,\phi_n)$ *of real-valued functions on an interval* $I$ *is totally positive (TP) if for any* $t_1 < \cdots < t_m$ *in* $I$, *the collocation matrix* $(\phi_i(t_j))_{0,1}^{n,m}$ *is totally positive.*

This is not standard terminology but we prefer to be succint. The significance of this definition for shape-preserving representations will be explained in the next section, but to prevent bewilderment and whet the reader's appetite, we now mention a connection with the previous section. Theorem 2 easily implies:

**Theorem 3.** *If* $A$ *is a totally positive matrix and* $v$ *is a vector, then*

$$V(Av) \le V(v). \tag{5}$$

This immediately implies

**Corollary 1.** *If* $(\phi_0,\dots,\phi_n)$ *is totally positive, then for any real numbers* $a_0,\dots,a_n$,

$$V(a_0\phi_0 + \cdots + a_n\phi_n) \le V(a_0,\dots,a_n). \tag{6}$$

But for the Bernstein basis

$$\phi_i(t) = \binom{n}{i}t^i(1-t)^{n-i}, \qquad 0 < t < 1, \quad i = 0,\dots,n, \tag{7}$$

inequality (6) is the same as (2) which, we recall, implied Theorem 1.

Fortunately, a wide variety of bases are TP. We now mention several. First, consider again the space $P_n$ of polynomials of degree $n$ on $[0,1]$. The following TP basis for $P_n$ was introduced in [24]. If $a_{-n} \le \cdots \le a_{-1} \le 0$ and $1 \le a_1 \le \cdots \le a_n$, then we define

$$\phi_i(t) = \prod_{j=i-n}^{-1} (t - a_j) \prod_{j=1}^{i} (a_j - t), \qquad i = 0,\dots,n. \tag{8}$$

Clearly (8) reduces, after suitable normalization, to the Bernstein basis (7) when $a_{-n} = \cdots = a_{-1} = 0, 1 = a_1 = \cdots = a_n$. In [40] the following basis for $P_{2k+1}$ was introduced, generalizing work in [1] for $k = 1$:

$$\phi_i(t) = \binom{k+i}{i}t^i(1-t)^{k+1}, \qquad i = 0,\dots,k,$$
$$\phi_i(t) = \phi_{2k+1-i}(1-t), \qquad i = k+1,\dots,2k+1. \tag{9}$$

This is shown to be TP in [33]. However, for CAGD, polynomials are often too inflexible, and it is better to use spline functions. A simple TP basis is given by the truncated powers [34]:

$$\phi_i(t) = (t - a_i)_+^k, \qquad t \in \mathbb{R}, \quad i = 0,\dots,n \tag{10}$$

for any $a_0, \ldots, a_n$. Most widely used though, because of their myriad elegant and useful properties, are B-splines [8]. Take $n \geq 0, k \geq 2$ and a sequence $t_0 \leq \cdots \leq t_{n+k}$ with $t_i < t_{i+k}, i = 0, \ldots, n$. Then for $i = 0, \ldots, n$, let $\phi_i$ be a B-spline of order $k$ with knots at $t_i, \ldots, t_{i+k}$; *i.e.*, a function (unique up to a positive multiple) which has support $[t_i, t_{i+k}]$, is a polynomial of degree $k - 1$ on any interval $[t_j, t_{j+1})$, and at $t_j$ has continuous derivatives up to order $k - 1 - |\{l : t_l = t_j\}|$. (By $|S|$ we mean the number of elements in $S$.) Then $(\phi_0, \ldots, \phi_n)$ is TP [34]. When $k = n + 1$ and $t_0 = \cdots = t_n = 0$ and $1 = t_{n+1} = \cdots = t_{2n+1}$, then $(\phi_0, \ldots, \phi_n)$ reduces, after suitable normalization, to the Bernstein basis (7).

B-splines can be generalised to Tchebycheffian B-splines [44, Chapter 9] whose restriction to any interval $[t_j, t_{j+1})$ lies in the span of some appropriate TP basis. Tchebycheffian B-splines provide TP bases, and using piecewise trigonometric polynomials lead to trigonometric B-splines [42,31].

Other TP bases can be obtained by keeping to algebraic polynomials on the intervals $[t_j, t_{j+1})$, but changing the continuity conditions at the knots $t_j$. A general condition at a knot $\tau$ can be expressed as

$$f^{(i)}(\tau^+) = \sum_{j=0}^{r} C_{ij} f^{(j)}(\tau^-), \qquad i = 0, \ldots, r. \tag{11}$$

It is shown in [20] that if the *connection matrix* $C = (C_{ij})_{0,0}^{r,r}$ at each knot is TP and non-singular, then one can construct a basis of functions (sometimes called $\beta$-splines) with the same supports as the usual B-splines and this basis is TP. This was first shown [25] for the special case when each matrix $C$ is positive and one-banded. Such bases may be useful for CAGD when the condition (11) at each knot is chosen so that a curve defined parametrically from this basis has geometric continuity of order higher than the continuity of the separate components. Thus, cubic $\beta$-splines, first introduced in [2,22], give a curve with continuous unit tangent and curvature, even though the seperate components need not have continuous first and second order derivatives.

In [7] it is shown that a TP local support basis can also be constructed when at each knot certain non-consecutive derivatives are constrained to be continuous; *i.e.*, when the matrix $C$ in (11) consists of ones in certain positions on the main diagonal and zeros elsewhere.

So far we have described a variety of TP bases without any proofs that they are TP. To finish this section we mention briefly some methods of showing that a basis is TP. One was given in [9] for a basis of B-splines. It depends on the following properties of the basis $(\phi_0, \ldots, \phi_n)$.

For $0 \leq j < k \leq n$, the function $S(t) = \sum_{i=j}^{k} a_i \phi_i(t)$ has at most $k - j$ zeros and the sign of $S$ at the left (or right) end of its support equals the sign of $a_j$ (or $a_k$).

The proof shows that the minors of the collocation matrix are positive by induction on their order. Defining $f(t_1) = \det(\phi_i(t_j))_{0,0}^{k,k}$ for $t_2 < \cdots < t_k$, the induction hypothesis and the above properties show that $f(t_1) \geq 0$ for $t_1 < t_2$ and this establishes the inductive step.

A different approach was introduced in [36], again for B-splines, and extended in [25,30]. In none of these was the approach used to prove total positivity directly, but the approach can easily be modified to do so, as we now briefly describe. Given a basis $(\phi_0, \ldots, \phi_n)$, we consider a new sequence $(\psi_0, \ldots, \psi_{n+1})$ such that for $i = 0, \ldots, n$, each $\phi_i$ is a positive combination of $\psi_i$ and $\psi_{i+1}$. (For B-splines this is done by inserting a knot.) Writing $\phi_i = \sum_{j=0}^{n+1} B_{ij} \psi_j$, the matrix $B = (B_{ij})_{0,0}^{n,n+1}$ is positive and one-banded and hence TP. By successive application of this process we reach a sequence $(\eta_0, \ldots, \eta_{n+l})$ so that

$$(\phi_0, \ldots, \phi_n)^T = C(\eta_0, \ldots, \eta_{n+l})^T, \tag{12}$$

where the matrix $C$ is TP. Now for any $t_1 < \cdots < t_m$ we choose $\eta_0, \ldots, \eta_{n+l}$ so that there are $0 \le j_1 < \cdots < j_m \le n + l$ such that for $k = 1, \ldots, m$,

$$\eta_i(t_k) = \begin{cases} 1, & i = j_k \\ 0, & \text{otherwise} . \end{cases}$$

(For B-splines of order $k$ this is done by inserting knots of multiplicity $k - 1$ at $t_1, \ldots, t_m$.) Then the collocation matrix of $\phi_0, \ldots, \phi_n$ at $t_1, \ldots, t_m$ is the submatrix of $C$ gained by taking columns $j_1, \ldots, j_m$. Since $C$ is TP, the submatrix is TP; *i.e.*, $(\phi_0, \ldots, \phi_n)$ is TP.

A variant of the above approach is to choose the sequence $(\eta_0, \ldots, \eta_{n+l})$ in (12) to be one that we already know to be TP. Since the collocation matrix of $(\phi_0, \ldots, \phi_n)$ is the product of $C$ with the collocation matrix of $(\eta_0, \ldots, \eta_{n+l})$, it is a product of TP matrices and so is TP. This method was used in [33], expressing the generalized Ball basis in terms of the Bernstein basis. In [22,4] cubic $\beta$-splines were constructed in this manner from the Bernstein basis on each subinterval. This immediately establishes that the basis is TP (although this is not mentioned in the papers). The construction is extended to torsion continuous quartics and rational cubics and quartics in [5,6].

## §3. Consequences of Total Positivity

Throughout this section we assume that $(\phi_0, \ldots, \phi_n)$ is a TP basis on an interval $I$ satisfying

$$\sum_{i=0}^{n} \phi_i(t) = 1, \qquad t \in I. \tag{13}$$

We note that if $(\psi_0, \ldots, \psi_n)$ is TP with $\sum_{i=0}^{n} \psi_i > 0$ on $I$, then defining

$$\phi_i = \frac{\psi_i}{\sum_{i=0}^{n} \psi_i}, \qquad i = 1, \ldots, n,$$

we see that $(\phi_i, \ldots, \phi_n)$ is TP on $I$ and satisfies (13). For example, if $\psi_0, \ldots, \psi_n$ are B-splines, then $\phi_0, \ldots, \phi_n$ are *rational B-splines* [45].

For our first result we define the *total variation* of a sequence of numbers $(a_0, \ldots, a_n)$ by

$$TV(a_0, \ldots, a_n) := \sum_{j=1}^{n} |a_j - a_{j-1}|.$$

Then the total variation of a function $f$ on an interval $I$ is defined by

$$TV(f) := \sup TV(f(t_1), \ldots, f(t_m)), \tag{14}$$

where the supremum is taken over all $t_1 < \cdots < t_m$ in $I$, all $m$.

**Theorem 4.** *With* $(\phi_0, \ldots, \phi_n)$ *as above and any real numbers* $a_0, \ldots, a_n$,

$$TV(a_0\phi_0 + \cdots + a_n\phi_n) \le TV(a_0, \ldots, a_n). \tag{15}$$

**Proof:** This was essentially proved in [41], where it was deduced from Corollary 1. We give a different proof which follows the same approach as the rest of this section. It is easily seen that if a matrix $A$ is positive, one-banded and stochastic, (*i.e.*, has row sums equal to 1), then for any vector $v$,

$$TV(Av) \le TV(v). \tag{16}$$

Now if $A$ is totally positive and stochastic it follows from Theorem 2 that it is a product of one-banded, positive stochastic matrices and so (16) still holds.

If $C$ denotes the collocation matrix of $(\phi_0, \ldots, \phi_n)$ at any points $t_1, \ldots, t_m$ in $I$ and $f = a_0\phi_0 + \cdots + a_n\phi_n$, then

$$(f(t_1), \ldots, f(t_m))^T = C^T(a_0, \ldots, a_n)^T. \tag{17}$$

Since $C$ is TP, $C^T$ is TP and stochastic. So from (16) and (17),

$$TV(f(t_1), \ldots, f(t_m)) \le TV(a_0, \ldots, a_n)$$

and thus from (14),

$$TV(f) \le TV(a_0, \ldots, a_n). \quad \blacksquare$$

Corollary 1 and Theorem 4 apply to a function $a_0\phi_0 + \cdots + a_n\phi_n$. Henceforth, we shall consider parametrically defined curves of form

$$q(t) = (q_1(t), q_2(t)) = \sum_{i=0}^{n} A_i \phi_i(t), \qquad t \in I, \tag{18}$$

where for $i = 0, \ldots, n$, $A_i = (x_i, y_i) \in \mathbb{R}^2$. Just as in the proof of Theorem 1, from Corollary 1 and (13) we can deduce:

**Theorem 5.** *The number of times any straight line crosses the curve $q$ given by (18) is no more than the number of times it crosses the polygonal arc $A_0 \ldots A_n$.*

As in the discussion after Theorem 1, we see that Theorem 5 implies that the curve $q$ preserves certain shape properties of the control polygon $A_0 \ldots A_n$. In order to prove further shape-preserving properties, we introduce the notion of *corner cutting*, see [32]. We say that the polygonal arc $B_0 \ldots B_{n+1}$ is obtained from the polygonal arc $A_0 \ldots A_n$ by *cutting a corner* if for some $j$,

$$
\begin{aligned}
B_i &= A_i, & 0 \leq i < j, \\
B_j &= \lambda A_{j-1} + (1 - \lambda) A_j, & \text{some } 0 \leq \lambda \leq 1, \\
B_{j+1} &= \mu A_j + (1 - \mu) A_{j+1}, & \text{some } 0 \leq \mu \leq 1, \\
B_{i+1} &= A_i, & j < i \leq n.
\end{aligned}
$$

**Lemma 1.** *For $q$ as in (18) and any $t_1 < \cdots < t_m$ in $I$, the polygonal arc $q(t_1) \ldots q(t_m)$ can be obtained by successively cutting corners of the polygonal arc $A_0 \ldots A_n$.*

**Proof:** If $C$ denotes the collocation matrix of $(\phi_0, \ldots, \phi_n)$ at $t_1, \ldots, t_m$, then from (18),

$$
(q(t_1), \ldots, q(t_m))^T = C^T (A_0, \ldots, A_n)^T. \tag{19}
$$

Now $C^T$ is TP and stochastic and hence is a product of positive one-banded, stochastic matrices. The result then follows from (19). ∎

The best-known example of Theorem 5 is when $m = 1$ and $(\phi_0, \ldots, \phi_n)$ is the Bernstein basis, in which case a process of cutting corners is given by the de Casteljau algorithm [12].

We shall now state a number of shape-preserving properties for (18). Each result can be proved by showing the inequality holds under cutting a corner and then applying Lemma 1. Now for a function $f$ on an interval $I$ we define

$$
V(\Delta f) := \sup V \left( \frac{f(t_2) - f(t_1)}{t_2 - t_1}, \ldots, \frac{f(t_m) - f(t_{m-1})}{t_m - t_{m-1}} \right),
$$
$$
TV(\Delta f) := \sup TV \left( \frac{f(t_2) - f(t_1)}{t_2 - t_1}, \ldots, \frac{f(t_m) - f(t_{m-1})}{t_m - t_{m-1}} \right).
$$

where the supremum is taken over all $t_1 < \cdots t_m$ in $I$, all $m$. If $f$ is $C^1$, then

$$
V(\Delta f) = V(f'),
$$
$$
TV(\Delta f) = TV(f').
$$

**Theorem 6.** *Suppose that $x_0 < \cdots < x_n$ and $q_1$ is continuous. Then $q_1$ is strictly increasing and writing $f(x) = q_2\big(q_1^{-1}(x)\big)$, for $x$ in $q_1(I)$,*

a) $V(\Delta f) \leq V \left( \dfrac{y_1 - y_0}{x_1 - x_0}, \ldots, \dfrac{y_n - y_{n-1}}{x_n - x_{n-1}} \right),$

b) $TV(\Delta f) \le TV \left( \frac{y_1 - y_0}{x_1 - x_0}, \dots, \frac{y_n - y_{n-1}}{x_n - x_{n-1}} \right).$

**Theorem 7.** *Suppose that for some vector* $V$, $V \cdot A_0 \le \dots \le V \cdot A_n$, *and if* $V \cdot A_{i-1} = V \cdot A_i = V \cdot A_{i+1}$, *that* $(A_i - A_{i-1}) \cdot (A_{i+1} - A_i) \ge 0$. *Then*

$$\text{number of inflections in } q \le \text{number of inflections in } A_0 \dots A_n. \qquad (20)$$

This result was proved in [29] for the case of B-splines. It is not true in general without a restriction on the control vertices, even for a cubic polynomial in Bézier form.

**Theorem 8.**

$$\text{length } q \le \text{length } A_0 \dots A_n.$$

Now for any polygonal arc $C_0 \dots C_m$, let $\theta_i$ denote the angle between $C_i - C_{i-1}$ and $C_{i+1} - C_i$, $(i = 1, \dots, m-1)$, where $0 \le \theta_i \le \pi$. We then write $\theta(C_0 \dots C_m) = \sum_{i=1}^{m-1} \theta_i$ and for any curve $q(t), t \in I$, define

$$\theta(q) := \sup \theta(q(t_1) \dots q(t_m)),$$

where the supremum is taken over all $t_1, \dots, t_m$ in $I$, all $m$. If $q$ is continuous with continuous tangent and curvature, then

$$\theta(q) = \int |K| ds,$$

where $K$ denotes the curvature of $q$ and $s$ denotes arc length.

**Theorem 9.**

$$\theta(q) \le \theta(A_0 \dots A_n). \qquad (21)$$

Clearly, some of the above results can be extended to curves in more than two dimensions. More interestingly, we have some analogous results for closed curves, defined as follows. Let $\phi_i (i \in \mathbb{Z})$ be a sequence of real-valued functions with compact support on $\mathbb{R}$ such that for some $T > 0$ and integer $n \ge 1$,

$$\phi_{i+n}(t) = \phi_i(t - T), \qquad i \in Z, \quad t \in \mathbb{R}.$$

We assume that

$$\sum_{i=-\infty}^{\infty} \phi_i(t) = 1, \qquad t \in \mathbb{R},$$

and that for any $m$, $(\phi_{-m}, \dots, \phi_m)$ is TP on $\mathbb{R}$. An example is a sequence of normalized B-splines on a periodic knot sequence.

Now for $A_i = (x_i, y_i) \in \mathbb{R}^2$, $A_{i+n} = A_i, i \in \mathbb{Z}$, we consider the closed curve

$$q(t) = (q_1(t), q_2(t)) = \sum_{i=-\infty}^{\infty} A_i \phi_i(t), \qquad 0 \le t \le T.$$

Then Theorems 5,8 and 9 still hold, where in (21) we replace $\theta(A_0 \dots A_n)$ by $\theta(A_0 \dots A_{n+1})$ and $\theta(q)$ by $\sup \theta(q(t_1) \dots q(t_m) q(t_1) q(t_2))$, where the supremum is taken over all $0 \le t_1 < \dots < t_m < T$, all $m$.

## §4. Other Properties

In this section we consider some shape-preserving properties which do not hold for a general TP sequence, but hold for some particular TP sequences of importance. For our first few results we consider the sequence of B-splines $N_i^k, i = 0, \ldots, n$, on $[a, b]$ for a knot sequence

$$a = t_0 = \cdots = t_{k-1} < t_k \leq \cdots \leq t_n < t_{n+1} = \cdots = t_{n+k} = b,$$

normalized so that $\sum_{i=0}^n N_i^k = 1$. As a special case of (18) we write

$$q(t) = \big(q_1(t), q_2(t)\big) = \sum_{i=0}^n A_i N_i^k(t), \qquad t \in [a, b], \tag{22}$$

where for $i = 0, \ldots, n, A_i = (x_i, y_i) \in \mathbb{R}^2$. For this we can extend Theorem 7 to

**Theorem 10.** *Suppose that for $i = 0, \ldots, n - k + 1$, the points $A_i, \ldots, A_{i+k-1}$ satisfy the conditions of Theorem 7 for some vector $V_i$. Then (20) holds.*

This is proved in [29] and also holds for more general $\beta$- splines. Following [43], in (22) we now choose

$$x_i = \sum_{j=i+1}^{i+k-1} t_j \tag{23}$$

so that, from Marsden's identity [37], we have

$$q_1(t) = t, \qquad a \leq t \leq b.$$

For $0 \leq m \leq n$ and $i = 0, \ldots, n - m$ we let $d_i^m$ denote the divided difference of $(y_i, \ldots, y_{i+m})$ at $(x_i, \ldots, x_{i+m})$ [8], e.g.

$$d_i^1 = \frac{y_{i+1} - y_i}{x_{i+1} - x_i}.$$

Then Theorem 6 can be extended to higher derivatives as

**Theorem 11.** *Take $0 \leq m \leq k - 1$ and suppose that the knots $t_k, \ldots, t_n$ have multiplicity at most $k - m$. Then*

$$V\left(q_2^{(m)}\right) \leq V(d_0^m, \ldots, d_{n-m}^m),$$
$$TV\left(q_2^{(m)}\right) \leq TV(d_0^m, \ldots, d_{n-m}^m).$$

This follows from applying the differentiation recurrence relation for B-splines [8] and using Corollary 1 and Theorem 4.

We now take $n = k - 1$ and, for simplicity, take $a = 0, b = 1$. Then (22),(23) gives the Bézier form

$$(t, p(t)) = \sum_{i=0}^{n} A_i \binom{n}{i} t^i (1-t)^{n-i}, \qquad 0 \le t \le 1, \qquad (24)$$

where

$$A_i = \left( \frac{i}{n}, y_i \right), \qquad i = 0, \ldots, n. \qquad (25)$$

From Theorem 5 we know that $p$ is convex provided $A_0 \ldots A_n$ is convex; i.e., $2p(a) \ge p(a - h) + p(a + h)$ for any $0 \le a - h < a + h \le 1$ provided $2y_i \ge y_{i-1} + y_{i+1}, i = 1, \ldots, n - 1$. We now give a corresponding result for log-convexity.

**Theorem 12.** *In (24), (25), suppose $y_i > 0, i = 0, \ldots, n$, and the polygonal arc with vertices $(i/n, \log y_i), i = 0, \ldots, n$, is convex; i.e., $y_i^2 \ge y_{i-1} y_{i+1}, i = 1, \ldots, n - 1$. Then $\log p$ is convex; i.e., $p(a)^2 \ge p(a - h)p(a + h)$ for any $0 \le a - h \le a + h \le 1$.*

**Proof:** This result was suggested to me by C. A. Micchelli. As I have not seen a proof in the literature, I sketch one here. Multiplying $p(t)$ by $(1 - t) + t$ we have

$$p(t) = \sum_{i=0}^{n+1} y_i^{(n+1)} \binom{n+1}{i} t^i (1-t)^{n+1-i},$$

where

$$y_i^{(n+1)} = \left( \frac{i}{n+1} \right) y_{i-1} + \left( \frac{n+1-i}{n+1} \right) y_i, \qquad i = 0, \ldots, n + 1. \qquad (26)$$

Not surprisingly this is known as *degree raising*. Now for $i = 1, \ldots, n$, we have from (26), after some manipulation,

$$(n+1)^2 \left( (y_i^{(n+1)})^2 - y_{i-1}^{(n+1)} y_{i+1}^{(n+1)} \right) = (y_i - y_{i-1})^2 + (i^2 - 1)(y_{i-1}^2 - y_{i-2} y_i)$$

$$+ \left( (n+1-i)^2 - 1 \right)(y_i^2 - y_{i-1} y_{i+1}) + (i-1)(n-i)(y_{i-1} y_i - y_{i-2} y_{i+1}) \ge 0,$$

since

$$y_i^2 \ge y_{i-1} y_{i+1}, \qquad i = 1, \ldots, n - 1.$$

Repeating this procedure, we can show that for any $m \ge n$,

$$p(t) = \sum_{i=0}^{m} y_i^{(m)} \binom{m}{i} t^i (1-t)^{m-i},$$

where

$$\left(y_i^{(m)}\right)^2 \geq y_{i-1}^{(m)} y_{i+1}^{(m)}, \qquad i = 1,\dots,m-1. \tag{27}$$

Now it is known [21] that the polygonal arc with vertices $\left(i/m, y_i^{(m)}\right), i = 0,\dots,m$, converges uniformly to the curve $(t, p(t)), 0 \leq t \leq 1$ as $m \to \infty$. But from (27), the polygonal arc with vertices $\left(i/m, \log y_i^{(m)}\right), i = 0,\dots,m$, is convex for all $m \geq n$ and thus the curve $(t, \log p(t))$ must be convex; *i.e.*, $\log p$ is convex. ■

To finish this section, we mention a result which has a superficial connection with Theorem 12 in that it also involves the sign of the expressions $y_i^2 - y_{i-1}y_{i+1}$ in terms of Bézier coefficients. It brings us full circle as it is a generalization of Descartes' rule of signs with which we started Section 1. Newton conjectured the result in his Universal Arithmetic of 1707, but did not prove it, this being left to Sylvester who published his proof in the first article of the first volume of the Proceedings of the London Mathematical Society, 1865. Although it was stated for a polynomial of form (1), by making the transformation as in Section 1, it holds also for a polynomial of form (3).

To motivate the result, we note that when $n = 2$ in equation (1) (or (3)), we can easily show that

$$V(p) = \begin{cases} 0, & \text{if } a_1^2 - a_0 a_2 \leq 0, \\ V(a_0, a_1, a_2), & \text{if } a_1^2 - a_0 a_2 > 0. \end{cases}$$

For general $n$, we have

**Theorem 13.** *In equation (1) (or (3)), let $D_i = a_i^2 - a_{i-1}a_{i+1}, i = 1,\dots,n-1$, and $D_0 = D_n = 1$. Then*

$$V(p) \leq V(a_0,\dots,a_n) - |\{j : 0 \leq j \leq n-1, a_j a_{j+1} < 0 \text{ and } D_j D_{j+1} \leq 0\}|.$$

## §5. Surfaces

Unfortunately, there appears to be no general property for surfaces which plays the role that total positivity plays for curves. However, various shape-preserving properties for curves can be extended to particular classes of surfaces. For simplicity, we consider only surfaces in three dimensions.

### 5.1. Polynomials on a Triangle

Our first example for curves was the Bézier representation of a polynomial on an interval, and so we now consider the Bézier representation of a polynomial on a triangle. Let $T$ be a triangle with vertices $P, Q, R$ in $\mathbb{R}^2$. We identify any point $x$ in $\mathbb{R}^2$ with its barycentric coordinates $(u, v, w)$, where

$$x = uP + vQ + wR, \qquad u + v + w = 1. \tag{28}$$

Then any polynomial of degree $n \geq 1$ on $T$ can be expressed in the form, analogous to (3),

$$p(x) = \sum_{\substack{i,j,k \geq 0 \\ i+j+k=n}} a_{ijk} \frac{n!}{i!\,j!\,k!} u^i v^j w^k, \quad u \geq 0, v \geq 0, w \geq 0. \tag{29}$$

Analogous to (24), (25), this can be written as

$$\bigl(x, p(x)\bigr) = \sum_{\substack{i,j,k \geq 0 \\ i+j+k=n}} A_{ijk} \frac{n!}{i!\,j!\,k!} u^i v^j w^k, \quad u, v, w \geq 0, \tag{30}$$

where the Bézier points $A_{ijk}$ in $\mathbb{R}^3$ are given by

$$A_{ijk} = \left( \left( \frac{i}{n}, \frac{j}{n}, \frac{k}{n} \right), a_{ijk} \right), \quad i,j,k \geq 0, \quad i+j+k = n. \tag{31}$$

Whereas for curves of form (24), (25) we defined the Bézier polygon to be the polygonal arc with vertices $A_0, \ldots, A_n$, so for the surface (30), (31) we define the *Bézier net* to be a polyhedral surface with vertices (31). To be precise, let $T_n$ denote the regular triangulation of $T$ formed by lines parallel to the sides of $T$ through the points $(i/n, j/n, k/n), i, j, k \geq 0, i + j + k = n$. Then the Bézier net is the surface $z = \hat{p}(x), x \in T$, where $\hat{p}$ is linear on each element of $T_n$ and satisfies

$$\hat{p}\left( \frac{i}{n}, \frac{j}{n}, \frac{k}{n} \right) = a_{ijk}, \quad i,j,k \geq 0, \quad i+j+k = n.$$

Analogous to some of the consequences of Theorem 1 we have

**Theorem 14.**
a) *If $\hat{p}$ is increasing in a certain direction, then so is $p$.*
b) *If $\hat{p}$ is convex, then so is $p$.*

Part a) is easily proved by differentiating $p$ in the given direction. Part b) was proved in [14], see also [15,16], and extended to higher dimensions in [19,46,3]. In contrast to curves, part b) is not true in the general parametric case [35]; *i.e.*, when the points $A_{ijk}$ in (30) are arbitrary points in $\mathbb{R}^3$.

Noting that for a suitably smooth function $f$ on an interval $[a, b]$ we have $TV(f) = \int_a^b |f'|$, a natural analogue of Theorem 4 for (29) would appear to be

$$V(p) \leq V(\hat{p}), \tag{32}$$

where for any suitable function $f$ on $T$,

$$V(f) := \int_T \left( f_x^2 + f_y^2 \right)^{\frac{1}{2}}. \tag{33}$$

However, it is shown in [27] that (32) need not be true.

A slight modification of the counterexample shows that the analogue of Theorem 8 is also false; *i.e.*, the area of the surface (30) is not always bounded by the surface area of the Bézier net $\hat{p}$. However, we do have the following analog of Theorem 6b. To make the analogy clearer we note that for a suitably smooth function $f$ on $[a, b]$,

$$TV(\Delta f) = \int_a^b |f''|.$$

Now let $S$ be any semi-norm on $\mathbb{R}^3$ and for any suitable function $f$ on $T$, define

$$V_1(f) := \int_T S\left(f_{xx}, f_{xy}, f_{yy}\right). \qquad (34)$$

**Theorem 15.** $V_1(p) \leq V_1(\hat{p})$.

Here the derivatives of $\hat{p}$ must be interpreted as distributions. A specific formula for $V_1(\hat{p})$ is given in [28], where the result is proved. The result was proved earlier in [27] and [17] for the special cases $S(x, y, z) = (x^2 + 2y^2 + z^2)^{\frac{1}{2}}$ and $S(x, y, z) = |x + z|$, respectively. With the latter choice of $S$, the result has been generalized to higher dimensions in [3].

### 5.2. Tensor Products

Suppose that $(\phi_0, \ldots, \phi_m)$ and $(\psi_0, \ldots, \psi_n)$ are sequences of positive functions on the intervals $I$ and $J$ respectively. By a *tensor-product surface* we mean a surface of the form

$$f(x, y) = \sum_{i=0}^m \sum_{j=0}^n a_{ij} \phi_i(x) \psi_j(y), \qquad x \in I, y \in J, \qquad (35)$$

for real coefficients $a_{ij}$. Then certain shape preserving properties of (35) follow easily from corresponding properties of $(\phi_0, \ldots, \phi_m)$ and $(\psi_0, \ldots, \psi_n)$. For example, suppose that $(\phi_0, \ldots, \phi_m)$ satisfies the property that if $(a_0, \ldots, a_m)$ is an increasing sequence, then $\sum a_i \phi_i$ is an increasing function. Then if, in (35), $(a_{0j}, \ldots, a_{mj})$ is an increasing sequence for each $j$, it follows that $f(x, y)$ is an increasing function of $x$ for each $y$. Similarly suppose that $\sum a_j \psi_j$ is a convex function whenever $(a_0, \ldots, a_n)$ is convex; *i.e.*, $2a_j \geq a_{j-1} + a_{j+1}, j = 1, \ldots, n-1$. Then if $(a_{i0}, \ldots, a_{in})$ is convex for each $i$, it follows that $f(x, y)$ is a convex function of $y$ for each $x$.

We now suppose $(\phi_0, \ldots, \phi_m)$ and $(\psi_0, \ldots, \psi_n)$ are Bernstein bases, where for simplicity we assume $I = J = [0, 1]$. Then (34) becomes the tensor-product Bézier form

$$p(x, y) = \sum_{i=0}^m \sum_{j=0}^n a_{ij} \binom{m}{i} x^i (1 - x)^{m-i} \binom{n}{j} y^j (1 - y)^{n-j},$$

for $0 \leq x \leq 1, 0 \leq y \leq 1$.

By analogy with the Bézier net for (29), we define the Bézier net $\hat{p}$ for (36) by

$$\hat{p}(x,y) = a_{ij}(i+1-mx)(j+1-ny) + a_{i+1,j}(mx-i)(j+1-ny)$$
$$+ a_{i,j+1}(i+1-mx)(ny-j) + a_{i+1,j+1}(mx-i)(ny-j),$$

for

$$\frac{i}{m} \leq x \leq \frac{i+1}{m}, \quad \frac{j}{n} \leq y \leq \frac{j+1}{n}, \quad 0 \leq i \leq m-1, \quad 0 \leq j \leq n-1.$$

Thus, $\hat{p}$ is bilinear on each square of a regular subdivision of $[0,1] \times [0,1]$ and

$$\hat{p}\left(\frac{i}{m}, \frac{j}{n}\right) = a_{ij}, \quad 0 \leq i \leq m-1, \quad 0 \leq j \leq n-1.$$

**Theorem 16.**

a) *If $\hat{p}$ is convex, then so is $p$.*

b) *Defining $V_1(f) = \int_0^1 \int_0^1 \left(f_{xx}^2 + 2f_{xy}^2 + f_{yy}^2\right) dxdy$, we have*

$$V_1(p) \leq V_1(\hat{p}).$$

The result is proved in [13] where a specific formula is given for $V_1(\hat{p})$.

### 5.3. Box Splines

For spline curves a very useful TP basis is provided by B-splines. For spline surfaces there are several challengers for the role analogous to B-splines, one of which is the box spline. On a rectangular mesh the box spline reduces to a tensor product B-spline and tensor products have already been mentioned. We now consider the next simplest example: a three-direction mesh; *i.e.*, a regular triangulation $T$ of $\mathbb{R}^2$ formed by sets of parallel lines in three different directions. Without loss of generality we can assume $T$ is formed by the lines

$$x = i, \quad y = i, \quad y - x = i, \quad i \in \mathbb{Z}.$$

We now let $B$ denote a box spline on $T$ which does not reduce to a tensor product B-spline. For details the reader should consult the literature on box splines; e.g., [10,18]. Here we simply mention that $B$ has compact support and its restriction to any element of $T$ is a polynomial. We now consider a surface of the form

$$f(x,y) = \sum_{i=-\infty}^{\infty} \sum_{j=-\infty}^{\infty} a_{ij} B(x-i, y-j) \tag{37}$$

for real coefficients $a_{ij}$. By analogy with the control polygon for (22), (23) and the Bézier nets for (29) and for (36), we define the *control net* $\hat{f}$ for (37) as the function on $\mathbb{R}^2$ which is linear on each element of $T$ and satisfies

$$\hat{f}(i,j) = a_{ij}, \quad i,j \in \mathbb{Z}.$$

Thus, the control net is a polyhedral surface with vertices $(i, j, a_{ij})$ for $i, j \in \mathbb{Z}$. Recalling definitions (33) and (34), for any suitable function $f$ on $\mathbb{R}^2$ we define

$$V(f) := \int_{\mathbb{R}^2} \left(f_x^2 + f_y^2\right)^{\frac{1}{2}},$$

$$V_1(f) := \int_{\mathbb{R}^2} S\left(f_{xx}, f_{xy}, f_{yy}\right),$$

where $S$ is any semi-norm on $\mathbb{R}^3$.

**Theorem 17.**

a) If $\hat{f}$ is increasing in a certain direction, then so is $f$.

b) If $\hat{f}$ is convex, then so is $f$.

c) $V(f) \le V(\hat{f})$.

d) $V_1(f) \le V_1(\hat{f})$.

This is proved in [26] and [28]. Part b) is proved independently in [19] where it is also extended to higher dimensions.

In addition to box splines, there are other locally supported multivariate spline functions for which analogous results could be investigated. The only results we know of concern half-box splines [23,38,39] for which properties analogous to some of those in Theorem 17 are derived in [26,28].

## 5.4. Conclusion

The study of shape-preserving representations for surfaces appears to be still in its infancy. It is to be hoped that many other results can be proved, even for simple cases such as the Bézier representation of a polynomial on a triangle or a rectangle. As such results would be of practical importance as well as of theoretical interest, we hope that this brief account will stimulate further interest in this area.

## References

1. Ball, A. A., CONSURF part one: introduction to conic lifting tile, Comput. Aided Design **6** (1974), 243–249.

2. Barsky, B. A., The beta-spline: a local representation based on shape parameters and fundamental geometric measures, Ph.D. dissertation, University of Utah, 1981.

3. Beśka, M., Convexity and variation diminishing property of multidimensional Bernstein polynomials, Ph.D. dissertation, University of Gdańsk, 1988.

4. Boehm, W., Curvature continuous curves and surfaces, Comput. Aided Geom. Design **2** (1985), 313–323.

5. Boehm, W., Smooth curves and surfaces, in *Geometric Modeling, Applications and New Trends*, G. Farin (ed.), SIAM, Philadelphia, 1987, 175–184.

6. Boehm, W., Rational geometric splines, Comput. Aided Geom. Design **4** (1987), 67–77.

7. Bojanov, B., B-splines with Birkhoff knots, C. R. Acad. Bulgare Sci. **40**, (1987), 11–14.

8. de Boor, C., Splines as linear combinations of B-splines. A survey, in *Approximation Theory II*, G. G. Lorentz, C. K. Chui, and L. L. Schumaker (eds.), Academic Press, New York, 1976, 1–47.

9. de Boor, C., Total positivity of the spline collocation matrix, Indiana Univ. Math. J. **25** (1976), 541–551.

10. de Boor, C. and K. Höllig, B-splines from parallelepipeds, J. Analyse Math. **42** (1982/3), 99–115.

11. de Boor, C. and A. Pinkus, The approximation of a totally positive band matrix by a strictly banded totally positive one, Linear Algebra Appl. **42** (1982), 81–98.

12. de Casteljau, F., Outillage méthodes calcul, André Citroën Automobiles SA, Paris, 1959.

13. Cavaretta, A. S. and A. Sharma, Variation diminishing properties and convexity for the tensor product Bernstein operator, to appear.

14. Chang, G. and P. J. Davis, The convexity of Bernstein polynomials over triangles, J. Approx. Theory **40** (1984), 11–28.

15. Chang, G. and Y. Feng, An improved condition for the convexity of Bernstein-Bézier surfaces over triangles, Comput. Aided Geom. Design **1** (1984), 279–283.

16. Chang, G. and Y. Feng, A new proof for convexity of Bernstein polynomials over triangles, Chinese Journal of Mathematics, Series B, to appear.

17. Chang, G. and J. Hoschek, Convexity and variation diminishing property of Bernstein polynomials over triangles, in *Multivariate Approximation Theory III*, W. Schempp and K. Zeller (eds.), Birkhäuser Verlag, Basel, 1985, 61–70.

18. Dahmen, W. and C. A. Micchelli, Recent progress in multivariate splines, in *Approximation Theory IV*, C. K. Chui, L. L. Schumaker and J. Ward (eds.), Academic Press, New York, 1983, 27–121.

19. Dahmen, W. and C. A. Micchelli, Convexity of multivariate Bernstein polynomials and box spline surfaces, Research Report 11176, T. J. Watson Research Center, 1985.

20. Dyn, N. and C. A. Micchelli, Piecewise polynomial spaces and geometric continuity of curves, Research Report 11390, T. J. Watson Research Center, 1985.

21. Farin, G., Subsplines über Dreiecken, Ph.D. dissertation, Technische Universität Braunschweig, 1979.

22. Farin, G., Visually $C^2$ cubic splines, Comput. Aided Design **14** (1982), 137–139.

23. Frederickson, P. O., Generalized triangular splines, Mathematics Report 7-71, Lakehead University, 1971.

24. Goldman, R. N., Polya's urn model and computer aided geometric design, SIAM J. Algebraic Discrete Methods **6** (1985), 1–28.

25. Goodman, T. N. T., Properties of $\beta$-splines, J. Approx. Theory **44** (1985), 132–153.

26. Goodman, T. N. T., Shape preserving approximation by splines, in *Multivariate Approximation Theory III*, W. Schempp and K. Zeller (eds.), Birkhauser Verlag, Basel, 1985, 61–70.

27. Goodman, T. N. T., Variation diminishing properties of Bernstein polynomials on triangles, J. Approx. Theory **50** (1987), 111–126.

28. Goodman, T. N. T., Further variation diminishing properties of Bernstein polynomials on triangles, Constr. Approx. **3** (1987), 297–305.

29. Goodman, T. N. T., Inflections on curves in two and three dimensions, University of Dundee report AA/881, 1988.

30. Goodman, T. N. T. and S. L. Lee, Interpolatory and variation-diminishing properties of generalized B-splines, Proc. Royal Soc. Edinburgh **96A** (1984), 249–259.

31. Goodman, T. N. T. and S. L. Lee, B-splines on the circle and trigonometric B-splines, in *Approximation Theory and Spline Functions*, S. P. Singh, J. H. W. Burry and B. Watson (eds.), Reidel, Dordricht, 1984, 297–325.

32. Goodman, T. N. T. and C. A. Micchelli, Corner cutting algorithms for the Bézier representation of free form curves, Linear Algebra Appl. **99** (1988), 225–258.

33. Goodman, T. N. T. and H. B. Said, Shape preserving properties of the generalized Ball basis, University Sains Malaysia report, Penang, 1988.

34. Karlin, S., *Total Positivity Vol.1*, Stanford University Press, Stanford, 1968.

35. Kuang, Z. and G. Chang, Remarks on convexity for parametric Bézier triangular patches, International Centre for Theoretical Physics report IC/85/171, Trieste, 1985.

36. Lane, J. M. and R. F. Riesenfeld, A geometric proof of the variation diminishing property of B-spline approximation, J. Approx. Theory **37** (1983), 1–4.

37. Marsden, M. J., An identity for spline functions with applications to variation diminishing spline approximation, J. Approx. Theory **3** (1970), 7–49.

38. Prautzsch, H., Unterteilungsalgorithmen für multivariate Splines-ein geometrischer Zugang, Ph.D. dissertation, Technische Universität Braunschweig, 1984.

39. Sabin, M. A., The use of piecewise forms for the numerical representation of shape, Ph.D. dissertation, Hungarian Academy of Science, Budapest, 1977.

40. Said, H. B., Recursive algorithm for the generalized Ball curve, to appear.

41. Schoenberg, I. J., On variation diminishing approximation methods, in *On Numerical Approximation*, R. E. Langer (ed.), University of Wisconsin Press, Madison, 1959, 249–274.

42. Schoenberg, I. J., On trigonometric spline interpolation, J. Math. Mech **13** (1964), 795–825.
43. Schoenberg, I. J., On spline functions, *Inequalities*, O. Shisha (ed.), Academic Press, New York, 1967, 255–291.
44. Schumaker, L. L., *Spline Functions: Basic Theory*, Wiley, New York, 1981.
45. Tiller, W., Rational B-splines for curve and surface representation, IEEE Comp. Graph. Appl. **3** (1983), 61–69.
46. Zhou, J., On convexity of Bernstein-Bézier surface over a tetrahedroid, J. of University of Science and Technology of China, to appear.

T. N. T. Goodman
Department of Mathematics and Computer Science
The University of Dundee
Dundee, DD1 4HN
SCOTLAND

EMAIL: t.goodman@ uk.ac.dundee (janet)

# Geometric Continuity

## John A. Gregory

**Abstract.** Geometric continuity concepts for parametric curves and surfaces are reviewed. Two different concepts for curve continuity are introduced which are called here "arc length" and "Frenet frame" continuity. The first of these is based on the idea of reparameterization, and this approach is used in the development of geometric continuity for surfaces.

## §1. Introduction

The purpose of this paper is to present a tutorial view of the concepts of *geometric continuity* within the subject of *computer-aided geometric design (CAGD)*. It is not intended to be an exhaustive survey but rather an introduction to the subject. However, an attempt has been made to collect together some of the current relevant material in the list of references [1-69]. A complementary paper by Boehm [12] gives a more historical perspective of this topic.

*Geometric* (sometimes called *visual*) *continuity* is concerned with how parametric (*i.e.*, free-form or sculptured) curves and surfaces should be pieced together in a smooth way. This concern might surprise the differential geometer, who is used to dealing with the concept of a $C^k$ continuous regular parametric curve or surface as one of the basic facts of life. However, our tools for the construction of parametric curves and surfaces in CAGD have their origins in the subject of approximation of real valued functions, for example in the use of Bernstein-Bézier and $B$-spline representations. The marriage between the theory of approximation of real functions and of the differential geometry of parametric functions is not yet complete, particularly in the area of piecewise defined surface patch representation.

For curves, there are now two distinct concepts of geometric continuity, and this has led to some confusion of terminology in the literature. The first we call geometric continuity $GC^k$ with respect to *arc length*. It is based on the existence of a $C^k$ (regular) reparameterization of the curve which is equivalent to

Mathematical Methods in Computer Aided Geometric Design
Tom Lyche and Larry L. Schumaker (eds.), pp. 353–371.
Copyright © 1989 by Academic Press, Boston.
ISBN 0-12-460515-X.

$C^k$ continuity with respect to the particular choice of arc length reparameterization. This accords with the definition of a $C^k$ curve in differential geometry and its use is now well established in CAGD. The second is a more recent addition to the subject, and is called here geometric continuity with respect to the *Frenet frame*, since it is based on the $C^0$ continuity of the Frenet frame and the curvatures of the curve. For this latter concept the definition is dependent on $n$, where $\mathbb{R}^n$ is the space in which the curve is defined. Thus, in the initial presentation of the material on geometric continuity it is easier to consider the case of general $n$, rather than taking the cases $n = 2$ or $n = 3$ of specific interest to CAGD.

For surfaces in $\mathbb{R}^3$ there is the one concept of geometric continuity. This is that two surface patches have a $GC^k$ join if they admit (locally) a reparameterization in which the composite surface is $C^k$. In the case of a $GC^1$ join this simply means that the surface patches join with position and tangent plane continuity. In the general case we shall see that conditions for a $GC^k$ join can be derived which are similar to those of $GC^k$ arc length continuity for curves. This is not surprising, since both share the common idea of reparameterization.

## §2. Geometric Arc Length Continuity for Curves

First let us recall some simple concepts for parametric curves in $\mathbb{R}^n$. Let $\mathbf{p} : [a, b] \to \mathbb{R}^n$ be a mapping of the real interval $[a, b]$ into $\mathbb{R}^n$. Then this is a *regular parametric representation of class $C^k$, $k \geq 1$*, if

$$\mathbf{p}^{(1)}(t) \neq \mathbf{0} \quad \forall \quad t \in [a, b], \tag{2.1}$$

$$\mathbf{p} \in C^k[a, b], \tag{2.2}$$

where by (2.2), we mean that each component of $\mathbf{p}$ is $k$ times continuously differentiable on $[a, b]$. Given a mapping $\phi : [\widehat{a}, \widehat{b}] \to [a, b], \phi \in C^k[\widehat{a}, \widehat{b}]$, which is such that $\phi^{(1)}(\tau) \neq 0$ for all $\tau \in [\widehat{a}, \widehat{b}]$, then the composite map

$$\widehat{\mathbf{p}}(\tau) := \mathbf{p}(\varphi(\tau)) : [\widehat{a}, \widehat{b}] \to \mathbb{R}^n \tag{2.3}$$

is called an *allowable reparameterization* of the regular curve, see Figure 1. An allowable reparameterization for which $\phi^{(1)} > 0$ ($\phi$ is monotonic increasing) is said to be *orientation preserving*. In particular, with

$$s := \varphi(t) := \int_{t_0}^{t} \left\| \mathbf{p}^{(1)}(t) \right\| dt \tag{2.4}$$

defining the arc length of the curve from a fixed point $t_0$, then

$$\widehat{\mathbf{p}}(s) := \mathbf{p}(\varphi^{-1}(s)) \tag{2.5}$$

defines an *arc length reparameterization* of the curve.

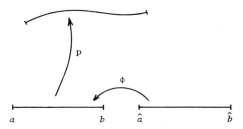

**Figure 1.** Pictorial representation of a reparameterization.

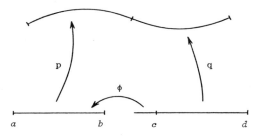

**Figure 2.** Reparameterization for a $C^k$ curve segment join.

We are now in a position to define and give appropriate conditions for the $GC^k$ (arc length) join of two curve segments. For this we follow the reparameterization approach of Barsky and DeRose [6] and Goodman [31]. In fact, the conditions for a $GC^k$ join are already known from the theory of contact of curves in differential geometry, and are given for $k = 1, \ldots, 6$ in Geise [30].

**Definition 2.1.** *Let* $\mathbf{p} : [a, b] \rightarrow \mathbb{R}^n$ *and* $\mathbf{q} : [c, d] \rightarrow \mathbb{R}^n$ *be two regular parametric representations of class* $C^k$. *Then* $\mathbf{p}$ *and* $\mathbf{q}$ *join with geometric (arc length) continuity* $GC^k$, *at* $b$ *and* $c$ *respectively, if there exists a* $C^k$ *mapping* $\varphi : \mathbb{R} \rightarrow \mathbb{R}$, *defined in a neighbourhood of* $c$, *which is such that*

$$\varphi(c) = b \text{ and } \varphi^{(1)}(c) > 0, \tag{2.6}$$

$$\frac{d^i}{dt^i}\mathbf{q}(t) \mid_{t=c} = \frac{d^i}{dt^i}\mathbf{p}(\varphi(t)) \mid_{t=c}, \qquad i = 0, \ldots, k. \tag{2.7}$$

The definition implies that $\mathbf{p}(\varphi(t))$, $t \leq c$, and $\mathbf{q}(t)$, $t > c$, defines a regular parametric representation of class $C^k$ in a neighbourhood of $c$, where $\mathbf{p}(\varphi(t))$ is an allowable reparameterization of the curve which is orientation preserving, see Figure 2. The particular choice of arc length parameterization is not required in the definition, since a curve is $C^k$ with respect to an arc length parameterization, $k \geq 1$, if and only if it has a regular parametric representation of class $C^k$.

The right hand sides of (2.7) can be expanded by the chain and product rules to give the equivalent conditions

$$\mathbf{q}^{(i)}(c) = \sum_{j=0}^{i} a_{ij}\mathbf{p}^{(j)}(b), \qquad i = 0, \ldots, k, \tag{2.8}$$

where (Goodman [31])

$$a_{i0} = \delta_{i0}, i = 0, \ldots, k,$$

$$a_{ij} = \sum_{i_1 + \cdots + i_j = i} \begin{bmatrix} i \\ i_1 \cdots i_j \end{bmatrix} \beta_{i_1} \ldots \beta_{i_j}, \qquad 1 \le j \le i \le k. \tag{2.9}$$

Here,

$$\beta_i = \varphi^{(i)}(c), \qquad i = 1, \ldots, k \tag{2.10}$$

and the summation in (2.9) is over positive integers, where if $\{i_1, \ldots, i_j\}$ comprises $r$ distinct elements with multiplicities $m_1, \ldots, m_r$, then

$$\begin{bmatrix} i \\ i_1 \cdots i_j \end{bmatrix} = \frac{i!}{i_1! \cdots i_j! m_1! \cdots m_r!}. \tag{2.11}$$

In particular, it follows that

$$a_{ii} = (\beta_1)^i, \tag{2.12}$$

where

$$\beta_1 = \varphi^{(1)}(c) > 0. \tag{2.13}$$

The $GC^k$ (arc length) continuity conditions (2.8) can be written in matrix form as

$$\left[ \mathbf{q}(c), \mathbf{q}^{(1)}(c), \ldots, \mathbf{q}^{(k)}(c) \right]^T = A \left[ \mathbf{p}(b), \mathbf{p}^{(1)}(b), \ldots, \mathbf{p}^{(k)}(b) \right]^T, \tag{2.14}$$

where the $(k+1) \times (k+1)$ lower triangular matrix $A = [a_{ij}]$ is called the *connection matrix* of the transformation. For example, the $GC^3$ connection matrix given by the above theory takes the form

$$A = \begin{bmatrix} 1 & & & \\ 0 & \beta_1 & & \\ 0 & \beta_2 & \beta_1^2 & \\ 0 & \beta_3 & 3\beta_1\beta_2 & \beta_1^3 \end{bmatrix}. \tag{2.15}$$

The importance of the $GC^k$ conditions (2.8) or (2.14) is that they are both necessary and sufficient for a $GC^k$ join since we have:

**Proposition 2.2.** *The curves* $\mathbf{p}$ *and* $\mathbf{q}$ *of Definition 2.1 join with geometric (arc length) continuity* $GC^k$ *if and only if there exist constants* $\beta_1 > 0$ *and* $\beta_2, \ldots, \beta_k$ *such that the constraints (2.8) hold, where the* $a_{ij}$ *satisfy (2.9).*

**Proof:** The necessity of this proposition has already been demonstrated. To prove sufficiency, a $C^k$ map $\varphi$ must be constructed such that (2.6) and (2.10) hold. This, however, is achieved trivially, for example by the Taylor interpolant

$$\varphi(t) := b + \sum_{j=1}^{k} \frac{\beta_j(t-c)^j}{j!}. \qquad \blacksquare \tag{2.16}$$

## §3. Differential Geometry of Curves

In Section 4 the concept of geometric continuity with respect to the Frenet frame will be discussed. For this it is necessary to review some basic concepts from differential geometry. We use the approach of Dyn and Micchelli [22], following that of Spivak [66], where the Frenet frame is introduced through a Gram-Schmidt orthogonalization process; see also Boehm [13]. This approach is not readily accessible in current texts, and thus it seems worthwhile to review it here, since it provides a concise and self-contained approach to the *Frenet frame* and *curvatures* of a curve in $\mathbb{R}^n$.

Let $\mathbf{p} : [a, b] \to \mathbb{R}^n$ be a regular parametric representation of class $C^n$ and suppose that the $n-1$ derivatives $\{\mathbf{p}^{(i)}(t)\}_{i=1}^{n-1}$ are linearly independent on $[a, b]$. The *Frenet frame* of the curve (see Figure 3) is the set of orthonormal vectors $\{\mathbf{v}_i(t)\}_{i=1}^n$ defined by the following construction:

(i) For $i = 1, ..., n-1$ the orthonormal system is created by the *Gram-Schmidt process*:

$$\mathbf{v}_i = \frac{\mathbf{u}_i}{\|\mathbf{u}_i\|}, \qquad \text{where} \qquad \mathbf{u}_i = \mathbf{p}^{(i)} - \sum_{j=1}^{i-1} (\mathbf{p}^{(i)}, \mathbf{v}_j)\mathbf{v}_j,$$

(ii) Given $\{\mathbf{v}_i\}_{i=1}^{n-1}$, $\mathbf{v}_n \in \mathbb{R}^n$ is added (uniquely) such that $\{\mathbf{v}_i\}_{i=1}^n$ is a *right handed* orthonormal system; *i.e.*, such that $\det \mathbf{v}_1, \ldots, \mathbf{v}_n = 1$.

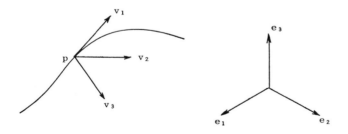

**Figure 3.** The Frenet frame in $\mathbb{R}^3$ relative to $\mathbf{p}$.

**Remark 3.1.** It follows that

$$\left[\mathbf{p}^{(1)}(t), \ldots, \mathbf{p}^{(n)}(t)\right]^T = L\left[\mathbf{v}_1(t), \ldots, \mathbf{v}_n(t)\right]^T, \tag{3.1}$$

where $L = [\ell_{ij}(t)]$ is a lower triangular matrix. In particular,

$$\ell_{ii}(t) = \|\mathbf{u}_i(t)\| > 0, \qquad i = 1, \ldots, n-1, \tag{3.2}$$

and

$$\ell_{nn}(t) = \pm\|\mathbf{u}_n(t)\|. \tag{3.3}$$

To obtain (3.3), the Gram-Schmidt process in (i) has been attempted for $i = n$, giving $\ell_{nn}(t) = 0$ if $\mathbf{p}^{(n)}(t) \in \text{span}\{\mathbf{p}^{(i)}(t)\}_{i=1}^{n-1}$ and $\ell_{nn}(t) \neq 0$ if $\{\mathbf{p}^{(i)}(t)\}_{i=1}^{n}$ are linearly independent. In this latter case, the sign in the normalization process, and hence the sign in (3.3), is chosen to give a right handed system. The initial element

$$\mathbf{v}_1(t) = \frac{\mathbf{p}^{(1)}(t)}{\ell_{11}(t)}, \qquad \ell_{11}(t) = \|\mathbf{p}^{(1)}(t)\| \tag{3.4}$$

is a unit tangent vector to the curve.

The *Frenet equations* are a system of differential equations satisfied by the Frenet frame which can be developed as follows. Since

$$\mathbf{v}_i^{(1)} \in \text{span} \left\{\mathbf{p}^{(j+1)}\right\}_{j=1}^{i} \subset \text{span} \{\mathbf{v}_j\}_{j=1}^{i+1}, \qquad i < n,$$

it follows that

$$\left[\mathbf{v}_1^{(1)}(t), \ldots, \mathbf{v}_n^{(1)}(t)\right]^T = K\left[\mathbf{v}_1(t), \ldots, \mathbf{v}_n(t)\right]^T, \tag{3.5}$$

where $K = [k_{ij}(t)]$ is a lower Hessenberg matrix. From (3.5), and the orthonormality of the frame, we have

$$k_{ij}(t) = \left(\mathbf{v}_i^{(1)}(t), \mathbf{v}_j(t)\right).$$

Also, differentiating the orthonormality conditions $(\mathbf{v}_i, \mathbf{v}_j) = \delta_{ij}$ gives

$$k_{ij}(t) + k_{ji}(t) = 0.$$

Thus $K$ is a lower Hessenberg, skew-symmetric matrix. Hence it is tri-diagonal and skew-symmetric.

The matrix $K$ of the Frenet equations (3.5) can now be written as

$$K = \|\mathbf{p}^{(1)}(t)\| \begin{bmatrix} 0 & \kappa_1(t) & & & & \\ -\kappa_1(t) & 0 & \kappa_2(t) & & & \\ & \ddots & \ddots & & \ddots & \\ & & -\kappa_{n-2}(t) & & 0 & \kappa_{n-1}(t) \\ & & & -\kappa_{n-1}(t) & & 0 \end{bmatrix}, \tag{3.6}$$

where the quantities

$$\kappa_i(t) = \frac{k_{i,i+1}(t)}{\|\mathbf{p}^{(1)}(t)\|}, \qquad i = 1, \ldots, n-1, \tag{3.7}$$

are invariant under reparameterization and are called the curvatures of the curve. In particular, in $\mathbb{R}^2$, $\kappa_1$ is the curvature. In $\mathbb{R}^3$, $\kappa_1$ is the curvature and $\kappa_2$ (the second curvature) is the torsion. Familiar geometrical interpretations of these quantities are provided by the Frenet equations, under the particular choice of arc length parameterization when $\|\mathbf{p}^{(1)}(t)\| = 1$; *e.g.*, see Hsiung [52].

Differentiating the equation for $\mathbf{p}^{(i)}(t)$ in (3.1), substituting for $\mathbf{v}_i^{(1)}(t)$ from the Frenet equations (3.5), and comparing the result with the equation for $\mathbf{p}^{(i+1)}(t)$ in (3.1), gives

$$\kappa_i(t) = \frac{\ell_{i+1,i+1}(t)}{(\ell_{ii}(t), \ell_{11}(t))}, \qquad \ell_{11}(t) = \|\mathbf{p}^{(1)}(t)\| \tag{3.8}$$

as an explicit expression for the curvatures. More familiar expressions for the curvatures in terms of $\{\mathbf{p}^{(i)}(t)\}_{i=1}^n$ can then be obtained from (3.1); *e.g.*, by observing that

$$L\,L^T = \left[\left(\mathbf{p}^{(i)}, \mathbf{p}^{(j)}\right)\right].$$

It should be noted that our definition of the Frenet frame requires that $\{\mathbf{p}^{(i)}(t)\}_{i=1}^{n-1}$ be linearly independent and hence $\kappa_i(t) > 0, i = 1, \ldots, n-2$. However, the $n-1^{\text{st}}$ curvature $\kappa_{n-1}(t)$ is zero when $\mathbf{p}^{(n)}(t) \in \text{span}\{\mathbf{p}^{(i)}(t)\}_{i=1}^{n-1}$. Otherwise the sign of $\kappa_{n-1}(t)$ is determined by the requirement that the Frenet frame is a right handed system. Thus, in $\mathbb{R}^2$ the curvature $\kappa_1$ is *signed*. In $\mathbb{R}^3$ the curvature $\kappa_1$ is positive and the torsion $\kappa_2$ is *signed*. The definition also gives us the freedom to view a plane curve as a special case of a space curve in $\mathbb{R}^3$ with zero torsion.

## §4. Geometric Frenet Frame Continuity for Curves

The second notion of geometric continuity is suggested by the work of Hagen [41] in $\mathbb{R}^3$ as generalized to $\mathbb{R}^n$ by Dyn and Micchelli [22].

**Definition 4.1.** *Let* $\mathbf{p} : [a, b] \to \mathbb{R}^n$ *and* $\mathbf{q} : [c, d] \to \mathbb{R}^n$ *be two regular parametric representations of class* $C^n$ *which are such that their first* $n - 1$ *derivatives are linearly independent. Then* $\mathbf{p}$ *and* $\mathbf{q}$ *join with geometric (Frenet frame) continuity at* $b$ *and* $c$ *respectively, if* $\mathbf{q}(c) = \mathbf{p}(b)$, *and if the Frenet frame and* $n - 1$ *curvatures of the composite curve are continuous.*

Following Dyn and Michelli, we now have

**Proposition 4.2.** *The curves* $\mathbf{p}$ *and* $\mathbf{q}$ *of Definition 4.1 join with geometric (Frenet frame) continuity if and only if*

$$\left[\mathbf{q}(c), \mathbf{q}^{(1)}(c), \ldots, \mathbf{q}^{(n)}(c)\right]^T = A\left[\mathbf{p}(b), \mathbf{p}^{(1)}(b), \ldots, \mathbf{p}^{(n)}(b)\right]^T, \tag{4.1}$$

*where* $A = [a_{ij}]$ *is an* $(n + 1) \times (n + 1)$ *lower triangular matrix such that (cf. (2.9))*

$$\begin{aligned} a_{i0} &= \delta_{i0}, \quad i = 0, \ldots, n, \\ a_{ii} &= (a_{11})^i, \quad i = 2, \ldots, n, \text{ where } a_{11} > 0, \end{aligned} \tag{4.2}$$

*(except that for zero $n - 1^{st}$ curvatures any $a_{nn}$ is allowed). Thus in $\mathbb{R}^n$ the geometric continuous connection matrix takes the form*

$$A = \begin{bmatrix} 1 & & & \\ 0 & a_{11} & & \\ 0 & a_{21} & (a_{11})^2 & \\ 0 & a_{31} & a_{32} & (a_{11})^3 \end{bmatrix}. \tag{4.3}$$

**Proof:** Let

$$\left[\mathbf{p}^{(1)}(b), \ldots, \mathbf{p}^{(n)}(b)\right]^T = L\left[\mathbf{v}_1(b), \ldots, \mathbf{v}_n(b)\right]^T$$
$$\left[\mathbf{q}^{(1)}(c), \ldots, \mathbf{q}^{(n)}(c)\right]^T = M\left[\mathbf{w}_1(c), \ldots, \mathbf{w}_n(c)\right]^T \tag{4.4}$$

define the transformation equations for the Frenet frames $\{\mathbf{v}_i(b)\}_{i=1}^n$ and $\{\mathbf{w}_i(c)\}_{i=1}^n$ of $\mathbf{p}$ and $\mathbf{q}$ at $b$ and $c$ respectively, where $L$ and $M$ are lower triangular matrices (see Remark 3.1). Suppose that the geometrical constraint equation (4.1) holds. Then $\mathbf{q}^{(1)}(c) = a_{11}\mathbf{p}^{(1)}(b)$, $a_{11} > 0$, and in general $\text{span}\{\mathbf{q}^{(j)}(c)\}_{j=1}^i = \text{span}\{\mathbf{p}^{(j)}(b)\}_{j=1}^i$, $i = 1, \ldots, n - 1$. This gives identical Frenet frames in the Gram-Schmidt process; *i.e.*, $w_i(c) = v_i(b)$, $i = 1, \ldots, n$. Substituting (4.4) in (4.1) now gives

$$m_{ii}(c) = a_{ii}\ell_{ii}(b). \tag{4.5}$$

Thus, with $a_{ii} = (a_{11})^i$, the curvatures given by (3.8) are identical. (Note any $a_{nn}$ is allowed for zero $n - 1^{st}$ curvature.) Conversely, suppose the composite curve is geometrically (Frenet frame) continuous. Then $\mathbf{w}_i(c) = \mathbf{v}_i(b), i = 1, \ldots, n$, in (4.4) and $\mathbf{q}(c) = \mathbf{p}(b)$ implies that (4.1) holds with $a_{i0} = \delta_{i0}, i = 0, \ldots, n$ and $a_{11} > 0$. (Note this argument also applies in the case $m_{nn}(c) = \ell_{nn}(c) = 0$ when $L$ and $M$ are singular, since then $\mathbf{p}^{(n)}(b) \in \text{span}\{\mathbf{p}^{(i)}(b)\}_{i=1}^{n-1}$ and $\mathbf{q}^{(n)}(c) \in \text{span}\{\mathbf{q}^{(i)}(c)\}_{i=1}^{n-1}$.) Finally (4.5), and the requirement that the curvatures given by (3.8) be identical at $b$ and $c$, respectively, give

$$a_{i+1,i+1} = a_{ii}a_{11}, \qquad i = 1, \ldots, n - 1,$$

as required (except that for zero $n - 1^{st}$ curvature any $a_{nn}$ is allowed). ■

## A Comparison of Geometric Continuities

We can observe from (2.14) and (4.1) that both the arc length and Frenet frame geometric continuity conditions can be represented by lower triangular matrix transformations. The Frenet frame connection matrix for $n > 2$ has a more general form that the $GC^n$ arc length connection matrix (compare (2.1) with (4.2) and, in particular, (2.15) with (4.3)). The Frenet frame condition is, however, dependent on the dimension $n$ of $\mathbb{R}^n$ whilst, with the arc length definition, $GC^k, k \neq n$, is allowed. We now summarize some of the differences:

(i) In $\mathbb{R}^n, GC^k$ arc length $k \neq n$ is allowed, whilst $GC$ Frenet frame is dependent on $n$.

(ii) In $\mathbb{R}^n, GC^n$ arc length implies $GC$ Frenet frame. The distinction is that $\kappa_i \in C^{n-i-1}$ for arc length continuity, whilst only $\kappa_i \in C^0$ is required for the Frenet frame condition.

(iii) In $\mathbb{R}^2, GC^2$ arc length and $GC$ Frenet frame are identical. $GC^k$ arc length, $k \neq 2$, is allowed and implies that locally (in the neighborhood of an arc length parameter value) the curve is a $C^k$ function with respect to an appropriately chosen Cartesian coordinate system.

(iv) In $\mathbb{R}^3, GC^3$ arc length implies $GC$ Frenet frame. $GC^2$ arc length does not imply $GC$ Frenet frame although the curvature $\kappa_1$ and the Frenet frame are continuous. It is the torsion $\kappa_2$ which will, in general, be discontinuous. However, a $CG^2$ arc length planar curve in $\mathbb{R}^3$ is Frenet frame continuous (it has zero torsion $\kappa_2$).

In a particular application, Barsky and Goldman observe, in these proceedings, that arc length continuity is preserved under certain multiplication and division operations on two composite curves (each having identical $GC^k$ joins). However, Frenet frame continuity is not preserved under these operations. It should also be observed that a linear combination of two composite curves, which have different geometric continuous joins but the same parameter domains, does not, in general, result in a geometric continuous curve (of the same order). This is due to the constraint (2.12) or (4.2) on the diagonal terms of the connection matrices. This constraint is not preserved by the linear combination (except when the diagonal terms of the two connection matrices are identical).

So, which of the two definitions is most appropriate? In $\mathbb{R}^2$ there is no problem since the arc length definition covers all possibilities. In $\mathbb{R}^3$ the situation is less clear, and is open to debate.

Finally, it should be noted that our discussion has assumed non-singular curves. Thus for arc length continuity we have assumed regular curves $\mathbf{p}$, for which $\mathbf{p}^{(1)}(t) \neq 0$. For Frenet frame continuity we have assumed

$$\{\mathbf{p}^{(1)}(t), \ldots, \mathbf{p}^{(n-1)}(t)\}$$

are linearly independent. Connection points at which these conditions do not hold are *singular points* and require special investigation.

## §5. Geometric Continuity for Surfaces

We now use the reparameterization approach of Section 2 to define a $GC^k$ geometrically continuous surface patch complex appropriate for CAGD. This will accord with the idea of a $C^k$ surface in differential topology built on manifold theoretic terms. This approach has been recognized by a number of authors, see for example DeRose [19] and Höllig [51]. Here we follow the exposition of Hahn [45] (see also Gregory and Hahn [39]).

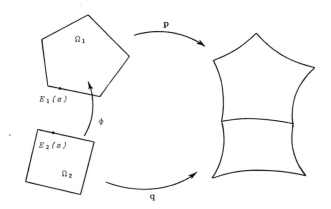

**Figure 4.** Reparameterization for a $C^k$ surface patch join.

A $C^k$ patch, $k \geq 1$, is a mapping $\mathbf{p} : \Omega \to \mathbb{R}^3$ of a closed polygonal domain into $\mathbb{R}^3$ which is a *regular parametric representation of class $C^k$*. Thus $\mathbf{p}$ is $k$ times continuously differentiable on $\Omega$ and its differential $\partial \mathbf{p}|_X : \Omega \to \mathbb{R}^3$ has rank 2 for all $X \in \Omega$. We have assumed a polygonal domain and hence an edge $E$ joining vertices $P$ and $Q$ can be parameterized as $E(s) = (1 - s)P + sQ$. More generally, a domain bounded by a finite number of edges with regular $C^k$ parameterizations is allowable. We now have:

**Definition 5.1.** *Let $\mathbf{p} : \Omega_1 \to \mathbb{R}^3$ and $\mathbf{q} : \Omega_2 \to \mathbb{R}^3$ be two $C^k$ patches defined on closed polygonal domains $\Omega_1$ and $\Omega_2$. Also, let $E_2 : [0, 1] \to \mathbb{R}^2$ be a regular $C^k$ parameterization of an edge of $\Omega_2$. Then $\mathbf{p}$ joins $\mathbf{q}$ with geometric continuity $GC^k$ (along the edge $E_2$) if there exists a $C^k$ diffeomorphism $\varphi$, defined in a neighborhood of $E_2$ such that:*

(i) *(Domain continuation) For $s \in [0, 1]$*

$$E_1(s) := \varphi(E_2(s)) \tag{5.1}$$

*is an edge of $\Omega_1$, and interior points of $\Omega_1$ in a neighborhood of $E_1$ are mapped from exterior points of $\Omega_2$,*

(ii) *(Patch continuation) For $s \in [0, 1]$*

$$\partial^i \mathbf{q}|_{E_2(s)} = \partial^i(\mathbf{p} \circ \varphi)|_{E_2(s)}, \qquad i = 0, \ldots, k. \tag{5.2}$$

The definition implies that the composite map

$$X \to \begin{cases} \mathbf{p} \circ \varphi(X) = \mathbf{p}(\varphi(X)), & X \notin \Omega_2, \quad \varphi(X) \in \Omega_2, \\ \mathbf{q}(X), & X \in \Omega_2, \end{cases} \tag{5.3}$$

is a regular parametric representation of class $C^k$ across the edge $E_2$, see Figure 4. The second condition (5.2) means that all derivatives up to and including order $k$ of $\mathbf{q}$ and the composed map $\mathbf{p} \circ \varphi$ agree along $E_2$, where we have used the convenient notation of total derivative multi-linear maps. With this notation we obtain the directional derivatives

$$
\begin{aligned}
\frac{\partial^i \mathbf{q}(X)}{\partial U_1 \dots \partial U_i} &= \frac{\partial^i}{\partial s_1 \dots \partial s_i} \mathbf{q}(X + s_1 U_1 + \dots + s_i U_i)\Big|_{s_1 = \dots = s_i = 0} \\
&= \partial^i \mathbf{q}\Big|_X (U_1, \cdots, U_i),
\end{aligned} \tag{5.4}
$$

where $U_j, j = 1, \dots, i$ are $i$ vectors (*directions*) in $\mathbb{R}^2$.

In fact, it is not necessary to check all derivatives up to and including order $k$, as implied by (5.2), since we have:

**Lemma 5.2.** *Let $U(s)$ be any non-zero $C^{k-1}$ vector field defined along the edge $E_2(s)$, which is transversal to that edge. Then (5.2) may be replaced by the requirement that for $s \in [0, 1]$*

$$
\frac{\partial^i \mathbf{q}(X)}{\partial U^i}\Big|_{X = E_2(s)} = \frac{\partial^i \mathbf{p}(\varphi(X))}{\partial U^i}\Big|_{X = E_2(x)}, \qquad i = 0, \dots, k. \tag{5.5}
$$

The proof of this lemma follows immediately from the observation that we can differentiate any of (5.5) an appropriate number of times along the edge direction $\dot{E}_2(s)$. Hence we can obtain all possible derivatives up to and including order $k$ in terms of derivatives along the linearly independent directions $U(s)$ and $\dot{E}_2(s)$

Conditions (5.1) and (5.5) are the surface analogs of (2.6) and (2.7) for curves. Furthermore, applying the chain and product rules to the right hand sides of (5.5) gives the surface analog of (2.8), namely

$$
\mathbf{q}(E_2(s)) = \mathbf{p}(E_1(s)) \tag{5.6}
$$

and

$$
\frac{\partial^i \mathbf{q}}{\partial U^i}\Big|_{E_2(s)} = \sum_{j=1}^{i} \sum_{i_1 + \dots + i_j = i} \begin{bmatrix} i \\ i_1 \dots i_j \end{bmatrix} \frac{\partial^i \mathbf{p}}{\partial V_{i_1} \dots \partial V_{i_j}}\Big|_{E_1(s)}, i = 1, \dots, k, \tag{5.7}
$$

where

$$
V_i(s) := \frac{\partial^i \varphi}{\partial U^i}\Big|_{E_2(s)}, \qquad i = 1, \dots, k. \tag{5.8}
$$

For example, the $GC^3$ conditions are

$$
\begin{aligned}
\mathbf{q}(E_2(s)) &= \mathbf{p}(E_1(s)) \\
\frac{\partial \mathbf{q}}{\partial U}\Big|_{E_2(s)} &= \frac{\partial \mathbf{p}}{\partial V_1}\Big|_{E_1(s)} \\
\frac{\partial^2 \mathbf{q}}{\partial U^2}\Big|_{E_2(s)} &= \frac{\partial \mathbf{p}}{\partial V_2}\Big|_{E_1(s)} + \frac{\partial^2 \mathbf{p}}{\partial V_1^2}\Big|_{E_1(s)} \\
\frac{\partial^3 \mathbf{q}}{\partial U^3}\Big|_{E_2(s)} &= \frac{\partial \mathbf{p}}{\partial V_3}\Big|_{E_1(s)} + \frac{3\partial^2 \mathbf{p}}{\partial V_2 \partial V_1}\Big|_{E_1(s)} + \frac{\partial^3 \mathbf{p}}{\partial V_1^3}\Big|_{E_1(s)}.
\end{aligned} \tag{5.9}
$$

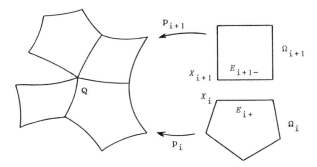

**Figure 5.** Patches meeting at a common vertex.

The direct equivalent of the curve conditions (2.8) are obtained in the special case where $V_i(s) = \beta_i(s)V(s)$; *i.e.*, where the $V_i(s), i = 1, \ldots, k$, lie along the common direction $V(s)$, but such an assumption is too restrictive in general.

The domain continuation condition on $\varphi$ of Definition 5.1 implies that if $U(s)$ is outward pointing on the side $E_2(s)$, then $V_1(s)$ is inward pointing to the side $E_1(s)$ (cf. (2.13)). We now have the surface analog to Proposition 2.2 which is:

**Proposition 5.3.** *Let $E_1 : [0,1] \to \mathbb{R}^2$ and $E_2 : [0,1] \to \mathbb{R}^2$ be regular $C^k$ parameterizations of boundary segments of $\Omega_1$ and $\Omega_2$, respectively, such that the $C^0$ continuity constraint (5.6) holds. Also, let $U : [0,1] \to \mathbb{R}^2$ be any non-zero $C^{k-1}$ vector field which is transversal to $E_2(s)$ in an outward direction. Then the patches $\mathbf{p}$ and $\mathbf{q}$ join with geometric continuity $GC^k$ if there exist $C^{k-i}$ vector fields $V_i : [0,1] \to \mathbb{R}^2, i = 1, \ldots, k$, such that the constraints (5.7) hold, where $V_1(s)$ is non-zero and transversal to $E_1(s)$ in an inward direction.*

The necessity of this proposition has been demonstrated, where, given a $C^{k-1}$ vector field $U(s)$, the continuity classes of $V_i, i = 1, \ldots, k$, follow from the definition (5.8). To prove sufficiency, a $C^k$ diffeomorphism $\varphi$ must be constructed which satisfies (5.1) and (5.8). This construction is given in Hahn [45], Lemma 3.2. Alternatively, when all vector fields are $C^k$, the diffeomorphism can be defined by the simple Taylor interpolant

$$\varphi(E_2(s) + tU(s)) := E_1(s) + \sum_{j=1}^{k} \frac{t^j}{j!} V_j(s). \qquad (5.10)$$

Having defined a $GC^k$ join of two patches across edges, we must next consider the situation where a number of polygonal patches $\mathbf{p}_i : \Omega_1 \to \mathbb{R}^3, i = 1, \ldots, n$, meet at a common vertex $\mathbf{Q} \in \mathbb{R}^3$ say. Suppose $X_i \in \mathbb{R}^2$ is the domain vertex of $\Omega_i$ such that $\mathbf{p}_i(X_i) = \mathbf{Q}, i = 1, \ldots, n$. Furthermore, suppose that $\mathbf{p}_{i+1}$ joins $\mathbf{p}_i$ with geometric continuity $GC^k$ across edges labelled $E_{i+1-}$

and $E_{i+}$, $i = 1, \ldots, n - 1$; see Figure 5. The *tangent sector* of $\mathbf{p}_i$ at $X_i$ is defined to be the set of tangent vectors $\frac{d}{ds}\mathbf{p}_i(c(s))|_{s=0}$ given by all regular curves $c : [0, 1] \to \Omega_i$ with $c(0) = X_i$. Following Hahn [45], we then say that the patches *join* with geometric continuity $GC^k$ at the vertex $\mathbf{Q}$, if the tangent sectors of the patches are non-overlapping and either (i) their union is a proper subset of the tangent plane at $\mathbf{Q}$, or (ii) their union is the tangent plane at $\mathbf{Q}$ and additionally $\mathbf{p}_1$ joins $\mathbf{p}_n$ with geometric continuity $GC^k$ across edges $E_{1-}$ and $E_{n+}$. In the latter case the patches are said to *surround* the vertex. Excluded, however, is the case where the patches wrap themselves more than once around the common vertex.

## $G^k$ Patch Complex

We are now in a position to define a $GC^k$ *patch complex* appropriate for CAGD. Such a complex is a collection of patches such that adjacent patches join with geometric continuity $GC^k$ along edges and at common vertices. To be precise, we should label each domain edge and define a connecting relation which identifies those edges along which there are $GC^k$ joins. This connecting relation must be symmetric, non-reflexive (an edge cannot have a $GC^k$ join with itself) and must be such that one edge is related to, at most, one other edge.

The definition of a $GC^k$ patch complex means that locally the surface admits a $C^k$ parameterization. This point is considered in more detail in Hahn [45]. In particular, the problem of patches which meet at a common vertex is tackled in much greater depth. Hahn also provides a parameterization-independent characterization of geometric continuity by the use of *covariant derivatives*. However, the reparameterization approach presented here should provide a more constructive method for tackling the problem of $GC^k$ patch complexes in CAGD.

## §6. Applications

So far we have presented an actor without a stage. Hence we conclude by briefly considering two application areas which have motivated much of the development of the theory of geometric continuity in CAGD.

## $GC^k$ Piecewise-defined Polynomials

The possibility of constructing piecewise defined curves with geometric arc length continuous joins is suggested by the work of Manning [56] and Nielson [57]. Nielson develops $GC^2$ cubic interpolatory parametric splines ($\nu$-splines) using a variational approach motivated by the theory of splines under tension. Barsky [3] considers local support bases for such splines ($\beta$-splines) which have been studied by a number of authors. In particular, Goodman [31] develops a $GC^k$ theory of $\beta$-splines, and Dyn and Micchelli [22] provide a more general analysis which includes the possibility of considering geometric Frenet frame continuous splines.

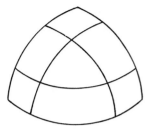 

**Figure 6.** Polygonal problems.

Let $t_0 < t_1 < \ldots < t_{N+1}$ be a knot partition in the parametric variable $t$ and let $A^{(i)}, i = 1, \ldots, N$, be $(k+1) \times (k+1)$ non-singular connection matrices. Then we can define the space of piecewise polynomials $\mathbf{p}|_{(t_i, t_{i+1})} \in \pi_{k+1}, i = 0, \ldots, N$ on $[t_0, t_{N+1}]$ such that

$$\left[\mathbf{p}(t_{i+}), \mathbf{p}^{(1)}(t_{i+}), \ldots, \mathbf{p}^{(k)}(t_{i+})\right]^T$$
$$= A^{(i)} \left[\mathbf{p}(t_{i-}), \mathbf{p}^{(1)}(t_{i-}), \ldots, \mathbf{p}^{(k)}(t_{i-})\right]^T, i = 1, \ldots, N. \tag{6.1}$$

Here $\pi_{k+1}$ is the space of parametric polynomials of degree $\leq k+1$ with range in $\mathbb{R}^n$. When $A^{(i)} = I, i = 1, \ldots, N$, the traditional space of parametric spline functions of degree $k+1$ (continuity $C^k$) is obtained. Geometric splines are obtained by choosing the $A^{(i)}$ of lower triangular form as in (2.9) (arc length) or (4.2) (Frenet frame, where $k = n$). In particular, with $k = 2$ (cubic $GC^2$ spline), the $\nu$-spline and $\beta$-spline connection matrices take the respective forms

$$A^{(i)} = \begin{bmatrix} 1 & 0 & 0 \\ 0 & 1 & 0 \\ 0 & \nu_i & 1 \end{bmatrix} \text{ and } A^{(i)} = \begin{bmatrix} 1 & 0 & 0 \\ 0 & \beta_1^{(i)} & 0 \\ 0 & \beta_2^{(i)} & (\beta_1^{(i)})^2 \end{bmatrix}, \quad \beta_1^{(i)} > 0. \tag{6.2}$$

(In fact, by considering the knots as free parameters, the two forms are equivalent, since one can be obtained from the other with a piecewise affine transformation onto a new knot partition.) Geometrical constructions of $GC^2$ cubic parametric splines are given in Farin [23] and Boehm [9].

## $GC^k$ Surface Patch Complexes

There are two situations for parametric surface patch complexes in CAGD, where the concept of a $GC^k$ join of two surface patches is an essential requirement. The first of these is where a *polygonal hole* can occur within a rectangular patch framework. Here, a parametrically defined surface is created as a complex of rectangular patches; *i.e.*, the patches are mappings of rectangular domains into $\mathbb{R}^3$. However, *polygonal holes* can occur within such a complex, as shown by the *triangular* and *pentagonal holes* in Figure 6. Thus a surface patch, or a number of patches, is required to fill the hole with appropriate $GC^k$ joins. For $k = 1$ (tangent plane continuity) a number of solutions to the problem have been suggested. For example, the construction of a polygonal patch as in Charrot and Gregory [15,37,38] and Varady [68], the use of recursive subdivision techniques as in Ball and Storey [2], or filling the hole with a number of rectangular patches, see Chiyokura [16] and Van Wijk [67].

The second situation where geometric continuity ideas are essential is the creation of parametric surfaces over more general mesh networks. Here, we do not wish the complete surface to be treated as a single map from a partition of $\mathbb{R}^2$. (Indeed, both the *polygonal hole* problem and this problem share the common theme of the wish to construct surface manifolds of a more complex structure than that of a single map from $\mathbb{R}^2$.) A number of $GC^1$ solutions to this problem have been proposed, based on triangular patch methods as in Herron [47], Nielson [60], Peters [61], and Piper [62]; see also Jensen [53].

## References

1. Ball, A. A., Reparametrisation and its application in computer aided geometric design, Int. J. Num. Meth. in Eng. **20** (1984), 197–216.
2. Ball, A. A. and D. J. T. Storey, Recursively generated $B$-spline surfaces, *Proceedings CAD84*, Butterworths, 1984, 112–119.
3. Barsky, B. A., The Beta-spline: a local representation based on shape parameters and fundamental geometric measures, Ph.D. dissertation, University of Utah, 1981.
4. Barsky, B. A., *Computer Graphics and Geometric Modeling using Beta-splines*, Springer-Verlag, Heidelberg, 1988.
5. Barsky, B. A. and J. C. Beatty, Local control of bias and tension in Beta-splines, ACM Trans. on Graphics **2** (1983), 109–134.
6. Barsky, B. A. and T. D. DeRose, Geometric continuity of parametric curves, Technical Report UCB/CSD 84/205, Computer Science Division, University of California, Berkely, California, 1984.
7. Bartels, R. H. and J. C. Beatty, Beta-splines with a difference, Technical Report CS-83-40, University of Waterloo, Ontario, 1984.
8. Bartels, R. H., J. C. Beatty, and B. A. Barsky., *An Introduction to Splines for Use in Computer Graphics and Geometric Modeling*, Morgan Kaufmann, Los Altos, 1987.
9. Boehm, W., Curvature continuous curves and surfaces, Comput. Aided Geom. Design **2** (1985), 313–323.
10. Boehm, W., Rational geometric splines, Comput. Aided Geom. Design **4** (1987), 67–77.
11. Boehm, W., Smooth curves and surfaces, in *Geometric Modeling: algorithms and new trends*, G. E. Farin (ed.), SIAM, Philadelphia, 1987, 175–184.

12. Boehm, W., Visual continuity, Technische Universität Braunschweig, preprint.

13. Boehm, W., Differential geometry I and II, in *Curves and Surfaces in CAGD* by G. E. Farin, Academic Press, N. Y., 1988.

14. de Boor, C., K. Höllig, and M. Sabin, High accuracy geometric Hermite interpolation, Comput. Aided Geom. Design **4** (1987), 269–278.

15. Charrot, P. and J. A. Gregory, A pentagonal surface patch for computer aided geometric design, Comput. Aided Geom. Design **1** (1984), 87–94.

16. Chiyokura, H., Localised surface interpolation method for irregular meshes, in *Advanced Computer Graphics*, T. L. Kunii (ed.), Springer-Verlag, Tokyo, 1986, 3–19.

17. Degen, W., Some remarks on Bézier curves, Comput. Aided Geom. Design **5** (1988), 259–268.

18. DeRose, T. D. and B. A. Barsky, Geometric continuity, shape parameters, and geometric constructions for Catmull-Rom splines, ACM Trans. on Graphics **7** (1988), 1–41.

19. DeRose, T. D., Geometric continuity: A parameterization independent measure of continuity for computer aided geometric design, Ph.D. dissertation, University of California, Berkeley, California (1985). Available as Technical Report UCB/CSD 86/255.

20. Doo, D. and M. A. Sabin, Behaviour of recursive division surfaces near extraordinary points, Computer Aided Design **10** (1978), 350–355.

21. Dyn, N., A. Edelman, and C. A. Micchelli, On locally supported basis functions for the representation of geometric continuous curves, Analysis **7** (1987), 313–341.

22. Dyn, N. and C. A. Micchelli, Piecewise polynomial spaces and geometric continuity of curves, Numerische Mathematik, to appear.

23. Farin, G. E., Visually $C^2$ cubic splines, Computer Aided Design **14** (1982), 137–139.

24. Farin, G. E., A construction for visual $C^1$ continuity of polynomial surface patches, Computer Graphics and Image Processing **20** (1982), 272–282.

25. Farin, G. E., Some remarks on $V^2$-splines, Comput. Aided Geom. Design **2** (1985), 325–328.

26. Farin, G. E., Piecewise rational quadratics, Arizona State University, preprint.

27. Farin, G. E., *Curves and Surfaces in CAGD*, Academic Press, N. Y., 1988.

28. Fritsch, F. N., The Wilson-Fowler spline is a $\nu$-spline, Comput. Aided Geom. Design **3** (1986), 155–162.

29. Foley, T. A., Interpolation with interval and point tension controls using weighted $\nu$-splines, ACM Trans. Math. Softw. **13** (1987), 68–96.

30. Geise, G., Über berührende Kegelschnitte einer ebenen Kurve, ZAMM **42** (1962), 297–304.

31. Goodman, T. N. T., Properties of $\beta$-splines, J. Approx. Theory **44** (1985), 132–153.

32. Goodman, T. N. T. and S. L. Lee, Geometrically continuous surfaces defined parametrically from piecewise polynomials, in *The Mathematics of Surfaces II*, R. Martin (ed.), Clarendon Press, Oxford, 1987, 343–361.

33. Goodman, T. N. T. and K. Unsworth, Generation of $\beta$-spline curves using a recurrence relation, in *Fundamental Algorithms for Computer Graphics*, R. A. Earnshaw (ed.), Springer-Verlag, Berlin, 1985, 325–357.

34. Goodman, T. N. T. and K. Unsworth, Manipulating shape and producing geometric continuity in $\beta$-spline curves, IEEE Computer Graphics and Applications **6** (1986), 50–56.

35. Goodman, T. N. T. and K. Unsworth, Shape preserving interpolation by parametrically defined curves, SIAM J. Num. Anal., to appear.

36. Goodman, T. N. T. and K. Unsworth, Shape preserving interpolation by curvature continuous parametric curves, Comput. Aided Geom. Design **4** (1988), 323–340.

37. Gregory, J. A. and P. Charrot, A $C^1$ triangular interpolation patch for computer-aided geometric design, Computer Graphics and Image Processing **13** (19890), 80–87.

38. Gregory, J. A., $N$-sided surface patches, in *The Mathematics of Surfaces*, J. A. Gregory (ed.), Clarendon Press, Oxford, 1986, 217–232.

39. Gregory, J. A. and J. M. Hahn, Geometric continuity and convex combination patches, Comput. Aided Geom. Design **4** (1987), 79–89.

40. Gregory, J. A. and J. M. Hahn, A $C^2$ polygonal surface patch, Comput. Aided Geom. Design **6** (1989), 69–76.

41. Hagen, H., Bézier-curves with curvature and torsion continuity, Rocky Mountain J. Math. **16** (1986), 629–638.

42. Hagen, H., Geometric spline curves, Comput. Aided Geom. Design **2** (1985), 223–227.

43. Hagen, H., Geometric surface patches without twist constraints, Comput. Aided Geom. Design **3** (1986), 179–184.

44. Hagen, H. and G. Schulze, Automatic smoothing with geometric surface patches, Comput. Aided Geom. Design **4** (1987), 231–235.

45. Hahn, J. M., Geometric continuous patch complexes, Comput. Aided Geom. Design **6** (1988), 55–68.

46. Hands, J. M., Reparametrisation of rational surfaces, in *The Mathematics of Surfaces II*, R. Martin (ed.), Clarendon Press, Oxford, 1987, 87–99.

47. Herron, G., Smooth closed surfaces with discrete triangular interpolants, Comput. Aided Geom. Design **2** (1985), 297–306.

48. Herron, G., Techniques for visual continuity, in *Geometric Modeling: Algorithms and New Trends*, G. E. Farin (ed.), SIAM, Philadelphia, 1987, 163–174.

49. Hosaka, M. and F. Kimura, Non-four-sided patch expressions with control points, Comput. Aided Geom. Design **1** (1984), 75–86.

50. Hoschek, J. and D. Liu, $GC^1$ continuity conditions between adjacent rectangular and triangular Bézier surface patches, Technische Hochschule Darmstadt, preprint.

51. Höllig, K., Geometric continuity of spline curves and surfaces, Computer Sciences Technical Report 645, University of Wisconsin, Madison, 1986.

52. Hsiung, C. C., *A First Course in Differential Geometry*, John Wiley, New York, 1981.

53. Jensen, T., Assembling triangular and rectangular patches and multivariate splines, in *Geometric Modeling: Algorithms and New Trends*, G. E. Farin (ed.), SIAM, Philadelphia, 1987, 203–220.

54. Kahmann, J., Continuity of curvature between adjacent Bézier patches, in *Surfaces in Computer Aided Geometric Design*, R. E. Barnhill and W. Boehm (eds.), North-Holland, Amsterdam, 1983, 65–75.

55. Liang, Y. D., Geometric continuity for curves and surface, Zhejiang University, Hangzhou, preprint.

56. Manning, J. R., Continuity conditions for spline curves, Computer J. **17** (1974), 181–186.

57. Nielson, G. M., Some piecewise polynomial alternatives to splines under tension, in *Computer Aided Geometric Design*, R. E. Barnhill and R. F. Riesenfeld (eds.), Academic Press, New York, 1975, 209–235.

58. Nielson, G. M., A locally controllable spline with tension for interactive curve design, Comput. Aided Geom. Design **1** (1984), 199–205.

59. Nielson, G. M., Rectangular $\nu$-splines, IEEE Computer Graphics and Applications **6** (1986), 35–40.

60. Nielson, G. M., A transfinite, visually continuous, triangular interpolant, in *Geometric Modeling: Algorithms and New Trends*, G. E. Farin (ed.), SIAM, Philadelphia, 1987, 235–246.

61. Peters, J., Local piecewise cubic $C^1$ surface interpolants for rectangular and triangular tessellations, University of Wisconsin, Madison, preprint.

62. Piper, B. R., Visually smooth interpolation with triangular Bézier patches, in *Geometric Modelling: Algorithms and New Trends*, G. E. Farin (ed.), SIAM, Philadelphia, 1987, 221–233.

63. Ramshaw, L., Blossoming: A connect-the-dots approach to splines, Research Report 19, Digital Systems Research Center, Palo Alto, 1987.

64. Sabin, M., Conditions for continuity of surface normals between adjacent parametric patches, Technical Report VSO/MS/151, British Aircraft Corporation, 1969.

65. Sarraga, R. F., $G^1$ interpolation of generally unrestricted cubic Bézier curves, Comput. Aided Geom. Design **4** (1987), 23–39.

66. Spivak, M., *Differential Geometry*, Publish or Perish Inc., Boston, 1975.

67. Van Wijk, J. J., Bicubic patches for approximating non-rectangular control-point meshes, Comput. Aided Geom. Design **3** (1986), 1–13.

68. Varady, T., Survey and new results in $N$-sided patch generation, in *The Mathematics of Surfaces II*, R. Martin (ed.), Clarendon Press, Oxford, 1987, 203–235.

69. Veron, M., G. Ris, and J. P. Musse, Continuity of biparametric surface patches, Computer Aided Design **8** (1976), 267–273.

John A. Gregory
Department of Mathematics and Statistics
Brunel University
Uxbridge, Middlesex UB8 3PH
ENGLAND

EMAIL: mastjag@ cc.brunel.ac.uk

Supported in part by SERC Grants GR/D/77148 and GR/E/25092.

# Curvature Continuous Triangular Interpolants

## Hans Hagen and Helmut Pottmann

**Abstract.** An interpolation scheme which assumes position values, tangent planes and curvature elements on the boundary of arbitrary triangles is presented. This new surface patch type can be used for modeling open and closed surfaces with second order geometric continuity.

## §1. Introduction

In this paper, we describe parametric triangular surface patches which assume position values, tangent planes as well as curvature elements (e.g., defined by osculating paraboloids or Dupin's indicatrices) on all three edges of an arbitrary triangular region. Both a transfinite interpolant and a discretized version are presented. This new surface patch type can be used for the representation of open or closed surfaces with second order geometric continuity. The geometric type of boundary information allows an easy assembling of the patches with other classes of surfaces; e.g., rectangular patches.

Our approach is an extended "side-vertex method" (cf. [7]) based upon the convex combination of interpolation operators which consist of univariate interpolation along lines joining a vertex and the opposing edge of a triangle. It was initiated by two recent developments: a triangular interpolant with first order geometric continuity due to Nielson [8], and Hagen's geometric surface patches [4]. In these publications the reader can find more details on the history of the subject and the underlying theoretical background.

## §2. Preliminary Remarks and Statement of the Problem

Surface patches are "results" of functions $F : T \to \mathbb{R}^3$

$$F(b_1, b_2, b_3) = \begin{pmatrix} x(b_1, b_2, b_3) \\ y(b_1, b_2, b_3) \\ z(b_1, b_2, b_3) \end{pmatrix}, \qquad (b_1, b_2, b_3) \in T,$$

Mathematical Methods in Computer Aided Geometric Design
Tom Lyche and Larry L. Schumaker (eds.), pp. 373–384.
Copyright © 1989 by Academic Press, Boston.
ISBN 0-12-460515-X.

where the domain $T$ is defined by barycentric coordinates as

$$T = \{(b_1, b_2, b_3) : 0 \le b_i \le 1 , i = 1, 2, 3 ; b_1 + b_2 + b_3 = 1\} .$$

Using the notation in [8], the vertices of $T$ are denoted by

$$V_1 = (1, 0, 0) , \qquad V_2 = (0, 1, 0) , \qquad V_3 = (0, 0, 1) ,$$

and the edges (cf. Figure 2) by

$$e_1 = \{(0, b_2, b_3) \in T\} , \qquad e_2 = \{(b_1, 0, b_3) \in T\} , \qquad e_3 = \{(b_1, b_2, 0) \in T\} .$$

It is convenient to use the set of indices

$$I = \{(1, 2, 3), (2, 3, 1), (3, 1, 2)\} .$$

We sometimes wish to refer to the boundary curves of the patch which are a result of restricting a function $F$ defined over $T$ to one of its edges. We use $F(e_i)$ to refer to this curve for the edge $e_i$ and $F(\partial T)$ to collectively refer to all three.

We will deal exclusively with oriented surfaces $F(T)$. The outward unit surface normal vector of $F(b_1, b_2, b_3)$ is denoted by $N[F](b_1, b_2, b_3)$. The second order behavior of a surface at a point $F(b_1, b_2, b_3)$ is completely determined if we know the Dupin indicatrix or an osculating paraboloid. We wish to describe that knowledge by the "curvature element" $C[F](b_1, b_2, b_3)$. Two surfaces $F$ and $F'$ possess an identical curvature element at a common point $P_0$, if and only if they have the same surface normal and the same Dupin indicatrix at $P_0$. We conclude that agreement of $C[F]$ is equivalent to second order contact. A surface with a continuous curvature element is called a visually $C^2$ ($VC^2$-) surface.

We now can make a formal statement of the properties of the interpolants we develop in this paper:

**Problem.** *Let* **F** *be a* **C$^2$** *surface defined over* **T$'$** $\supset$ **T**. *Find an interpolant* **P[F]** *which is defined and continuous over* **T** *and has a continuous curvature element such that*

$$P[F](\partial T) = F(\partial T) ,$$

$$C[P[F]](\partial T) = C[F](\partial T) .$$

## §3. The Geometric Hermite-operator

For the development of our surface patches we need a univariate operator which produces a quintic interpolant to arbitrary end points $V_0, V_1$ as well as first and second derivative vectors $V_0', V_1'$ and $V_0'', V_1''$, respectively. This *quintic Hermite-operator* has the representation

$$\begin{aligned} H_5[V_0, V_1, V_0', V_1', V_0'', V_1''](t) &= H_0^5(t)V_0 + H_1^5(t)V_0' + H_2^5(t)V_0'' + \qquad (2.1) \\ &\quad + H_3^5(t)V_1'' + H_4^5(t)V_1' + H_5^5(t)V_1 , \quad t \in [0, 1] , \end{aligned}$$

with the Hermite polynomials

$$H_0^5(t) = -6t^5 + 15t^4 - 10t^3 + 1 \ ,$$
$$H_1^5(t) = -3t^5 + 8t^4 - 6t^3 + t \ ,$$
$$H_2^5(t) = (-t^5 + 3t^4 - 3t^3 + t^2)/2 \ ,$$
$$H_3^5(t) = (t^5 - 2t^4 + t^3)/2 \ ,$$
$$H_4^5(t) = -3t^5 + 7t^4 - 4t^3 \ ,$$
$$H_5^5(t) = 6t^5 - 15t^4 + 10t^3 \ .$$

Often, we don't know $V_i', V_i''$, but instead have the unit tangent vectors $T_0, T_1$ and the "curvature vectors" $K_0, K_1$

$$K_0 = \kappa_0 \cdot E_2(V_0)$$
$$K_1 = \kappa_1 \cdot E_2(V_1), \tag{2.2}$$

where $\kappa_0$ and $\kappa_1$ are the curvature values of the surface curve in $V_0$ and $V_1$. Here $E_2$ is the principal normal vector (for more details see [3]).

If we want to interpolate to these geometric end conditions, we can use

$$V_0' = \lambda_0 T_0 \ , \qquad V_0'' = \lambda_0^2 K_0 + \mu_0 T_0 \ ,$$
$$V_1' = \lambda_1 T_1 \ , \qquad V_1'' = \lambda_1^2 K_1 + \mu_1 T_1 \ , \tag{2.3}$$
$$\lambda_0, \lambda_1 > 0 \ , \qquad \lambda_0, \lambda_1, \mu_0, \mu_1 \in \mathbb{R} \ .$$

The values $\lambda_0, \lambda_1, \mu_0, \mu_1$ can be used like tension parameters to affect the shape of $H_5(t)$. We don't recommend taking them all to be unity or zero. A careful selection is necessary to obtain good results.

## §4. A Transfinite VC²-patch

For the present situation, we need an operator

$$g[V_0, V_1, C_0, C_1](t) = g(t) \ ,$$

that models a curve with endpoints $V_0, V_1$ compatible to the curvature elements $C_0, C_1$ at these points. $C_0, C_1$ include the knowledge of the corresponding outward surface normals $N_0, N_1$. We want to have the osculating plane $\sigma_0$ at $V_0$ passing through $N_0$ and $V_1$, and, conversely, the osculating plane $\sigma_1$ at $V_1$ containing $N_1$ and $V_0$ (cf. Figure 1). Under these assumptions we wish to obtain a curve $g$ which is situated near a geodesic curve of the surface $F$, because a geodesic is characterized by the property that its osculating planes contain the corresponding surface normals. The geodesics will tend to be

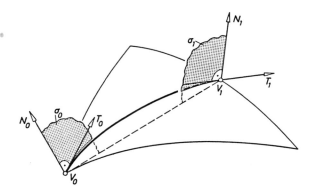

**Figure 1.** Osculating planes.

planar, especially for almost spherical patches. Therefore, we require $V_1$ to be contained in $\sigma_0$ and vice versa.

Hence, under the weak restriction that neither $N_0$ nor $N_1$ is parallel to $V_1 - V_0$, the tangent vectors $T_0, T_1$ at $V_0, V_1$ are defined (cf. G. Nielson [8]) by

$$T_0 = \frac{N_0 \times (V_1 - V_0) \times N_0}{\|N_0 \times (V_1 - V_0) \times N_0\|} \,, \qquad T_1 = \frac{N_1 \times (V_1 - V_0) \times N_1}{\|N_1 \times (V_1 - V_0) \times N_1\|} \,, \qquad (3.1)$$

where $\times$ denotes the cross product in $\mathbb{R}^3$. Let $\kappa_0^N, \kappa_1^N$ be the oriented normal curvatures for the directions $T_0$ and $T_1$ respectively. The curvature vectors of $g$ are then

$$K_0 = \kappa_0^N N_0 \,, \qquad K_1 = \kappa_1^N N_1 \,. \qquad (3.2)$$

Using the operator $H_5$ and four shape parameters $\lambda_0, \lambda_1, \mu_0, \mu_1$, we now define

$$g[V_0, V_1, C_0, C_1](t) := H_5[V_0, V_1, \lambda_0 T_0, \lambda_1 T_1, \lambda_0^2 K_0 + \mu_0 T_0, \lambda_1^2 K_1 + \mu_1 T_1](t) \,. \qquad (3.3)$$

The above preparations allow a description of our transfinite interpolant. It is based upon the ideas of the side-vertex method and the operator $g$. The arguments of $g$ are a vertex and the point on the opposing edge where a ray starting from the vertex and passing through the point $(b_1, b_2, b_3)$ intersect (cf. Figure 2). These boundary points have the representation

$$\frac{b_j V_j + b_k V_k}{1 - b_i} \,, \qquad (i, j, k) \in I \,.$$

**Theorem 1.** *Let*
$$P_i[F](b_1, b_2, b_3) =$$
$$g\left[F(V_i), F\left(\frac{b_j V_j + b_k V_k}{1 - b_i}\right), C[F](V_i), C[F]\left(\frac{b_j V_j + b_k V_k}{1 - b_i}\right)\right](1 - b_i) \,.$$
$$(3.4)$$

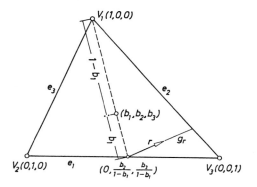

**Figure 2.** The domain $T$.

Then

$$P[F] = W_1 P_1[F] + W_2 P_2[F] + W_3 P_3[F], \qquad (3.5)$$

where

$$W_i = \frac{b_j^3 b_k^3}{b_1^3 b_2^3 + b_2^3 b_3^3 + b_3^3 b_1^3} \ , \qquad (i, j, k) \in I$$

satisfies the interpolation conditions

$$P[F](\partial T) = F(\partial T) \ , \qquad C[P[F]](\partial T) = C[F](\partial T) \ .$$

**Proof:** We consider directional derivatives with respect to an arbitrary direction $r$ of the domain $T$. The weight functions $W_i$ have the properties

$(a) \quad \displaystyle\sum_{i=1}^{3} W_i = 1$

$(b) \quad W_i(e_k) = \delta_{ik} \qquad\qquad\qquad\qquad\qquad\qquad (3.6)$

$(c) \quad \dfrac{\partial W_i}{\partial r}(e_k) = 0 \ , \quad \dfrac{\partial^2 W_i}{\partial r^2}(e_k) = 0 \ ; \qquad i, k \in \{1, 2, 3\} \ .$

Due to our construction, $P_i$ interpolates to $F$ on $e_i$. Condition $(b)$ now implies that $P$ interpolates to $F$ on the entire boundary of $T$.

The directional derivatives $\frac{\partial P_i}{\partial r}(e_i)$, $\frac{\partial^2 P_i}{\partial r^2}(e_i)$ are the first and second derivative vectors of the curve $P_i(g_r) \subset P_i(T)$ which are starting from points of $F(e_i)$ and which are the $P_i$-images of straight lines $g_r \subset T$ with the direction $r$ (cf. Figure 2). Using $(b)$ and $(c)$ we find

$$\frac{\partial P}{\partial r}(e_i) = \frac{\partial P_i}{\partial r}(e_i) \ , \qquad \frac{\partial^2 P}{\partial r^2}(e_i) = \frac{\partial^2 P_i}{\partial r^2}(e_i) \ , \qquad i = 1, 2, 3 \ ,$$

and conclude

$$C[P[F]](e_i) = C[P_i[F]](e_i) , \qquad i = 1, 2, 3 . \qquad (3.7)$$

Based upon the definition of $g$ and the fact that $P_i$ interpolates to $F$ on $e_i$, we have

$$N[P_i[F]](e_i) = N[F](e_i) , \qquad i = 1, 2, 3 .$$

The envelope of the family of common tangent planes of $P_i[F]$ and $F$ along $F(e_i)$ is a developable ruled surface $\psi_i$. The rulings of $\psi_i$ determine the conjugate directions (see [1]) to the tangents of the boundary curve $F(e_i)$. Hence, the Dupin indicatrices of $P_i[F]$ and $F$ at a point $X$ of $F(e_i)$ share a common diameter on the tangent $t(X)$ of $F(e_i)$ with common tangents (parallel to the corresponding ruling of $\psi_i$) at the end points (cf. Figure 3).

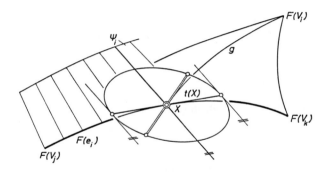

**Figure 3.** Dupin indicatrix.

Another common diameter is due to the side-vertex curve $g_r$. Therefore, the two indicatrices have to be identical. Also, in the case of an asymptotic direction $t(X)$ and a hyperbolic point $X$ this conclusion is true because the two indicatrices will now have a contact of order $\geq 3$ at the infinite point of $t(X)$. We have just proved

$$C[P_i[F]](e_i) = C[F](e_i) , \qquad i = 1, 2, 3 . \qquad (3.8)$$

Together with (3.7) the interpolation condition

$$C[P[F]](\partial T) = C[F](\partial T)$$

is verified.  ■

Note that the tension parameters have to be chosen properly to obtain geometrically $C^2$-surfaces $P_i[F](T)$. We can take $C^2$-functions $\lambda_0^i, \lambda_1^i : T \to \mathbb{R}^+$ and $\mu_0^i, \mu_1^i : T \to \mathbb{R}$ for $i = 1, 2, 3$ , which satisfy the conditions

$$\frac{\partial \lambda}{\partial r}(\partial T) = 0 \ ; \qquad \frac{\partial \mu}{\partial r}(\partial T) = 0 \ ; \qquad \frac{\partial^2 \lambda}{\partial r^2}(\partial T) = 0 \ ; \qquad \frac{\partial^2 \mu}{\partial r^2}(\partial T) = 0.$$

## §5. Discretization of the Transfinite VC²-patch

We now describe a $VC^2$-interpolant that depends upon the position and curvature element at the three vertices of $T$. We denote these values and outward surface normals by

$$
\begin{aligned}
F_1 &= F(1,0,0) \ , & N_1 &= N[F](1,0,0) \ , & C_1 &= C[F](1,0,0) \ , \\
F_2 &= F(0,1,0) \ , & N_2 &= N[F](0,1,0) \ , & C_2 &= C[F](0,1,0) \ , \\
F_3 &= F(0,0,1) \ , & N_3 &= N[F](0,0,1) \ , & C_3 &= C[F](0,0,1) \ .
\end{aligned}
$$

For each of the three boundary position curves, we will use the operator $g$ defined in (3.3). Thus, we have

$$
\begin{aligned}
F(1-t,t,0) &= g[F_1, F_2, C_1, C_2](t) \ , \\
F(0,1-t,t) &= g[F_2, F_3, C_2, C_3](t) \ , \\
F(t,0,1-t) &= g[F_3, F_1, C_3, C_1](t) \ .
\end{aligned}
$$

In the next step, we define surface normals along these boundary curves. As noted in [8], direct interpolation to the surface normals seems to be difficult, because the tangent vectors on an edge must be perpendicular to the outward surface normal. In order to overcome this inconsistency, we interpolate to certain cross boundary tangent vectors $S$. Along the curve $F(e_k)$ we define the tangent vectors

$$
\begin{aligned}
S_k(t) :=& (1 - f_k(t))S_k(0) + f_k(t)S_k(1) \ , \\
& f_k(0) = 0 \ , \ f_k(1) = 1 \ , \qquad\qquad t \in [0,1] \ , \qquad\qquad (4.1)
\end{aligned}
$$

where $S_k(0)$ and $S_k(1)$ are perpendicular to the boundary curve $F(e_k)$ at $F_i$ and $F_j$ respectively $((i, j, k) \in I)$ and $F_k$ is a function to be determined. Furthermore, these vectors have to be perpendicular to the corresponding surface normals $N_i, N_j$ (cf. Figure 4). Using the tangent vectors $E_k(t) := \frac{\partial F}{\partial e_k}(t)$ of the boundary curve, we get

$$S_k(0) = N_i \times E_k(0) \ , \qquad S_k(1) = N_j \times E_k(1) \ , \qquad (i, j, k) \in I \ .$$

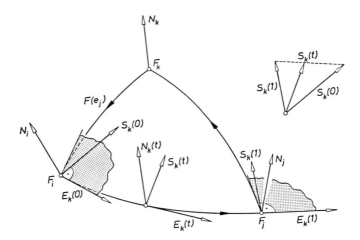

**Figure 4.** Definition of the surface normals.

In [8], we find this method with $f(t) = t$. But now linear interpolation would be incompatible with the curvature elements $C_i, C_j$ for the following reason: if the vectors $S_k$ and consequently the normals $N_k$ along $e_k$ have been selected, we know the envelope of the family of tangent planes along the boundary curve $F(e_k)$. This ruled surface $\psi_k$ describes with its rulings the conjugate directions to the tangents of the boundary curve $F(e_k)$. At the endpoints $F_i, F_j$ we are given the conjugate directions $R_k(0), R_k(1)$. This knowledge is contained in $C_i, C_j$. The normal vectors along $e_k$ are

$$N_k(t) = \frac{E_k(t) \times S_k(t)}{\|E_k(t) \times S_k(t)\|}. \tag{4.2}$$

The conjugate directions $R_k(t)$ to $E_k(t)$ satisfy

$$\langle N_k(t), R_k(t) \rangle = \langle N'_k(t), R_k(t) \rangle = 0 , \tag{4.3}$$

where $N'_k(t) = \frac{\partial N_k}{\partial t}(t)$. Equations (4.2) and (4.3) yield a necessary condition for $R_k(t)$

$$\langle E'_k(t) \times S_k(t) + E_k(t) \times S'_k(t), R_k(t) \rangle = 0 . \tag{4.3a}$$

Using

$$S'_k(t) = f'_k(t)A , \quad A := S_k(1) - S_k(0) ,$$

we have

$$\det\left(E'_k(t), S_k(t), R_k(t)\right) + f'_k(t) \det\left(E_k(t), A, R_k(t)\right) = 0. \tag{4.4}$$

At $t = 0$ and $t = 1$ we can use this equation in connection with the known values $R_k(0)$, $R_k(1)$ (derived from $C_i, C_j$) for the computation of $f_k'(0)$ and $f_k'(1)$. We are now in position to define the function $f_k$ by cubic Hermite-interpolation:

$$f_k(t) := 3t^2 - 2t^3 + f_k'(0)(t - 2t^2 + t^3) + f_k'(1)(t^3 - t^2) . \qquad (4.5)$$

Equations (4.1) and (4.2) then describe the outward surface normals $N_k(t)$ along $e_k$, where we assume that $\|E_k(t) \times S_k(t)\| \neq 0$. Difficulties arise in the case

$$\det (E_k(t), A, R_k(t)) = 0 ,$$

where $t = 0$ or $t = 1$. Assuming $\{R_k, E_k\}$ are linearly independent, we take solutions $S_k'(0)$, $S_k'(1)$ from (4.3a) — the same values for adjacent patches — and define

$$S_k(t) = (1 - 3t^2 + 2t^3)S_k(0) + (3t^2 - 2t^3)S_k(1) \\ + (t - 2t^2 + t^3)S_k'(0) + (t^3 - t^2)S_k'(1) . \qquad (4.6)$$

Linear dependence of $R_k$ and $E_k$ is due to an asymptotic direction $E_k$, and will result in $E_k' = 0$. Then (4.3a) is satisfied automatically, and we can set $S_k' = 0$. Moreover, we can take $S_k' = 0$, if

$$\det (E_k', S_k, R_k) = \det (E_k, A, R_k) = 0 .$$

The last step of discretization is the definition of curvature elements along $e_k$. The conjugate directions $R_k(t)$ can be taken from

$$R_k(t) = N_k(t) \times [E_k'(t) \times S_k(t) + E_k(t) \times S_k'(t)] . \qquad (4.7)$$

At $F_i$ and $F_j$ we know the normal curvatures $\kappa^N(R_k(0))$ and $\kappa^N(R_k(1))$ for the directions $R_k(0)$ and $R_k(1)$, respectively. In order to obtain $\kappa^N(R_k(t))$, we use linear interpolation:

$$\kappa^N(R_k(t)) = (1 - t)\kappa^N(R_k(0)) + t\kappa^N(R_k(1)) . \qquad (4.8)$$

So far, at the points of the boundary $F(\partial T)$ we can compute the normal curvatures for the boundary tangent directions $E_k(t)$ (by Meusnier's formula) and the conjugate directions $R_k(t)$. If these directions are different, the corresponding curvature elements $C_k(t)$ are completely determined, and the curvatures of our side-vertex curves can be computed using well-known formulas of differential geometry.

The case of points with $E_k(t) \times R_k(t) = 0$ has to be treated separately. If we have distinct points of that type only, we can use numerical methods to define the curvature of our curves $g_r$ by the curvatures of curves $g_r$ in a neighborhood of this special point.

It remains to consider the case of a straight boundary line $F(e_k)$. We can now define the curvature elements along $e_k$ using an osculating ruled surface $\phi_k$. For more details on this approach see [5].

Since the surface normals and curvature elements are uniquely determined by data at the endpoints of the edges only, any two patches which are joined along a common edge and which have been discretized in this fashion, will have a common surface normal and curvature element along this edge.

Based upon the above choices for the boundary data, we may write down the discretized form of each of the three radial projectors

$$P_i(b_1, b_2, b_3) = g\left[F_i, g[F_j, F_k, C_j, C_k]\left(\frac{b_j V_j + b_k V_k}{1 - b_i}\right), C_i,\right.$$

$$\left. C_i\left(\frac{b_j V_j + b_k V_k}{1 - b_i}\right)\right](1 - b_i) . \tag{4.9}$$

Note that $P_i$ interpolates to the boundary position data on all three edges and to curvature elements on the edge $e_i$. Similar to Theorem 2 in [8], we can now use some simpler weight functions than those used previously for the transfinite interpolant. We state this fact in the following theorem:

**Theorem 2.** *If $A_1, A_2, A_3$ are three operators with the properties that*

$$A_i[F](\partial T) = F(\partial T) ,$$
$$C[A_i[F]](e_i) = C[F](e_i) , \qquad i = 1, 2, 3 ,$$

*then*

$$A[F] = \sum_{i=1}^{3} \beta_i A_i[F] ,$$

*where*

$$\beta_i = \frac{b_j^2 b_k^2}{b_1^2 b_2^2 + b_1^2 b_3^2 + b_2^2 b_3^2} , \qquad (i, j, k) \in I ,$$

*interpolates to $F$ and its curvature element to the entire boundary of $T$.*

**Proof:** Since the curvature element contains the knowledge of the surface normal, we have

$$N[A_i[F]](e_i) = N[F](e_i) .$$

It is well-known (cf. [8]), that the weight functions $\beta_i$ will form an interpolant $A[F]$ with

$$A[F](\partial T) = F(\partial T) , \qquad N[A[F]](\partial T) = N[F](\partial T) .$$

The second order directional derivatives of $A$ can be expressed as

$$
\begin{aligned}
\frac{\partial^2 A[F]}{\partial r^2}(e_i) &= \frac{\partial^2 \beta_1}{\partial r^2}(e_i) A_1[F](e_i) + 2\frac{\partial \beta_1}{\partial r}(e_i)\frac{\partial A_1[F]}{\partial r}(e_i) + \\
&+ \beta_1(e_i)\frac{\partial^2 A_1[F]}{\partial r^2}(e_i) + \frac{\partial^2 \beta_2}{\partial r^2}(e_i) A_2[F](e_i) + \\
&+ 2\frac{\partial \beta_2}{\partial r}(e_i)\frac{\partial A_2[F]}{\partial r}(e_i) + \beta_2(e_i)\frac{\partial^2 A_2[F]}{\partial r^2}(e_i) + \\
&+ \frac{\partial^2 \beta_3}{\partial r^2}(e_i) A_3[F](e_i) + 2\frac{\partial \beta_3}{\partial r}(e_i)\frac{\partial A_3[F]}{\partial r}(e_i) + \\
&+ \beta_3(e_i)\frac{\partial^2 A_3[F]}{\partial r^2}(e_i) \,.
\end{aligned}
$$

Since

$$
\beta_i(e_j) = \delta_{ij} \,, \quad \frac{\partial \beta_i}{\partial r}(e_k) = 0 \,, \quad A_i[F](\partial T) = F(\partial T) \,, \quad i,j,k \in \{1,2,3\} \,,
$$

this reduces to

$$
\frac{\partial^2 A[F]}{\partial r^2}(e_i) = \frac{\partial^2 A_i[F]}{\partial r^2}(e_i) + F(e_i)\left[\frac{\partial^2 \beta_1}{\partial r^2}(e_i) + \frac{\partial^2 \beta_2}{\partial r^2}(e_i) + \frac{\partial^2 \beta_3}{\partial r^2}(e_i)\right] \,.
$$

We now use $\beta_1 + \beta_2 + \beta_3 = 1$ to conclude that the last term is zero. Thus, we have

$$
C[A[F]](e_i) = C[A_i[F]](e_i) \,,
$$

and together with $C[A_i[F]](e_i) = C[F](e_i)$,

$$
C[A[F]](\partial T) = C[F](\partial T) \,. \quad \blacksquare
$$

## §6. Curvature Estimation for Smooth Surface Design

The normal curvatures $\kappa_0^N$ and $\kappa_1^N$ are essential for applications using this method. Appropiate "curvature input" can be supplied by an automatic smoothing process based upon the calculus of variations.

The functional $\int_S (k_1^2 + k_2^2)ds$ is a standard fairness criterion for surfaces in engineering (see [9] and [10]). The quantities $k_1$ and $k_2$ are the principal normal section curvatures (see [4]). This functional is equivalent to the strain energy of flexure and torsion in a thin rectangular elastic plate of small deflection.

Hagen and Schulze [6] used this functional for a variation formulation of the surface fairing problem under the assumption of orthogonal parameter lines. Just recently Farin and Hagen [2] proved the following result without any regularity constraints: A surface is smooth in the sense that $\int_S (k_1^2 + k_2^2)ds$ is minimized provided that

$$
h_{12} := N^T \cdot F_{uw} = \frac{g_{12}(g_{11}h_{22} + g_{22}h_{11})}{g_{11}g_{22} + g_{12}^2},
$$

where

$$F_{uw} := \frac{\partial^2}{\partial u \partial w} F \; ; \quad g_{11} := F_u^T \cdot F_u \; , \qquad g_{12} := F_u^T \cdot F_w \; , \quad g_{22} := F_w^T \cdot F_w$$

$$h_{11} := N^T \cdot F_{uu} \; , \quad h_{22} := N^T \cdot F_{ww}.$$

This gives smooth normal components of twist vectors as an output of an automatic smoothing process. The appropriate values for $h_{22}$ and $h_{11}$ can be supplied by a smooth network of curves.

## References

1. do Carmo, M., *Differential Geometry of Curves and Surfaces*, Prentice Hall, Englewood Cliffs, NJ, 1976.
2. Farin, G., and H. Hagen, A local twist estimator, Trans. Graph., to appear.
3. Hagen, H., Geometric spline curves, Computer Aided Geometric Design **2** (1985), 223–227.
4. Hagen, H., Geometric surface patches without twist constraints, Computer Aided Geometric Design **3** (1986), 179–184.
5. Hagen, H., and H. Pottmann, Curvature estimates for geometric surface-patches, preprint.
6. Hagen, H., and G. Schulze, Automatic smoothing with geometric surface patches, Computer Aided Geometric Design **4** (1987), 231–235.
7. Nielson, G. M., The side-vertex method for interpolation in triangles, J. Approx. Theory **25** (1979), 318–336.
8. Nielson, G. M., A transfinite, visually continuous, triangular interpolant, in *Geometric Modeling: Algorithms and New Trends*, G. E. Farin (ed.), SIAM Publications, Philadelphia, 1987, 235–246.
9. Nowacki, H. and R. Reese, Design and fairing of ship surfaces, in *Surfaces in CAGD*, B. Barnhill and W. Boehm (eds), North Holland, 1983, 121–134.
10. Walter, W., Numerical representation of surfaces using an optimum principle, Ph.D. thesis, TU München, 1971.

Hans Hagen and Helmut Pottmann
Institut für graph. Datenverarbeitung und Computergeometrie
Universität Kaiserslautern
D–6750 Kaiserslautern
W. GERMANY

This research was supported by a NATO Collaborative Research Grant under contract number 0097/88.

# Box-Spline Surfaces

## Klaus Höllig

**Abstract.** An introduction to bivariate box-splines with particular emphasis on algorithms for the representation of surfaces is given. This includes a discussion of basic properties, recurrence relations and subdivision algorithms. As an illustration of the more advanced mathematical theory, a few theoretical results, such as the construction of box-spline tilings and interpolation with box-splines, are also described.

## §1. Introduction

In recent years, a rather beautiful mathematical theory for box-splines has been developed. While, to a large extent, this theory is motivated by Schoenberg's classical treatment of univariate cardinal splines, a number of multivariate results do not have a direct analog in the univariate theory. Examples are results on diophantine equations, approximation order, and difference equations.

The present report is primarily concerned with the algorithmic aspects of box-splines. In Sections 2 and 3, basic properties and recurrence relations are derived, and the parametric representation of surfaces with cardinal splines is discussed. Subdivision algorithms, which play the key role for applications in computer aided geometric design, are described in Section 4. These algorithms are natural genalizations of uniform knot refinement for tensor product B-splines, and have been independently developed by Boehm, Cohen–Lyche-Riesenfeld and Dahmen–Micchelli. Section 5 is a small disgression, which gives a few examples of interesting "box-spline theorems".

Mathematical Methods in Computer Aided Geometric Design
Tom Lyche and Larry L. Schumaker (eds.), pp. 385–402.
Copyright ⊖ 1989 by Academic Press, Boston.
ISBN 0-12-460515-X.

**Figure 1.** B-splines with uniform knots

**Figure 1.** B-splines with uniform knots.

## §2. Definition and Basic Properties

The univariate B-Spline $B_n$ with uniform knot sequence $\{0, 1, \ldots, n\}$ satisfies

$$B_n(x) = \int_0^1 B_{n-1}(x - t)\, dt. \tag{1}$$

Starting with $B_1 := \chi_{[0,1)}$, the characteristic function of the unit interval, (1) yields an inductive definition of $B_n$.

The (bivariate) box-spline is a natural generalization of this definition. The role of the knot sequence is played by a $2 \times n$ integer matrix

$$\Xi = [\xi^1 \quad \cdots \quad \xi^n],$$

the columns of which generate the bivariate mesh. Denote by

$$A_\xi f(x) := \int_0^1 f(x - t\xi)\, dt$$

the average of a function $f$ in the direction $\xi$. The bivariate box-spline

$$B_\Xi : \mathbb{R}^2 \mapsto \mathbb{R}$$

is defined by averaging the characteristic function of the parallelogram spanned by the vectors $\xi^1$, $\xi^2$ in the direction of the vectors $\xi^3, \ldots, \xi^n$. More precisely, one has the following

**Inductive Definition.** *Assume that the columns of $\Xi$ span $\mathbb{R}^2$. If $n = 2$, then $|\det \Xi| B_\Xi$ is defined as the characteristic function of the parallelogram*

$$\{t_1 \xi^1 + t_2 \xi^2 : 0 \leq t_\nu < 1\}.$$

*If $n > 2$, then*

$$B_\Xi := A_\xi B_{\Xi \setminus \xi}, \tag{2}$$

*where $\Xi \setminus \xi$ is the $2 \times (n-1)$ matrix obtained from $\Xi$ by deleting the column $\xi$.*

This definition is illustrated in Figure 2 which shows the piecewise linear and quadratic box-spline obtained by averaging the characteristic function of the unit square in the directions $\begin{bmatrix} 1 \\ 1 \end{bmatrix}$ and $\begin{bmatrix} -1 \\ 1 \end{bmatrix}$,

$$B_{\begin{bmatrix} 1 & 0 \\ 0 & 1 \end{bmatrix}} \quad \longrightarrow \quad B_{\begin{bmatrix} 1 & 0 & 1 \\ 0 & 1 & 1 \end{bmatrix}} \quad \longrightarrow \quad B_{\begin{bmatrix} 1 & 0 & 1 & -1 \\ 0 & 1 & 1 & 1 \end{bmatrix}}.$$

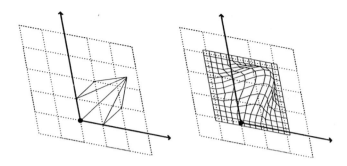

**Figure 2.** A linear and quadratic box-spline.

First, this yields the piecewise linear "hat-function", which is equal to 1 at $\begin{bmatrix}1\\1\end{bmatrix}$ and 0 outside the hexagon with vertices $\{\ \begin{bmatrix}0\\0\end{bmatrix}, \begin{bmatrix}1\\0\end{bmatrix}, \begin{bmatrix}2\\1\end{bmatrix}, \begin{bmatrix}2\\2\end{bmatrix}, \begin{bmatrix}1\\2\end{bmatrix}, \begin{bmatrix}0\\1\end{bmatrix}\ \}$, and then the piecewise quadratic "Zwart-element".

To justify the definition (2), it remains to show that the box-spline $B_\Xi$ does not depend on the order of the columns of the matrix $\Xi$. This follows from the

**Integral Formula.** *For any smooth function $\varphi$,*

$$\int_{\mathbb{R}^2} B_\Xi(x)\varphi(x)\,dx = \int_\square \varphi(\Xi t)\,dt, \tag{3}$$

*where $\square := [0,1)^n$. In particular, setting $\varphi = 1$ gives $\int B_\Xi = 1$.*

**Proof:** For $n = 2$, this just requires a change of variables,

$$\int B_\Xi \varphi = |\det \Xi|^{-1} \int_{\Xi\square} \varphi = \int_\square \varphi \circ \Xi.$$

Assuming by induction that (3) holds with $\Xi$ replaced by $\Xi\backslash\xi$, one obtains for $n > 2$ that

$$\int B_\Xi \varphi = \int_{\mathbb{R}^2} \int_0^1 B_{\Xi\backslash\xi}(x - t\xi)\,\varphi(x)\,dt dx$$

$$= \int_0^1 \int_{\mathbb{R}^2} B_{\Xi\backslash\xi}(x)\,\varphi(x + t\xi)\,dx dt$$

$$= \int_0^1 \int_{\square'} \varphi([\Xi\backslash\xi]t' + t\xi)\,dt' dt = \int_\square \varphi \circ \Xi,$$

where $\square' := [0,1)^{n-1}$. ∎

**Notation.** *It will be convenient to "treat the matrix $\Xi$ as a set"; i.e., to write $\{\xi \in \Xi\}$ for the columns of $\Xi$ counting multiplicities. Thus, $Z \subset \Xi$ means that*

$Z$ is a submatrix of $\Xi$. The submatrix of $\Xi$ obtained by deleting (adding) the columns of $Z$ is denoted by $\Xi\backslash Z$ ($\Xi \cup Z$). In particular, $Z$ can be a single column $\xi$ of the matrix $\Xi$. The phrase "$Z$ spans" is used as abbreviation for "the columns of $Z$ span $\mathbb{R}^2$". Finally, the number of columns of $\Xi$ is denoted by $n(\Xi)$.

As an example, consider

$$\Xi = \begin{bmatrix} 1 & 0 & 1 & 2 & 1 \\ 0 & 1 & 1 & 0 & 0 \end{bmatrix},$$

and let

$$\xi = \begin{bmatrix} 1 \\ 0 \end{bmatrix}, \quad Z = \begin{bmatrix} 1 & 1 \\ 0 & 1 \end{bmatrix}.$$

Then one has, e.g.,

$$\Xi\backslash\xi = \begin{bmatrix} 0 & 1 & 2 & 1 \\ 1 & 1 & 0 & 0 \end{bmatrix}, \quad \Xi \cup Z = \begin{bmatrix} 1 & 0 & 1 & 2 & 1 & 1 & 1 \\ 0 & 1 & 1 & 0 & 0 & 0 & 1 \end{bmatrix}.$$

It follows directly from either the inductive definition or the integral formula that $B_\Xi$ is nonnegative and

$$B_\Xi(x) > 0 \iff x \in \Xi\square = \{x = \Xi t : \ t \in [0, 1)^n\}.$$

It is less obvious (cf. Propositions 2, 3 below) that $B_\Xi$ is a piecewise polynomial of degree $n(\Xi) - 2$ and smoothness $m(\Xi) - 2$, where

$$m(\Xi) := \min_{Z \text{ does not span}} n(\Xi\backslash Z). \tag{4}$$

The mesh for $B_\Xi$ is contained in the union of the lines in the directions $\xi$ translated over the integer grid $\mathbb{Z}^2$; *i.e.*, in the set

$$\Gamma(\Xi) := \cup \{\alpha + \mathbb{R}\xi : \ \alpha \in \mathbb{Z}^2, \ \xi \in \Xi\}. \tag{5}$$

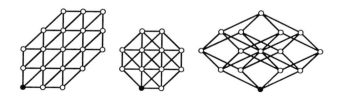

**Figure 3.** Meshes for $\Xi = \begin{bmatrix} 1 & 1 & 0 & 0 & 1 & 1 \\ 0 & 0 & 1 & 1 & 1 & 1 \end{bmatrix}, \begin{bmatrix} 1 & 0 & 1 & -1 \\ 0 & 1 & 1 & 1 \end{bmatrix}, \begin{bmatrix} 1 & -1 & 2 & -2 \\ 1 & 1 & 1 & 1 \end{bmatrix}.$

**Differentiation.** *Denote by $D_\xi$ the derivative in the direction of the vector $\xi$ and by $\nabla_\xi$ the corresponding backward difference; i.e.,*

$$D_\xi f = [\partial_1 f \quad \partial_2 f] \cdot \xi, \quad \nabla_\xi f = f - f(\cdot - \xi).$$

*More generally, define $D_\Xi f := \prod_{\xi \in \Xi} D_\xi$ and $\nabla_\Xi f := \prod_{\xi \in \Xi} \nabla_\xi$.*

Then,

$$D_Z B_\Xi = \nabla_Z B_{\Xi \setminus Z}. \tag{6}$$

It is sufficient to prove (6) for $Z = \xi$. In this case, it follows from the inductive definition that

$$D_\xi B_\Xi = D_\xi \int_0^1 B_{\Xi \setminus \xi}(\cdot - t\xi) \, dt = -\int_0^1 \frac{d}{dt} B_{\Xi \setminus \xi}(\cdot - t\xi) \, dt$$

$$= B_{\Xi \setminus \xi} - B_{\Xi \setminus \xi}(\cdot - \xi) = \nabla_\xi B_{\Xi \setminus \xi}.$$

With the aid of identity (6), one can describe the local structure of $B_\Xi$. The basic tool is the following

**Lemma 1.** *For any $w \in \mathbb{R}^2$,*

$$D_w^r = \sum_{\substack{Z \text{ spans, } n(\Xi \setminus Z) = r}} a_Z D_{\Xi \setminus Z} + \sum_{\substack{Z' \text{ does not span}}} a_{Z'} D_w^{r-n(\Xi \setminus Z')} D_{\Xi \setminus Z'}. \tag{7}$$

**Proof:** Since the columns of $\Xi$ span $\mathbb{R}^2$, $w$ can be written as a linear combination $w = \sum a_\xi \xi$, and, correspondingly,

$$D_w = \sum a_\xi D_\xi.$$

This gives (7) for $r = 1$ since $\xi = \Xi \setminus [\Xi \setminus \xi]$ and $\Xi \setminus \xi$ either does or does not span. Using induction, assume that (7) is valid for some $r$ and apply $D_w$ to both sides,

$$D_w^{r+1} = \sum a_Z D_w D_{\Xi \setminus Z} + \sum a_{Z'} D_w^{r+1-n(\Xi \setminus Z')} D_{\Xi \setminus Z'}. \tag{8}$$

If $Z$ spans, $D_w$ can be expressed as linear combination of the derivatives $D_\zeta$ with $\zeta \in Z$,

$$D_w = \sum_\zeta a_{Z,\zeta} D_\zeta.$$

Substituting this into (8), and using that $\zeta \cup \Xi \setminus Z = \Xi \setminus [Z \setminus \zeta]$, the first sum on the right hand side equals

$$\sum_Z \sum_\zeta a_Z a_{Z,\zeta} D_{\Xi \setminus (Z \setminus \zeta)}.$$

As before, $Z\backslash\zeta$ either does or does not span. In any case, the corresponding summands are of the type appearing on the right hand side of (7); hence the lemma holds with $r$ replaced by $r+1$. ∎

**Proposition 2.** *In any connected component of the complement of the mesh; i.e., the set* $\mathbb{R}^2\backslash\Gamma(\Xi)$, $B_\Xi$ *is a polynomial of degree* $\leq n(\Xi) - 2$.

**Proof:** For $r = n(\Xi) - 1$, the first sum on the right hand side of (7) is empty, since $r = n(\Xi\backslash Z)$ implies that $n(Z) = 1$. Therefore,

$$D_w^r B_\Xi = \sum_{Z' \text{ does not span}} a_{Z'} D_w^{r-n(\Xi\backslash Z')} D_{\Xi\backslash Z'} B_\Xi. \tag{9}$$

Fix a particular matrix $Z'$. Since $Z'$ does not span, the columns of $Z'$ are scalar multiples of some vector $\xi \in \Xi$. Choose a vector $\xi'$ in $\Xi\backslash Z'$ which is not a scalar multiple of $\xi$. Then, by the differentiation formula (6),

$$D_{\Xi\backslash Z'} B_\Xi = D_{\xi'} D_{[\Xi\backslash Z']\backslash \xi'} B_\Xi = D_{\xi'} \nabla_{[\Xi\backslash Z']\backslash \xi'} B_{\xi' \cup Z'},$$

since $\Xi\backslash[[\Xi\backslash Z']\backslash \xi'] = \Xi\backslash[\Xi\backslash[\xi' \cup Z']] = \xi' \cup Z'$. By the inductive definition, $B_{\xi' \cup Z'}$ is obtained by averaging the characteristic function of the parallelogram spanned by scalar multiples of the vectors $\xi$, $\xi'$ in the direction of $\xi$ only; i.e.,

$$B_{\xi' \cup Z'}(t\xi + t'\xi') = f(t) \chi_{[0,1)}(t')$$

for some function $f$. Therefore, $D_{\xi'} B_{\xi' \cup Z'} = 0$ on any set not cut by the lines $\mathbb{R}\xi$ and $\xi' + \mathbb{R}\xi$. Since $D$ and $\nabla$ commute, it follows that all terms on the right hand side of (9) vanish on the complement of $\Gamma(\Xi)$. ∎

**Proposition 3.** $B_\Xi$ *is* $m(\Xi) - 2$ *times continuously differentiable.*

**Proof:** For $r = m - 1$, the second sum on the right hand side of (7) is empty by definition (4) of $m$ (the exponent of $D_w$ would be negative). Therefore, for any $w$,

$$D_w^r B_\Xi = \sum_{Z \text{ spans}} a_Z D_{\Xi\backslash Z} B_\Xi = \sum a_Z \nabla_{\Xi\backslash Z} B_Z,$$

which shows that all $r$-th derivatives of $B_\Xi$ are bounded and implies continuity of the derivatives of order less than $r$. ∎

By definition of $m$, multiplicities in $\Xi$ reduce the smoothness of the corresponding box-spline. For example, for

$$\Xi = \begin{bmatrix} 1 & 0 & 1 & 1 & 0 & -2 \\ 0 & 1 & 2 & 2 & 1 & -4 \end{bmatrix},$$

one has

$$m(\Xi) = n(\Xi\backslash Z) = 3, \quad Z = \begin{bmatrix} 1 & 1 & -2 \\ 2 & 2 & -4 \end{bmatrix};$$

i.e., $B_\Xi$ is only once continuously differentiable. On the other hand, if any two columns of $\Xi$ are linearly independent, then $B_\Xi$ is of maximal smoothness; i.e., $m(\Xi) = n(\Xi) - 1$.

**Recurrence Relation.** If $x = \Xi t = \sum_{\xi \in \Xi} t_\xi \xi$ and the box-splines $B_{\Xi \setminus \xi}$, $\xi \in \Xi$, are continuous at $x$, then

$$(n(\Xi) - 2) \, B_\Xi(x) = \sum_{\xi \in \Xi} t_\xi B_{\Xi \setminus \xi}(x) + (1 - t_\xi) B_{\Xi \setminus \xi}(x - \xi). \qquad (10)$$

**Proof:** Since $x = \Xi t$,

$$(D_x B_\Xi)(x) = \sum_{\nu=1}^{2} x_\nu (\partial_\nu B_\Xi)(x) = \sum_{\xi \in \Xi} t_\xi D_\xi B_\Xi,$$

with $\partial_\nu$ the partial derivative with respect to $x_\nu$. Therefore, in view of the differentiation formula (6), the recurrence relation is equivalent to the identity

$$(n - 2) B_\Xi = D_x B_\Xi + \sum_{\xi \in \Xi} B_{\Xi \setminus \xi}(\cdot - \xi).$$

Because of the continuity assumption, one has to verify only the weak form of this identity; *i.e.*, it is sufficient to show that for any smooth function $\varphi$,

$$\int_{\mathbb{R}^2} \Big( (n-2) B_\Xi(x) - D_x B_\Xi(x) \Big) \, \varphi(x) \, dx = \sum \int_{\mathbb{R}^2} B_{\Xi \setminus \xi}(x) \varphi(x + \xi) \, dx. \quad (11)$$

Integrating by parts, gives

$$-\int D_x B_\Xi \varphi = \sum_\nu \int B_\Xi(x) \partial_\nu (x_\nu \varphi(x)) \, dx$$

$$= \int B_\Xi(x) \Big( 2\varphi(x) + \sum x_\nu (\partial_\nu \varphi)(x) \Big) \, dx.$$

Hence, using the integral formula (3), (11) can be written as

$$\int_\square (n\varphi(\Xi t) + \sum_\nu (\Xi t)_\nu (\partial_\nu \varphi)(\Xi t)) \, dt = \sum_{\xi \in \Xi} \int_{\square'} \varphi([\Xi \setminus \xi] t' + \xi) \, dt', \qquad (12)$$

where $\square' := [0, 1)^{n-1}$. Noting that, by the chain rule,

$$\sum_\nu (\Xi t)_\nu \, (\partial_\nu \varphi)(\Xi t) = \sum_{\mu=1}^{n} t_\mu \, \partial'_\mu \varphi(\Xi t)$$

with $\partial'_\mu := \partial / \partial t_\mu$, the left hand side of (12) simplifies to

$$\int_\square \sum_\mu \partial'_\mu (t_\mu \varphi(\Xi t)) \, dt.$$

The validity of (12) follows now from the fundamental theorem of calculus, applied in the form

$$\int_0^1 \partial'_\mu f(t', t_\mu) \, dt_\mu = f(t', 1) - f(t', 0)$$

with $f(t', t_\mu) := \int_{\square'} t_\mu \varphi([\Xi \setminus \xi^\mu] t' + \xi^\mu t_\mu) \, dt'$. ∎

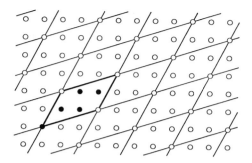

**Figure 4.** Sublattice and elements of the factor group.

## §3. Cardinal Splines

A *cardinal spline* $s$ is, by definition, a linear combination of translates of box-splines $B_\Xi$ over the integer lattice $\mathbb{Z}^2$; *i.e.*,

$$s(x) = \sum_{\alpha \in \mathbb{Z}^2} c(\alpha) B_\Xi(x - \alpha), \quad x \in \mathbb{R}^2, \tag{13}$$

with coefficients $c(\alpha) \in \mathbb{R}$. Because of the local support and the positivity of the box-splines, the function $s$ is well approximated by the coefficients $c$. For example, monotonicity (convexity) of the grid function $c : \mathbb{Z}^2 \mapsto \mathbb{R}$ in a particular direction $\xi$ implies monotonicity (convexity) of the corresponding cardinal spline in this direction. A more fundamental property of the box-spline basis is that the translates form a

**Partition of Unity.** *For all $x \in \mathbb{R}^2$,*

$$1 = \sum B_\Xi(x - \alpha). \tag{14}$$

**Proof:** By (2),

$$A_\xi \left( \sum B_\Xi(\cdot - \alpha) \right) = \sum B_{\Xi \cup \xi}(\cdot - \alpha).$$

Therefore, in view of the inductive definition of $B_\Xi$, (14) has to be proved for $n(\Xi) = 2$ only. In this case,

$$B_\Xi = \chi_{\Xi \square}/|\det \Xi|,$$

and, since the translates of the parallelograms $\Xi \square$ over the sublattice $\Xi \mathbb{Z}^2 = \{\beta = \Xi \alpha : \alpha \in \mathbb{Z}^2\}$ form a partition $\mathbb{R}^2$, it follows that

$$\sum_{\beta \in \Xi \mathbb{Z}^2} B_\Xi(\cdot - \beta) = 1/|\det \Xi|.$$

This implies (14) since $\mathbb{Z}^2$ is the disjoint union of $\gamma + \Xi \mathbb{Z}^2$ with $\gamma$ in the factor group $\mathbb{Z}^2/\Xi \mathbb{Z}^2$ which has exactly $|\det \Xi|$ elements. ■

A box-spline surface $S$, by definition, can be parametrized by a cardinal spline with coefficients $c(\alpha) \in \mathbb{R}^3$; *i.e.*,

$$S = \{s(x): \ x \in \mathcal{R}\}$$

with $s$ given by (13). Usually, the parameter domain $\mathcal{R}$ is a rectangle with integer boundaries, and then the range of summation in (13) can be restricted to

$$a(\mathcal{R}, \Xi) := \{\alpha: \ B_\Xi(x - \alpha) > 0 \text{ for some } x \in \mathcal{R}\}.$$

For practical purposes, $a(\mathcal{R}, \Xi)$ can be replaced by a rectangle $a'$ in $\mathbb{Z}^2$ containing $a$ if one defines

$$c(\alpha) := 0, \quad \text{for } \alpha \in a' \backslash a.$$

Of course, it is possible to choose $a' = \mathbb{Z}^2$, which is the most convenient convention for theoretical purposes and which will be adopted in the sequel.

The piecewise bilinear surface $S_c$, which interpolates the coefficients

$$c(\alpha), \quad \alpha \in a(\mathcal{R}, \Xi),$$

is called the *control net* of $S$. More precisely, $S_c$ is parametrized by

$$x \mapsto s_c(x) = \sum c_\alpha B_E(x - \alpha), \quad E := \begin{bmatrix} 1 & 1 & 0 & 0 \\ 0 & 0 & 1 & 1 \end{bmatrix};$$

*i.e.*, is a bilinear cardinal spline. Since the translates of the box-spline are nonnegative and sum to one, a point on the box-spline surface $S$ lies in the convex hull of the coefficients,

$$s(x) \in \text{conv}\{c(\alpha): \ \alpha \in a(x, \Xi)\}.$$

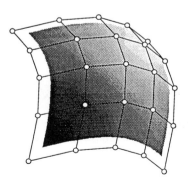

**Figure 5.** Box-spline surface with control net.

## §4. Subdivision Algorithms

A box-spline surface can be evaluated by means of the recurrence relation for $B_\Xi$. However, if only a sufficiently good approximation is needed, then subdivision algorithms are considerably more efficient. The idea is to express $B_\Xi$ in terms of the box-splines $B_\Xi(\cdot/h - \alpha)$ of the refined lattice $h\mathbb{Z}^2$,

$$B_\Xi(x) = \sum_{\alpha \in \mathbb{Z}^2} b(\alpha, h, \Xi) B_\Xi(x/h - \alpha). \tag{15}$$

The corresponding refinement of the control nets yields a rapidly converging approximation procedure.

**Notation.** *It will be convenient to use the following conventions and abbreviations. The Dirac sequence is denoted by $\delta$; i.e.,*

$$\delta(\alpha) = \begin{cases} 1, & \text{if } \alpha = 1; \\ 0, & \text{otherwise.} \end{cases}$$

*Any grid function $f : \mathbb{Z}^2 \mapsto \mathbb{R}$, is extended to a function on $\mathbb{R}^2$ by setting*

$$f(\alpha) := 0, \quad \text{for } \alpha \notin \mathbb{Z}^n.$$

*For $1/h \in \mathbb{N}$,*

$$\sum_\alpha^h \cdots$$

*denotes the sum over all $\alpha \in \mathbb{Z}^n$ with $\alpha_\nu \in [0, 1/h)$; i.e., with $h\alpha \in \square$. The dimension $n$ will always be clear from the context. For example, if $\alpha$ appears in the form $\ldots \Xi\alpha \ldots$, then $n = n(\Xi)$.*

The coefficients

$$b(\cdot, h, \Xi) : \mathbb{Z}^2 \mapsto \mathbb{R},$$

which are referred to as *discrete box-splines*, are easily computed from the inductive definition of $B_\Xi$.

**Lemma 4.**

$$b(\alpha, h, \Xi) = h^{n-2} \sum_\beta^h \delta(\alpha - \Xi\beta). \tag{16}$$

**Proof:** If $Z \subset \Xi$ with $n(Z) = 2$, then $B_Z$ is the normalized characteristic function of the parallelogram $Z\square$. Since $Z\square$ can be partitioned by the scaled parallelograms $hZ\square$ shifted over the grid

$$\{Zh\beta : \beta \in \mathbb{Z}^2 \text{ and } h\beta \in \square\},$$

it follows that

$$B_Z(x) = \sum_\beta^h B_Z(x/h - Z\beta).$$

Averaging both sides in the direction $\xi$ gives

$$B_{Z \cup \xi}(x) = \sum{}^h \int_0^1 B_Z((x - t\xi)/h - Z\beta) \, dt.$$

With $y := x/h - Z\beta$, the integral in the sum equals

$$\int_0^1 B_Z(y - t\xi/h) \, dt = h \int_0^{1/h} B_Z(y - t\xi) \, dt = h \sum_\gamma{}^h \int_0^1 B_Z(y - (t + \gamma)\xi) \, dt$$

$$= h \sum{}^h B_{Z \cup \xi}(y - \gamma\xi).$$

Hence, with $\Xi := Z \cup \xi$, one obtains

$$B_\Xi(x) = h \sum_\beta{}^h \sum_\gamma{}^h B_\Xi(x/h - Z\beta - \xi\gamma) = h \sum_{\beta'}{}^h B_\Xi(x/h - \Xi\beta'). \tag{17}$$

Repeating the averaging process shows that (17) holds for general $\Xi$ with $h$ replaced by $h^{n(\xi)-2}$. Identity (16) follows by counting the number of $h\beta' \in \square$ for which $\alpha = \Xi\beta'$. ∎

As a consequence of Lemma 4, one obtains the coefficients for representing a cardinal spline with respect to a scaled box-spline basis.

**Corollary.** *For any integer $1/h$, a box-spline surface has the equivalent representations*

$$\sum_\alpha c(\alpha)B_\Xi(x - \alpha) = \sum_\alpha c(\alpha, h, \Xi)B_\Xi(x/h - \alpha), \tag{18}$$

*where the coefficients with respect to the scaled basis are defined as*

$$c(\alpha, h, \Xi) := h^{n(\Xi)-2} \sum_\beta{}^h c(h\alpha - h\Xi\beta). \tag{19}$$

**Proof:** Substituting (15) with $b$ given by (16) into the left hand side of (18) yields

$$\sum_\alpha c(\alpha)B_\Xi(x - \alpha) = h^{n-2} \sum_\alpha \sum_\beta \sum_\gamma{}^h c(\alpha)\delta(\beta - \Xi\gamma)B_\Xi((x - \alpha)/h - \beta).$$

Changing the summation index $\beta$ to $\alpha' := \alpha/h + \beta$ and evaluating the sum over $\alpha$, leaves, by definition of $\delta$, only terms with $\alpha = h(\alpha' - \beta) = h(\alpha' - \Xi\gamma)$. Hence the triple sum simplifies to

$$\sum_{\alpha'} \sum_\gamma{}^h c(h(\alpha' - \Xi\gamma))B_\Xi(x/h - \alpha')$$

which proves (19). ■

For $h = 2^{-r}$, the expression for $c(\alpha, h, \Xi)$ can be computed recursively by repeated application of the refinement procedure with $h = 1/2$; *i.e.*, by computing successively the coefficients

$$c^{[\ell]}(\alpha) := c(\alpha, 2^{-\ell}, \Xi).$$

**Subdivision Algorithm.** *Choose any basis $Z \subset \Xi$ and compute*
    (i) $c^{[\ell]}(\alpha) := \sum_{\beta \in \{0,1\}^2} c^{[\ell-1]}(\alpha/2 - Z\beta/2)$
    (ii) *for $\xi \in \Xi \backslash Z$ do:*
$$c^{[\ell]}(\alpha) \leftarrow (c^{[\ell]}(\alpha) + c^{[\ell]}(\alpha - \xi))/2.$$

For the derivation of this algorithm one has to show that the coefficients $c^{[1]}(\cdot)$ satisfy (19) with $h = 1/2$. For $n(\Xi) = 2$; *i.e.*, for $Z = \Xi$, only the first step of the algorithm is applied, and definitions (19) and (i) are identical. The general case follows by induction. Assume that $c^{[1]}(\alpha) = c(\alpha, 1/2, \Xi)$, as defined by the algorithm, equals

$$2^{2-n} \sum_{\beta}^{1/2} c(\alpha/2 - \Xi\beta/2).$$

Adding one more direction $\xi$, the algorithm yields

$$c^{[1]}(\alpha) \leftarrow 2^{1-n} \left( \sum_{\beta}^{1/2} c(\alpha/2 - \Xi\beta/2) + \sum_{\beta}^{1/2} c(\alpha/2 - \xi/2 - \Xi\beta/2) \right)$$

$$= 2^{1-n} \sum_{\beta}^{1/2} \sum_{\gamma}^{1/2} c(\alpha/2 - \Xi\beta/2 - \xi\gamma/2)$$

which, again, agrees with (19).

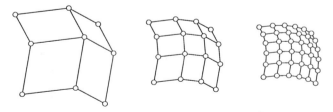

**Figure 6.** Subdivision of control nets.

The subdivsion algorithm becomes particularly simple if $\Xi$ contains the unit matrix; *i.e.*, if one can choose

$$Z = \begin{bmatrix} 1 & 0 \\ 0 & 1 \end{bmatrix}$$

in step (i) of the algorithm. In this case, for

$$\alpha = 2\alpha' + \alpha'', \quad \alpha'' \in \{0,1\}^2,$$

there is a unique $\beta$, namely $\beta = \alpha''$, for which $(\alpha/2 - \mathbb{Z}\beta/2) \in \mathbb{Z}$. Therefore, the first step of the algorithm can be written as

(i') $c^{[\ell]}(2\alpha' + \alpha'') = c^{[\ell-1]}(\alpha'), \quad \alpha'' \in \{0,1\}^2.$

Further, combining the steps in the do-loop yields an alternate form of (ii), namely

(ii') $c^{[\ell]}(\alpha) \leftarrow \sum_\beta w_{\Xi \backslash \mathbb{Z}}(\beta) c^{[\ell]}(\alpha - \beta),$

with appropriate weights $w$.

**Example.** For $\Xi = \begin{bmatrix} 1 & 0 & 1 & -1 \\ 0 & 1 & 1 & 1 \end{bmatrix}$ one has

$$4 \, w_{\begin{bmatrix} 1 & -1 \\ 1 & 1 \end{bmatrix}} = \begin{bmatrix} 0 & 1 & 0 \\ 1 & 0 & 1 \\ 0 & 1 & 0 \end{bmatrix},$$

where the entry corresponding to the index $\begin{bmatrix} 0 \\ 0 \end{bmatrix}$ is printed bold. Applying the algorithm to the rectangular array of control points

$$\ldots \begin{matrix} p & q \\ r & s \end{matrix} \ldots,$$

step (i') yields

$$\ldots \begin{matrix} p & p & q & q \\ p & p & q & q \\ r & r & s & s \\ r & r & s & s \end{matrix} \ldots$$

and step (ii')

$$\ldots \begin{matrix} \frac{r+2p+q}{4} & \frac{p+2q+s}{4} \\ \frac{p+2r+s}{4} & \frac{r+2s+q}{4} \end{matrix} \ldots$$

The display below shows two further examples, the second of which is recognized as Chaikin's algorithm for tensor product B-splines.

$$8 \, w_{\begin{bmatrix} 1 & 0 & 1 \\ 0 & 1 & 1 \end{bmatrix}} = \begin{bmatrix} 0 & 1 & 1 \\ 1 & 2 & 1 \\ 1 & 1 & 0 \end{bmatrix}, \qquad 16 \, w_{\begin{bmatrix} 1 & 1 & 0 & 0 \\ 0 & 0 & 1 & 1 \end{bmatrix}} = \begin{bmatrix} 1 & 2 & 1 \\ 2 & 4 & 2 \\ 1 & 2 & 1 \end{bmatrix}.$$

Subdivision masks

**Convergence of Subdivision.** *Assume that for any $\xi$, the matrix $\Xi \backslash \xi$ spans and that*

$$\Xi \mathbb{Z}^n = \mathbb{Z}^2. \tag{20}$$

Then, for $s$ defined by (13),

$$|c(\alpha, h, \Xi) - s(x)| \leq \text{const } h, \quad \text{for } x/h - \alpha \in \Xi\square, \tag{21}$$

with const depending on $\Xi$ and $\max_{\xi, \alpha} |\nabla_\xi c(\alpha)|$.

While the assumption (20) can be shown to be necessary, the assumption that $\Xi\backslash\xi$ spans merely excludes the essentially univariate situation when the parametrization is constant in one direction. The proof requires several auxiliary Lemmas.

**Lemma 5.** *For $\xi \in \Xi$,*

$$\nabla_\xi c(\alpha, h, \Xi) = h^{n-2} \sum_\beta^h \nabla_\xi c(h\alpha - h[\Xi\backslash\xi]\beta). \tag{22}$$

**Proof:** Let $Z := \Xi\backslash\xi$. By (19), the left hand side of (22) equals

$$h^{n-2} \sum_{\sigma=0}^1 (-1)^\sigma \sum_\beta^h c(h\alpha - \sigma h\xi - h\Xi\beta) =$$

$$h^{n-2} \sum_{\beta'}^h \sum_{\sigma=0}^1 \sum_\gamma^h c(h\alpha - \sigma h\xi - hZ\beta' - h\gamma\xi).$$

The two innermost sums can be rewritten as

$$\sum_{\gamma=0,\ldots,1/h-1} c(h\alpha - hZ\beta' - h\gamma\xi) - \sum_{\gamma'=1,\ldots,1/h} c(h\alpha - hZ\beta' - h\gamma'\xi)$$

$$= c(h\alpha - hZ\beta') - c(h\alpha - hZ\beta' - h(1/h)\xi) = (\nabla_\xi c)(h\alpha - hZ\beta')$$

which proves (22). ∎

**Lemma 6.** *If $\Xi\backslash\xi$ spans, then*

$$|\nabla_\xi c(\alpha, h, \Xi)| \leq \text{const } h \max_\beta |\nabla_\xi c(\beta)|$$

with const depending on $\Xi$.

**Proof:** It is sufficient to show that at most $h^{3-n}$ summands contribute to the sum on the right hand side of (22). To this end, let $\Xi\backslash\xi = Z \cup Z'$ with $Z$ a basis. The number of these summands equals the number of indices $\beta$ with $h\beta \in \square$ for which

$$j := h\alpha - h[\Xi\backslash\xi]\beta = h\alpha - hZ\gamma - hZ'\gamma' \in \mathbb{Z}^2.$$

For $[\gamma \ \ \gamma'] \in [0, 1/h)^{n-1}$, the index $j$ varies in the bounded set

$$J := h\alpha - Z\square - Z'\square.$$

Therefore, since for each $j$ and $\gamma'$ there is at most one $\gamma$, the number of summands is bounded by

$$\#(J \cap \mathbb{Z}^2) \times h^{-n(Z')} = \#(J \cap \mathbb{Z}^2) \times h^{-(n(\Xi)-n(\xi)-n(Z))} \leq \text{const } h^{-(n-3)}.$$

**Proof of (21).** By Lemma 6,

$$\max_{\xi,\alpha} |\nabla_\xi c(\alpha, h, \Xi)| \leq \text{const } h.$$

Since the translates of $B_\Xi$ form a partition of unity,

$$c(\alpha, h) - s(x) = \sum_\beta (c(\alpha, h) - c(\beta, h)) B_\Xi(x/h - \beta), \tag{23}$$

where the sum needs to be taken only over all $\beta$ for which $x/h - \beta \in \Xi\square$. Since also $x/h - \alpha \in \Xi\square$,

$$|\alpha - \beta| \leq \text{const}'$$

for those $\beta$. The assumption (20) implies that any vector $y$ can be written as linear combination of the vectors $\xi \in \Xi$ with integer coefficients,

$$y = \sigma_1 \xi^1 + \ldots + \sigma_r \xi^n,$$

where one may assume that $\sigma = \pm 1$ by allowing the vectors from $\Xi$ to be repeated. In other words, any two points in the lattice $\mathbb{Z}^2$ can be connected by a path using directions from $\Xi$ and $-\Xi$ only. This implies in particular that the difference

$$c(\alpha, h) - c(\beta, h)$$

can be written as a sum of backward differences corresponding to the path connecting $\alpha$ and $\beta$. This shows that the relevant terms in (23) are of order $O(h)$ uniformly in $\alpha$ and $\beta$. ∎

## §5. Selected Theorems

In this section a few examples of the rich mathematical theory for box-splines are given. This is a small disgression from the main topic of this paper, intended to stimulate the interest of the reader in multivariate splines and, perhaps, in some of the references below.

**Partition of the Support** [9]. Denote by $\mathcal{B}(\Xi)$ the set of all bases $Z \subset \Xi$, counting multiplicities. Then there exists points $\alpha_Z$ such that $\Xi\square$ is partitioned by the parallelograms

$$\alpha_Z + Z[0, 1)^2, \quad Z \in \mathcal{B}(\Xi).$$

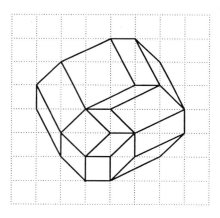

**Figure 7.** Partition for $\Xi = \begin{bmatrix} 1 & 0 & 1 & -1 & 2 & -1 \\ 0 & 1 & 1 & 1 & 1 & 2 \end{bmatrix}$.

**Tilings of the Plane** [3]. For the function

$$f_\Xi(x) := \prod_{\xi \in \Xi} \xi x,$$

the translates of the set

$$\Omega(\Xi) := \{x : |f(x)| < |f(x + \alpha)|, \; \forall \; \alpha \in \mathbb{Z}^2 \backslash 0\}$$

over the lattice $\mathbb{Z}^2$ form a tiling (*i.e.*, an essentially disjoint partition) of $\mathbb{R}^2$.

While the sets $\Omega$ can be defined under rather mild assumptions on the function $f$, for the specific $f$ defined above, these sets play the key role in the characterization of functions of exponential type as limits of cardinal series [4].

**Cardinal Interpolation** [5]. For any box-spline $B_\Xi$ there exists a "Lagrange spline"

$$Q(x) := \sum_\alpha q(\alpha) B_\Xi(x - \alpha)$$

which interpolates the data $\delta$ on $\mathbb{Z}^2$ with at most polynomial growth; *i.e.*, with

$$|Q(x)| = O(|x|^r), \quad |x| \to \infty,$$

for some $r > 0$.

Since, in general, the translates of the box-splines are not linearly independent, cardinal interpolation is not well posed in the classical sense. The above theorem shows that an interpolant does exist also in the "ill posed case" under appropriate assumptions on the data.

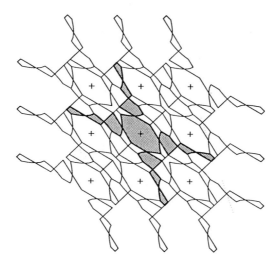

**Figure 8.** Tiling for $\Xi = \left[\begin{smallmatrix} 1 & 3 \\ 3 & 1 \end{smallmatrix}\right]$.

## §6. Bibliographic Comments.

Most of the material in this survey article is taken from [2,6,10]. The section on subdivision algorithms is based on [1,7,8,11]. But, the convergence theorem is proved under a slightly weaker assumption, using the method in [6].

## References

1. Boehm, W., Subdividing multivariate splines, Comput. Aided Design **15** (1983), 345–352.
2. de Boor, C. and K. Höllig, B-splines from parallelepipeds, J. Analyse Math. **42** (1982/83), 99–115.
3. de Boor, C. and K. Höllig, Box-spline tilings, preprint.
4. de Boor, C., K. Höllig, and S.D. Riemenschneider, Convergence of cardinal series, Proc. Amer. Math. Soc. **98** (1986), 457–460.
5. de Boor, C., K. Höllig, and S. Riemenschneider, Fundamental solutions for multivariate difference equations, Amer. Math. J., to appear.
6. de Boor, C., K. Höllig, and S. Riemenschneider, Box-splines, preprint.
7. Cohen, E., T. Lyche and R. Riesenfeld, Discrete box-splines and refinement algorithms, Comput. Aided Geom. Design **1** (1984), 131–148.
8. Dahmen, W. and C. A. Micchelli, Subdivision algorithms for the generation of box-spline surfaces, Comput. Aided Geom. Design **1** (1984), 115-130.
9. Dahmen, W. and C. A. Micchelli, On the solution of certain systems of partial difference equations and the linear independence of translates of box-splines, Trans. Amer. Math. Soc. **292** (1985), 305-320.

10. Höllig, K., Box-splines, in *Approximation Theory V*, C. K. Chui, L. L. Schumaker, and J. Ward (eds.), Academic Press, N. Y., 1986, 71–95.

11. Prautzsch, H., Unterteilungsalgorithmen für Multivariate Splines – ein geometrischer Zugang, Dissertation, TU Braunschweig, 1984.

Klaus Höllig
Mathematisches Institut A
Universität Stuttgart
Pfaffenwaldring 57
7000 Stuttgart 80
W. GERMANY

Supported by the United States Army under Contract No. DAAG29-80-C-0041
Sponsored by the National Science Foundation under Grant No. DMS-8351187

EMAIL: bitnet: labj @ ds0rus1i

# Parallelization of the Subdivision Algorithm for Intersection of Bézier Curves on the FPS T20

## A. Kaufmann

**Abstract.** The subdivision algorithm[1,4] is well-known in sequential programming, but it is defined as a parallel process. What is the performance of this algorithm on a parallel computer? I will try to answer this question by discussing a few experimental results.

### §1. Introduction

The parallelization of the subdivision algorithm entails defining:

- processes which make up the algorithm,
- the processors network,
- strategies to share *basic-inputs* in the network,
- vectorial parts of processes in the algorithm.

Since it is difficult to study the algorithm theoretically, here we give results for a particular implementation on the FPS T20.

### §2. The FPS T20

The parallel computer FPS T20 of Floating Point System Inc. is made up of sixteen processors, connected in a four dimensional hypercube [2] (cf. Figure 1). This computer has no shared-memory, but each processor has its own memory. Moreover, it has no synchronization between processors, and communication is expensive. With the hypercube, we can build three different networks: the ring, the torus, and obviously the hypercube. For the vectorization, each processor owns two *pipe-lines*, one for additions, and the other for multiplications.

Mathematical Methods in Computer Aided Geometric Design
Tom Lyche and Larry L. Schumaker (eds.), pp. 403–411.

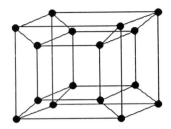

**Figure 1.** A four dimensional hypercube.

## §3. Parallelization of an Algorithm

In order to parallelize an algorithm on this type of computer, we must:

- write the sequential algorithm as a set of processes,
- classify this set with the partial order relationship: *the process $P_1$ is greater than the process $P_2$ if $P_1$ must be computed before $P_2$.* The processes must be chosen in order to reduce the number of communications.
- choose the "best" network.
- find, in each process, the vectorial parts, and implement them in *pipe-lines*.

**Definition 3.1.** *A pipe-line is an architecture specially designed to quickly compute operations on vectors (additions, or mutiplications term by term). It is composed of a few stages (cf. Figure 2) which work in parallel. Each stage computes a piece of the final operation, and sends its results to the next stage.*

## §4. The Bézier Algorithm [4]

Let $\Gamma(t) = \sum_{i=0}^{m} B_m^i(t) P_i$ be a polynomial curve, where $P_i$ are elements of $\mathbb{R}^2$, and $B_m^i(t)$ are the Bernstein polynomials $\binom{m}{i} t^i (1-t)^{m-i}$. Then, we have several interesting properties:

**Property 4.1.** $B_m^i(t) \geq 0$ for $t \in [0, 1]$.

**Property 4.2.** $\sum_{i=0}^{m} B_m^i(t) \equiv 1$.

**Property 4.3** (*Subdivision property*). *From the polygon $P = \{P_0, ..., P_m\}$ defined for $t \in [0, 1]$, we can obtain two polygons $P_g = \{P_0^0, ..., P_m^m\}$, and $P_d = \{P_m^m, ..., P_m^0\}$ defined respectively for $u \in [0, 0.5]$ and $v \in [0.5, 1]$ (cf. Figure 3). $P_g$ and $P_d$ define the same curve as $P$, and they are given by*

$$
P_i^k = \begin{cases} P^i, & \text{if } k=0 \\ \frac{P_i^{k-1} + P_{i-1}^{k-1}}{2}, & \text{otherwise.} \end{cases}
$$

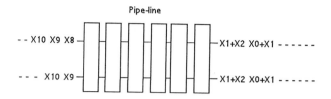

**Figure 2.** A pipe-line with six stages.

The intersection algorithm [4] is based on Property 4.3. Let P and Q be polygons defining two curves. Then,

- compute the min-max boxes of these polygons,
- study the intersection of min-max boxes. if we have no intersection, the algorithm is finished, else, we split P and Q in $(P_g, P_d, Q_g, Q_d)$, and we apply the algorithm recursively for pairs of polygons $(P_i, Q_j)$.

**Definition 4.4.** *The pairs $(P_i, Q_j)$ are called basic-inputs.*

## §5. Parallelization

### 5.1. Definition of Processes

**Hypothesis 5.1.** *The min-max boxes of P and Q have an intersection.*

Under Hypothesis 5.1, a *process* is defined as follows:

1) the subdivision of (P,Q) in $(P_g, P_d, Q_g, Q_d)$,
2) the computation of min-max boxes of $(P_g, P_d, Q_g, Q_d)$,
3) the storage, in a stack, of basic-inputs whose min-max boxes have an intersection.

**Theorem 5.2.** *The process with basic-input (P,Q) is greater than processes with basic-inputs $(P_i, Q_j)$. But, these processes are independent.*

**Proof:** The proof is obvious by definition of the subdivision. ■

For this algorithm, the best network is a tree. Since this network requires too many processors, it cannot be used. Hence, I chose a ring of processors where data circulates clockwise.

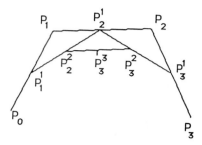

**Figure 3.** Example of the subdivision property.

## 5.2. Strategies to Share Basic-inputs

As communications are expensive, I searched for a compromise between communications and calculations. For this I studied four strategies to share basic-inputs in the network. For all of them, I classified processors in three classes: *the importing processors* which have no basic-input, *the neutral processors* which have a basic-input, and *the exporting processors* which have more than one basic-input.

**Definition 5.3.** *Let exp be a exporting processor, and imp an importing one, in the network.*

**Definition 5.4.** *Let $k$ be the number of exportable basic-inputs owned by exp.*

**Definition 5.5** (*First strategy*). *Exp will satisfy imp only if imp=exp+1.*

**Definition 5.6** (*Second strategy*). *Exp will satisfy imp if*

1. *we have no exporting processors between exp and imp,*
2. *we have at the most $k-1$ importing processors between exp and imp.*

**Definition 5.7** (*Third strategy*). *Here, I modify the classification of processors. A big importing processor has no basic-input, and it needs two. A normal importing processor has a basic-input, and it needs another one. A neutral processor has two basic-inputs. And, an exporting processor has more than two basic-inputs. Then, Exp will satisfy imp only if:*

1. *we have no exporting processor between them,*
2. *$2*I+i < k$, where $I$ (resp. $i$) is the number of big (resp. normal) importing processors between exp and imp.*

**Definition 5.8** (*Fourth strategy*). *For this strategy, I try to use the maximum number of processors. For this, I apply the second strategy while I have exporting processors and importing processors.*

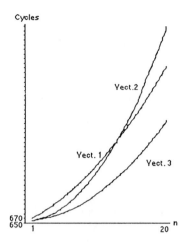

**Figure 4.** Comparison of algorithms.

## §6. Vectorization

Before describing the possible algorithms, we must choose the data structure. The more convenient data structure is point by point storage, where polygons are adjacent in memory.

**Definition 6.1.** $C^+$ *is the cost of an addition,* $C^*$ *is the cost of a multiplication,* $n$ *is the degree of the curve associated to* $P$, *and* $m$ *is the degree of the curve associated to* $Q$.

**Hypothesis 6.2.** $n \leq m$.

**Definition 6.3.** $P_{+1}$ *is the polygon* $P$ *without its first point,* $P_{-1}$ *is the polygon* $P$ *without its last point, and* $P^k$ *is* $k$-*th subdivision step of* $P$.

### 6.1. Algorithms

We have three possible algorithms:

**Algorithm 6.4.** *$P$ and $Q$ are subdivided separately. Then, the input data vectors are $P^k_{-1}$ and $P^k_{+1}$, or $Q^k_{-1}$ and $Q^k_{+1}$. The complexity of this is $(C^+ + C^*)(m + n) + n^2 + m^2$.*

**Algorithm 6.5.** *$P$ and $Q$ are subdivided in the same pass. For this, the input data vectors are $(PQ)^k_{-1}$ and $(PQ)^k_{+1}$. But, in this case, the computer makes useless calculations because $(PQ)$ is considered as a single polygon. Its complexity is $(C^+ + C^*)m + 2n^2 + m^2$.*

**Algorithm 6.6.** *For this last algorithm, I tried to suppress the useless calculations of the previous algorithm. For this, the input data vectors are $(P^k_{-1}Q^k_{+1})$ and $(P^k_{+1}Q^k_{-1})$. Its complexity is $(C^+ + C^*)m + n(n + 1) + m^2$.*

## 6.2. Comparison of Algorithms

**Hypothesis 6.7.** $(C^+ + C^*) = 13$, $m = 20$, and $n$ is between 1 and 20.

Under Hyphothesis 6.7, I obtain the comparison graph of Figure 4.

## §7. Experimental Results

**Definition 7.1.** *The speed-up of a parallel algorithm is the sequential time divided by the parallel time.*

## 7.1. General Speed-up

In Figure 5, we can see the speed-up compared to the ring length for the four strategies. This figure shows that the first and third strategies are not interesting, and the optimal network has eight processors. But, for the other two strategies, the optimal network seems be at thirty-two or sixty-four processors. The speed-up is not high because the values are averages of various examples, with different degrees of curves, and different numbers of intersection points.

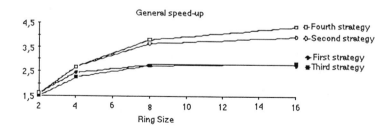

**Figure 5.** General speed-up.

## 7.2. Sequential Time

In Figure 6, we can see that sequential time is linear by comparison with the number of intersection points. The dotted line is the approximation line. The parallel time by comparison with the number of intersection points is also linear.

## 7.3. First and Third Strategies

In Figures 7 and 8, we find once more that the optimal network is made up of eight processors. We remark also that the growth of speed-up very quickly becomes slow.

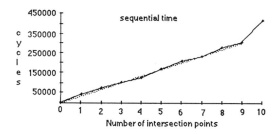

**Figure 6.** Sequential time.

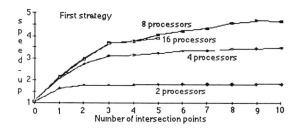

**Figure 7.** First strategy.

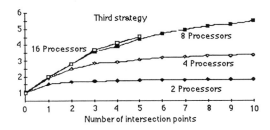

**Figure 8.** Third strategy.

## 7.4. Second and Fourth Strategies

Figures 9 and 10 show results for the second and fourth strategies. We see that for these strategies, the speed-up grows a longer time than in the previous strategies.

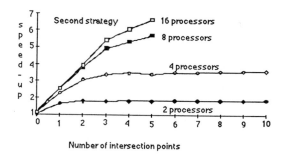

**Figure 9.** Second strategy.

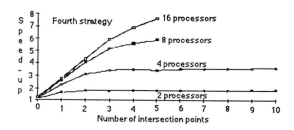

**Figure 10.** Fourth strategy.

## §8. Conclusion

On parallel computers whose processors can be organized in rings, the subdivision algorithm is interesting if we have only a few processors. In this case, the speed-up by comparison of the number of intersection points is linear if we choose a strategy of repartition which satisfies the maximum of processors.

We cannot hope for the speed-up to be equal to the number of processors because,

1) the cost of communications is not negligible, and communications are made in sequential with calculations.

2) secondly, we must wait for all processors having a job.

Here, I have presented a particular application of parallelism in CAGD. There are indeed many other applications which can be parallelized. For instance, we can parallelize surface intersection. However, in this case, designing parallel algorithms seems to be a more difficult task than for curve intersection.

## References

1. Boehm, W., G. Farin, and J. Kahmann, A survey of curves and surfaces methods in CAGD, Comput. Aided Geom. Design **1** (1984), 1–60.
2. FPS Inc., *Understanding the FPS series: system introduction and publications guide*, June, 1988.
3. Kaufmann, A., Parallelization of the subdivision algorithm for Bézier curves intersection, Technical Report RT-43-IMAG, Lab. TIM3, Univ. J. Fourier, Grenoble, France, 1988.
4. Lane, J. M. and R. F. Riesenfield, A theoretical development for the computer generation and display of piecewise polynomial surfaces, IEEE Trans. on Pattern Anal. and Machine Intelligence **2** (1980), 35–46.

A. Kaufmann
Lab. TIM3-IRMA
Université J. Fourier
BP 53X
38041 Grenoble Cédex
FRANCE

EMAIL: kaufmann@ afp.imag.fr

# Composite Quadrilateral Finite Elements
# of Class $C^r$

## M. Laghchim-Lahlou and P. Sablonnière

**Abstract.**     Let $\pi$ be some partition of a polygonal domain $D$ into quadrilaterals whose set of vertices is $A = \{A_i, \ 1 \leq i \leq N\}$. Given a smooth function $u$, we construct piecewise polynomial functions (ppf) $v \in C^r(D)$ of degree $n = 3r$ for $r$ odd and $n = 3r + 1$ for $r$ even on the so called FVS (after Fraeijs de Veubeke and Sander) subtriangulation $\tau_4$ of $\pi$ obtained by drawing diagonals in each $Q \in \pi$. These functions $v$ interpolate the derivatives $D^\alpha u(A_i)$ for $|\alpha| \leq r$ and $1 \leq i \leq N$. For each $Q \in \pi$, $v|_Q$ is a composite quadrilateral finite element generalizing the classical $C^1$-cubic $FVS$ quadrilateral.

## §1. Introduction

Let $\pi$ be some partition of a bounded polygonal domain $D$ of $\mathbb{R}^2$ into quadrilaterals whose set of vertices is $A = \{A_i, \ 1 \leq i \leq N\}$. Let $\tau_4$ be the subtriangulation of $\pi$ obtained by drawing diagonals in each $Q \in \pi$. We call $\tau_4$ the FVS (after Fraeijs de Veubeke and Sander) subtriangulation of $\pi$. Let

$$P_n^r(D, \tau_4) := \{v \in C^r(D) : v|_T \in P_n \text{ for all } T \in \tau_4\},$$

where $P_n$ is the space of bivariate polynomials of total degree at most $n$. Given $u \in C^s(D)$, $s \geq r$, and $V_r$ a finite dimensional subspace of $C^r(D)$, we consider the following Hermite interpolation problem:

**Problem 1.** $(H^r(A, V_r))$. *Construct* $v \in V_r$ *such that*

$$D^\alpha v(A_i) = D^\alpha u(A_i), \text{ for } |\alpha| \leq r \text{ and } 1 \leq i \leq N.$$

There exist, of course, many solutions to this problem, belonging to some spaces of type $P_n^r(D, \tau_4)$ or subspaces of them. Some of these solutions are

Mathematical Methods in Computer Aided Geometric Design
Tom Lyche and Larry L. Schumaker (eds.), pp. 413–418.
Copyright © 1989 by Academic Press, Boston.
ISBN 0-12-460515-X.

*globally* defined and cannot be obtained by assembling finite elements. Our aim here is first construct *local* quadrilateral composite finite elements and then to prove that the global ppf obtained by putting them together is a solution of the above problem $H^r(A, V_r)$. The goal is to use polynomials of the *lowest possible degree* and data derivatives of the *lowest possible order*. Therefore, we generalize the $C^1$-cubic case of FVS quadrilateral finite elements (see e.g. [2,3]).

Since the complete proofs are rather technical because they involve algebraic manipulations of numerous coefficients, we have chosen to describe the basic ideas for the cases $(n, r) = (7, 2)$ and $(9, 3)$ as examples of the general cases $(3r, r)$ for $r$ odd and $(3r + 1, r)$ for $r$ even. The detailed proofs will be given in further papers, together with similar results on composite elements of HCT type. We also prove that our results are optimal in some sense.

We assume that the reader is somewhat familiar with the Bernstein-Bézier representation of ppf on triangulations (see e.g. [1, 4]). In addition, we use the following notations : the generic quadrilateral $Q$ of $\pi$ has vertices $A_1, A_2, A_3, A_4$ and edges $\Gamma_1 = A_1 A_2, \Gamma_2 = A_2 A_3, \Gamma_3 = A_3 A_4$ and $\Gamma_4 = A_4 A_1$. For $1 \le i \le 4$, let $\Gamma'_i, \Gamma''_i$, etc., denote the first, second, etc., rows of B-coefficients of $v|_Q$ parallel to $\Gamma_i$ . In general, $\nu_i$ is a direction not parallel to the edge $\Gamma_i$. We write $Dv(M_i) \cdot \nu_i$, $D^2 v(M_i) \cdot \nu_i^2$, etc. for the first, second, etc., derivatives of $v$ at the point $M_i \in \Gamma_i$ in the direction $\nu_i$.

## §2. FVS Quadrilaterals of Class $C^{2s}$

**Theorem 1.** *For* $Q = A_1 A_2 A_3 A_4$ *an arbitrary quadrilateral of* $\pi$, *the set* $P_7^3(Q, \tau_4)$ *is a vector space of dimension 56. Each* $v \in P_7^3(Q, \tau_4)$ *is completely defined by the following data:*

*(i) the partial derivatives* $D^\alpha v(A_i)$ *for* $|\alpha| \le 3$ *and* $1 \le i \le 4$

*(ii) the directional derivatives*

$$Dv(M_i).\nu_i, \quad D^2 v(N_i).(\nu_i)^2, \quad D^2 v(P_i).(\nu_i)^2, \quad D^3 v(M_i).(\nu_i)^3,$$

*where* $\nu_i$ *is some vector not colinear to* $\Gamma_i$, *and* $M_i$ *and* $N_i \ne P_i$ *are arbitrary points on the interior of the edge* $\Gamma_i$ *for* $1 \le i \le 4$.

**Proof:** See Figure 1. As an immediate consequence of the BB representation, the B-coefficients are computed from the partial derivatives $D^\alpha v(A_i)$, for $|\alpha| \le 3$ and $1 \le i \le 4$. The B-coefficients ① are then computed from the $Dv(M_i).\nu_i$, and from the black B-coefficients on $\Gamma_i$ and $\Gamma'_i$. Similarly, the B-coefficients ② are computed from the black B-coefficients on $\Gamma_i$, $\Gamma'_i$, $\Gamma''_i$ and the preceding ones. Now, the ⊗ B-coefficients are deduced from $C^3$-continuity across diagonals, and they allow the computation of the B-coefficients ③ from the black ones on $\Gamma_i$, $\Gamma'_i$, $\Gamma''_i$, $\Gamma'''_i$ and the data $D^3 v(M_i).(\nu_i)^3$. Now, look at the B-coefficients in $Q$ except the black ones. They can be considered as those of a bi-cubic surface and can be completely determined by the four B-coefficients ① , ② and ③ at each corner. ∎

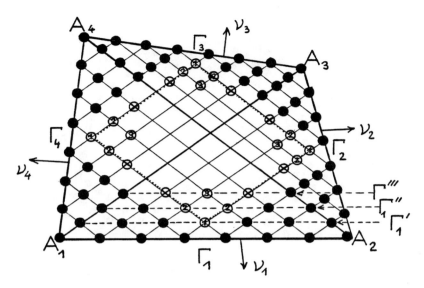

**Figure 1.** The data used in Theorem 1.

**Corollary 2.** *A reduced FVS quadrilateral* $\tilde{P}_7^3(Q, \tau_4)$ *of dimension 40 can be deduced from the above by adding the following conditions on each side* $\Gamma_i$ *of* $Q$.

$$(1) \qquad Dv.\nu_i|_{\Gamma_i} \in P_5(\Gamma_i)$$
$$(2) \qquad D^2v.(\nu_i)^2|_{\Gamma_i} \in P_3(\Gamma_i)$$
$$(3) \qquad D^3v.(\nu_i)^3|_{\Gamma_i} \in P_3(\Gamma_i)$$

**Proof:** The proof is obvious because these new conditions allow the computation of B-coefficients ①, ② and ③. ∎

**Theorem 3.** *Given* $u \in C^3(D)$, *let* $v$ *be the ppf defined on* $D$ *by putting together the finite elements* $v|_Q$ *described in Theorem 1 (or Corollary 2) and interpolating the derivatives of* $u$ *(with the convention that* $\nu_i = \nu_i'$ *on the edge* $\Gamma_i$ *common to adjacent quadrilaterals* $Q$ *and* $Q'$, *and that the derivatives of* $u$ *in this direction are interpolated at the same points of* $\Gamma_i$). *Then* $v \in C^2(D)$ *is a solution of the problem* $H^2(A, V_2)$, *where* $V_2$ *is a proper subspace of* $P_7^2(D, \tau_4)$.

**Proof:** The proof is a straightforward consequence of the verification of the $C^2$-continuity of $v$ across each $\Gamma_i$. ∎

More generally, given $u \in C^{4s-1}(D)$, it is possible to construct a quadrilateral finite element $v \in P_{6s+1}^{2s+1}(Q, \tau_4)$ from the following data.

(i) the partial derivatives $D^\alpha v(A_i) = D^\alpha u(A_i)$ for $1 \le i \le 4$ and $|\alpha| \le 3s$

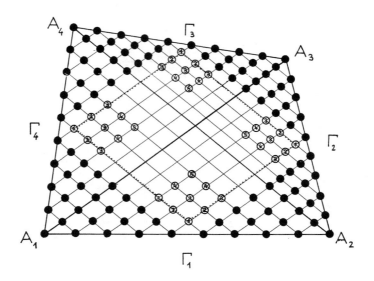

**Figure 2.** The data used in Theorem 4.

(ii) directional derivatives $D^\ell v.(\nu_i)^\ell$ on the edges $\Gamma_i$ of $Q$, for $1 \le i \le 4$, at distinct points of the interior of $\Gamma_i$. For $1 \le \ell \le 2s$, $\ell$ of these derivatives are needed. For $2s + 1 \le \ell \le 4s - 1$, $4s - \ell$ values of these derivatives are needed.

**Remark.** There exists a reduced finite element constructible from the first set (i) of data only.

The function $v$, defined by assembling the above finite elements $v|_Q$ interpolating the derivatives of $u$, is a solution of the problem $H^{2s}(A, V_{2s})$, where $V_{2s}$ is a proper subspace of $P^{2s}_{6s+1}(D, \tau_4)$. Moreover, no such construction is possible in a subspace of $P^{2s}_{6s}(D, \tau_4)$. The detailed proofs will be given elsewhere [5].

## §3. FVS Quadrilaterals of Class $C^{2s+1}$

**Theorem 4.** Let $\hat{P}^3_9(Q, \tau_4)$ be the subspace of those functions $v \in P^3_9(Q, \tau_4)$ whose partial derivatives of order 4 are continuous at the vertices of $Q = A_1 A_2 A_3 A_4$. Then $\hat{P}^3_9(Q, \tau_4)$ is completely defined by the following set of 96 data:

(i) the 60 partial derivatives $D^\alpha v(A_i)$, for $|\alpha| \le 4$ and $1 \le i \le 4$.

(ii) the 36 directional derivatives

$$Dv(M_i).\nu_i, \quad D^2 v(N_{i,j}).(\nu_i)^2, \quad D^3 v(P_{ik}).(\nu_i)^3,$$

$$D^4 v(N_{ij}).(\nu_i)^4, \quad D^5 v(M_i).(\nu_i)^5,$$

where $\nu_i$ is a vector not colinear to the edge $\Gamma_i$, and $M_i$, $N_{i1} \neq N_{i2}$, and $P_{i1} \neq P_{i2} \neq P_{i3}$ are distinct points of the interior of $\Gamma_i$, for $i = 1, 2, 3, 4$.

**Proof:** See Figure 2. The proof is similar to that of Theorem 1. The black B-coefficients are computed from the data derivatives at vertices. The B-coefficients numbered ①, ②, ③, ④, ⑤, are computed from the derivative data on edges and black ones. Finally the non-black B-coefficients of $v|_Q$ are considered as those of a biquartic spline surface of class $C^3$ whose dimension is 36. Therefore the 36 numbered B-coefficients uniquely define this surface. ∎

**Corollary 5.** *A reduced FVS quadrilateral* $v \in P_9^3(Q, \tau_4)$ *of dimension 60 can be deduced from the above by adding the following conditions on each edge* $\Gamma_i$ *of $Q$:*

$$(1) \qquad Dv.\nu_i|_{\Gamma_i} \in P_7(\Gamma_i)$$

$$(2) \qquad D^2v.(\nu_i)^2|_{\Gamma_i} \in P_5(\Gamma_i)$$

$$(3) \qquad D^3v.(\nu_i)^3|_{\Gamma_i} \in P_3(\Gamma_i)$$

$$(4) \qquad D^4v.(\nu_i)^4|_{\Gamma_i} \in P_3(\Gamma_i)$$

$$(5) \qquad D^5v.(\nu_i)^5|_{\Gamma_i} \in P_3(\Gamma_i).$$

**Theorem 6.** *Given* $u \in C^4(D)$, *let* $v$ *be the ppf defined on $D$ by putting together the finite elements* $v|_Q$ *described in Theorem 4 (or its corollary) and interpolating the derivatives of $u$ (with the same convention on normal derivatives as in Theorem 3). Then* $v \in C^3(D)$ *is a solution to the problem* $H^3(A, V_3)$, *where $V_3$ is a proper subspace of* $P_9^3(D, \tau_4)$.

More generally, given $u \in C^{4s+1}(D)$, it is possible to construct a quadrilateral finite element $v|_Q$ in $P_{6s+3}^{2s+1}(Q, \tau_4)$ from the following data:

(i) partial derivatives $D^\alpha v(A_i) = D^\alpha u(A_i)$, for $1 \leq i \leq 4$ and $|\alpha| \leq 3s + 1$

(ii) directional derivatives $D^l v.(\nu_i)^l$ on the edges $\Gamma_i$ of $Q$ at distinct points in the interior of $\Gamma_i$. For $1 \leq l \leq 2s + 1$, we have that $l$ values of these derivatives are needed, and for $2s + 2 \leq l \leq 4s + 1$ we have that $4s + 2 - l$ values of these derivatives are needed.

We remark that there exists a reduced finite element constructible from the first set (i) of data only. Then the function $v$, obtained by assembling these finite elements $v|_Q$, is a solution of the problem $H^{2s+1}(A, V_{2s+1})$, where $V_{2s+1}$ is a proper subspace of $P_{6s+3}^{2s+1}(D, \tau_4)$. Moreover, such a construction is impossible in $P_{6s+2}^{2s+1}(D, \tau_4)$. The detailed proofs will be given elsewhere [5].

### References

1. de Boor, C., B–net basics, in *Geometric Modeling: Algorithms and New Trends*, G. E. Farin (ed.), SIAM Publications, Philadelphia, 1987, 131–148.
2. Ciarlet, P. G., *The Finite Element Method for Elliptic Problems*, North Holland, Amsterdam, 1978.

3. Ciavaldini, J. F. and J. C. Nedelec, Sur l'élément de Fraeijs de Veubeke et Sander, RAIRO, Anal. Numér **R2** (1974), 29–45.

4. Farin, G., Triangular Bernstein–Bézier patches, Comput. Aided Geom. Design **3** (1986), 83–127.

5. Lagchim–Lahlou, M. and P. Sablonnière, Eléments finis composites quadrilatéraux de classe $C^r$, preprint.

Paul Sablonnière
INSA Rennes
Laboratoire LANS
20 Av. des Buttes de Coësmes
35043 Rennes Cédex
FRANCE

# A Knot Removal Strategy
# for Scattered Data in $\mathbb{R}^2$

## A. J. Y. Le Méhauté and Y. Lafranche

**Abstract.** We present a strategy for reducing the number of nodes for the representation of a piecewise polynomial approximation of a function defined on scattered data, without perturbing the approximation more than a given tolerance. The method removes some (or all) of the interior knots. The number and the location of these knots are determined automatically.

## §1. Introduction

Recently, Lyche and Mørken [8,9] presented a data reduction strategy for splines in one variable, and extended their scheme to tensor product surfaces. To remove knots from a spline approximation of a function, they made extensive use of the properties of discrete univariate B-splines and the knot-insertion algorithm. Unfortunately, it is not possible to use the same techniques for scattered data in $\mathbb{R}^2$, and we propose a different approach to a removal strategy in this case.

Given a set of $N$ scattered data points

$$\mathcal{A} = \{A_1, A_2, ..., A_N\} \subset \mathbb{R}^2$$

and a triangulation $\Delta$ based on $\mathcal{A}$, we assume that we know all the data needed for the construction of a piecewise polynomial $C^1$ surface $S$ that interpolates the data. Given a tolerance $\varepsilon$, we successively remove one after the other of those $A_i$ whose contribution to $S$ is not significant; that is to say, those points such that, if we remove them, the surface $S'$ built upon the remaining points satisfies $\text{dist}(S, S') \leq \varepsilon$.

Let $\mathcal{A}$ be the set of all the data points, hereafter called *knots*; and let $\Delta$ be the (unique) Delaunay triangulation based on $\mathcal{A}$ (by this, we mean that

Mathematical Methods in Computer Aided Geometric Design
Tom Lyche and Larry L. Schumaker (eds.), pp. 419–426.
Copyright © 1989 by Academic Press, Boston.
ISBN 0-12-460515-X.

the vertices of $\Delta$ are points $A_i$ in $\mathcal{A}$, and all the $A_i$ are vertices of $\Delta$). For properties of Delaunay's triangulation, see [4].

Let $\Omega = \cup\{T \; : \; T \text{ is a triangle}, T \in \Delta\}$, $\Omega$ not necessarily convex. Let us assume that either we know the boundary $\partial\Omega$ of $\Omega$, or $\Delta$ is a triangulation of the convex hull of $\mathcal{A}$. In both cases, we know all of the points $A_i$ that define the boundary of $\Omega$.

For simplicity, we assume that

$$\mathcal{A} = \{A_1, A_2, ..., A_I, A_{I+1}, ..., A_N\},$$

where $A_1, A_2, ..., A_I$ are strictly interior points in $\Omega$ and $A_{I+1}, ..., A_N$ are the vertices of the polygonal boundary $\partial\Omega$.

Let us write

$$A^0 = \{A_1, A_2, ..., A_I\} \quad \text{and} \quad \Delta^0 = \Delta,$$

and let $S^0$ be the finite element spline of class $C^1$, degree 5, constructed using Bell's approximant on every triangle $T \in \Delta^0$ (for the precise definition, see Section 5 below). Let $\varepsilon > 0$ be given. We will now describe the procedure to eliminate those points $A_j, j \in \{1, ..., I\}$ whose influence on $S^0$ is negligible.

## §2. Measure of the Significance of Each Point

For each $j = 1, ..., I$, let

$$\mathcal{A}_{(j)} = A^0 \backslash \{A_j\} = \{A_1, ..., A_{j-1}, A_{j+1}, ..., A_I\},$$

and let $\Delta^0_{(j)}$ be the Delaunay triangulation of $\mathcal{A}_{(j)}$.

From the properties of Delaunay's triangulations, we know that $\Delta^0_{(j)}$ and $\Delta^0$ differ only on the insertion polygon $P_j$ of $A_j$ [10], where $P_j$ is the polygon union of all the triangles that share $A_j$ as a common vertex

$$P_j = \cup\{T, T \in \Delta^0, A_j \text{ is a vertex of } T\}.$$

In [5], $P_j$ is called the *platelet* related to $A_j$. It is not necessarily convex, but is star-shaped relative to $A_j$. There are two different triangulations of $P_j$ :

- in $\Delta^0_{(j)}$, $P_j$ is triangulated using only its boundary points, with $(n-2)$ triangles if $P_j$ has $n$ points on its boundary,
- in $\Delta^0$, $P_j$ is triangulated with $n$ triangles, all of them having $A_j$ as a vertex.

We intersect these two triangulations in order to obtain a new one, $\mathcal{T}$, which is a refined triangulation of both: each triangle, from one or the other, is a union of triangles from $\mathcal{T}$, and

$$P_j = \cup\{\tau \in \mathcal{T}\}.$$

We make two remarks. First, when we intersect the two triangulations, we obtain only two types of intersections: a side from $\Delta^0_{(j)}$ cut a side from $\Delta^0$ in either one or two points, outside the vertex of $P_j$. Secondly, $\mathcal{T}$ is not necessarily a Delaunay triangulation.

Let $S^0_{(j)}$ be the finite element spline of class $C^1$ and degree 5 constructed with Bell's approximant on every triangle in $\Delta^0_{(j)}$. As $\Delta^0$ and $\Delta^0_{(j)}$ differ only on $P_j$, $S^0$ and $S^0_{(j)}$ differ only by their values on $P_j$, and thus

$$\|S^0 - S^0_{(j)}\|_\Omega = \sum_{\tau \in \mathcal{T}} \|S^0 - S^0_{(j)}\|_\tau$$

for any norm.

### §3. A Discrete Norm

Let $p$ be a polynomial of degree $k$ defined on a triangle $\Sigma$. Associated with $\Sigma$, there is a Bernstein basis; more precisely,

$$p = B_k[c, \lambda(\cdot, \Sigma)] = \sum_{|\alpha|=k} c(\alpha) B^k_\alpha(\lambda),$$

where $\{c(\alpha), |\alpha| = k\}$ denotes the set of control points (or Bézier coefficients) of the polynomial $p$, and

$$B^k_\alpha(\lambda) = \frac{k!}{\alpha!}\lambda^\alpha = \frac{k!}{\alpha_1!\alpha_2!\alpha_3!}\lambda_1^{\alpha_1}\lambda_2^{\alpha_2}\lambda_3^{\alpha_3}.$$

Here $\lambda = (\lambda_1, \lambda_2, \lambda_3)$ denotes the barycentric coordinate relative to $\Sigma$.

**Lemma.** $\|c\|_{\ell^\infty} = \max\limits_{|\alpha|=k} |c(\alpha)|$ *is a norm on* $\Pi_k$, *the set of all polynomials of degree* $\leq k$.

The expression

$$\|B_k[c, \lambda(\cdot, \Sigma)]\|_{L^\infty} = \max_{x \in \Sigma} |p(x)|$$

is also a norm on $\Pi_k$, and these two norms are equivalent; *i.e.*, there exist constants $C_1$ and $C_2$ such that, for any $p \in \Pi_k$,

$$C_1\|c\|_{\ell^\infty} \leq \|B_k[c, \lambda(\cdot, \Sigma)]\|_{L^\infty} \leq C_2\|c\|_{\ell^\infty}$$

and $C_2$ is trivially equal to 1.

To compare $S^0$ and $S^0_{(j)}$, we will use the discrete norm defined in the above lemma. In order to do so, we recall that $S^0$ and $S^0_{(j)}$ are piecewise polynomials, and we can compare their respective Bézier set only if they are associated with the same triangle. This explains why we defined a refined triangulation $\mathcal{T}$ of $\Delta^0 \cap P_j$ and $\Delta^0_{(j)} \cap P_j$.

## §4. Control Points From One Triangle to Another

Let $\{c(\alpha), |\alpha| = k\}$ be the Bézier net associated with a polynomial $p$ and relative to a triangle $\Sigma$, and let $\{c'(\alpha), |\alpha| = k\}$ be the Bézier net associated with the same polynomial, but relative to another triangle $\Sigma'$. Thus, $p = B_k[c, \lambda(\cdot, \Sigma)] = B_k[c', \lambda'(\cdot, \Sigma')]$. Without loss of generality, we may assume that $\Sigma$ and $\Sigma'$ have two common vertices. (If $\Sigma$ and $\Sigma'$ have no common vertex, we can proceed in three steps). Let $\Sigma = [s_1, s_2, s_3]$ and $\Sigma' = [s_1', s_2, s_3]$, and let

$$\alpha = (\alpha_1, \alpha_2, \alpha_3) \text{ be such that } |\alpha| = k \text{ and}$$
$$\underline{\alpha} = (0, \alpha_2, \alpha_3) = \alpha - (\alpha_1, 0, 0).$$

Then, for any $\ell = 1, 2, ..., k$, for the triangle $\Sigma$,

$$p = B_k[c, \lambda(\cdot, \Sigma)] = \sum_{|\alpha|=k-\ell} P_\alpha(\lambda(\cdot, \Sigma)) B_\alpha^{k-\ell}(\lambda(\cdot, \Sigma)),$$

where

$$P_\alpha(\lambda) = \sum_{|\beta|=\ell} c(\alpha + \beta) B_\beta^\ell(\alpha), \qquad \ell = k - |\alpha|$$

is a subpolynomial of degree $\ell$ of $P$ ([3]). On the other hand, for the triangle $\Sigma'$,

$$p = B_k[c', \lambda'(\cdot, \Sigma')] = \sum_{|\beta|=k-\alpha_1} P_\beta(\lambda'(\cdot, \Sigma')) B_\beta(\lambda'(\cdot, \Sigma')),$$

where

$$P_\beta(\lambda'(\cdot, \Sigma')) = \sum_{\delta=\alpha_1} c'(\beta + \delta) B_\delta(\lambda'(\cdot, \Sigma')).$$

But $(\alpha_1, 0, 0)$ is associated with the vertex $s_1'$ of $\Sigma'$ on the Bézier net relative to $\Sigma'$ and degree $\alpha_1$. Thus, $P_\beta(\lambda'(s_1', \Sigma')) = c'(\beta + (\alpha_1, 0, 0)) = c'(\beta_1 + \alpha_1, \beta_2, \beta_3)$.

Let us now consider the particular choice

$$\beta = \underline{\alpha} = \alpha - (\alpha_1, 0, 0) = (0, \alpha_2, \alpha_3).$$

Then

$$c'(\beta + (\alpha_1, 0, 0,)) = c'(\alpha) = P_{\underline{\alpha}}(\lambda'(s_1', \Sigma')).$$

Moreover, $\underline{\alpha}$ has its support in $[\Sigma] \cap [\Sigma'] = [s_2, s_3]$, and we get

$$P_{\underline{\alpha}}(\lambda'(s_1', \Sigma')) = P_{\underline{\alpha}}(\lambda(s_1', \Sigma)).$$

This implies that

$$c'(\alpha_1, \alpha_2, \alpha_3) = \sum_{|\beta|=\alpha_2+\alpha_3} c(\beta_1, \beta_2 + \alpha_2, \beta_3 + \alpha_3) \alpha_1^{\beta_1}(s_1') \lambda_2^{\beta_2}(s_1') \lambda_3^{\beta_3}(s_1') \frac{k!}{\beta!},$$

which can be easily evaluated by the de Casteljau algorithm.

## §5. On Bell's Approximant

It is well known that, in order to provide a $C^1$ finite element spline, one may use Argyris or Bell's approximant. Let us recall some results (see [6] and references therein). Suppose that we want to interpolate a function $f$. Associated with any triangle $\Sigma = [a_1, a_2, a_3]$ in $\Delta$, let us consider the following 18 degrees of freedom:

$$\{\partial^\alpha f(a_i), \quad |\alpha| \leq 2, \quad i = 1, 2, 3\}$$

and the 3 normal derivatives:

$$\{\frac{\partial}{\partial \nu_i} f(b_i), \quad i = 1, 2, 3\},$$

where $b_i$ is the midpoint of $[a_{i+1}, a_{i+2}]$.

Then, the Argyris polynomial [1] is the polynomial of degree 5 which interpolates these 21 quantities, defined as

$$p(M) = \Pi_\Sigma^5[f](M) = T_\Sigma^5[f](M) + R_\Sigma^5[f](M),$$

where

$$T_\Sigma^5[f](M) = \sum_{i=1}^{3} \lambda_i^3 \sum_{j=0}^{2} \frac{(2+j)!}{2!j!} (1 - \lambda_i)^j T_{a_i}^{2-j} f(M)$$

and

$$R_\Sigma^5[f](M) = \sum_{i=1}^{3} \alpha_i \lambda_i \lambda_{i+1}^2 \lambda_{i+2}^2.$$

Here the $\lambda_i$ are the barycentric coordinates in $\Sigma$, $T_{a_i}^p f$ is the (usual) Taylor expansion of degree $p$ about $a_i$ of $f$, and $\alpha_i = \frac{16}{\nabla_{ii}} [\frac{\partial}{\partial \nu_i} (T_\Sigma^5[f])(b_i)]$, with $\nabla_{ii} = \frac{\partial}{\partial \nu_i} \lambda_i$.

Bell's polynomial [2] is the polynomial of degree 5 which interpolates the 18 degrees of freedom defined on the vertices of $\Sigma$, obtained from Argyris' when one replaces $\frac{\partial}{\partial \nu_i} f(b_i)$ by

$$\frac{1}{4} \sum_{\substack{k=i+1 \\ k=i+2}} \{T_{a_k}^1 \frac{\partial}{\partial \nu_i} (a_k)\}.$$

The associated Bézier net (cf. [7]) is

$$a_{500} = f(a_1)$$
$$a_{410} = 4f(a_1) + T_{a_1}^1 f(a_2)$$
$$a_{401} = 4f(a_1) + T_{a_i}^1 f(a_3)$$
$$a_{320} = 6f(a_1) + 3T_{a_1}^1 f(a_2) + T_{a_1}^2 f(a_2)$$
$$a_{311} = 12f(a_1) + 4T_{a_1}^1 f(a_2) + 4T_{a_1}^1 f(a_3) + D^2 f(a_1) \cdot (a_1 a_2, a_1 a_3)$$
$$a_{302} = 6f(a_1) + 3T_{a_1}^1 f(a_3) + T_{a_1}^2 f(a_3)$$
$$a_{122} = \alpha_1,$$

where the other coefficients can be obtained by a circular permutation.

**Remark.** *It is obvious that the best choice of the degrees of freedom, from the standpoint of computation, is not $\partial^\alpha f(a_i)$, $|\alpha| \leq 2$, but*

$$\{f(a_i); T_{a_i}^1 f(a_j), T_{a_i}^2 f(a_j), \ j = i+1, i+2; D^2 f(a_i) \cdot (a_i a_{i+1}, a_i a_{i+2})\}.$$

## §6. Knot Removal

We are now able to evaluate the significance of each node $A_j \in A^0$. Let

$$\omega_j = \sum_{\tau \in \mathcal{T}} \|c(S^0, \tau) - c(S_{(j)}^0, \tau)\|_{\ell^\infty},$$

where $c(S^0, \tau)$ (resp: $c(S_{(j)}^0, \tau)$) denotes the Bézier set associated with $S^0$ (respectively, $S_{(j)}^0$), evaluated as a Bell's polynomial on the triangle $\tau \in \mathcal{T}$.

Then it is possible to rank the vertices $A_1, A_2, ..., A_I$ by the increasing order of the $\omega_i, i = 1, ..., I$. Let $A_1^*, A_2^*, ..., A_I^*$ be the re-ordered points. On account of the properties of the Delaunay triangulation, $P_j$ and $P_k$, $k \neq j$, have no triangle in common if and only if $[A_j^*, A_k^*]$ is not an edge in the triangulation $\Delta^0$. Then we remove those points $A_j$ such that $\omega_j \leq \varepsilon$ (where $\varepsilon$ is the given tolerance), in increasing order of $\omega_j$, in such a way that we do not remove two neighbors $A_j^*$ and $A_k^*$. At the end of the process, we remove $q$ points, say $A_1^*, A_2^*, ..., A_q^*$. Let $A^1 = A^0 \backslash \{A_1^*, ..., A_q^*\}$ be the set of all remaining knots, and let $\Delta^1$ be the Delaunay triangulation of $\Omega$ based on $A^1$. Note that $\Delta^0$ and $\Delta^1$ differ only on $\bigcup\limits_{j=1}^{q} P_j$.

On $\Delta^1$, we are able to construct a new piecewise polynomial surface $S^1$ which is a finite element spline of class $C^1$ and degree 5, and such that

$$\|S^0 - S^1\|_\Omega \leq \varepsilon,$$

where $S^1$ is the desired surface.

## §7. Remarks and Comments

1) We can iterate the process and remove points which were neighbors of already removed knots. But we have to keep in mind that we have to compare the resulting surface with $S^0$.

2) The boundary $\partial\Omega$ is entirely preserved. It is possible to use extra information (such as points on the same line, etc.) to remove knots from the boundary.

3) We use Bell's triangle because it is very simple, but one can use others, such as Clough & Tocher.

4) It is possible to use this removal strategy in higher dimensions, the only complicated step being the refinement of the triangulations in $P_j$.

## References

1. Argyris, J. M., I. Fried, and D. W. Scharpf, The TUBA family of plate elements for the matrix displacement method, Aer. J. Royal Aeronautical Society **72** (1968), 701–709.

2. Bell, K., A refined triangular plate bending element, Internat. J. Numer. Methods. Engrg. **1** (1969), 101–122.

3. de Boor, C., B form basics, in *Geometric Modeling: Algorithms and New Trends*, G. E. Farin (ed.), SIAM Publications, Philadelphia, 1987, 131–148.

4. Lafranche, Y., Application de l'interpolation polynomiale au dépouillement graphique de valeurs dans $\mathbb{R}^3$, Thèse $3^e$ cycle, Université de Rennes, 1984.

5. Le Méhauté, A. J. Y., Approximation of derivatives in $\mathbb{R}^n$. Applications: construction of surfaces in $\mathbb{R}^2$, in *Approximation Theory and Spline Functions*, S. P. Singh, J. H. W. Burry and B. Watson (eds.), Reidel, Dordrecht, 1984, 361–378.

6. Le Méhauté, A. J. Y., Interpolation et approximation par des fonctions polynomiales par morceaux dans $\mathbb{R}^n$, Thèse d'Etat, Université de Rennes, 1984.

7. Le Méhauté, A. J. Y., An efficient algorithm for $C^k$ simplicial finite element interpolation in $\mathbb{R}^n$, C.A.T. Report 111, Texas A&M University, March, 1986.

8. Lyche, T., and K. Mørken, Knot removal for parametric B-splines curves and surfaces, Comput. Aided Geom. Design **4** (1987), 217–230.

9. Lyche, T., and K. Mørken, A data-reduction strategy for splines with applications to the approximation of functions and data, IMA J. Numer. Anal. **8** (1988), 185–208.

10. Watson, D.F., ACORD = Automatic contouring of raw data, Computer & Geoscience **8** (1981), 97–101.

A. J. Y. Le Méhauté and Y. Lafranche
Laboratoire d'Analyse Numérique et Optimisation
Université des Sciences et Techniques de Lille
59655 Villeneuve D'Ascq Cédex
FRANCE

EMAIL: lemehaut@ frcitl71

# Interpolation Systems
# and the Finite Element Method

## J. Lorente and V. Ramirez

**Abstract.** In this paper we study a problem in bivariate interpolation associated with the finite element method, using an interpolation technique called *interpolation systems*. We give a necessary and sufficient condition for obtaining a finite element of the type $(k, 4k + p + 1, k, p)$ (following the notation of A. Le Méhauté [6]).

## §1. Introduction

Many papers (cf. [1,2,5,6,7,9,10], etc.) dealing with multivariate interpolation give special attention to the construction of different kinds of *finite elements* (in $\mathbb{R}^2$) either of triangular or of rectangular shape; see Le Méhauté [6].

The finite element method is a technique of local approximation where the following concept is defined:

**Definition 1.1.** *A finite element in $\mathbb{R}^n$ is a triplet $(T, P(T), \Sigma(T))$, where $T$ denotes an $n$-polyhedron, $P(T)$ is a space of functions contained in $C^k(T)$, $k \in N$, and $\Sigma(T)$ is a class of functionals supported in $T$ and linearly independent, so that one obtains $P(T)$-univolvency.*

Therefore, the finite element method solves, in a local sense, the problem of interpolating a function $f$ on a triangulated domain of $\mathbb{R}^2$ with polygonal boundary; that is, on each element of the triangulation, a function $P \in P(T)$ is constructed which is the solution of the interpolation problem:

$$L_i(P) = L_i(f) \text{ for every } L_i \in \Sigma(T). \tag{1.1}$$

It is from this point of view that the study of the $P(T)$-unisolvency of $\Sigma(T)$ and obtaining functions solving the problem become important.

Mathematical Methods in Computer Aided Geometric Design
Tom Lyche and Larry L. Schumaker (eds.), pp. 427–434.

In this paper we apply the technique of *interpolation systems* to problem (1.1). This technique was introduced by M. Gasca and J. I. Maeztu in [3]. This line of ideas was continued and extended by V. Ramirez in [4]. Basically, it consists of constructing a set of functions $S$, a space of functions $\langle B(S) \rangle$, and a set of linear functionals or *associated data* $L(S)$ in such a way that this set of data is equivalent to the initial one and, at the same time, one can assure the unisolvency of the problem in the space $\langle B(S) \rangle$.

## §2. Notation, Definitions, and Previous Results

Let $I$ be a nonempty set of indices of the form

$$I = \{(0,0), \ldots, (0, n(0)), \ldots, (m,0), \ldots, (m, n(m))\}.$$

We define an *interpolation system* (in $\mathbb{R}^2$) as a set

$$S = \{(f_i, f_{ij}), (i,j) \in I\},$$

where $f_i, f_{ij}$ are functions from $\mathbb{R}^2$ into $\mathbb{R}$ of the type

$$f_i(x,y) = a_i x + b_i y + c_i$$

and

$$f_{ij}(x,y) = a_{ij} x + b_{ij} y + c_{ij}.$$

Moreover, the following condition should be satisfied for each $(i,j) \in I$

$$a_i b_{ij} \neq a_{ij} b_i.$$

Thus, given a fixed couple $(i,j) \in I$,

a) There exists a unique point $u_{ij} \in \mathbb{R}^2$ such that

$$f_i(u_{ij}) = f_{ij}(u_{ij}) = 0;$$

b) The following vectors are linearly independent in $\mathbb{R}^2$:

$$\rho_i = (-b_i, a_i), \qquad \rho_{ij} = (-b_{ij}, a_{ij}).$$

c) We denote by $t$ (respectively $s$) the number of functions in the set

$$\{f_0, f_1, \ldots, f_{i-1}, f_{i0}, f_{i1}, \ldots, f_{ij-1}\}$$

vanishing at the point $u_{ij}$ and such that their graphs coincide (respectively, do not coincide) with the graph of $f_i$.

**Definition 2.1.** *Given an interpolation system, $S$, we shall say that the set of functions*

$$B(S) = (\phi_{ij})_{(i,j)\in I}, \text{ with } \phi_{ij} = f_0 \cdot f_1 \ldots f_{i-1} \cdot f_{i0} \cdot f_{i1} \ldots f_{ij-1},$$

*from $\mathbb{R}^2$ into $\mathbb{R}$ is the associated basis, $B(S)$, for $S$. (When $i = 0$ or $j = 0$ in the previous product, the corresponding factors take the value 1.)*

**Definition 2.2.** *We define the associated data as the family $L(S), L(S) = \{L_{ij}\}_{(i,j)\in I}$, where each $L_{ij}$ is the functional defined on $f : \mathbb{R}^2 \to \mathbb{R}$ by*

$$L_{ij}(f) = \left. \frac{\partial^{s+t} f}{\partial \rho_i^s \partial \rho_{ij}^t} \right|_{u_{ij}}.$$

*(The values $s$ and $t$ are computed for the index $(i, j)$.)*

We denote by $\Pi_m$ the real vector space of polynomials with total degree less or equal than $m$. It is known that the dimension of $\Pi_m$ is given by $(m + 1)(m + 2)/2$. The proof of the following results can be found in [3,4].

**Theorem 2.3.** *Det $\{L_{ij}(\phi_{hk})\}_{(i,j);(h,k)\in I} \neq 0$. Moreover, if the pairs $(i, j)$ and $(h, k)$ are arranged in lexicographical order, the corresponding matrix is triangular.*

**Corollary 2.4.** *The interpolation problem: find $p \in \langle B(S) \rangle = Sp\{B(S)\}$ such that $L_{ij}(p) = W_{ij}$ for each $(i, j) \in I$ with $W_{ij} \in \mathbb{R}$ admits a unique solution.*

**Theorem 2.5.** *$\langle B(S) \rangle = \Pi_m(x, y)$ if and only if $I = \{(i, j) \in Z_+^2 ; 0 \le i + j \le m\}$. (In this case, $S$ is called a system of order $m$ (cf. [3]).)*

## §3. Triangular Finite Elements of Class k and Type $(\mathbf{k, N, \chi, p})$

Now we are going to construct an interpolation system for a particular class of finite elements studied by A. Le Méhauté in [6].

**Definition 3.1.** *(cf. [6]) Let $T$ be a triangle with vertices $A_1, A_2, A_3$ and $\Sigma$ be a set of functionals associated with $T$ in such a way that $(T, P(T), \Sigma)$ is a finite element. Then one can distinguish two types of functionals (or degrees of freedom) in $\Sigma$:*

    a) *The functionals given in order to define the finite element are called of first type. They appear on the vertices and sides of the triangle $T$.*
    b) *The functionals which, jointly with those of the first type, assure $P(T)$-unisolvency for $\Sigma$ are called of second type.*

**Definition 3.2.** *(See [6]) We say that $(T, P(T), \Sigma)$ is a finite element of type $(k, N, \chi, p)$ if the degrees of freedom of the first type are*

a)

$$\ell_i(f) \in \{D^\alpha f(A_s) \text{ with } |\alpha| \le k + \chi, s = 1, 2, 3\} \qquad (3.1)$$

b)

$$\ell_i(f) \in \left\{ \frac{\partial^j}{\partial \overline{\mu}_s^j} \left( Q_{rs}^j \right), s = 1, 2, 3; j = 0, \dots, k; r = 1, \dots, p+j \right\} \quad (3.2)$$

where $Q_{rs}^j$ are given points on the side opposite to $A_s$ (different depending on $r$) and $\overline{\mu}_s$ is the normal direction to the side opposite to $A_s$.

Here we shall only describe the case $\chi = k$ and $N = 4k + p + 1$, although the general case can be treated in an analogous way. We shall obtain an interpolation system with a set of associated data equivalent to the set given by (3.1) and (3.2) with $\langle B(S) \rangle \subseteq \Pi_{4k+p+1}$.

Let $T$ be the triangle in Figure 1 with vertices $A_1, A_2, A_3$, and let $r_1, r_2, r_3$ be the lines supporting the sides opposite to $A_1, A_2, A_3$, respectively.

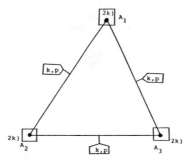

**Figure 1.** A finite element of type $(k, 4k + p + 1, k, p)$.

We define the following set of functions, $S$, from $\mathbb{R}^2$ into $\mathbb{R}$

$$S = \{(f_i, f_{ij}, u_{ij}) : (i, j) \in I\}$$

where, for $i = 0, 1, \dots, k$, $f_i, f_{ij}$ are defined as:

$$f_{3i} \equiv r_1; \qquad f_{3i+1} \equiv r_2; \qquad f_{3i+2} \equiv r_3$$

$$f_{3i,j} \equiv \begin{cases} r_2, & 0 \le j \le 2(k-i) \text{ at } A_3 = u_{3i,j} \\ \mu_{r1}, & j = 2(k-i) + r \text{ for } r = 1, \dots, p+i \text{ at } Q_{r1}^i = u_{3i,j} \\ r_3, & 2k + p + 1 - i \le j \le 4k + p + 1 - 3i \text{ at } A_2 = u_{3i,j} \end{cases}$$

$$f_{3i+1,j} \equiv \begin{cases} r_3, & 0 \le j \le 2(k-i) \text{ at } A_1 = u_{3i+1,j} \\ \mu_{r2}, & j = 2(k-i) + r \text{ for } r = 1, \dots, p+i \text{ at } Q_{r2}^i = u_{3i+1,j} \\ r_1, & 2k + p + 1 - i \le j \le 4k + p - 3i \text{ at } A_3 = u_{3i+1,j} \end{cases}$$

$$f_{3i+2,j} \equiv \begin{cases} r_1, & 0 \le j \le 2(k-i)-1 \text{ at } A_2 = u_{3i+2,j} \\ \mu_{r3}, & j = 2(k-i)-1+r \text{ for } r=1,\ldots,p+i \text{ at } Q^i_{r3} = u_{3i+2,j} \\ r_2, & 2k+p-i \le j \le 4k+p-3i-1 \text{ at } A_1 = u_{3i+2,j} \end{cases}$$

where by $\mu_{rs}$ we denote the line passing through $Q^*_{rs}$ with direction $\overline{\mu}_s$. Next we shall describe the functions of $B(S)$.

Let $i \in \{0,1,\ldots,k\}$ be fixed. Then one has

$$\phi_{3i,j} = (r_1 r_2 r_3)^i \begin{cases} r_2^j, & 0 \le j \le 2(k-i) \\ r_2^{2(k-i)+1} \mu_{11} \cdots \mu_{r-11}, & j = 2(k-i)+r \\ & r = 1,\ldots,p+i \\ r_2^{2(k-i)+1} r_3^{j+i-2k-p-1} \mu_{11} \cdots \mu_{p+i1}, & 2k+p+1-i \le \\ & j \le 4k+p+1-3i. \end{cases}$$

$$\phi_{3i+1,j} = r_1(r_1 r_2 r_3)^i \begin{cases} r_3^j, & 0 \le j \le 2(k-i) \\ r_3^{2(k-i)+1} \mu_{12} \cdots \mu_{r-12}, & j = 2(k-i)+r \\ & r = 1,\ldots,p+i \\ r_3^{2(k-i)+1} r_1^{i+j-2k-p-1} \mu_{12} \cdots \mu_{p+i2}, & j \le 4k+p-3i \end{cases}$$

$$\phi_{3i+2,j} =$$

$$r_1 r_2 (r_1 r_2 r_3)^i \cdot \begin{cases} r_1^j, & 0 \le j \le 2(k-i)-1 \\ r_1^{2(k-i)} \mu_{13} \cdots \mu_{r-13}, & j = 2(k-i)+r-1 \\ & r = 1,\ldots,p+1 \\ r_1^{2(k-i)} r_2^{i+j-2k-p} \mu_{13} \cdots \mu_{p+i3}, & j \le 4k+p-3i-1. \end{cases}$$

It is easy to prove the following result:

**Theorem 3.3.** *Let $P$ be the space spanned by $B(S)$. Then the following statements hold:*

   *i)* $\Pi_{3k+2} \subseteq P \subseteq \Pi_{4k+p+1}$ *if $k \ge 1$.*
   *ii)* $L(S)$ *is equivalent to $\Sigma$ as given by (3.1) and (3.2).*
   *iii) The space $P^*$ spanned by the functions*

$$\left\{ (r_1 r_2 r_3)^{k+1} \cdot \pi_i \quad i = 1, \ldots, \frac{(k+p-1)(k+p)}{2} \right\}$$

*is orthogonal to $P$ with respect to $L(S)$ (where by $\pi_i$ we denote the elements of a basis of $\Pi_{k+p-2}$). Moreover, $P \oplus P^* \equiv \Pi_{4k+p+1}$.*

Taking into account the previous discussions the following interesting result is obtained.

**Theorem 3.4.** Let $l_i, i = 1, \ldots, (k+p-1)(k+p)/2$, be functionals of second type for $T$ and $\Sigma = L(S) \cup \{l_i\}$. Then the triplet $(T, \Pi_{4k+p+1}, \Sigma)$ uniquely defines a finite element of the type $(k, 4k+p+1, k, p)$ if and only if the class of functionals $\{l_i\}$ is $P^*$-unisolvent.

**Proof:** The matrix of unisolvency of $\Sigma$ in $\Pi_{4k+p+1}$ is given by

$$M = M(\Sigma, P + P^*) = \begin{pmatrix} L(B(S)) & L(P^*) \\ \{l_i\}(B(S)) & \{l_i\}(P^*) \end{pmatrix},$$

where $L = L(S)$ is the class of functionals associated with $S$, and therefore the matrix $L(B(S))$ is a lower triangular matrix which is regular by Theorem 2.3, and $L(P^*) \equiv (0)$ from Theorem 3.3iii. Hence $M$ is a regular matrix if and only if the matrix $\{l_i\}(P^*)$ is regular; or in other words $\{l_i\}$ is $P^*$-unisolvent. ∎

## §4. Remarks

**Remark 4.1.** The construction of the solution of the interpolation problem associated with a finite element of type $(k, 4k+1, k, p)$ is accomplished by the process $P = P_1 + P_2$, where $P_1$ is constructed in a recurrent way as the solution of the problem

$$L_{ij}(P_1) = L_{ij}(f), \quad \text{for all} \quad L_{ij} \in L(S) \tag{4.1}$$

and $P_2$ is the solution of the interpolation problem

$$l_i(P_2) = l_i(f) - l_i(P_1), \qquad i = 1, \ldots \frac{(k+p)(k+p-1)}{2}. \tag{4.2}$$

**Remark 4.2.** Once $P_1$ has been constructed, the system to solve is of order

$$\frac{(k+p)(k+p-1)}{2};$$

while in [6], once the Taylor polynomial associated with $T$ was constructed, one had to solve a system of the order

$$\frac{(k+p)(k+p-1)}{2} + \frac{3(2p+k)(k+1)}{2}.$$

**Remark 4.3:** In order to evaluate the functionals $L_{ij}$, the algorithm of Carnicer and Gasca [1] is useful.

## §5. $C^k$-continuity of Finite Elements of Type $(k, 4k + p + 1, k, p)$

Finally, we are going to obtain the $C^k$-continuity by applying the technique of interpolation systems.

**Lemma 5.1.** *Let $T$ be the triangle in Figure 1. Let us assume that the associated data which are prescribed on the side $r_1$ vanish (if $u_{ij} \in r_1$, then $L_{ij}(f) = 0$). Then the solution of the interpolation problems (4.1) and (4.2) is given as follows:*

$$P(x, y) = r_1^{k+1} Q(x, y).$$

**Proof:** Let $S$ be the interpolation system described in §3. We can consider a new interpolation system $S'$ which yields the functionals $L'_{i'j'} = L_{ij}$ which were defined on the side $r_1(f'_{i'} \equiv f_{3i'} \equiv r_1, i' = 0, 1, \ldots, k)$. In this way the associated basis to $S'$ will be $B(S') = \{\phi'_{i'j'}\}$ where $\phi'_{i'j'} = r_1^{i'} \cdot f'_{i'0} \cdots f'_{i'j'-1}$, $(i', j') \in I'$, for $i' = 0, \ldots, k + 1$, and $L(S') \equiv L(S)$.

Therefore, from Theorem 3.3 and Remark 4.1, the solution of (4.1) and (4.2) is given by

$$P(x, y) = P_1 + P_2 = \sum a_{i'j'} \phi'_{i'j'} + (r_1 \cdot r_2 \cdot r_3)^{k+1} \cdot \left( \sum b_i \cdot \pi_i \right),$$

where $a_{i'j'} = 0$ for $i' = 0, 1, \ldots, k$. Indeed, $L'_{i'j'}(P) = 0$, and hence

$$P(x, y) = r_1^{k+1} \cdot Q(x, y). \quad \blacksquare$$

The $C^k$-continuity of the finite element of type $(k, 4k + p + 1, k, p)$ follows immediately from this lemma.

### References

1. Carnicer, J. and M. Gasca, On finite element interpolation problems, in *Mathematical Methods in Computer Aided Geometric Design*, T. Lyche and L. Schumaker (eds.), Academic Press, N. Y., 1989, 105–113.
2. Ciarlet, P. G. and P. A. Raviart, General Lagrange and Hermite interpolation in $\mathbb{R}^k$ with applications to finite element methods, Arch. Rational Mech. An. **46** (1972), 177–199.
3. Gasca, M. and J. I. Maeztu, On Lagrange and Hermite interpolation in $\mathbb{R}^k$, Numer. Math. **39** (1982), 1–14.
4. Gasca, M. and V. Ramirez, Interpolation systems in $\mathbb{R}^k$, J. Approx. Theory **42** (1984), 36–52.
5. Le Méhauté, A., Taylor interpolation of order $n$ at the vertices of a triangle. Applications for Hermite Interpolation and Finite Elements, *Symposium on Applied Theory*, Safed, Israel, May, 1980.
6. Le Méhauté, A., Interpolation et approximation par des fonctions polynomiales par Morceaux dans $\mathbb{R}^n$, Université de Rennes I, Thése d'état, 1984.

7. Lorente, J., Funciones splines: interpolación conservativa. Interpolación Multivariada, Ph.D. dissertation, Universidad de Granada, 1987.

8. Lorente J. and V. Ramirez, On interpolation systems and $H$-reducible interpolation problems in *Topics in Multivariate Approximation*, C. Chui, L. L. Schumaker, and F. Utreras (eds.), Academic Press, New York, 1987, 153–163.

9. Ženíšek, A., Interpolation polynomials on the triangle, Numer. Math. **15** (1970), 283–296.

10. Ženíšek, A., A general theorem on triangular finite $C^{(m)}$-elements, RAIRO Rech. Opér. **R2** (1974), 119–127.

J. Lorente and V. Ramirez
Departamento de Matemática Aplicada
Universidad de Granada
18071 Granada
SPAIN

Supported in part by DGICYT.PT 86-0458.

# Uniform Bivariate Hermite Interpolation

## R. A. Lorentz

**Abstract.** We consider the Hermite interpolation problem of interpolating all derivatives up to a given order at each point of a point set in the plane by bivariate polynomials of a given total degree. Such interpolations are called *uniform* if the order to which derivatives are interpolated is the same at each point. We show that all such schemes interpolating derivatives up to order two are almost regular.

## §1. Introduction

There are many ways of generalizing Hermite interpolation by univariate polynomials to two dimensions. Here one of the simplest and most natural of these possibilities is treated: uniform Hermite interpolation by bivariate polynomials of a given total degree.

**Problem 1.1.** *(Uniform bivariate Hermite interpolation with polynomials of given total degree). Let $n, p$ and $m$ be nonnegative integers with*

$$\frac{(n+1)\,(n+2)}{2} = m \cdot \frac{(p+1)\,(p+2)}{2}\,, \tag{1.1}$$

*and let*

$$\Pi_n = \{P(x,y) \ : \ P(x,y) = \sum_{i+k\leq n} a_{ik}x^i y^k\} \tag{1.2}$$

*be the space of bivariate polynomials of total degree $n$. Given real numbers $c_{q,j,l}$ with $1 \leq q \leq m$, $0 \leq j+l \leq p$ and a knot set $Z = \{z_q\} = \{(x_q, y_q)\}$, $q = 1,\ldots,m$, find a polynomial $P \in \Pi_n$ satisfying*

$$\frac{\partial^{j+l}}{\partial x^j \partial y^l} P(x_q, y_q) = c_{q,j,l} \tag{1.3}$$

Mathematical Methods in Computer Aided Geometric Design
Tom Lyche and Larry L. Schumaker (eds.), pp. 435–444.

*for all* $1 \le q \le m$ *and* $0 \le j + l \le p$.

Compared to the general bivariate Hermite interpolation problem, three simplifications have been made here. The space of interpolation polynomials has been chosen to be a space of polynomials of given total degree. The derivatives to be interpolated are all derivatives up to a given order and, lastly, this order is the same at each point. It is a consequence of these simplifications that both the space of interpolation polynomials as well as the set of derivatives to be interpolated are invariant under affine transformations of the plane. In [10], another kind of uniform Hermite interpolation is studied, where these components resemble those of tensor–product interpolations.

In two dimensions, the uniform Hermite interpolation problem is not automatically solvable for all right–hand–sides as it is in one dimension. Indeed, trying to use quadratic polynomials to interpolate the function value and both first derivatives at each of two knots leads to a linear system of equations whose determinant is zero no matter where the knots are located.

For this reason, a new classification of such interpolation schemes has been introduced in [7,8]. Let $D(Z)$ be the determinant of the linear system of equations to be solved for the coefficients of the interpolating polynomial.

**Definition 1.2.** *We say that the interpolation scheme of Problem 1.1 is regular if $D(Z)$ vanishes for no choice of knots $Z$; singular if $D(Z) = 0$ for all knot sets $Z$; and almost regular if $D(Z)$ vanishes only on a subset of $\mathbb{R}^{2m}$ of measure zero.*

It is easy to see that an interpolation scheme is almost regular as soon as $D(Z) \ne 0$ for *some* knot set $Z$.

We will restrict our investigations here to showing which uniform Hermite interpolations are almost regular. In particular, we will not touch upon the interesting and equally difficult question of characterizing those knot sets $Z$ for which $D(Z) \ne 0$ once it has been determined that they exist. The author, together with G.G. Lorentz, has shown, [9], that the problem of uniform bivariate Hermite interpolation is regular for $p = 1$ with any $m$ and $n$ satisfying (1.1) with two exceptions. They are the cases $m = 2$, $n = 2$ and $m = 5$, $n = 4$ which are singular. Here it will be shown that for $p = 2$, such interpolations are almost regular for any $m$ and $n$ satisfying (1.1). This result, in itself, is not new (see Hirschowitz [4]). Using methods of algebraic geometry, Hirschowitz proves both of these results and the almost regularity of the three–dimensional version of uniform Hermite interpolation of function values and first derivatives. In the latter case, the interpolations are almost regular for ten or more knots. He also makes the conjecture that there exists an $M$ such that uniform Hermite interpolation is almost regular if M or more knots are used. Experimental evidence supports this conjecture. In fact, the author knows of no case of failure of almost regularity for interpolations with more than five knots.

Others working along the same lines are Waldschmidt [12] and Chudnovsky [1]. In the latter paper, one can find applications to the theory of transcendental numbers via multidimensional Schwarz lemmas.

The techniques used here are completely different. This work was carried out as part of a program, formulated by G. G. Lorentz and the author, to apply the results of the general theory of bivariate Birkhoff interpolation to specific problems. The basic concepts and tools were developed in [7,8] and applied in [9,10]. With these techniques, it is almost certain that one can answer the question of almost regularity of such interpolation schemes for a few more values of $p$ (say $3 \leq p \leq 10$) and perhaps even for all values of $p$.

There is other related work generalizing univariate Hermite interpolation. For example, Gasca and Maeztu [2] have introduced generalized Newton–type interpolation schemes which also interpolate derivatives. Yet another approach is that of Hakopian [3] and that of Kergin [5]. However, both of these methods differ from that of uniform bivariate Hermite interpolation. Whereas the first one uses different interpolation spaces, the latter interpolates functionals which are integral means of function values and derivatives.

## §2. Interpolations with Few Knots

Before treating the general case, interpolations with few knots will be considered. They are different because they tend to be singular, whereas interpolations with many knots tend to be almost regular. The following lemma completely classifies all uniform bivariate Hermite interpolations with up to five knots. A similar lemma (for up to three knots) with tensor product–type interpolations was proved in [10].

**Lemma 2.1.** *Uniform bivariate Hermite interpolation (as described in Problem 1.1) with $m$ knots is*
  a) *regular for $m = 1$*
  b) *singular for $m = 2$*
  c) *singular for $m = 3$ except for the case of Lagrange interpolation ($n = 1, p = 0$) which is almost regular*
  d) *cannot be properly posed for $m = 4$; i.e., (1.1) has no integer solution*
  e) *singular for $m = 5$.*

**Proof:** Case a) is just the bivariate Taylor expansion of a polynomial. To show case b), we let $P(x, y) = 0$ be the line passing through both knots. Then $Q = P^{p+1}$ is a polynomial of degree easily shown not to exceed $n$. All derivatives of $Q$ up to order $p$ vanish at each of the two points. Thus, $Q$ is a non–trivial solution of the homogeneous interpolation problem and so the determinant $D(z_1, z_2)$ vanishes identically.

Case c) will be proved under the assumption that two of the three points lie on the $x$–axis. This does not restrict the generality since both the interpolation space and the set of functionals to be interpolated are affinely invariant. Then, among other things, the polynomial must interpolate two function values and $2p$ partial derivatives in the $x$ direction. Since for $y = 0$, there are only $n + 1$ coefficients available, $n + 1 \geq 2(p + 1)$. But this is a contradiction to (1.1) with $m = 3$ if $p \geq 1$. Finally, Lagrange interpolation can be carried out on the three points $(0, 0), (0, 1)$ and $(1, 0)$ which shows that this case is almost regular.

If $m = 4$, then $(n + 1)(n + 2) = 4(p + 1)(p + 2)$. Making the change of variables $u = n + 1, v = p + 1$ and solving for $v$,

$$v = \frac{-1 \pm \sqrt{1 + u(u + 1)}}{2} .$$

For this equation to have an integer solution, the radicand must be a perfect square. Thus, $1 + u(u + 1) = d^2$ for some integer $d$. Clearly $d > u$; i.e., $d \geq u + 1$. But then

$$d^2 \geq (u + 1)^2 = u^2 + 2u + 1 > 1 + u(u + 1),$$

so that this equation combined with the original equation has no solution.

Case e) is proved as in case b) by producing a non–trivial solution of the homogeneous equations. For any five points, there always exists a quadratic polynomial $P$ such that the points lie on the curve $P(x, y) = 0$. Then $Q = P^{p+1}$ vanishes with all of its derivatives up to order $p$ at each of the five points. The degree of $Q$ is $2(p + 1)$. From $(n + 1)(n + 2) = 5(p + 1)(p + 2)$, it follows that $2(p + 1) \leq n$. In fact, one calculates that

$$2(p + 1) + 12(p + 2) + 2 = 4p^2 + 14p + 12,$$

and that this quantity does not exceed

$$5(p + 1)(p + 2) = 5p^2 + 15p + 10$$

for $p \geq 1$. Thus, $Q$ is a non–trivial solution of the homogeneous interpolation problem. ∎

The singularity of three–node uniform Hermite interpolation problems was shown by Le Méhauté [6] with a completely different proof.

As mentioned in the introduction, no singular uniform Hermite interpolation problems are known with $m > 5$. It would be interesting to know if Lemma 2.1 includes all of the singular cases.

## §3. Uniform Hermite Interpolation with Second Derivatives

One of the concepts we will be using is that of a shift. We will describe only a restricted version of this general concept here. Given a distribution of 1's located at the lattice points of the plane (i.e., at points with integer coordinates) a *simple shift* $\Lambda$ moves one of these 1's to a neighboring lattice point which is not already occupied by a 1. Such a simple shift is called a *right* (respectively *upper* shift if the 1 is moved a unit length to the right (respectively upwards). One can also shift sets of 1's. Given a set $T$ of 1's, a *multiple shift* $\Lambda^*$ of $T$ is the repeated application of simple shifts of the 1's of $T$. If $\Lambda^* = \Lambda_k \dots \Lambda_1$, where the $\Lambda_i$ are simple shifts, then the *order* of $\Lambda^*$ is $(\alpha, \beta)$ if $\alpha$ of the shifts are right shifts and $\beta$ of them are upper shifts.

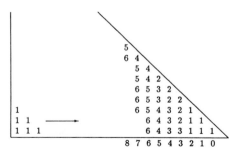

**Figure 1.** Location of the shifted 1's.

In the following proofs, the location of the 1's of the lattice will be restricted to either the finite triangle

$$S_n = \{(i, k) : 0 \le i + k \le n\}$$

or to the half–open triangle which is shown in Figure 1. In each of these cases, shifts cannot move 1's over the diagonal. Then one can speak of *maximal* shifts. Given a set $T$ of 1's, $\Lambda^*$ is a maximal (upper–right) shift of $T$ if $\Lambda^*$ shifts $T$ as far to the right as possible and then as as far upward as possible. Note that no matter what the distribution of the other 1's inside the triangle is, the image of a maximal shift applied to $T$ is uniquely defined.

We are now in a position to prove the main theorem of this section. Values of $n$ which satisfy (1.1) for $p = 2$ and some value of $m$ are given by $n = 2, 7, 10, 11 \pmod{12}$.

**Theorem 3.1.** *For all $n$ with $n = 2, 7, 10, 11 \pmod{12}$, uniform Hermite interpolation of function values, first and second derivatives at each knot by polynomials of total degree $n$ is almost regular.*

**Proof:** Applying a theorem from [8] to our case, one obtains the following geometric proof of the almost regularity of our uniform interpolation of $S_n$ with respect to $S_2$:

Step 0. Start with $m$ copies of $S_2$ and the empty triangle $S_n$.

Step 1. Move a copy of $S_2$ from the lower left–hand corner of $S_n$ maximally to the right and maximally upward (in this first step there is no possibility for upward shifts).

Step 2. Move the next copy of $S_2$ maximally to the right and maximally upward but so that it does not overlap the previous shifted copy of $S_2$.

Step i. Move a copy of $S_2$ maximally to the right and maximally upward but so that it does not overlap the previously shifted copies of $S_2$ (see Figure 1 for the resulting location of the points from the first shift (denoted by 1's) to the sixth shift (denoted by 6's)).

| $n$ | 1 | 2 | 3 | 4 | 5 | 6 | 7 | 8 | 9 | 10 | 11 | 12 | 13 | 14 | 15 | 16 | 17 | 18 | 19 | 20 | 21 | 22 | 23 | 24 |
|---|---|---|---|---|---|---|---|---|---|---|---|---|---|---|---|---|---|---|---|---|---|---|---|---|
| $r_n$ | 3 | 0 | 5 | 3 | 2 | 6 | 5 | 6 | 8 | 5 | 8 | 9 | 7 | 3 | 10 | 11 | 11 | 11 | 9 | 11 | 13 | 13 | 14 | 13 |
| $s_n$ | 0 | 0 | 3 | 0 | 1 | 2 | 1 | 3 | 3 | 1 | 4 | 2 | 2 | 3 | 4 | 4 | 4 | 3 | 3 | 4 | 4 | 5 | 4 | 4 |

| $n$ | 25 | 26 | 27 | 28 | 29 | 30 | 31 | 32 | 33 | 34 | 35 | 36 | 37 | 38 | 39 | 40 | 41 |
|---|---|---|---|---|---|---|---|---|---|---|---|---|---|---|---|---|---|
| $r_n$ | 15 | 14 | 15 | 16 | 16 | 15 | 18 | 16 | 17 | 18 | 18 | 21 | 21 | 18 | 23 | 21 | 20 |
| $s_n$ | 6 | 4 | 5 | 5 | 5 | 5 | 6 | 5 | 6 | 6 | 6 | 8 | 6 | 6 | 9 | 6 | 7 |

**Table 1.** Values of $r_n$ and $s_n$.

Then if $m$ steps of this procedure fill $S_n$ completely, a certain condition called the Pólya condition (see [8]) is satisfied after each shift, and if the shifts are unique, it follows that $S_n$ is almost regular with respect to $S_2$.

The key to the proof of Theorem 3.1 is the following lemma which is also an interesting combinatorial result in itself. It describes the properties of an auxilliary construction (similar to phase 1 above) which is that of filling up a triangle extending infinitely far to the left by shifting copies of $S_2$ maximally to the right and then maximally upward (see Figure 1).

The columns will now be numbered from right to left starting with column 0. The two numbers which will interest us are $r_n$, which is the number of 1's in column $n+1$, when column $n$ is completely filled, and $s_n$, which is the number of 1's in column $n+2$ when column $n$ is completely filled. From Figure 1 one can, for example, see that $r_4 = 3, s_4 = 0, r_5 = 2, s_5 = 1$ and $r_6 = 6, s_6 = 2$.

It is remarkable that although these numbers appear to behave chaotically, they are actually periodic in a certain sense. In fact, if we define $f(n) = r_{2n}$ and $g(n) = s_{6n}$, then both $f(n)$ and $g(n)$ are periodic with period 36. This follows from

**Lemma 3.2.** Let $r_n$ and $s_n$ be defined as above. Then for $n \geq 3$,

$$r_{n+36} = r_n + 18 \tag{3.1}$$

and

$$s_{n+36} = s_n + 6. \tag{3.2}$$

**Proof:** Table 1 shows the values of $r_n$ and $s_n$ for $1 \leq n \leq 41$. It was obtained by carrying out these shifts explicitly (with the help of a computer) until the $41^{st}$ column was full. From this table, we can see that $r_{41} = r_5 + 18$, $s_{41} = s_5 + 6$ and that $r_n$ and $s_n$ have the following properties for $5 \leq n \leq 41$:

a) $s_n \leq r_n$

b) $n + 2 - r_n > 0$

c) $n + 3 - s_n > 0$.

Our proof will be by induction on $n$, starting with $n = 5$. At each step of the induction, we will assume that (3.1) and (3.2) hold for an $n$ and that conditions a) – c) hold for all $i$ with $n \leq i \leq n+36$. Then it will be shown that (3.1) and (3.2) hold for $n+1$ and a) – c) hold for all $i$ with $n+1 \leq i \leq n+37$.

While filling column $n+1$, most of the time each maximally right and then maximally upward shift will move a triple of 1's to the top of the available space left in column $n+1$, a pair of 1's to column $n+2$ and a single 1 to column $n+3$. It is only when there is only room enough for a pair of 1's or a single 1 in column $n+1$, that one has to distinguish the cases. If $n+2-r_n = 2 \pmod 3$, then the last shift filling column $n+1$ puts two 1's in column $n+2$, three 1's in column $n+2$ and a single 1 into column $n+3$. If, on the other hand, $n+2-r_n = 1 \pmod 3$, then the last shift moves a single one into column $n+1$, a triple of 1's into column $n+2$ and a pair of 1's into column $n+3$.

Thus, if $\lfloor a \rfloor$ is the integer part of $a$, then

$$\left\lfloor \frac{n+2-r_n}{3} \right\rfloor$$

triples will fit into column $n+1$. After that, there is

$$\varepsilon_{n+1} = n+2-r_n - 3\left\lfloor \frac{n+2-r_n}{3} \right\rfloor$$

room left with $0 \leq \varepsilon_{n+1} \leq 2$. If $\varepsilon_{n+1} = 0$, column $n+1$ is full. Otherwise, the next shift will fill this column with $\varepsilon_{n+1}$ 1's.

While filling column $n+1$, column $n+2$ gets

$$\left\lfloor \frac{n+2-r_n}{3} \right\rfloor$$

pairs of 1's and, if $\varepsilon_{n+1} \neq 0$, an additional triple of 1's. Thus,

$$r_{n+1} = s_n + 2\left\lfloor \frac{n+2-r_n}{3} \right\rfloor + \delta_{n+1}, \tag{3.3}$$

where

$$\delta_{n+1} = \begin{cases} 0, & \text{if } \varepsilon_{n+1} = 0 \\ 3, & \text{otherwise.} \end{cases}$$

This formula for $\delta_{n+1}$ is valid if there is enough room in column $n+2$ to accommodate these 1's. But this follows from the induction assumption b).

Carrying out the same calculation for $r_{n+37}$, we obtain

$$\begin{aligned} r_{n+37} &= s_{n+36} + 2\left\lfloor \frac{n+2+36-r_{n+36}}{3} \right\rfloor + \delta_{n+37} \\ &= s_n + 2\left\lfloor \frac{n+2-r_n}{3} \right\rfloor + 18 + \delta_{n+37} . \end{aligned} \tag{3.4}$$

The induction hypothesis was used.

Again, this formula is only valid if there is enough room in column $n + 38$ to accommodate these 1's. The room available is

$$n + 39 - r_{n+36} = n + 23 - r_n$$

while the number of 1's shifted in is

$$2 \left\lfloor \frac{n + 2 + 36 - r_{n+36}}{3} \right\rfloor + \delta_{n+37} = 2 \left\lfloor \frac{n + 2 - r_n}{3} \right\rfloor + 12 + \delta_{n+37}$$

$$\leq \frac{2}{3}(n + 2 - r_n) + 15 \ .$$

The difference between these two numbers is $(1/3)(n+20-r_n)$ which is positive by the induction hypothesis b).

Thus (3.4) is valid. It follows that

$$\varepsilon_{n+37} = n + 2 + 36 - r_{n+36} - 3 \left\lfloor \frac{n + 2 + 36 - r_{n+36}}{3} \right\rfloor$$

$$= n + 2 - r_n - 3 \left\lfloor \frac{n + 2 - r_n}{3} \right\rfloor = \varepsilon_{n+1} \ .$$

Therefore $\delta_{n+37} = \delta_{n+1}$ and comparing (3.3) and (3.4), we see that

$$r_{n+37} = r_{n+1} + 18 \ .$$

Moreover,

$$n + 37 + 2 - r_{n+37} = n + 21 - r_{n+1} > 0$$

so that b) holds for $r_{n+37}$.

Using the same considerations for $s_{n+1}$, we obtain

$$s_{n+1} = 1 \cdot \left\lfloor \frac{n + 2 - r_n}{3} \right\rfloor + \gamma_{n+1},$$

where

$$\gamma_{n+1} = \begin{cases} 0, & \text{if } \varepsilon_{n+1} = 0 \\ 2, & \text{if } \varepsilon_{n+1} = 1 \\ 1, & \text{if } \varepsilon_{n+1} = 2. \end{cases}$$

Similarly,

$$s_{n+37} = 1 \cdot \left\lfloor \frac{n + 2 + 36 - r_{n+36}}{3} \right\rfloor + \gamma_{n+37}$$

$$= \left\lfloor \frac{n + 2 - r_n}{3} \right\rfloor + 6 + \gamma_{n+37} \ . \tag{3.5}$$

As before, it can be shown that there is enough room in column $n+39$ (the difference between $n + 40 - s_{n+36}$ and the number of 1's put into that column being at most $(2/3)\{n + 23 - s_n + (1/3)(r_n - s_n)\}$) and that $\gamma_{n+37} = \gamma_{n+1}$. Thus,

$$s_{n+37} = s_{n+1} + 6.$$

Moreover,

$$n + 37 + 2 - s_{n+37} = n + 33 - s_{n+1} > 0$$

so that c) holds for $s_{n+37}$. Finally comparing (3.4) and (3.5), it is clear that $r_{n+37} > s_{n+37}$ which finishes the proof. ∎

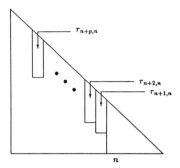

**Figure 2.** The remainders $r_{n+i,n}$.

**Continuation of the Proof of Theorem 3.1:**

The construction mentioned at the beginning of the proof will be carried out in two phases. In the first phase, which lasts until all but the first three columns are filled, the construction of Lemma 3.2 will be carried out without paying attention as to whether the Pólya condition is satisfied. This will guarantee that these shifts are unique. It remains to be shown that the distribution of 1's obtained after filling all but the first three columns satisfies the Pólya condition and, for the last three rows, one must check the Pólya condition and the uniqueness for each individual shift. The details may be found in [11]. ∎

## §4. The General Case

A very large part of the proofs of Theorem 3.1 and Lemma 3.2 can be carried over to the case of the almost regularity of $S_n$ with respect to $S_p$ for arbitrary $p$. When carrying out the construction of shifting copies of $S_p$ maximally to the right and then upwards, the $p$ columns numbered $n+1, \ldots, n+p$ would contain 1's when column $n$ is filled. Denote these numbers by $r_{n+i,n}, i = 1, \ldots, p$ (see Figure 2). If one can show that the numbers $r_{n+i,n}$ repeat themselves once with a period $T_p$, then it can be shown that they are periodic in the sense that

$$r_{n+T_p+i,n+T_p} = r_{n+i,n} + \frac{(p-i+1)(p-i+2)}{(p+1)(p+2)}T_p$$

for $1 \le i \le p$.

And indeed, such periods have been found computationally for $p$ between 1 and 6. If $|S|$ is the number of points in $S$, then they are $T_1 = 9$, $T_2 = 36$, $T_3 = 20$, $T_4 = 45$, $T_5 = 63$ and $T_6 = 56$. It is to be expected that such periods also exist for higher $p$. We can write them as $T_1 = 3|S_1|$, $T_2 = 6|S_2|$, $T_3 = 2|S_3|$, $T_4 = 3|S_4|$, $T_5 = 3|S_5|$ and $T_6 = 2|S_6|$. In each of these cases $T_p \le |S_p|^2$ and $T_p = c_p|S_p|$, where $c_p$ is a divisor of $|S_p|$. However, we have no proof of this fact in general. In any case, to prove the almost regularity of $S_n$ with respect to $S_p$ for $3 \le p \le 6$, it remains to be shown that some certain inequalities hold for the last $p$ columns. They are needed to show that the final shifts of the construction are unique and that the resulting incidence matrices satisfy the Pólya condition.

## References

1. Chudnovsky, G. V., Singular points on complex hypersurfaces and multi-dimensional Schwarz lemma, Seminaire de Théorie des Nombres, 1979–80, Marie Jose Bertin (ed.), Progress in Mathematics **12** (1981), 29–69.
2. Gasca, M. and J. I. Maeztu, On Lagrange and Hermite interpolation in $R^n$, Numer. Math. **39** (1982), 1–14.
3. Hakopian, H. A., Multivariate divided differences and multivariate interpolation of Lagrange and Hermite type, J. Approx. Theory **34** (1982), 286–305.
4. Hirschowitz, A., La méthode d'Horace pour l'interpolation à plusieurs variables, Man. Math. **50** (1985), 337–388.
5. Kergin, P., A natural interpolation of $C^K$ functions, J. Approx. Theory **29** (1980), 278–293.
6. Le Méhauté, A., Interpolation et approximation par des fonctions polynomiales par morceaux dans $R^n$, Doctoral Dissertation, Université de Rennes, 1984.
7. Lorentz, G. G. and R. A. Lorentz, Multivariate interpolation, in *Rational Approximation and Interpolation*, P. R. Graves–Morris, E. B. Saff, and R. S. Varga (eds.), Lecture Notes in Mathematics, No. 1105, Springer Verlag, Berlin, 1984, 136–144.
8. Lorentz, G. G. and R. A. Lorentz, Solvability problems of bivariate interpolation I, Constr. Approx. **2** (1986), 153–169.
9. Lorentz, G. G. and R. A. Lorentz, Solvability problems of bivariate interpolation II: Applications, Approx. Theory Appl. **3** (1987), 79–97.
10. Lorentz, R. A., Uniform bivariate Hermite interpolation I: Coordinate degree, Arbeitspapiere der GMD No. 286, 1988, Math. Z., to appear.
11. Lorentz, R. A., Uniform bivariate Hermite interpolation II: Total degree, Arbeitspapiere der GMD No. 323, 1988.
12. Waldschmidt, M., Nombres transcendants et groupes algébriques, Astérisque, **69–70** (1979), 1–217.
13. Ženíšek, A., general theorem on triangular finite $C^m$ elements, RAIRO, Rech. Opér., **R2**, (1974), 119–127.

R. A. Lorentz
Gesellschaft für Mathematik und Datenverarbeitung
Schloß Birlinghoven, Postfach 1240
5205 St. Augustin 1
W. GERMANY

EMAIL: gmap27@ dbngmd21.bitnet

# A Survey of Applications of an Affine Invariant Norm

## Gregory M. Nielson and Thomas A. Foley

**Abstract.** A survey of applications of an affine invariant norm to several areas of Computer Aided Geometric Design is presented. The main purpose for using an affine invariant norm is to obtain methods and techniques which are not affected by affine transformations of the input data. This means, for example, that the artificial choices of the origin or the units of measurement should have no effect on the final results of the method. Applications in the areas of scattered data interpolation, knot spacing for parametric curve interpolation, and triangulations and tessellations are covered.

## §1. Introduction

Many of the well known and widely used methods of Computer Aided Geometric Design are not invariant with respect to affine transformations of the input data. In some cases, this means that if the data is rotated the results of the method do no reflect this rotation in the proper way. In other cases, this means that the choice of the units of measurement used for the input data will have an effect on the results of the method. If inches and seconds are used, the results could be different than if meters and minutes were used. We consider this lack of affine invariance to be a deficiency. In some cases, this situation can be remedied by certain modifications to the method. The modifications covered in this paper are based upon replacing the conventional method of measuring the distance between two points by a norm which has the property of being affine invariant. We discuss applications of this affine invariant norm to scattered data interpolation, knot spacing for parametric spline curves and characterizations of optimal triangulations.

All of the various techniques that we discuss utilize a collection of data points $V_i, i = 1, \ldots, n$. While much of what we cover holds true for points in $N$-dimensional space, most of our discussion is restricted to the case of $E^2$

Mathematical Methods in Computer Aided Geometric Design
Tom Lyche and Larry L. Schumaker (eds.), pp. 445–467.
Copyright © 1989 by Academic Press, Boston.
ISBN 0-12-460515-X.

where $V_i = (x_i, y_i)$. Also, since each of the techniques we discuss requires that the points be distinct and not collinear, we assume this for the remainder of the paper. In $E^2$, an affine transformation takes the form

$$T(V) = \begin{pmatrix} t_{11} & t_{12} \\ t_{21} & t_{22} \end{pmatrix} V + \begin{pmatrix} c_1 \\ c_2 \end{pmatrix}. \tag{1.1}$$

An affine invariant norm will depend upon the data. We indicate this dependence by the use of the notation

$$\|\ \|_{\mathbf{V}}, \quad \text{where} \quad \mathbf{V} = \begin{pmatrix} V_1 \\ V_2 \\ \vdots \\ V_n \end{pmatrix}.$$

**Definition 1.1.** *Assume that $P$ and $Q$ are any two points in the domain of the norm $\|\ \|_{\mathbf{V}}$. This norm is said to be affine invariant provided*

$$\|P - Q\|_{\mathbf{V}} = \|T(P) - T(Q)\|_{T(\mathbf{V})} \tag{1.2}$$

*for any affine transformation $T$.*

The following affine invariant norm, $\|\|\ \|\|_{\mathbf{V}}$ was first introduced in [17]:

$$\|\|P\|\|_{\mathbf{V}}^2 = (x, y) \begin{pmatrix} \dfrac{\Sigma_{\mathbf{Y}}^2}{\Sigma_{\mathbf{X}}^2 \Sigma_{\mathbf{Y}}^2 - (\Sigma_{\mathbf{XY}})^2} & \dfrac{-\Sigma_{\mathbf{XY}}}{\Sigma_{\mathbf{X}}^2 \Sigma_{\mathbf{Y}}^2 - (\Sigma_{\mathbf{XY}})^2} \\ \dfrac{-\Sigma_{\mathbf{XY}}}{\Sigma_{\mathbf{X}}^2 \Sigma_{\mathbf{Y}}^2 - (\Sigma_{\mathbf{XY}})^2} & \dfrac{\Sigma_{\mathbf{X}}^2}{\Sigma_{\mathbf{X}}^2 \Sigma_{\mathbf{Y}}^2 - (\Sigma_{\mathbf{XY}})^2} \end{pmatrix} \begin{pmatrix} x \\ y \end{pmatrix}, \tag{1.3}$$

where

$$P = \begin{pmatrix} x \\ y \end{pmatrix},$$

$$\Sigma_{\mathbf{X}}^2 = \frac{\sum_{i=1}^n (x_i - \bar{x})^2}{n}, \qquad \bar{x} = \frac{\sum_{i=1}^n x_i}{n}$$

$$\Sigma_{\mathbf{Y}}^2 = \frac{\sum_{i=1}^n (y_i - \bar{y})^2}{n}, \qquad \bar{y} = \frac{\sum_{i=1}^n y_i}{n}$$

and

$$\Sigma_{\mathbf{XY}} = \frac{\sum_{i=1}^n (x_i - \bar{x})(y_i - \bar{y})}{n}.$$

It is quite easy to verify that this norm is actually affine invariant once it is observed that

$$\|\|P\|\|_{\mathbf{V}}^2 = (x, y)\, n [\bar{\mathbf{V}}^* \bar{\mathbf{V}}]^{-1} \begin{pmatrix} x \\ y \end{pmatrix}, \tag{1.4}$$

where

$$\bar{V} = \begin{pmatrix} x_1 - \bar{x}, & y_1 - \bar{y} \\ x_2 - \bar{x}, & y_2 - \bar{y} \\ \vdots & \vdots \\ x_n - \bar{x}, & y_n - \bar{y} \end{pmatrix}.$$

This observation also makes it obvious what the generalization of this norm is for points of $E^N$.

One way to study a norm is to examine its unit disks. For a general quadratic norm, we use the notation

$$||P||_A^2 = (x, y) A \begin{pmatrix} x \\ y \end{pmatrix} = (P, P)_A, \tag{1.5}$$

where A is a symmetric, positive definite, $2 \times 2$ matrix

$$A = \begin{pmatrix} a_{11} & a_{12} \\ a_{21} & a_{22} \end{pmatrix}.$$

The level curve consisting of all points satisfying

$$||P||_A = \rho$$

is an ellipse rotated from standard position by the angle

$$\alpha = \frac{1}{2} \tan^{-1}\left(\frac{2a_{12}}{a_{22} - a_{11}}\right),$$

and with lengths of the major and minor axes given by

$$a^2 = \frac{\rho^2}{c^2 a_{11} - 2cs a_{12} + s^2 a_{22}},$$

$$b^2 = \frac{\rho^2}{c^2 a_{11} + 2cs a_{12} + s^2 a_{22}},$$

where

$$c = \cos(\alpha) \quad \text{and} \quad s = \sin(\alpha).$$

These values are further illustrated in Figure 1.

For the affine invariant norm of (1.3), we have that

$$\alpha = \frac{1}{2} \tan^{-1}\left(\frac{2\Sigma_{\mathbf{XY}}}{\Sigma_{\mathbf{X}}^2 - \Sigma_{\mathbf{Y}}^2}\right).$$

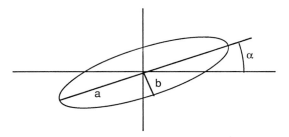

**Figure 1.** Unit disk of a quadratic norm.

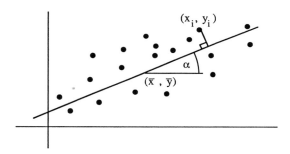

**Figure 2.** Normal regression line.

It is interesting to note that this angle $\alpha$ is the slope of the regression line obtained by minimizing the sum of the perpendicular distances. This is further illustrated in Figure 2.

We now present some examples of this affine invariant norm. In Figure 3, we show four data sets each being affine images of each other. Starting in the upper left corner, this data is rotated in the counter clockwise direction by 44 degrees to yield the data in the upper right corner. This data is then scaled by a factor of 2 in the y-component to yield the data of the lower right corner. Scaling by a factor of .5 in the x-component leads to the data in the lower left corner. The four concentric ellipses in each case represent the points which are .25, .50, .75 and 1.00 units from the center of the ellipse as measured by the affine invariant norm. Even though the conventional Euclidean distance between two points changes from data set to data set, the distance measured by the affine invariant norm remains constant.

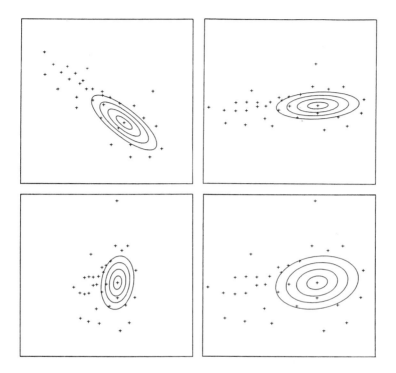

**Figure 3.** Four affine related data sets.

## §2. Applications to Scattered Data Interpolation

The term scattered data interpolation was first used by Schumaker [22] in his survey of this topic over twelve years ago. Since that time, a great deal of research has been published on this topic. Franke [10] has given an excellent survey and critical comparison of various methods. Recently, he has updated his survey [11]. For the discussion here, a method of scattered data interpolation is an operator that accepts independent data values $\mathbf{V} = (V_1, \ldots, V_n)$ and associated dependent values $f_i, i = 1, \ldots, n$ and produces a function $S[\mathbf{V}](V) = S(V) = S(x, y)$ such that $S(x_i, y_i) = f_i, i = 1, \ldots, n$. We assume that the independent data values are distinct and that they do not all lie on a line. It seems reasonable that the happenstance of the selection of the units of measurement or the location of the coordinate axes for the dependent data should not affect the final results of the interpolation method. But, unfortunately, for a great number of the methods, this is not the case. In general, it would be desirable if a scattered data interpolation technique were to be affine invariant.

**Definition 2.1.** *A scattered data interpolation method is said to be affine invariant provided*

$$S[T(\mathbf{V})](T(V)) = S[\mathbf{V}](V) \tag{2.1}$$

*for any affine transformation $T$.*

It is interesting to identify certain less restrictive classes of scattered data interpolation methods. Namely, those that are *translation invariant*, those that are *rotation invariant* and those that are *scale* and *scalar* invariant. It is clear what the definition of the first two would be, but the difference between scale and scalar is not standard and so we elaborate. By scale invariance, we mean that $S[\begin{pmatrix} \alpha & 0 \\ 0 & \beta \end{pmatrix} \mathbf{V}](\begin{pmatrix} \alpha & 0 \\ 0 & \beta \end{pmatrix} V) = S[\mathbf{V}](V)$, where $\alpha, \beta \neq 0$. By scalar invariance, we mean the special case of scale invariance where $\alpha = \beta$. The reason we distinguish these two cases is that a number of methods that are scalar invariant are not scale invariant. The difference between scale invariance and scalar invariance is related to the problem of the choice of units of measurement used for the independent data. This distinction is clarified by the following example.

Given five data points, an interpolant of the form $S(x, y) = a + bx + cy + dxy + e(x^2 + y^2)$ is determined. With the data of Table 1, the interpolant is easily verified to be $S_1(x, y) = 2(x+y-x^2-y^2)$. If we think of the units for the $x$-variable to be feet and those of the $y$-variable to be minutes, then the same data in the units of inches and seconds is given in Table 2. The interpolant is, in this case, $S_2(x, y) = (12x + 60y - x^2 - y^2)/936$. Now if one were to use this interpolant to estimate the dependent argument at, say, .75 feet and .5 minutes, we get in the first case, $S_1(.75, .50) = 0.875$ and in the second case $S_2(9, 30) = \frac{103}{104} \neq 0.875$.

| $x_i$ | $y_i$ | $z_i$ |
|-------|-------|-------|
| 1.0   | 1.0   | 0     |
| 1.0   | 0.0   | 0     |
| 0.5   | 0.5   | 1     |
| 0.0   | 1.0   | 0     |
| 0.0   | 0.0   | 0     |

**Table 1.**

| $x_i$ | $y_i$ | $z_i$ |
|-------|-------|-------|
| 12    | 60    | 0     |
| 12    | 0     | 0     |
| 6     | 30    | 1     |
| 0     | 60    | 0     |
| 0     | 0     | 0     |

**Table 2.**

The reason these two estimates are different is that the basis functions $1, x, y, xy, x^2 + y^2$ are not closed under affine transformations. The space of bivariate polynomials $P_m = \langle x^i y^j : i + j \leq m \rangle$ **is** affine invariant and consequently approximations based on these functions will be translation, rotation,

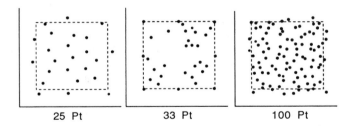

25 Pt     33 Pt     100 Pt

**Figure 4.** Data sets.

and scale invariant. Unfortunately, polynomial basis functions are not appropriate for scattered data interpolation due to a variety of reasons including the lack of unisolvence for most data configurations. Because of the need to have basis functions that are unisolvent over the independent data values, most scattered data interpolation methods use basis functions that depend upon the data. Usually this dependence is such that the span of the basis functions is **not** closed under affine transformations and so the resulting methods are not affine invariant. A number of the more popular and effective methods (see for example [13], [14] and [4]) utilize basis functions which involve $||V - V_i||$. While this expression is invariant with respect to rotations and translations, it is not invariant with respect to scale and shear transformation. The use of the affine invariant norm $|||\ |||_{\mathbf{V}}$ (see equation $(1.3)$) in lieu of the conventional Euclidean norm will take care of the lack of affine invariance for this expression and may possibly lead to scattered data interpolation method which is affine invariant. The reason that it is not immediately obvious that the resulting method will be affine invariant is that, for most methods, there are additional basis functions. For example, the basis functions for the thin plate [4] or surface [13] spline are $||V - V_i||, i = 1, \ldots, n$ **and** $1, x, y$. It has been shown in [17] that the modification of this method which involves the affine invariant norm

$$S[\mathbf{V}](V) = \sum_{j=1}^{n} b_j |||V - V_j|||_{\mathbf{V}}^2 \log |||V - V_j|||_{\mathbf{V}} + c_1 x + c_2 y + c_3,$$

where the coefficients $c_1, c_2, c_3$ and $b_j, j = 1, \ldots, n$ are determined from the system of $n + 3$ equations

$$\sum_{j=1}^{n} b_j |||V_i - V_j|||_{\mathbf{V}}^2 \log |||V_i - V_j|||_{\mathbf{V}} + c_1 x_i + c_2 y_i + c_3 = f_i, \quad i = 1, \ldots, n$$

$$\sum_{j=1}^{n} b_j = 0, \quad \sum_{j=1}^{n} b_j x_j = 0, \quad \sum_{j=1}^{n} b_j y_j = 0,$$

is affine invariant.

The question now arises as to what effect this modification has on the performance of the method. One way to assess this is to compare the ability of these two methods, the original and the modified, to reproduce a given function based upon sampled values. The errors of the first row of Table 3 are based upon the difference between a function, $F$, and the spline approximation obtained by evaluating this function at the independent data sites. The function is

$$F(x,y) = .75\exp\left[-\frac{(9x-2)^2+(9y-2)^2}{4}\right] + .75\exp\left[-\frac{(9x+1)^2}{49} - \frac{9y+1}{10}\right]$$
$$+ .5\exp\left[-\frac{(9x-7)^2+(9y-3)^2}{4}\right] - .2\exp\left[-(9x-4)^2-(9y-7)^2\right]$$

$$(2.2)$$

and the data sets are shown in Figure 4.

|                      | 25 Pt. Data Set | 33 Pt. Data Set | 100 Pt. Data Set |
|----------------------|-----------------|-----------------|------------------|
| Original             | .03480          | .04210          | .00947           |
| Aff. Inv.            | .03380          | .04150          | .00942           |

**Table 3.** RMS errors for three data sets.

Also shown in Table 3 are the errors for the modified, affine invariant method. The errors are not very different in this case because the methods are not very different. This is due to the fact that the affine invariant norm is not much different than the Euclidean norm for these data sets. The unit disks of the affine invariant norm are very close to circles. This is often the case for a large number of data sets that one encounters in applications. But it is possible for the results to be quite different; particularly if the units of measurement of the data are very different. In order to illustrate this, we show in Table 4 the results of applying the original method to three more data sets where we have artificially scaled the $x$ component by a factor of 10. The errors are significantly larger compared to the errors for the original method.

|                      | Scaled 25 Pt. | Scaled 33 Pt. | Scaled 100 Pt. |
|----------------------|---------------|---------------|----------------|
| Original             | .14609        | .15041        | .07887         |
| Aff. Inv.            | .03380        | .04150        | .00942         |

**Table 4.** RMS errors for scaled data sets ($x \leftarrow 10x$).

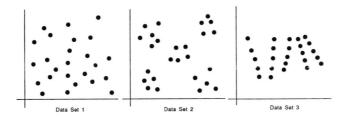

**Figure 5.** Three data sets.

In Table 5 we show the results of further comparisons. Here the the ratio of the RMS errors of the original method and the affine invariant modification for three data sets and three functions are given. The three data sets are shown in Figure 5 and the three functions are

$$F_1(x,y) = \frac{1}{3}\exp\left[-\frac{81}{16}((x-\frac{1}{2})^2 + (y-\frac{1}{2})^2)\right],$$

$$F_2(x,y) = \frac{1.25 + \cos(5.4y)}{6[1 + (3x-1)^2]},$$

and

$$F_3(x,y) = \text{same as in equation (2.2)}$$

The graphs of these three functions are shown in Figure 6. The results of this table indicate that for typical data sets and typical functions, the affine invariant modification often gives slightly better results than the original method. So, by the use of this affine invariant norm, one can obtain an affine invariant method of scattered data interpolation with very little additional computational costs and probably no loss to the methods ability to reproduce given functions based upon evaluations.

|              | Data Set 1 | Data Set 2 | Data Set 3 |
|--------------|------------|------------|------------|
| Function $F_1$ | 1.05       | 1.28       | 1.08       |
| Function $F_2$ | 0.98       | 1.13       | 1.01       |
| Function $F_3$ | 0.96       | 1.04       | 0.99       |

**Table 5.** $\dfrac{\text{RMS error surface spline}}{\text{RMS error affine invariant surface spline}}$.

We now discuss some results on the use of the affine invariant norm in conjunction with Hardy's multiquadric method (see [14] and [10]). The form of this interpolant is

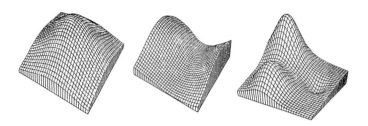

**Figure 6.** Graphs of $F_1, F_2$ and $F_3$.

$$H[\mathbf{V}](V) = \sum_{i=1}^{n} a_i \sqrt{||V - V_i||^2 + R^2},\qquad(2.3)$$

where $R^2 > 0$ is a user defined parameter and the coefficients $a_i, i = 1, \ldots, n$ are determined by the solution of the linear system of equations

$$H[\mathbf{V}](V_j) = f_j, \quad j = 1, \ldots, n.$$

If the parameter $R^2$ is chosen in a manner that depends only on the distances between data points, then Hardy's multiquadric method is invariant with respect to rotations, translations and scalar (but not scale) transformations. If the Euclidean norm of (2.3) is replaced by the affine invariant norm of (1.3), then the method will be affine invariant. The effect this has on the performance of the method is indicated by the results of the following example.

Using the function $F$ of (2.2) and the 100 point data set of Figure 4, the results of either the original method or the affine invariant modification are approximately the same because the data is uniformly distributed. However, if the $x$-coordinates are scaled by 5 or by 50, then we observe a significant difference in the error. Since the interpolant depends on the parameter $R^2$ and since the optimal choice of the value is an open question, we consider several values and plot the RMS error as a function of $R^2$. This is shown in Figure 7 where it should be noted that a log-log scale is being used. The long dashed curve is the error for the data scaled by 50 in $x$ using the Euclidean norm; the short dashed curve represents the same interpolant applied to the data scaled by 5 in $x$; and the solid curve represents the error on each of these data sets when the multiquadric method uses the affine invariant norm. For $R^2 < 10^{-3}$ all three of these error curves are approximately constant and we conclude that, for this example, using the affine invariant norm yields smaller errors for all choices of $R^2 < 1$.

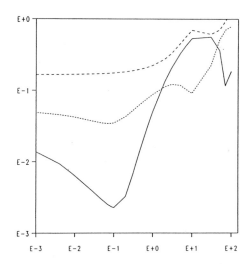

**Figure 7.** Errors for multiquadric method.

## §3. Applications to Knot Selection

Parametric curves play an important role in many areas of CAGD. Most applications utilize piecewise defined curves and so a knot sequence is involved. It is well known that the choice of the knots can have a tremendous effect on the curve (see [5,6,7,16,2,9]). In this section, we discuss several methods of knot selection and the effects of using the affine invariant metric of (1.3). We will restrict our discussion to the case of planar, natural cubic interpolating splines. Given the data $V_i = (x_i, y_i), i = 1, \ldots, n$ and a knot sequence $t_1 \leq t_2 \leq \cdots \leq t_n$, we denote by $S(t) = (x(t), y(t))$ the cubic spline with natural end conditions such that $S(t_i) = V_i, i = 1, \ldots, n$. We consider the method of knot selection as part of the overall curve interpolation operation. We use the notation $S[\mathbf{V}](t)$ for the operator which accepts the input data $\mathbf{V} = (V_1, \ldots, V_n)$, applies some knot selection algorithm, and produces the interpolating cubic spline. Based upon the results of [8] we may assume, without loss of generality, that $t_1 = 0$ and $t_n = 1$ and make the following definition.

**Definition 3.1.** *A method $S[\mathbf{V}](t)$ of planar, natural, cubic spline interpolation is said to be affine invariant provided*

$$T(S[\mathbf{V}](t)) = S[T(\mathbf{V})](t), \quad 0 \leq t \leq 1, \tag{3.1}$$

*where $T$ is any affine transformation as defined in (1.1).*

Two particular methods of knot selection are very well known. These are *uniform*, where $t_i = \frac{i-1}{n-1}$ and *chord-length* where $t_i = t_{i-1} + d_i/d$ and

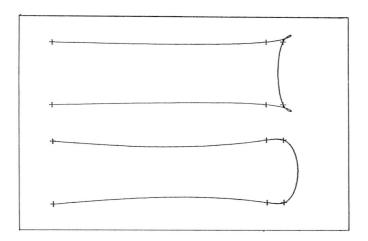

**Figure 8.**   Uniform (top) and chord-length knot selection.

$d_i = \|V_{i-1} - V_i\|$ and $d = \sum d_i$. The main advantage of uniform knots is the simplicity of the resulting numerical algorithms. Also, this method of knot selection leads to a curve fitting operator which is affine invariant. A major problem with this method is that it can yield some very undesirable curves when the distance between data points is not nearly constant. A simple example of this is shown in Figure 8. The choice of chord-length knot selection tends to eliminate this problem as shown in the second example of Figure 8. The problem with the chord-length method of knot selection is that it is not affine invariant. It is invariant with respect to rotations, translations and scalar transformation, but not with respect to scale and shear transformations. This drawback is illustrated by the simple example of Figure 9 where the data has been scaled in the $y$-direction only.

It is easy to correct the problem of the lack of affine invariance for the chord-length method by using the affine invariant norm of (1.3) in place of the standard Euclidean norm; that is,

$$t_i = t_{i-1} + \frac{\||V_i - V_{i-1}|\|_{\mathbf{v}}}{\sum \||V_i - V_{i-1}|\|_{\mathbf{v}}}, \quad i = 2, \ldots, n.$$

While this modification does cure the problem of lack of affine invariance and works quite well in most situations, it does introduce the possibility of poor results in some cases. This is illustrated in Figure 10. The problem is the shape of the curve near the implied "bump" on the curve. A method recently developed by Foley and Nielson [8] alleviates this problem while maintaining the property of being affine invariant. It not only utilizes the affine invariant norm of (1.3), it also takes into consideration the "bending" of the curve implied

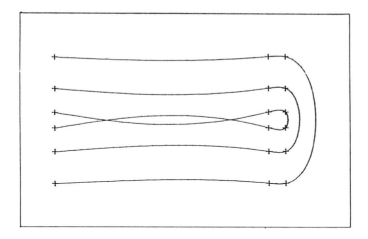

**Figure 9.** Effect of scaling on chord-length knot selection.

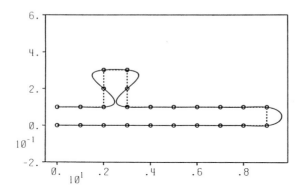

**Figure 10.**   Chord-length knot spacing using affine invariant norm.

by the data. The example of Figure 11 uses this method.

## §4. Applications to Triangulations

Several areas of CAGD involve triangulations. Basically, the problem of triangulating planar data sets requires the partitioning of the convex hull into a collection of triangles with vertices from the data set. As before, the vertices $V_i$, $i = 1, \ldots, n$, are assumed to be distinct and not all lie on a line. The convex

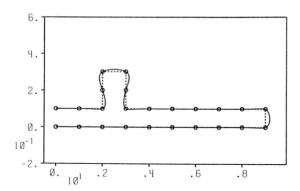

**Figure 11.**   Knot spacing method of Foley and Nielson.

hull is denoted by $CH\langle(V_1, V_2, \ldots, V_n)\rangle = CH\langle \mathbf{V} \rangle$. For three vertices $V_i$, $V_j$, $V_k$, the convex hull is a triangle which is denoted by $T_{ijk}$. This is a closed set, and the open set consisting of the interior of this triangle is denoted by $\mathring{T}_{ijk}$.

**Definition 4.1.** *Given the vertices* $V_i$, $i = 1, \ldots, n$ , *we say a collection of triple indices* $I_t = \{ijk : 1 \leq i, j, k \leq n, i \neq j \neq k \neq i\}$ *represents a triangulation provided:*

i)   $\mathring{T}_{ijk} \neq \emptyset$

ii)   $\mathring{T}_{abc} \cap \mathring{T}_{\alpha\beta\gamma} = \emptyset, \quad abc, \alpha\beta\gamma \in I_t, \quad abc \neq \alpha\beta\gamma$

iii)   $V_m \notin T_{ijk}, \quad m \neq i, j, k$

iv)   $\displaystyle\bigcup_{ijk \in I_t} T_{ijk} = CH\langle \mathbf{V} \rangle.$

For any given data set, there are a number of possible triangulations. For certain applications, a preference for one triangulation over the other may exist. Usually, an optimal criteria attempts to avoid long thin triangles [12]. Two optimal criteria have been discussed quite extensively: 1) the *max-min* criteria of Lawson [15], and 2) the *min-max* criteria of Little and Barnhill [1]. Both of these optimal triangulations have a similar method of characterization. Associated with each triangulation there is a vector with $n_t$ entries representing either the largest or smallest angle of each triangle. The entries of each vector are ordered and then a lexicographic ordering of the vectors is used to impose an ordering on the set of all triangulations. In the case of the min-max criteria, $A_i$ is the largest angle of a triangle and the entries of each vector, $\mathbf{A}_t$ , are ordered so that $\mathbf{A}_t = (A_1, A_2, \ldots, A_{n_t})$, with $A_i \geq A_j$, $i < j$. The smallest of these vectors based on their lexicographic ordering associates

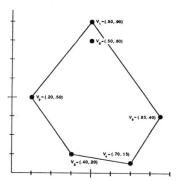

**Figure 12.** Six data points.

with the optimal triangulation. In the case of the max-min criteria, $a_i$ is the smallest angle and the entries of each vector are ordered the other way so that $\mathbf{a}_t = (a_1, a_2, \ldots, a_{n_t}), \quad a_i \leq a_j, \quad i \leq j$. The largest of these vectors represents the optimal triangulation in max-min sense. The following example helps to illustrate these ideas. In Figure 12, there are six data points which have a total of ten possible triangulations which are shown in Figure 13. Based upon the max-min criteria we have the ordering:

$$\tau_1 < \tau_2 < \tau_5 < \tau_3 < \tau_0 < \tau_6 < \tau_7 < \tau_4 < \tau_8 < \tau_9,$$

and so $\tau_9$ is the optimal triangulation in this sense. It is interesting to note that each triangulation is obtainable from one with a smaller associated vector by swapping the diagonal of a convex quadrilateral. In fact, this basic operation forms the basis of the algorithm of Lawson for computing the optimal triangulation. Lawson[15] has shown that any triangulation can be obtained from any other triangulation by a sequence of these operations. Furthermore, Lawson has proved that if the choice of the diagonal is made on the basis of the max-min criteria for the quadrilateral only, eventually the optimal triangulation will be obtained. In other words, for this criterion, a local optimum is a global optimum. It is interesting to note that this is not the case for the min-max criterion. This same example points this out. It turns out that based upon the min-max criteria, $\tau_4$ is optimal and $\tau_8$ is a local minimum. More details on this example and related results can be found in [18].

In many applications, the choice of the location of the coordinate axes or the choice of the units for measured data is rather arbitrary. Consequently, these choices should not affect the final results. Since the above criteria for an optimal triangulation is based upon angles only, it is clear that a translation or rotation of the data would not affect the triangulation, but unfortunately, a change of scale can affect matters. The following example shows this. In the left portion of Figure 14, we show the optimal max-min triangulation of some data whose units of measurement are inches and seconds. In the right portion, we show the optimal triangulation of this same data except the units of measurement have been changed to feet and minutes. Even though both triangulations

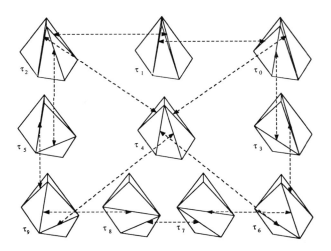

**Figure 13.** Ten triangulations of six points.

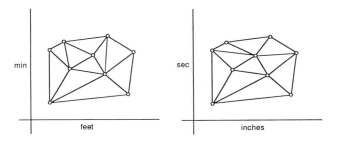

**Figure 14.** Different optimal triangulations of the same data.

are optimal in the min-max sense, they are different. This anomalous behavior is a drawback which can be eliminated by the use of the affine invariant norm of (1.3).

At the outset, the characterization of an optimal triangulation analogous to those mentioned above seems unlikely. The min-max triangulation is based upon angles, and angles are certainly affected by scale transformations. The basic idea of the characterization of [19] is based upon the duality of the min-max triangulation and the Dirichlet tessellation. Since the tessellation is based solely upon distance, the problem of the angles is circumvented. Before we discuss this approach, we review some background information on Dirichlet

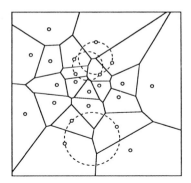

**Figure 15.** The Dirichlet tessellation of a set of points.

tessellations.

The *Dirichlet tessellation* based on the vertices $V_i$, $i = 1, \ldots, n$, is a partition of the plane into $n$ regions $R_i$, $i = 1, \ldots, n$, called the *Thiessen regions*. The Thiessen region $R_k$ consists of all points in the plane whose closest point among $V_i$, $i = 1, \ldots, n$, is $V_k$. A Dirichlet tessellation is usually illustrated by drawing the boundaries of the regions $R_i, i = 1, \ldots, n$. An example is shown in Figure 15. There are several interesting properties that can be noted. The edges of the boundaries of these regions consist of points which are equidistant to two vertices and are therefore perpendicular bisectors of two vertices. Points of intersection of edges are points that are equidistant to three (or more) points and are, therefore, the centers of circles specified by these points. Two vertices which have Thiessen regions with a common edge are called neighbors and if neighbors are joined together, then a triangulation of the convex hull is obtained. This is often referred to as the *Delaunay triangulation* [20,3] or the *Thiessen triangulation* [15,21,25]. An example based on the same points as in Figure 15 is given in Figure 16. Lawson [15], as well as Sibson [24], has shown that this particular triangulation is the same as the optimal triangulation characterized by the max-min criterion. Each of the triangles of this optimal triangulation is characterized by the property that the interior of the circumscribing circle contains no vertices. The centers of these circumscribing circles are, of course, at the triads of the Dirichlet tessellation.

When a general quadratic norm, as given by (1.5), is used, the idea of a circumscribing circle can be extended to a "circumscribing ellipse". Given three distinct points $V_i, V_j$ and $V_k$ it can be shown [19] that there is a unique *center point*, $C(V_i, V_j, V_k)$ which is equally distant ( in the $|| \ ||_A$ sense) to all three points.

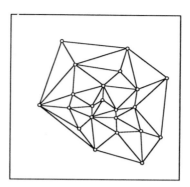

**Figure 16.** A triangulation of a set of points.

**Definition 4.2.** *Let $V_i, V_j$ and $V_k$ be three non-collinear points. The set of points*

$$E_A(V_i, V_j, V_k) = \{V : \|V - C(V_i, V_j, V_k)\|_A \leq \|V_j - C(V_i, V_j, V_k)\|_A\}$$

*is called a circumscribing A-ellipse.*

We normally think of the information representing a tessellation as consisting of a list of points along with the edge connection information. Since the points of a tessellation are equidistant to (at least) three vertices, it would be equivalent to represent this information with a list of triples, each one leading to a circumcenter as defined above. The edge information is also represented by this list of triples; for if two triples share a pair of indices, then there is an edge joining the two associated circumcenters. If a pair of indices $ij$ of a particular triple are not shared by some other triple, then there is an infinite edge ( ray ) emanating from the center and in the direction of the perpendicular bisector of $V_i$ and $V_j$. In this more general case the "perpendicular bisector" will consist of all points which are of equal A-norm distance to $V_i$ and $V_j$, and this has a direction vector given by

$$D = \begin{pmatrix} A_{12}(x_i - x_j) + A_{22}(y_i - y_j) \\ A_{11}(x_j - x_i) + A_{12}(y_j - y_i) \end{pmatrix}$$

which has the property that

$$(V_j - V_i, D)_A = 0,$$

or in other words, D is "perpendicular" to $V_j - V_i$ with respect to the A-innerproduct.

**Definition 4.3.** *An A-norm tessellation consists of a list of triples* $D_A = D_A(\mathbf{V})$ *created in the following manner:*

i) *The triple* $ijk \in D_A$, *provided the set of vertices equidistant ( using the A-norm ) to* $C(V_i, V_j, V_k)$ *consists of exactly the three vertices* $V_i, V_j$ *and* $V_k$, *and the interior of* $E_A(V_i, V_j, V_k)$ *contains no other vertices.*

ii) *In the event that there are more than three vertices on the boundary of* $E_A(V_i, V_j, V_k)$ *(say,* $V_{i_1}, V_{i_2}, \ldots, V_{i_m}$ *) and no other vertices in the interior of* $E_A(V_i, V_j, V_k)$, *we require that one of* $i, j$ *or* $k$ *be the minimum index of* $i_1, i_2, \ldots, i_m$ *and that the remaining two vertices be contiguous neighbors on the boundary of* $E_{ijk}$. *This will account for* $m - 1$ *entries in* $D_A$.

The second condition of the above definition of an A-norm tessellation deals with the analog of what is often called the neutral case.

Some examples of $A$-norm Dirichlet tessellations are given in Figure 17. In the lower right, we have included the unit disks associated with each tessellation. The fact that the dual of this type of tessellation is actually a triangulation is established in [19]. The triangulations which are dual to the tessellations of Figure 17 are shown in Figure 18.

Thus far, what we have said holds for a general quadratic norm. If the affine invariant norm of (1.3) is used, then an affine invariant tessellation and a dual triangulation will result. Examples of this type of tessellation are shown in Figure 19. The data is the same as that of Figure 3. The triangulations which are dual to the tessellations of Figure 19 are shown in Figure 20.

## Acknowledgments

A portion of this work was done while the authors were visiting Lawrence Livermore National Laboratory. We wish to thank Fred Fritsch for being the host for these visits and for many interesting and useful discussions. The first author received support from an Associated Western Universities Grant (AWU/DOE ) during his visit to LLNL. We wish to extend our appreciation to Dick Franke for his assistance and in particular for providing the data for Tables 3,4 and 5. We wish to thank the CAGD group at ASU for their support.

We appreciate the support of the North Atlantic Treaty Organization under grant NATO RG. 0097/88 and the U. S. Department of Energy under research contract DOE DE-FG02-87ER25041 to Arizona State University.

We wish to thank the organizers of this conference, Tom Lyche and Larry Schumaker, for the opportunity to present our work and for their very kind and generous hospitality during our days in Oslo.

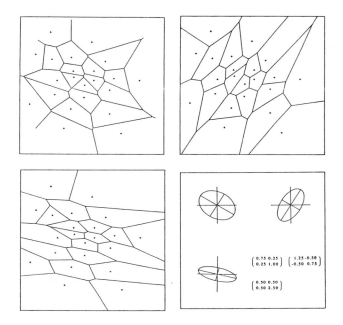

**Figure 17.** Some *A*-norm tessellations.

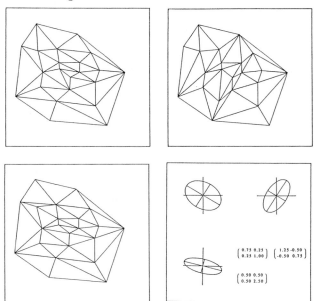

**Figure 18.** Some triangulations from *A*-norm tessellations.

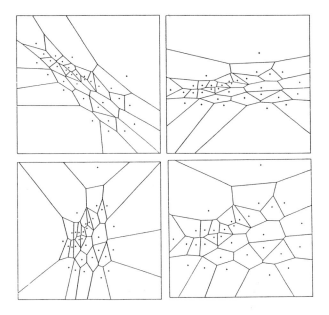

**Figure 19.** Tessellations based upon an affine invariant norm.

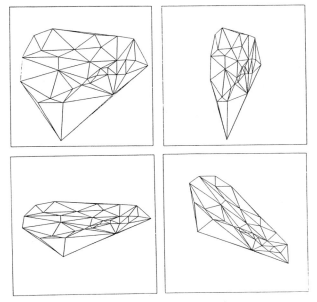

**Figure 20.** Affine invariant triangulations.

# References

1. Barnhill, R. E. and F. F. Little, Three- and four-dimensional surfaces, Rocky Mountain J. Math. **14** (1984), 77–102.

2. de Boor, C., *A Practical Guide to Splines* , Springer-Verlag, New York, 1978.

3. Delaunay, B., Sur la sphère vide, Bull. Acad. Sci. U.S.S.R.(VII), Classe Sci. Mat. Nat. (1934),793–800.

4. Duchon, J., Splines minimizing rotation invariant semi-norms in Sobolev spaces, in *Multivariate Approximation Theory*, W. Schempp and K. Zeller (eds.), Birkhäuser, Basel, 1979, 85–100.

5. Epstein, M. P., On the influence of parameterization in parametric interpolation, SIAM J. Numer. Anal. **13** (1976), 261–268.

6. Farin, G. F., *Curves and Surfaces in Computer Aided Geometric Design*, Academic Press, New York, 1988.

7. Foley, T. A., Interpolation with interval and point tension controls using cubic weighted $\nu$ -splines, ACM Transactions on Mathematical Software, **13** (1987), 68–96.

8. Foley, T. A. and G. M. Nielson, A knot selection method for parametric splines, in *Mathematical Methods in Computer Aided Geometric Design*, T. Lyche and L. Schumaker (eds.), Academic Press, N. Y., 1989, 261–271.

9. Fritsch, F., The Wilson-Fowler spline is a $\nu$ -spline, Comput. Aided Geom. Design **3** (1986), 155–162

10. Franke, R., Scattered data interpolation: Tests of some methods, Math. Comp. **38** (1982), 181–200.

11. Franke, R., Recent advances in the approximation of surfaces from scattered data, in *Topics in Multivariate Approximation*, L. L. Schumaker, C. Chui and F. Utreras (eds.), Academic Press, New York, 1987, 175–184.

12. Gregory, J. A., Error bounds for linear interpolation on triangles, in *The Mathematics of Finite Elements and Applications II*, J. Whiteman (ed.), Academic Press, London, 1975, 163–170.

13. Harder, R. L. and R. N. Desmarais, Interpolation using surface splines, Journal of Aircraft **9** (1972), 189–197.

14. Hardy, R. L., Multiquadric equations of topography and other irregular surfaces, J. Geophysical Res. **76** (1971), 1905–1915.

15. Lawson, C. L., Software for $C^1$ surface interpolation, in *Mathematical Software III*, J. R. Rice (ed.), Academic Press, New York, 1977, 161–194.

16. Marin, S. P., An approach to data parameterization in parametric cubic spline interpolation problems, J. Approx. Theory **41** (1984), 64–86.

17. Nielson, G. M., Coordinate free scattered data interpolation, in *Topics in Multivariate Approximation*, L. L. Schumaker, C. Chui and F. Utreras (eds.), Academic Press, New York, 1987, 175–184.

18. Nielson, G. M., An example with a local minimum for the MinMax ordering of triangulations, Technical Report TR87-014, Arizona State University, 1987.

19. Nielson, G. M., Affine invariant triangulations and tessellations, Technical Report TR88-023, Arizona State University, 1988.
20. Preparata, F. P. and M. I. Shamos, *Computational Geometry: An Introduction*, Springer-Verlag, New York, 1985.
21. Rhynsburger, D., Analytic delineation of Thiessen polygons, Geograph. Anal. **5** (1973), 133–144.
22. Schumaker, L. L., Fitting surfaces to scattered data, in *Approximation Theory II*, G. G. Lorentz, C. K. Chui and L. L. Schumaker (eds.), Wiley, New York, 1976, 203–268.
23. Schumaker, L.L., Triangulation methods, in *Topics in Multivariate Approximation*, L. L. Schumaker, C. Chui and F. Utreras (eds.), Academic Press, New York, 1987, 219–232.
24. Sibson, R., Locally equiangular triangulations, Computer J. **21** (1978), 243–245.
25. Thiessen, A. H., Precipitation averages for large areas, Monthly Weather Review **39** (1911), 1032–1034.

Thomas A. Foley and Gregory M. Nielson
Computer Science Department
Arizona State University
Tempe, Arizona 85287-5406
USA

Supported by NATO RG. 0097/88, AWU/DOE and DOE DE-FG02-87ER25041

EMAIL: foley@ asuvax.csnet
EMAIL: nielson@ asuvax.csnet

# An Algorithm for Smooth Interpolation
# to Scattered Data in $\mathbb{R}^2$

P. R. Pfluger and R. H. J. Gmelig Meyling

**Abstract.** The algorithm presented here determines a smooth bivariate piecewise polynomial interpolant for given function values at scattered points in $\mathbb{R}^2$. After choosing an appropriate triangulation $\Delta$, the interpolant will be determined in the spline space $S_{2m+1}^m(\Delta)$ so that a high degree of polynomial precision is achieved. For the case $m = 2$ (quintic splines of class $C^2$), several numerical tests are performed.

## §1. Notation

We describe an algorithm to find a smooth piecewise polynomial interpolant to scattered data in the plane. In order to state the problem we use the following standard notation. Let $\Delta = \{\Delta_i\}_{i=1}^T$ be a triangulation of a simply connected, closed subset $\Omega$ of $\mathbb{R}^2$ with a polygonal boundary $\delta\Omega$. We require that the triangulation $\Delta$ consist of T open, non-empty triangles $\Delta_i$, satisfying the following conditions:

1. $\Delta_i \cap \Delta_j = \emptyset$    for $i \neq j$
2. $\bigcup_i \overline{\Delta_i} = \Omega$
3. No vertex of any triangle $\Delta_i$ lies in the interior of an edge of any triangle $\Delta_j$.

    The V vertices of $\Delta$ will be denoted by $\underline{x}^1, \underline{x}^2, \ldots, \underline{x}^V$. For any triangulation T, the number of interior edges $E_o$, respectively boundary edges $E_b$ ($E = E_o + E_b$), and the number of interior vertices $V_o$ resp. boundary vertices $V_b$ ($V = V_o + V_b$) are related through the following formulas

Mathematical Methods in Computer Aided Geometric Design      469
Tom Lyche and Larry L. Schumaker (eds.), pp. 469–480.
Copyright © 1989 by Academic Press, Boston.
ISBN 0-12-460515-X.

$$T = 2V_o + V_b - 2$$
$$E_o = 3V_o + V_b - 3 \tag{1.1}$$
$$E_b = V_b.$$

The relations (1.1) follow from the formula of Euler ($E - V = T - 1$) and trivial identities.

In this paper we will use the following function spaces:

$$\Pi_k = \{\pi : \ \pi(\underline{x}) = \sum_{i=0}^{k} \sum_{j=0}^{k-i} x_1^i x_2^j, \quad \underline{x}^T = (x_1, x_2)\} \tag{1.2}$$

$$S_k^m(\Delta) = \{s \ : \ s \in C^m(\Omega), \ s|_{\Delta_i} = \pi_i, \ \pi_i \in \Pi_k; \ i = 1, \ldots, T\} \tag{1.3}$$

$$P_k^m(\Delta) = \{p \ : \ p \in S_k^0(\Delta), p \in C^m[\underline{x}^j]; \ j = 1, \ldots, V_o\}. \tag{1.4}$$

## §2. Interpolation Problem

Now we can formulate the *Lagrange interpolation problem* which we will try to solve:

> For a given nonnegative integer m, find a spline s of class $C^m$ which inter-
> polates function values $f_i = f(\underline{x}^i)$ at distinct points $\underline{x}^i, i = 1, \ldots, V$, scattered
> in a simply connected, closed subset $\Omega$ of $\mathbb{R}^2$.

The triangulation $\Delta$ is specifically chosen such that the vertices of $\Delta$ are identical with the points $\underline{x}^i$. The spline $s$ will have to belong to the space $S_k^m(\Delta)$ for a suitably chosen $k$. Algorithms to solve the stated interpolation problem are of increasing importance for the design of 3D-surfaces. Various approaches have been proposed in the literature. Some are based on local methods interpolating in $S_5^1(\Delta)$ (see Farin and Barnhill [3]) or in $S_9^2(\Delta)$ (see Whelan [13] and Rescorla [11]). It has been indicated by Ženišek that for a given $m$, there is no straightforward local calculation of a $C^m$-smooth spline $s \in S_k^m(\Delta)$ for $k < 4m+1$ (see [14]). If we want to use polynomials $\pi_i$ of a lower degree we will have to apply a global method, which in general involves the solution of a large linear system. Several such approaches have been described in the literature (cf. [6]). All of these methods determine an interpolating spline which minimizes a certain functional, or which passes through additional interpolation points. Grandine [9] chooses a particular interpolating spline $s \in S_3^1(\Delta)$, which is in some sense close to the interpolating spline $p \in S_1^0(\Delta)$. The interpolating spline p can be determined locally. The modification of $p$, that is the actual calculation of $s \in S_3^1(\Delta)$, leads to a minimum norm problem where the constraints are the smoothness conditions on $s$. The algorithm has a polynomial precision of degree 1 and is in some way shape-preserving.

However, in many cases it is desirable to interpolate by functions of class $C^2$. Curvature-continuity is often required. The purpose of our investigation is to solve the interpolation problem using splines of class $C^m$ for any nonnegative integer $m$, while keeping the degree $k$ of the polynomials $\pi_i$ as small as possible. In analogy with Grandine's approach, we start with a non-smooth interpolant $p \in P_k^m(\Delta)$ which we can determine locally. Then we will change $p$ slightly in order to obtain the desired smoothness and at the same time preserve as high a degree of polynomial precision as possible. For practical purposes, the case $m = 2$ will be the most interesting, and we restrict our numerical experiments to this situation.

## §3. Choice of the Degree k

In our algorithm we have chosen the degree k of the polynomials $\pi_i$ to be equal to $2m + 1$. This choice was suggested by considerations on the dimension of the space $S_k^m(\Delta)$. Namely, a solution of the interpolation problem can only exist if the dimension of the space $S_k^m(\Delta)$ is greater or equal to the number of interpolating conditions, in other words greater or equal to the number of vertices $V$. It was shown by Schumaker [13] that $lb \leq \dim S_k^m(\Delta) \leq ub$, where

$$lb = (\alpha - 3\beta) + \beta V_b + (3\beta - \gamma)V_o + \sum_{i=1}^{V_o} \sigma_i, \tag{3.1}$$

$$ub = (\alpha - 3\beta) + \beta V_b + (3\beta - \gamma)V_o + \sum_{i=1}^{V_o} \tilde{\sigma}_i. \tag{3.2}$$

For our purpose it seemed most appropriate to express the upper- and lower-bound in terms of the number of vertices using formulae (1.1). The parameters $\alpha, \beta, \gamma$ depend in the following way on $m$ and $k$:

$$\alpha = \binom{k+1}{2}, \qquad \beta = \binom{k-m+1}{2}, \qquad \gamma = \alpha - \binom{m+2}{2}. \tag{3.3}$$

However, the values $\sigma_i$ and $\tilde{\sigma}_i$ depend in a more complicated way on the triangulation $\Delta$. To explain this, we number all interior vertices $\underline{x}^1, \ldots, \underline{x}^{V_o}$ in such a way that every vertex $\underline{x}^i$ is connected by an edge to at least one vertex $\underline{x}^j (j < i)$. Hence, the boundary vertices get the numbers $V_o + 1, \ldots, V_o + V_b = V$. For every interior vertex $\underline{x}^i$ we define the nonnegative integers $\sigma_i$ and $\tilde{\sigma}_i$:

$$\sigma_i = \sum_{j=1}^{k-m} (m + j + 1 - je_i)_+, \tag{3.4}$$

$$\tilde{\sigma}_i = \sum_{j=1}^{k-m} (m + j + 1 - j\tilde{e}_i)_+, \tag{3.5}$$

where $e_i$ equals the number of edges of different slope connected to vertex $\underline{x}^i$, and $\tilde{e}_i$ equals the number of edges of different slope connecting $\underline{x}^i$ to vertices $\underline{x}^j$ with $j > i$. In the definition (3.4), respectively (3.5), the following standard notation is used:

$$(a)_+ = \begin{cases} a, & \text{for } a \geq 0 \\ 0, & \text{for } a < 0. \end{cases}$$

While the values of $e_i$ depend on the triangulation $\Delta$ only, the values $\tilde{e}_i$ depend also on the numbering of the vertices. Although $e_i$ is always greater or equal to 2, $\tilde{e}_i$ may become 0. The following inequalities hold trivially for $i = 1, \ldots, V_o$:

$$e_i \geq \tilde{e}_i \qquad\qquad \sigma \leq \tilde{\sigma}_i. \tag{3.6}$$

Let us now choose $k = 2m$. Using (3.2) we obtain the following expression for the upper bound ub:

$$\dim S_{2m}^m \leq ub = \binom{m+2}{2} V_b + \binom{m+2}{2} + \sum_{i=1}^{V_o} \tilde{\sigma}_i. \tag{3.7}$$

In this case the upper bound is independent of $V_o$. The dimension of $S_{2m}^m(\Delta)$ will most likely not increase sufficiently if we add interior vertices, that is if we add interpolation conditions. However, if we increase the degree of the polynomials $\pi_i$ by one (i.e., $k = 2m + 1$), the lower bound on the dimension of the spline space becomes larger than $V$. Using (3.1) we obtain in this case the following expression for the lower bound:

$$lb = (m+1)V + \binom{m+1}{2}(V_b + 1) + \Sigma_m \quad \text{with} \quad \Sigma_m = \sum_{i=1}^{V_o} \sigma_i. \tag{3.8}$$

Hence, we expect that the interpolation problem can always be solved in the space $S_{2m+1}^m(\Delta)$ even though the existence of a solution is not guaranteed. In the following table we list the lower bounds on the dimension of $S_{2m+1}^m(\Delta)$ for several values of $m$ as a function of $V$:

| $m$ | lb |
|---|---|
| 0 | $V$ |
| 1 | $2V + V_b + 1 + \Sigma_1$ |
| 2 | $3V + 3V_b + 3 + \Sigma_2$ |
| 3 | $4V + 6V_b + 6 + \Sigma_3.$ |

The additional term $\Sigma_m$ will increase with increasing $m$. If we use the notation $M_p =$ number of interior vertices where $p$ edges of different slope meet ($p \geq 2$), then we can express $\Sigma_m$ in the following formula:

$$\Sigma_m = \sum_{p=2}^{m+1} \{(m+1)r(m,p) - (p-1)\binom{r(m,p)+1}{2}\} M_p, \tag{3.9}$$

where $r(m,p)$ is the largest integer (strictly) less than $\frac{m+1}{p-1}$.

## §4. A Representation for Elements of the Space $S_{2m+1}^m(\Delta)$

All computations in $S_{2m+1}^m(\Delta)$ are inherently difficult since in general no local basis is known for these spaces, except for the trivial case $m = 0$. Therefore, a suitable representation for the polynomial pieces $\pi_i$ of a spline is essential. We have chosen to represent every polynomial $\pi_i$ in Bernstein-Bézier form. We will first review some standard notation (see [4] or [5]).

Let $\Delta_i$ be an arbitrary triangle in $\Delta$ having vertices $\underline{x}^1, \underline{x}^2, \underline{x}^3$. Any point $\underline{x}$ in $\Delta$ can be expressed in terms of the (nonnegative) *barycentric coordinates*

$$\underline{\lambda} = (\lambda_1(\underline{x}), \lambda_2(\underline{x}), \lambda_3(\underline{x})),$$

which form the unique solution of the linear system

$$\sum_{j=1}^{3} \lambda_j(\underline{x})\underline{x}^j = \underline{x} \qquad \sum_{j=1}^{3} \lambda_j(\underline{x}) = 1. \tag{4.1}$$

The *Bernstein polynomials* of degree $k$ over triangle $\Delta_i$ are defined by

$$B_{\underline{\alpha}}^k(\underline{x}) = \frac{k!}{\underline{\alpha}!}\underline{\lambda}^{\underline{\alpha}}, \qquad |\underline{\alpha}| = k. \tag{4.2}$$

Here $\underline{\alpha} = (\alpha_1, \alpha_2, \alpha_3) \in Z_+^3$ is a multi-index, with

$$|\underline{\alpha}| = \sum_{j=1}^{3} \alpha_j, \qquad \underline{\alpha}! = \prod_{j=1}^{3} \alpha_j!, \qquad \underline{\lambda}^{\underline{\alpha}} = \prod_{j=1}^{3} \lambda_j^{\alpha_j}. \tag{4.3}$$

The $\binom{k+2}{2}$ functions $B_{\underline{\alpha}}^k(\underline{x})$ with $|\underline{\alpha}| = k$ are linearly independent and form a basis for the space $\Pi_k$. Thus, any bivariate polynomial $\pi_i$ of degree at most $k$ can be expressed as a linear combination of the Bernstein polynomials

$$\pi_i(\underline{x}) = \sum_{|\underline{\alpha}|=k} c_{\underline{\alpha}} B_{\underline{\alpha}}^k(\underline{x}). \tag{4.4}$$

This is called the *Bernstein-Bézier form* or simply *B-form* of a bivariate polynomial. The coefficients $c_{\underline{\alpha}}$ are the *Bézier ordinates* of $\pi_i$ which can be associated with domain points

$$\underline{v}_{\underline{\alpha}} = \frac{1}{k}\sum_{j=1}^{3} \alpha_j\underline{x}^j, \tag{4.5}$$

defining a mesh in $\Delta_i$. The points $(\underline{v}_{\underline{\alpha}}, c_{\underline{\alpha}}) \in \mathbb{R}^3$, with $|\underline{\alpha}| = k$, are the *control points* of the surface patch $\{(\underline{x}, \pi_i(\underline{x})); \underline{x} \in \Delta_i\}$.

We now investigate the relationship between Bézier ordinates and the directional derivatives at the vertices in the case $k = 2m + 1$. Let $\underline{u}_2 =$

$\underline{x}^2 - \underline{x}^1, \underline{u}_3 = \underline{x}^3 - \underline{x}^1$ be vectors in the direction of those edges of $\Delta_i$ which are attached to $\underline{x}^1$. We denote the mixed directional derivatives of $\pi_i$ at $\underline{x}^1$ by

$$D_{\underline{u}_2}^r D_{\underline{u}_3}^s \pi_i(\underline{x}^1), \qquad 0 \le r + s \le m. \tag{4.6}$$

Here the derivative is taken $r$ times with respect to $\underline{u}_2$ and $s$ times with respect to $\underline{u}_3$. Exactly $\binom{m+2}{2}$ specific Bézier ordinates are determined by the $\binom{m+2}{2}$ directional derivatives (4.6) at vertex $\underline{x}^1$. This relationship is explicitly given in the following expression:

$$D_{\underline{u}_2}^r D_{\underline{u}_3}^s \pi_i(\underline{x}^1) = \frac{k!r!s!}{(k-r-s)!} \sum_{\underline{\beta}} \sum_{\underline{\gamma}} (-1)^{\beta_1+\gamma_1} \frac{1}{\underline{\beta}!\underline{\gamma}!} c_{\underline{\beta}+\underline{\gamma}+(k-r-s)\underline{e}^1}. \tag{4.7}$$

In formula (4.7) the summation is taken over

$$|\underline{\beta}| = r, \quad \underline{\beta} = (\beta_1, \beta_2, 0); \quad |\underline{\gamma}| = s, \quad \underline{\gamma} = (\gamma_1, 0, \gamma_3)$$

for $0 \le r + s \le m, k = 2m + 1$. From the $\binom{m+2}{2}$ directional derivatives (see (4.6)) we can recursively compute the $\binom{m+2}{2}$ Bézier ordinates $c_{\underline{\alpha}}, |\underline{\alpha}| = k, \alpha_1 = m+1, \dots, k$ using (4.7). These are precisely the Bézier ordinates belonging to the domain points $\underline{v}_{\underline{\alpha}}$ in the so-called $m$-th disk around vertex $\underline{x}^1$ (see [2]). The directional derivatives (4.6) are uniquely determined by the function value and the $1^{st}$ through $m^{th}$ order partial derivatives of $\pi_i$ at $\underline{x}_1$; i.e., the vertex data at $\underline{x}^1$:

$$\frac{\partial^{r+s} \pi_i(\underline{x}^1)}{\partial_{\underline{x}_1}^r \partial_{\underline{x}_2}^s}, \qquad 0 \le r + s \le m. \tag{4.8}$$

Thus the vertex data at $\underline{x}^1, \underline{x}^2, \underline{x}^3$ uniquely determines $3\binom{m+2}{2}$ Bézier ordinates of triangle $\Delta_i$, namely

$$c_{\underline{\alpha}} \quad \text{with} \quad |\underline{\alpha}| = 2m + 1, \quad \alpha_1, \alpha_2, \alpha_3 \ge m + 1. \tag{4.9}$$

Note that in our case $(k = 2m + 1)$ the derivatives up to order $m$ of the polynomial $\pi_i$ can be specified independently at the different vertices $\underline{x}^1, \underline{x}^2, \underline{x}^3$. There remain $\binom{m+1}{2}$ Bézier ordinates which are independent of the vertex data, namely the ordinates

$$c_{\underline{\alpha}} \quad \text{with} \quad |\underline{\alpha}| = 2m + 1, \quad \alpha_1, \alpha_2, \alpha_3 \le m + 1 \tag{4.10}$$

belonging to domain points $\underline{v}_{\underline{\alpha}}$ in the interior of triangle $\Delta_i$. Over the entire triangulation $\Delta$ we obtain in this way

$$\binom{m+2}{2} V + \binom{m+1}{2} T \tag{4.11}$$

parameters. Compare the expression (4.11) to the formula for the dimension of $P_{2m+1}^m(\Delta)$ given by Alfeld [1]:

$$\dim P_{2m+1}^m(\Delta) = \binom{m+2}{2} V + \binom{m+1}{2} T. \tag{4.12}$$

Even if all partial derivatives up to the order $m$ agree for all polynomials $\pi_i$ in the common vertices, the resulting function need not be of class $C^m$, but it will be a function $p$ belonging to the space $P_{2m+1}^m(\Delta)$. However, we can enforce $C^m$ continuity by linear constraints on the Bézier ordinates. To explain this, we consider two vectors $\underline{t}$ and $\underline{n}$, which are tangential, respectively transversal, to a specific interior edge $e$. If we choose all polynomials $\pi_i$ such as to interpolate the vertex data (function values and partial derivatives up to order $m$ at the vertices) then the continuity of the global function $p$ and of all its derivatives in the direction of $\underline{t}$ is guaranteed along edge $e$. This function will be of class $C^m$ if all cross-boundary derivatives (up to order $m$) are continuous along all interior edges. Considering the specific interior edge $e$, we have to ensure that the restriction of the cross-boundary derivatives

$$D_{\underline{n}}^j \pi_i, \quad j = 1, \ldots, m$$

are uniquely determined either by the data at the vertices, or by additional constraints across $e$. Since the derivatives

$$D_{\underline{t}}^l D_{\underline{n}}^j \pi_i, \quad l = 0, 1, \ldots, m - j$$

at the vertices incident to edge e are prescribed by the vertex data, the $(k - j)^{th}$ degree univariate polynomial $D_{\underline{n}}^j \pi_i$ restricted to $e$ is uniquely defined by $(2m + 1 - j + 1) - 2(m - j + 1) = j$ additional constraints across the edge $e$. Hence, for the continuity of $D_{\underline{n}}^j p$ along $e$ $(j = 1, \ldots, m)$, it is sufficient to impose

$$\sum_{j=1}^m j = \binom{m+1}{2}$$

conditions on $p$ and for the continuity over the whole triangulation $\Delta$,

$$\binom{m+1}{2} E_o \tag{4.13}$$

conditions will be imposed. This leads to a linear system in the Bézier ordinates based on a theorem of Farin [5]. For details we refer to [7].

A function $p \in P_{2m+1}^m(\Delta)$ is $C^m$-smooth throughout the domain $\Omega$ if all $\binom{m+1}{2}$ smoothness-conditions across each of the $E_o$ interior edges $e$ of $\Delta$ are satisfied. The difference between the number of parameters (4.12) and the number of linear constraints (4.13) can be compared to the lower bound on $\dim S_{2m+1}^m(\Delta)$ given in (3.8):

$$\binom{m+2}{2}V + \binom{m+1}{2}T - \binom{m+1}{2}E_o = lb - \Sigma_m. \qquad (4.14)$$

One can verify this by using the identity $T = V_b + 2(V_o - 1)$. In other words, the linear system composed of all cross-edge smoothness constraints contains at least $\Sigma_m$ *redundant* equations. For the case $m \leq 2$ these redundancies, caused by special interior vertices, can easily be removed from the linear system.

## §5. Outline of the Algorithm

In this section, we discuss the construction of an interpolating piecewise polynomial function of degree $2m + 1$ to scattered positional data which is of class $C^m$ . We should mention that we use a Dirichlet triangulation $\Delta$ with vertices at the given data points $\underline{x}^i, i = 1, \ldots, V$. Since for $m \geq 1$ the dimension of the space $S_{2m+1}^m(\Delta)$ exceeds the number of interpolation conditions, there is in general more than one spline $s \in S_{2m+1}^m(\Delta)$, with $s(\underline{x}^i) = f_i, i = 1, \ldots, V$. We will determine a well-defined particular spline interpolant.

The algorithm consists of two stages:

1. The construction of an *initial* interpolant $p \in P_{2m+1}^m(\Delta)$.
2. The construction of a *modified* interpolant $s \in S_{2m+1}^m(\Delta)$, where $s$ can be viewed as a $C^m$-smooth perturbation of $p$.

Our interpolation scheme will be *exact* for data from polynomials of degree at most $m$ over $\Omega$. For $m = 1$ a similar interpolation method was developed by Grandine [9].

**Initial interpolant $p$:**

Given vertex data (4.8) and Bézier ordinates (4.10) uniquely define a spline $p \in P_{2m+1}^m(\Delta)$. The derivatives which are not available have to be generated from the positional data. Reasonably accurate estimates for the derivatives of $p$ at the vertices can be determined using the following technique suggested by Lawson [10]: At every vertex $\underline{x}^i = (x_1^i, x_2^i)$ one computes a bivariate $m$-th degree polynomial $q_i$ which interpolates $f_i$ at the data point $\underline{x}^i$ and approximates the values $f_j$ at a number of adjacent vertices $\underline{x}^j$ in the least squares sense. We use as weights the inverse distance of data point $\underline{x}^j$ to data point $\underline{x}^i$. In other words, the polynomial $q_i$ given by

$$q_i(x_1, x_2) = f_i + \sum_{r,s} \frac{d_{r,s}^i}{r!s!}(x_1 - x_1^i)^r(x_2 - x_2^i)^s, \qquad (5.1)$$

(where we sum over all integers $r,s$ satisfying $1 \leq r + s \leq m$) minimizes the following function:

$$\sum_{\underline{x}^j \in N_i} w_j(q_i(x_1^j, x_2^j) - f_j)^2 \quad \text{with} \quad w_j = 1/\text{dist } (\underline{x}^i, \underline{x}^j)^2, \tag{5.2}$$

where $N_i$ is a set of cardinality larger than $\binom{m+2}{2} - 1$. Now the coefficients $d_{r,s}^i$ provide estimates for the partial derivatives of $p$ at $\underline{x}^i$, namely the vertex data at $\underline{x}^i$. Clearly, the estimates will be *precise* if the positional data are all drawn from a bivariate polynomial of degree $\leq m$. Given the function values and the estimated derivatives of $p$ at the vertices, it is possible to choose the remaining Bézier ordinates defining $p$ in such a way that we obtain $m$-th degree polynomial precision. For details we refer to [7].

**Modified Interpolant s:**

As a next step of the interpolation process, we compute a perturbation $s$ of the initial interpolant $p$, such that $s$ satisfies the $C^m$-smoothness condition and remains of $m$-th degree polynomial precision.

Every function $p \in P_{2m+1}^m(\Delta)$ is defined by a vector consisting of all Bézier ordinates of all polynomials $\pi_i$. Since we are interested in an interpolant, precisely $V$ of these Bézier ordinates are given. Therefore, we consider the vector $\underline{x}_p$ of the remaining Bézier ordinates. The vector $\underline{x}_p$ consists of

$$\nu = \left(\binom{m+2}{2} - 1\right)V + \binom{m+1}{2}T \tag{5.3}$$

components (see (4.11)).

As we have seen in (4.12), the Bézier ordinates have to satisfy

$$\mu = \binom{m+1}{2}E_o \tag{5.4}$$

smoothness conditions such that the corresponding spline function belongs to $S_{2m+1}^m(\Delta)$. Let us now denote the linear system of these smoothness conditions by

$$A\underline{x} = \underline{b} \quad \text{with} \quad A \in \mathbb{R}^{\mu \times \nu}, \quad \underline{x} \in \mathbb{R}^\nu, \underline{b} \in \mathbb{R}^\mu. \tag{5.5}$$

Although the coefficient matrix $A$ is very sparse, its sparsity pattern is in general quite irregular and depends on the geometry of $\Delta$.

In Section 3 it was shown that the space $S_{2m+1}^m(\Delta)$ provides a sufficiently large number of degrees of freedom for the interpolation of scattered positional data. However, it is unknown whether the linear system (5.5) is always solvable. Thus far, no triangulation $\Delta$ has been found for which smoothness constraints and interpolation conditions are inconsistent (for $m = 1$ see [9]; for $m = 2$ see [7]).

Unless $p$ happens to be in $S_{2m+1}^m(\Delta)$, we have to find a perturbation $\underline{x}_s$ of $\underline{x}_p$ which satisfies the equation (5.5). It is now our objective to solve the following problem

$$\underline{x}_s = \underline{x}_p + \underline{e} \quad \text{with} \quad A\underline{x}_s = \underline{b}. \tag{5.6}$$

The components of $\underline{x}_s$ uniquely define the modified interpolant $s \in S_{2m+1}^m(\Delta)$.

We determine $\underline{x}_s$ by calculating a *minimum norm correction* $\underline{e}$; *i.e.*, we solve the constrained optimization problem

$$\text{minimize } \|\underline{e}\|_2, \qquad \text{subject to} \quad A\underline{e} = \underline{r}, \quad \underline{r} = \underline{b} - A\underline{x}_p. \tag{5.7}$$

Clearly, the proposed updating technique does not affect the $m$-th degree polynomial precision of the interpolation method. If $\underline{x}_p$ defines a polynomial of degree $\leq m$ throughout $\Omega$, then we have $\underline{e} = \underline{0}$ and thus $s(\underline{x}) = p(\underline{x})$, for all $\underline{x} \in \Omega$.

Since the minimum norm solution $\underline{e}$ can be expressed as $\underline{e} = A^T \underline{y}$, we solve problem (5.7) through the computation of the vector $\underline{y} \in \mathbb{R}^m$ given by the linear system

$$AA^T \underline{y} = \underline{r}. \tag{5.8}$$

For the solution of the sparse linear system, we used the iterative method of *conjugate gradients* [8].

## §6. Numerical Experiments

In this section we present some numerical experiments with the interpolation method described in Section 5. The interpolating spline $p \in P_5^2(\Delta)$ is defined by $5V + 3T$ parameters, namely function values and partial derivatives through order 2 at the vertices as well as the Bézier ordinates associated with 3 domain points in the interior of every triangle in $\Delta$. The function values are given. Estimates for the first and second order partial derivatives are generated by solving linear least squares problems of type (5.2). In each problem only positional data from eight adjacent vertices (including the immediate neighbors of $\underline{x}^i$) are taken into account. The three Bézier ordinates defining $p$ are finally determined by the requirement of quadratic precision of the interpolation scheme. At the next stage, the parameters of $p$ are distorted in such a way that we obtain a globally $C^2$-smooth quintic spline interpolant $s$. In other words, we impose all $3E_o$ smoothness constraints across the interior edges of $\Delta$.

We used five test functions on different triangulations. Tests were also performed on cardinal interpolation in order to show the almost local behavior of the interpolation method. For a report on the results of all the tests we refer to [7]. Here we will only mention the behavior of the convergence we could observe using uniform triangulations with increasingly finer mesh size. Since the interpolation method is of an almost local character and it reproduces all quadratic polynomials ($m = 2$), we expect a *rate of convergence* of the *third order*. In other words we expect the interpolation error

$$\epsilon = \frac{\|s - f\|_\infty}{\|f\|_\infty} \tag{6.1}$$

to behave like $O(h^3)$. Here $h$ stands for the mesh size of $\Delta$ which tends to zero. We consider a $N \times N$ *uni-diagonal* mesh $\Delta(N)$ (see [12]) with the following characteristic properties

$$
\begin{aligned}
V_o &= (N-2)^2 & E_o &= (N-1)(3N-5) \\
V_b &= 4(N-1) & \Sigma_2 &= V_o & (6.2) \\
T &= 2(N-1)^2 & V &= N^2.
\end{aligned}
$$

The dimension of the spline space $S_5^2(\Delta(N))$ equals the lower bound given by $lb = 4(N+1)^2 - 9$. We have run our programs for the values $N = 4, 6, 8, 10, \ldots, 20$. Generally, the experiments confirm the third order convergence although the behavior is less clear in the case of Franke's function. For details, we refer once again to [7].

## References

1. Alfeld, P., On the dimension of multivariate piecewise polynomial functions, in *Numerical Analysis*, Longman Scientific & Technical, D. F. Griffiths and G. A. Watson (eds.), 1985, Pitman, London, 1–23.
2. Alfeld, P., B. Piper, and L. L. Schumaker, An explicit basis for $C^1$ quartic bivariate splines, SIAM J. Numer. Anal. **24** (1987), 891–911.
3. Barnhill, R. E. and G. Farin, $C^1$ quintic interpolation over triangles: two explicit representations, Int. J. Numer. Methods in Engineering **17** (1981),1763–1778.
4. Dahmen, W., Bernstein-Bézier representation of polynomial surfaces, Vorlesungsreihe SFB 72, no. 31, Univ. Bonn, 1986.
5. Farin, G., Triangular Bernstein-Bézier patches, Comput. Aided Geom. Design **3** (1986), 83–127.
6. Gmelig Meyling, R. H. J., Approximation by piecewise cubic $C^1$-splines on arbitrary triangulations, Numer. Math. **51** (1987), 65–85.
7. Gmelig Meyling, R. H. J. and P. R. Pfluger, Smooth interpolation to scattered data by bivariate piecewise polynomials of odd degree, to appear.
8. Golub, G. H. and C. F. Loan, *Matrix Computation*, North Academic, London, 1983.
9. Grandine, T. A., An iterative method for computing multivariate $C^1$ piecewise polynomial interpolants, Comput. Aided Geom. Design **4** (1987), 307–319.
10. Lawson, C. L., $C^1$ surface interpolation for scattered data on a sphere, Rocky Mountain J. Math. **14** (1977), 177–202.
11. Rescorla, K. L., Cardinal interpolation: a bivariate polynomial example, Comput. Aided Geom. Design **3** (1986), 313–321.
12. Schumaker, L. L., Bounds on the dimension of spaces of multivariate piecewise polynomials, Rocky Mountain J. Math. **14** (1984), 251–264.
13. Whelan, T., A representation of a $C^2$ interpolant over triangles, Comput. Aided Geom. Design **3** (1986), 53–66.

14. Ženíšek, A., Interpolation polynomials on the triangle, Numer. Math. **15** (1970), 283–296.

Pia P. Pfluger
Dept. of Mathematics
University of Amsterdam
Roetersstraat 15
1018 WB  Amsterdam
THE NETHERLANDS

R. H. J. Gmelig Meyling
Dept. of Mathematics
Twente Univeristy of Technology
P. O. Box 217
7500 AE Enschede
THE NETHERLANDS

# Some Remarks on
# Three B-Spline Constructions

## Hartmut Prautzsch

**Abstract.** This paper makes evident that de Boor's algorithm, the new construction of B-splines in [3], and Boehm's or Sablonnière's algorithm for computing the Bézier points of a B-spline curve are merely different representations of the same structure.

## §1. Introduction

In [3], basic B-spline properties are derived directly from corresponding properties of Bézier curves. De Casteljau's construction together with Stärk's interpretation [5] is all that is used in that development of B-splines.

The construction in [3] is similar to the inverse of the algorithm given by Boehm [1] and also Sablonnière [4]. As it turns out, both constructions are also linked to de Boor's algorithm. The intent of this paper is to uncover the exact relationship among all three constructions.

The paper is organized as follows. First, in order to introduce some notation, a few useful facts about Bézier curves are recalled. Secondly, de Boor's algorithm [2], and Boehm's idea [1] are presented. Finally, the construction in [3] is outlined and its relationship to both of the above algorithms is shown.

## §2. Bézier Polynomials

An $n$ sided Bézier polygon $\mathbf{b}$, see Figure 1, can be given by the ordered sequence of its $n+1$ vertices. These vertices are denoted by $\mathbf{b}_0, \mathbf{b}_1, \ldots, \mathbf{b}_n$; usually these are points in $\mathbb{R}^m, m \in \mathbb{N}$.

For convenience, $\mathbf{b}$ is also identified with the matrix $[\mathbf{b}_0 \mathbf{b}_1 \ldots \mathbf{b}_m]$. Then the algorithm of de Casteljau can be described by the operator $C_t$, defined for $t \in \mathbb{R}$ by

$$C_t \mathbf{b} := (1-t)[\mathbf{b}_0 \mathbf{b}_1 \ldots \mathbf{b}_{n-1}] + t[\mathbf{b}_1 \mathbf{b}_2 \ldots \mathbf{b}_n]. \tag{2.1}$$

Mathematical Methods in Computer Aided Geometric Design
Tom Lyche and Larry L. Schumaker (eds.), pp. 481–487.

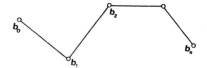

**Figure 1.** An $n$ - sided Bézier polygon.

If this operator is applied $n$ times to $\mathbf{b}$, it yields the single point $C_t^n \mathbf{b}$. One readily verifies the identity

$$C_t^n \mathbf{b} = \sum_{i=0}^{n} \mathbf{b}_i \binom{n}{i} t^i (1-t)^{n-i}, \tag{2.2}$$

which shows that $C_t^n \mathbf{b}$ is a polynomial in $t$. It is a so called Bézier polynomial of degree $n$. It is also useful to use the notation

$$\mathbf{b}(t) := C_t^n \mathbf{b}. \tag{2.3}$$

Since $\mathbf{b}(0) = \mathbf{b}_0$ and $\mathbf{b}(1) = \mathbf{b}_1$, the Bézier polygon $\mathbf{b}$ is naturally associated with the interval [0,1] or, after the substitution $t = \frac{u-a}{b-a}$ with the interval $[a, b]$, $a < b$. In order to stress the crucial information of this transformation, the abbreviation

$$\mathbf{b}(a, b) := \mathbf{b}\left(\frac{u - a}{b - a}\right) \tag{2.4}$$

is introduced.

## §3. de Boor's Algorithm

In the following paragraphs, let $u_k$, $k \in \mathbb{Z}$, be knots on the real line with $u_{k-1} \leq u_k < u_{k+n+1}$, and let $N_k^n(u)$ be the corresponding B-splines of degree $n$. We consider the linear combination

$$\mathbf{s}(u) := \sum_{i \in \mathbb{Z}} \mathbf{c}_i^{(0)} N_i^n(u) \tag{3.1}$$

of $n$-th degree B-splines.

The spline $s$ can be evaluated recursively by de Boor's algorithm [2]. Suppose $\mathbf{s}(u)$ is to be computed for some fixed number $u$. Assuming without loss of generality that $u \in [u_0, u_1]$, the triangular scheme in Figure 2, generated with the relation

$$\mathbf{c}_i^{(k)} = (1 - \alpha)\mathbf{c}_{i-1}^{(k-1)} + \alpha \mathbf{c}_i^{(k-1)}, \qquad \alpha = \frac{u - u_i}{u_{i+n-k+1} - u_i}, \tag{3.2}$$

yields

$$\mathbf{c}_o^{(n)} = \mathbf{s}(u). \tag{3.3}$$

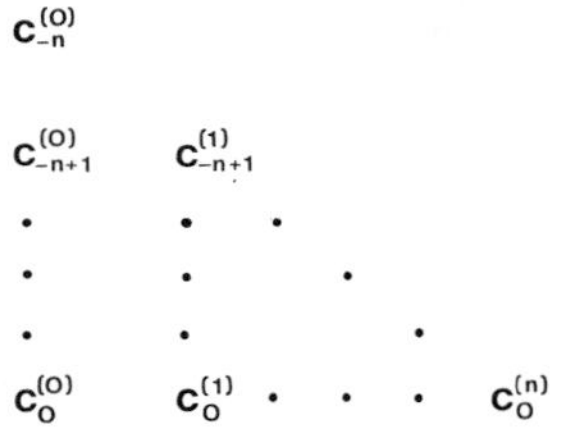

$$\mathbf{c}_{-n}^{(0)}$$

$$\mathbf{c}_{-n+1}^{(0)} \quad \mathbf{c}_{-n+1}^{(1)}$$

$$\cdot \qquad \cdot \quad \cdot$$
$$\cdot \qquad \cdot \qquad \cdot$$
$$\cdot \qquad \cdot \qquad \quad \cdot$$

$$\mathbf{c}_{0}^{(0)} \quad \mathbf{c}_{0}^{(1)} \quad \cdot \quad \cdot \quad \cdot \quad \mathbf{c}_{0}^{(n)}$$

**Figure 2.** de Boor's scheme.

## §4. Boehm's Construction

Because of (3.3), the points $\mathbf{c}_i^{(k)}$ in the scheme (3.2) are polynomials of degree $k$ in $u$. In particular, $\mathbf{c}_0^{(n)}(u)$ agrees with $\mathbf{s}(u)$ for all $u \in [u_0, u_1]$. Boehm [1] has made use of this and the additional fact that each polynomial has a unique Bézier representation over any fixed interval of reference. This means that there is a unique $k$-sided Bézier polygon $\mathbf{b}^{(i,k)}$ satisfying

$$\mathbf{c}_i^{(k)}(u) = \mathbf{b}^{(i,k)}(u_0, u_1). \tag{4.1}$$

Now it is easy to establish a recursive construction for the polygons $\mathbf{b}^{(i,k)}$ using (3.2). This construction can also be found with a different derivation in Sablonnière [4].

## §5. A New Development of B-splines

We now outline the method in [3] for constructing B-splines from Bézier curves. For sake of conciseness, we begin by defining an operator $*$, and defer its explanation until later.

Let $\mathbf{p} = [\mathbf{p}_0 \mathbf{p}_1 \ldots \mathbf{p}_m]$ be a Bézier polygon associated with the knot interval $[u_k, u_\ell]$. The operator $*$ to be defined depends on $u_k$ and $u_\ell$ and maps the $m$-sided polygon $\mathbf{p}$ onto an $(m-1)$–sided Bézier polygon. It is defined by the equations

$$(*\mathbf{p})(u_k, u_{\ell+1}) = [\mathbf{p}_1 \mathbf{p}_2 \ldots \mathbf{p}_m](u_k, u_\ell) \tag{5.1}$$

and

$$(\mathbf{p}*)(u_{k-1}, u_\ell) = [\mathbf{p}_0 \mathbf{p}_1 \ldots \mathbf{p}_{m-1}](u_k, u_\ell), \tag{5.2}$$

respectively. Thus, the operator $*$ provides the new Bézier representation of a Bézier polynomial after a reparametrization. This operation is also known as subdivision. The constructive counterpart of the operator $*$ is de Casteljau's construction, cf. Figure 3.

In order to facilitate multiple applications of $*$, the polygons $*\mathbf{p}$ and $\mathbf{p}*$ are associated with the respective intervals $[u_k, u_{\ell+1}]$ and $[u_{k-1}, u_\ell]$. The operator

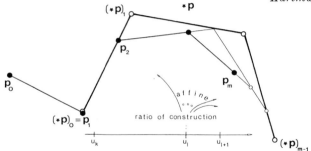

**Figure 3.** The construction $*$

$*$ is valuable for the description of the smoothness conditions of the spline $\mathbf{s}$ in (3.1). In order to elaborate, for every non-empty knot interval $[u_k, u_{k+1}]$, let $\mathbf{b}^{(k)}$ be the unique $n$-sided Bézier polygon that satisfies

$$\mathbf{b}^{(k)}(u_k, u_{k+1}) = \mathbf{s}(u) \tag{5.3}$$

for all $u \in [u_k, u_{k+1}]$. Then, the assumption, $u_{k+1} = u_{k+2} = \cdots = u_{k+p} < u_{k+p+1}$, $p \in \mathbb{N}$; *i.e.*, $\mathbf{s} \in C^{n-p}(u_{k+1})$, is equivalently expressed by the identity

$$*^p \mathbf{b}^{(k)} = \mathbf{b}^{(k+p)} *^p, \tag{5.4}$$

(see [5,3]). Note, that each of the first $p-1$ applications of $*$ mean only that an endpoint of a polygon is discarded.

The smoothness condition (5.4) together with the commuting property $*(p*) = (*p)*$ allows building the scheme of Figure 4, (see [3]).

The polygons $\mathbf{p}^{k,k+n+1}$ of the scheme are single points and coincide with the control points $\mathbf{c}_k^{(0)}$. Moreover,

$$\mathbf{p}^{k,k+n} = [\mathbf{c}_{k-1}^{(0)}, \mathbf{c}_k^{(0)}]. \tag{5.5}$$

The next theorem (cf. [3]) reflects the part of the scheme marked with heavy lines in Figure 4.

**Theorem 1.** (cf. [3]) *The spline control points can be constructed with the aid of the* $*$ *operation. For example,*

$$\mathbf{s}(u) = \sum_{i=0}^{n} (*^i \mathbf{b}^{(k)} *^{n-i}) N_{k-n+i}^n(u)$$

for all $u = [u_k, u_{k+1})$.

To conclude this section, we mention that the operator $*$ provides a tool to quickly derive and prove various B-spline properties such as the knot insertion algorithm, derivative formula, basis property, the recurrence relation and others (cf. [3]).

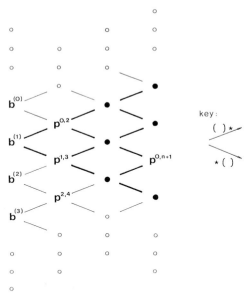

**Figure 4.** Calculating the B-spline control points.

## §6. Proving de Boor's Algorithm

de Boor's algorithm as given in Section 3 may be derived from de Castel-jau's algorithm through applications of the operator $*$. In order to do so, let $t := \frac{u - u_o}{u_1 - u_0}$. Then for fixed $t$, every intermediate polygon $C_t^k \mathbf{b}^{(0)}$; $k = 0, 1, \ldots, n$, of de Casteljau's construction can be seen as a representation of a Bézier poly-nomial with respect to the interval $[u_0, u_1]$. Thus, as Theorem 1 shows, the points

$$\mathbf{d}_i^k := *^{n-k+i}(C_t^k \mathbf{b}^{(0)}) *^{-i}, \quad i = -n + k, -n + k + 1, \ldots, 0, \qquad (6.1)$$

are the B-spline control points of these polynomials. In order to draw further conclusions, the following commuting property (cf. [3]) is crucial:

**Lemma 2.** *Let* $\mathbf{p}$ *be a Bézier polygon associated with* $[u_k, u_\ell]$ *and for any* $u \in \mathbb{R}$, *let* $\alpha, \beta, \gamma$ *be the numbers*

$$\alpha := \frac{u - u_k}{u_\ell - u_k}, \quad \beta := \frac{u - u_k}{u_{\ell+1} - u_k}, \quad \gamma := \frac{u - u_{k-1}}{u_\ell - u_{k-1}}.$$

*Then*

$$*(C_\alpha \mathbf{p}) = C_\beta(*\mathbf{p})$$

*and*

$$(C_\alpha \mathbf{p})* = C_\gamma(\mathbf{p}*).$$

Applying Lemma 2 to equation (6.1) results in

$$\mathbf{d}_i^k = C_s *^{n-k+i} (C_t^{k-1}\mathbf{b}^{(0)})*^{-i}, \tag{6.2}$$

where

$$s = \frac{u - u_i}{u_{n-k+i+1} - u_i}.$$

From (6.2), (5.5) and (6.1) it follows that

$$\mathbf{d}_i^k = C_s[\mathbf{d}_{i-1}^{k-1}, \mathbf{d}_i^{k-1}], \tag{6.3}$$

which is identical to de Boor's recursion (3.2). From Theorem 1 and (6.1), the identity $\mathbf{d}_i^0 = \mathbf{c}_i^{(0)}$ becomes evident. Equation (6.3) further implies that

$$\mathbf{d}_i^k = \mathbf{c}_i^{(k)}, \quad i = 0, -1, \ldots, -n + k. \tag{6.4}$$

## §7. Relation to the Construction of Boehm and Sablonniere

Exchanging all operators $C_t$ in (6.1) with the operators $*$ leads to the equation

$$\begin{aligned}
\mathbf{c}_i^{(k)} &= C_s^k *^{n-k+i} \mathbf{b}^{(0)} *^{-i} \\
&= C_s^k \mathbf{p}^{i,n-k+i+1}.
\end{aligned} \tag{7.1}$$

Obviously, (7.1) holds for all $u$ or $s \in \mathbb{R}$ respectively. Comparing (7.1) with (2.1) proves that $\mathbf{p}^{i,n-k+i+1} = *^{n-k+i}\mathbf{b}^{(0)}*^{-i}$ is the unique Bézier polygon of the polynomial $\mathbf{c}_i^{(k)}(u)$ with respect to the interval $[u_i, u_{n-k+i+1}]$.

This result is comparable to [1]. Bézier polygons have been established for the polynomials $\mathbf{c}_i^{(k)}(u)$ of de Boor's algorithm. The difference here is that the interval of reference is $[u_i, u_{n-k+i+1}]$ as opposed to $[u_0, u_1]$ in [1].

Thus, the final conclusion is that de Boor's algorithm, the $*$ construction of B-splines, and the algorithm of Boehm and Sablonnière are three different realizations of a single structural property, which, however, stem from two inverse developments.

### References

1. Boehm, W., Über die Konstruktion von B-Spline - Kurven, Computing **18** (1977), 161–166.
2. de Boor, C., On calculating with B-splines, J. Approx. Theory **6** (1972), 50–62.
3. Prautzsch, H., A round trip to B-splines via de Casteljau, Trans. Graph., to appear.
4. Sablonnière, P., Spline and Bézier polygons associated with a polynomial spline curve, Computer-Aided Design **10** (1978), 257–261.

5. Stärk, E., Mehrfach differenzierbare Bézier - Kurven und Bézier - Flächen, Dissertation, TU Braunschweig, 1976.

Hartmut Prautzsch
Department of Mathematical Sciences
Rensselaer Polytechnic Institute
Troy, NY 12180-3590
USA

EMAIL: user fswl@ rpitsmts.bitnet

# Modified B-Spline Approximation
# for Quasi-Interpolation or Filtering

## Christophe Rabut

**Abstract.** We use "modified B-splines" (linear combination of neighborhood B-splines) to adapt the usual B-spline approximation of discrete data, in order to quasi-interpolate or to filter the data. A very good tool to analyze the global properties is the transfer function of the associated filter, which is also used to determine the coefficients of the above linear combination.

## §1. Introduction

Given data $\{(x_i, y_i)\}_{i=1}^{N}$, let $B_i$ be the usual B-spline (of degree $2m-1$) associated with the knots $x_{i-m}, ..., x_{i+m}$. Let $\sigma(x) = \sum_{i=1}^{N} y_i B_i(x)$; see for example [1]. The function $\sigma$ is called the *usual B-spline approximation* of the data.

For many applications, the approximation $\sigma$ may seem to lack flexibility, and particularly in CAGD, we may prefer to get a spline which better fits the data. We will call such a spline $\sigma$ a *quasi-interpolating spline*. On the other hand, we may prefer to get a spline which filters out some of the noise in the data, in which case we call $\sigma$ a *filtering spline*.

First, we must distinguish the coefficients $Y_i^n$ of the B-spline approximation from the data $y_i$. Thus, we write $\sigma^n(x) = \sum_{i=1}^{N} Y_i^n B_i(x)$. Now we need some criterium so that we can easily determine $Y_i^n$ from the $y_i$'s so that the spline function $\sigma^n(x)$ has the desired properties such as quasi-interpolation, filtering, etc.

In order to get rid of boundary effects and to be able to analyse the properties of the approximation as a filter, we will use infinite equidistant data: $\forall i \in \mathbb{Z}, x_i = ih$ and $y = (y_i)_{i \in \mathbb{Z}}$. In this case, we can use $B_i(x) = B(x - x_i)$, where $B$ is the usual B-spline centered at 0. Of course if we have (as usual) only a finite number of (regularly spaced) data, it is always possible to extend

Mathematical Methods in Computer Aided Geometric Design
Tom Lyche and Larry L. Schumaker (eds.), pp. 489–498.
Copyright © 1989 by Academic Press, Boston.
ISBN 0-12-460515-X.

it in an appropriate way (the influence of such an extension is then limited to a small band near $x_1$ and $x_N$).

The coefficients $Y_i^n$ will always be a linear combination of $y_j$ for small $|j - i|$. We will set $Y_i^n = \sum_{j=-n}^{n} a_j y_{i-j}$, the real values $a_j$ being some coefficients (independent of the vector $y$) to be determined so that $\sigma$ has the desired properties. As we will always choose symmetrical coefficients ($\forall j \in [-n, n], a_{-j} = a_j$), we can also use the equivalent form $Y_i^n = \sum_{j=0}^{n} b_j (\delta^{2j} y)_i$, where $\delta^2$ is the symmetrical second difference ($(\delta^2 y)_i = y_{i+1} - 2y_i + y_{i-1}$). Let $\sigma^n$ be the B-spline approximation of the data $(x_i, Y_i^n)_{i \in \mathbb{Z}}$; *i.e.*, $\sigma^n(x) = \sum_{i \in \mathbb{Z}} Y_i^n B(x - x_i)$. Let $B^n(x) = \sum_{j=-n}^{n} a_j B(x - x_j)$. Then $B^n(x) = \sum_{j=0}^{n} b_j (\delta_h^{2j} B)(x)$, where $(\delta_h^2 B)(x) = B(x + h) - 2B(x) + B(x - h)$, and $\sigma^n(x) = \sum_{i \in \mathbb{Z}} y_i B^n(x - x_i)$.

The spline $\sigma^n$ can be regarded in two different but equivalent ways:

(a) *Modified B-spline approximation* : the data $y_i$ are modified to $Y_i^n$, (where $Y_i^n = \sum_{j=0}^{n} b_j (\delta^{2j} y)_i$ ), and the function $B$ is unchanged.

(b) *Modified B-spline approximation*: the function $B$ used for the B-spline approximation is modified to $B^n$, where $B^n = \sum_{j=0}^{n} b_j (\delta_h^{2j} B)$, and the coefficients of the approximation remain as the data $y_i$.

Both of these approaches are important. In particular, the shape of $B^n$ is most often worth studying; indeed, $B^n$ is actually the B-spline approximation of data $y_i = \varepsilon_i$, where $\varepsilon_0 = 1, \forall i \in \mathbb{N}^*, \varepsilon_i = 0$.

We now have to determine the coefficients $a_j$ (or $b_j$), in order to satisfy some properties for the approximation. To do so, two approaches are particularly efficient :

- looking at the values of $B^n$ at knots

- looking at the transfer function of the filter which can be associated to the modified B-spline approximation.

We present here only the second approach. In the next section we define the transfer function and present its main properties.

## §2. Transfer Function

The first idea is to study the result of the approximation scheme at the data. We will work only on $(\sigma(x_i))_{i \in \mathbb{Z}}$, and not on $\sigma(x)$ for $x \neq x_i$ . In other words we will study the transformation $T : y \in \mathbb{R}^{\mathbb{Z}} \to z \in \mathbb{R}^{\mathbb{Z}}$ defined by

$$z_j = \sigma^n(x_j) = \sum_{i \in \mathbb{Z}} y_i B^n(x_j - x_i) = \sum_{i \in \mathbb{Z}} y_{j-i} B^n(x_i),$$

for all $j \in \mathbb{Z}$. Since we know how $\sigma(x)$ behaves from the behavior of the values $\sigma(x_i)$ at the knots, studying this discrete transformation will give us good information on the whole approximation process.

Obviously, $T$ is a linear transformation, and for some appropriate norm, $T$ is continuous for the norm $\| \cdot \|_\tau$ defined by

$$\| y \|_\tau = \max \left( | y_0 |; \quad \frac{| y_i |}{| i |^\tau}, \quad i \in \mathbb{Z} \right)$$

for any

$$y \in Y^\tau = \{ y \in \mathbb{R}^{\mathbb{Z}} : | y_i | = \mathcal{O}(| i |^\tau), \quad i \to \pm\infty \}.$$

Moreover, $T$ is translation invariant; *i.e.*, if $y'$ is such that $y'_i = y_{i+k}$ for some $k \in \mathbb{Z}$ and all $i \in \mathbb{Z}$, then $z' = T(y')$ satisfies $z'_i = z_{i+k}$ for all $i \in \mathbb{Z}$.

For these reasons, $T$ is a so-called *filter*. In fact, it is a very simple filter as it is a convolution of $y$ with the $2n + 1$ nonzero components of the vector $(B(x_i))_{i \in \mathbb{Z}}$. It is easy to see that for any $\alpha \in \mathbb{Z}$, the vector $y = e_\alpha = (e^{2i\pi\alpha k})_{k \in \mathbb{Z}}$ is an eigenvector of the transformation $T$. (Here $i^2 = -1$).

**Definition 2.1.** *Let $H(\alpha)$ be the eigenvalue associated with the eigenvector $e_\alpha$ . The mapping $H : \alpha \to H(\alpha)$ is called the* transfer function *(or in some papers,* attenuation function*) of the filter $T$. $H$ is an even, real valued function whenever $a_{-j} = a_j$ for all $j \in [-n, n]$. Furthermore, $H$ is periodic (with period $1/h$).*

Before going further, it is of interest to focus our attention on the meaning of the transfer function of the filter $T$. Taking the real part (respectively, the imaginary part) of the equation $T(e_\alpha) = H(\alpha)e_\alpha$, we see that if the data $y$ is such that $y_i = \cos(2\pi i\alpha)$, respectively, $y_i = \sin(2\pi i\alpha)$, for all $i \in \mathbb{Z}$, then the output $z = T(y)$ is such that $z_i = H(\alpha)\cos(2\pi i\alpha)$, respectively, $z_i = H(\alpha)\sin(2\pi i\alpha)$, for all $i \in \mathbb{Z}$. Thus, $H(\alpha)$ is the *coefficient of amplification* or attenuation of a (co)sinusoïdal signal of frequency $\alpha$. As a particular case, $H_n(0)$ is the amplification coefficient of constants (we will always require $H_n(0) = 1$). As any periodical data may be written as a sum of cosinusoïdal (and sinusoïdal) data of different frequencies, the shape of H is indicative of the response of the filter to any periodic data. Furthermore, as any support-bounded data may be extended in a periodic way, and as any support-unbounded data may be considered as the limit of support-bounded data when the support tends to $\infty$, it is understandable that the shape of $H$ is indicative of the response of the filter to any data. As a particular case, if $H(\alpha) = 1$ for all $\alpha \in \mathbb{R}$, then the filter $T$ is the identity.

**Theorem 2.2.** *Let $Y_n^i = \sum_{j=0}^{n} b_j (\delta^{2j} y)_i$ and let $b_{n+1} = 0$. Let $H_n$ be the transfer function of the associated B-spline approximation $\sigma_n(x) = \sum_{i \in \mathbb{Z}} Y_i^n B_i(x)$, i.e., the transfer function of the filter $y \to z$ defined by*

$$z_j = \sigma_n(x_j) = (Y_{j+1}^n + 4Y_j^n + Y_{j-1}^n)/6$$

for all $y \in \mathbb{Z}$. Then

$$H_n(\alpha) = b_0 + \sum_{j=1}^{n+1} (b_j + b_{j-1}/6) \left[ -4\sin^2(\pi\alpha h) \right]^j.$$

**Proof:** The proof is quite easy, since $H_n$ is obviously the product of the transfer function $G_1$ of the filter $y \to Y$ and of the transfer function $G_2$ of the filter $Y \to z$. It is easy to prove that $G_1(\alpha) = \sum_{j=1}^{n} b_j[-4\sin^2(\pi\alpha h)]^j$ and that $G_2(\alpha) = 1 - (4/6)\sin^2(\pi\alpha h)$. ∎

**Theorem 2.3.** *Let $g$ and $h$ be two filters with respective transfer functions $G$ and $H$. Let $g : y \to z$ and $h : y \to z$. For any periodic function $f$ of period $P$, let*

$$\|f\|_2 = \left( \int_P [f(x)]^2 dx. \right)^{1/2}.$$

*Then*

$$\|z - z'\|_{\ell^\infty} \leq \|z - z'\|_{\ell^2} \leq \|G - H\|_\infty \|y\|_{\ell^2}, \qquad \text{if } y \in \ell^2,$$

*and*

$$\|z - z'\|_{\ell^\infty} \leq \|z - z'\|_{\ell^2} \leq \|G - H\|_2 \|y\|_{\ell^1}, \qquad \text{if } y \in \ell^1.$$

**Proof:** For the proof, we first note that the transfer function $H_n(\alpha)$ is nothing else but the Fourier transform of the vector $(B^n(x_j))_{j \in \mathbb{Z}}$. We then use Parseval's identity and bound the involved sums in a quite standard way. ∎

Sharper bounds are available with suitable norms.

## §3. Choosing the Coefficients $b_j$

We now need some way to determine the interesting values of $b_j$, depending on the type of approximation we want. Given an even transfer function $G$, we want to determine $b_j$ so that the associated transfer function $H_n$ is as close to $G$ as possible, and so, by Theorem 2.3, the B-spline approximation output, at the knots, is as close to the filter $g$ output as possible, for the same data sets. In the remainder of this section we list some criteria to accomplish this.

### 3.1. First Criterium: Truncated Development

Since $G$ is an even periodic function, with period $P = 1/h$, it can be written in the form $G(\alpha) = \sum_{j \in \mathbb{N}} c_j[-4\sin^2(\pi\alpha h)]^j$. We identify $H_n$ with the first terms of $G$ and so obtain

$$b_0 = c_0, \qquad b_j + b_{j-1}/6 = c_j, \quad \text{for} \quad j = 1, ..., n; \qquad b_j = 0, \quad j \geq n+1.$$

If we want to quasi-interpolate data, we choose $G(\alpha) = 1$, so we get

$$b_j = (-1/6)^j, \qquad \forall j \in [0, n].$$

If we want to get a high-pass filter, it is better to write

$$H_n(0) = 1 \quad \text{and} \quad H_n^{(2j)}(1) = 0, \quad \forall j \in [0, n-1].$$

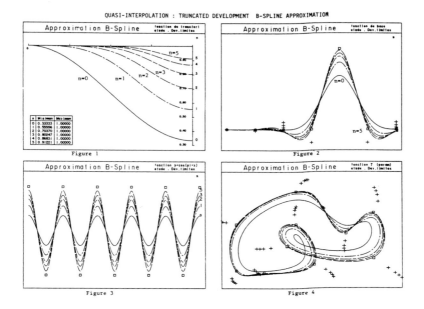

QUASI-INTERPOLATION : TRUNCATED DEVELOPMENT   B-SPLINE APPROXIMATION

Figure 1

Figure 2

Figure 3

Figure 4

We then obtain

$$b_j = \binom{n}{j}(\frac{1}{4})^j, \qquad \forall j \in [0, n],$$

which is equivalent to

$$a_j = \binom{2n}{n+j}(1/4)^j \qquad \forall j \in [0, n].$$

We illustrate the performance of the methods in several figures. Figures 1 to 4 are for quasi-interpolating B-spline approximation (where $b_j = (-1/6)^j$), for $n = 1, \ldots, 5$. Figure 1 shows the transfer function, Figure 2 shows $B^n$, and Figures 3 and 4 show the response to data (the data points are marked with squares, and the computed coefficients $Y_i^n$ are marked with pluses). Figure 4 is a parametric curve; each component is worked out separatedly (with equidistant knots).

Figure 9 shows the results for the transfer function of the high pass filter, while Figure 10 shows the corresponding $B^n$. In all the figures of this paper, the curves for different $n$ are marked with distinct types of dotted lines.

As we can see, when $n$ increases, the transfer function comes nearer and nearer to the value 1 (nearer and nearer 0 for the high cut filter); the $B^n$ function is a better approximation of $\sigma^n$ (flatter and flatter for the high-cut filter); and the approximation functions are more and more quasi-interpolating.

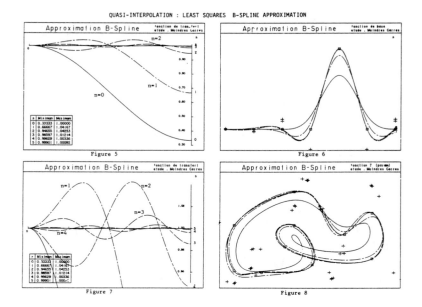

QUASI-INTERPOLATION : LEAST SQUARES  B-SPLINE APPROXIMATION

Figure 5

Figure 6

Figure 7

Figure 8

**Theorem 3.1.** *Let* $n \in \mathbb{N}$, *and let* $b_j = (-1/6)^j$ *for all* $j \in [0, n]$ *and* $b_j = 0$ *for all* $j \notin [0, n]$. *Let*

$$\sigma^n(x) = \sum_{i \in \mathbb{Z}} y_i B^n(x - x_i) = \sum_{i \in \mathbb{Z}} Y_i^n B(x - x_i).$$

*Then*

$$\sigma^n(x_j) = y_j - (-1/6)^{n+1}(\delta^{2n+2}y)_j$$

*for all* $j \in \mathbb{Z}$.

**Proof:** Induction. ■

It is easy to see that $\sigma^n$ interpolates any polynomial of degree at most $2n+1$. Moreover, using this theorem, it is easy to get bounds on $|\sigma^n(x_j) - y_j|$. We now present some properties of $B^n$ and $\sigma$.

**Theorem 3.2.** *Let* $\sigma$ *be the basic cardinal spline satisfying* $\sigma(x_j) = \delta_{0j}$ *for all* $j \in \mathbb{Z}$, *where* $\delta$ *is the usual Kronecker delta with* $\delta_{00} = 1$ *and* $\delta_{0j} = 0$ *if* $j \neq 0$. *Then, with the same hypothesis as Theorem 3.1,*

$$(i) \qquad B^n(x_j) = \begin{cases} \delta_{0j} + (-1)^{j+1}(1/6)^{n+1}\binom{2n+2}{n+j+1}, & j \in [-n-1, n+1] \\ 0, & j \notin [-n-1, n+1] \end{cases}$$

(ii) $$\| \sigma - B^n \|_\infty < \frac{2(2/3)^{n+1}}{\sqrt{\pi(n+1)}}$$

(iii) $$\sigma = \lim_{n\to\infty} B^n = \sum_{i\in \mathbb{N}}(-1/6)^i \delta^{2i} B$$

(iv) Let $\hat{\sigma}$ be the Fourier transform of $\sigma$. Then,

$$\hat{\sigma}(\omega) = h\frac{\sin^4(\omega h/2)}{(\omega h/2)^4}\cdot\frac{3}{2+\cos\omega h}.$$

**Proof:** Part (i) is the particular case of Theorem 3.1 when $y_j = \delta_{0j}$. Statement (ii) follows from

$$|\sigma(x) - B^n(x)| = \left|\sum_{i\in\mathbb{Z}}(\sigma(x_i) - B^n(x_i))\,\sigma(x - x_i)\right|$$

$$\leq \sup_{i\in\mathbb{Z}}|\sigma(x_i) - B^n(x_i)|\cdot\sum_{i\in\mathbb{Z}}|\sigma(x-x_i)|$$

$$\leq 2(1/6)^{n+1}\binom{2n+2}{n+1} < \frac{2(2/3)^{n+1}}{\sqrt{\pi(n+1)}}.$$

Assertion (iii) is a direct consequence of (ii). Finally, (iv) is obtained by taking the Fourier Transform of both sides of the equality (iii). ∎

| $n$ | $d$ | $b_0$ | $b_1$ | $b_2$ | $b_3$ | $b_4$ |
|---|---|---|---|---|---|---|
| 1 | | 1 | -8/23 | | | |
| 2 | 474 | 1 | -30/$d$ | 47/$d$ | | |
| 3 | 8838 | 1 | -1890/$d$ | -351/$d$ | -240/$d$ | |
| 4 | 15443 | 1 | -22776/$d$ | 11320/$d$ | 4002/$d$ | 1137/$d$ |

**Table 1.** Values for quasi-interpolation

## 3.2. Second Criterion: Least Squares

In most cases, other criteria give much better results than the one discussed above. We give an example of one such in this section. Looking at Theorem 2.3, the idea now is to minimize $\| H_n - G \|_2$. This is quite simple as $E_n = \int_0^{1/2h}(G(\alpha) - H_n(\alpha))^2 d\alpha$ is a quadratic function of the $b_j$ coefficients. Minimizing $E_n$ leads to a linear system with unknowns $b_j$. We can, of course, add some additional constraints; such as, for example:

- reproduction of constants: we require $H_n(0) = 1$, or equivalently $b_0 = 1$

- reproducing polynomials of degree $\leq 3$: require $H_n(0) = 1$ and $H_n''(0) = 0$ which is equivalent to $b_0 = 1$ and $b_1 = -1/6$
- no frequency amplified: here we require $H_n(\alpha) \leq 1$ for all $\alpha \in \mathbb{R}$
- no frequency inversed: we require $H_n(\alpha) \geq 0$ for all $\alpha \in \mathbb{R}$.

Table 1 gives some values obtained for quasi- interpolation (*i.e.*, $G(\alpha) \equiv 1$), with the reproducing constants constraint:

We notice that for $n = 1$ with $\alpha_0 = (1/\pi h)\sin^{-1}(5/8) \simeq (1/h)0.215$, we have

$$\max_{\alpha \in \mathbb{R}}(H_1(\alpha)) = H_1(\alpha_0) \simeq 1.1415,$$

which may be considered as too much amplification of the frequencies around $\alpha_0$. Thus, for $n = 1$, we suggest using $b_1 = -1/4$, which is between the truncated development case and the least squares one, and gives considerably better results.

The results of quasi-interpolating B-spline approximation using the least squares criterion are shown in Figures 5–8. Each figure shows the cases $n = 1, \ldots, 5$, where for $n = 1$, $b_1 = -1/4$.

Figure 5 shows the transfer function $H_n(\alpha)$, while Figure 7 shows the the transfer function $H_n(\alpha)$ (enlarging the scale around $H_n(\alpha) = 1$). Figure 6 depicts $B^n$, and Figure 8 shows the response to the same parametric data as in Figure 4. When comparing Figures 5–8 with Figures 1–4, we can see how much more quasi-interpolating the least squares B-spline approximation is than the truncated development B-spline approximation. Figure 11 shows the transfer function for the low-pass filtering B-spline approximation, obtained for $G(\alpha) = 0$ with the constraint $H_n(0) = 1$.

Using a sharper form of Theorem 2.3, (with $G(\alpha) \equiv 1$), we can prove the following:

**Theorem 3.3.** *Let* $n \in \mathbb{N}$, *and let* $b_j^n$ *be defined as above. Let*

$$\sigma^n(x) = \sum_{i \in \mathbb{Z}} y_i B^n(x - x_i) = \sum_{i \in \mathbb{Z}} Y_i^n B(x - x_i).$$

*Then, if* $y \in \ell^\infty$, *there exists some constant* $C_n$ *such that*

$$\mid \sigma^n(x_j) - y_j \mid \leq C_n \parallel y \parallel_\infty.$$

*Furthermore,* $C_1 < 0.3$, $C_2 < 0.064$, $C_3 < 0.02$, $C_4 < 0.06$, $C_5 < 0.0018$.

We can easily see that these estimates are much sharper than those obtained in Theorem 3.1 for the truncated development case. Unhappily, due to the need to solve the linear system, we do not have a general value for $C_n$, which seems to grow exponentially at a rate less than $\sqrt{1/10}$, which is much better than the truncated development case.

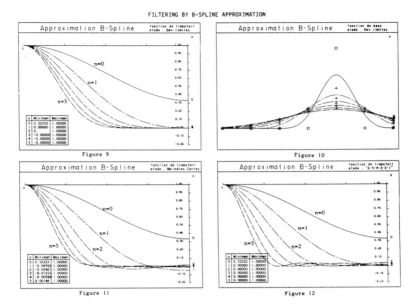

FILTERING BY B-SPLINE APPROXIMATION

Figure 9

Figure 10

Figure 11

Figure 12

## 3.3. Appraisal

The truncated development criterion leads to very simple formulae and to easy estimates. Furthermore, as a consequence of it, we can get some interesting theoretical results concerning the basis function $\sigma$ (Theorem 3.2). But the least squares criterion gives much sharper results, whatever transfer function $G$ we want to approach, and so we suggest using it.

For quasi-interpolation problems, it is of interest to note that the common criterion, which is *interpolating polynomials of degree as high as possible* (see [2]), which is equivalent to the *truncated development* criterion (Theorem 3.1), is **not** the best for getting quasi-interpolating approximation.

We have worked on other criteria, which, due to space limitations, cannot be presented in detail here. We quickly mention two of them:

-   for quasi-interpolation: let $a_j^n$ be the coefficients $a_j$ (see introduction) obtained by the truncated development criterion, at level $n$. Taking $a_j = a_j^\infty = \lim_{n \to \infty} a_j^n$ for all $j \leq n$, and using some normalization such that $H_n(0) = 1$, which is equivalent to $\sum_{j=-n}^n a_j = 1$, we get very good results, which seem even better than the least squares case.

-   for filtering: let $a_j = (n + 1 - |j|)_+/(n + 1)^2$ for all $j \in \mathbb{Z}$.

The resulting approximation is a very good low-pass filter. The transfer function of this last approximation is shown in Figure 12.

## §4. Conclusions

4.1. The *transfer function* is a most efficient way to get a global view of an approximation process. For quasi-interpolation, it is much better than *an order of convergence in $h^q$ (or interpolating polynomials of degree at most $q - 1$).*

4.2. We think that these methods are useful for CAGD. It is helpful for the operator to give *good* coefficients so that the curve goes near the interesting points (quasi-interpolation), or filters some noisy data. Furthermore, this method is very handy to use for *closed curves*, and most efficient for $d$ dimensional surfaces obtained by tensor products (which are very much smoothed by the usual tensor product B-spline approximation).

4.3. This method is very easy to introduce in existing algorithms: we only have to add a line to compute the coefficients $Y_i^n$; everything else remains unchanged !

4.4. The *modified B-splines $B^n$* can certainly be used in place of the usual B-splines in other applications (such as rational splines). This allows one (or even many) degrees of freedom.

4.5. Work is presently underway for determining *best low-pass filters* by cross-validation. Other work is also underway to extend our method to *thin plate splines*.

## References

1. de Boor, C. *A Practical Guide to Splines*, Springer Verlag, 1978.
2. Lyche, T., Local spline approximation methods and osculatory interpolation formulae, in *Approximation Theory*, R. Schaback and K. Scherer (eds.), Springer Lecture Notes in Mathematics 556, 1976, 305–319.

Christophe RABUT
I.N.S.A., Service de mathématiques
Avenue de Rangueil
31077 Toulouse Cédex
FRANCE

# Design Tools for Shaping Spline Models

## R. F. Riesenfeld

**Abstract.** A survey of high level methods for specifying tensor product splines is presented. Although relatively little work has occurred in this area, such methods are very important to give users effective means for rapidly specifying spline representations of geometric models. The need for more new methods is clear since good shape operators for specifying splines are used whenever possible and displace lower level techniques.

## §1. Introduction

Researchers in spline modeling have made great advances in the last twenty years. For most of the last two decades, the major emphasis of mathematical research in this field has been centered around the problem of finding suitable spline representations and associated computational algorithms to make them numerically tractable. This central focus has dealt with developing a plethora of basic, fundamental spline formulations that have various desirable properties and characteristics which lend themselves to applications in representing the shapes that typically occur in the design of mechanical parts. Ensuing numerical analysis research has greatly contributed to the efficiency, stability, and robustness of the diverse algorithms that are currently available.

A system for designing geometric shapes, including sculptured surfaces, which adequately models mechanical parts with spline representations must have several critical components in addition to the modules that implement the fundamental algorithms and representations for splines. This is necessary to achieve a functional capability that is attractive to mechanical designers. An important aspect of geometric modeling systems deals with the specification tools with which a designer is presented. These tools are usually packaged in terms of something that is often called a geometric editor. The function of these tools is to interface the designer with the spline representations that the system provides.

Mathematical Methods in Computer Aided Geometric Design
Tom Lyche and Larry L. Schumaker (eds.), pp. 499–519.

The lowest level of possible functionality of tools for the designer is obviously that of requiring the designer to specify individual coefficients. At this level there is little of analytical interest, nor much leverage given to the powerful computing environments that typically host this kind of activity today. But at a higher level, one more removed from the fundamental mathematical representation but more intuitive and helpful to a designer, the problem becomes rich. It challenges us in our creative understanding of the mathematical issues, as well as in our understanding of the design process and the implementational difficulties. This paper is concerned with summarizing the current state and indicating some directions for needed further research. We also note that relatively little work and progress have been committed to this critical, eclectic area which is becoming more importan' as we achieve greater success in the fundamental area of representation, and must develop more effective methods of communicating shape descriptions from the user to mathematical representations.

Any mathematical method for representing a spline can be equivalently thought of as a user operator for CAGD. In this sense, interpolation is a design method, as is least squares approximation (see Cohen [6]). So are the popular methods of curve definition like Bézier and B-spline methods, in which moving a single vertex redefines a single coefficient. This paper is mostly concerned with methods where the mapping of the user action to the spline representation is not a straightforward mapping. We also narrow the discussion mostly to tensor product B-splines, because they are the forms for which we have succeeded in building systems of general utility. That is, this paper is primarily concerned with the problem of effectively building, from the viewpoint of the user, tensor product B-splines models that accurately represent parts common to mechanical engineers. Efficient operations typically lead to the specification of multiple spline coefficients simultaneously. Hence the term "high level" operators.

## §2. Surfaces from Curves

Some well known mathematical formulations for specifying certain shape requirements can also be thought of as implementations of high level shape operators. For the purposes of this overview and gaining insight beyond the current state, we will look only at methods beyond the lowest level of shape operators.

### Surface Of Revolution

The widespread use of surfaces of revolution in practical situations has made it one of the most basic and natural design tools. Mathematically, the user specifies a profile curve and an axis of revolution, and then asks for a surface of revolution. Since the circle can be represented as a rational spline curve, then the surface of revolution can be represented as a spline if the profile curve is also a spline curve. With this mathematical representation, a designer with a CAD system has more freedom than a machinist with a lathe or a potter with a potter's wheel. He can specify that he wants the profile curve to be rotated through only a certain arc of the circle. He might then want to blend this surface with other rational surfaces to make a more complex part. The flexibility has its drawbacks, for the designer can accidentally specify a profile curve which crosses the axis, and then the surface of revolution has the characteristic of a double cone. It "encloses" a single point at the apex, where the profile crosses the axis. An object with such a boundary is clearly unrealizable. Even with that caution, this simple operation is highly useful, for many objects have radial symmetry, in the first approximation.

## Lofting

One of the oldest lofting methods which has existed since the early days of CAGD is the "lofting" operator, a function which derives its name from the large architectural spaces (lofts) where ship hull designers traditionally were located. Lofting deals with fitting a smooth patch through two parametric boundary curves that are to become embedded on two parametrically opposite sides of a patch or surface. The lofted surface $L(s,t)$ has the form

$$L(s,t) = b_1(s)\gamma_1(t) + b_2(s)\gamma_2(t),$$

where the boundary curves are $\gamma_1$ and $\gamma_2$, and the blend curves are $b_1$ and $b_2$ with $b_1, b_2 \geq 0$ and $b_1 + b_2 = 1$. A *ruled surface*, that is, when $b_1 = (1-s)$ and $b_2 = s$, is perhaps the simplest lofted surface. Although it is not motivated by geometrical considerations, a topological homotopy function from elementary topology is exactly the same as a lofting function. Recall that a homotopy is simply a parametrized surface that transitions smoothly between two space curves, precisely the role of a lofted surface.

A simple generalization of this is an operation that generates a surface that interpolates a family of parametrically parallel curves. This is exactly the operation that is done by traditional lofters when they seek a surface that passes smoothly through the cross-sectional curves of a ship's hull. A corresponding problem exists in defining the fuselage of an airplane from its cross-sectional curves. This can be thought of as a higher level design operation, especially if it is used to determine a tensor product spline surface. It is an efficient method of specifying several coefficients simultaneously through a single, coherent and geometrically meaningful and intuitive operation.

Conceptually this operation is rather straightforward, but its application is rather more complicated. First, appropriate parametric correspondences between the two curves must be established. One can normalize the two curves so that both have parametric ranges over the unit interval, but the lofted surface that is defined between two curves depends on the individual parametrizations of both curves. This situation is readily illustrated by an example. Consider two unit circles in the $z = 0$ and $z = 1$ planes. One might expect to get a uniformly ruled cylinder as a loft without any other complications or subtleties, but some unanticipated variations can occur all within the context of the definition provided. First, suppose that the two circles are identically parametrized but in a nonuniform (non-arclength) manner. Then the resulting cylinder will be correspondingly nonuniformly parametrized. This case is not too severe a deviation from a simple cylinder, but it deserves mention.

The next situation, also determined by the previous two unit circles, reveals a greater problem. Suppose the two circles are uniformly parametrized, but differ in phase by 180 degrees. Now the lofted surface does not yield a cylinder, at least in the mechanical design sense. It yields a cone, because antipodal points on the two circles get connected. This problem is serious. Parametrizations, which are not unique, are critically important, especially when combining surfaces to make more complicated ones.

Second, interpolation with piecewise polynomials can result in shapes which have undesirable characteristics away from the constrained points or curves. In those cases, intuition and the interpolation operator do not give the same surface. It is sometimes possible to improve results by reparametrizing or adding knots and constraint conditions. However, dealing with nonintuitive interpolating surfaces continues to be an area of research.

### Coons-Type Operators

The traditional Coons' Patch, or Boolean sum surface, harks back to the earliest days of CAD itself. It was motivated by the requirement of interpolating a smooth surface through four connected boundary curves. Considerable freedom is allowed in the interior of such a patch after it meets the constraint of interpolating the boundary curves as well as some optional normal derivative information. Let $h_{i,j}(u)$ be the cubic polynomial such that $h_{i,j}(k) = \delta_{k,i}\delta_{0,j}$, $h'_{i,j}(k) = \delta_{k,i}\delta_{1,j}$, and let $\sigma(s,t)$ represent the function whose boundary curves and cross boundary derivatives will be used as the boundary information to form $C$. The cubically blended Coons' patch is defined as

$$
C(s,t) = \sum_{i=0}^{1} h_{i,0}(t)\sigma(s,i) + \sum_{i=0}^{1} h_{i,1}(t)\frac{\partial\sigma(s,i)}{\partial t}
$$

$$
+ \sum_{i=0}^{1} h_{i,0}(s)\sigma(i,t) + \sum_{i=0}^{1} h_{i,1}(s)\frac{\partial\sigma(i,t)}{\partial s}
$$

$$
- \sum_{i=0}^{1}\sum_{p=0}^{1} h_{i,0}(s)h_{p,0}(t)\sigma(i,p)
$$

$$
- \sum_{i=0}^{1}\sum_{p=0}^{1} h_{i,0}(s)h_{p,1}(t)\frac{\partial\sigma(i,p)}{\partial t}
$$

$$
- \sum_{i=0}^{1}\sum_{p=0}^{1} h_{i,1}(s)h_{p,0}(t)\frac{\partial\sigma(i,p)}{\partial s}
$$

$$
- \sum_{i=0}^{1}\sum_{p=0}^{1} h_{i,1}(s)h_{p,1}(t)\frac{\partial^2\sigma(i,p)}{\partial s\partial t}.
$$

The *bilinearly blended* Coons' Patch uses the simple linear blending functions, and does not require normal derivative information. This general form allows $\sigma$ to be any parametric bivariate function which has well defined cross boundary derivatives. Inspired by the widespread utility and applicability of the Coons' Patch even in a highly restricted form, a "Boolean sum" operator can be based on the idea of generally filling in a spline surface in a region bounded by four curves (see Cobb [5]), where the blending functions are written as spline blending functions.

Using the homotopy analogy, a Boolean sum surface is a double homotopy. As we remarked above, a loft is a homotopy between two curves. A Boolean sum surface satisfies the homotopy requirements in both directions, so it is a special kind of function homotopic in both variable directions. Building such functions constructively was studied by Coons and Gordon in the early years of CAGD.

In many instances during a design process, the critical features of a region are the boundary curves, with the interior being rather flexible in its specification. In research applications, it has been discovered that the 2D use of the Boolean sum can be a surprisingly helpful operation for defining a spline surface in a convex region bounded by four opposing curves. It can be used in cases for which the bounding curves resemble a quarter annulus, for example, where the boundary curves are the quarter arcs and the radial line segments that make up the part of an annulus centered at the origin that lies in the first quadrant. If the four planar curves do not bound a convex set, the Coons' operator makes a flat surface that has as its parametric boundary the four specified curves. However, those curves do not form the geometric boundary, which must be a convex set. While such a surface is an extreme simplification of the general problem attacked by Coons, the Boolean sum operator is a useful tool in a modeling world where one is constantly called upon to impose a system of rectangular, tensor product patches on objects not naturally modeled in this "topology."

## Capping Operator

The so-called "capping problem," which occurs most naturally as a result of sweep or an extrusion, gives impetus to the need for a "capping operator," that is, an operator which solves the capping problem. We present the capping operator here as a natural generalization of the last operator, although its need in application is most easily developed subsequent to the sweep or extrusion operators, which will be discussed later. Nonetheless, we will describe the capping operation here where it fits as a mathematical sequel.

The general capping problem loosely consists of defining a filling, or capping, surface in a region defined by a single closed boundary curve. An extremely simple example might be a case in which one wants to close a cylindrical construction, that is, "capping" a pipe, or a generalized cylindrical or generalized pipe. The problem has several interesting particularizations. One is the case in which the cap is planar. "Capping" a circular pipe would give a disc as the standard solution. One could also ask for a cap that blends the surface normals smoothly along the boundary curves. In either case, it is clear that when the boundary curves consist of four connected but logically distinct pieces, topologically the boundary of a square, that the capping problem can be solved by the above Boolean sum surface.

The general capping problem is far more difficult, especially in the setting where the cap is not necessarily convex and one is further restricted to finding a quilt of tensor product splines that form the cap. One can approach this in several ways. If one allows triangular elements with curved boundaries, one could apply a standard triangularization method to the capping region, and then try to build a nonplanar quilt of triangular elements defined over the triangular domains. If carried out in a general parametric way, this approach has formidable implementational and systems difficulties when the pieces are reassembled, but this is mentioned as an obvious approach. This paper is concerned with methods that apply to tensor product surfaces, so this will not be discussed further herein.

The capping problem has by no means been satisfactorily solved, however some interesting work has been initiated and forms the basis of this discussion (see Donahue [9]). Essentially one has to find some automatic scheme for breaking up the cap region into a quilt of adjoining 4-sided pieces or subregions. Then the problem is conceptually reduced to imposing a reasonable subdivision method that produces 4-sided subregions, using Boolean sum operators as above or some other similarly straightforward technique, and then associating the patches defined over subregions to form a coherent, logically connected, reasonably parametrized, overall region to generate a cap in an automatic manner.

The first step of the Donahue approach, which is restricted to planar regions, is to compute the *skeleton* of the capping region $R$. The skeleton of a region is defined as the locus of the centers of all largest inscribed circles so that every point on the boundary is touched by at least one inscribed circle. Intuitively one can think of the equivalent definition of "setting fire to the boundary of a region $R$" and letting it burn inward. The skeleton is the set of points where the fires burning inward from the boundaries meet. This is a kind of generalization to the more common concept of center of mass toward the notion of a "center line of mass." The skeleton can be thought of as the (curved) line of mass, instead of the point of mass, that captures the essential shape character of an object. In general a skeleton will have multiple branches, but in most practical cases there is a central "spine" or "trunk" that is associated with the major center line of the region just as a tree trunk can be associated with the major shape of a (natural) tree.

Once the skeleton is established computationally, then each point along the boundary curve is paired with its nearest skeletal point. This allows the construction of ruled surfaces between the skeleton as one curve and the boundary curve as the other.

Multivariate splines are extremely interesting theoretically, but expensive to compute, more difficult to implement, and hard for the user to specify in an intuitive way. Nonetheless, there are many reasons why tensor product splines are inadequate, and multivariate splines are a natural candidate as proper generalizations of tensor product B-splines. The capping problem is an application sufficiently difficult to justify the extra burdens associated with using multivariate splines. Mueller demonstrated in his thesis [12] that the box spline formulation of multivariate splines can be applied to the capping problem. The multidirectional symmetry together with the multi-sided boundaries make such surfaces intriguing and tempting for such applications, although the specifics of defining an appropriate user interface remains a formidable research topic. Because of this seemingly natural fit of a multi-sided box spline to the problem of capping, the general technical unsolved difficulties notwithstanding, we mention its potential for the future and include an illustration of its successful application for the present. Color Plate 16 shows Mueller's box spline cap applied with appropriate symmetry to a six sided region.

## Extrusions

The "extrusion operation", inspired by the common manufacturing process, is relatively established as a method of describing a certain class of shapes. In modeling systems that allow only primitive shapes and their Boolean combinations, and disallow freeform surfaces, the extrusion operation is straightforward to implement. An extrusion operation is characterized by a profile shape. The profile shape is defined by Boolean operations combining named 2D shapes. Formally, the extruded shape is the cross product of the cross-sectional shape with an orthogonal line. A fixed profile shape (region) in the $x - y$ plane can then be used as the basis of defining a solid shape in three dimensions by extruding it along the $z$-direction. The resulting shape is the cross product of the cross-sectional shape in $x - y$ and the length in $z$. A canonical, simple extrusion is the I-beam example. The beam cross-section is described at the origin in the $x - y$ plane, and then the length of the beam is specified in the $z$-direction.

In the "stick figure world" the cross product definition of an extrusion leads to a direct construction of an extrusion. An instance of the profile is defined at each end of the extrusion, and then corresponding vertices are connected with straight lines. If the original profile is closed, then the extrusion will be a closed, well-defined solid with the defining cross-sectional shape occurring at any internal cut orthogonal to the $z$-axis.

A similar construction applied to the control points of a B-spline profile curve leads to an extruded spline surface. If it is desired to extrude a B-spline curve defined about the origin in the $x - y$ plane through a distance $h$ in the $z$-direction, a second instance of the cross-section curve is copied from the origin to the $z = h$ plane. Then the extruded surface is defined as the lofted surface, usually linearly ruled, between the two instances of the end profile curves. The extruded B-spline surface is defined as only the surface lofted between the profile curves. It is always ruled in the direction of the extrusion.

This differs a bit from the "stick world" example, where a closed object might be considered the result of the extrusion, depending to some extent on local culture and tradition. In the world of freeform surfaces, only the surface is defined. Note that an open curve can be extruded by this definition. The result is simply an open, ruled surface defined by the profile curve, not the boundary of a solid object.

Another useful generalization is to allow the profile curve to be in a plane that is not orthogonal to the trajectory curve. A simple practical case of this occurs if one wants to model a piece of French bread that has come from cutting a loaf with a series of parallel cuts that are on a bias, that is, not orthogonal to the longitudinal axis of the loaf. This is the usual way of cutting French bread. Each piece is a simple extrusion of a profile curve that lies in parallel planes not orthogonal to the major axis of the loaf. The above form has a simple generalization which encompasses that also. Such shapes frequently occur in mechanical design as well.

Extruded lettering of various kinds is tediously pervasive in computer generated television logos and many advertisements. This has become one of the most common examples of the use of extrusion to generate shapes.

### Sweeps

There are many possible generalizations to the extrusion operation. One can generalize the extrusion direction to be along an arbitrary curve instead of along a fixed orthogonal direction to define a "space curve sweep." A familiar example using this kind of sweep construction is a torus, which is defined as a profile circle swept through a trajectory circle. This is the ordinary cross product definition of a torus from elementary topology.

The "space curve sweep" is an abstraction of a snug washer that can slide along a flexible rod, in such a manner that it always remains normal to the rod. At every point, the washer always remains in the moving plane normal to the tangent vector of the curve defined by the rod. There are certainly many examples in practice for which such a generalization is already quite useful. Suppose one wants to define a shape like a drawer handle, which is topologically similar to a half torus. This kind of sweep operation is very useful for defining shapes that are essentially forms that can be thought of as bent pipes, or bent extrusions with more complicated profile sections. There are manifold occurrences of these shapes in the everyday world of mechanical design.

We can represent this form analytically using the following definitions (cf. Bloomenthal [2]). If the profile curve is denoted $p(v) = (x(v), y(v))$ and $T$ represents the unit tangent to the axis curve, $\gamma(u)$, let $X$ and $Y$ represent unit vectors such that the triple $X, Y, T$ forms a right-handed orthonormal coordinate system. Note that since $T$ is a function of the parameter $u$, so are $X$ and $Y$. Also note that $X$ and $Y$ still must be further specified. The new sweep function can be represented as

$$\sigma(u, v) = \gamma(u) + [X(u) \quad Y(u) \quad T(u)] [x(v) \quad y(v) \quad 0]^t .$$

Since the profile curve is defined relative to the $x-y$ origin, the origin of the profile curve will always be on the axis, or sweep curve, in this construction. Now, consider in the $x-y$ plane, the radius of the smallest circumscribing circle centered at the origin that contains the profile curve. If the radius of curvature of the axis curve locally exceeds the radius of the circumscribing circle of the profile curve, then the sweep construction can be implemented in a straightforward way. Otherwise the sweep will self-intersect locally.

A further useful generalization with apparent utility is one in which the profile section is allowed to vary as a function of the distance along the extruded direction. In this manner one can define a duct or channel that smoothly blends from a square hole to a round hole, for example. Note that such shapes cannot be described as surfaces of revolution. This "blended sweep" can be combined with the space sweep to produce a highly general compound sweep. It can be represented as (cf. [2])

$$\sigma(u, v) = \gamma(u) + [X(u) \quad Y(u) \quad T(u)] [x(u,v) \quad y(u,v) \quad 0]^t.$$

Other useful generalizations of sweeps exist. It is not necessary conceptually to make the profile curve planar. Suppose one wants to define a duct that connects two nonplanar openings. This situation makes physical sense, and one ought to be able to define a mathematical operation that captures this notion. In the above equation we need only modify the 0 to be a $z(u,v)$ function.

While the intuitive motivations for sweeps are often quite clear, there are many issues of larger and smaller detail to consider when actually trying to implement a sweeps package. First of all, one must decide on clear mathematical meanings that correspond with the above imaginary actions.

For example, the Frenet frame is frequently thought of as being mathematically the correct coordinate system to use for defining sweep operations. However, the normal vector flips sides when a curve has an inflection point. Similar difficulties can arise for space curves with high torsion. The normal can rotate rapidly causing the Frenet frame to gyrate wildly. The Frenet frame is not defined for a linear segment of a curve either, although the geometrical concept of a sweep still seems to make sense there. The proper CAGD generalization is still a matter of research, but one can certainly develop heuristic techniques to deal with the difficulties mentioned in [2,9].

## Offset

The offset operator is important for the process of defining a spline model of a mechanical part, and also for defining the surfaces needed for defining a process plan for manufacturing as well. An offset surface, in the simplest form, is simply a translate of a surface by a fixed amount in a fixed given, typically normal, direction. If the unit normal to a surface $\sigma$ is defined as $n = \left(\frac{\partial \sigma}{\partial u} \times \frac{\partial \sigma}{\partial v}\right) / \left\| \frac{\partial \sigma}{\partial u} \times \frac{\partial \sigma}{\partial v} \right\|$, then the offset surface of distance $d$ from $\sigma$ is defined as

$\sigma(u, v) + dn(u, v)$. In the I-beam example, we can define the sides of an I-beam as an extrusion of the I-profile. The end caps can then be given as simple offsets of each other in the extruded direction. This is a useful, frequently needed operation, albeit a trivial one to define mathematically. However, the offset surface has self-intersections and loops if the radius of curvature is less than the offset distance. If a surface neighbors itself (nonlocally) by less than twice the offset distance, its offset surface will clearly intersect itself.

An "offset surface" is a concept that comes up naturally in developing a process plan for many manufacturing processes. When one is concerned with milling a surface with a ball end cutter, one usually has to specify the machining operation in terms of a surface through which the tool center passes. When using either a flatend or ball end mill, the "tool path surface" is defined as a surface that is offset by a fixed amount at each point of the surface in the direction normal to the original surface. This form of the "normal offset operator" produces a translate only when the original surface is planar. Normal offset surfaces also arise in manufacturing processes like plastic injection molding for which shrinkage is a factor. The mold has to be larger than the designed artifact to account for final shrinkage in the cooling stage of the process.

No real process can tolerate the mathematical offset surface with its loops and self-intersections, so research continues into modified offset surfaces which satisfy real process needs. If loops are generated in the offset toolpath space for a milling machine, they should be eliminated to save valuable machine time. Detecting such loops, however, is not simple. Additionally, the offset of a B-spline surface is not another tensor product B-spline surface. In a system that supports only tensor product B-spline representations, it then becomes necessary to define an approximate normal offset surface that comes close enough to the correct offset in order to serve the intended purposes. Spline approximations can be derived from the original surface with sufficient accuracy to meet the needs of the processes.

## Booleans and Trimmed Surfaces

From the nonspline culture of "constructive solid geometry" (CSG) models, which uses algebraic assemble of simple shapes as its main modeling operators, we inherit the notion of performing Boolean operations with geometric entities. In the simple, primitive world, a pipe can be defined as the difference of two concentric cylinders, one with slightly smaller radius. To implement volumetric algebra in the primitive world, one can store a parsed, unevaluated expression tree, called a CSG tree, and then compute analytic intersections and perform the evaluations only as required. While this task is not simple, it is still much easier than trying to work with objects whose boundaries are defined by sculptured spline surfaces. Regardless, the idea of union, intersection, and difference is attractive and powerful, and can be extended to objects made up of spline surfaces. Moreover, using Boolean operations to specify shape is a paradigm that users have accepted in the world of simple, primitive building blocks, and also want to have available in a spline-based system. In the more complex environment of spline objects, the intuitive meaning of Boolean operations is relatively clear. Sometimes, however, the designer wants to perform Booleans on objects that are only partially specified. Then ambiguities can arise when surfaces are not parts of closed objects. The mathematical and computational aspects become more problematic, and strategies must be developed to overcome them (see Thomas [23,24]).

First we should restate the context of the problem. It is generally implicitly understood that when Boolean operations are applied to objects defined by splines, that we are working with a boundary representation of the objects. This means that the characteristic function of an object, or the *classification function* as it is more commonly called in this context, is applied to the boundaries, that is, the spline surfaces that determine the boundaries of the object. Since the surfaces are oriented, it is possible to define (only implicitly) the interior of an object as those points in space that are interior to all the local boundary surfaces which specify the object. Since this is not an explicit definition, classifying a point according to whether it is inside, outside, or on the boundary of an object is normally expensive.

A full implementation of a Boolean operation is technically complex, as reflected in [23,24]. Here we outline the approach. As the above discussion explains, in a boundary representation we seek the boundary representation of the resulting object. The boundary result can be computed by performing basic Boolean operations on the boundary elements of each object involved, and then connecting selected pieces appropriately. In analyzing the construction of Boolean operators on objects represented by spline boundaries, we find that all of them can be made up of more elementary operations. One such lower level operation which also has general user utility is the "cut" operation [23]. "Cut" operates on two oriented spline surfaces $S_1$ and $S_2$. The cut operation returns the portion of $S_2$ which lies on the inside of $S_1$, that is, surface $S_1$ cuts $S_2$ and gives back the part of $S_2$ that is inside the cutting surface. This operation is based entirely on the physical analog.

Through modeling experience we have found that the low level, more elementary, cut operation is often useful, especially in the early stages of building a model when it may not yet be closed. It often makes perfect sense to "cut" (or "trim") one surface by another surface even if no Boolean operation is indicated. At this point, it should be noted that a "cut" or "trim" operation has taken us outside the world of tensor product B-spline surfaces defined over rectangular regions. If we wish to continue to perform modeling operations with the results of a cut operation, and hence for any Boolean operation, as they can all be implemented using combinations of cuts, we must allow for the "trimmed surface" data type. More formally, a *trimmed surface* is an ordinary tensor product (B-spline) surface that has a restricted parameter domain. The restriction usually occurs in the form of a (B-spline) curve, or maybe a simple piecewise linear curve that delineates the restricted region. By allowing trimmed surfaces, we can now admit the result of a cut operation in the system.

The cut operation is too formidable to implement in an analytic manner, so it is usually approached by invoking one or more numerical methods. Essentially a root finding problem, the cut operation is equivalent to finding the intersection curve of two surfaces. Two fundamental approaches based on subdivision or incremental techniques are typically used in practice. Subdivision methods tend to be more stable and are nearly certain not to miss any parts of the solution curve, but are also relatively slow. Incremental methods involving standard Newton iteration provide a faster, but less certain alternative. Hybrid schemes are obviously possible, as well. In general this is a difficult computational problem, one which is not at all being satisfactorily dealt with. There are fundamental issues to discover concerning basic representations for geometric entities, algorithms that operate on such entities, and methods for making geometric decisions with greater assurance of correctness in light of known numerical inaccuracies (see Hoffmann *et al* [10]).

For sake of brevity and integrity of purpose, a major digression on implementing Boolean operations is omitted here. The cut operation can be used to directly support the elementary classification functions defined by,

$$A \text{ in } B = \{p \in \partial A : p \in B\}$$
$$A \text{ out } B = \{p \in \partial A : p \notin B\}$$
$$A \text{ on } B = \{p \in \partial A : p \in \partial B\},$$

where $\partial$ means "boundary of". It is well known that when objects are defined by their boundaries, then classification of the boundaries with respect to each object allows one to generate the classification of the new "Booleaned" object. Finding a robust, practical implementation of the Boolean operations remains a formidable task confronting the world of spline geometers at this juncture.

## Fillets and Chamfers

The terms "fillets" and "chamfers" are derived from manufacturing operations, where *filleting* corresponds to providing extra material to fill an inside corner to make it round, and *chamfering* corresponds to removing (grinding off) some material to smooth an outside edge. We use the direct analogy for the terms in geometric modeling. For both aesthetic and functional reasons, filleting and chamfering are pervasive operations in many areas of mechanical design. Fillets are particularly common in injection molded pieces, but they also appear in many objects manufactured with other processes. A ball end mill can be used naturally to define a fillet of constant radius equal to that of the cutter. Fillets are useful for avoiding accumulation of foreign matter on a part, and for leading to stronger joints with better stress distributions in regions where two surfaces meet. Chamfers occur for similar reasons, as well as for safety. Rounded edges pose less threat to humans in contact with a part. They can also be specified to make assembly easier. There are many other reasons that make fillets and chamfers commonplace in mechanical design, so having them as modeling operations is useful. We will only discuss fillets, as chamfers are mathematically equivalent.

A *fillet operator* is a compound operator that can be built up from some of the previously mentioned operators. Often a fillet is not an intrinsically critical dimension, although one may be required to give strictness to the interpretation of a drawing, regardless. So long as some smooth feature is present that basically follows the shape of the designated fillet, the functional need is often met. But in the traditional settings of engineering drawings the most expedient way to specify a fillet is with a fixed radius. Perhaps when computer models replace paper definitions, the intrinsic freedoms that exist will be properly conveyed in the specifications.

Today a fillet is usually specified in terms of a fixed radius. This can be thought of as a "rolling ball surface" formed by the "bottom" silhouette of ball bearing of corresponding radius which is being rolled between the surfaces that need to be filleted. This is a generalization of the familiar "quarter round" concave (not convex) molding that is sometimes used between the walls and the ceiling of a room or between two walls of a house.

There are various ways to define mathematical fillets, but here again we are restricting ourselves to fillets of a similar representation as the spline model. We are trying to define a spline fillet for spline models so as to reduce the overall representational complexity of matters. All other modules of a system must be able to operate on the fillet representation as well as the original defining surfaces themselves (cf. [11]).

In the general case, the fillet cannot be represented exactly as a rational spline. However, it can be approximated as closely as necessary. One relatively direct way of thinking of a fillet is the following. Consider two spline surfaces $A$ and $B$ that meet in an intersection curve $C$. Now suppose it is necessary to fillet the interior angle where $A$ and $B$ meet. Let the "inside" of each surface be defined as being the side toward the fillet. Before blending the fillet surface into the two original surfaces, it is first necessary to eliminate the corner definition from each original surface. For each original surface $A$ and $B$, define a spline approximation to the offset surface which is offset from its original on the inside by a distance $d$, called $A'$ and $B'$, respectively. This process uses the "offset" operation defined earlier. Now let each offset surface $A'$ and $B'$ intersect the other corresponding original surface, that is, find $A' \cap B$ and $A \cap B'$. This construction can be used as a reasonable approximation under nonextreme conditions to where the "rolling ball" would be tangent to the original surfaces $B$ and $A$, respectively, so that the corner can be cut away from that curve "out". Further, the intersection curve defined by $A' \cap B'$, where the two offset surfaces meet, is a good approximation to the curve traced by the center of the "rolling ball" as it moves along. Clearly counterexamples can be generated to show this construction is not exact, but in practice it is a useful approach which works on a large class of mechanical shapes.

So far we have used the cut operator and the offset operator to define some reference constructions for the fillet and to "trim" the two constituent surfaces. Now, at this point, defining a circular loft of radius $d$ between the two intersection curves completes the fillet. The cross boundary tangent direction of each point along the intersection curves with the trimmed surface is necessary. All of these operations make sense and define "reasonable" approximations when the surfaces to which they are applied do not have large dynamic range in their curvatures in the vicinity of the filleting location. It is easy to find counterexamples for which the process outlined above will not generate a reasonable surface, but mechanical parts, in general, are well behaved in filleting regions.

Generalizations are possible and necessary to cover wider applications. There are cases where variable radius filleting is more appropriate, especially for aesthetic purposes. For example, consider the join where a cylinder meets a plane obliquely. Suppose we are interested in filleting around the join. By choosing an oblique angle far from the normal, we can see that a fixed radius fillet would produce an odd looking result. A more aesthetically pleasing fillet is produced by selecting a larger radius for filleting where the cylinder makes an oblique angle (the outside angle), and a smaller radius on the inside, the side of the cylinder that makes an acute angle with the plane. The more extreme the angle, the more obvious this phenomenon becomes. In fact, it can be seen in a simpler construction. Let two straight lines intersect at, say, a 30 degree angle. Now study what fillets look good for both the inside angle and the outside angles. As observed above, the radii will not be the same.

Other generalizations of the fillet operation allow for different amounts of offset from each surface, and allow the radius to vary as a function of position along the fillet. And, of course, one can use shapes for the fillet profile other than circular arcs. Elliptical fillets are common in the specification of some bolts, as a common example. An implementationally convenient profile to use is a Hermite spline where the end conditions are extracted from each surface at the appropriate point of contact.

## §3. Making Solids from Surfaces

Mechanical parts tend to be modeled best with "solid models," so somehow we must eventually develop closed models from spline surfaces. Building a closed, coherently oriented spline model by hand, as is frequently done, is a tedious and labor intensive process that runs against the general spirit of CAD. Making spline models should be done with facility. Hence we need operators to assist in making closed models.

Two approaches are mentioned that facilitate building a closed model. One is to begin with a simple spline shape that corresponds to a common primitive shape. This is similar in philosophy to the way the constructive solid geometry modeling has done things. If one anticipates having a need for a spline definition ultimately, it has simplifying implementational advantages to represent some basic primitive shapes, the building blocks of CSG systems, as splines. Hence, a block can be represented as a spline.

As Stay [22] showed in his thesis, if one is using splines to represent primitive shapes, one can go a step further and extend the definition of simple shapes to objects he called "rounded edge primitives." Constructing such models presents problems beyond the usual consideration of spline theory, per se. For example, suppose one represents a cylinder as a rolled up rectangle with opposite sides identified. This works without difficulties until one applies a bend operation, for example, to such a primitive. At that point, there is an additional problem to account for. The seam of the cylinder, where the two edges meet, will behave differently than the rest of the spline surface unless considerable care is taken to impose additional restrictions on the seam. This has profound implications on the design of data structures for such a system and for ways of enforcing geometric constraints of this type. All of these topics are unsolved research topics. We only mention them here to remark on some of the difficulties with this approach, which otherwise seems rather an attractive way to develop spline models rapidly.

The building block approach to creating solids requires that the user specify, or at least consider, a large number of parameters at once. This is especially true if the sides are not parallel, and "draft angles" are part of the specification, along with several different radii corresponding to the various edges. Of course, this does accomplish a large geometric task once all the parameters are provided, and one can develop the model rather rapidly.

Sometimes there is a preference for working in a 2D domain as much as possible, before moving into a truly 3D environment where all interface issues become more complex. Working in the 2D environment draws on a long tradition of engineering design where users have very good understanding of the issues. The building block approach to building up a spline model has the effect of thrusting the user into considering 3D aspects of the model at an earlier stage. This is really a matter of idiosyncratic choice of design paradigm, so no attempt is made to place particular value on one approach relative to the other.

Another effect of using 3D primitives to develop complex spline models is that it seems to have the effect of involving a greater number of Boolean operations in the final model. Primitives are built up, modified, and combined with standard Boolean operations. With the current state of affairs, this is generally regarded as a liability of this approach because Boolean operations are not always satisfactorily robust. In the current world of computing, where Boolean operations are expensive at best and unstable at worst, they should not be used indiscriminately. Hence, modelers tend to choose alternative forms of modeling that involve fewer Booleans operations.

A second fundamental approach to creating solids is to apply operators like "thicken" to a surface shape that has been carefully designed. This is an approach that works better when the specifications are somewhat flexible in the thickness of a 3D part. This operator takes a basic spline surface, defines an offset of it, and then closes the space between the two surfaces with a band around the offset. This operator is appropriate for objects having a similar top and bottom surface with a surface band connecting the top and bottom, at least to a first order approximation

This gives only loose specification to the band that connects the two surfaces. Should the band be a ruled surface that yields sharp corners on the edges where the bands meet the top and bottom surfaces? Or should the band be a more complex loft that picks up normal derivative information from the join where it meets the top and bottom? Examples of both styles of definition are easy to find, so this may be best offered to the designer as options. The spoon that appeared in Cobb's thesis [5] and shown in Section 6 below was designed with this operator.

## §4. Modifying Surface Shapes

### Warp, Bulge, Flatten, Bend, Taper

There is a collection of useful shape operators for splines which were developed in [5], including "taper," " bend," "flatten," and "warp," each of whose names associates them with an intuitive action. The taper operator applies a scaling function to a surface in one direction. "Bend" is the analog of the physical operation. One simply has to specify the final bend angle and how sharp (how local) the bend should be. "Flatten" has the effect of applying a flat plane to a clay model, for example. Flatten has the effect of depressing a surface in a specified direction by a variable, unimodal, well function. The physical analog similarly motivates "warp," which has the opposite effect of "flatten" in the sense that "flatten" can be used to undo a warp. Warp has the effect of puffing up a region by pushing with a (virtual) thumb. The "bulge" operation of Shirman and Sequin [21] is also in this group of highly intuitive shape operators and has similar motivation.

All of these operators can be implemented in a direct and straightforward manner by simply applying the corresponding actions to the control points of the B-splines themselves. All of these operators exploit the local support property of B-splines. Deciding on which control points these operators should be applied to makes the specification difficult. The relationship between visual effect and parameter values, or even geometry, is poorly understood. The operators only become truly tractable in an interactive environment where one can apply the operations for one set of parameters, see the effect, and then reapply them again for slightly different values until the desired results are achieved. The ability of the user to apply them interactively until the right shape is defined is very important. Much of the scientific contribution in developing them is actually in identifying them and their importance rather than in their particular implementation.

### Distortion Operators

Many aesthetically appealing shapes are defined by a variety of transformations that we can collectively call "distortion" operations (see Barr [1] and Parry [13]). These are operations that can mildly deform a model, or can be applied in ways that create Salvidor Dali-type images. They can take a well constructed model of a glass bottle, say, and make it look as though it has been exposed to intense heat. Other operations apply curvilinear transformations to make objects take on a serpentine form or shape. So far these deformation operations have tended to be more applicable to the artistic domain, partly because such tools are somewhat hard to control precisely for many mechanical applications. Perhaps with greater experience, these operators will find more widespread use in mechanical design.

Nearly any such wild transformation can be made into an operator by applying it to the space itself or to the control points of the spline. In engineering applications one normally prefers to preserve the Euclidean integrity of the coordinate space, so one would apply these transformations to the model and not warp the entire space. One could warp the entire space if the visual image were the designer's end result, as is normally the case in computer art.

## §5. Examples

The following figures offer examples of interesting splines shapes modeled with the Alpha_1 system developed at the University of Utah. All of the examples are typical of a wide class of modeling problems, and all of them are good candidates to be modeled with design tools.

In the logo for Alpha_1 in Color Plate 9, we can immediately make the observation that the body of the logo can be formed by a sweep operation. Sweeping a fixed circular profile along an axis curve is a standard method for modeling artifacts that resemble bent pipe. We can also see a good example of two kinds of self-intersections in the body of the logo. One is a global self-intersection where the letter alpha normally crosses itself. Other local self-intersections occur at the three sharp corners. The self-intersection at the peak of the 1 is formed by an angle so acute that it would not look good without mitring the corner to eliminate any excess surface that would bulge through. The lower two corners do not require mitring, since the angles are not as acute, and the self-intersections are simply absorbed internal to the surface. Finally, the sweep that forms the letter is finished with a capping operation that meets the swept body with surface normal continuity. One might try to use a bend operation to form the fundamental axis curve, or it could be designed with other, more traditional methods.

Color Plate 10 shows the versatility and power of a general, variable profile sweep. Not only are the handles done with sweeps, but so are the other two major sections of the scissors, namely, the central portion and the pointed part. Without using a powerful design tool of this kind, the design would result in a far more copious description.

The jet engine hollow turbine blade root portrayed in Color Plate 11 is a model rich in diverse shape. It has simple flat surfaces, fixed radius fillets, and rather complex sculptured surfaces around the opening. The "tree" portion of the root part, the part pointed to by the root arrow in the picture, is generated with an extrusion that is then capped with a flat surface. The platform area shows shapes that could be modeled with a non-normal extrusion.

The Boolean operations used to scoop out the pockets, trim the platform, and trim the passage bottom are particularly interesting in Color Plate 11.

The trimming surfaces do not come from a closed object. One can think of the pictures as either depicting a sequence of cut operations, or of performing subtractions with partially defined objects. These are difficult constructions to resolve correctly. Observe that the platform does not intersect the boundary of the trimming surface. However the implied action is clear to any observer, and that inference should be made by the CAD system.

The complexities of Color Plate 12 are discussed in [6]. The body is an example of a rather more complicated loft with tremendously varying cross sections. Sweeps and bends are appropriate tools for the landing skids. A "cookie cutter" developed by extruding the profile of the vent window was used to cut a hole in the body, and then cut a piece of glass to the exact size of the hole. Then the top canopy was modeled separately and had to be unioned to the main fuselage. Other more detailed shape operations will not be discussed here.

Color Plate 13 has received considerable circulation as an example of several successive applications of shape operators, which are more instructively seen in a video presented at the conference. First a 2D Boolean sum spline surface the size of the bowl was created. Then it was warped to make a bowl surface. A tab was bent up to generate a site from which the handle was extruded, tapered, and bent. Finally thicken was applied to the top surface to build a solid from the spoon's top surface. The spoon was chosen to demonstrate the compounding of several operators to yield a complex sculptured part.

Another good example of the use of a compound shape operator appears in Color Plate 14. A basic surface of revolution was used to generate a bottle. The sides were flattened, warped inwardly, and finally the bottle was thickened. An object of this kind is extremely tedious to model without such high level operators.

In both Color Plates 15 and 16, we see capping operations. The gear-like part in Color Plate 15 can be modeled as a variable, nonplanar sweep. It was capped using an algorithm that computes the skeleton and then generates a suitable tensor product spline cap. The cap in Color Plate 16 is not a tensor product; it is a 3-directional multivariate box spline. While modeling with multivariate splines is a research endeavor, the results of a successful application are (perhaps overly) auspicious.

## §6. Conclusions

This paper has dealt with the "computer aided" part of CAGD. Powerful methods of representation cannot be brought to bear unless we derive good ways of asking the user to specify (design with) them. In presenting an overview of high level methods for designing spline surfaces, we note that the repertoire is limited. The level of activity in this area has been slight over the years. More research is needed in defining new, more creative operators. The environment for carrying out design activities has changed dramatically and has outpaced our thinking in this area. To balance this subject, more (computer aided) "design research" is necessary to find better and more powerful paradigms that lend themselves more appropriately to the next era of design environments.

Some specific near-term achievements are possible. One concerns the robustness problem in performing Boolean operations with spline objects. Often this process of computing Boolean operations is fraught with numerical difficulties that can undermine the overall robustness of the evaluation. Nonetheless, such operations are necessary, and we must advance to the point of being able to perform such operations with greater confidence and reliability. This is a relatively deep matter which goes to the heart of how the most basic entities and values are represented in a computer, and how we perform operations using them. The state-of-the-art must make progress here to increase the level of satisfaction among the users of the latest systems.

Beyond lack of attention, another major reason for the general absence of high level operators is probably due to the lack of a "super-computing" environment for the task. Repetitive operator computation can be enormously compute intensive, especially when an interactive, real-time effect is sought. We are entering a new era of massively parallel and cheap computing at the disposal of the designer in his normal working environment. This era of "desktop supercomputing" is just beginning, so research is timely in developing such aids. To rapidly achieve a complex sculptured shape, a designer should be able to mold spline entities with the aid of (possibly expensive) high level operators. Beyond mere feasibility of representing form, we must gain much greater facility in defining complex spline shapes.

We can think of the process of trying to invent new and powerful design operators as essentially trying to determine a new vocabulary list for this field. What are the right "verbs" of CAGD? When is a design system good and effective? What are good, concise ways to communicating shape information when ordinary language is not adequate? We must give quantitative meaning to intuitive concepts which are entirely qualitative in natural language. Advances in this subject will require some aspects of psychology as well as a keen understanding of the underlying mathematical and computing issues, and the subtle process of mechanical design.

## Acknowledgements

Appreciation is expressed to Beth Cobb and Elaine Cohen for their many insightful discussions and contributions on this topic. Special thanks are due to the editors and organizers of the conference for their efforts in bringing together such a stimulating conference, and for their generous help communicating this paper. I am grateful to the Alpha_1 Group and the Alpha_1 System for the examples and many ideas presented here.

## References

1. Barr, A., Global and local deformations of solid primitives, Proceedings of Siggraph 84, ACM, 1984, 21–30.

2. Bloomenthal, M. , Approximation of sweep surfaces by tensor product B-splines, Computer Science Technical Report, Univ. of Utah, 1988.

3. de Boor, C., *A Practical Guide to Splines*, Springer-Verlag, New York, 1978.

4. Chiyokura, H., *Solid Modeling with Designbase*, Addison-Wesley, 1988.

5. Cobb, E. S., Design of sculptured surfaces using the B-spline representation, Ph.D. dissertation, University of Utah, 1984.

6. Cohen, E., Some mathematical tools for a modeller's workbench, IEEE Comp. Graph. Appl. **3** (1983), 63–66.

7. Coquillart, S. Computing offsets of B-spline curves, Comput. Aided Design **19** (1987), 305–309.

8. Coquillart, S., A control-point based sweeping technique, IEEE Comp. Graph. Appl. **19** (1987), 36–45.

9. Donahue, B., Modeling objects with generalized sweeps, Master's Thesis, University of Utah, 1985.

10. Hoffmann, C., J. E. Hopcroft, and M. S. Karasick, Robust set operations on polyhedral solids, Cornell TR 87-875, 1987.

11. Hoffmann, C. and J. E. Hopcroft, Quadratic blending surfaces Comput. Aided Design **18** (1986), 301–306.

12. Mueller, T. I., Geometric modeling with multivariate B-splines, Ph.D. dissertation, University of Utah, 1986.

13. Parry, S. , Freeform deformations in a constructive solid geometry modeling system, Ph.D. dissertation, Brigham Young University, 1986.

14. Pegna, J., Variable sweep geometric modeling, Ph.D. dissertation, Stanford University, 1987.

15. Requicha, A. A. G. and H. B. Voelcker, Solid modeling: current status and research directions, IEEE Computer Graphics and Applications **7** (1983), 25–37.

16. Riesenfeld, R. F., A view of spline-based solid modeling, in *Proceedings of Autofact-5*, Assoc. SME, 1983, 2.75–2.83.

17. Rossignac, J. and A. A. G. Requicha, Constant-radius blending in solid modeling, Computers in Mechanical Engineering **3** (1984), 65–73.

18. Rossignac, J. and A. A. G. Requicha, Offsetting operations in solid modeling, Comput. Aided Geom. Design **3** (1986), 129–148.

19. Schumaker, L. L., *Spline Functions: Basic Theory*, Wiley, New York, 1981.

20. Sederberg, T. W. and S. R. Parry, Free-Form deformation solid geometric models, Proceedings of Siggraph 8, ACM (1986), 151–160.

21. Shirman L. A., and C. H. Sequin, Local surface interpolation with shape parameters between adjoining Gregory patches, preprint.

22. Stay, P. R., Rounded edge primitives and their use in Computer Aided Geometric Design, Master's Thesis, University of Utah, 1984.

23. Thomas, S. W., Modeling volumes bounded by B-spline surfaces, Ph.D. dissertation, University of Utah, 1984.

24. Thomas, S. W., Set operations on sculptured solids, Technical Report UUCS-87-0004, Computer Science, University of Utah, 1987.

Richard F. Riesenfeld
Department of Computer Science
University of Utah,
Salt Lake City, Utah 84112
USA

Supported in part by DARPA (DAAK11-84-K0017 and N00014-88-K-0688). All opinions, findings, conclusions or recommendations expressed are those of the authors and do not necessarily reflect the views of the sponsoring agencies.

EMAIL: rfr @ cs.utah.edu

# A Process Oriented Design Method
# for Three-dimensional CAD Systems

## D. Roller and E. Gschwind

**Abstract.** Efficiency of CAD systems has usually been seen in the context of algorithmic performance of the implementation. However, other aspects can also be very important for the overall efficiency of 3D CAD systems. In this paper, we introduce an input method that has the potential to considerably increase the efficiency of 3D CAD systems due to its ease of use and understanding. The proposed method is based on the recently introduced workplane and machining concept for solid modeling, and expands this technique toward modeling of more complex shapes in a process oriented way.

## §1. Introduction

Efficiency is a very important aspect of CAD systems, particularly for 3D systems, which have been considered slow and unproductive in the past [2]. Of course there is no single parameter to influence efficiency; however, efficiency and productivity can be seen as the result of two groups of aspects: functionality and usability [6].

In the past, most of the development effort for 3D systems was spent in enhancing the basic functionality. Dependent on the data structure and stored model information, 3D systems are usually classified as wireframe, surface, and solid modelers. Among these, the solid modelers carry the most complete geometric description of a model. However, solid modelers are still rather complicated to use, in general, and are typically limited in either complexity or accuracy of geometry. These are probably the main reasons why solid modeling is not yet the predominant technology in industrial CAD installations [4].

Significant improvements in the usability of solid modelers were made recently by the introduction of the workplane and machining concept [7] for solid model generation. In combination with enhanced general interaction principles, the efficiency of solid modeling design can be increased dramatically.

Mathematical Methods in Computer Aided Geometric Design
Tom Lyche and Larry L. Schumaker (eds.), pp. 521–528.
Copyright © 1989 by Academic Press, Boston.
ISBN 0-12-460515-X.

We will now introduce an improved method that extends solid model generation to an additional class of complex shaped mechanical parts. It can be viewed as a generalization of the mentioned workplane and machining concept, and will be called "process oriented solid modeling" here.

## §2. Process Oriented Solid Modeling

In order to better understand the advantages of the proposed process oriented solid modeling technique, let us first have a brief look at conventional methods. The dominant method for solid model creation is the use of Boolean or set operations. Using Boolean operations is a general method, and does not assume a particular internal data structure of the underlying solid modeler like constructive solid geometry [5] or boundary representation [1]. Figure 1 shows five example parts and the principle steps to create them.

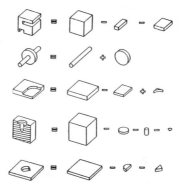

**Figure 1.** Conventional solid modeling using Boolean operations.

This construction technique forces the user to think in terms of mathematical set theory and three-dimensional coordinate systems. Creating a slot in a block as in the first example requires the positioning of a properly sized block in 3D space as well as calling a DIFFERENCE function to subtract it from the basic block.

This is certainly not the way designers think about a step-wise design. As opposed to modeling with Boolean operations, process oriented solid modeling is based on higher level commands that are oriented toward manufacturing processes, like EXTRUDE, TURN, MILL, DRILL or PUNCH.

Figure 2 illustrates how the same example parts as shown in Figure 1 would be designed using the process oriented solid modeling method. In general, the principle here is to use rotation and translation of planar profiles for model creation and modification. The profile can be seen as tool geometry or better still as a cross-section of a tool. Translation or rotation of a profile

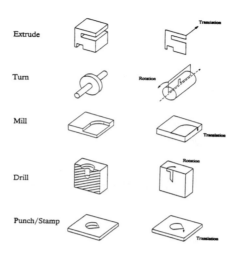

**Figure 2.** Examples using the process oriented design method.

is interpreted as a modeling operation that has similar effects on the object shape as a comparable manufacturing operation moving the tool.

Note that EXTRUDE, TURN, MILL etc. as design commands do not necessarily have to determine the technology used for the actual manufacturing of the part. Rather, these commands, called *machining commands*, are meant to be very powerful and easily understood shape creation and modification commands for design work. The examples chosen in Figures 1 and 2 are very simple ones. There are of course known modeling techniques, such as SWEEP, to facilitate the process oriented design method for such simple objects.

In order to make this type of construction process as natural and easily understood as possible, a so-called *workplane concept* was developed. A workplane is a plane in 3D space that is being used for the profile construction. A selection of a workplane automatically results in a specific view transformation of the object; now ordinary 2-D commands can be used for profile construction in 3D space. This transformation is performed in such a way that the workplane is perpendicular to the viewing direction (cf. Figure 3).

Figures 4 and 5 demonstrate how process oriented solid modeling can be applied to designing mechanical parts effectively. The final part shown in Figure 5 is constructed using just three 3D commands (EXTRUDE, MILL and LIFT) and simple two-dimensional profile construction. Starting from a block that has been generated by EXTRUDEing a profile, Figure 4 shows the use of a MILL command to generate pockets in the block. Figure 4 demonstrates how a mounting plate can be constructed to the block using a LIFT operation (adding material to already existing material).

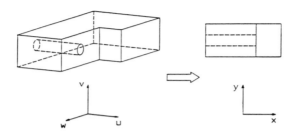

**Figure 3.** Workplane concept.

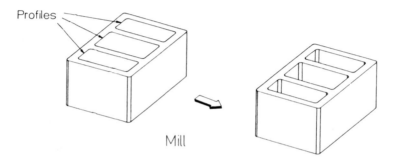

**Figure 4.** Process oriented design using machining commands.

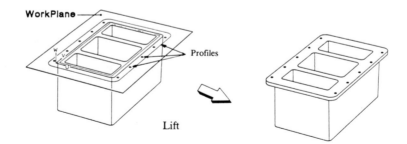

**Figure 5.** Setting the workplane for a LIFT operation.

## §3. Modeling of Complex Shaped Bodies

The workplane and machining concept as introduced in [7] only supports the design of a limited class of parts. These parts are characterized by successive employment of rotation or translation of profiles.

We are now going to expand this concept to cover the design of more complex shaped and relatively frequently occurring parts in mechanical design. Examples of such kind of parts are gears, springs, screws and nuts with threads.

As a motivation for this extension, we are going to look at a lathe from a manufacturing point of view, and develop an abstraction for our design method (cf. Figure 6). As can be seen, we have three superimposed movements of tool and work piece respectively.

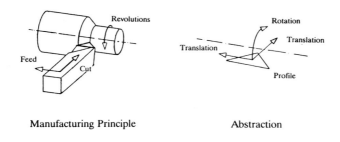

Manufacturing Principle    Abstraction

**Figure 6.** Operation principle of a lathe and its abstraction.

Tool profile movements that can be expressed by superimposed transformations, combined with existing modeling techniques are the basic idea of our method. The definition of objects is performed in three stages:

1. Definition of the tool cross-section P with simple 2-D methods, utilizing the workplane concept.
2. Depending on the selected command, the associated manufacturing-like process defines the tool motion. Multiple simple motions can be superimposed to define complex transformations. Transformations $\mathbf{M}$ are applied to a tool profile $\mathbf{P}$ in order to generate a set of profiles $\{\mathbf{P}_1, \mathbf{P}_2, \ldots, \mathbf{P}_n\}$.
3. Known modeling techniques like Boolean operations, Sweep, and Loft are then used internally to perform the manufacturing-like operations.

The result of such modeling operations obviously can lead to objects with complex boundary surfaces.

The main advantage of this concept is that only a few parameters are needed to define geometrically complex objects like screws, gears, springs etc. Designers are not normally familiar with all manufacturing aspects. However, they have a good understanding of the principal operation of machine tools. Therefore process oriented solid modeling is natural and very easy for designers to learn. Consequently, expensive training time for a solid modeling system based on this technique could be kept to a minimum.

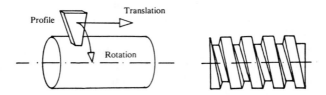

**Figure 7.** Modeling of a screw thread.

## §4. Examples

The following examples have been implemented as a software prototype system on an HP 9000 workstation computer, in order to demonstrate the feasibility of the proposed method [3].

### 4.1. Screw Thread

The motion **M** of a suited profile for generating a screw thread can be formulated as a rotation **R** and a superimposed translation **T**

$$\mathbf{M}(\alpha, s) = \mathbf{T}(s) \circ \mathbf{R}(\alpha). \tag{4.1}$$

The dependency between the rotation angle $\alpha$ and the translation parameter $s$ is given by the feedrate

$$\mathbf{F} = \frac{\alpha}{s} = \text{constant} \ \left[\frac{\text{turns}}{\text{inch}}\right]. \tag{4.2}$$

Thus the complete transformation that describes the motion of the profile is given by

$$\mathbf{M}(\alpha) = \tilde{\mathbf{T}}(\alpha) \circ \mathbf{R}(\alpha). \tag{4.3}$$

### 4.2. Circular Spring

For the circular spring shown in Figure 8, the tool profile movement **M** can be described as a global rotation **R** and a superimposed local rotation $\mathbf{R_L}$:

$$\mathbf{M}(\alpha, \beta) = \mathbf{R_L}(\beta) \circ \mathbf{R}(\alpha). \tag{4.4}$$

The dependency between the angles $\alpha$ and $\beta$ is

$$\alpha = k\beta, \tag{4.5}$$

where $k$ is the number of windings.

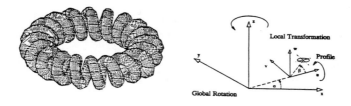

**Figure 8.** Generation of a circular spiral spring.

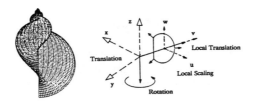

**Figure 9.** Design of a snail shell.

## 4.3. Snail Shell

This is of course just an academic example; however, it explains in an easily understood way how process oriented solid modeling works with more complex profile transformations. Similar technical objects would be custom springs with variable wire diameter.

Figure 9 shows the composition of the profile transformation for the generation of this example. This profile transformation $\mathbf{M}$ is defined as a local scaling $\mathbf{S_L}$ plus a local translation $\mathbf{T_L}$ plus a global rotation $\mathbf{R}$ plus a global translation $\mathbf{T}$:

$$\mathbf{M}(f, r, \alpha, z) = \mathbf{S_L}(f) \circ \mathbf{T_L}(r) \circ \mathbf{R}(\alpha) \circ \mathbf{T}(z). \qquad (4.6)$$

The dependency of the local translation distance $r$ perpendicular to the rotation axis and the global rotation angle is

$$r = ae^{k\alpha}. \qquad (4.7)$$

This equation describes a logarithmic spiral, where $a$ and $k$ are basically shape parameters of the spiral. Similar dependencies were chosen for the scaling factor $f$ and the offset $z$ parallel to the rotation axis.

## §5. Conclusion

The process oriented solid modeling construction concept introduced in this paper combines a natural design approach with high end functionality and ease of use.

In particular, an extension of the category of shapes conventional solid modelers are capable of has been achieved. The developed method supports the design of frequently occurring complex mechanical parts with high level geometry generation commands.

Experience with a software prototype of this method has shown that it is very easy to learn and understand. Thus a complete CAD system based on this technique potentially could provide a more efficient design of complex parts.

## References

1. Braid, I. C., R. C. Hillyard, and I. A. Stroud, Stepwise construction of polyhedra in geometric modeling, in *Mathematical Methods in Computer Graphics and Design*, K. W. Brodlie (ed.), Academic Press, New York, 1980, 123–141.
2. Solid Modeling Applications ... The Real Payback. Proceedings of CAM-I's 3rd Geometric Modeling Seminar, PM- 85-MM-01, Computer Aided Manufacturing International, Inc., Arlington, Texas, 1985.
3. HP 9000 Series 800 Model 835 Turbo SRX Hardware Technical Data, Hewlett-Packard Co., Palo Alto, 1988.
4. Johnson, R. J., Solid Modeling: A state-of-the-art report, CAD/CIM Alert, Management Roundtable, Inc., Chestnut Hill, Massachusetts, 1985.
5. Requicha, A. A. G. and H. B. Voelker, Mathematical models of rigid solid objects, Technical Memo TM-28, Production Automation Project, University of Rochester, Rochester, New York, 1977.
6. Roller, D., J.-P. Mainguy, and W. Kurz, Internal design of design automation software and its consequences for the user, in *Proceedings of the Fifth European Conference on CAD/CAM and Computer Graphics*, Hermes-Verlag, Paris, 1986, 765–783.
7. Roller, D., Benutzbarkeitsaspekte von CAD-Systemen, CAD/CAM Manual 1988, Institute of Industrial Innovation, Linz.

Dieter Roller and Ernst Gschwind
Hewlett Packard GmbH
Mechanical Design Division
Herrenberger Strasse 130
D-7030 Boeblingen
W. GERMANY

# Open Questions in the Application of Multivariate B-splines

## Malcolm Sabin

**Abstract.** There was a great interest a few years ago in the multivariate $B$-spline ideas which were opened by Schoenberg's geometric analogy. These have turned out so far to be a beautiful insight without direct practical application. This paper identifies two rather obvious potential applications, and explores the problems which yet need to be solved to bring them to fruition.

## §1. Introduction

This paper has three main sections. Section 2 recapitulates the multivariate $B$-spline concepts, focusing in particular on the simplex spline. Section 3 examines the scattered data contouring problem, identifies the advantage which the simplex spline approach ought to bring, and suggests some targets for research, giving some reasons why there may be difficulties. Section 4 examines a possible new field analysis method analogous to finite element, finite difference and boundary element methods. Section 5 looks at the $B$-spline-like methods which are not yet unified with the multivariate theory, in the hope that some mathematician will be stimulated to bridge the gap.

## §2. Multivariate B-splines

The univariate $B$-spline is a familiar concept to this audience. The actual $B$-spline functions may be approached from a number of different definitions:

- the piecewise polynomial functions of minimum support for a given continuity,
- convolution of the next lower order function,
- averaging of two instances of the next lower order function.

Mathematical Methods in Computer Aided Geometric Design
Tom Lyche and Larry L. Schumaker (eds.), pp. 529–537.
Copyright © 1989 by Academic Press, Boston.
ISBN 0-12-460515-X.

529

We took this into bivariate theory mainly by the tensor product concept, though certain bivariate non-tensor product forms were known ([4,13]).

Curry and Schoenberg [2] (as cited by Dahmen [3] and Boehm [1]) pointed out that the univariate $B$-splines could also be reached by taking a simplex, and associating, with each point on a line, the cross-sectional hyperarea of the simplex cut by the hyperplane of a parallel family which passed through that point.

From this insight came the natural generalisation of projection onto a plane or hyperplane, to give the bivariate or multivariate theory, and it was very pleasing that almost all the previous bivariate forms fell very naturally into this theoretical framework, though the tensor products and the forms defined over the semiregular St. Andrews grid and the hexagonal grid turned out to be projections of a box rather than of a simplex ([16]).

## §3. Scattered Data Contouring

The production of a contour map from data values at specific points is a process happening regularly and frequently in computer centres all over the world. There are sufficient ideas to fill numerous books, as almost every scientific discipline has felt the need for methods to achieve this, and very many scientists have felt moved to invent or develop methods and algorithms to cater for their immediate needs. Most ingenuity has been applied to the scattered data problem, where the known points do not lie on a regular grid, but are scattered wherever the data was actually available ([15]).

One of the popular methods in the bivariate case uses a triangulation joining the data points (the Delaunay triangulation is deservedly regarded as a good one for this purpose) and then fills in the triangles so formed either with plane triangular facets, with higher order triangular patches or with piecewise patches to give continuity of first (or higher) derivatives.

The simplest such piecewise patch giving a $C^1$ surface uses Powell-Sabin triangles ([12]), each of which contains six quadratic pieces. Because, on average, there are twice as many triangles in a plane lattice as there are data points, this gives about twelve times as many quadratic triangles to contour as there are data points. The robustness of contouring of quadratic triangles makes this very effective.

However, $C^1$ continuity is achieved in this method by estimating the derivatives at the data points, and imposing those derivatives on the interpolated surface. It is therefore a Hermite method, with the advantage of locality of definition. We know, in the univariate and tensor product cases, that Hermite methods pay for this locality the price of using either more pieces than the spline, or else pieces of higher order, or else achieving a lower continuity.

It therefore seems an obvious question to ask whether a $C^1$ spline interpolant could be found with either lower order pieces, or else fewer pieces per data point, and multivariate $B$-spline theory is the obvious place to look. We need not look at lower order, since the only order less than quadratic is linear, and that will certainly not give $C^1$. Can we use fewer than twelve pieces per data point?

Looking for $C^1$ with quadratic pieces means taking simplices of five vertices in $\mathbb{R}^4$.

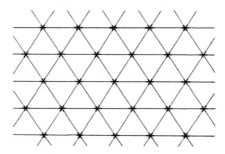

**Figure 1.** A regular triangular grid.

In the regular triangular grid case most of such a method is obvious. Divide the data points into threes, such that each triple forms a equilateral triangle of the grid. Each vertex of such a triangle points towards the base of a neighboring triangle. The choice of division is arbitrary within six possibilities, three of which point up, the other three down (sorry, this is an inelegance I don't like either). Place a vertex at the centroid of each triple.

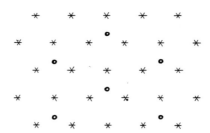

**Figure 2.** Vertices at the centroid of triples.

Construct simplex splines by taking five out of the six vertices surrounding each vertex, in such a way that the long side of the pentagon so formed lies near a side of the triple wholly inside the pentagon. There are three of these pentagons round each vertex. Each pentagon is the support of a quadratic simplex spline function whose maximum lies near one of the original data points.

Solve for the $B$-spline amplitudes. There is one equation for each original data point, and one coefficient for each $B$-spline function, and these are in one-to-one correspondence. In fact, the equations form a well-conditioned set, and so it will probably be satisfactory to solve by relaxation.

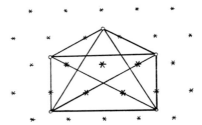

**Figure 3.** A simplex with its maximum near a data point.

The missing part of this method is the handling of the boundary. The nice property is that it gives a $C^1$ interpolant using only four triangles per data point, a factor of three better than the Powell-Sabin method.

The scattered data analog is much harder to see. There are two stages in the method as described above, though these need not necessarily have the same sequence in a more general technique:

(i) Choose a set of vertices for the support of the simplices.

The general technique of grouping data points into threes and using the centroids of the triples may still work, but one can imagine data distributions where it would be very artificial. Franke ([11]) has described ways of generating data sets with local density a given function of that of the given data.

(ii) Pick sets of five among them.

This is perhaps the better place to start, as the grouping into five generates functions, which we can then move so that the data points are covered in a well-conditioned fashion. Dahmen [3] has an elegant staircase argument for this, which relies on vertices being close to coincident. I had two further ideas for this, neither of which has been developed beyond the gleam-in-the-eye stage.

The first method chose a single simplex by some arbitrary choice, and then worked out, filling a four-dimensional Toblerone bar in the same way that the unequal interval quadratic univariate splines may be regarded as filling a three-dimensional bar. The purpose of this construction is to ensure by construction that the functions generated sum to unity. Filling the outer product of unit area with the abscissa space does ensure this.

The actual filling process involved labelling the vertices, edges and faces of each simplex with its relationship to the enclosing bar. Stepping across any (3D) face of the starting simplex to the nearest point beyond it produces another simplex whose relationship to the bar may be deduced from the labelling of the crossed face.

I do not have enough four-dimensional insight to evaluate this possibility. I could not even relate the regular grid case above to this idea by labelling it, though I am not convinced it is impossible.

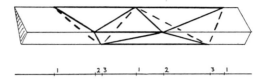

**Figure 4.** Labelling of vertices.

The second idea was to use higher order Voronoi diagrams to choose fives from the vertex set.

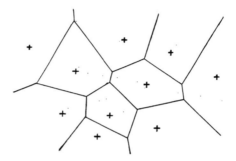

**Figure 5.** First order Voronoi diagram.

The first order Voronoi diagram divides a domain into regions, each of which contains those points which are closer to one corresponding vertex than to any other.

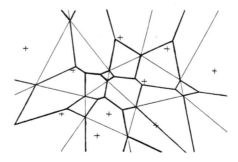

**Figure 6.** Second order Voronoi diagram.

The second order diagram divides the domain into pieces each of which contains those points which have a particular pair of vertices as closest two. Not every pair of vertices has a corresponding region. In fact, there will be such a region if and only if the first order regions for those two vertices abut.

Similarly, the third order diagram divides the domain into pieces with a particular triple as the three closest. Only those triples have regions for which two second order regions abut.

The fifth order Voronoi diagram by this same mechanism identifies quintuples of vertices on the basis of locality. I thought this was a lovely idea until I discovered that it would not produce the regular grid example. Indeed, it is difficult to imagine any plausible locality-based selection of fives (and I want the locality base in order to achieve good conditioning of the result), which would omit the vertex in the middle of the regular grid house-shape from the quintuple on that base.

Even if my first ideas fail, the challenge is still there, to produce a scattered data contouring method which uses hopefully only four, but certainly less than twelve, quadratic triangles per data point.

## §4. Field Analysis

Suppose that the first challenge has been solved. It will then be obvious to some of us that there is another application which can build on the same ideas. Instead of interpolating a scalar function over a multivariate domain, we could interpolate a vector function, merely by treating the components independently. If this vector function represented a displacement field, we could use the method to solve strength and stiffness problems.

The strain energy of the interpolated field could be evaluated, and the displacements of the control points chosen to minimize it subject to the boundary conditions. In fact this problem is considerably simpler, because we do not have to worry about interpolated points at all. We can just minimize the strain energy by choosing the coefficients of the B-spline functions.

Such an approach will give a large linear system of equations, which may be solved to give the minimum. In that sense, it will look exactly like finite elements, finite differences, finite volumes, and boundary elements. It will differ in that

- it can match arbitrary boundaries

- it has a $C^1$ solution, and is therefore efficient for elliptic problems whose solutions themselves have high continuity. (Don't try it on hyperbolic problems with shock waves)

- subdivision of the simplices gives relatively easy adaption to the spatial frequencies found in the solution, so that a coarse initial mesh can give information about where finer discretisation is necessary. This property holds for tetrahedral meshing in 3D, which unfortunately is a long way from having the previous property

– the bandwidth is no worse than conventional quadratic finite elements, and probably somewhat less than tensor product quadratic B-spline elements.

I do not suppose that this method will completely supplant the four existing methods, but there may well be a niche for it, just as each of the four has its own applications now. So far, I have only heard of one experiment with this, that of Tom Grandine ([7]) at Wisconsin. He reports that the solution itself was a very good one, but in his implementation he found that the time taken to set up the system matrix was prohibitive. However, I suspect that he was identifying all of the pieces of every basis function and using closed form integration for the evaluation of the stiffness terms. A numerical integration based on a regular grid not much denser than the mesh might give a different story. I have not had the opportunity to read Grandine's dissertation ([8]), in which full details are discussed. The papers by Grandine, [9] and [10], are more accessible and describe specific optimizations in the computation.

At the conference where this paper was presented, Wolfgang Dahmen pointed out that:

(i) *subdivision of a simplex cannot be carried out by joining the faces to a point in its interior, since this produces a linear dependence in the set of basis functions.* This is correct. However, division into sub–simplices can be performed without loss of rank by creating a new point on an edge which projects onto the boundary of the region of support, and joining that point to all faces not meeting the split edge. The subdivision does NOT have to propagate into adjacent simplices, as it would if the simplices were themselves conventional finite elements.

(ii) *work has already been done in this area by Gmelig Meyling, Pfluger and Traas of the University of Twente, Netherlands.* Since the conference I have received copies of Gmelig Meyling's publications, including [5] and [6], and I commend them to the attention of anyone considering working in this area. The paper of Traas [17] in this volume may also be of interest.

## §5. Multivariate B-splines Still Outside the Multivariate Theory

Preceding sections of this paper have dealt with applications of the multivariate B-spline theory. This section identifies a direction in which the theory itself could well be extended.

The main limitation of the multivariate theory in my view is that it provides only functions over manifolds of topological genus 1, the hyperplane and the hypertorus. There exist B-spline-like functions over other manifolds. For example, associating vector coefficients with

$$(1 \pm x)^2, \quad (1 \pm y)^2, \quad (1 \pm z)^2 \quad \text{over} \quad x^2 + y^2 + z^2 = 1$$

maps the sphere into a distorted sphere. These functions are continuous in all derivatives (Bézier-ish), but one can put together eight instances of the triangle I described in [14] to form a sphere from piecewise cubics (B-spline-like).

We require methods for scattered data interpolation of, for example, skin temperatures or boundary layer thicknesses over a complete aircraft. How may the theory be extended to generate functions over such manifolds? I do not pretend to be able to address this one myself, but I do commend it to the attention of others, because I have a sneaking suspicion that making this extension may well provide insights necessary for proper solution of the other questions.

This suspicion stems from the fact that an irregular mesh may have some regions which are almost regular: regions which are slightly less regular may well have five neighbors round a vertex instead of six, and B-splines over an icosahedron cannot fail to be relevant.

## References

1. Boehm, W., Subdividing Multivariate Splines, Comput. Aided Design **15** (1983), 345–352.
2. Curry, H. B. and I. J. Schoenberg., Polya frequency functions IV: The fundamental spline functions and their limits, J. Analyse Math. **17** (1966), 71–107.
3. Dahmen, W. and C. A. Micchelli, Multivariate splines – a new constructive approach, in *Surfaces in Computer Aided Design*, R. Barnhill and W. Boehm (eds.), North Holland, Amsterdam, 1983, 191–215.
4. Frederickson, P. O., Quasi-interpolation, extrapolation, and approximation on the plane, Conf. Numerical Math., Winnipeg, 1971, 159–167.
5. Gmelig Meyling, R. H. J., Polynomial spline approximation in two variables, dissertation, University of Amsterdam, 1986.
6. Gmelig Meyling, R. H. J., On algorithms and applications for bivariate B-splines, in *Algorithms for Approximation*, J. C. Mason and M. G. Cox (eds.), Clarendon Press, Oxford, 1985, 83–96.
7. Grandine, T. A., Private communication, 1988.
8. Grandine, T. A., Computing with multivariate simplex splines, dissertation, University of Wisconsin, Madison, 1985.
9. Grandine, T. A., Computational cost of simplex spline functions, SIAM J. Numer. Anal. **24** (1987), 887–890.
10. Grandine, T. A., The evaluation of inner products of multivariate simplex splines, SIAM J. Numer. Anal. **24** (1987), 882–886.
11. McMahon, J. R. and R. Franke, Knot selection for least squares thin plate splines, preprint.
12. Powell, M. J. D. and M. A. Sabin, Piecewise quadratic approximations on triangles, ACM Trans. Math. Software **3** (1977), 316–325.
13. Sabin, M. A., The use of piecewise forms for the numerical representation of shape, dissertation, Budapest, 1977.
14. Sabin, M. A., Non-rectangular surface patches suitable for inclusion in a B-spline surface., *Proc. Eurographics 83*, Ten Hagen (ed.), North Holland, Amsterdam, 1984, 57–69.

15. Sabin, M. A., Contouring: the state of the art, in *Fundamental Algorithms for Computer Graphics*, R. A. Earnshaw (ed.), Springer-Verlag, Heidelberg, 1985, 411–482.
16. Sablonnière, P., A catalog of B-splines of degree ≤ 10 on a three direction mesh, Rpt. ANO-132, Univ. Lille, 1984.
17. Traas, C. R., Approximation of surfaces constrained by a differential equation, using bivariate quadratic simplex splines, in *Mathematical Methods in Computer Aided Geometric Design*, T. Lyche and L. Schumaker (eds.), Academic Press, N. Y., 1989, 593–599.

Malcolm Sabin
Fegs Ltd., Oakington
Cambridge, CB4 5BA
ENGLAND

# On Global $GC^2$ Convexity Preserving Interpolation of Planar Curves by Piecewise Bézier Polynomials

R. Schaback

**Abstract.** For sequences of planar data points whose piecewise linear interpolant has the property that two successive direction changes add up to at most an acute angle, there is a unique global $GC^2$ interpolant consisting of convex quadratic polynomial pieces where the data allow a convex interpolant. Cubic pieces are used where the data require inflection points. Collinear data points are interpolated by straight lines embedded on both sides by cubic pieces. Not-a-knot boundary conditions are possible.

## §1. Global Parametric Spline Interpolation

In the nonparametric case, the standard construction of a polynomial spline function $s(x)$ interpolating planar data

$$b_i = (x_i, y_i),\ 1 \leq i \leq n, \qquad x_i < x_{i+1} \quad \text{for} \quad 1 \leq i \leq n-1$$

is carried out by taking the data points as *knots* or *breakpoints*. The degree of the polynomial pieces between the knots is then determined by continuity requirements for $s$ and its derivatives. For $C^2$ continuity of $s$, this leads to cubic polynomials, but two additional boundary conditions must be specified to yield a fully determined solution.

In the parametric case, an analogous *standard* interpolant to a given sequence of data points

$$b_i \in \mathbb{R}^2,\ 1 \leq i \leq n, \qquad b_i \neq b_{i+1} \quad \text{for} \quad 1 \leq i \leq n-1 \qquad (1)$$

should also have breakpoints at the data points $b_i$, and the degree of the parametric polynomial curve between $b_i$ and $b_{i+1}$ should also be determined

Mathematical Methods in Computer Aided Geometric Design
Tom Lyche and Larry L. Schumaker (eds.), pp. 539–547.
Copyright © 1989 by Academic Press, Boston.
ISBN 0-12-460515-X.

by the continuity requirements. For visual or geometric $C^2$ continuity, two scalar conditions at each inner breakpoint have to be satisfied (continuity of tangent direction and curvature) and therefore the parametric interpolating piece should have only two additional degrees of freedom between the specified endpoints $b_i$ and $b_{i+1}$. This implies that the interpolant should be a piecewise *quadratic* Bézier polynomial defined by triplets of control points $b_i, \tilde{b}_i, b_{i+1}$ for $1 \leq i \leq n-1$. As in the nonparametric case, two remaining degrees of freedom have to be fixed by certain boundary conditions. For example, tangent directions at $b_1$ and $b_n$ can be prescribed by two additional points $b_0 \neq b_1$ and $b_{n+1} \neq b_n$ with the requirement that the lines $L(b_0, b_1)$ and $L(b_n, b_{n+1})$ through $b_0, b_1$ and $b_n, b_{n+1}$, respectively, are tangents to the solution at $b_1$ and $b_n$.

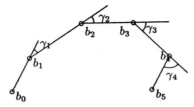

**Figure 1.** Data set $(n = 4)$ with prescribed tangent directions.

The following facts about the interpolant were proven in [3]:

1. A solution of the interpolation problem cannot have an inflection point, and therefore the *chord angles*

$$\gamma_i = \angle(b_{i+1} - b_i, b_i - b_{i-1}), \ 1 \leq i \leq n,$$

measured by arc length values in $(-\pi, \pi]$, must necessarily all be in $(0, \pi)$ or all in $(-\pi, 0)$. That is, the piecewise linear interpolant of the data always *turns left* or always *turns right* in the sense of an observer moving along the curve. This is a necessary condition depending on the data only. For the rest of this section, we restrict ourselves to the case $\gamma_i \in (0, \pi)$.

2. The interpolation problem is *solvable* if

$$\gamma_i + \gamma_{i+1} < \pi \quad \text{for} \quad 1 \leq i \leq n-1. \tag{2}$$

There are unsolvable cases where (2) is not satisfied.

3. The interpolation problem is *uniquely* solvable, if

$$\gamma_i + \gamma_{i+1} < \pi/2 \quad \text{for} \quad 1 \leq i \leq n-1. \tag{3}$$

There are cases with multiple solutions where (3) is not satisfied.

This paper extends [3] by dealing with

1. cubic pieces to be inserted where the data require inflection points;
2. straight lines interpolating sections of collinear data, with cubic pieces at ends;
3. not–a–knot boundary conditions.

The interpolation problem can be written as a system of equations involving the *tangent angles*

$$\alpha_i = \text{ angle between chord } b_{i+1} - b_i \text{ and tangent at } b_i$$

and *chord lengths* $h_i = \|b_{i+1} - b_i\|_2$. Equating curvature at both sides of $b_i$ (see [3]) yields the tridiagonal system

$$\frac{\sin(\gamma_i - \alpha_i)\sin^2(\gamma_i - \alpha_i + \alpha_{i-1})}{2h_{i-1}\sin^2\alpha_{i-1}} = \frac{\sin\alpha_i \sin^2(\gamma_{i+1} - \alpha_{i+1} + \alpha_i)}{2h_i \sin^2(\gamma_{i+1} - \alpha_{i+1})} \qquad (4)$$

for $2 \leq i \leq n - 1$. The tangent angles $\alpha_i$ are variables for $2 \leq i \leq n - 1$ satisfying $0 < |\alpha_i| < |\gamma_i|$, while the boundary conditions fix $\alpha_1 = \gamma_1$, $\alpha_n = 0$. An equivalent formulation of the interpolation problem can be given by fixing $b_1, \ldots, b_n$ as interpolation points and using two angles $\gamma_1 = \alpha_1$ and $\gamma_n$ to describe directions of boundary tangents, leaving $\alpha_2, \ldots, \alpha_{n-1}$ as variables in the system (4) with $\alpha_n = 0$.

If (4) is solved, the interior control point $\widetilde{b}_i$ of a quadratic piece defined by control points $b_i, \widetilde{b}_i, b_{i+1}$ simply is constructed as the intersection of the tangents at $b_i$ and $b_{i+1}$ defined by the corresponding tangent angles. However, (4) was not used in [3] to prove existence and uniqueness of a solution; certain geometrical arguments (a *shooting strategy*) proved to be more powerful.

## §2. Cubic Pieces at Inflection Points

**Definition 2.1.** *A section* $b_{i-1}b_i$, $3 \leq i \leq n-1$, *of a data set (1) is called an inflection piece, if the chord angles satisfy* $\gamma_{i-1} \cdot \gamma_i < 0$.

We intend to use a cubic Bézier polynomial to interpolate in an inflection piece, but we want to retain the standard construction for the rest of the interpolation. This will automatically yield a convexity preserving interpolant. In view of (2) and (3), we tacitly assume all chord angles $\gamma_i$ at inflection pieces to be acute.

**Algorithm 2.2.**

**Step 1.** *Let* $b_{i-1}b_i$ *be an inflection piece for the data set (1). Fix angles*

$$\alpha_j^* = \gamma_j h_j / (h_j + h_{j-1}), \qquad j = i - 1, i \qquad (5)$$

*for boundary tangents at* $b_{i-1}$ *and* $b_i$. *This defines two subproblems by*

a) *interpolation points* $b_1, \ldots, b_{i-1}$ *and tangent directions* $\alpha_1^*, \alpha_{i-1}^*$,

b) interpolation points $b_i, \ldots, b_n$ and tangent directions $\alpha_i^*, \gamma_n$.

**Step 2.** Assume $|\alpha_i^*| \leq |\alpha_{i-1}^*|$. If the condition

$$\|b_i - b_{i+1}\| \sin |\alpha_i^*| \sin^2(|\alpha_{i-1}^*| - |\alpha_i^*|) < \frac{3}{4} \|b_i - b_{i-1}\| \sin^2 |\alpha_i^*| \sin(|\gamma_i| - |\alpha_i^*|) \quad (6)$$

is satisfied, solve both subproblems and proceed to Step 3. Otherwise replace $\alpha_{i-1}^*$ by a value that satisfies both restrictions, e.g. $\alpha_{i-1}^* := -\alpha_i^*$, and proceed as before.

**Step 3.** Find a cubic Bézier polynomial that interpolates data points, tangent directions and curvature values of the two partial solutions of Step 2 at $b_{i-1}$ and $b_i$. This can be done by solving a system of two quadratic equations, as will be shown later.

**Remark :** Asymptotically,

$$\alpha_j = \gamma_j h_j / (h_j + h_{j-1}) + \mathcal{O}(h^2)$$

$$\tan \alpha_j = 1/2 \cdot h_j \cdot \kappa(b_j) + \mathcal{O}(h^2)$$

hold for sufficiently dense data samples from smooth curves, where $h :=$ $\max_j h_j$ tends to zero and where $\kappa(b_j)$ is the curvature of the curve at the data point $b_j$. This makes the choice (5) of tangent angles in Step 1 reasonable, and implies that (6) is automatically satisfied for large data sets sampled with bounded mesh ratio $h_j / h_{j+1}$ from a smooth curve.

Step 3 requires the solution of a Hermite–type interpolation problem by a cubic Bézier polynomial, where function values, tangent directions, and curvature values at two points $A$ and $D$ have to be reproduced. As was already pointed out by de Boor, Höllig, and Sabin in [1], a solution does not necessarily exist. Unfortunately, the approach of [1] does not carry over directly to this situation (in their terminology we would need $\rho_0 \cdot \rho_1 < 0$), but we use a similar method to prove

**Theorem 2.3.** Under the conditions of Step 2, a unique solution of Step 3 exists.

**Proof:** Let $A, B, C, D$ be the control points of the required cubic Bézier polynomial that interpolates at $A$ and $D$ and has tangent angles $\alpha_A$ and $\alpha_D$ defined as in Figure 2.

Curvature values $\kappa_A$ and $\kappa_D$ at $A$ and $D$ are expressed by two points $B'$ and $C'$ on the tangents $T_A$ and $T_D$ at $A$ and $D$ such that the quadratic Bézier polynomials with control points $A, B', D$ and $A, C', D$ attain $\kappa_A$ and $\kappa_D$ at $A$ and $D$, respectively. That is,

$$|\kappa_A| = \frac{\|A - D\| \sin \alpha_A}{2\|A - B'\|^2}, \qquad |\kappa_D| = \frac{\|A - D\| \sin \alpha_D}{2\|D - C'\|^2}.$$

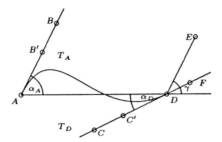

**Figure 2.** Local insertion of a cubic piece with an inflection point.

Now the curvature of the cubic piece must be

$$|\kappa_A| = \frac{2\,\mathrm{dist}(C, T_A)}{3\|A - B\|^2}, \qquad |\kappa_D| = \frac{2\,\mathrm{dist}(B, T_D)}{3\|D - C\|^2}.$$

Introducing the variables

$$x := \|A - B\|/\|A - B'\|, \qquad y := \|D - C\|/\|D - C'\|$$

and the constants

$$u := \frac{\|D - C'\|\sin(\alpha_A - \alpha_D)}{\|A - D\|\sin\alpha_A}, \qquad v := \frac{\|A - B'\|\sin(\alpha_A - \alpha_D)}{\|A - D\|\sin\alpha_D}$$

a little calculation produces the system

$$\frac{3}{4}x^2 - 1 = -uy, \qquad \frac{3}{4}y^2 - 1 = vx. \tag{7}$$

In case of $\alpha_A = \alpha_D$, we have $u = v = 0$, and find $x = y = 2/\sqrt{3}$ as unique positive solutions.

If we assume $\alpha_A > \alpha_D$, a straightforward discussion of the parabolae (7) yields existence of a unique positive solution whenever $u < \sqrt{3}/2$. Since

$$u^2 = \frac{\sin\alpha_D\sin^2(\alpha_A - \alpha_D)}{\|A - D\|\sin^2\alpha_A \cdot 2|\kappa_D|}$$

depends on $\kappa_D$, we try to express $\kappa_D$ by angles. If $D, F, E$ are the control points of the next quadratic piece (see Figure 2), we have

$$|\kappa_D| = \frac{\|D - E\|\sin(\gamma - \alpha_D)}{2\|D - F\|^2} \geq \frac{\sin(\gamma - \alpha_D)}{2\|D - E\|},$$

because (3) makes the angle at the control point $F$ obtuse. Then

$$u^2 \leq \frac{\|D - E\|\sin\alpha_D\sin^2(\alpha_A - \alpha_D)}{\|A - D\|\sin^2\alpha_A\sin(\gamma - \alpha_D)},$$

and $u < \sqrt{3}/2$ is satisfied if (6) holds in the form

$$\|D - E\|\sin\alpha_D\sin^2(\alpha_A - \alpha_D) < \frac{3}{4}\|A - D\|\sin^2\alpha_A\sin(\gamma - \alpha_D). \quad \blacksquare$$

When an inflection point is enforced by a boundary condition (*i.e.*, $i = 2$ or $i = n$ in Definition 2.1), a similar strategy is possible.

## §3. Straight Sections

**Definition 3.1.** *If a data set (1) contains collinear points*

$$b_i, b_{i+1}, \ldots, b_{i+k}, \qquad k \geq 2, \quad 1 \leq i \leq n - k, \tag{8}$$

*we call $b_i, \ldots, b_{i+k}$ a straight section of the data set.*

Straight sections should be interpolated by straight lines. Each straight section splits the interpolation problem and requires *patching* to a neighboring standard solution.

**Algorithm 3.2.** *Assume $i > 1$ for a straight section (8) and the solvability of the piecewise quadratic interpolation problem in $b_1, \ldots, b_i$ with prescribed tangent direction $b_{i+1} - b_i$ at $b_i$. First, solve this problem. The last piece of the solution has control points $b_{i-1}, \widetilde{b_{i-1}}, b_i$. Then, with*

$$\widehat{b_{i-1}} := \frac{1}{4}\widetilde{b_{i-1}} + \frac{3}{4}b_i,$$

*replace the last section of the solution by the cubic Bézier polynomial defined by control points $b_{i-1}, \widetilde{b_{i-1}}, \widehat{b_{i-1}}, b_i$.*

**Theorem 3.3.** *The algorithm produces a geometrically $C^2$ patch between the first $i - 2$ pieces of the interpolant of $b_1, \ldots, b_i$ and the linear interpolant of $b_i, \ldots, b_{i+k}$.*

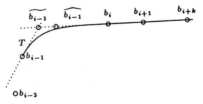

**Figure 3.** Local insertion of a cubic piece near a straight section.

**Proof:** If $T$ is the tangent at $b_{i-1}$; *i.e.*, the line through $b_{i-1}$ and $\widetilde{b_{i-1}}$, the absolute value $\kappa$ of the curvature at $b_{i-1}$ can be expressed as

$$\kappa = \frac{1}{2}\frac{\text{dist}(b_i, T)}{\|b_{i-1} - \widetilde{b_{i-1}}\|^2} = \frac{2}{3}\frac{\text{dist}(\widehat{b_{i-1}}, T)}{\|b_{i-1} - \widehat{b_{i-1}}\|^2},$$

using a quadratic and a cubic piece. The algorithm's choice of the additional control point $\widehat{b_{i-1}}$ for the cubic piece on the line through $b_i, \ldots, b_{i+k}$ guarantees

$$\text{dist}(\widehat{b_{i-1}}, T) = \frac{3}{4}\text{dist}(b_i, T),$$

as required for reproduction of $\kappa$ at $b_{i-1}$. ∎

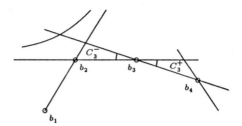

**Figure 4.** Local behavior of the shooting method.

## §4. Not–a–knot Boundary Conditions

If no tangent direction in the first point of a data set (1) is available, one can try to interpolate $b_1, b_2, b_3$ by a single quadratic Bézier polynomial, placing the first breakpoint at $b_3$. We do not prescribe the parameter $t$ at which $b_2$ is to be interpolated.

**Theorem 4.1.** *Let $b_1, b_2, b_3$ be three different and non–collinear points, and let $b_1, B, b_3$ be the control points of a quadratic Bézier polynomial $Q$ that interpolates $b_1, b_2, b_3$ successively. Then $B$ lies on the hyperbola*

$$b_2 + u(b_1 - b_2) + v(b_3 - b_2), \qquad u, v \in \mathbb{R}, \qquad u \cdot v = 1/4, \qquad u < 0. \qquad (9)$$

*Conversely, $Q(t) = b_2$ holds for $t \in (0, 1)$, if $B$ is taken as*

$$B(t) = b_2 - \frac{1-t}{2t}(b_1 - b_2) - \frac{t}{2(1-t)}(b_3 - b_2). \qquad (10)$$

**Proof:** Write the condition $Q(t) = b_2$ in the barycentric coordinates used in (9). ∎

**Theorem 4.2.** *For a data set satisfying (3) the usual boundary conditions may be replaced by not–a–knot–conditions, and there will still be a unique solution.*

**Proof:** We use the shooting technique of [3] and consider the image $F(B(t))$ of the hyperbola (10) under the mapping $F$ defined by the property that the quadratic Bézier polynomials with control points $b_1, B, b_3$ and $b_3, F(B), b_4$ are geometrically $C^2$ continuous at $b_3$. Some simple monotonicity arguments imply that $F(B(t))$ is a (radially) monotonic transversal curve in the sense of [3] contained in the cone $C_3^+$ (see Figure 4). This proves feasibility of the not–a–knot–condition at one end of the data set.

If a shooting strategy is carried out from the other end, a curve starting from $b_3$ results, extending monotonically (in the sense of [3]) into the cone $C_3^-$, and reaching the line through $b_3, b_4$ asymptotically. Such a curve uniquely intersects $B(t)$, proving feasibility of the not-a-knot condition at both ends. ∎

Since the shooting strategy is numerically unstable, we have to reformulate the not–a–knot boundary condition in terms of the system (4). For $i = 3$ the left–hand–side of (4) has to be replaced by the curvature $\kappa_3$ at $b_3$ of the quadratic piece interpolating $b_1, b_2$, and $b_3$. Then $t$ has to be expressed by the variable $\alpha_3$. Introducing the angle $\delta = \gamma_3 - \alpha_3$ in Figure 5, we want to write $B(t)$ as a function $B(t(\delta))$ of $\delta$. Then the left–hand side of (4) for $i = 3$ becomes

$$\kappa_3 = \frac{\|b_3 - b_1\| \sin(\beta + \gamma_3 - \alpha_3)}{2\|B(t(\gamma_3 - \alpha_3)) - b_3\|^2},$$

where we used the notations defined in Figure 5.

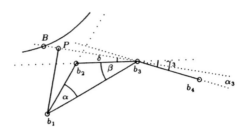

**Figure 5.** Reformulating the not-a-knot boundary condition.

We drop the arguments $\delta$ and $t$ for simplicity and first use the fact that $B, b_3$, and the projection $P$ of $b_1$ to the tangent are collinear:

$$B - b_3 = \lambda(P - b_3). \tag{11}$$

Then we express $B$ and $P$ in barycentric coordinates

$$B = b_2 + u_B(b_1 - b_2) + v_B(b_3 - b_2), \quad P = b_2 + u_P(b_1 - b_2) + v_P(b_3 - b_2),$$

eliminate $\lambda$ from (11) as

$$\lambda = \frac{u_B}{u_P} = \frac{1 - v_B}{1 - v_P},$$

and use $u_B \cdot v_B = 1/4$ to express $u_B$ and $v_B$ as functions of $u_P$ and $v_P$. With $w_P := u_P/(1 - v_P) = u_B/(1 - v_B) < 0$, we get

$$u_B = \frac{1}{2} w_P(1 + \sqrt{1 - w_P^{-1}}), \qquad 1 - v_B = \frac{1}{2}(1 + \sqrt{1 - w_P^{-1}}).$$

Having eliminated $B$, we are left with $P$, and some trigonometric reasoning gives the result

$$w_P = \frac{-\sin\delta}{\cos(\pi/2 - \alpha - \beta - \delta)} \frac{\|b_3 - b_2\|}{\|b_1 - b_2\|}.$$

This can be used to express $B - b_3$ via $u_B$ and $v_B$ as functions of $\delta$. ■

### References

1. de Boor, C., K. Höllig, and M. Sabin, High accuracy geometric Hermite interpolation, Comput. Aided Geom. Design **4** (1987), 269–278.
2. Schaback, R., Adaptive rational splines, Constr. Approx. , to appear.
3. Schaback, R., Interpolation in $\mathbb{R}^2$ by piecewise quadratic visually $C^2$ Bézier polynomials, NAM–Bericht 61, Univ. Göttingen, 1988.

Robert Schaback
Institut für Numerische und Angewandte Mathematik
Universität Göttingen
D–3400 Göttingen
W. GERMANY

EMAIL: rscmbab@ dgogwdg1.bitnet

# Best Interpolation with Free Nodes
# by Closed Curves

Karl Scherer

**Abstract.** Best interpolation with free nodes addresses the problem of designing a curve through prescribed points in $\mathbb{R}^d$ such that some smoothness functional is minimized; e.g., the $k^{th}$ derivative in the least square sense. In addition the nodes are allowed to vary freely. Here we consider closed curves; *i.e.*, the periodic counterpart of the problems considered in [7,6]. We prove existence of an optimal curve in the general case and uniqueness in the cubic case $k = 2$.

## §1. Introduction

Given data $\{y_i\}_{i=1}^n \in \mathbb{R}^d$ with $y_1 = y_n$ and nodes

$$\underline{t}: \qquad 0 = t_1 < t_2 < \ldots < t_n = 1, \qquad (1.1)$$

the problem is to find a curve $s(x) = (s_1(x), \ldots, s_d(x))$ attaining

$$\inf_{\underline{t}} \inf \{ \int_0^1 \|f^{(k)}\|^2 : f(t_i) = y_i, \quad 1 \le i \le n, \quad f \in \mathcal{L}_2^k(0,1) \}. \qquad (1.2)$$

Here $\mathcal{L}_2^k(0,1)$ is the space of all $\mathbb{R}^d$ - valued *periodic* functions whose components are $(k - 1)$ times differentiable with derivative in $L_2(0,1)$, and it is assumed that $k \le n$. A solution of (1.2), if one exists, must therefore be an interpolating periodic spline curve of degree $2k - 1$ and smoothness $C^{2k-2}$. This is well known from classical spline theory. The corresponding optimal set $\underline{t}$ of nodes reflects a kind of optimal parametrization. As a result, the solution curve has nice shape preserving properties and thus is well suited for design purposes (cf. the discussion at the end of this paper).

Mathematical Methods in Computer Aided Geometric Design
Tom Lyche and Larry L. Schumaker (eds.), pp. 549–559.

The above problem (for non-periodic curves) was introduced by Toepfer [9] and Marin [2] in the most important case $k = 2$ of cubic splines. They pointed out its usefulness for design purposes. Existence and uniqueness has been shown in [2] for scalar data. In the general case, existence has been proved in Scherer and Smith [7] under the assumption

$$y_i \neq y_{i+1}, \tag{1.3}$$

as well as some additional restrictions on the data. Uniqueness for data in $\mathbb{R}^d$ and $k = 2$ has been shown recently by the author. Here it is shown that the periodic problem (1.2) always has a solution which is unique if $k = 2$.

## §2. Existence

A standard approach to finding the solution of the inner infimum problem in (1.2) uses Bernoulli polynomials which appear as certain reproducing kernels. The idea is to consider for $r = 1, 2, \ldots$ the functions

$$B_r(t) := r! {\sum_l}' \frac{e^{2\pi l t}}{(i 2\pi l)^r}, \tag{2.1}$$

where the sum $\sum'$ is extended over all nonzero integers. It is well known that the restrictions to $(0, 1)$ satisfy

$$B_1(t) = t - 1/2, \qquad 0 < t < 1,$$

$$B_r'(t) = r B_{r-1}(t)$$

$$\int_0^1 B_r(t) dt = 0.$$

These are the defining properties of the Bernoulli polynomials. Also, it is easy to see that

$$\int_0^1 B_r(t - u) f^{(r)}(u) du = r!(-1)^r f(t)$$

for all $[0, 1]$ periodic functions with $r^{th}$ derivative in $L_2(0, 1)$ such that

$$\int_0^1 f(u) du = 0. \tag{2.2}$$

Hence, for $t_j \in (0, 1]$ and $k = 1, 2, \ldots$, the kernel

$$G_j(t) := B_{2k}(t_j - t)/k! \tag{2.3}$$

has the reproducing property

$$\int_0^1 G_j^{(k)}(u) f^{(k)}(u) = f(t_j) \tag{2.4}$$

for all functions satisfying (2.2). Now one can prove

**Lemma 2.1.** *Let $\gamma$ and $\gamma_1, \ldots, \gamma_n$ belong to $\mathbb{R}^d$. Then the function*

$$s(t) := \sum_{j=1}^{n} \gamma_j G_j(t) + \gamma \tag{2.5}$$

*is a $[0,1]$ periodic spline curve of degree $2k-1$ and knots $t_j$, and is the unique solution of the inner infimum problem in (1.2) iff the coefficients satisfy*

$$\sum_{j=1}^{n} \gamma_j G_j(t_l) + \gamma = y_l, \qquad 1 \le l \le n,$$

$$\sum_{i=1}^{n} \gamma_i = 0. \tag{2.6}$$

We do not prove this standard result, but remark only that the degree of $s(t)$ is actually $2k-1$ (rather than $2k$) since the leading term of $G_j(t)$ is $t^{2k}/k!$ independently of $j$, and is cancelled by the second equation in (2.6). The minimum property of $s(t)$ follows from the relation

$$\int_0^1 (s^{(k)}(t), f^{(k)}(t))dt = \sum_{j=1}^{n} (\gamma_j, f(t_j)) = 0, \tag{2.7}$$

which by (2.4) and the second equation in (2.6) holds for all functions $f$ in $\mathcal{L}_2^k(0,1)$ interpolating the zero data. Here $( \, , \, )$ denotes the scalar product in $\mathbb{R}^d$.

After these preparations it is not hard to prove

**Theorem 2.2.** *There exists a solution of problem (1.2); i.e., a sequence $\underline{t}^*$ of type (1.1) such that the corresponding spline curve defined by (2.3), (2.5) and (2.6) attains the infimum in (1.2).*

**Proof:** Let

$$\underline{t}^{(N)}: \qquad 0 = t_1^{(N)} < \ldots < t_n^{(N)} = 1$$

be sequences of knots such that the corresponding spline curves

$$S_N(t) := \sum_{j=1}^{n} \gamma_j^{(N)} B_{2k}(t_j^{(N)} - t) + \gamma^{(N)} \tag{2.8}$$

satisfy (2.6) and

$$I = \lim_{N \to \infty} \int_0^1 \|S_N^{(k)}(t)\|^2 dt,$$

where $I$ denotes the value of the infimum in (1.2). From

$$y_{l+1} - y_l = S_N(t_{l+1}^{(N)}) - \gamma^{(N)} - (S_N(t_l^{(N)}) - \gamma^{(N)})$$

$$= \int_0^1 S_N^{(k)}(t)(B_k(t_{l+1}^{(N)} - t) - B_k(t_l^{(N)} - t))dt/k!$$

and Schwarz's inequality, it follows that

$$(k! \, ||y_{l+1} - y_l||)^2$$

$$\leq \int_0^1 ||S_N^{(k)}(t)||^2 dt \int_0^1 |B_k(t_{l+1}^{(N)} - t) - B_k(t_l^{(N)} - t)|^2 dt$$

$$\leq M \int_0^1 |B_k(u) - B_k(u + t_l^{(N)} - t_{l+1}^{(N)})|^2 dt,$$

where $M$ is a constant independent of $N$. Therefore the assumption

$$\lim_{N \to \infty} |t_l^{(N)} - t_{l+1}^{(N)}| = 0$$

leads to a contradiction to (1.3). Consequently, there exists a subsequence of the $\underline{t}^{(N)}$, again denoted by $\underline{t}^{(N)}$, such that $\lim_{N \to \infty} t_l^{(N)} = t_l^*$ and

$$\underline{t}^* : \qquad 0 = t_1^* < t_2^* < \ldots < t_n^* = 1. \tag{2.9}$$

This implies uniform convergence of

$$\lim_{N \to \infty} B_{2k}(t_j^{(N)} - t) = B_{2k}(t_j^* - t), \qquad 1 \leq j \leq n.$$

In view of (2.9), the resulting functions are linearly independent so that the matrices in the systems (2.6) formed with respect to $\underline{t}^{(N)}$ tend to the non-singular matrix formed with respect to $\underline{t}^*$ . Hence the coefficients $\gamma_j^{(N)}$ and $\gamma^{(N)}$ of the $S_N(t)$ in (2.8) tend to vectors $\gamma_j^*, \gamma^*$ in $\mathbb{R}^d$. Finally, it follows that the spline curve

$$s^*(t) = \sum_{j=1}^n \gamma_j^* B_{2k}(t_j^* - t) + \gamma^*$$

satisfies (2.6) with respect to the knots $t^*$ and that

$$\lim_{N \to \infty} \int_0^1 ||s^{*(k)}(t) - S_N^{(k)}(t)||^2 dt = 0.$$

This shows that $s^*(t)$ is a solution of problem (1.2). ∎

For the actual computation of $s^*(t)$, there exists a more advantageous system than (2.6). It uses $B$-splines, and has a nearly band structure. We use it here for the cubic case $k = 2$ since the uniqueness proof will be based on it. In view of (2.5), we can represent $s''(t)$ for $t \in [0, 1]$ by

$$s''(t) = \sum_{i=1}^{n-2} a_i N_{i,2}(t) + a_{n-1} \tilde{N}_{n-1,2}(t), \tag{2.10}$$

where the $N_{i,2}(t)$ for $1 \leq i \leq n - 2$ are the unique piecewise linear functions with knots in $\underline{t}$ satisfying

$$N_{i,2}(t_j) = \delta_{i+1,j}.$$

To define $\tilde{N}_{n-1,2}(t)$, we extend the sequence $\underline{t}$ periodically by

$$t_{j(n-1)+i} := j + t_i, \qquad 1 \le i \le n-1, \quad j \in \mathbb{Z}, \tag{2.11}$$

and take it as the periodic extension of the $B$-spline $N_{n-1,2}(t)$ formed with respect to these knots. Setting

$$a_0 := a_{n-1}, \quad a_n := a_1, \quad w_j := y_{j+1} - y_j, \quad w_n := w_1, \tag{2.12}$$

we obtain the $(n-1) \times (n-1)$ system

$$(1/6)(h_j a_{j-1} + 2(h_j + h_{j+1})a_j + h_{j+1}a_{j+1}) = w_{j+1}h_{j+1}^{-1} - w_j h_j^{-1}, \tag{2.13}$$

with $1 \le j \le n-1$ for the coefficients in (2.10), where $h_i := t_{i+1} - t_i$ is defined with respect to (2.11) so that $h_n = h_1$. This system of equations is well known (cf. Section 2.4 of [8]). For short, we write it as

$$GA = Z, \tag{2.14}$$

where $A = (a_1, \ldots, a_{n-1})^t$ with $a_i \in \mathbb{R}^d$ and $Z = (z_1, \ldots, z_{n-1})^t$ with $z_j := w_{j+1}h_{j+1}^{-1} - w_j h_j^{-1}$. The matrix $G$ is a tridiagonal matrix except for the first and $(n-1)^{st}$ row where additionally entries $h_1$ and $h_n = h_1$ appear in the last and first column, respectively. We remark that the equations (2.13) are obtained by evaluating

$$\int_0^1 s''(t)N_{j,2}(t)dt \quad \text{for} \quad 1 \le j \le n-2 \quad \text{and} \quad \int_0^1 s''(t)\tilde{N}_{n-1,2}(t)dt$$

which guarantees the minimum property of $s(t)$ in a similar way as in (2.7).

The value of the inner infimum in (1.2) for $k = 2$ is now computed as

$$\int_0^1 \|s''(t)\|^2 dt = \langle A, Z \rangle,$$

where the scalar product $\langle \, , \, \rangle$ is defined by

$$\langle A, Z \rangle := \sum_{j=1}^{n-1} (a_j, z_j),$$

and $( \, , \, )$ is the scalar product in $\mathbb{R}^d$. Problem (1.2) is therefore equivalent to

$$\inf_{\underline{h} \in K} \{F(\underline{h}) := \langle A, Z \rangle : GA = Z\}, \tag{2.15}$$

with the set $K$ being defined by

$$K := \{\underline{h} = (h_1, \ldots, h_{n-1}) : \quad h_i > 0, \quad \sum_{i=1}^{n-1} h_i = 1\}.$$

## §3. Uniqueness

The treatment of the uniqueness question follows along the same lines as the proof given in [6] for the nonperiodic case and $k = 2$ . A basic observation is that problem (2.15) is equivalent to the min - max problem

$$\inf_{\underline{h} \in K} \sup_A \phi(A, \underline{h}) := -\langle A, G, A \rangle + 2\langle A, Z \rangle. \tag{3.1}$$

The supremum is attained iff the gradient of $\phi$ with respect to A vanishes; *i.e.*,

$$0 = \frac{\partial \phi}{\partial A} = -2GA + 2Z, \tag{3.2}$$

which coincides with (2.14). In this case, one has $\phi(A, \underline{h}) = \langle A, Z \rangle = F(\underline{h})$. A critical point of (3.1) is then given by

$$0 = \mu + \frac{d\phi}{dh_j} = \frac{\partial \phi}{\partial A} \frac{dA}{dh_j} + \frac{\partial \phi}{\partial h_j}, \quad \sum_{j=1}^{n-1} h_j = 1,$$

where $\mu$ is a Lagrangian parameter. In view of (3.2), this is equivalent to

$$0 = \mu + \frac{\partial \phi}{\partial h_j} \quad , \quad 1 \le j \le n-1 \quad ; \quad \sum_{j=1}^{n-1} h_j = 1. \tag{3.3}$$

Hence the critical points of (2.15) and (3.1) are the same. For the following it is important to consider also the "dual" problem to (3.1); *i.e.*,

$$\sup_A \inf_{\underline{h} \in K} \phi(A, \underline{h}). \tag{3.4}$$

One easily notes that the critical points are again the same, since such a point in (3.4) must necessarily satisfy (3.3), and then

$$0 = \frac{d\phi}{dA} = \frac{\partial \phi}{\partial A} + \sum_{i=0}^{n-1} \frac{\partial \phi}{\partial h_i} \frac{dh_i}{dA} =$$

$$= \frac{\partial \phi}{\partial A} - \mu \sum_{i=1}^{n-1} \frac{dh_i}{dA} = \frac{\partial \phi}{\partial A}.$$

By the existence result of the previous section, there exists at least one solution pair $\underline{h}, A$ of the equations (3.2), (3.3) which is provided by a solution of (1.2) via

$$A = (s''(t_2), \dots, s''(t_n)),$$

since by (2.9) the corresponding $\underline{h}$ lies in the interior of $K$. The problem is then to single out this solution from the other critical points which may enter through the nonlinear part (3.3) of the equations.

In the cubic case $k = 2$, the above equations have a particularly simple form. This is due to the relations

$$\langle A, GA \rangle = \sum_{i=1}^{n-1} h_i \alpha_i, \quad \alpha_i := \frac{1}{3}[\|a_i\|^2 + \|a_{i-1}\|^2 + (a_i, a_{i-1})], \tag{3.5}$$

$$\langle A, Z \rangle = \sum_{i=1}^{n-1} T_i / h_i, \quad T_i := -(a_i - a_{i-1}, w_i) \tag{3.6}$$

which can be verified under the convention (2.12) in the same manner as in [6] for the nonperiodic case. Hence the equations (3.3) take the form

$$0 = \mu - \alpha_i - 2T_i h_i^{-2}, \quad 1 = \sum_{i=1}^{n-1} h_i. \tag{3.7}$$

If all $T_i$ with $1 \le i \le n - 1$, are positive, they have a simple unique solution with $\mu > 0$ and $\underline{h} \in K$ given by

$$h_i = \sqrt{2T_i/(\mu - \alpha_i)}, \quad 1 = \sum_{i=1}^{n-1} \sqrt{2T_i/(\mu - \alpha_i)} \ .$$

Thus, in this case the function

$$\psi(A) := \inf_{\underline{h} \in K} \phi(A, \underline{h}) = \inf_{\underline{h} \in K} \sum_{i=1}^{n-1} (-\alpha_i h_i + 2T_i h_i^{-1})$$

can be calculated via these formulae. In [6] it is shown that $\psi(A)$ is well defined and continuous in $A$ on the closure $\overline{B}$ of the set

$$B := \{A \in (\mathbb{R}^{n-1})^d : T_i > 0, 1 \le i \le n - 1\}. \tag{3.8}$$

Obviously, one has $\psi(A) = -\infty$ outside of $\overline{B}$. In [6] it is proved that $\psi(A)$ can attain the supremum in (3.4) only for $A \in B$. The crucial property of $\psi(A)$ is then that $\psi$ has a negative definite Hessian on $B$ and hence is concave in $A$ on the convex closed set $\overline{B}$. With the help of these assertions one obtains quite easily

**Theorem 3.1.** *There exists exactly one solution $A^*, \underline{h}^*$ of problem (3.4) which has the properties that $A^* \in B$ and $\min_i h_i^* \equiv \delta > 0$. Every solution of problem (2.14) or (3.1) must be equal to it. Hence,*

$$\inf_{\underline{h} \in K} F(\underline{h}) = \inf_{\underline{h} \in K} \sup_A \phi(\underline{A}, \underline{h}) = \sup_{\underline{h} \in K} \phi(\underline{A}, \underline{h}), \tag{3.9}$$

*and the original infimum problem (1.2) has a unique solution.*

This theorem is proved in the same manner as in [6] since all the formulae which are needed have the same structure. We remark that this theorem does not guarantee that the infimum problem (2.14) possesses only one critical point satisfying (2.13) and the equations

$$0 = \lambda + \frac{\partial F}{\partial h_i} = \lambda - \alpha_i - 2T_i h_i^{-2}; \quad 1 = \sum_{i=1}^{n-1} h_i. \tag{3.10}$$

These equations are equivalent to (3.2), (3.3) or (3.7), respectively, and form the basis for the computation of the solution of (1.2). It is therefore interesting that in the scalar case $d = 1$, the stronger result is true that they possess only one solution. Before proving this, we note that the Hessian of $F$ has the form (cf. [6])

$$\frac{\partial^2 F}{\partial h_i \partial h_j} = \langle \frac{\partial A}{\partial h_i}, G \frac{\partial A}{\partial h_j} \rangle + 4\delta_{ij} T_i h_i^{-3}. \tag{3.11}$$

Now one observes that the equations (3.10) can be rewritten in still another equivalent form; namely,

$$0 = \partial F/\partial h_i - \partial F/\partial h_{i-1} = 2(s'''(t_i+) - s'''(t_i-), s'(t_i)) \tag{3.13}$$

for $i = 2, \ldots, n-1$, together with $\sum_{i=1}^{n-1} h_i = 1$. This follows from the formulae

$$s'(t_i+) = w_i h_i^{-1} - (2a_{i-1} + a_i)h_i/6$$

$$s'(t_i-) = w_{i-1} h_{i-1}^{-1} + (2a_{i-1} + a_{i-2})h_{i-1}/6,$$

valid for a cubic interpolating spline curve. Because of the periodicity of $s(t)$, one has the further condition

$$0 = (s'''(t_n+) - s'''(t_n-), s'(t_n)) \tag{3.13a}$$

which results from $0 = \partial F/\partial h_{n-1} - \partial F/\partial h_1 = \partial F/\partial h_{n-1} - \partial F/\partial h_n$. Here convention (2.12) has been used. Now we can prove

**Theorem 3.3.** *In the scalar case $d = 1$, the equations (3.10), where $A$ is determined by (2.14), have only one solution.*

**Proof:** Suppose $\underline{h}$ is a solution of (3.10) under the constraint (2.14), and suppose that the corresponding periodic function defined via (2.10) has the property

$$s'(t_i) = \begin{cases} 0, & \text{for } i = i_1 < i_2 < \cdots < i_r \in \{1, \ldots, n-1\} \\ \text{nonzero}, & \text{otherwise}. \end{cases}$$

Then (3.13) implies that $s(t)$ has knots only at the points $t_{i_1}, \ldots, t_{i_r}$, where $s'(t)$ has a zero. There can exist no other zeros of $s'(t)$, since otherwise $s'(t)$ would have at least 3 zeros in a segment $[t_{i_j}, t_{i_{j+1}}]$ and hence would vanish identically there as a polynomial of degree 2. But this would contradict (1.3) in view of the interpolating property.

Here we have taken into account the periodicity of $s(t)$ via (3.13a). Hence we conclude that $s(t)$ is a cubic periodic spline function which is strictly monotone between any two knots with $s'(t)$ alternating in sign. Furthermore, $s''(t)$ can be written in the form

$$s''(t) = \sum_{j=0}^{r} \hat{a}_j \hat{N}_{j,2}(t), \qquad (3.15)$$

where the $\hat{N}_{j,2}$ are formed as in (2.10) but with respect to the reduced set $t_1, t_{i_1}, \ldots, t_{i_r}, t_n$ (in case $t_{i_1} = t_1$ there appear only $r$ B-splines in (3.15)). Now the data $\{y_i\}_{i=1}^{n}$ must show the same pattern as $s(t)$; *i.e.*,

$$\operatorname{sgn} w_{i_j} w_{i_j+1} < 0, \qquad 1 \le j \le r. \qquad (3.16)$$

Suppose then that $\underline{\tilde{h}} \in K$ is a second solution of (3.10) and (2.14) and that the corresponding cubic interpolating spline function satisfies (3.14) for another set of integers $i'_1 < \ldots < i'_s \in \{1, \ldots, n-1\}$. Then the data must satisfy (3.16) with respect to this set of integers. But this can only be the case if $s = r$ and $i'_j = i_j$ for $1 \le j \le r$. Hence any solution of (3.10), (2.14) must give rise to a spline function of the form (3.15). If $t_{i_1} > t_1$, the vector

$$\underline{\hat{h}}: \qquad \hat{h}_j := t_{i_{j+1}} - t_{i_j}, \quad 0 \le j \le r; \quad t_{i_0} \equiv t_1, t_{i_{r+1}} \equiv t_n,$$

satisfies (3.13) with respect to the reduced set of knots and $\sum_{j=0}^{r} \hat{h}_j = 1$. Together with the obvious interpolating property, we therefore have for $s''(t)$ in (3.15) an equivalent system of equations constituted by (3.10) and (2.14) with respect to $\underline{\hat{h}}$ and $\hat{A} := (\hat{a}_0, \ldots, a_r)$. This system describes the critical points of the function $F(\underline{\hat{h}}) \equiv \int_0^1 |s''(t)|^2 dt$ which is defined for any cubic interpolating spline function of the form (3.15), where $\hat{A}$ satisfies (2.14). We then show that $F(\underline{\hat{h}})$ is strictly convex in $\underline{\hat{h}}$ under the assumption (3.16) on the data. Then there can exist only one critical point of $F(\underline{\hat{h}})$ and the theorem will be established.

First we remark that due to the periodicity of data, one has

$$\operatorname{sign} w_n = (-1)^{r+1} \operatorname{sign} w_1 = (-1)^{r+1} \operatorname{sign} w_n;$$

*i.e.*, r must be an odd number. Then we observe that between any two knots there is a point such that $s'(t)$ has alternating signs in these points. Due to periodicity there must exist $r + 1$ zeros of $s'(t)$ in $(t_1, t_n)$. By Rolle's theorem, $s''(t)$ possesses at least $r$ zeros in $(t_1, t_n)$. But if it had only $r$ zeros in $(t_1, t_n)$, its sign between the smallest zero and $t_1$ would be opposite to that of $s''(t_n) = s''(t_1)$, a contradiction. Hence, the piecewise linear function $s''(t)$ must have $r + 1$ zeros in $(t_1, t_n)$, which can only be the case when $s''(t)$ changes sign between any two knots. Therefore, the $\hat{a}_j$ in representation (3.15 ) must alternate in sign, too.

Now we consider the Hessian of $F(\hat{\underline{h}})$. According to (3.11) it suffices to show that the $T_i$ defined by (3.6) are positive in order that $F(\underline{h})$ is strict convex. But since the $\hat{a}_j$ alternate in sign, so do the numbers $\hat{a}_j - \hat{a}_{j-1}$ and also the numbers $w_{i_j}$ by (3.16). Hence, all $T_i$ have constant sign which must be positive in view of the relation in (3.6).  ∎

## §4. Discussion

On the basis of the preceding uniqueness result, convergent algorithms can be developed in order to compute the solution of (1.2). They find that solution of the nonlinear system (3.7) and its linear part (2.14) which gives the infimum in (1.2). In this respect one must remark that there are other solutions possible (for $T_i's$ with different sign) which are then critical points of $F(\underline{h})$, but which do not give the infimum in (1.2). Such an example has been found in the case of open curves by numerical experimentation. A report on this will appear elsewhere (cf. [5]).

Finally, we want to discuss the shape preserving properties in the case $k = 2$ of cubic splines. The basic comment here is, as has already been emphasized in [2,9], that (1.2) provides a well-defined optimality principle for selecting an interpolating curve. This is in contrast to most of the other methods where some *ad hoc* principle is used. In this respect, it should be noted that if in (1.2) with $k = 2$ we replace the second derivative by the curvature, the value of the new infimum is not less than the old one (cf. [6]). This meets somewhat the objective in [1], where curves with smooth curvature are considered to be "fair".

More specific requirements concerning curvature are continuity and in case $d = 2$ the sign preserving property, thus preserving convexity/concavity where the data indicate this behavior. This latter property is not fullfilled by the method given here, as test examples with data in "U" form show. The first continuity property may be violated for exceptional data. It should be possible to characterize such cases with the optimality principle considered here.

Further shape preserving properties can be observed in the scalar case. The argument of Theorem 2 shows that the solution curve is comonotone; *i.e.*, has exactly the same extrema as the data and is strictly increasing /decreasing between two extrema. Also, there is only one inflection point between two extrema. These nice properties are somewhat affected by the fact that the data must satisfy (1.3). Otherwise the optimal location of knots according to (1.2) would recognize them as one point only.

Finally, I mention as a general property of the solution of (1.2) that it is invariant under orthogonal transformations $U$ of the data in $\mathbb{R}^d$; in particular, it is rotation invariant. This is seen from the following equalities:

$$\inf\{\int_0^1 ||f^{(k)}||^2 : f(t_i) = Uy_i, \quad 1 \le i \le n, \quad f \in \mathcal{L}_2^k(0,1)\}$$

$$= \inf\{\int_0^1 ||(Ug)^{(k)}||^2 : (Ug)(t_i) = Uy_i, \quad 1 \le i \le n, \quad g \in \mathcal{L}_2^k(0,1)\}$$

$$= \inf\{\int_0^1 ||g^{(k)}||^2 : g(t_i) = y_i, \quad 1 \le i \le n, \quad g \in \mathcal{L}_2^k(0,1)\}.$$

Moreover, it is easily seen to be invariant under translation and scalar multiplication of the data. However, it is not invariant under scaling the data differently in each component, and thus is not affine invariant in the sense of [3].

## References

1. Farin, G., G. Rein, N. Sapidis, and A. J. Worsey, Fairing cubic B-splines curves, Comput. Aided Geom. Design **4** (1987), 91–103.
2. Marin, S., An approach to data parametrization in parametric cubic spline-interpolation problems, J. Approx. Theory **41** (1984), 64–86.
3. Nielson, G., Coordinate free scattered data interpolation, in *Topics in Multivariate Approximation*, C. K. Chui, L. L. Schumaker, and F. I. Utreras (eds.), Academic Press, N. Y., 1987, 175–184.
4. Ortega, J. M. and W. C. Rheinboldt, *Iterative Solution of Nonlinear Equations in Several Variables*, Academic Press, London and New York, 1970.
5. Rademacher, C., and K. Scherer, Algorithms for computing best cubic parametric interpolation, preprint, 1988.
6. Scherer, K., Uniqueness of best parmetric interpolation by cubic spline curves, preprint, 1988.
7. Scherer, K. and P. W. Smith, Existence of best parametric interpolation by curves, preprint, 1987.
8. Stoer, J., *Einführung in die Numerische Mathematik I*, Springer, Heidelberg, 1979.
9. Toepfer, H. J., Models for curve fitting, in *Numerische Methoden der Approximationstheorie 6*, L. Collatz (ed.), ISNM 59, Birkhäuser, Basel 1981, 209–216.

Karl Scherer
Institut für Angewandte Mathematik
Universität Bonn
Wegelerstrasse 6
5300 Bonn
W. GERMANY

# Segmentation Operators on Coons' Patches

## Guido Schulze

**Abstract.** Segmentation properties of Coons' patches are derived using an approach based on operators of special types on the patches. The set of all segmentation operators of this kind is determined, and in particular, segmentation operators are derived which yield surface segments with boundary curves that are not coordinate lines of the input surface.

## §1. Introduction

The surface equations derived by S.A. Coons [3] in 1964 characterize parametric surfaces that take given space curves as boundary curves and – if wanted – fit certain cross partial derivatives along these curves.

In 1969, W. J. Gordon pointed out that the surfaces described by Coons can be obtained by the Boolean sum $P_x \oplus P_y$ of parametric extensions $P_x$, $P_y$ of one-dimensional operators [4]. Since that time, the transfinite interpolation methods treated by Coons and Gordon have become more and more important in theory (blending-function methods in approximation theory) as well as in practice (design of industry products like car bodies and ship hulls with Coons' patches).

Further developments of Coons' method came up in applying transfinite interpolation methods to various fields. These include

- interpolation of curve networks by Gordon surfaces [5]
- interpolation of non-rectangular curve meshes [1,6]
- removal of twist incompatibilities using:
    - rational correction terms [7,2]
    - convex combination of Coons' patches [11,8]
    - geometric Coons' patches [9,10].

Mathematical Methods in Computer Aided Geometric Design
Tom Lyche and Larry L. Schumaker (eds.), pp. 561–572.
Copyright ⊝ 1989 by Academic Press, Boston.
ISBN 0-12-460515-X.

In the present paper, the concept of a Coons' patch of type $n$ is developed consistently from the invariance property of a Coons' patch under application of Boolean sums of interpolation operators. Here the main relations of Coons' patches to surface patches which are obtained by (tensor-) products of interpolation operators (tensor product surfaces, which we abbreviate as TP-surfaces) are given. In the case of polynomial blending-functions, the stated characterizations of these two surface classes are valid.

In the following sections, the segmentation properties of Coons' patches and TP-surfaces are investigated. For this we outline the concept of an automatic segmentation process which applied on an arbitrary Coons' patch yields a surface segment which itself belongs to the class of Coons' patches. The desired *"segment generators"* are mathematically represented by segmentation operators on the set $G^n$ of Coons' patches of type $n$. As a main result of the second section, we derive explicitly all segmentation operators $S$ on $G^n$ which allow a representation as composition $S(x) = x \circ \varphi$ of the surface parametrization $x$ and proper transformations $\varphi : \mathbb{R}^2 \to \mathbb{R}^2$ .

In Section 4 we determine all segmentation operators of the above kind which map a subclass $D^{(0,n)} \subset G^n$ onto $G^n$ . These operators allow us to create surface segments with boundary curves that are not coordinate lines of the input surface.

As concluding results we determine in the last section all segmentation operators on the set $T^n$ of TP-patches of type $n$, and we also give a segment generator that creates Coons-type surface segments on an arbitrary TP-surface.

## §2. Introduction to the Theory of Coons' Patches

**Definition 2.1.** *The linear operator* $H^n : C^n[0, 1] \longrightarrow C^n[0, 1]$ $(n \in \mathbb{N}_0)$

$$H^n f(u) = \sum_{k=0}^{n} \frac{\partial^k}{\partial u^k} f(0) F_{0,k}(u) + \frac{\partial^k}{\partial u^k} f(1) F_{1,k}(u)$$

*with*

$$F_{i,k} \in C^n[0, 1] \qquad \text{for} \quad i \in \{0, 1\} , \qquad k \in \{0, 1, \dots, n\}$$

*and*

$$F_{i,k}^{(\nu)}(j) = \delta_{ij} \cdot \delta_{\nu k} \qquad \text{for } i, j \in \{0, 1\}, \quad k, \nu \in \{0, 1, \dots, n\}$$

*is called the $n^{th}$ Hermite-Operator on $[0, 1]$ with blending functions $F_{i,k}$, $i \in \{0, 1\}$,   $k \in \{0, 1, \dots, n\}$ .*

**Definition 2.2.** *If $X$ is a vector space and $P : X \longrightarrow X$ is a linear operator, then we call the set Prec $P := \{x \in X \mid P(x) = x\}$ the precision set of $P$ .*

**Example 2.3.** *Because of its idempotence, the operator $H^n$ is a projector from $C^n[0, 1]$ into the vector space $V = sp(F_{0,0}, F_{1,0}, \dots, F_{0,n}, F_{1,n})$, and therefore*

$$Prec\ H^n = Im(H^n) = V .$$

**Definition 2.4.** *The parametric extensions $H_u^n$ and $H_v^n$ of the operator $H^n$ to $v$, respectively to $u$, are defined by*

$$H_u^n : C^{n,\ell}([0,1]^2) \longrightarrow C^{n,\ell}([0,1]^2) \qquad (\ell \in \mathbb{N}_0)$$

$$H_u^n f(u,v) := \sum_{k=0}^{n} \frac{\partial^k}{\partial u^k} f(0,v) \cdot F_{0,k}(u) + \frac{\partial^k}{\partial u^k} f(1,v) \cdot F_{1,k}(u)$$

*and*

$$H_v^n : C^{\ell,n}([0,1]^2) \longrightarrow C^{\ell,n}([0,1]^2)$$

$$H_v^n f(u,v) := \sum_{k=0}^{n} \frac{\partial^k}{\partial v^k} f(u,0) \cdot F_{0,k}(v) + \frac{\partial^k}{\partial v^k} f(u,1) \cdot F_{1,k}(v).$$

**Definition 2.5.**

i) *A parametric surface $x : [0,1]^2 \longrightarrow \mathbb{R}^3$ is called a Coons' patch of type $n$ ($n \in \mathbb{N}$) with blending functions $F_{0,0}, F_{1,0}, \ldots, F_{0,n}, F_{1,n}$, if the component functions $x^i$ of $x$ $(i = 1,2,3)$ satisfy the condition*

$$x^i \in Prec\,(H_u^{n-1} \oplus H_v^{n-1}) \qquad \text{for } i = 1,2,3\,,$$

*where the operator $H_u^{n-1} \oplus H_v^{n-1}$ is defined in general by $H_u^m \oplus H_v^m = H_u^m + H_v^m - H_u^m H_v^m$ $(m \in \mathbb{N}_0)$.*

ii) *$x$ is called a tensor product surface of type $n$ with blending functions $F_{0,0}, F_{1,0}, \ldots, F_{0,n}, F_{1,n}$, if the component functions $x^i$ satisfy*

$$x^i \in Prec\,(H_u^{n-1} \cdot H_v^{n-1}) \qquad \text{for } i = 1,2,3\,.$$

The definitions of Coons- and TP-surfaces lead to certain representation formulas.

**Theorem 2.6.** *(Representation theorem)*

i) *A Coons' patch of type $n$ $(n \in \mathbb{N})$ with blending functions*

$$F_{i,\nu},\, F_{j,\mu} \qquad i,j \in \{0,1\}\,, \quad \nu,\mu \in \{0,1,\ldots,n-1\}$$

*has a representation of the form*

$$x(u,v) = \sum_{i=0}^{1} \sum_{\nu=0}^{n-1} \frac{\partial^\nu}{\partial u^\nu} x \Big|_{(i,\nu)} F_{i,\nu}(u) + \sum_{j=0}^{1} \sum_{\mu=0}^{n-1} \frac{\partial^\mu}{\partial v^\mu} x \Big|_{(\mu,j)} F_{j,\mu}(v)$$

$$- \sum_{i,j=0}^{1} \sum_{\nu,\mu=0}^{n-1} \frac{\partial^\nu}{\partial u^\nu} \frac{\partial^\mu}{\partial v^\mu} x \Big|_{(i,j)} F_{i,\nu}(u) F_{j,\mu}(v)\,. \tag{2.1}$$

*A parametric surface $x \in C^{(2n,2n)}([0,1]^2)$ is a Coons' patch of type $n$ with blending functions $F_{i,\nu},\, F_{j,\mu} \in \Pi_{2n-1}$ if and only if*

$$\frac{\partial^{4n}}{\partial u^{2n} \partial v^{2n}} x(u,v) = 0 \quad \text{for all } (u,v) \in [0,1]^2. \tag{2.2}$$

ii) *A TP-surface of type n with blending functions $F_{i,\nu}$, $F_{j,\mu}$ has a representation of the form*

$$x(u,v) = \sum_{i,j=0}^{1} \sum_{\nu,\mu=0}^{n-1} \frac{\partial^\nu}{\partial u^\nu} \frac{\partial^\mu}{\partial v^\mu} x \Big|_{(i,j)} F_{i,\nu}(u) F_{j,\mu}(v). \qquad (2.3)$$

*A parametric surface $x \in C^{(2n,2n)}([0,1]^2)$ is a TP-surface of the type n with blending functions $F_{i,\nu}$, $F_{j,\mu} \in \Pi_{2n-1}$ if and only if*

$$\frac{\partial^{2n}}{\partial u^{2n}} x(u,v) = 0 \text{ and } \frac{\partial^{2n}}{\partial v^{2n}} x(u,v) = 0 \text{ for all } (u,v) \in [0,1]^2. \qquad (2.4)$$

**Proof:**

i) The representation formula (2.1) follows directly from the definition of a Coons' patch. The additional statement is obtained by determining the set

$$Prec\left(H_u^{n-1} \oplus H_v^{n-1}\right) \cap C^{(2n,2n)}([0,1]^2) \ .$$

For this we use the following equations. If $P$ and $Q$ are commutative projectors, and $\bar{P}$ and $\bar{Q}$ denote the corresponding remainder projectors, then the equation

$$Prec\left(P \oplus Q\right) = Im\left(P \oplus Q\right) = Im\left(P\right) + Im\left(Q\right) = Ker\left(\bar{P}\right) + Ker\left(\bar{Q}\right)$$

holds, where $Ker\, R$ denotes the Kernel of the operator $R$ . To determine the desired precision set, use the above equations and the following well-known statement:

$$Ker\left(\bar{H}^{n-1}\right) \cap C^n[0,1]$$
$$= \left\{ f \in C^n[0,1] : \frac{d^n}{dt^n} f(u) = 0 \text{ for all } u \in [0,1] \right\}.$$

ii) The proof in this case is analogous to i) . ∎

Before we turn our attention to the segmentation problem, we use the representation theorem to summarize the fundamental relations between Coons' patches and TP-surfaces.

**Theorem 2.7.**

i) *A TP-surface of type n is a Coons' surface of the same type.*

ii) *A TP-surface of type n $(n > 1)$ is a Coons' patch of type $(n-1)$ if the equation*

$$\frac{\partial^{2(n-1)}}{\partial u^{n-1} \partial v^{n-1}} x \Big|_{(i,j)} = 0 \qquad (2.5)$$

*holds for $i,j \in \{0,1\}$ .*

iii) *A Coons' surface of type n is a TP-surface of the same type if and only if the following equations hold for $\mu = 0, 1, \ldots, n - 1$:*

$$\frac{\partial^\mu}{\partial v^\mu} x \Big|_{(u,j)} = \sum_{\nu=0}^{n-1} \frac{\partial^\nu}{\partial u^\nu} \frac{\partial^\mu}{\partial v^\mu} x \Big|_{(0,j)} F_{0,\nu}(u) + \frac{\partial^\nu}{\partial u^\nu} \frac{\partial^\mu}{\partial v^\mu} x \Big|_{(1,j)} F_{1,\nu}(u)$$
(2.6a)

for $j = 0, 1$ and

$$\frac{\partial^\mu}{\partial u^\mu} x \Big|_{(i,v)} = \sum_{\nu=0}^{n-1} \frac{\partial^\nu}{\partial v^\nu} \frac{\partial^\mu}{\partial u^\mu} x \Big|_{(i,0)} F_{0,\nu}(v) + \frac{\partial^\nu}{\partial v^\nu} \frac{\partial^\mu}{\partial u^\mu} x \Big|_{(i,1)} F_{1,\nu}(v)$$
(2.6b)

for $i = 0, 1$.

iv) *A Coons- (TP-) patch of type n is a Coons- (TP-) patch of type $(n + 1)$ if the blending functions satisfy*

$$F_{i,k}^{(\nu)}(j) = \delta_{ij} \cdot \delta_{\nu k} \quad \text{for} \quad i, j \in \{0, 1\} \ , \ k \in \{0, 1, \ldots, n - 1\}$$
$$\text{and} \quad \nu \in \{0, 1, \ldots, n\}.$$
(2.7)

**Proof:**

i) The first statement follows directly from

$$Prec\,(H_u^n \cdot H_v^n) =$$
$$Prec\,(H_u^n) \cap Prec\,(H_v^n) \subset Prec\,(H_u^n) + Prec\,(H_v^n) =$$
$$Prec\,(H_u^n \oplus H_v^n) \ .$$

ii) To prove the second statement, start with a TP-scheme of type $n$ and combine proper summands to get expressions of the form $x(u, j)$, $x_v(u, j)$, etc. and $x(i, v)$, $x_u(i, v)$ etc. Adding missing terms, and considering (2.5) leads to a Boolean scheme of type $(n - 1)$.

iii) On the one hand, putting the equations (2.6) into the representation (2.1) of a Coons' patch of type $n$ yields a representation of the form (2.3). On the other hand, the equations (2.6) follow from putting the parameters $(u, j)$, respectively $(i, v)$, into a TP-scheme of the form (2.3).

iv) Let $\tilde{H}^{n-1}$ denote the operator $H^{n-1}$, assuming that the blending functions satisfy (2.14). Then it is easy to verify that

$$Prec\,(\tilde{H}_u^{n-1} \oplus \tilde{H}_v^{n-1}) \subset Prec\,(H_u^n \oplus H_v^n)$$

and

$$Prec\,(\tilde{H}_u^{n-1} \cdot \tilde{H}_v^{n-1}) \subset Prec\,(H_u^n \cdot H_v^n)$$

which are equivalent to the assertions. ■

**Remark 2.8.** *Every Coons' patch of type $(n - 1)$ with blending functions $F_{i,k}^{(\nu)}(j) = \delta_{ij} \cdot \delta_{\nu k}$ for $i, j \in \{0, 1\}$ , $k \in \{0, 1, \ldots, n - 2\}$ and $\nu \in \{0, 1, \ldots, n - 1\}$ satisfies (2.5).*

## §3. Segmentation Operators on Coons' Patches

In this section we investigate the segmentation properties of Coons' patches with polynomial blending functions. To this end, we use the following mappings between surfaces.

**Definition 3.1.** *Let $G^n$ be the set of all Gordon-Coons' surfaces $x \in C^{(2n,2n)}$ $([0,1]^2)$ of type $n$ with polynomial blending functions $F_{i,\nu} \in \Pi_{2n-1}$ $(i = 0,1$ , $\nu = 0,1,\ldots,n-1)$. A transformation $S : G^n \longrightarrow G^n$ with the property that*

$$Im(S(x)) \subseteq Im(x) \tag{3.1}$$

*holds for all $x \in G^n$ is called a segmentation operator on $G^n$ .*

**Remark 3.2.** *This concept corresponds to the intuitive idea of an automatic process which applied on an arbitrary Coons' patch yields a surface segment which itself belongs to the class of Coons' patches.*

Because of the property (3.1), every segmentation operator is of the form $S(x) = x \circ \varphi_x$, where $\varphi_x : [0,1]^2 \longrightarrow [0,1]^2$ denotes a transformation which may depend on the input surface $x$.

In the following, we derive statements about the segmentation properties of Coons' patches (or proper subclasses) by determining regular transformations $\varphi : [0,1]^2 \longrightarrow [0,1]^2$ such that a mapping $S : G^n \longrightarrow G^n$ defined by

$$S(x) = x \circ \varphi \tag{3.2}$$

is a segmentation operator on $G^n$. The set of all segmentation operators of the form (3.2) is a set of linear operators on $G^n$ and will be denoted by $\mathcal{L}_{G^n}$ .

**Theorem 3.3.** *The set $\mathcal{L}_{G^n}$ of all segmentation operators of the form (3.2) on $G^n$ is given by*

$$\mathcal{L}_{G^n} = \{\, S : G^n \longrightarrow G^n : \ S(x) = x \circ \varphi_i \ \ (i = 1,2) \qquad \text{where}$$
$$\varphi_1(u,v) = (a \cdot u + b \,, \, c \cdot v + d) \,,$$
$$\varphi_2(u,v) = \varphi_1(v,u) \,, \ a,b,c,d \in [0,1] \,, \ a \cdot c \neq 0\}$$

**Proof:**

a) Each element of $\mathcal{L}_{G^n}$ is a segmentation operator on $G^n$ because $x \circ \varphi_i$ satisfies

$$\frac{\partial^{4n}}{\partial u^{2n} \partial v^{2n}}(x \circ \varphi_i) = \frac{\partial^{4n}}{\partial u^{2n} \partial v^{2n}} x \left(\frac{\partial \varphi_i^1}{\partial u}\right)^{2n} \cdot \left(\frac{\partial \varphi_i^2}{\partial v}\right)^{2n} = 0$$

(which means that $x \circ \varphi_i$ is a Coons' patch) and the subsurface property by construction.

b) Let $S$ be a segmentation operator on $G^n$ of the form $S(x) = x \circ \varphi$. According to Theorem 2.6, the segmentation property $S(x) \in G^n$ for all $x \in G^n$ is equivalent to

$$\frac{\partial^{4n}}{\partial u^{2n} \partial v^{2n}} S(x) = 0 \ \text{ for all } \ x \in G^n \,.$$

Hence for the component function $x^i$, $i = 1, 2, 3$, we get the condition

$$\frac{\partial^{4n}}{\partial u^{2n} \partial v^{2n}} (x^i \circ \varphi) = 0 \quad \text{for all} \quad x^i \in Prec\left(H_u^{n-1} \oplus H_v^{n-1}\right). \tag{3.3}$$

For polynomial blending functions $F_{i,\nu} \in \Pi_{2n-1}$, the precision set of the Boolean sum operator $H_u^{n-1} \oplus H_v^{n-1}$ is given by

$$Prec\left(H_u^{n-1} \oplus H_v^{n-1}\right) = \{ g : [0,1]^2 \to \mathbb{R} :$$
$$g(u, v) = \sum_{i=0}^{2n-1} \left(A_i(v)u^i + B_i(u)v^i\right), \; A_i, B_i \in C^{2n}[0,1]\}. \tag{3.4}$$

Therefore, the component function $x^i(u, v) = f(u)$ where $f \in C^\infty[0,1]$ is arbitrarily chosen is an element of the above precision set, and we get from (3.3) the condition

$$\frac{\partial^{4n}}{\partial u^{2n} \partial v^{2n}} (f \circ \varphi^1) = 0 \quad \text{for all} \quad f \in C^\infty[0,1] \tag{3.5}$$

($\varphi^1$ denotes the first component function of $\varphi$). By direct calculation we find

$$\frac{\partial^{4n}}{\partial u^{2n} \partial v^{2n}} (f \circ \varphi^1) = (f^{(4n)} \circ \varphi^1) \cdot (\varphi_u^1)^{2n} \cdot (\varphi_v^1)^{2n}$$
$$+ (f^{(4n-1)} \circ \varphi^1) \cdot S_{4n-1} + \cdots + (f' \circ \varphi^1) \cdot S_1,$$

where we use the notation $\dfrac{d^k}{dt^k} f = f^{(k)}$ and $\dfrac{\partial \varphi^1}{\partial u} = \varphi_u^1$ , and the symbols $S_1, \ldots, S_{4n-1}$ represent sums of partial derivatives of $\varphi^1$. By proper choice of functions $f_i$ with $f_i^{(i+1)} = 0$ for $i = 1, \ldots, 4n-1$, we conclude from (3.5) that $S_1 = 0$, $S_2 = 0$, $\ldots$, $S_{4n-1} = 0$ and finally $\left(\varphi_u^1\right)^{2n} \cdot \left(\varphi_v^1\right)^{2n} = 0$ . Therefore, for each pair $(u, v) \in [0,1]^2$ , one of the equations $\varphi_u^1(u, v) = 0$ , $\varphi_v^1(u, v) = 0$ holds.

Because of the regularity of $\varphi$ and the relation $det \; \varphi_* = \varphi_u^1 \varphi_v^2 - \varphi_u^2 \varphi_v^1$ , there exists no $(u, v) \in [0,1]^2$ such that $\varphi_u^1(u, v)$ and $\varphi_v^1(u, v)$ both vanish. For continuity reasons, we conclude the validity of one of the identities $\varphi_u^1 = 0$ or $\varphi_v^1 = 0$. In analogy to the above, we find also the validity of one of the equations $\varphi_u^2 = 0$ or $\varphi_v^2 = 0$. Hence, the transformation $\varphi$ has one of the following representations

(i) $\varphi(u, v) = (\varphi^1(u), \varphi^2(v))$ or (ii) $\varphi(u, v) = (\varphi^1(v), \varphi^2(u))$ .

We first consider case i) : By examining (3.4), we find that the component functions $x^1$ with $x^1(u, v) = u \cdot f(v)$, where $f \in C^\infty[0,1]$ are also elements of the precision set of $H_u^{n-1} \oplus H_v^{n-1}$ . Therefore, from (3.3) we get

$$\frac{\partial^{4n}}{\partial u^{2n} \partial v^{2n}} \left((f \circ \varphi^2) \cdot \varphi^1\right)(u, v) = (f \circ \varphi^2)^{(2n)}(v) \cdot (\varphi^1)^{(2n)}(u) = 0$$

for all $f \in C^\infty[0,1]$ and all $u \in [0,1]$. By proper choice of $f$ such that $(f \circ \varphi^2)^{(2n)}(v) \neq 0$ for one $v \in [0,1]$, this yields $(\varphi^1)^{(2n)}(u) = 0$ for all $u \in [0,1]$. Therefore, $\varphi^1$ is a polynomial of degree $2n - 1$ in $u$.

By using elements $x^1$ of the precision set of $H_u^{n-1} \oplus H_v^{n-1}$ of the form $x^1(u,v) = f(v) \cdot u^{2n-1}$, one shows that $\varphi^1$ is linear in $u$. The linearity of $\varphi^2$ in $v$ follows in complete analogy to the above. The case (ii) can be treated in the same way. ∎

The following statements are immediate consequences of Theorem 3.3.

**Corollary 3.4.** *Every Coons' patch of $G^n$ allows segmentation along coordinate lines.*

**Corollary 3.5.** *There is no segmentation operator of the form (3.2) on $G^n$ that yields surface segments which are not bounded by coordinate lines of the input surface.*

## §4. Segmentation of Subclasses

In Section 3 we determined all segmentation operators of the form (3.2) on the set $G^n$ of Coons' patches. In order to derive further "*segment generators*", we have to restrict the set of input surfaces to a proper subset of Coons' surfaces. This gives us more available information of the surfaces to be segmented. In the following, $D^{(2n,0)} \subset G^n$ denotes the set of parametric surfaces $x : [0,1] \longrightarrow \mathbb{R}^3$ which satisfy the differential equation $\dfrac{\partial^{2n}}{\partial \bar{u}^{2n}} x = 0$. The following theorem gives segmentation operators from $D^{(2n,0)}$ into $G^n$ .

**Theorem 4.1.** *Every mapping* $S : D^{(2n,0)} \longrightarrow G^n$ *of the form* $S(x) = x \circ \varphi_i$ , $(i = 1, 2)$ *where* $\varphi_i$ *denotes the transformations*

$$\varphi_i : [0,1]^2 \longrightarrow [0,1]^2 ,$$
$$\varphi_1(u,v) = \big(h_1(v) \cdot u + h_2(v), \, h_3(v)\big) ,$$
$$\varphi_2(u,v) = \varphi_1(v,u)$$

*with* $h_i \in C^{2n}[0,1]$, $h_1(t) \neq 0$, $h_3'(t) \neq 0$ *for all* $t \in [0,1]$ *is a segmentation operator from* $D^{(2n,0)}$ *into* $G^n$ .

**Proof:** The statement follows for $\varphi_1$ from the equation

$$\frac{\partial^{2n}}{\partial u^{2n}} (x \circ \varphi_1) = \frac{\partial^{2n}}{\partial \bar{u}^{2n}} x \cdot \left(\frac{d\varphi_1}{du}\right)^{2n} .$$

For $\varphi_2$ the corresponding equation holds. ∎

In analogy to Theorem 3.3, all segmentation operators from $D^{(2n,0)}$ into $G^n$ are determined.

**Theorem 4.2.** *Every segmentation operator $S : D^{(2n,0)} \longrightarrow G^n$ of the form (3.2) is listed in Theorem 4.1.*

**Proof:** First one shows, in analogy with the proof of Theorem 3.3, that one of the identities $\varphi_u^2 = 0$ or $\varphi_v^2 = 0$ holds. Hence $\varphi$ is of the form

(i) $\varphi(u, v) = \left(\varphi^1(u, v), \varphi^2(v)\right)$     or     (ii) $\varphi(u, v) = \left(\varphi^1(u, v), \varphi^2(u)\right)$ .

The additional assumption $x \in D^{(2n,0)}$ implies that one cannot derive the relation $\varphi_u^1 = 0$ or $\varphi_v^1 = 0$ which we got in the proof of Theorem 3.3. Instead, we show by proper choice of mappings $x^1$ with $x^1(u, v) = f(v) \cdot u$ and $f \in C^\infty[0, 1]$ that $\varphi^1$ is a polynomial of degree $2n - 1$ in $u$. For this we differentiate $x^1 \circ \varphi$ as follows:

$$\frac{\partial^{4n}}{\partial u^{2n}\, \partial v^{2n}} \left(x^1 \circ \varphi\right) = \frac{\partial^{4n}}{\partial u^{2n}\, \partial v^{2n}} \left(\left(f \circ \varphi^2\right) \cdot \varphi^1\right)$$

$$= \left(f \circ \varphi^2\right)^{2n} \cdot \left(\varphi^1\right)^{(2n,0)}$$

$$+ \binom{2n}{1} \left(f \circ \varphi^2\right)^{2n-1} \cdot \left(\varphi^1\right)^{(2n,1)}$$

$$+$$

$$\vdots \qquad\qquad\qquad (4.1)$$

$$+ \binom{2n}{2n-1} \left(f \circ \varphi^2\right)' \cdot \left(\varphi^1\right)^{(2n,2n-1)}$$

$$+ \left(f \circ \varphi^2\right) \cdot \left(\varphi^1\right)^{(2n,2n)}$$

$$= \left(f^{(2n)} \circ \varphi^2\right) \cdot \left(\varphi^{2'}\right)^{(2n)} \cdot \left(\varphi^1\right)^{(2n,0)}$$

$$+ \left(f^{(2n-1)} \circ \varphi^2\right) \cdot S_{2n-1} + \cdots + \left(f' \circ \varphi^2\right) \cdot S_1$$

$$+ \left(f \circ \varphi^2\right) \cdot \left(\varphi^1\right)^{(2n,2n)},$$

where $S_1, S_2, \ldots, S_{2n-1}$ denote sums of products of derivatives of $\varphi^1$ and $\varphi^2$. Choosing functions $f_i$ such that $f_i^{(i)} = 0$ for $i = 1, \ldots, 2n - 1$, from (4.1) we get

$$\left(\varphi^1\right)^{(2n,2n)} = 0, \; S_1 = 0, \; S_2 = 0, \; \ldots, \; S_{2n-1} = 0,$$

and finally

$$\left(\varphi^{2'}\right)^{2n} \cdot \left(\varphi^1\right)^{(2n,0)} = 0.$$

Therefore, we have $\left(\varphi^1\right)^{(2n,0)} = 0$ because $\varphi^{2'}(v) = 0$ for one $v \in [0, 1]$ is contradictory to the regularity of $\varphi$ . Hence $\varphi^1$ is a polynomial in $u$ of degree $2n - 1$. Choosing elements $x^1$ in $Prec\left(H_u^{n-1} \oplus H_v^{n-1}\right)$ of the form $x^1(u, v) = f(v) \cdot u^{2n-1}$, one further shows that $\varphi^1$ is linear in $u$. The case (ii) can be treated analogously. ∎

**Remark 4.3.** *The corresponding statements to those in Theorems 4.1 and Theorem 4.2 hold for a surface* $x \in D^{(0,2n)}$ ; *i.e.,* $\dfrac{\partial^{2n}}{\partial v^{2n}} x = 0$ .

With the segmentation operators listed in Theorem 4.1, one can obviously get segments on surfaces of the subset $D^{(2n,0)}$ (or $D^{(0,2n)}$ ) which are not bounded by coordinate lines of the input surface.

**Example 4.4.** *Consider the cylindric surface* $x$ *defined for* $u, v \in [0,1]$ *by* $x(u,v) = (\cos(\pi \cdot u), \sin(\pi \cdot u), v)$. *From the validity of the differential equation* $\dfrac{\partial^{4n}}{\partial u^2 \, \partial v^2} x = 0$ *we conclude:* $x$ *is a Coons' patch of type 1. Furthermore, the relation* $x \in D^{(0,2)}$ *holds and therefore we can create surface segments which are themselves Coons' patches of type 1 by using the transformation*

$$\varphi(u,v) = \big(h_1(u), \, h_2(u) \cdot v + h_3(u)\big) \, .$$

*Let* $P_0$, $P_1$, $P_2$, $P_3$ *be four points in the* $u$–$v$ *plane which satisfy the constraints* $P_i \in [0,1]^2$ *and* $P_0^1 = P_3^1$ , $P_1^1 = P_2^1$ .

*A transformation of the form* $\varphi(u,v) = \big(h_1(u), \, h_2(u) + v \cdot h_3(u)\big)$ *which maps the unit square* $[0,1]^2$ *onto the quadrangle formed by* $P_0$, $P_1$, $P_2$, $P_3$ *is given by*

$$h_1(u) = P_0^1 + u \cdot (P_1^1 - P_0^1)$$
$$h_2(u) = P_3^2 - P_0^2 + u \cdot (P_2^2 + P_0^2 - P_3^2 - P_1^2)$$
$$h_3(u) = P_0^2 + u \cdot (P_1^2 - P_0^2) \, ;$$

*i.e., the surface curves*

$$
\begin{aligned}
\bar{x}_1(u) &= \big(\cos(\pi \cdot h_1(u)), \, \sin(\pi \cdot h_1(u)), \, h_3(u)\big) \\
\bar{x}_2(u) &= \big(\cos(\pi \cdot h_1(u)), \, \sin(\pi \cdot h_1(u)), \, h_2(u) + h_3(u)\big) \\
\bar{x}_3(v) &= \big(\cos(\pi \cdot h_1(0)), \, \sin(\pi \cdot h_1(0)), \, h_2(0) \cdot v + h_3(0)\big) \\
\bar{x}_4(v) &= \big(\cos(\pi \cdot h_1(1)), \, \sin(\pi \cdot h_1(1)), \, h_2(1) \cdot v + h_3(1)\big)
\end{aligned}
\tag{4.2}
$$

*are proper to 'cut' a Coons-type surface segment of type 1 out of the cylinder surface. The curves* $\bar{x}_1$, $\bar{x}_2$ *are not coordinate lines of* $x$. *To get a parametrization of the above segment, one only has to put the formulas (4.2) into the scheme of a Coons' segment of type 1.*

## §5. Segmentation of Tensor-Product Surfaces

In this section we investigate the segmentation properties of TP-patches. We denote by $T^n$ the set of all TP-surfaces $x \in C^{(2n,2n)}[0,1]$ of type $n$ with polynomial blending functions $F_{i,\nu} \in \Pi_{2n-1}$ , $(i = 0,1; \; \nu = 0,1,\ldots,n-1)$. In addition, let $\mathcal{L}_{T^n}$ denote the set of all segmentation operators $S : T^n \longrightarrow T^n$ of the form (3.2).

**Theorem 5.1.** *The set of segmentation operators on $T^n$ of the form (3.2) is identical to $\mathcal{L}_{G^n}$; i.e.,*

$$\mathcal{L}_{T^n} = \mathcal{L}_{G^n}.$$

**Proof:**

a) Each element of $\mathcal{L}_{T^n}$ is a segmentation operator on $T^n$. This follows for $\varphi_1$ from the equation

$$\frac{\partial^{2n}}{\partial u^{2n}}\,(x \circ \varphi_1) = \frac{\partial^{2n}}{\partial \bar{u}^{i\,2n}}\,x \cdot \left(\frac{\partial}{\partial \bar{u}^i}\,\varphi_1^i\right)^{2n}.$$

For $\varphi_2$ the corresponding equation holds.

b) We verify that every segmentation operator of the form (3.2) on $T^n$ is an element of $\mathcal{L}_{T^n}$. First, using elements $x^1(u,v) = u$ and $x^1(u,v) = v$ of the precision set of $H_u^{n-1} \cdot H_v^{n-1}$, one shows that $\varphi$ is a polynomial in $u$ and $v$ of degree $2n-1$. The statement follows by comparing the coefficients of $x \circ \varphi$ with the coefficients of arbitrary polynomials in $u$ and $v$ of degree $2n-1$. ∎

From Theorem 5.1 we derive the following corollary:

**Corollary 5.2.**

(i) Every TP-surface $x \in T^n$ allows segmentation along coordinate lines

(ii) There is no segmentation operator of the form (3.2) on $T^n$ which yields surface segments which are not bounded by coordinate lines of the input surface.

According to Theorem 5.1, every segmentation operator $S : T^n \longrightarrow T^n$ of the form (3.2) is an element of $\mathcal{L}_{T^n}$. In addition, we can derive further segment generators if we admit surface segments which are themselves not TP-surfaces but are instead Coons' patches.

**Theorem 5.3.** *The mappings $S : T^n \longrightarrow G^n$ defined by $S(x) = x \circ \varphi$, where*

$$\varphi(u,v) = a \cdot u + b \cdot v + c; \qquad a, b, c \in \mathbb{R}^2, \tag{5.1}$$

*are segmentation operators from $T^n$ into $G^n$.*

**Proof:** By construction of $S$, the segmentation property of $S$ holds. Now the fact that $\dfrac{\partial^{m+\ell}}{\partial u^m \partial v^\ell}\,(x \circ \varphi)$ with $\varphi$ as in (5.1) consists of a sum of products, where every summand has a derivative of the form $\dfrac{\partial^{i+j}}{\partial u^i \partial v^j}\,x$ with $i + j = m + \ell$, and the fact that $x$ is an element of $T^n$, implies $S(x) \in G^n$. ∎

Theorem 5.3 implies:

**Corollary 5.4.** *Consider on a TP-patch $x \in T^n$ four surface curves $\bar{x}_i = x \circ c_i$, $i = 1, 2, 3, 4$, where the mappings $c_i : [0, 1] \longrightarrow [0, 1]^2$ are linear parametrizations of a parallelogram $P \in [0, 1]^2$ . Then there exists a surface segment $y \in G^n$ of $x$ which fits the curves $\bar{x}_i$ as boundary curves.*

## References

1. Barnhill, R. E., Smooth Interpolation over triangles, in *Computer Aided Geometric Design*, R. Barnhill and R. Riesenfeld (eds.), Academic Press, New York, 1974, 45–70.

2. Barnhill, R. E., Computer aided surface representation and design, in *Surfaces in Computer Aided Design*, R. E. Barnhill and W. Boehm (eds.), North–Holland, Amsterdam, 1983, 1–24.

3. Coons, S. A., Surfaces for the computer aided design of space forms, Project MAC, MIT. Revised to Mac-Tr-41, June 1967.

4. Gordon, W. J., Distributive Lattices and the approximation of multivariate functions, in *Approximations with special Emphasis on Spline Functions*, I. J. Schoenberg (ed.), Academic Press, New York, 1969, 223–277.

5. Gordon, W. J., Spline–blended surface interpolation through curve networks, Report GMR-799, July, 1968.

6. Gregory, J. A., A blending function interpolant for triangles, in *Multivariate Approximation*, D. Handscomb (ed.), Academic Press, New York, 1979, 279–287.

7. Gregory, J. A., Smooth interpolation without twist constraints, in *Computer Aided Geometric Design*, R. Barnhill and R. Riesenfeld (eds.), Academic Press, New York, 1974, 71–87.

8. Gregory, J. A., $C^1$ Rectangular and non–rectangular surface patches, in *Surfaces in CAGD*, R. E. Barnhill and W. Boehm (eds.), North–Holland Publishing Company, 1983, 25–33.

9. Hagen, H., Geometric Coons' patches, preprint.

10. Hagen, H. and G. Schulze, Automatic smoothing with geometric surface patches, Comput. Aided Geom. Design , to appear.

11. Nielson, G., The side–vertex method for interpolation in triangles, J. Appr. Theory **25** (1979), 318–336.

Guido Schulze
Institut für graph. Datenverarbeitung
und Computergeometrie
Universität Kaiserslautern
D–6750 Kaiserslautern
W. GERMANY

# A General Subdivision Theorem
# for Bézier Triangles

## H.-P. Seidel

**Abstract.** The subdivision of Bézier triangles is studied from the view-point of multiaffine mappings. Using the principle that polynomials of degree $n$ and symmetric $n$-affine maps are equivalent to each other, a theorem is derived that provides simultaneous closed form solutions for the various recursive algorithms due to Goldman [12]. From this, the major properties of subdivision algorithms for Bézier triangles are readily deduced.

## §1. Introduction

Pioneered by the work of de Casteljau [5,6] and Ramshaw [14], the use of multiaffine mappings has recently gained a lot of attention within the context of computer aided geometric design [1,15,16,17,18], and has led to considerable simplifications in the theory of Bézier and B-spline curves and surfaces. In this paper we wish to apply multiaffine mappings to the study of subdivision algorithms for triangular Bézier surfaces [2,7,8,9,10,12,13]. In particular, we will use multiaffine maps to construct simultaneous closed form solutions for the various recursive subdivision algorithms due to Goldman [12]. From this we obtain a simple derivation for the de Casteljau algorithm for computing the control points of a Bézier curve on a Bézier triangle, and for expressing a Bézier polynomial with respect to different reference triangles. Furthermore, the major properties of subdivision algorithms for Bézier triangles are readily deduced.

Mathematical Methods in Computer Aided Geometric Design
Tom Lyche and Larry L. Schumaker (eds.), pp. 573–581.

## §2. The Blossoming Principle

To start our development, we first have to introduce the notion of a symmetric multiaffine map. Recall that a map $f : \mathbb{R}^2 \to \mathbb{R}^d$ is called *affine* if it preserves affine combinations; *i.e.*, if $f$ satisfies

$$f(\sum_{i=1}^{m} a_i \cdot U_i) = \sum_{i=1}^{m} a_i \cdot f(U_i)$$

for all real numbers $a_1, ..., a_m \in \mathbb{R}$ and points $U_1, ..., U_m \in \mathbb{R}^2$ satisfying $\sum_{i=1}^{m} a_i = 1$. A map $f : (\mathbb{R}^2)^n \to \mathbb{R}^d$ is called *n-affine* (or just *multiaffine*) if it is affine in each argument when the others are held fixed. Therefore, $f$ is *n*-affine if and only if for every sequence $A_1, ..., A_{j-1}, A_{j+1}, ..., A_n \in \mathbb{R}^2$, the map from $\mathbb{R}^2$ to $\mathbb{R}^d$ defined by

$$f_{A_1,...,A_n}(U) = f(A_1, ..., U, ..., A_n)$$

is affine. Finally, a map $f : (\mathbb{R}^2)^n \to \mathbb{R}^d$ is *symmetric* if $f$ keeps its value under any permutation of its arguments.

   With this notation we are now able to state the following *blossoming principle* [14] that is central in our treatment:

**Theorem 2.1.** *For every polynomial $F : \mathbb{R}^2 \to \mathbb{R}^d$ of degree $n$ there exists a unique symmetric $n$-affine map $f : (\mathbb{R}^2)^n \to \mathbb{R}^d$ satisfying*

$$f(\underbrace{U, ..., U}_{n}) = F(U).$$

**Proof:** A proof may be found in [5,6,14,15,19] as well as in many standard textbooks on algebra or complex analysis. Usually, the existence of a blossom $f$ is verified by writing down an explicit formula. Then a derivative formula is obtained by using the fact that $f$ is symmetric and multiaffine. Finally, this derivative formula is used to show that $f$ is unique. ■

**Notation:** Following de Casteljau and Ramshaw, the unique symmetric $n$-affine map $f$ corresponding to $F$ will be called the *symmetric polar form* or the *blossom* of $F$, while $F$ is referred to as the *diagonal* of $f$.

**Example 2.2.** *Consider a quadratic bivariate polynomial*

$$F(s,t) = a \cdot s^2 + b \cdot st + c \cdot t^2 + d \cdot s + e \cdot t + h.$$

*Then the map from $\mathbb{R}^2 \times \mathbb{R}^2$ to $\mathbb{R}$ defined by*

$$f((s_1, t_1), (s_2, t_2)) = a \cdot s_1 s_2 + \frac{b}{2} \cdot (s_1 t_2 + s_2 t_1) + c \cdot t_1 t_2$$
$$+ \frac{d}{2} \cdot (s_1 + s_2) + \frac{e}{2} \cdot (t_1 + t_2) + h$$

*is symmetric, affine in each component, and satisfies $f((s,t),(s,t)) = F(s,t)$. Hence, $f$ is the blossom of $F$ according to Theorem 2.1.*

   Theorem 2.1 immediately yields the following corollary [5,6,14,15]:

**Corollary 2.3.** *Let $\triangle(R, S, T)$ be a reference triangle in $\mathbb{R}^2$, and let the points $U \in \mathbb{R}^2$ be given in barycentric coordinates $U = r \cdot R + s \cdot S + t \cdot T$ with respect to $\triangle(R, S, T)$. We consider a polynomial $F : \mathbb{R}^2 \to \mathbb{R}^d$ of degree $n$ with corresponding blossom $f$. Then*

$$b_{i,j,k} := f(\underbrace{R, ..., R}_{i}, \underbrace{S, ..., S}_{j}, \underbrace{T, ..., T}_{k})$$

*are the Bézier points of $F$ with respect to $\triangle(R, S, T)$, and*

$$F(U) = \sum_{i+j+k=n} B^n_{i,j,k}(U) \cdot f(\underbrace{R, ..., R}_{i}, \underbrace{S, ..., S}_{j}, \underbrace{T, ..., T}_{k})$$

*is the corresponding Bézier representation.*

**Proof:** Making use of the fact that $f$ is symmetric and affine in every component, the standard multinomial theorem yields

$$F(U) = f(\underbrace{U, ..., U}_{n})$$

$$= r \cdot f(R, U, ..., U) + s \cdot f(S, U, ..., U) + t \cdot f(T, U, ..., U)$$

$$= \sum_{i+j+k=n} \binom{n}{ijk} r^i s^j t^k \cdot f(\underbrace{R, ..., R}_{i}, \underbrace{S, ..., S}_{j}, \underbrace{T, ..., T}_{k}),$$

and the assertion follows from the linear independence of the Bernstein polynomials $B^n_{i,j,k}(U)$. ∎

**Example 2.4.** *The Bézier points of a quadratic bivariate polynomial*

$$F(s, t) = a \cdot s^2 + b \cdot st + c \cdot t^2 + d \cdot s + e \cdot t + h$$

*with respect to the standard triangle $\triangle((0, 0), (1, 0), (0, 1))$ are obtained as*

$$b_{2,0,0} = f((0,0), (0,0)) = h$$

$$b_{1,1,0} = f((0,0), (1,0)) = \frac{d}{2} + h$$

$$\vdots$$

$$b_{0,0,2} = f((0,1), (0,1)) = c + e + h.$$

## §3. Subdivision Algorithms for Bézier Triangles

We are now ready to state the following general subdivision theorem for Bézier triangles:

**Theorem 3.1.** Let $F(U) = \sum_{i+j+k=n} B_{i,j,k}^n(U) \cdot b_{i,j,k}$ be a bivariate Bézier polynomial with respect to a reference triangle $\triangle(R, S, T)$ in $\mathbb{R}^2$, and let $f$ be the corresponding blossom. Given $m$ points $U_i := r_i \cdot R + s_i \cdot S + t_i \cdot T$ in barycentric coordinates with respect to $\triangle(R, S, T)$, we consider the recursively defined $(m + 2)$-dimensional simplicial array of points

$$b_{i,j,k}^{0,\ldots,0} := b_{i,j,k}$$

$$b_{i,j,k}^{l_1+1,l_2,\ldots,l_m} := r_1 \cdot b_{i+1,j,k}^{l_1,l_2,\ldots,l_m} + s_1 \cdot b_{i,j+1,k}^{l_1,l_2,\ldots,l_m} + t_1 \cdot b_{i,j,k+1}^{l_1,l_2,\ldots,l_m}$$

$$b_{i,j,k}^{l_1,l_2+1,\ldots,l_m} := r_2 \cdot b_{i+1,j,k}^{l_1,l_2,\ldots,l_m} + s_2 \cdot b_{i,j+1,k}^{l_1,l_2,\ldots,l_m} + t_2 \cdot b_{i,j,k+1}^{l_1,l_2,\ldots,l_m}$$

$$\vdots$$

$$b_{i,j,k}^{l_1,l_2,\ldots,l_m+1} := r_m \cdot b_{i+1,j,k}^{l_1,l_2,\ldots,l_m} + s_m \cdot b_{i,j+1,k}^{l_1,l_2,\ldots,l_m} + t_m \cdot b_{i,j,k+1}^{l_1,l_2,\ldots,l_m}$$

with $i + j + k + l_1 + \cdots + l_m = n$. Then

$$b_{i,j,k}^{l_1,\ldots,l_m} := f(\underbrace{R, ..., R}_{i}, \underbrace{S, ..., S}_{j}, \underbrace{T, ..., T}_{k}, \underbrace{U_1, ..., U_1}_{l_1}, ..., \underbrace{U_m, ..., U_m}_{l_m})$$

yields a closed form solution for the above recurrence. In particular, the different recursion steps commute.

**Proof:** The equation $b_{i,j,k}^{0,\ldots,0} = b_{i,j,k}$ follows directly from Corollary 2.3. Using the fact that $f$ is symmetric and affine in each component, for the remaining equations we get

$$b_{i,j,k}^{l_1,\ldots,l_\mu+1,\ldots,l_m} =$$

$$= f(\underbrace{R, .., R}_{i}, \underbrace{S, .., S}_{j}, \underbrace{T, .., T}_{k}, \underbrace{U_1, .., U_1}_{l_1}, .., \underbrace{U_\mu, .., U_\mu}_{l_\mu+1}, .., \underbrace{U_m, .., U_m}_{l_m})$$

$$= r_\mu f(\underbrace{R, .., R}_{i+1}, \underbrace{S, .., S}_{j}, \underbrace{T, .., T}_{k}, \underbrace{U_1, .., U_1}_{l_1}, .., \underbrace{U_\mu, .., U_\mu}_{l_\mu}, .., \underbrace{U_m, .., U_m}_{l_m})$$

$$+ s_\mu f(\underbrace{R, .., R}_{i}, \underbrace{S, .., S}_{j+1}, \underbrace{T, .., T}_{k}, \underbrace{U_1, .., U_1}_{l_1}, .., \underbrace{U_\mu, .., U_\mu}_{l_\mu}, .., \underbrace{U_m, .., U_m}_{l_m})$$

$$+ t_\mu f(\underbrace{R, .., R}_{i}, \underbrace{S, .., S}_{j}, \underbrace{T, .., T}_{k+1}, \underbrace{U_1, .., U_1}_{l_1}, .., \underbrace{U_\mu, .., U_\mu}_{l_\mu}, .., \underbrace{U_m, .., U_m}_{l_m})$$

$$= r_\mu \cdot b_{i+1,j,k}^{l_1,\ldots,l_\mu,\ldots,l_m} + s_\mu \cdot b_{i,j+1,k}^{l_1,\ldots,l_\mu,\ldots,l_m} + t_\mu \cdot b_{i,j,k+1}^{l_1,\ldots,l_\mu,\ldots,l_m},$$

and the assertion follows. ∎

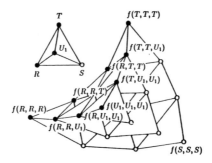

**Figure 1.** The first subdivision algorithm.

Note that in the special case $m = 1$, the above theorem provides a closed form solution for the familiar de Casteljau algorithm [3,4]. For $m \geq 2$ the recursive array $\{b_{i,j,k}^{l_1,\ldots,l_m} : i + j + k + l_1 + \ldots + l_m = n\}$ was first considered by Goldman [11,12].

To demonstrate the strength of the above theorem, we now discuss various special cases separately. We start with the case $m = 1$.

**Corollary 3.2.** *(de Casteljau) In the special case $m = 1$ of the above theorem, the function value $F(U_1)$ is given by*

$$F(U_1) = b_{0,0,0}^n.$$

**Proof:** $F(U_1) = f(\underbrace{U_1, \ldots, U_1}_{n}) = b_{0,0,0}^n.$ ∎

**Corollary 3.3.** *(First Subdivision Algorithm) In the special case $m = 1$ of the above theorem, the points on the 2-dimensional subsimplices of the tetrahedral array $\{b_{i,j,k}^{l} : i + j + k + l_1 = n\}$ can be used for subdividing the Bézier triangle $F(U)$ with respect to the point $U_1$. In particular:*

- *$\{b_{i,j,0}^{l_1} : i + j + l_1 = n\}$ contains the Bézier points w.r.t. $\triangle(R, S, U_1)$*
- *$\{b_{0,j,k}^{l_1} : j + k + l_1 = n\}$ contains the Bézier points w.r.t. $\triangle(S, T, U_1)$*
- *$\{b_{i,0,k}^{l_1} : i + k + l_1 = n\}$ contains the Bézier points w.r.t. $\triangle(T, R, U_1)$.*

**Proof:** It suffices to consider the triangle $\triangle(R, S, U_1)$. According to Theorem 3.1, we have

$$b_{i,j,0}^{l_1} = f(\underbrace{R, \ldots, R}_{i}, \underbrace{S, \ldots, S}_{j}, \underbrace{U_1, \ldots, U_1}_{l_1}),$$

and Corollary 2.3 yields the assertion. ∎

Next, we turn to the case $m = 2$.

**Corollary 3.4.** (*Bézier curves on a Bézier triangle*) *In the special case* $m = 2$ *of the above theorem, let* $G$ *be the restriction of* $F$ *to the line segment* $\overline{U_1 U_2}$, *and let* $B^n_{l_1, l_2}(U)$, *with* $l_1 + l_2 = n$ *be the Bernstein polynomials with respect to* $\overline{U_1 U_2}$. *Then*

$$G(U) = \sum_{l_1 + l_2 = n} B^n_{l_1, l_2}(U) \cdot b^{l_1, l_2}_{0,0,0}$$

*can be written as a Bézier polynomial with Bézier points* $\{b^{l_1, l_2}_{0,0,0} : l_1 + l_2 = n\}$.

**Proof:** Writing $U \in \overline{U_1 U_2}$ as an affine combination $U = u_1 \cdot U_1 + u_2 \cdot U_2$ with $u_1 + u_2 = 1$, and using the fact that the blossom $f$ of $F$ is symmetric and affine in each component, the standard binomial theorem yields

$$G(U) = F(U) = f(\underbrace{U, ..., U}_{n})$$

$$= u_1 \cdot f(U_1, U, ..., U) + u_2 \cdot f(U_2, U, ..., U)$$

$$= \sum_{l_1 + l_2 = n} \binom{n}{l_1 l_2} \cdot f(\underbrace{U_1, ..., U_1}_{l_1}, \underbrace{U_2, ..., U_2}_{l_2})$$

$$= \sum_{l_1 + l_2 = n} B^n_{l_1 l_2}(U) \cdot f(\underbrace{U_1, ..., U_1}_{l_1}, \underbrace{U_2, ..., U_2}_{l_2}),$$

and Theorem 3.1 completes the proof. ∎

Figure 2 shows a Bézier curve on a Bézier triangle. The figure depicts the Bézier points with respect to the line segment $\overline{U_1, U_2}$. The underlying figure comes from [2].

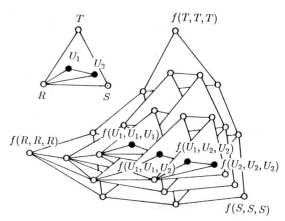

**Figure 2.** Bézier curve on a Bézier triangle.

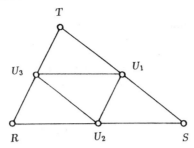

**Figure 3.** Subdivision of a Bézier triangle into four subtriangles.

**Corollary 3.5.** *(Second Subdivision Algorithm) In the special case $m = 2$ of Theorem 3.1 the points on the 2-dimensional subsimplices of the 4D-simplicial array $\{b_{i,j,k}^{l_1 l_2} : i + j + k + l_1 + l_2 = n\}$ can be used for subdividing the Bézier triangle $F(U)$ with respect to $U_1$ and $U_2$. In particular,*

- $\{b_{i,0,0}^{l_1 l_2} : i + l_1 + l_2 = n\}$ *contains the Bézier points w.r.t. to $\triangle(R, U_1, U_2)$*
- $\{b_{0,j,0}^{l_1 l_2} : j + l_1 + l_2 = n\}$ *contains the Bézier points w.r.t. $\triangle(S, U_1, U_2)$*
- $\{b_{0,0,k}^{l_1 l_2} : k + l_1 + l_2 = n\}$ *contains the Bézier points w.r.t. to $\triangle(T, U_1, U_2)$*

**Proof:** The proof follows directly from Theorem 3.1 in connection with Corollary 2.3. ∎

Finally, we consider the case $m = 3$:

**Corollary 3.6.** *(Third Subdivision Algorithm) In the special case $m = 3$ of the above theorem, the points on the 2-dimensional subsimplices of the 5-D-simplicial array $\{b_{i,j,k}^{l_1,l_2,l_3} : i+j+k+l_1+l_2+l_3 = n\}$ can be used for subdividing the Bézier triangle $F(U)$ with respect to $U_1, U_2, U_3$. In particular, the Bézier points of $F$ with respect to a different domain triangle $\triangle(U_1, U_2, U_3)$ are given by the points $b_{0,0,0}^{l_1,l_2,l_3}$ with $l_1 + l_2 + l_3 = n$.*

**Proof:** By Corollary 2.3, the Bézier points $c_{l_1,l_2,l_3}$ of $F$ with respect to $\triangle(U_1, U_2, U_3)$ are given as

$$c_{l_1,l_2,l_3} = f(\underbrace{U_1, ..., U_1}_{l_1}, \underbrace{U_2, ..., U_2}_{l_2}, \underbrace{U_3, ..., U_3}_{l_3}) = b_{0,0,0}^{l_1,l_2,l_3}. \quad \blacksquare$$

**Remark 1:** As has been pointed out by Boehm and Farin [2], to achieve a change of domain, it suffices to apply the simple de Casteljau algorithm three times instead of computing the whole 5-D-simplicial array $\{b_{i,j,k}^{l_1,l_2,l_3} : i + j + k + l_1 + l_2 + l_3 = n\}$. This follows from the fact that both the Bézier points $b_{i,j,k}$ of $F$ with respect to $\triangle(R, S, T)$ and the Bézier points $b_{0,0,0}^{l_1,l_2,l_3}$ of $F$ with respect to $\triangle(U_1, U_2, U_3)$ lie on 2-dimensional subsimplices, and that moving between two adjacent 2-dimensional-subsimplices may be achieved by a single application of the de Casteljau algorithm.

**Remark 2:** A similar remark holds for the problem of subdividing a Bézier triangle into four subtriangles according to Figure 3. As shown by Prautzsch [13], four applications of the de Casteljau algorithm suffice to solve this problem, since all necessary points are contained in the four tetrahedral arrays $\{b_{i,j,k}^{l_1,0,0} : ...\}$, $\{b_{i,j,0}^{l_1,l_2,0} : ...\}$, $\{b_{i,0,0}^{l_1,l_2,l_3} : ...\}$ and $\{b_{0,0,k}^{l_1,l_2,l_3} : ...\}$. This follows directly from Corollary 2.3.

## §4. Conclusions

We have given new proofs for the various subdivision algorithms for Bézier triangles from the viewpoint of multiaffine mappings. Using the so called *blossoming principle*, a closed form solution for the various recursive algorithms can be derived and from this the results follow readily.

Although we have restricted ourselves to surfaces in this paper, this restriction is by no means essential. In fact, since the blossoming principle holds for arbitrary multivariate polynomials $F : \mathbb{R}^c \rightarrow \mathbb{R}^d$, our proofs carry over to higher dimensional Bézier simplices almost word by word.

### References

1. Boehm, W., On de Boor-like algorithms and blossoming, Comput. Aided Geom. Design **5** (1988), 71–79.
2. Boehm, W. and G. Farin, Letter to the editor, Comput. Aided Design **15** (1983), 260–261.
3. Boehm, W., G. Farin and J. Kahmann, A survey of curve and surface methods in CAGD, Comput. Aided Geom. Design **1** (1984), 1–60.
4. de Casteljau, P., Courbes et surfâces à pôles, André Citroën Automobiles, Paris, 1963.
5. de Casteljau, P., *Formes à pôles*, Hermes Publishing, Paris, 1985.
6. de Casteljau, P., *Shape Mathematics and CAD*, Kogan Page Ltd, London, 1986.
7. Farin, G., Subsplines über Dreiecken, Diss. TU Braunschweig, 1979.
8. Farin, G., Bézier polynomials over triangles and the construction of piecewise $C^r$ polynomials, TR/91, Dept. of Mathematics, Brunel University, 1980.
9. Farin, G., Triangular Bernstein-Bézier patches, Comput. Aided Geom. Design **3** (1986), 83–127.
10. Filip, D., Practical Considerations for Triangular Patch Surfaces, Thesis, UC Berkeley, 1985.
11. Goldman, R., Using degenerate Bézier triangles and tetrahedra to subdivide Bézier curves, Comput. Aided Design **14** (1982), 307–311.
12. Goldman, R., Subdivision algorithms for Bézier triangles, Comput. Aided Design **15** (1983), 159–166.
13. Prautzsch, H., Unterteilungsalgorithmen für multivariate Splines, Diss. TU Braunschweig, 1984.

14. Ramshaw, L., Blossoming: A Connect-the-Dots Approach to Splines, SRC Report 19, Digital Systems Research Center, Palo Alto, 1987.
15. Ramshaw, L., Bézier and B-splines as multiaffine maps, in *Theoretical Foundations of Computer Graphics and CAD*, Springer, Berlin, 1988, 757–776.
16. Ramshaw, L., On restoring polynomial curves with spline curves of lesser degree, Symposium on CAGD, Jerusalem, 1988.
17. Seidel, H.-P., Knot insertion from a blossoming point of view, Comput. Aided Geom. Design **5** (1988), 81–86.
18. Seidel, H.-P., A new multiaffine approach to B-splines, Comput. Aided Geom. Design **6** (1989), 23–32.
19. Seidel, H.-P., Class lecture notes on Geometric Modeling, Wilhelm-Schickard-Institut für Informatik, Universität Tübingen, 1988.

H.-P. Seidel
Graphisch-Interaktive Systeme
Wilhelm-Schickard-Institut für Informatik
Universität Tübingen
D-7400 Tübingen
W. GERMANY

EMAIL: igsr001@ dtuzdv5a.bitnet

# Cardinal Interpolation with Translates of Shifted Bivariate Box-Splines

## Joachim Stoeckler

**Abstract.** We study cardinal interpolation by integer translates of shifted bivariate box-splines on the 3-directional mesh. For splines of low degree we obtain a complete characterization of all admissible shift parameters such that cardinal interpolation is correct.

## §1. Introduction

The bivariate three-directional box-spline $M_{r,s,t}$ is defined by its Fourier transform

$$\widehat{M_{r,s,t}}(x_1, x_2) = \left(\frac{\sin\frac{x_1}{2}}{\frac{x_1}{2}}\right)^r \left(\frac{\sin\frac{x_2}{2}}{\frac{x_2}{2}}\right)^s \left(\frac{\sin\frac{x_1+x_2}{2}}{\frac{x_1+x_2}{2}}\right)^t;$$

here $r, s, t \in \mathbb{N}_0$ and $\rho := \rho(r, s, t) := \min\{r + s, r + t, s + t\} \geq 1$. $M_{r,s,t}$ is symmetric with respect to the origin, has compact support, polynomial degree $r + s + t - 2$ and is $\rho - 2$-times continuously differentiable [2]. With $\phi := M_{r,s,t}$ the discrete Fourier transform

$$\tilde{\phi}(x) := \sum_{\alpha \in \mathbb{Z}^2} \phi(\alpha) e^{-i\alpha \cdot x}$$

does not vanish for any $x \in \mathbb{R}^2$. This property, proved by de Boor, Höllig and Riemenschneider [3], is necessary and sufficient for the correctness of *cardinal interpolation* by integer translates of $\phi$, cf. [3,6,8]: For any bounded data sequence $(y_\alpha)_{\alpha \in \mathbb{Z}^2}$ there is one and only one bounded sequence $(d_\alpha)_{\alpha \in \mathbb{Z}^2}$ satisfying

$$\sum_{\alpha \in \mathbb{Z}^2} d_\alpha \phi(\beta - \alpha) = y_\beta \quad \text{for all} \quad \beta \in \mathbb{Z}^2.$$

Mathematical Methods in Computer Aided Geometric Design
Tom Lyche and Larry L. Schumaker (eds.), pp. 583–592.

Moreover, the spline function interpolating the sequence $\delta = (\delta_{0\beta})$ (Kronecker symbol) decays exponentially [3,6,8].

In this paper we are concerned with suitable choices for the shift parameter $y \in \mathbb{R}^2$ such that cardinal interpolation with the shifted box-spline $M_{r,s,t}(\cdot+y)$ is again correct. A general result for the univariate case was proved by Micchelli [9]: Cardinal interpolation by integer translates of $M_n(\cdot+y), y \in [-1/2,+1/2]$, with $M_n$ the centered cardinal $B$-spline of order $n$, is correct if and only if $|y| < 1/2$. For bivariate box-splines of low degree, it also turns out that the region of all admissible shift parameters $y$ does not depend on the multiplicities $r, s$ and $t$.

This paper can be viewed as a contribution to finding more general configurations for the nodes in bivariate box-spline interpolation. Our results were announced earlier in the survey on cardinal interpolation of Jetter [8].

## §2. Exponential Euler Splines

In order to study the discrete Fourier transform $\tilde{\phi}_y$ of $\phi_y = M_{r,s,t}(\cdot + y)$, we define the functions

$$A_{r,s,t}(y;z) := \sum_{\alpha \in \mathbb{Z}^2} M_{r,s,t}(y - \alpha)z^\alpha, \qquad z = (z_1, z_2) \in (\mathbb{C}\backslash\{0\})^2. \qquad (1)$$

Similar functions, called *exponential Euler splines*, were introduced by Dahmen and Micchelli [7]. The name is partly due to the functional equation

$$A_{r,s,t}(y + \beta; z) = z^\beta A_{r,s,t}(y; z), \qquad \beta \in \mathbb{Z}^2. \qquad (2)$$

Since the relation

$$\tilde{\phi}_y(x_1, x_2) = A_{r,s,t}(y; e^{ix_1}, e^{ix_2}) \qquad (3)$$

holds for any $x_1, x_2 \in \mathbb{R}$, for our purposes we need only deal with complex arguments $|z_1| = |z_2| = 1$ in (1).

We list a few of the properties of $A_{r,s,t}$ which carry over from the box-spline $M_{r,s,t}$ (see [2,3,6,8]). First, $A_{r,s,t}$ is a piecewise polynomial function of degree $r+s+t-2$ with respect to the real variable $y$. It satisfies the recursion

$$A_{r,s,t}(y; z) = \int\limits_{-1/2}^{+1/2} A_{r,s,t-1}(y_1 + \tau, y_2 + \tau; z)d\tau, \qquad (4)$$

if $\rho(r, s, t - 1) \geq 1$. Furthermore, by the symmetries of $M_{r,s,t}$ (cf. [3]), for any $z_1, z_2 \in \mathbb{C}$ with $|z_1| = |z_2| = 1$ we have

$$A_{r,s,t}(y_1, y_2; z_1, z_2) = A_{r,s,t}(-y_1, -y_2; \bar{z}_1, \bar{z}_2), \qquad (5)$$

$$\begin{aligned}
A_{r,s,t}(y_1, y_2; z_1, z_2) &= A_{s,t,r}(y_1 - y_2, y_1; \bar{z}_2, z_1 z_2) \\
&= A_{t,r,s}(y_2, y_2 - y_1; z_1 z_2, \bar{z}_1) = A_{s,r,t}(y_2, y_1; z_2, z_1) \\
&= A_{t,s,r}(y_1, y_1 - y_2; z_1 z_2, \bar{z}_2) = A_{r,t,s}(y_2 - y_1, y_2; \bar{z}_1, z_1 z_2).
\end{aligned} \qquad (6)$$

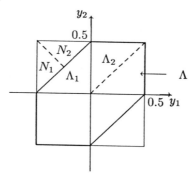

**Figure 1.** The set $\Lambda$ of admissible shift parameters.

Note that the symmetry relations (6) permute the indices $r, s$ and $t$. The coordinate transformations of the real parameters $y_1, y_2$ in (6) leave the set

$$\Lambda := \{(y_1, y_2) \in \mathbb{R}^2 \ : \ -1/2 \leq y_1, y_2, y_1 - y_2 \leq +1/2\} \tag{7}$$

given in Figure 1 fixed, while each component of $[-1/2, +1/2]^2 \backslash \Lambda$ is reflected or shifted by an integer vector. The transformations of the complex parameters $z_1, z_2$ are automorphisms of the torus group.

By (2) and (5) we can specify the location of certain values of $A_{r,s,t}$.

**Proposition 1.** *For any* $x = (x_1, x_2) \in \mathbb{R}^2$ *and any* $y \in \{\pm(\frac{1}{2}, 0), \pm(0, \frac{1}{2}),$ $\pm(\frac{1}{2}, \frac{1}{2}), \pm(\frac{1}{2}, -\frac{1}{2})\}$ *we have*

$$A_{r,s,t}(y; e^{ix_1}, e^{ix_2}) \in \mathbb{R} \cdot e^{i(y_1 x_1 + y_2 x_2)}.$$

## §3. Correctness of Cardinal Interpolation: General Results

In order to discuss correctness of cardinal interpolation with integer translates of $\phi_y = M_{r,s,t}(\cdot + y)$, we have to locate the roots of the function $A_{r,s,t}(y; z_1, z_2)$ on the torus $|z_1| = |z_2| = 1$, cf. (3). As a tool, we consider the corresponding functions for the univariate case

$$A_n(u; w) := \sum_{k \in \mathbb{Z}} M_n(u - k) w^k, \qquad u \in \mathbb{R}, w \in \mathbb{C} \backslash \{0\},$$

where $M_n$ is the centered cardinal $B$-spline of order $n$. By Micchelli's result [9], the following property of $A_n$ is known.

**Proposition 2.** *For arbitrary* $n \in \mathbb{N}$, *the only roots of* $A_n(u; w)$ *with* $u \in [-1/2, +1/2], w \in \mathbb{C}$ *and* $|w| = 1$ *are given by*

$$A_n(-1/2, -1) = A_n(+1/2, -1) = 0.$$

Furthermore, $A_n(u; -1)$ is even with respect to $u = 0$ and odd with respect to $u = 1/2$.

Now for the bivariate case the product structure

$$A_{r,s,0}(y; z) = A_r(y_1; z_1) A_s(y_2; z_2)$$

and the relations (6) lead to

**Theorem 1.** *Cardinal interpolation by translates of $M_{r,s,t}(\cdot + y)$ with $y \in [-1/2, 1/2]^2$, is correct*

> *for $r = 0$, if and only if $|y_2| \neq 1/2$ and $|y_1 - y_2| \neq 1/2$,*
> *for $s = 0$, if and only if $|y_1| \neq 1/2$ and $|y_1 - y_2| \neq 1/2$,*
> *for $t = 0$, if and only if $|y_1| \neq 1/2$ and $|y_2| \neq 1/2$.*

Furthermore, we can give the following extension of Sivakumar's result [10] concerning non-correctness along the boundary lines of the set $\Lambda$ in (7).

**Theorem 2.** *Let $y \in [-1/2, +1/2]^2$ and $r, s, t > 0$. Then cardinal interpolation with $M_{r,s,t}(\cdot + y)$ is **not** correct if $|y_1| = 1/2, |y_2| = 1/2$ or $|y_1 - y_2| = 1/2$.*

**Proof:** Because of (6), it is sufficient to deal with points $y = (u, u + 1/2), u \in \mathbb{R}$. Using Proposition 2 one can easily show

$$A_{r,s,1}(u, u + 1/2; -1, -1) = 0 \quad \text{for all} \quad u \in \mathbb{R}. \tag{8}$$

For general $t > 0$ the assertion follows from (8) and the recursion (4). ∎

## §4. Correctness of Cardinal Interpolation: Low Order Splines

For box-splines $M_{r,s,t}$ of degree up to 3 with none of the multiplicities $r, s, t$ vanishing we have a complete characterization of all shift parameters $y$ such that cardinal interpolation with translates of $M_{r,s,t}(\cdot + y)$ is correct.

**Theorem 3.** *Let $y \in [-1/2, +1/2]^2$ and $r, s, t \in \mathbb{N}$ with $r + s + t \leq 5$. Then cardinal interpolation with translates of $M_{r,s,t}(\cdot + y)$ is correct if and only if $y$ lies in the interior of the set $\Lambda$ given in (7).*

By the symmetry relations (5) and (6), for the proof of Theorem 3 we have only to deal with multiplicities $(r, s, t) \in \{(1, 1, 1), (1, 1, 2), (1, 1, 3), (2, 2, 1)\}$, and with shift parameters $y \in \Lambda_1 \cup \Lambda_2 \cup N_1$, cf. Figure 1. Since the method of the proof is similar for each set of multiplicities, we restrict ourselves to a detailed description of the cubic case $(r, s, t) = (2, 2, 1)$. The three sets $\Lambda_1, \Lambda_2$ and $N_1$ are treated separately.

(a) Correctness for all parameters $y \in \Lambda_1$ with $y_2 - y_1 \neq 1/2$:

We introduce barycentric coordinates $\mu_0(y) := -2y_1, \mu_1(y) := 2y_2$, $\mu_2(y) := 1 + 2y_1 - 2y_2$ on $\Lambda_1$. With the cubic Bernstein-Bézier basis polynomials

$$B_{k\ell m} := \frac{6}{k!\ell!m!} \mu_0^k \mu_1^\ell \mu_2^m, \quad k + \ell + m = 3, \quad k, \ell, m \geq 0,$$

the function $A_{2,2,1}(\cdot, z)|_{\Lambda_1}$ can be written in the form

$$A_{2,2,1}(y; z) = \sum_{k+\ell+m=3} c_{k\ell m}(z) B_{k\ell m}(y), \quad y \in \Lambda_1;$$

here $c_{k\ell m}(z)$ are complex coefficients given by

$$48 \cdot \begin{bmatrix} c_{003} \\ c_{012} \\ c_{021} \\ c_{030} \\ c_{102} \\ c_{111} \\ c_{120} \\ c_{201} \\ c_{210} \\ c_{300} \end{bmatrix} = \begin{bmatrix} 28 & 4 & 4 & 4 & 4 & 2 & 2 & 0 \\ 28 & 5 & 3 & 1 & 7 & 1 & 3 & 0 \\ 24 & 6 & 2 & 0 & 12 & 0 & 4 & 0 \\ 18 & 5 & 1 & 0 & 18 & 0 & 5 & 1 \\ 28 & 7 & 1 & 3 & 5 & 3 & 1 & 0 \\ 26 & 9 & 1 & 1 & 9 & 1 & 1 & 0 \\ 22 & 9 & 1 & 0 & 14 & 0 & 1 & 1 \\ 24 & 12 & 0 & 2 & 6 & 4 & 0 & 0 \\ 22 & 14 & 0 & 1 & 9 & 1 & 0 & 1 \\ 18 & 18 & 0 & 1 & 5 & 5 & 0 & 1 \end{bmatrix} \begin{bmatrix} 1 \\ \overline{z_1} \\ z_1 \\ \overline{z_2} \\ z_2 \\ \overline{z_1 z_2} \\ z_1 z_2 \\ z_1 \overline{z_2} \end{bmatrix} \quad (9)$$

The entries of the above matrix are found by using the algorithms given in [4] for computing the Bernstein-Bézier representation of $M_{r,s,t}$ on the translates of $\Lambda_1$.

Now the shift parameter $y \in \Lambda_1$ is cancelled in our consideration using the well known convex hull property of Bernstein-Bézier polynomials and the following lemma.

**Lemma 1.** *Let* $|z_1| = |z_2| = 1$, *and let* $c_{k\ell m}(z)$ *be as in (9). Then*

$$0 \in C(z) := \text{convex hull} \left( c_{k\ell m}(z) : \quad k + \ell + m = 3 \right)$$

*can only hold in one of the following cases:*

(i) $c_{k\ell m}(z) = 0$ *if* $m = 0$, *and* $\mathcal{R}e(c_{k\ell m}(z)) > 0$ *otherwise,*
(ii) $c_{300}(z) = 0$, *and* $\mathcal{R}e(c_{k\ell m}(z)) > 0$ *if* $k < 3$,
(iii) $c_{030}(z) = 0$, *and* $\mathcal{R}e(c_{k\ell m}(z)) > 0$ *if* $\ell < 3$.

(Here and in the following, $\mathcal{R}e$ and $\mathcal{I}m$ denote the real and the imaginary part of a complex number.)

In each of the above cases the point 0 is an extremal point of $C(z)$, and $A_{2,2,1}(y; z) = 0$ implies $\mu_2(y) = 0$, hence $y_2 - y_1 = 1/2$. Thus Lemma 1 gives the correctness assertion in Theorem 3 for all shift parameters $y \in \Lambda_1$, $y_2 - y_1 \neq 1/2$.

**Proof of Lemma 1:** Direct computations lead to the assertion of Lemma 1 if $z_1 = -1$ or $z_2 = -1$. Hence we have to consider the trigonometric polynomials

$$u_{k\ell m}(x_1, x_2) := 48 \, \mathcal{R}e(c_{k\ell m}(z_1, z_2)),$$
$$v_{k\ell m}(x_1, x_2) := 48 \, \mathcal{I}m(c_{k\ell m}(z_1, z_2)),$$

where $z_1 = e^{ix_1}$, $z_2 = e^{ix_2}$ and $x_1, x_2 \in (-\pi, +\pi)$. A study of these functions leads to

$$u_{k\ell m}(x_1, x_2) > 0 \quad \text{for all} \quad (k, \ell, m) \notin \{(3, 0, 0), (0, 3, 0)\}. \tag{10}$$

Let us consider the functions

$$u_{300}(x_1, x_2) = 18 + 18 \cos x_1 + 6 \cos x_2 + 5 \cos(x_1 + x_2) + \cos(x_1 - x_2)$$
$$= (18 + 6 \cos x_2)(1 + \cos x_1) - 4 \sin x_1 \sin x_2, \tag{11}$$
$$u_{030}(x_1, x_2) = u_{300}(x_2, x_1) \tag{12}$$

in more detail:

**Case 1:** ($u_{300}(x_1, x_2) > 0$ and $u_{030}(x_1, x_2) > 0$). Then by (10) the set $C(z)$ is contained in $\{w \in \mathbb{C} \mid \mathcal{R}e(w) > 0\}$. Hence 0 is not an element of $C(z)$.

**Case 2:** ($u_{300}(x_1, x_2) \leq 0$ and $0 \leq x_1 < \pi$). Some easy computations on (11) give in this case

$$0 < 3(\pi - x_1) < x_2 < x_1 < \pi \quad \text{and} \quad x_1 > \frac{5\pi}{6}. \tag{13}$$

In particular we can conclude

$$0 < \sin x_1 < \sin x_2. \tag{14}$$

Now if $u_{300}(x_1, x_2)$ vanishes, Proposition 1 and $|x_1| < \pi$ give $c_{300}(z_1, z_2) = 0$. Furthermore, by (12) and (13) we have

$$u_{030}(x_1, x_2) = u_{300}(x_2, x_1) > 0,$$

which in connection with (10) leads to the desired assertion, *i.e.*, to case (ii) of Lemma 1. If, however, $u_{300}(x_1, x_2)$ is strictly negative (which does happen!), then Proposition 1 and $0 \leq x_1 < \pi$ give

$$v_{300}(x_1, x_2) > 0. \tag{15}$$

Furthermore, inequality (14) leads directly to

$$v_{k\ell m}(x_1, x_2) > 0, \text{ if } (k, \ell, m) \in \{(0, 1, 2), (0, 2, 1), (1, 1, 1), \tag{16}$$
$$(0, 3, 0), (1, 2, 0)\}.$$

The positivity of the remaining trigonometric polynomials $v_{k\ell m}$ can be seen using

$$v_{003}(x_1, x_2) = 0,$$

$$v_{201}(x_1, x_2) = 2v_{102}(x_1, x_2) > \frac{2}{3}v_{300}(x_1, x_2) > 0, \tag{17}$$

$$v_{210}(x_1, x_2) > v_{300}(x_1, x_2) > 0.$$

Hence by (15), (16), (17) the set $C(z)$ lies in the upper half of the complex plane with only the point $c_{003}(z_1, z_2)$, a positive number, on the real axis. So $0$ cannot be an element of $C(z)$.

**Case 3** $(u_{300}(x_1, x_2) \leq 0$ and $-\pi < x_1 < 0)$. This case is similar.

**Case 4** $(u_{030}(x_1, x_2) \leq 0)$. This case is treated analogously using the symmetry relation (12).

This concludes the proof of Lemma 1. ∎

(b) The correctness for all parameters $y \in \Lambda_2, y_2 \neq 1/2$, is shown with the same method as above.

(c) To show the non-correctness for all parameters $y \in N_1$, we again use the Bernstein-Bézier form of $A_{2,2,1}$ on the triangle $N_1 \cup N_2$ (cf. Figure 1) with barycentric coordinates $\mu_0(y) = 1 - 2y_2, \mu_1(y) = 1 + y_1, \mu_2(y) = 2y_2 - 2y_1 - 1$. The control points are given by

$$48 \begin{bmatrix} d_{003} \\ d_{012} \\ d_{021} \\ d_{030} \\ d_{102} \\ d_{111} \\ d_{120} \\ d_{201} \\ d_{210} \\ d_{300} \end{bmatrix} = \begin{bmatrix} 8 & 16 & 0 & 0 & 16 & 0 & 0 & 8 \\ 12 & 12 & 0 & 0 & 20 & 0 & 0 & 4 \\ 16 & 8 & 0 & 0 & 20 & 0 & 2 & 2 \\ 18 & 5 & 1 & 0 & 18 & 0 & 5 & 1 \\ 12 & 20 & 0 & 0 & 12 & 0 & 0 & 4 \\ 18 & 14 & 0 & 0 & 14 & 0 & 0 & 2 \\ 22 & 9 & 1 & 0 & 14 & 0 & 1 & 1 \\ 16 & 20 & 0 & 0 & 8 & 2 & 0 & 2 \\ 22 & 14 & 0 & 1 & 9 & 1 & 0 & 1 \\ 18 & 18 & 0 & 1 & 5 & 5 & 0 & 1 \end{bmatrix} \begin{bmatrix} 1 \\ z_1 \\ \overline{z_1} \\ z_2 \\ \overline{z_2} \\ z_1 z_2 \\ \overline{z_1 z_2} \\ z_1 \overline{z_2} \end{bmatrix} \tag{18}$$

For fixed $y \in N_1$ let us consider the trigonometric functions

$$u(x_1, x_2) := \mathcal{R}e\left(A_{2,2,1}(y; e^{ix_1}, e^{ix_2})\right),$$

$$v(x_1, x_2) := \mathcal{I}m\left(A_{2,2,1}(y; e^{ix_1}, e^{ix_2})\right).$$

For the non-correctness proof we have to find a common root of $u$ and $v$. The main tool is given in

**Lemma 2.** For fixed $y \in N_1$ there is a continuous mapping $\alpha: [0, \pi] \to [0, \pi]$ with $\alpha(x) \geq \max\{x, \pi - x\}$, such that

$$v(\alpha(x), x) = 0.$$

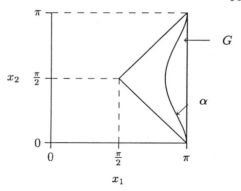

**Figure 2.** The construction of Lemma 2.

The region $G \subset [0, \pi]^2$ containing the curve $(\alpha(x), x)$ and a typical mapping $\alpha$ are shown in Figure 2.

Now we define the real-valued continuous function $a(x) := u(\alpha(x), x)$, $x \in [0, \pi]$. Using (18) it can be easily checked that $a$ changes sign in $[0, \pi]$, and this yields the existence of a common root of $u$ and $v$.

**Proof of Lemma 2:** Using (18) and the relation $\mu_0(y) \geq \mu_1(y)$ for all $y \in N_1$, we obtain the following properties of $v|_G$, where $G$ is given in Figure 2:

$$v(\pi, x) \leq 0, \quad \text{with equality if and only if } x = 0 \text{ or } x = \pi,$$
$$v(\pi - x, x) \geq 0, \quad \text{with equality if and only if } x = 0,$$
$$v(x, x) \geq 0, \quad \text{with equality if and only if } x = \pi \text{ or } \mu_0(y) = \mu_1(y).$$

These relations prove the existence of a root $(\tilde{\alpha}(x), x)$ of $v$ for any $x \in [0, \pi]$. Furthermore, some lengthy computations yield that at a root of $v$ which is interior to $G$, the partial derivative $\partial v / \partial x_2$ does not vanish. Furthermore, $\partial v / \partial x_2$ does not vanish at the corners $(\pi, 0)$ and $(\pi, \pi)$ of $G$.

Now if the strict inequality $\mu_0(y) > \mu_1(y)$ holds, then by the implicit function theorem the above choice of $\tilde{\alpha}(x)$ must be unique, and the mapping $x \mapsto \tilde{\alpha}(x)$ is differentiable on $[0, \pi]$. If, however, $\mu_0(y) = \mu_1(y)$ holds then we find a differentiable mapping $x \mapsto \tilde{\alpha}(x)$ on an interval $[0, x^*] \subset [0, \pi]$ with $\tilde{\alpha}(x^*) = x^*$. Hence the continuous mapping we are looking for is given by

$$\alpha(x) := \begin{cases} \tilde{\alpha}(x), & \text{if } x \in [0, x^*] \\ x, & \text{if } x \in [x^*, \pi]. \end{cases} \quad \blacksquare$$

These considerations complete the proof of Theorem 3 for the box-spline $M_{2,2,1}$.

## §5. Further Remarks

(a) In [10] Sivakumar develops the correctness assertion of Theorem 3 for all multiplicity vectors $(r, s, t) = (2n, 2n, 2n), n \in \mathbb{N}$.

(b) The approximation order of the scaled interpolation scheme for the shifted box-spline $M_{r,s,t}(\frac{1}{h}(\cdot + y))$ is the same as for the centered box-spline (cf. [1,6]). This is due to the fact that the order of the commutator does not change, see [5].

## Acknowledgement

I wish to express my gratitude to Prof. Dr. K. Jetter for the initiation of this study and for many valuable suggestions.

## References

1. Binev, P. G., Error estimate for box spline interpolation, in *Constructive Theory of Functions '87*, B. Sendov, P. Petrushev, K. Ivanov, and R. Maleev (eds.), Bulgarian Academy of Sciences, Sofia, 1988, 50–55.

2. de Boor, C. and R. DeVore, Approximation by smooth multivariate splines, Trans. Amer. Math. Soc. **276** (1983), 775–788.

3. de Boor, C., K. Höllig and S. D. Riemenschneider, Bivariate cardinal interpolation by splines on a three direction mesh, Illinois J. Math. **29** (1985), 533–566.

4. Chui, C. K., *Multivariate Splines, Theory and Applications*, CBMS Publications, SIAM, Philadelphia, 1988.

5. Chui, C. K., K. Jetter and J. D. Ward, Cardinal interpolation by multivariate splines, Math. Comp. **48** (1987), 711–724.

6. Dahmen, W. and C. A. Micchelli, Recent progress in multivariate splines, in *Approximation Theory IV*, C. K. Chui, L. L. Schumaker, and J. D. Ward (eds), Academic Press, New York, 1983, 27–121.

7. Dahmen, W. and C. A. Micchelli, On the multivariate Euler-Frobenius polynomials, in *Constructive Theory of Functions '87*, B. Sendov, P. Petrushev, K. Ivanov, and R. Maleev (eds.), Bulgarian Academy of Sciences, Sofia, 1988, 237–243.

8. Jetter, K., A short survey on cardinal interpolation by box splines, in *Topics in Multivariate Approximation*, C. K. Chui, L. L. Schumaker, and F. I. Utreras (eds), Academic Press, New York, 1987, 125–139.

9. Micchelli, C. A., Cardinal L-splines, in *Studies in Spline Functions and Approximation Theory*, S. Karlin, C. A. Micchelli, A. Pinkus, and I. J. Schoenberg (eds), Academic Press, New York, 1976, 163–202.

10. Sivakumar, N., On bivariate cardinal interpolation by shifted splines on a three-direction mesh, J. Approx.Theory, to appear.

Joachim Stoeckler
Department of Mathematics
Texas A&M University
College Station, Texas 77843
USA

# Approximation of Surfaces Constrained by a Differential Equation Using Simplex Splines

## C. R. Traas

**Abstract.** We investigate the utility of bivariate quadratic simplex splines for the approximation of surfaces. In the present application the surface is constrained to satisfy a differential equation. It is shown that with a fair amount of automatization these splines can be used very well.

## §1. Introduction

Over the past years a fairly complete theory of multivariate simplex splines (also called B-splines) has been developed by many authors. These splines are suitable for a wide range of applications, such as smooth surface fitting, solution of partial differential equations and computer-aided design.

Numerical experience is rather limited. This is a consequence of the expected high computational cost of the multivariate simplex spline, and of the complexity of grid partitions in higher dimensions. However, by automatization of certain processes in the various actions that precede an actual calculation (knot placement, boundary conditions), the weight of these objections can be reduced. In particular when choosing quadratic splines in two variables only, which can be arranged to be of class $C^1$, there are no serious practical limitations with respect to applications.

This article is concerned with the approximation of surfaces which are constrained to satisfy a differential equation. The problem is posed as an extremal problem over a suitable space of functions. Using the space of quadratic simplex splines over a given knot partition as an approximation space, the problem is reformulated as an extremal problem over a space of finite dimensional (coefficient) vectors.

Mathematical Methods in Computer Aided Geometric Design
Tom Lyche and Larry L. Schumaker (eds.), pp. 593–599.
Copyright ⊖ 1989 by Academic Press, Boston.
ISBN 0-12-460515-X.

An essential part in the optimization process is the computation of inner-products of *low-order* splines. In the test case considered in this article (corresponding physically with a thin bending plate), this concerns splines which are piecewise constant and have triangular support. The problem of finding an inner product therefore reduces to the determination of the area of the intersection of two arbitrarily shaped and oriented triangles. The problem of finding a first vertex of this intersection can be formulated as a *linear programming problem* for which the simplex method applies.

It is shown that bivariate quadratic simplex splines can be applied very well, and that they give numerical results comparable in accuracy with results of other methods which are based on piecewise quadratic polynomials.

## §2. Bivariate Simplex Splines

Let $x_0, \ldots, x_m$ be $m + 1$ points in $m$-space, having a convex hull with non-vanishing $m$-dimensional volume. The set of all points inside and on the convex hull is called the $m$-simplex $S$ based on the vertices $x_0, \ldots, x_m$:

$$S = \{x : x \in \mathbb{R}^m, \ x = t_0 x_0 + \cdots + t_m x_m, \ t_j \in \mathbb{R}^+, \ j = 0, \ldots, m, \ \sum_{j=0}^{m} t_j = 1\}.$$

For the special situation where $x_0 = 0$ and $x_i = (0, \ldots, 0, 1, 0, \ldots, 0)$ is the $i^{th}$ unit vector for $i = 1, \ldots, m$, the simplex is called the *standard $m$-simplex*. The $s$-variate simplex spline of degree $d$, over the knots $y_j$ is the function

$$M(y|y_0, \ldots, y_m) = \frac{\text{vol}_d\{x \ : \ x \in S, \quad \text{first } s \text{ components of } x = y\}}{\text{vol}_m(S)},$$

with $y, y_j \in \mathbb{R}^s$ and $y_j$ equal to the first $s$ components of $x_j$, $j = 0, \ldots, m$ and $d + s = m$.

In a sense, therefore, the spline can be considered as a projection onto $\mathbb{R}^s$ of an $m$-simplex. In the present article we consider, in particular, $s = 2$ (bivariate splines) and $d = 2$ (piecewise quadratics), and thus $m = 4$ (4-simplices as generators of the splines). The support of such a spline is given by the convex hull of the five knots $y_0, \ldots, y_4$ in $\mathbb{R}^2$. A straight line passing through any two of the knots separates quadratic polynomial pieces within the support of the spline. If the knots are in "general position" (*i.e.*, no three knots are on one straight line), then these quadratic pieces match in a $C^1$ sense. For special purposes, e.g. modeling discontinuities or satisfying boundary conditions, certain knots in one support are intentionally placed with three or four on a straight line. Nice pictures of simplex splines can be found in [5].

Our objective is, given a region $\Omega \subset \mathbb{R}^2$, to construct a set of simplex splines such that their *linear span* contains the space of all quadratic polynomials over the region $\Omega$. The construction of such a set proceeds as follows. Let $\Omega$ be properly triangulated; *i.e.*, partitioned into triangles such that any two of these triangles are either disjoint, or have an edge or a vertex in common. Consider every triangle of the triangulation as a **special** projection of a 4-simplex, in six different ways, namely, with different knot multiplicities: with two double knots and one simple knot, in three different ways, and with one three-fold knot and two simple knots, also in three different ways. The six simplex splines, corresponding to these configurations, are exactly (apart from a normalizing constant) the six quadratic Bernstein polynomials which can be defined on the triangle. The total collection of these splines over the entire triangulation can be considered to be generated by a collection of 4-simplices in the four-dimensional space which is defined by the direct product of $\Omega$ with the *standard 2-simplex*. These 4-simplices are carefully arranged: they precisely fill the four-dimensional space defined above, they are mutually disjoint or share a lower-dimensional face and, as described above, with each triangle of the triangulation six 4-simplices are associated.

Taking linear combinations of the splines, constructed in this manner, will not result, in general, in smooth surfaces. Only *special* linear combinations, as expressed in the Bézier-Bernstein formalism, will give smooth results. In order to obtain smooth results with arbitrary linear combinations, the simplex splines themselves should be smooth; *i.e.*, the multiplicity of the knots should be removed and the resulting five knots should be in general position. This can be achieved by applying the so-called process of *pulling apart the knots*. This process can be interpreted as a process of (slightly) *deforming* the four-dimensional space in which the generating 4-simplices are placed, deforming the 4-simplices collectively and in a coherent way. The simplices then still are generators of splines, and if care has been taken that no 3 or 4 knots in any one support are on one straight line, then all splines are (local-support) $C^1$ functions and, hence, any linear combination of them will result in a surface of class $C^1$.

The practical computation of a simplex spline can be performed by using a recurrence relation, which in the bivariate case reads as follows:

$$M(x|x_0,\ldots,x_m) = \frac{m}{m-2} \sum_{j=0}^{m} \lambda_j M(x|\{x_0,\ldots,x_m\} \setminus x_j). \qquad (1)$$

Here the $x_j \in \mathbb{R}^2$ are the knots which define the spline, and $x \in \mathbb{R}^2$ is the position at which its value is computed. In the quadratic case, $m = 4$. The $\lambda_j$ are barycentric coordinates, defined by

$$x = \sum_{j=0}^{m} \lambda_j x_j, \qquad \sum_{j=0}^{m} \lambda_j = 1.$$

The $\lambda_j$ are not defined uniquely in this way; there is some freedom of choice. The start of the recursion is a set of lowest order splines $M(x|x_{i_0}, x_{i_1}, x_{i_2})$, which are constants equal to $1/\mathrm{vol}_2[x_{i_0}, x_{i_1}, x_{i_2}]$ inside the convex hull of their knots, and zero otherwise.

The directional derivative $y^T$ grad $M$ of the simplex spline $M$ in the direction $y$, for which we use the notation $D_y M$, can also be expressed as a linear combination of lower order splines:

$$D_y M(x|x_0, \ldots, x_m) = m \sum_{j=0}^{m} \mu_j M(x|\{x_0, \ldots, x_m\} \setminus x_j), \qquad (2)$$

where the $\mu_j$ are defined by

$$y = \sum_{j=0}^{m} \mu_j x_j, \qquad \sum_{j=0}^{m} \mu_j = 0.$$

A more detailed treatment of the theory of simplex splines can be found in [1]. Practical processes for realizing the pulling apart are described in [2], and the treatment of boundary conditions is described in [7].

## §3. Surfaces Constrained by a Differential Equation

The aim is to construct a function $u(x, y)$ which satisfies given boundary conditions and, in addition, satisfies a given partial differential equation in a region $\Omega \subset \mathbb{R}^2$. Assume that a variational principle exists for the problem considered; *i.e.*, let a functional $J[u]$, defined on the function space in which the solution is sought, be associated with the differential problem, attaining an extremum for the element $u$ which is a solution of this problem. Then a derived problem is to compute *inner products*; *i.e.*, to evaluate integrals which, in case of a fourth order differential equation, look like

$$\int \int_{\Omega} \frac{\partial^2 u}{\partial x^p \partial y^q} \cdot \frac{\partial^2 u}{\partial x^r \partial y^s} \, dx dy, \qquad p + q = r + s = 2.$$

Introducing the space of quadratic simplex splines over a given knot partition (obtained by pulling apart) in $\Omega$ as an approximation space, the problem becomes an extremal problem over a finite-dimensional space of coefficient vectors. The inner products then have to be evaluated for these splines. By using (2) twice, a second order partial derivative of a bivariate quadratic simplex spline can be written as a linear combination of at most nine bivariate constant splines. The evaluation of the inner product, therefore, reduces to summing up at most 81 inner products of lowest order splines; *i.e.*, splines which are constant within their supports consisting of three points. Evaluating these latter inner products means computing the area of the intersection of two triangles, each being oriented arbitrarily in the plane.

A first problem in this connection is to find a first vertex of the intersection of two triangles in the plane. Several approaches to a solution of this problem exist; a practical way is to use the *linear programming method*, which is quite natural because of the fact that the problem can be formulated as a problem involving linear inequalities.

## §4. Inner Products of Lowest Order Splines

The problem of the computation of inner products of lowest order splines (in two variables) can be reduced to the determination of the area of the intersection of two triangles, oriented arbitrarily in the plane. Let the vertices $(x_1, x_2, x_3)$ and $(x_4, x_5, x_6)$, respectively, represent two such triangles. All points of the intersection of the triangles satisfy the relations $\lambda_i \geq 0$, $i = 1, \ldots, 6$, where $\{\lambda_1, \lambda_2, \lambda_3\}$ and $\{\lambda_4, \lambda_5, \lambda_6\}$ are barycentric coordinates w.r.t. the first triangle and the second triangle, respectively. Introduce a local Cartesian system of coordinates $\xi, \eta$, with one of the six vertices $x_i$ as the origin and such that the other vertices of the associated triangle have nonnegative coordinates in this system (then all points of the intersection of the two triangles will certainly have nonnegative coordinates). Following the formalism of the *simplex method*, introduce *slack variables* $y_1, \ldots, y_6$ to convert inequalities to equalities:

$$\lambda_i - y_i = 0, \qquad i = 1, \ldots, 6,$$

and, as far as the initial vector $y$ (consisting of the components $y_1, \ldots, y_6$) is not feasible (e.g. $y_p < 0$ for some $p \in \{1, 2, 3, 4, 5, 6\}$) for the starting point (the origin of the local system), introduce *artificial variables* $z_p$ (two at most) and the equality constraint(s),

$$\lambda_p - y_p + z_p = 0.$$

The (auxiliary) objective function is defined by $z = -\sum_p z_p$, and the initial basic vector in the linear programming tableau consists of the $y_i$ components with $i \neq p$, together with the artificial variable(s) $z_p$ . The initial non-basic vector consists of the variables $\xi, \eta$ and $y_p$, which all are zero in the starting point. At most three simplex steps are required to find a first vertex of the intersection of the two triangles.

Once a first vertex has been found, the other vertices of the intersection can be found by simply stepping from a vertex to its neighbor by pushing the relevant barycentric coordinate to zero, taking care that all barycentric coordinates remain nonnegative. Some special attention is needed during this latter process in case of certain special configurations, e.g. triangles with (partially) coinciding edges or with coinciding vertices. Finally, the area of the intersection is readily computed.

## §5. Evaluation of a Model Problem

The differential equation chosen is the one describing the deflection of a thin, loaded plate. This problem has been solved already in many ways, so good computational material is available for comparison (see e.g. [6]). For this problem a variational principle exists. The high order of the occurring derivatives requires the approximative description of the deflection to be of class $C^1$. In this respect the space of quadratic simplex splines, as described above, is a suitable tool.

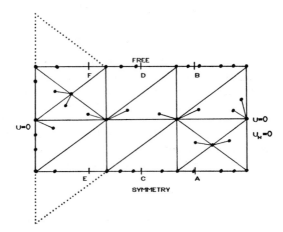

**Figure 1.** Upper half of bending plate.

The configuration adopted is given in Figure 1. It represents a thin, square plate, bending under its own weight. One side of the plate is clamped (boundary condition $u = 0$, $\frac{\partial u}{\partial n} = 0$) and the opposite side is simply supported (boundary condition $u = 0$). The two other sides are free. This configuration contains a line of symmetry; therefore only one half of the plate needs to be analyzed. The triangulation chosen is given in the figure, together with the pulled knots. The flaps at the left are extensions, outside the plate, of the triangulation. They only serve the purpose to match the symmetry condition and the free boundary condition, respectively, with the simply supported boundary condition; see [7]. These cornerpoints cannot be taken as multiple points, otherwise non-regularities will propagate into the interior of the plate. From each of the flaps three of the six associated splines are used. (Another way to prevent an inward propagation of non-regularities is to avoid diagonals which depart from multiple cornerpoints. We did not make this choice here).

The results of the computation can be compared with the results presented in [6] and [3]. These results are available in the points A through F, indicated in Figure 1. Table 1 gives a survey.

|  | simplex splines | split triangle | "exact" |
|---|---|---|---|
| $u_A$ | 3.6208 | 3.6268 | 3.8600 |
| $u_B$ | 3.8702 | 3.8806 | 4.0780 |
| $u_C$ | 7.9348 | 7.9696 | 8.2410 |
| $u_D$ | 8.4300 | 8.5065 | 8.8081 |
| $u_E$ | 6.7535 | 6.7561 | 6.9554 |
| $u_F$ | 7.1179 | 7.2292 | 7.4573 |

**Table 1.** Computed deflections of thin plate ($*10^2$ ).

The quoted results from [3] were obtained with a split-triangle quadratic element, see [4], by partitioning the upper half of the thin plate into 16 triangles (a uniform, unidiagonal "type 1" grid). The fineness of this grid is comparable with that of the grid used in Figure 1, and also the numerical results are very comparable. The quoted results from [6] have been obtained with a bicubic rectangular conforming element and are considered, on the basis of convergence results with decreasing mesh width, to be correct to four digits.

## References

1. Dahmen, W. and C. A. Micchelli, Multivariate splines - a new constructive approach, in *Surfaces in CAGD*, R. E. Barnhill and W. Boehm (eds.), North-Holland, 1983, 191–215.
2. Gmelig Meyling, R. H. J., An algorithm for constructing configurations of knots for bivariate B-splines, SIAM J. Numer. Anal. **24** (1987), 706–724.
3. Gmelig Meyling, R. H. J., Numerical solution of the biharmonic equation using different types of bivariate spline functions, in *Algorithms for Approximation II*, J. C. Mason and M. G. Cox (eds.), Chapman and Hall, London, 1989.
4. Heindl, G., Interpolation and approximation by piecewise quadratic $C^1$-functions of two variables, in *Multivariate Approximation Theory*, W. Schempp and K. Zeller (eds.), 1979, 146–161.
5. Micchelli, C. A., On a numerically efficient method for computing multivariate B-splines, in *Multivariate Approximation Theory*, W. Schempp and K. Zeller (eds.), 1979, 211–248.
6. Schwarz, H. R., *Methode der Finiten Elemente*, Teubner Studienbücher, 1980.
7. Traas, C. R., Boundary conditions with bivariate quadratic B-splines, in *Approximation Theory V*, C. K. Chui, L. L. Schumaker and J. D. Ward (eds.), Academic Press, 1986, 595–598.

C. R. Traas
Faculty of Applied Mathematics
University of Twente
P. O. Box 217
7500 AE Enschede
THE NETHERLANDS

EMAIL: traas1@ henut5.bitnet

# A Construction for VC$^1$ Continuity
# of Rational Bézier Patches

## A. Vinacua and P. Brunet

**Abstract.** The literature on rational Bézier patches focuses mostly on their algebraic definition and manipulation; it is our opinion that a geometrical approach should be sought, along similar lines to what has been done in the nonrational case. In this paper we show how a natural geometric representation for the weights already used by Farin for rational curves allows a geometric construction for VC$^1$ stitching of rectangular and triangular rational patches to be defined. The resulting procedure generalizes a known construction for the nonrational case, also due to Farin.

## §1. Introduction

One of the reasons why Bézier curves and surface patches are so popular is the rich interplay between geometrical properties of the control net and the resulting curve or surface. For polynomial surfaces there is an abundant literature on these kind of connections (see for example [2] and references therein). However, not much has been done in this connection for their rational counterparts. Rational curves are treated in [1,4], for example, but we know of no such work dealing with rational surfaces from this point of view.

In this paper we search for these kinds of results in connection with the sewing together of surface patches with visual continuity (see e.g. [5,6]) of the first order, thus extending the results in [3]. To do this, one needs to have information on the weights associated with each control node attached to the control net in a manner suitable for the intended geometric approach. We find that the practical way to do this is using points analogous to the auxiliary points used by Farin in [4], together with appropriate compatibility conditions that are needed in the case of surfaces.

In Sections 2 and 3 we compute a pair of tangent directions —spanning the tangent plane— to a rectangular and a triangular patch. Using these

Mathematical Methods in Computer Aided Geometric Design
Tom Lyche and Larry L. Schumaker (eds.), pp. 601–611.

computations, in Section 4 we obtain a procedure to determine the first row of control points (and the corresponding weights) of a neighboring patch in order to have continuity of the tangent plane across the boundary. The row obtained is just one of many that would achieve this, under certain stringent hypotheses (which are nonetheless common in the related literature) necessary to be able to carry out the computations. In Section 5 we go back to the non-rational case and revisit Farin's transition principle (see [4]).

## §2. Tangential Directions for Rectangular Patches

Consider a rectangular patch of the standard form

$$S(u,v) = \frac{\sum\limits_{i,j=0}^{n} \beta_{ij} \mathbf{P}_{ij} B_i^n(u) B_j^n(v)}{\sum\limits_{i,j=0}^{n} \beta_{ij} B_i^n(u) B_j^n(v)},$$

and let us concentrate on its boundary. The boundary curve along, say, $u = 0$, is given by

$$C_{u=0}(v) = S(0,v) = \frac{\sum\limits_{j=0}^{n} \beta_{0j} \mathbf{P}_{0j} B_j^n(v)}{\sum\limits_{j=0}^{n} \beta_{0j} B_j^n(v)}.$$

The derivative along the direction of this curve is then given by $\frac{d}{dv} C_{u=0}(v)$. Since we are only interested in the direction of this derivative, we need not evaluate it completely. We are free to discard any scalar factors. Keeping this in mind, we compute the numerator of this derivative, which is, after the usual simplifications,

$$n \left[ \sum_{i=0}^{n} \sum_{j=0}^{n-1} \left( \beta_{0\,j+1} \mathbf{P}_{0\,j+1} - \beta_{0j} \mathbf{P}_{0j} \right) B_j^{n-1}(v) \beta_{0i} B_i^n(v) - \right.$$
$$\left. - \sum_{i=0}^{n} \sum_{j=0}^{n-1} \beta_{0i} \mathbf{P}_{0i} B_i^n(v) \left( \beta_{0\,j+1} - \beta_{0j} \right) B_j^{n-1}(v) \right],$$

and dividing this by $n$, $\left( \sum_{i=0}^{n} \beta_{0j} B_j^n(v) \right)$ and $\left( \sum_{j=0}^{n-1} (\beta_{0\,j+1} - \beta_{0j}) B_j^{n-1}(v) \right)$ we obtain

$$\frac{\sum\limits_{j=0}^{n-1} \left( \beta_{0\,j+1} \mathbf{P}_{0\,j+1} - \beta_{0j} \mathbf{P}_{0j} \right) B_j^{n-1}(v)}{\sum\limits_{j=0}^{n-1} \left( \beta_{0\,j+1} - \beta_{0j} \right) B_j^{n-1}(v)} - \frac{\sum\limits_{i=0}^{n} \beta_{0i} \mathbf{P}_{0i} B_i^n(v)}{\sum\limits_{i=0}^{n} \beta_{0i} B_i^n(v)}, \qquad (1)$$

which can be regarded as the difference between two rational Bézier curves; *i.e.*, as the vector joining equiparametric points of these two curves.

Analogously we compute the transversal derivative $\frac{\partial}{\partial u}S(0,v)$, which after similar transformations, yields the tangential direction given by

$$\frac{\sum\limits_{j=0}^{n}\beta_{1j}\mathbf{P}_{1j}B_j^n(v)}{\sum\limits_{j=0}^{n}\beta_{1j}B_j^n(v)}-\frac{\sum\limits_{i=0}^{n}\beta_{0i}\mathbf{P}_{0i}B_i^n(v)}{\sum\limits_{i=0}^{n}\beta_{0i}B_i^n(v)}. \tag{2}$$

Again the direction is given by a vector joining points of equal parameter value on two rational Bézier curves. Note also that the second terms in (1) and (2) are the same, namely the boundary curve itself. This last formula also shows that scaling the weights of the second row has no effect on the direction of these two derivatives, and hence on the first order visual continuity along this boundary, although it may change the shape of the patch if the other weights are not scaled by the same factor.

## §3. Tangential Directions for Triangular Patches

Let us consider now the case of triangular patches. Using the standard barycentric coordinates $u$, $v$, $w$, $u+v+w=1$, the parametric equation of a triangular rational Bézier patch of degree n can be written as

$$S(u,v,w)=\frac{\sum\limits_{i+j+k=n}\beta_{ijk}\mathbf{P}_{ijk}B_{ijk}^n}{\sum\limits_{i+j+k=n}\beta_{ijk}B_{ijk}^n}. \tag{3}$$

As is well known, boundary curves are standard rational Bézier curves. For instance, when $u=0$, $w=1-v$,

$$C_{u=0}(v)=S(0,v,1-v)=\frac{\sum\limits_{j=0}^{n}\beta_{0j\,n-j}\mathbf{P}_{0j\,n-j}B_j^n(v)}{\sum\limits_{j=0}^{n}\beta_{0j\,n-j}B_j^n(v)}. \tag{4}$$

Along the boundary $u=0$, we will assume in what follows that the curve $C_{u=0}(v)$ is degree-elevated; in other words, it can also be written in terms of a reduced set of control vertices, $\mathbf{P}_{00n-1}^*\cdots\mathbf{P}_{0n-10}^*,$

$$C_{u=0}(v)=\frac{\sum\limits_{j=0}^{n-1}\beta_{0j\,n-1-j}^*\mathbf{P}_{0j\,n-1-j}^*B_j^{n-1}}{\sum\limits_{j=0}^{n-1}\beta_{0j\,n-1-j}^*B_j^{n-1}}. \tag{5}$$

In this case, comparing equations (4), (5) and using the properties of the Bernstein polynomials, it is easy to derive the following relations between both sets of control vertices and weights:

$$\beta_{0j\ n-j}\mathbf{P}_{0j\ n-j} = \frac{j}{n}\beta^*_{0\ j-1\ n-j}\mathbf{P}^*_{0\ j-1\ n-j} + \frac{n-j}{j}\beta^*_{0j\ n-1-j}\mathbf{P}^*_{0j\ n-1-j}$$

$$\beta_{0j\ n-j} = \frac{j}{n}\beta^*_{0\ j-1\ n-j} + \frac{n-j}{j}\beta^*_{0j\ n-1-j}.$$

In the following, we will use the abridged notations $\beta_{0j}$ and $\mathbf{P}_{0j}$ for $\beta_{0j\ n-j}$ and $\mathbf{P}_{0j\ n-j}$. Similarly, we will write $\beta^*_{0j}$ , $\mathbf{P}^*_{0j}$ instead of $\beta^*_{0j\ n-1-j}$ , $\mathbf{P}^*_{0j\ n-1-j}$, and $\beta_{1j}$ , $\mathbf{P}_{1j}$ instead of $\beta_{1j\ n-1-j}$ , $\mathbf{P}_{1j\ n-1-j}$.

Obviously, the tangential derivative along the boundary of a triangular rational patch has the same expression as the corresponding derivative in rectangular patches. In order to compute an expression for the transversal derivative, let us first compute the directional derivative of (3) in a generic direction $\xi = (u', v', w')$, with $u' + v' + w' = 0$. After several manipulations and neglecting the constant denominator, it can be written in terms of univariate Bernstein polynomials as

$$D_\xi\Big|_{u=0} = \sum_{i=0}^{n-1}\left(n\sum_{j=0}^{n}u'\beta_{0j}\beta_{1i}\mathbf{P}_{1i}B_i^{n-1}B_j^n + H_i\beta^*_{0i}\mathbf{P}^*_{0i}\right), \qquad (6)$$

where we assume that $B^{n-1}_{-1} = B^{n-1}_n = 0$ and

$$H_i = (n-i)\sum_{j=0}^{n}\left(v'\frac{j-i}{i}B_j^n B_{i-1}^{n-1} + w'\frac{i-j}{n-i}B_j^n B_i^{n-1}\right)\beta_{0j} -$$

$$- (n-i)\sum_{j=0}^{n-1}u'\beta_{1j}B_i^n B_j^{n-1} +$$

$$+ (i+1)\sum_{j=0}^{n}\left(v'\frac{j-i-1}{i+1}B_j^n B_i^{n-1} + w'\frac{i+1-j}{n-i-1}B_j^n B_{i+1}^{n-1}\right)\beta_{0j} -$$

$$- (i+1)\sum_{j=0}^{n-1}u'\beta_{1j}B_{i+1}^n B_j^{n-1}.$$

In the general case, $H_i$ contains weights from the first and second row of control vertices of the patch, $\beta_{0j}$ and $\beta_{1j}$. However, for the particular choice of the vector $\xi = (-1, v, 1-v)$, the terms containing weights from the first row vanish, and the expression for the transversal derivative $D_\xi\Big|_{u=0}$ becomes symmetric. In this case,

$$H_i = -(n-i)\sum_{j=0}^{n-1}u'\beta_{1j}B_i^n B_j^{n-1} - (i+1)\sum_{j=0}^{n-1}u'\beta_{1j}B_{i+1}^n B_j^{n-1}. \qquad (7)$$

From (6) and (7), regrouping terms and dividing by $n$, $(\sum_{s=0}^{n-1} \beta_{0s}^* B_s^{n-1})$ and by $(\sum_{s=0}^{n-1} \beta_{1s} B_s^{n-1})$, the following expression for the direction of $D_\xi\big|_{u=0}$ is obtained:

$$
D_\xi\Big|_{u=0} = \frac{\sum\limits_{j=0}^{n-1} \beta_{1j}\mathbf{P}_{1j}B_j^{n-1}}{\sum\limits_{j=0}^{n-1} \beta_{1j}B_j^{n-1}} - \frac{\sum\limits_{j=0}^{n-1} \beta_{0j}^*\mathbf{P}_{0j}^*B_j^{n-1}}{\sum\limits_{j=0}^{n-1} \beta_{0j}^*B_j^{n-1}}.
$$

Comparing with equation (2), it can be observed that the transversal derivative along the boundaries in rational triangular Bézier patches has the same expression as the corresponding derivative in rectangular patches.

## §4. The VC¹ Construction

Let us now consider two neighboring patches; from the preceding two sections we learn that it does not matter what kind of patches they are, because the formal expressions for the two tangential directions —under the hypothesis made— are the same for triangular and rectangular patches. We may thus be in any of the possible combinations: rectangular–rectangular, triangular–rectangular or triangular–triangular. In what follows, if any of the intervening patches is triangular, we will assume that its boundary has been degree-reduced, and the weights and control points that we will refer to will be, along the boundary, these degree-reduced weights and control points. After things have been sewn together in an appropriate manner, we can easily degree-elevate these boundaries to get a standard control net for the triangular patches.

As in [3], we will say that the two patches match each other with first order visual continuity (VC¹) if they share the tangent plane along the common boundary. This, according to our computations in Sections 2 and 3, means that for each value of the parameter $v \in [0,1]$, the four points

$$
\frac{\sum\limits_{j=0}^{n} \beta_{1j}\mathbf{P}_{1j}B_j^n(v)}{\sum\limits_{j=0}^{n} \beta_{1j}B_j^n(v)}, \qquad \frac{\sum\limits_{j=0}^{n-1}\left(\beta_{0\,j+1}\mathbf{P}_{0\,j+1} - \beta_{0j}\mathbf{P}_{0j}\right)B_j^{n-1}(v)}{\sum\limits_{j=0}^{n-1}\left(\beta_{0\,j+1} - \beta_{0j}\right)B_j^{n-1}(v)},
$$

$$
\frac{\sum\limits_{j=0}^{n} \beta_{-1j}\mathbf{P}_{-1j}B_j^n(v)}{\sum\limits_{j=0}^{n} \beta_{-1j}B_j^n(v)} \qquad \text{and} \qquad \frac{\sum\limits_{j=0}^{n} \beta_{0j}\mathbf{P}_{0j}B_j^n(v)}{\sum\limits_{j=0}^{n} \beta_{0j}B_j^n(v)}
$$

are coplanar. Here the subindices $0j$ correspond to weights and control points on the shared boundary, and $1j$ and $-1j$ to those on the first row into each of the two patches.

As $v$ varies, these four points describe four rational Bézier curves. These curves are projections of polynomial Bézier curves in $\mathbb{R}^4$, and the condition that these four points be coplanar is equivalent to the condition that the corresponding points in $\mathbb{R}^4$, given by

$$
\mathcal{P} = \begin{bmatrix} \sum\limits_{j=0}^{n} \beta_{1j}\mathbf{P}_{1j}B_j^n(v) \\ \sum\limits_{j=0}^{n} \beta_{1j}B_j^n(v) \end{bmatrix}, \quad
\mathcal{Q} = \begin{bmatrix} \sum\limits_{j=0}^{n-1} \left(\beta_{0\,j+1}\mathbf{P}_{0\,j+1} - \beta_{0j}\mathbf{P}_{0j}\right)B_j^{n-1}(v) \\ \sum\limits_{j=0}^{n-1} \left(\beta_{0\,j+1} - \beta_{0j}\right)B_j^{n-1}(v) \end{bmatrix},
$$

$$
\mathcal{R} = \begin{bmatrix} \sum\limits_{j=0}^{n} \beta_{-1j}\mathbf{P}_{-1j}B_j^n(v) \\ \sum\limits_{j=0}^{n} \beta_{-1j}B_j^n(v) \end{bmatrix} \quad \text{and} \quad
\mathcal{S} = \begin{bmatrix} \sum\limits_{j=0}^{n} \beta_{0j}\mathbf{P}_{0j}B_j^n(v) \\ \sum\limits_{j=0}^{n} \beta_{0j}B_j^n(v) \end{bmatrix}
$$

lie on a hyperplane passing through the origin. That is, we must require that the four position vectors for $\mathcal{P}(v)$, $\mathcal{Q}(v)$, $\mathcal{R}(v)$ and $\mathcal{S}(v)$ be linearly dependent for each value of the parameter in $[0,1]$. Therefore, there must exist four functions $\alpha(v)$, $\beta(v)$, $\gamma(v)$ and $\xi(v)$ such that

$$
0 \equiv \alpha(v)\mathcal{P}(v) + \beta(v)\mathcal{Q}(v) + \gamma(v)\mathcal{R}(v) + \xi(v)\mathcal{S}(v). \tag{8}
$$

To make computations feasible, we need to make some hypothesis on the nature of these functions. We take here —as has been done elsewhere— the simplest possible case, namely that these functions are also polynomials and that their degree is 1. Then obviously $\alpha$, $\beta$ and $\gamma$ must be constants, and $\xi(v) = \xi_0(1 - v) + \xi_1 v$. Substituting these in (8), and doing some algebra, one easily sees that $\forall j = 0, \ldots, n$,

$$
\alpha\mathcal{P}_{1j} + \gamma\mathcal{P}_{-1j} + \xi_0\frac{n-j}{n}\mathcal{P}_{0\,j+1} + \left[\beta - \xi_0\frac{n-j}{n} + \xi_1\frac{j}{n}\right]\mathcal{P}_{0j} - \xi_1\frac{j}{n}\mathcal{P}_{0\,j-1} = 0,
$$

where $\mathcal{P}_{ij} = \begin{bmatrix} \mathbf{P}_{ij} \\ \beta_{ij} \end{bmatrix} \in \mathbb{R}^4$. Taking $\gamma$ to be $-1$, this can be rewritten as

$$
\begin{aligned}
\mathcal{P}_{-1j} = \; & \frac{n-j}{n}\left[\alpha\mathcal{P}_{1j} + \xi_0\mathcal{P}_{0\,j+1} + \left[\beta - \xi_0\right]\mathcal{P}_{0j}\right] + \\
& \frac{j}{n}\left[\alpha\mathcal{P}_{1j} + \left[\beta + \xi_1\right]\mathcal{P}_{0j} - \xi_1\mathcal{P}_{0\,j-1}\right].
\end{aligned} \tag{9}
$$

For the corner $j = 0$, for instance, (9) reduces to

$$
\mathcal{P}_{-10} = \alpha\mathcal{P}_{10} + \xi_0\mathcal{P}_{01} + \left[\beta - \xi_0\right]\mathcal{P}_{00}. \tag{10}
$$

Notice that this condition is less stringent than the condition for the visual continuity of the two patches in $\mathbb{R}^4$. If $\alpha + \beta \neq 1$, the previous formula gives for $\mathcal{P}_{-10}$ a point which does not lie on the plane determined by $\mathcal{P}_{00}$, $\mathcal{P}_{10}$ and

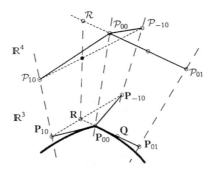

**Figure 1.** Computing the cross ratio (11).

$\mathcal{P}_{01}$, and therefore the two patches *do not* meet smoothly in $\mathbb{R}^4$. However, this singularity will be killed by the projection.

The main point now is how to obtain the coefficients in (9). Noting that neighboring patches may already have fixed these, one can use (10) and the corresponding formula for the corner $j = n$ to find these coefficients from given $\mathcal{P}_{-10}$ and $\mathcal{P}_{-1n}$. To see how one can do this, let us concentrate on the case $j = 0$. Consider the point $\mathcal{R}$ given by the intersection of the plane determined by the origin, $\mathcal{P}_{10}$ and $\mathcal{P}_{-10}$ and the line through $\mathcal{P}_{00}$ and $\mathcal{P}_{01}$ (see Figure 1).

From (10) one sees that

$$\mathcal{R} = \frac{\mathcal{P}_{-10} - \alpha \mathcal{P}_{10}}{\beta} = \frac{\xi_0}{\beta} \mathcal{P}_{01} + \frac{\beta - \xi_0}{\beta} \mathcal{P}_{00}$$

from which one easily computes the cross ratio

$$\text{Cr}\left(\mathcal{P}_{00}, \mathcal{R}, \frac{\mathcal{P}_{00} + \mathcal{P}_{01}}{2}, \mathcal{P}_{01}\right) = \text{ratio}\left(\mathcal{P}_{00}, \mathcal{R}, \mathcal{P}_{01}\right) = \frac{\xi_0}{\beta - \xi_0}. \qquad (11)$$

Here we have taken $\text{Cr}(\mathbf{a}, \mathbf{b}, \mathbf{c}, \mathbf{d})$ to mean $\dfrac{\text{``}\mathbf{b} - \mathbf{a}\big/\mathbf{d} - \mathbf{b}\text{''}}{\text{``}\mathbf{c} - \mathbf{a}\big/\mathbf{d} - \mathbf{c}\text{''}}$. Notice that this quantity has geometrical meaning even in $\mathbb{R}^3$, since the cross ratio is invariant under projections. The midpoint $\frac{\mathcal{P}_{00} + \mathcal{P}_{01}}{2}$ is projected down to some point $\mathbf{Q}$ in $\overline{\mathbf{P}_{00}\mathbf{P}_{01}}$ which carries all the information about the ratio of the weights $\beta_{00}$ and $\beta_{01}$. In fact $Q = \left(\beta_{00}\mathbf{P}_{00} + \beta_{01}\mathbf{P}_{01}\right)\big/\left(\beta_{00} + \beta_{01}\right)$. One can regard it as the position at which an imaginary wedge should be placed to balance the segment $\overline{\mathbf{P}_{00}\mathbf{P}_{01}}$ if the weights at the endpoints were physical weights. These points were introduced by Farin in [4]. Here they arise naturally as the best way to geometrically represent the weights. However, there is a slight constraint, since, as opposed to the case of curves, one is now not free to place them anywhere.

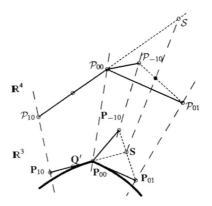

**Figure 2.** Computing the cross ratio (12).

Since they represent ratios of weights, it is obvious that along any closed path in the control net it is enough to fix all but one of these wedge positions, and the last one will already be uniquely determined. A simple geometrical relation can be found between these points. If we look at a triangle with a wedge fixed on each side, then the lines joining each vertex with the position of the wedge of the opposite side are the projections of the medians of a triangle in $\mathbf{R}^4$, and must thus meet at a point.

Returning to the problem of computing the coefficients in (10), similar constructions to the previous one give (see Figure 2)

$$\mathrm{Cr}\left(\mathcal{P}_{00}, \mathcal{S}, \frac{\mathcal{P}_{00} + \mathcal{P}_{10}}{2}, \mathcal{P}_{10}\right) = \frac{\alpha}{\beta - \xi_0} \tag{12}$$

and (see Figure 3)

$$\mathrm{Cr}\left(\mathcal{P}_{00}, \frac{\mathcal{P}_{00} + \mathcal{P}_{-10}}{2}, \mathcal{T}, \mathcal{P}_{-10}\right) = \xi_0 - \beta, \tag{13}$$

from which $\alpha$, $\beta$ and $\xi_0$ are easily determined.

At the corner corresponding to $j = n$, one finds that

$$\mathcal{P}_{-1n} = \alpha \mathcal{P}_{1n} + \left[\beta + \xi_1\right]\mathcal{P}_{0n} - \xi_1 \mathcal{P}_{0\,n-1}.$$

Since $\alpha$ and $\beta$ are already fixed, there is only one degree of freedom for the position of $\mathcal{P}_{-1n}$. This is a consequence of the hypothesis that the coefficient functions $\alpha$, $\beta$, $\gamma$ and $\xi$ are linear in the parameter $v$. If higher degree is accepted, much more flexibility is attained, although the problem becomes, of course, more involved. Nonetheless, $\xi_1$ can again be determined by computing

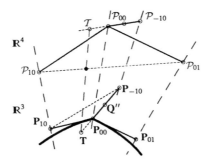

**Figure 3.** Computing the cross ratio (13).

the appropriate cross ratio. All the intermediate points $\mathbf{P}_{-1j}$ can now be found; one must only observe that the structure of (9), in which each intermediate point $\mathcal{P}_{-1j}$ is the result of a linear blend between the points —let's say— $\mathcal{P}^1_{-1j}$ and $\mathcal{P}^2_{-1j}$ that result from certain combinations (with fixed coefficients) of $\mathcal{P}_{0j}$, $\mathcal{P}_{0\,j+1}$, $\mathcal{P}_{0\,j-1}$ and $\mathcal{P}_{1j}$. The projections $\mathbf{P}^1_{-1j}$ and $\mathbf{P}^2_{-1j}$ and their weights can easily be determined by finding points in $\mathbb{R}^3$ with the appropriate cross ratios, and then $\mathbf{P}_{-1j}$ can also be computed (see Figure 4) by noting that

$$\mathrm{Cr}\left(\mathcal{P}^1_{-1j}, \mathcal{P}_{-1j}, \frac{\mathcal{P}^1_{-1j} + \mathcal{P}^2_{-1j}}{2}, \mathcal{P}^2_{-1j}\right) = \frac{j}{n-j}. \qquad (14)$$

The projection of $(\mathcal{P}^1_{-1j} + \mathcal{P}^2_{-1j})/2$ can easily be found because we already know the positions of the other two wedges on the sides of the triangle $\mathbf{P}^1_{-1j}\mathbf{P}_{0j}\mathbf{P}^2_{-1j}$.

## §5. Farin's Transition Principle

In [4] Farin states a transition principle to translate properties of nonrational curves to rational curves. Application of this principle requires just that we express whatever property we are interested in as a set of ratios. Then substitution of cross ratios instead of ratios yields the "corresponding" projective property valid for rational curves.

For the problem dealt with here, Farin [3] gave a construction for the case of nonrational surfaces. It is interesting to note that the same form of transition is valid to translate the construction given there into ours: just note that finding a point with certain barycentric coordinates implies looking at lines from a vertex of the base triangle through a point on the opposite edge that splits the edge in the desired ratio. Keeping this in mind, a look at Figures 1, 2 or 3 will show how our construction reduces to Farin's in the case of nonrational patches, and can be deemed a daughter of the same transition principle.

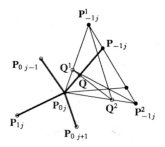

**Figure 4.** The cross ratio of the solid dots is $\dfrac{j}{n-j}$.

## §6. Conclusions

A geometric construction for the control points of a neighboring patch that matches with $VC^1$ continuity a given patch has been presented for rational Bézier surfaces. This construction is more general than that for the polynomial case, since discontinuous patches in $\mathbb{R}^4$ may be projected onto $VC^1$ surfaces.

The necessary information about the weights is included in the control net by means of positions of imaginary wedges on the edges. This allows a simple geometrical construction; these wedge positions, being scale invariant, seem to be the natural way to handle weights.

The presented construction determines the first two rows of control vertices and weights of a patch, as a function of the last two rows of the adjacent patch. Using this method, it is very simple to generate a surface sheet by sequentially patching —with either rectangular or triangular patches— provided that no holes are left.

Triangular and rectangular patches can be handled in the same way because the formal expressions of certain tangential directions are identical for both.

## References

1. Boehm, W., On cubics: a survey, Computer Graphics and Image Processing **19** (1982) 201–226.
2. Boehm, W., G. Farin, and J. Kahmann, A survey of curve and surface methods in CAGD, Comput. Aided Geom. Design **1** (1984) 1–60.
3. Farin, G., A construction for visual $C^1$ continuity of polynomial surface patches, Computer Graphics and Image Processing **20** (1982), 272–282.
4. Farin, G., Algorithms for rational Bézier curves, Comput. Aided Design **15** (1983), 73–77.
5. Herron, G., Techniques for visual continuity, in *Geometric Modeling: Algorithms and new trends*, G. Farin, (ed.), SIAM, 1987, 163–174.

6. Kahmann, J., Continuity of curvature between adjacent Bézier patches, in *Surfaces in Computer Aided Geometric Design*, R. E. Barnhill and W. Boehm, (eds)., North-Holland, 1983, 65–75.

P. Brunet and A. Vinacua
Universitat Politècnica de Catalunya
Departament de Llenguatges i Sistemes Informàtics
Secció d'Informàtica Gràfica
Avinguda Diagonal 647, $8^{ena}$ planta
08028 Barcelona
SPAIN

EMAIL: ealvar@ ebrupc51.bitnet
EMAIL: vinacua% fib.upc.es@ mcvax